THE
BAMPTON LECTURES
1889

THE

ORIGIN AND RELIGIOUS CONTENTS

OF

THE PSALTER

IN THE LIGHT OF OLD TESTAMENT CRITICISM
AND THE HISTORY OF RELIGIONS

WITH AN INTRODUCTION AND APPENDICES

Eight Lectures

PREACHED BEFORE THE UNIVERSITY OF OXFORD IN THE YEAR 1889
ON THE FOUNDATION OF THE LATE REV. JOHN BAMPTON, M.A.
CANON OF SALISBURY

BY

THOMAS KELLY CHEYNE, M.A., D.D.

ORIEL PROFESSOR OF THE INTERPRETATION OF HOLY SCRIPTURE
CANON OF ROCHESTER

WIPF & STOCK · Eugene, Oregon

Wipf and Stock Publishers
199 W 8th Ave, Suite 3
Eugene, OR 97401

The Origin and Religious Contents of The Psalter
In the Light of Old Testament Criticism and the History of Religions
By Cheyne, T. K.
ISBN 13: 978-1-60608-257-7
Publication date 8/5/2009
Previously published by Kegan Paul, Trench, Trubner & Co., 1891

TO THE

RIGHT REV. JAMES MOORHOUSE, D.D.
LORD BISHOP OF MANCHESTER

WHO HAS NOT DESPAIRED OF PRESENT AND FUTURE BENEFIT TO THE CHURCH
FROM THE MORE HISTORICAL STUDY OF THE OLD TESTAMENT
AND WHO OPENED WIDE THE DOOR OF PROGRESS AT THE MANCHESTER
CHURCH CONGRESS IN MDCCCLXXXVIII

EXTRACT

FROM THE LAST WILL AND TESTAMENT

OF THE LATE

REV. JOHN BAMPTON,

CANON OF SALISBURY.

—— 'I give and bequeath my Lands and Estates to the Chancellor, Masters, and Scholars of the University of Oxford for ever, to have and to hold all and singular the said Lands or Estates upon trust, and to the intents and purposes hereinafter mentioned; that is to say, I will and appoint that the Vice-Chancellor of the University of Oxford for the time being shall take and receive all the rents, issues, and profits thereof, and (after all taxes, reparations, and necessary deductions made) that he pay all the remainder to the endowment of eight Divinity Lecture Sermons, to be established for ever in the said University, and to be performed in the manner following:

'I direct and appoint, that, upon the first Tuesday in Easter Term, a Lecturer be yearly chosen by the Heads of Colleges only, and by no others, in the room adjoining to the Printing-House, between the hours of ten in the morning and two in the afternoon, to preach eight Divinity Lecture Sermons, the year following, at St. Mary's in Oxford, between the commencement of the last month in Lent Term, and the end of the third week in Act Term.

'Also I direct and appoint, that the eight Divinity Lecture Sermons shall be preached upon either of the following Subjects—to confirm and establish the Christian Faith, and to confute all heretics and schismatics—upon the divine authority of the holy

Scriptures—upon the authority of the writings of the primitive Fathers, as to the faith and practice of the primitive Church—upon the Divinity of our Lord and Saviour Jesus Christ—upon the Divinity of the Holy Ghost—upon the Articles of the Christian Faith, as comprehended in the Apostles' and Nicene Creeds.

'Also I direct, that thirty copies of the eight Divinity Lecture Sermons shall be always printed, within two months after they are preached; and one copy shall be given to the Chancellor of the University, and one copy to the Head of every College, and one copy to the Mayor of the city of Oxford, and one copy to be put into the Bodleian Library; and the expense of printing them shall be paid out of the revenue of the Land or Estates given for establishing the Divinity Lecture Sermons; and the Preacher shall not be paid, nor be entitled to the revenue, before they are printed.

'Also I direct and appoint, that no person shall be qualified to preach the Divinity Lecture Sermons, unless he hath taken the degree of Master of Arts at least, in one of the two Universities of Oxford or Cambridge; and that the same person shall never preach the Divinity Lecture Sermons twice.'

INTRODUCTION.

(I.–III.) EXPLAINING THE ORIGIN AND CRITICAL BASIS, AND (IV.) ILLUSTRATING SOME FEATURES IN THE CONTENTS OF THESE LECTURES.

I.

THE present work may at least claim to be comprehensive. The first part of it might be enlarged, with the help of the underlying researches, into a synthetic Introduction to the Old Testament; the second into a historical sketch of post-Exilic Jewish religion down to the time of Christ. There would be only one hindrance, the same which has delayed the appearance of this work, namely, the continued necessity of not overworking my sight. As each fragment of long-planned work is finished, I cannot withhold the expression of deep thankfulness. But—*semper amari aliquid.* I have already had a foretaste of the rough treatment to which these Lectures are exposed through a misapprehension of their object,[1] and I fear that even with the printed page before them some readers may not find it easy to give it a fair consideration. It may be worth while in an Introduction to assist such to understand both the author and his point of view. And first, what is the object of this book, which is so much more than a collection of actually spoken discourses?

---

[1] Even Mr. Gore misapprehends, not, I am sure, my object, but my theory, to judge from his somewhat unkind and premature reference to it (*Lux Mundi*, ed. 10, Preface, p. xxi.).

It is primarily historical, but also in a very real sense apologetic. At the present juncture we seem to need a more critical study of the facts which condition the outward form of Christianity. Some of the most important of these are of course to be found in the Old Testament, as the crown of which we may justly regard the Psalms. The history of the growth of the Psalter must therefore first of all be studied, and if the whole of it, practically, should prove to belong to the great post-Exilic period, we shall have to compare the religious ideas of the Psalter, obtained by a careful exegesis, with those of the peoples with whom the Israelites came into the closest contact.

I am far from expecting or even desiring to make at once a large number of converts to my theories (mine, not in any invidious sense). I wish to help, not to force, my fellow-students. Of most I would only ask that they would keep my argument in view for a long time, and ponder first one part of it and then another again and again. They must remember that many subordinate problems are involved, the solution of which, though always important for critical accuracy, may sometimes without serious loss be postponed. And in the study both of these and of the main problem they must be so fair as to suppose that the objections to my solutions which may occur to them have most probably occurred to me, and should not be too hastily presumed to be insurmountable. In a word or a sentence, or, more often, a note, these objections may prove to have been met, though I must regretfully confess that even with the aid of notes I have not always been able to exhibit the full strength of my arguments. May I suggest that the best way to study the book (if it should be so fortunate as to find students) would be, first to read it without and next with the notes, and with the appendices; and that possibly some of my older readers would do well to read the second part (beginning at Lect. VI.) before the first? I should like to add that by the patient use of the Index of Passages this volume may to some extent serve as a critical commentary on the Psalms and on related passages of the Bible. It is, I know, but too probable that this may seem to many an extravagant request. They may wish that I had selected some far simpler critical problem, and treated of the difficulties which it may have caused to belief from the most developed dogmatic point of view. Some future Bampton Lecturer may adopt such a course, which would be both modest and safe. That one who addresses not only Hebraists but the religious public at large, to which he appears to be only known as a recent writer, should act differently, doubtless demands some justification, which I will now in the second place proceed to give.

Yes; the problem of the origin of the Psalter (not to speak now of the problem of the development of its ideas) is certainly a complicated one. But to a competent scholar that will be its strongest recommendation. In the light of the history of Old Testament criticism, this is the very moment to attack it. Why have there been hitherto such great differences of opinion respecting its solution ? Because it has been treated without sufficient reference to collateral problems. This was excusable on the ground that the examination of those problems was still in an early stage. Of late however solutions of many of them, approximately certain, have been obtained, and critics can return to the problem of the Psalter in the sure hope that, if it can be solved in a manner historically intelligible, the solutions of those other problems will become all the more convincing. The cautious reader will therefore ask now to be assured whether the Lecturer who in 1889 adopted so novel a course was a recent fledgeling or a critic of fully adequate experience.

The antecedents of a student are only important in so far as they explain the road by which he has travelled. The taste for Biblical problems is with me, so to speak, an inherited one; I deserve no credit for it. I could not be disloyal to my earliest teacher, whose spirit is in me still, and whose work, which faintly shone in a dark period, it is my privilege to continue. To other teachers I have incurred far greater intellectual debts. But to him I owe the example of a mild and yet fervent Johannine religion, and a Pauline love of the Scriptures. One thing more he both taught and practised—the disregard of luxury. No credit then is due to me for being content to study for ten years in silence and poverty till the college of Scott and Jowett for the first time opened a fellowship (Nov. 1869) to Semitic and Biblical scholarship; much less for the enthusiasm with which, fresh from Göttingen, I looked forward to the day when native Biblical scholars should resume the work of Lowth, so fruitful in Germany, so fruitless for the time in England. There was then another dreamer too in Oxford, whose enthusiasm was more practical than mine, the late Dr. Appleton, who aspired to promote critical theology not less than other studies, and used to discuss and give clearness to my ideas at the time of the foundation of the *Academy* (1869–1870). It was largely owing to this friend that I persevered in free Old Testament criticism, when alone in Oxford and probably in the Anglican Church. It might not be impossible, he thought, in course of years for me and for others to make even a smaller weight of learning than Pusey's available for progress by the sedulous polishing of the critical faculty. Neither of us knew then that outside my own communion I had a powerful and brilliant fellow-worker in distant Aberdeen. Nor that in my own neighbourhood a younger scholar was being matured to take his share at first in the purely linguistic but at last also with growing firmness in the fully critical treatment of the Old Testament.

Thrown once more on my own resources since the sad death of my friend Appleton, I entered on a fresh phase of experience. I felt isolated, like so many overzealous students, and began to doubt whether I had not valued research too highly, and whether my inner life was not suffering from a sometimes too keen and unsympathetic criticism. Those doubts were not altogether unfounded. But though I should now soften some too incisive statements of earlier days, I have written nothing which in the light of further experience I can wish absolutely to retract. The thought of a palinode, which has been imputed to me, has never entered my head. Some of the work begun between 1870 and 1876 has quite lately been finished; some more will yet, if health be granted, find its completion. I am thankful for the task long since committed to me, and am not less strict a critic than of old because now more of a church-teacher. I had however to pass through a difficult experience in order to gain or regain full sympathy with brethren left behind. There are many traces of this in my third work on Isaiah, which I confess surprise me now and then a little myself. The reader must not misinterpret this. Those who sympathize with critical progress, and remember how cold Oxford and the Church apparently were between 1870 and 1880, will admit that I have some right to be surprised. During those bitter years a piercing and reconciling word on the subject of the Bible was impossible, because Church and university would none of those things which criticism had discovered. In its self-suppression and in its irenic and apologetic attitude the *Isaiah* of 1880–1881 was a strong effort of faith in the unseen. Many younger students were, it is true, being prepared to meet me, but I did not know of their existence. Yet no credit is due either to me for my advances towards them, or to them for their advances towards me. We were all of us being gently led forward by different routes. A high tide of God's Spirit had been sweeping over Oxford and the Church. In one obscure student its influence showed itself in this—that Johannine religion reasserted its supremacy over criticism and speculation. He came to realize the full meaning of words which he had himself penned in his first book, 'Rationalism and mysticism have been hitherto the poles of exegesis; yet each of these, exclusive as they seem, may serve to indicate a higher region where contradictions repose in the light of God's truth.'[1] He ceased to require to see for himself the full reconciliation of seemingly opposed truths, though determined to do his best both as a finder of truths and as an inquirer after *the* truth. Without subscribing to Goethe's sentence 'Grau, theurer Freund, ist alle Theorie,' he felt that he needed for himself, both inwardly and outwardly, a fuller experience of truth. And so he was unconsciously prepared to receive a new and unexpected call. On the eve of a journey to the East, he turned back, and bound himself by the obligations of a country pastor. He had his reward; the sense of spiritual isolation passed from him and he gained the pastoral spirit. But was this a reward to rest in? Was there not another priesthood, not less of divine appointment than that of the Church—the priesthood of study and of teaching? And in this student's life ought not the latter to take the precedence of the former? Meantime it became evident enough that the long frost which had bound up the study of the Bible, was breaking. The religious temper at Oxford seemed to be becoming more irenic and in the best sense Christian. Partizanship seemed to be diminishing; there might possibly be room for one who ventured to combine what men call or miscall rationalism and mysticism. When therefore in 1887 a new academical prospect opened before him, he went hopefully to meet it.

II.

This third period of ten years begins with the *Prophecies of Isaiah*, and ends with the *Lectures on the Psalms*. Is there any noteworthy difference between these books, beyond

[1] *Notes and Criticisms on the Heb. Text of Isaiah*, 1869, p. ix.

the fact that the one is primarily exegetical, the other mainly critical and historical? To be frank, there is. That extreme self-suppression which marks the former work throughout, and that willingness to concede to tradition all that could with any plausibility be conceded, it would be scarcely proper to exhibit in the altered circumstances of the Church. In 1880 it was still a heresy to accept with all its consequences the plurality of the authorship of the Book of Isaiah; in 1890, to a growing school of church-students this has become an indubitable fact. In 1880, seeing too much with the eyes of my expected readers, I adopted a possible but not sufficiently probable view of certain psalms, and a possible but not sufficiently probable view of the central prophecy of the Second Isaiah. In 1890, seeing entirely with my own eyes not less as an apologist than as a critic, I offer my readers the truest solution which I can find of these and of all other problems, believing that this course is now, for the Church itself, both necessary and right. Let those Church-teachers cast a stone at me for this seeming inconsistency, who were able in 1880 to act as I have done in 1890.

The reader will, I think, have seen that my outer and inner history was preparing me to produce exactly such a book as this. Each part of these Bampton Lectures has grown out of work already done, and its mental attitude is the result of my whole experience. It still remains for me to indicate the researches on which the present volume is partly based, and which are not merely personal, but express views to which many, both here and in America, have of late been drawing nearer. It was in 1869 that a small book of *Notes and Criticisms on the Hebrew Text of Isaiah* announced the principles to which I hoped, and still hope, to be true, viz. that preconceived theological notions ought to be rigorously excluded from exegesis. In 1870, in *The Book of Isaiah Chronologically Arranged*, I adopted what many now regard as the best way of promoting the assimilation of critical ideas. The work condescends too little to the general reader, and there are too many gaps in the commentary. The limits of the work, its date, and the circumstances of the writer will explain this. But there are some evident signs of progress. In criticism the book is by no means a servile copy of Ewald, and in the stress which it lays on the development of religious ideas and on the illustration of Isaiah by Assyriology, it takes a clear step beyond him. Both in these two latter points and in its acceptance of the unity of Isa. xl.–lxvi. (a theory easier than any other to commend to beginners) it anticipates a recent work with similar objects from the able pen of Dr. Driver. I have had to refer to this book at p. 275 on Isa. liii. My next subjects of special but (as will be seen) not exclusive study were the Books of Genesis and Jeremiah. It was no doubt rash, considering the state of the public mind, to meddle with the former, but I had caught from Germany the idea of disinterested study, and I believed in the force of truth. Just then my own disinterestedness was put to a severe test. The English idea of consistency was, and to a great extent perhaps still is, that having chosen your school and your leader, you should stick to them. With all their faults I loved Ewald's works and Ewald himself. Schleiermacher and he were to me what Maurice and Stanley were at that time to so many of my brethren. Ewald's works, in particular, had lifted me to a higher plane of knowledge, and he himself, the 'rückschauender Prophet,' seemed to me a great even though very imperfect personality. Yet in 1870–1871 I passed into the school of Graf and Kuenen. I hesitated, indeed, to accept the full conclusions of the latter, who appeared to me not to allow enough for the freedom of development,[1] and I was still in some points a follower of Ewald. My course of study involved this. Unlike some of my younger friends at the present day, I was not so fascinated by the Pentateuch as to

---

[1] *Academy*, Dec. 25, 1875 (review of Duhm's *Theologie der Propheten*).

neglect the study of the prophets. Jeremiah lay open before me beside Genesis, and Kuenen on Jeremiah seemed to me cold compared with Ewald. But I have said enough elsewhere (see pp. 191, 209) to explain my attitude towards these two great critics. Suffice it to add that the appearance in 1871 of Part VI. of Colenso on the Pentateuch (a faulty but at that time thankworthy book) strengthened the impetus towards Genesis-studies which I had received from foreign teachers. I examined this book, first for myself and then for the readers of the original *Academy*, and ventured to prophesy,[1] five years before the appearance of Wellhausen's *Geschichte Israels*, that the most important results common to Graf, Kuenen, and Colenso would be confirmed by an increasing number of critics, 'though theological prejudices in England, combined in Germany with prepossessions induced by a long critical tradition, [might] for some time retard the conclusion.' Many another able work or article on the Old Testament, proceeding most often from Germany or Holland, also exercised my powers of criticism and assimilation. I indulged the not wholly vain hope that I was getting nearer and nearer to the centre of problems, but I am not ashamed to admit that by Christmas 1875 I had satisfied myself that the most immediately fruitful field of work lay, not in the criticism of the Pentateuch, but in that of the prophets and Hagiographa. Something of course had been won by the restless energy of Kuenen, but doubts grew upon me, first, as to the complete post-Exile origin of the priestly legislation, and then as to that of the narratives, and the eager interest with which I followed the recent Assyrian discoveries opened my eyes to the difficulty of dating even the narrative of the Yahvist as it stands. With fresh archæological and Assyriological evidence I hoped to return some day to a problem which as yet 'baffled' me. For the present, in spite of the seductions of Wellhausen (1878), I devoted myself to other departments of

[1] *Academy*, March. 1, 1873.

study, and not least (as long as health allowed me) to learning the Assyrian language. My *Genesis* remained unfinished, but out of this fragment grew five articles published in 1876–1877 in the *Encyclopædia Britannica* on 'Canaan' and 'Canaanites,' 'Cherubim,' 'Circumcision,' 'Cosmogony,' and 'Deluge.' All these exhibit an interest in the mythic substratum[1] of narratives and phrases in the Old Testament which is, I suppose, peculiarly though not exclusively English, and is not unexpressed in this volume. The reader will also find me in 1877, in a discussion of the Babylonian Deluge-story, asking a question which in one of these Lectures is answered in the affirmative,[2] viz. 'Can the Yahvistic narrative in [the early chapters of Genesis] be safely broken up into several?' I have to add that in 1877 an article on Daniel (see p. 106), in 1878 one on Esther (see p. 298), and in 1881 articles on the Hittites, Isaiah, Jeremiah, and Jonah appeared in the same work.

These articles were none of them written to order, but grew out of the plan, formed about 1875, of a historical sketch of the growth of the Old Testament literature from the advanced, and yet not extreme, point of view which I had adopted. Of course, disputable points would have been mentioned, and some documents would have been referred to in different chapters; of the partly provisional character of such a sketch I was well aware. The task was too great for me, and it has since been accomplished on a larger scale than I thought of by that honoured veteran, Reuss. But I learned, in preparing my material, to treat Old Testament subjects in a large and comprehensive way, which may be the hardest but is, I believe, the best way. Among other articles, I will here only speak of two—those on Isaiah and on Jonah.

---

[1] Ewald, out of a too passionate opposition to Strauss, sought to banish the words 'myth' and 'mythic' from Biblical criticism. This appeared to me to be flying in the face of facts.

[2] See pp. 270, 279, and cf. *Job and Solomon*, p. 6, where this answer is anticipated.

The former is perhaps more interesting now than it was at the time, because of its analysis of the so-called Second Isaiah, by which it not only takes, as I believe, a step in advance, but a step which other critics are only just beginning to take. Of course, I do not forget that my honoured teacher Ewald had pointed the way, but how vague and hesitating his criticism is, no one can fail to see. Half the phenomena were hidden from him, and of the rest he has no sufficiently plausible account to give. It appeared to me when completing my commentary on Isaiah that the time had come for a keener analysis. I had long lived as it were in the Exilic and post-Exilic period of Hebrew literature, and certain conclusions forced themselves upon me as they would hardly have done upon a special student of the separate book of Isaiah. I took care that the data upon which I worked should appear in my commentary, but through the deliberate self-suppression which is the soul of that work I reserved my results for the Encyclopædia. The consequence was that few scholars met with them, and that not till 1888 did Stade begin to take steps unknowingly in my own direction, and only in 1889 did Kuenen independently adopt nearly my own views. Mr. G. A. Smith, in vol. ii. of *Isaiah* (just published) in the 'Expositor's Bible,' is the only English scholar who has as yet conceded the principle of the separability of Isa. xl.–lxvi. into parts of distinct origin. When the question is debated more widely here and in Germany, it will be impossible for generous students to ignore either my article or its date; it must however be taken in connexion with the alterations of view indicated in this volume, and to which I hope to return elsewhere.[1] The latter of the abovementioned articles ('Jonah') had to be of narrow compass in consideration of the smallness of the book. It must be grouped with an article entitled 'Jonah, a Study in Jewish

---

[1] First of all in notices of Mr. G. A. Smith's work in the *Expositor* (Feb. 1891) and the *Academy* (Feb. 21). To the former I ask the attention of critics.

Folklore and Religion' in the *Theological Review* for 1877 (pp. 211-219), in which I endeavour to show that the Book of Jonah is not a mere romance, as we might infer from Nöldeke,[1] but an edifying story, adapted to the writer's times, and founded, like some of those in Gen. i.-xi., on Semitic mythology. I may add that this article was written before the appearance of Goldziher's *Hebrew Mythology*,[2] which indeed is somewhat meagre in its treatment of 'Jonah.' Two other books of the prophetic canon, of special interest for the critic, I also touched upon in articles, though not in the *Encyclopædia*,—Joel incidentally in various reviews of books, and Zechariah in an essay read before a theological society in London in 1879, though only published (without alteration) in the *Jewish Quarterly Review* for Oct. 1888. I had pointed out in a review of Baudissin's *Studien* (*Academy*, Nov. 25, 1876) that Joel and at any rate Zech. xii.-xiv. must be studied together, but had not felt it safe to draw the most obvious conclusion, viz. that these writings are about contemporaneous. In 1873 I still thought that by disintegrating Joel we might show it to be pre-Exilic; in 1876 I admitted that this book was post-Exilic, but hesitated as to 2 Zechariah.[3] Not till 1879 did I formulate views on Zechariah which, compared with the more recent utterances of Stade and Wellhausen, are moderate, and are substantially those put forth by Kuenen in 1889 in his *Onderzoek* (ed. 2, vol. ii.).[4]

In referring to these articles on the present occasion I am of course not claiming for them more than a relative degree

---

[1] *Die alttestamentliche Literatur* (1868), p. 72. Nöldeke uses the word 'romance,' but explains '*almost entirely* a free production of the imagination.'

[2] The most appreciative and certainly not the least detailed and discriminating of the English reviews of Goldziher was from my own pen (*Academy*, March 10 and 17, 1877).

[3] Prof. Driver has been equally cautious. He has now, I believe, arrived at a result respecting Joel. But in 1880 he saw difficulties in a post-Exile date which he could not at that time overcome (see his thorough review of Merx's *Joel*, in the *Academy*, 1880).

[4] Cf. Stade, *Geschichte*, ii. (1888), p. 70.

of accuracy. There is much said in them which I should now, not retract, but modify, and much unsaid which must be gathered from other works. The 'unsaid' matters relate mostly to the linguistic argument. Linguistic studies have always keenly interested me, and a desire for fresh stimulus in them took me when poor and unknown to Göttingen. Against two 'prevalent errors' I pleaded in 1876, when a large measure of university reform seemed imminent ; one was 'the supposition that the Old Testament [could] be fruitfully treated from a purely linguistic point of view,' the other 'too narrow a conception' of the linguistic preparation required by an Old Testament critic.[1] And again in 1880 I complained that 'though keenly interested in criticism, the public takes wonderfully little pains to master the preliminaries.'[2] A large and thorough criticism rests on an equally large and thorough exegesis, and exegesis itself rests ultimately on the grammar and the lexicon. The linguistic argument is unfortunately not often of primary importance in the higher criticism of the Old Testament. But it is very often of at least subsidiary value, and I must regret that condensed summaries even in the best of Encyclopædias did not permit me to do it justice.

A small group of works mainly exegetical must now be mentioned, every one of which has helped to form the basis of these Lectures. The group opens with notes on the Old Testament in the so-called Variorum edition of the Authorized Version, the labour of preparing which was shared with me by my friend Mr. (now Professor) Driver. Then follows in 1880-1881 *Isaiah*, in 1882 *Micah* (see below, p. 224), in 1884 *Hosea* (see p. 378), in 1883-1885 *Jeremiah* and *Lamentations* (see p. 100). My plan in these latter books was, upon educational grounds, to give more or less fully the exegetical facts upon which critical conclusions

---

[1] *Essays on the Endowment of Research*, p. 192.
[2] *The Prophecies of Isaiah*, ed. 3, ii. 224.

were based, without generally drawing these conclusions myself. An exception is however made in the treatment of Jer. x. 1-16 and Jer. l., li., and this exception marks my dawning consciousness that the necessity for minimizing the results of literary criticism even in addressing clerical students was passing away. The transitional period however is not yet quite over, and so my commentaries (especially those on Isaiah and Jeremiah) need not yet be reconstructed. Modifications of my views on Isaiah will be found on pp. 35, 182, 184, 264, 275 of this work, and some of the special problems of Jeremiah I have examined more freely in a volume to be noticed presently. I indulge a faint hope that a larger critical treatment of this great prophet may yet be open to me. Meantime I am not ashamed to have offered in my commentary on Jeremiah one more sacrifice as a teacher to the temporary needs of the Church. I have therefore ventured to refer to it at p. 376 in speaking of Jer. vii. 22, 23, my comment upon which supplies the only frank and yet considerate discussion of a stumbling-block to orthodoxy, and the only provisional standing-ground, which I am myself able to point out to perplexed students.

Another small group of writings opens with a new version of the Psalms with introduction and notes ('Parchment Library,' 1884), on which the larger commentary of 1888 was based. My attention had been much directed to the Hagiographa, as the volume called *Job and Solomon, or, The Wisdom of the Old Testament* (1887), further shows. The latter work is a real Ben-oni (Gen. xxxv. 18). During its preparation I proved by personal experience how thoroughly faith and free historical criticism of the Bible can be reconciled, and how the one can be strengthened by the other. Nothing but the certainty of the fundamental Old Testament truths, reasserted and developed by Jesus Christ, could have supported me in my sore trial, when, not indeed my life, but my twofold ministry, seemed closed. I trust that this is, in no narrow sense of the word, an evangelical work. But it is none the less uncompromisingly critical, and as such is necessarily appealed to in these Lectures. The two remaining books are popular in form, but I hope that the *Jeremiah* of 1888 ('Men of the Bible') is a contribution to the psychological as well as critical reading of the times of the great prophet. A mere life of an individual prophet it certainly is not, nor does it appeal merely to a popular audience. It is, so far as its limits allow, a summing up of many critical and historical questions, and a synthesis of many sure and some at least probable results. *Elijah, or, The Hallowing of Criticism* (1888) is also referred to in these Lectures in support of my belief in the permanent religious value of mythic and legendary narratives in the Old Testament.

III.

Upon the results of these works, modified wherever necessary and developed, I have ventured to build, but upon the results of how many other scholars too, need hardly be said. My predecessors are of course chiefly German; I can no more ignore them than if I were myself a German. But what a pleasure it has been to me to refer to some English workers! Professor Sayce's recent attitude towards Old Testament criticism causes me, I must confess, some little surprise. It seems a poor return for the general willingness of critics to learn from Assyriology. But to the stimulating character of my friend's books and conversation I gratefully own my indebtedness. Prof. Robertson Smith, since we first met on the way to Germany, has always been to me a valued ally. His *Religion of the Semites* was not yet out when these Lectures were in preparation, so that the coincidences are perhaps the more interesting. To another true friend of my second period, Prof. Driver, my references would have been more frequent, had his expected book on the Old Testament literature appeared in time. As a student of the language and grammatical sense of the Old Testament, I have long since had a high respect for his opinion; as a critic I do not yet know to what extent we agree. Slowly have time and study melted his conscientious reserve, and made him in a double sense my comrade. But his excellent though in some points over-cautious handbook to Isaiah and his recent article in the *Contemporary Review* (Feb. 1890) leave no doubt to which side upon the whole his judgment inclines, and his known fairness and candour, and the solidity of his exegetical basis, will give special value to his book at the present juncture. To two other scholars, Prof. Davidson and Prof. Briggs, I would also willingly have referred oftener. In my youth I looked to the former for teaching, but in vain; in riper years I welcome his luminous but too rare contributions to Biblical theology.[1] Nor can I forget that from his classroom have proceeded the most promising of our younger workers. With the latter, who is also happily the founder of a school, I am in full accord on the expediency of a bolder church-policy towards historical criticism, and among other points on the interpretation of Ps. xvi. (*Messianic Prophecy*, p. 151). It is pleasant to add the names of Mr. C. J. Ball and Mr. G. A. Smith, the one the author of *Jeremiah* (vol. i., 1890), the other of *Isaiah* (2 vols., 1889-1890) in the 'Expositor's Bible.' That the former is very much less fair to my own work than the latter (doubtless from imperfect knowledge of it) need make no difference in my estimate of his ability.

Is there anything else of mine worth mentioning as contributing to the basis of these Lectures? Yes; but only in the department of apologetic. It is something perhaps to have pointed out again and again how criticism assists the discovery of the more permanent elements in the religion of the Old Testament, and in *The Prophecies of Isaiah* to have

---

[1] See his articles in the *Expositor* on Hosea (1879), the Second Isaiah (1883-84), Amos (1887), Joel (1888). See also his *Job* and *Hebrews*.

given more than one apologetic essay which has a bearing on the Psalms as well as on Isaiah, also in two Church Congress papers[1] to have sketched a programme both theoretic and practical for apologetic workers. The theoretic portion of the latter is of course the most important. The principle of the *Kenōsis* (or, as it has been lately paraphrased, the self-limitation) of the Divine Son, and that of the continual guidance both of the Church and of each faithful Christian by the Holy Spirit, seemed to me in 1883 and 1888 (as they still seem to me in 1890) the only possible foundation for a reform of apologetic suited to our English orthodoxy. The development of these principles in their application to Biblical criticism is a delicate work, for which the combination of several or even many minds is required, but I ventured to offer carefully expressed suggestions, and to appeal most earnestly to the clergy to consider them. Nor were these the first *conciones ad clerum* which, not uninvited, I had ventured to deliver. Before the members of the London Biblical Society I read in 1881 a paper on the Progressive Revelation of the Doctrine of the Holy Spirit (*Clergyman's Magazine*, March 1880) which urged the increasing importance of fearless faith in the Paraclete. It seemed too much to hope to see results, when, who could have believed it?—in the autumn of 1889 a very able reassertion of both fundamental principles proceeded from the pen of the Principal of Pusey House (see his fine essay in *Lux Mundi*). Now I will not accuse Mr. Gore, who is a ripe theological thinker, of borrowing from me without acknowledgment. But fairness and brotherly feeling must impel him to recognize that the movement which he advocates for the reform of the Old Testament section of apologetic theology was initiated in the Anglican Church on almost the same lines by another.

Still, deeply thankful as I am for the support of one who has done so much high-toned work both for Oxford and

[1] See *Job and Solomon*, pp. 1-9; *The Hallowing of Criticism*, pp. 183-207.

Calcutta, I earnestly wish that some Church-students, whose position is somewhat different from Mr. Gore's, would rally to the same banner. Professor Driver's paper at the Derby Diocesan Conference in 1888 on the relation of the Church to Bible-criticism was such as we might have expected from the author of the helpful handbook on Isaiah published in the same year. Its tendency is similar to that of my own addresses. The recommendation to begin Biblical study by seeking a vivid realization of the Gospel picture of our Lord is an echo (I would rather say, a sanction) of my own advice to hallow criticism by the love of Christ, and to study with reverent care the facts of Christ's humanity reported in the Gospels. But Professor Driver's ecclesiastical position is so independent that I must still look out eagerly for champions who represent a school. When will some young adherent, I will not say of Evangelicalism, but of Evangelical principles set himself to think out in his own way the relation of Biblical criticism to vital Christian truth? Let me explain briefly what I mean.

It is, I suppose, of the essence of evangelical Protestantism that the religious teaching received from without should be submitted by the individual Christian to the test of its agreement with the 'living oracles.' Vast as his debt to the Church may be, he must not rest satisfied till he can say, 'Now we believe, not because of thy saying' (John iv. 42). It is incumbent upon him to take nothing upon authority, but in humble reliance upon the Spirit's all-powerful help, by the critical study of the Scriptures and by personal experience, to discover for himself, and to help his fellows to discover for themselves, what are the really vital elements of Church doctrine. I do not say that he will soon come to an end of that study, but I do say that, from the Protestant point of view, he must begin it. And that which is the duty of ordinary evangelical Churchmen must surely be still more the duty of those who are in high Church-positions. It is for them not

Evangelicals, the importance of adopting, not indeed Mr. Gore's estimate of the positive results of criticism, but at least his view of the needs of apologetic theology. Evangelicals will naturally find it somewhat harder than Mr. Gore to follow the critics to their more advanced conclusions, because they cannot say with him, ' It is becoming more and more difficult to believe in the Bible without believing in the Church ' (in the sense of the writers of *Lux Mundi*). It was to a great extent in their interest that I ventured at Lambeth[1] to entreat some of our learned Church-dignitaries to unite in recommending the most certain results of Old Testament criticism ' first of all, for study and assimilation, and in due time for use in public teaching, as conducive to the interests of edification.' That appeal for a compromise has not been responded to ; even a fair-minded neutral,[2] who rightly guesses that in my heart I addressed it to Nonconformists as well as Anglicans, reads into my words his own ideas of what I must have meant, and clings to his own view. I wish that it could have been otherwise, though in that case I should have had to restrict my own freedom, not indeed as a critic, but as a Church-teacher. Let us then, if it must be so, go on as before, tolerating much difference of opinion, and freely recognizing the provisional character of most apologetic arguments, but vying with each other in the love of Christ and His Church.

Yes ; our arguments must for the most part bear the stamp of provisionalness. Of those two fundamental principles of which I have spoken it is the first alone which is absolutely certain : ' He shall guide you into all the truth.' Helpful as the idea transferred from a fervid exhortation of St. Paul to orthodox theology certainly is, it is exposed, as the great German constructive theologians found, to serious objections

---

[1] See paper on 'Reform in the Teaching of the Old Testament,' in *Contemporary Review*, Aug. 1889.

[2] Principal Cave, *Contemporary Review*, April 1890.

to be continually appealing to the letter of Church-formularies, but first to study the Scriptures both critically and spiritually, and then to initiate a higher exegesis of the formularies to correspond to the higher criticism and exegesis of the Scriptures. I am very far from desiring another 'Tract XC.,' but I do desire, as one who springs from an Evangelical stock, that the formularies should be interpreted by the Scriptures, and not the Scriptures by some current view of the formularies. A true Evangelical begins, not with the Prayer-book and Articles, but with the Holy Scriptures. And a reforming Evangelical should prove his Protestant sincerity by adopting modern historical principles of Bible-criticism. With singular prescience Mr. H. B. Wilson, late Fellow and Tutor of St. John's College, Oxford, expressed these ideas in the Bampton Lectures for 1851, the historical importance of which has perhaps not yet been fully recognized :—

In appealing to Scripture sense, I mean not necessarily, as the Scripture has been interpreted in some times and places, even by the then authorized interpreters, who may, nevertheless, have been, not only the authorized, but also the best interpreters of their day; but the sense of Scripture, as it *shall be* interpreted, under the best lights of the present and future times (p. 28).

The sense of formularies founded on Scripture must be sought in the declarations and history of Scripture rightly understood, and interpreted according to the best lights of those who in each age are responsible for their judgment upon it (p. 32).

The appeal therefore which on June 4, 1889, I addressed to a clerical meeting at Lambeth Palace Library to 'some Evangelicals and some High Churchmen' I now with all brotherly frankness renew. I have no secret wish to exalt Evangelical over Catholic theologians. Both can be equally fervent Christians and earnest Anglican Churchmen. I only urge upon those who, though deeply appreciative of much that is in the old Catholic theology, are both by education and by the stress of personal experience essentially Protestant both from the elder orthodoxy and from the more negative criticism. It remains to be seen whether it will hold its ground here, as a dogmatic principle, in a more advanced stage of criticism and exegesis, whether in short our English Liebners will not be pushed either backward or forward— backward to the elder orthodoxy, or forward to a view of the Church-dogmas as not to all intents and purposes infallible theories, binding on the Christian intellect, but logical and imperfect renderings of the imaginative Biblical symbols of superlogical phenomena. Speculative orthodoxy will perhaps regard this as a needless alarm, but critical historians who have to supply facts to the speculative theologians, must keep their minds in suspense. Let them not be hindered in their useful work, but rather encouraged to take some steps in advance. We want fresh Lightfoots, as thorough as the great Bishop but critically more versatile, who will not disdain the use of new methods, and who, if I may, under a sense of duty, again affectionately say so, will 'enter more sympathetically into the labours of the Old Testament critics.'[1]

IV.

A few words in conclusion on the contents of these Lectures. Some may perhaps wish to know whether I have retreated at all from the position taken up in the spoken discourses. For an adequate reason I should have been willing either to go forward or to go backward; but I have not found such a reason. Passages omitted in delivery have been restored; notes and appendices have been added; corrections have been introduced throughout; and in the eighth Lecture the relation of Judaism to Zoroastrianism has received a much more elaborate treatment. This is the sum of the changes in the printed volume. I venture to ask that the contents may be judged, not only from the point of view of

[1] *Contemp. Rev.* Aug. 1889, p. 232 (see note on p. 218).

criticism, but from that of education. It is my hope that I have brought together much that is useful to the Bible-student quite apart from my argument. The notes abound in historical and exegetical matter, and the store of facts in the linguistic appendix can hardly fail to be helpful to the Hebraist. I have still a word to say respecting the first of the two appendices. I feel that conservative readers may neglect it, because the external evidence is treated in it from my own special point of view, and because it involves careful reference to parts of the Lectures. I respectfully deprecate this. Again and again have hasty arguments been drawn from the external evidence; I have endeavoured to show how little comparatively this external evidence is worth, and how scanty are the conclusions which, so far as it is real, can be drawn from it. I should be glad, however, if some younger scholar would give a more detailed but a not less keen examination to the supposed allusions to the Psalms in Ecclesiasticus and Baruch, in connexion with a fresh inquiry into the date of these books.

Turning now to the Lectures, and first of all to the 'higher criticism' in them, the reader will observe that, while in Lects. VI.–VIII. I have referred now and then to the Priestly Code as upon the whole a post-Exilic work, in the earlier Lectures I have not assumed for it any date whatever. Not that I had any uncertainty on this point; but I thought it best to let the reader find out how well the results of Psalm-criticism agree with a late date. That the Psalter as a whole presupposes the Law, is not to be doubted; it has in fact been sufficiently shown by such a conservative critic as Prof. Bissell. Now the psalms are, as has been said before, the response of the worshipping congregation to the demands made upon it in the Law. If the Law as a whole were pre-Exilic, the Psalter, or at any rate a considerable part of it, should be pre-Exilic too, unless indeed we go so far as to conjecture that a pre-Exilic Psalter, akin to though possibly not so fine as our Psalter, has been lost. It may of course be maintained that a number of the extant psalms which I have taken to be post-Exilic should rather be referred to the age of Josiah. I cannot wonder if this should occur to many of my readers, because my own opinion has not always been the same. Before I had given a sufficiently thorough study to the various *groups* of psalms, and before I had sufficiently viewed the psalms, both singly and in groups, in the light of other Old Testament productions, the date of which has been approximately fixed, I had thought it possible that not a few psalms might belong to the period of Josiah and Jeremiah, and that nearly all the psalms which I now refer to the Greek or Maccabæan period might be placed in the Persian age. I have now given up these views for reasons which will be found in these Lectures. Suffice it to observe here that the new conservative school is apt to fill the reign of Josiah with more literary works than it can bear; and that the early Maccabæan enthusiasm ought to have produced an appreciable effect on sacred poetry. But what I specially wish to bring home to the orthodox reader is this —that if, putting aside Ps. xviii., and possibly lines or verses imbedded here and there in later psalms (see pp. 108, 203, 205), the Psalter as a whole is post-Exilic, the Christian apologist of the nineteenth century has everything to gain. Take Ps. xvi. for instance. If this be pre-Exilic, nay even if it be an early post-Exilic work, it is impossible to find in it anticipations worth mentioning of Christianity, except indeed upon the hypothesis of a 'heaven-descended theology.' As Gruppe has well said,[1] ' Es liegt den älteren Sängern fern, das Unbegreifbare, oder wie man richtiger sagen würde, das Ungreifbare zu fassen.' But if Ps. xvi. falls within that part of the post-Exilic period when immortality began to take form as the highest hope of believers, how full of Christian significance does it become! I say this not without an effort, remember-

[1] *Griechische Culte und Mythen*, i. 221.

ing how violently Max Müller was attacked by a German philologist for finding traces of the hope of immortality in the Old Testament.¹ But the effort is more than compensated by the help which I have derived from my critical results as a Christian teacher. Throughout the Psalter indeed I have been able to draw a fulness of spiritual meaning from the Psalms which was impossible to me before, as I hope that my eleven Psalm-studies in the *Expositor* (1888–1890) prove.² But have you not, it may be asked, condescended unduly to the cravings of orthodoxy? I cannot see that I have. Orthodoxy and heterodoxy were alike far from my thoughts, nor did I at all anticipate these exegetical results. They are based not merely on literary criticism, but on a long and careful examination of the Old Testament in the light of Babylonian and (especially) Persian religion.³ For this I would diffidently ask the attention of students, as I have tried to fill up provisionally a lacuna in historical theology. It will be found that my conclusions are not those of most previous critics, and that they tend to diminish the amount of Hellenic and to increase that of Oriental influence on the Jews in the period which preceded Christianity. I have no antecedent prejudice myself against the view that Hellenic ideas and sentiments have filtered to some as yet uncertain extent into the New Testament (cf. p. 312), but I think that this infiltration, so far as it took place, was only possible because similar purely Oriental influences had gone before. Certainly I cannot join with Mr. Owen in the theory, derived apparently from M. Havet, that the Judaism

---

[1] Lehrs, essay on Greek ideas on the future life, *Aufsätze*, p. 303.

[2] These Studies represent as many cathedral sermons on the Psalms.

[3] I regret that I am no Zend and Pahlavi scholar, but I have at least practised caution. That we have among us such eminent specialists as Drs. Mills and West is a subject for much congratulation. What Dr. Mills has printed in the Supplementary Introduction to Vol. I. of his great work on the Gâthâs fully justifies the non-specialist in trusting his guidance. America and England may both claim a share in him. Dr. West, however, as a native English scholar, needs not my poor eulogy. For other authorities see pp. 395, 433–435.

amidst which Jesus Christ lived 'was already permeated by Hellenizing teaching.'[1] Nor even with such an eminent scholar as Professor Pfleiderer[2] in the view that 'Hellenic eschatology had probably influenced the general popular belief of the Jews in the time of Jesus through the channel of Essenism.'

The view which I have given of the development of the belief in immortality among the Jews appears to me to be strongly confirmed by the accepted results of scholarship respecting the parallel development in Greece. It is most interesting to trace upon the monuments how the gradual extension of the Hellenic cult of heroes converted immortality from an aristocratic into a popular possession.[3] A similar phenomenon is visible, as I think, in the Old Testament. At first only great men like Enoch, Elijah, and doubtless (see Isa. xxix. 22, 23, lxiii. 16, Jos., *Ant.* i. 13, 3) Abraham, Isaac, and Jacob, were regarded as the denizens of Paradise. But, partly through deeper religious thought and experience, and partly through Zoroastrian influence, what the ordinary man had formerly not dared to dream of, might become the assured hope of each believer. In the period of the Psalter there were no doubt differences of sentiment on the future lot of man; so there were also in Greece and in Egypt. But the road along which Jewish religion was henceforth to travel, was now definitely marked out. I trust that those parts of my book which deal with the history of religion will not be rejected by theological students. They will find many illustrations derived from ethnic religions, and contributions to a survey of Jewish thought down to the time of Christ.

---

[1] Review of Hatch's *Hibbert Lectures* (*Academy*, Dec. 13, 1890).

[2] *Philosophy of Religion*, iv. 162. I only refer to this statement (which the author would now probably alter) because of the deservedly wide circulation of the work in which it occurs.

[3] See Lehrs, *Aufsätze*, p. 337 &c.; Weil, review of Rohde's *Psyche*, *Journal des Savants*, Oct. 1890. Prof. Max Müller's third volume of *Gifford Lectures* will, I believe, deal with this subject.

Those interested in missions may also be invited to glean from these Lectures. When for instance our Oxford friends in Calcutta have again to oppose Mr. Dutt's statements on the indebtedness of Christianity to 'a Palestinian Buddhism,'[1] they may perhaps be assisted by my pages on the Essenes, which contain some fresh material. And to all students, whatever their special tastes may be, the Index will, I hope, reveal many interesting features of the book.

And so I bid farewell to a volume in which I have spoken more frankly, but I am sure not less considerately and charitably than ever. May it be blessed, in spite of its manifold imperfections, to the good of the Church at large! To me at any rate the exercise of the critical faculty and of the historic imagination has been as truly a religious work as joining in the worship of the sanctuary. I have found that to be true which an old Oxford friend has recently expressed in earnest words,—

All such research adds interest to the record, as it opens out to us the action of the Divine Intimacy, in laying hold of its material. We watch it by the aid of such criticism, at its work of assimilation; and, in uncovering its principles of selection, we apprehend its inner mind; we draw closer to our God.—(H. S. Holland, *Lux Mundi*, p. 43.)

[1] See *The Epiphany* (edited by the Oxford missionaries), Aug. 21, 1890.

CHRONOLOGICAL TABLE.

[N.B. On the chronological problems of this period, cf. Kuenen, *De chronologie van het Perzische tijdvak der Joodsche Geschiedenis* (Amsterdam, 1890), and Schürer, *The Jewish People in the Time of Christ*, Div. I., vol. i. (Edinburgh, 1890). Events in foreign history contemporary with those in Jewish are printed in italics.]

	B.C.
Captivity of Jehoiachin and Ezekiel	597
Fall of Jerusalem	586
First return of the Jews	536
Pythagoras	540–510
Foundation of second temple	535
Haggai and Zechariah prophesy, under Zerubbabel and Joshua (pp. 21, 52)	520
Capture of Babylon by Darius Hystaspis (p. 73)	520
Completion of second temple	515
Revolt of Egypt and Persian reconquest (cf. p. 52, foot)	486–484
Capture of Babylon by Xerxes (p. 73)	481
Artaxerxes I. Longimanus (p. 163)	465–425
Revolt of Inarus in Egypt	462–456
Second return of Jews under Ezra	458
Revolt of Megabyzus in Syria (p. 71)	448
Nehemiah the Tirshatha (p. 228)	445
Fortification of Jerusalem (pp. 50, 231, 232)	444
Artaxerxes II. Mnemon	405-359
Murder by Johanan the high priest; tyranny of Bagōses (p. 52)	383 (?)
Artaxerxes III. Ochus (captivity of Jews, pp. 53, 229)	359–338
Battle of Issus (Jaddua, high priest, p. 59)	333
Foundation of Alexandria (p. 10)	331
Ptolemy I. Soter, king of Egypt (Onias I., Simon I., high priests)	323–285
Capture of Jerusalem by Ptolemy	320
Ptolemy II. Philadelphus (Eleazar and Manasseh, high priests, p. 170)	285–247
Ptolemy III. Euergetes (Onias II., high priest, p. 127)	247–222
Antiochus III. Magnus, king of Syria (Simon II., high priest)	223-187
Capture of Jerusalem by Antiochus (cf. p. 114)	203
Seleucus IV. Philopator	187–175

CHRONOLOGICAL TABLE.

B.C.

Scopas recovers Jerusalem for Ptolemy V. Epiphanes, but is
   defeated by Antiochus at Paneas (p. 114) 199-198
Sacrilege of Heliodorus (p. 123) 187
Composition of Wisdom of Ben Sira in Hebrew . . . 180 (?)
Accession of Antiochus IV. Epiphanes (Onias III., high priest, p.
   123) 175
Onias III. deposed, and succeeded by Joshua or Jason . . . 174
Jason outbid and supplanted by Menelaus 171
Murder of Onias III. (pp. 123, 137) 170
Massacres of Antiochus and Apollonius at Jerusalem (p. 94) 170, 168
The 'abomination of desolation' (pp. 94, 105) set up . . 168 (Dec.)
Persecution of faithful Jews (pp. 19, 66); revolt under Mattathias
   (pp. 48, 57); the leader's death 167-166
Judas Maccabæus organizes his army with solemn prayer at Mizpah
   (pp. 18, 94); victory at Emmaus (pp. 94, 199) . . . 166-165
Victory at Beth-zur (p. 199); re-dedication of the temple (Dec.; see
   pp. 16-18, 33) 165
Composition of Book of Daniel, probably in Jan. (p. 94); successful
   war against the Edomites &c. (p. 98); *death of Antiochus
   Epiphanes* 164
Judas defeated at Beth-Zacharia (p. 92) 163-162
Alcimus (Jakim) appointed high priest (p. 27); his massacre of the
   Asidæans (pp. 56, 93) 162
Victory of Judas at Adasa (pp. 48, 178); his defeat and death at
   Eleasa (pp. 93, 96) 161
Death of Alcimus 160
Jonathan begins to rule from Michmash (p. 68) 158
Occupies Jerusalem, and is invested with the high priesthood (p. 68) 153
Destruction of Carthage by the Romans (p. 23) 146
Assassination of Jonathan, who is succeeded by Simon; capture of
   the citadel (p. 25); fortification of Jerusalem (p. 50) . . 142
Popular decree in favour of Simon and his family (p. 26) . . 141
Assassination of Simon, who is succeeded by John Hyrcanus (p. 24) 135
First appearance of parties called Pharisees and Sadducees (p. 39) 135 &c.
Translation of Wisdom of Ben Sira into Greek . . . . 132 (?)
Hyrcanus destroys Shechem and the temple on Gerizim, and con-
   quers the Edomites; his sons destroy Samaria (p. 96) . 109-108
Aristobulus I. assumes title of king (pp. 28, 39) 105
Alexander Jannæus (p. 24) 104-78
Salome Alexandra (p. 61); adopts a Pharisæan policy . . 78-69
Hyrcanus II. and Aristobulus II. refer their claims to Pompeius
   (pp. 143, 219); Jerusalem surrenders to the latter, who captures
   the temple and forces his way into the Most Holy Place . . 63
Battle of Pharsalia; death of Pompeius 48
Composition of Psalms of Solomon in Hebrew 63-48
Herod the Great 37-4

CONTENTS.

INTRODUCTION.

	PAGE
THE ORIGIN, CRITICAL BASIS, AND CONTENTS OF THESE LECTURES	ix

LECTURE I.

PART
I. THE PSALTERS WITHIN THE PSALTER 3
II. ANALYSIS OF BOOKS IV. AND V. 15

LECTURE II.

I. ANALYSIS OF BOOKS IV. AND V. CONTINUED . . . 47
II. CONCLUSION OF THE ANALYSIS 63

LECTURE III.

I. MACCABÆAN PSALMS IN BOOKS II. AND III. . . . 89
II. PSALMS OF THE PRE-MACCABÆAN GREEK AND OF THE PERSIAN PERIOD IN BOOKS II. AND III. . . . 112

LECTURE IV.

I. PSALMS LXXII., LXXIII., XLIX., L., ETC. 141
II. PSALMS LI., LXV.–LXVII., XLV., ETC. 161

LECTURE V.

I. THE EARLIEST OF THE MINOR PSALTERS 190
II. LARGER GROUPS OF PSALMS IN BOOK I. 226

LECTURE VI.

PART   PAGE
I. THE RELIGIOUS IDEAS OF THE PSALTER NOT BORROWED . 258
II. WHO IS THE GOD OF THE PSALTER? 285

LECTURE VII.

I. JEHOVAH'S SPHERE OF WORKING AND HIS AGENCIES . 312
II. HOW JEHOVAH WORKS, AND WITH WHAT RESULTS . . 338

LECTURE VIII.

I. HUMAN OBEDIENCE AND DIVINE LOVINGKINDNESS . . 363
II. RISE OF DOCTRINE OF JUDGMENT AFTER DEATH . . 381

APPENDICES.

APPENDIX
I. LAST WORDS ON MACCABÆAN PSALMS AND OTHER POINTS 455
II. THE LINGUISTIC AFFINITIES OF THE PSALMS . . . 461

INDICES 485

⁎ The reader will kindly remember that the numbering of the verses in references to the Old Testament is in accordance with the Hebrew Bible.

LECTURE I.

And they came into the house and saw the young child with Mary his mother; and they fell down and worshipped him; and opening their treasures they offered unto him gifts, gold and frankincense and myrrh.—Matt. ii. 11 (R.V.).

LECTURE I.

PART I.—Need of reform in that part of orthodox theology which relates to the Old Testament.—New facts have come and are coming to light, new critical results have been and are being obtained, which will contribute some essential elements to the new apologetic theology. Some of these arise out of the historical study of the Psalter. The criticism of the earlier Lectures will furnish a basis for the historico-theological outlines of the later ones.—The error of the older interpreters—their neglect of the Psalters within the Psalter.—How Carpzov opened the door to criticism; importance of the colophon, Ps. lxxii. 20.—We must argue backwards from the date of Books IV. and V. to that of any earlier groups of psalms.—Three strongly marked features of these books enable us to determine their period.—The argument leads up to the view that the collection of Books IV. and V. is contemporaneous with a reorganization of the temple music under Simon the Maccabee.

PART II.—Books IV. and V. must now be analyzed into groups.—Why such groups can be discovered here with special ease.—Are there any which require a Maccabæan date for their adequate explanation?—*A priori* historical reasons for expecting such.—Immediately available criteria of Maccabæan psalms.—Application of these to the three psalms which are most plausibly viewed as Maccabæan, viz., cxviii., cx., cxlix., and first to Ps. cxviii., the most striking psalm of the group (Pss. cxv.–cxviii.), which forms the second part of 'the Hallel.'—Both this psalm and the rest of the group shown to be Maccabæan; occasion of Ps. cxviii., the purification of the temple.—A fresh canon of criticism.—Theories of the origin of Ps. cx. examined.—The Maccabæan theory preferred.—The subject, Simon the Maccabee; see 1 Macc. xiv. 8–15, and for the impression produced by Simon's career, *Orac. Sib.* iii. 652–660.—The occasion, the capture of the Acra; comp. Ps. cx. 3.—Why 'the order of Melchizedek'?—An answer to the objections brought against the high priesthood of Simon.—Can Simon's eulogist have been inspired? A twofold answer: (1) Inspiration recognizes the limitations of human nature; (2) Ps. cx. is 'germinally Messianic,' and the indirect Messianic prediction which underlies the psalm was not based on illusion.

PART I.

THE PSALTERS WITHIN THE PSALTER.

MAY the spirit of these words sink into my mind, and so perfume with its fragrance every critical detail, that the youngest student may feel the Christian earnestness of these inquiries. There are some who tell us that criticism is without sympathies, and cares not to become interesting to those who have. For my own part, I think that sympathy is one condition of historical insight, and if I had no sympathy with that Old Testament religion, as the ripe fruit of which I regard primitive Christianity, I should know that my labours would be smitten with sterility. As for being interesting, that is an object which perhaps I may not always gain, but which I shall most assuredly continue to aim at. I have tried to take the step myself from knowing to imagining, and I shall endeavour to help others both to know more and to imagine better. With such principles, I invite you to-day into a far-off land, like that from which the Magi came, the land of Israel's religious antiquity. We will study the products of the soil, and gather such precious gifts as we can for Him to whom the star will point us. You will follow me sometimes at a distance, for I cannot put before you the whole of a complicated argument. Preserve your independence, but grant me at least the respect which belongs to a native English worker. A lost leader of old Oxford has told us how, after twenty years in a new spiritual climate, he felt no delicacy in speaking with some authority.[1] Those words I may venture to apply to myself. After more than twenty years of deepening experience of free Bible-study, I have earned a right to another title than that of 'Germanizer.' The

[1] Newman, *Difficulties felt by Anglicans*, p. 372.

phrase 'German criticism,' in the sense in which it is commonly used, is, indeed, scarcely accurate. Enthusiastic as one's regard must be for the past and present Biblical scholars of Germany, it remains true that Biblical science did not begin with them; nor can it, even in the Old Testament, be by them exhausted.

I have said that I would fain be interesting, and it is especially to churchmen in the widest sense, both in England and in America, that I make my appeal. Reforms in that part of orthodox theology which relates to the Old Testament are, as many think, urgent, for to neglect them would mean the unchecked progress of the great spiritual revolt. Will these reforms be ungrudgingly conceded? Gleams of hope have lately visited us in the English-speaking countries; but I am well aware of the remaining hindrances. Not yet have the workers sufficiently realized that the time for compromise on certain points is over,[1] and that you must not 'put a piece of new cloth upon an old garment.' Let us at least in Oxford not confound inconsistency with reverence, nor deny to Old Testament subjects the complete revision which they need. Let St. Paul be our model—St. Paul, that great reviser of exegesis, and yet steeped in reverence. The truths of the past, let us, like him, revere, but not its errors. Imposing enough were those errors in the past; St. Paul himself in the field of criticism could not but be subject to them. A poetic attractiveness they had, which ensured their supremacy, and the Christian ideas of which they were the vehicle gave them the semblance of truth. But by degrees religion has outgrown its shelter. Fancied knowledge respecting the Old Testament has been weighed in the balances and found wanting. The old house has fallen, and great has been the fall of it.

To us, teachers of historical theology, and cramped by no theory of the inspiration of books, younger students look for guidance in the seeming chaos.[a] They need first a true statement of the present position of criticism, and next an assignment of the share of work which belongs to them.

---

[1] The precise meaning of this qualification has been explained elsewhere (see Preface).

[a] For all notes referred to by *letters* see at end of the Part.

The chaos indeed is no longer absolute; it would be misleading to say that we are only now beginning to reconstruct. Sound results have already been obtained, which are definite enough to modify very largely our view of the Old Testament. These results must be popularized with wise discretion. But there are others which are only in course of being obtained, and the sufficient demonstration of which is still future. It is these which call for the renewed research of young scholars who have passed through a faithful apprenticeship. The genuine student has a large faith in the future. Historical truth is not 'like a sinking star,' and if we band ourselves together in manly modesty and in general agreement as to principles, we shall accomplish a serviceable though still imperfect reconstruction.

I think that this prospect ought to allure fresh labourers, and to revive the courage of the old. Our work ought to show by its brighter and more buoyant style the new and hopeful stage upon which we are entering. The false facts and mistaken inferences of the past should be brushed aside with a proper impatience. Dulness, conventionality, and repetition, are qualities out of date, now that the Hebrew Scriptures are fully recognized as a literature, and have taken their fitting place alone, yet not alone, at the head of the sacred books of the East.

To explore the recesses of this literature, so like and yet so unlike every other, in a free but sympathetic spirit, and show the importance of the results for the historical comprehension of our religion, would supply themes for a goodly company of Bampton lecturers. I have chosen the Psalter for myself, because the study of this book in England has hardly kept pace with that of the narrative books of the Old Testament. It is indeed a favourite with all classes; as many winged words from it have passed into common use as from any other part of the Scriptures. But it is only beginning to attract the attention of Bible-students, and the language in which St. Chrysostom stirs up the Christians of his own day to a more intelligent use of the Psalter is still but too applicable to ourselves.[1] It is surely no unworthy ambition to enable the English-speaking peoples to love and honour

---

[1] *Hom. in Ps. cxl. (cxli.).*

the Psalms not less heartily but more wisely and in a more historical spirit. Kay and Perowne in England and De Witt in America have prepared the way. Their admirable works have been little short of a revelation to many, though the 'quiet in the land' do not 'lift up their voice' and proclaim the treasure that they have found. I will not blame these silent friends of the Psalter, but may point out that the criticism and the exegesis not less than the translation of the Psalms need to be modernized. There is a growing and dangerous tendency of English Biblical critics to concentrate themselves upon the Pentateuch—dangerous, because they are not all sufficiently aware that their historical induction will be premature until they have included in its basis the facts supplied by the Psalter.[b]

The work before me, then, is twofold: firstly, critical and historical; secondly, exegetical and theological. A modernization of the study of the Psalter is needed in both these aspects, but more especially in the former. Dean Jackson, a luminary of the best age of Anglican theology, 'bewails the negligence of most interpreters in not inquiring into the occasion and authorship of the psalms.'[1] The complaint is even now more justified than one could wish. I hope that I do not undervalue an exegesis which, so far as it can, evades critical decisions, but such exegesis must be incomplete, and the view of the Old Testament to which it leads is neither a satisfactory nor an inspiring one. Let me then seek to furnish by criticism a solid basis for the historico-theological outlines which will conclude these lectures, and which will, as I hope, contribute some essential elements to the new apologetic theology.

I have remarked elsewhere that the Hebrew Psalter came together, not as a book, but as a Pentateuch.[2] In spite of this undoubted fact, a thick darkness settled down on the older interpreters, for want of a critical and analytic study of the Psalters within the Psalter. Hammond, for instance, the contemporary of Bishop Walton, after alluring us with a title referring to the Books of the Psalms, expects us to be contented with explanatory notes which do indeed incidentally indicate where each book begins and ends, but attach no

---

[1] *Works*, viii. 84.　　[2] *The Book of Psalms* (1888), Introd. p. xiii.

critical reflections to the notice. As Dr. Briggs truly says, 'One looks in vain in the commentaries of this period (the seventeenth century) for a critical discussion of literary questions.'[1] It is noteworthy, that this same Henry Hammond, who retains the fivefold division of the Psalms with utter unconsciousness of its critical significance, has no scruple in denying the unity of the book of Zechariah. You will remind me, of course, that he denies it, not as a critic, but as a theologian. He does so, and the same temper upon the whole pervades all the older expositors. Even Lowth, who did so much for opening the eyes of men to the literary character of the Old Testament, is still as uninterested in critical questions as his predecessors, and treats the Psalter simply as a lyrical anthology. And yet twenty years before Lowth delivered his famous lectures, a German professor, J. G. Carpzov, had discovered the historical importance of the colophon attached to Ps. lxxii., 'The prayers of David, son of Jesse, are ended,' of which even Calvin, the most modern of the Reformation expositors, so entirely misses the meaning.[2] In his *Introductio in Libros V. T.* (1721), part ii., p. 106, the first germ of the later Psalm-criticism appears. Carpzov there expresses the view that the Book of Psalms was brought into its present form by Ezra, but that Hezekiah had already made a smaller collection which contained Pss. i.–lxxii.^c This observation is destructive of the view that the Psalter is a chaotic anthology which, but for a reverential awe ('Wake not David from his slumbers,' said a Bath Qōl, or oracular echo[3]), its Jewish custodians might have been well pleased to rearrange.

This colophon or subscription in Ps. lxxii. 20 is the starting-point of my present inquiry into the origin of the Psalter. It shows convincingly that the Psalter as we have it was preceded by one or more minor Psalters. It shows this, and more than this. The colophon, 'The prayers of David, the son of Jesse, are ended,' must originally have been appended to a collection of psalms, each of which was headed *l'dāvīd*, i.e., written by David. We actually find a number of

---

[1] *Biblical Study, its Principles, Method, and History* (1883), p. 168.
[2] Cf. my *Commentary*, Introduction, p. xiv.
[3] *Midrash Tillin*, c. 27.

such poems in what is now the second Book of the Psalms. These poems, then, formed the collection; for it is most improbable that any psalms headed *l'dāvīd* were omitted by the editor. But the colophon now stands at the end of a psalm bearing the title *lish'lōmōh*, i.e., written by Solomon. How came it to be transferred thither? A reason is suggested by the case of the prophecy in Jer. l., li., the colophon of which, though it now stands at the end of *v.* 64, must once have stood at the end of *v.* 58. This is clear from the fact that the words, 'and they shall be weary,' which at present precede the colophon in *v.* 64, occur again at the end of *v.* 58, where alone they have a sense. That early scribe to whom the current text of Jeremiah is due, having accidentally omitted the subscription in its proper place, supplied it at the close of the brief appended narrative, taking with it a word (וַיִּעָפוּ), which stood in the same line with it in *v.* 58. The case may be similar with the colophon in Ps. lxxii. 20, which probably stands where it does by a clerical error, Ps. lxxii. being a late appendix to the Davidic hymn-book. The colophon is therefore a witness to the gradual enlargement of small psalm-collections. Is there anything else to mark Ps. lxxii. as the last member of a large group of psalms? Obviously there is—the blessing or doxology (*v.* 19). How, then, can we help assuming at least provisionally that the five books of the Psalter once constituted as many independent collections? I say, provisionally; because an inspection of Pss. cvi. and cvii. will presently suggest that Pss. xc.–cl. were divided into two books only by an afterthought.

It is to the fourth and fifth Books of the Psalter (which were originally but one Book) that I would first invite your attention. Book IV. contains two psalms, and Book V. fifteen, which are headed *l'dāvīd*. You will admit that there is a strong presumption that the collections which include these psalms were brought together subsequently to that which contains the great body of so-called Davidic psalms, or let us say, to Psalms i. (or iii.)–lxxii. Psalms attested by a comparatively old tradition as Davidic would not have had to wait for an official sanction. If, therefore, we can establish the period when these collections were respectively made, we shall be in a position to argue backwards to the date of any large or small earlier groups. Of these groups I shall have much to say; the psalms must be studied not merely singly but by groups, and the use of the comparative method will give our results greater definiteness and sureness. We have now to ask, Have Books IV. and V., taken as wholes, any strongly marked features which enable us to determine their date or dates? Yes; for instance (*a*) the paucity of authors' names, (*b*) the almost complete absence of musical phrases in the titles, and (*c*) the many distinct references to a congregational use of the psalms—characteristics which presuppose, the first that the psalms of Books IV. and V. are not much older than the collections themselves, the second that the temple music had undergone a radical change in (or near) the time of the collectors, and the third that while the temple services had become more precious than ever, the older psalms were found to be from a later point of view not in all points sufficiently adapted to congregational use.[1] We have therefore to study the long space of time between the Return from the Exile and the Septuagint translation of the psalms (say between 537 and the second half of the second century B.C.); does history suggest a period in which the stationary civilization of Judæa received such an impulse from without that the old music became intolerable to cultivated ears? I have as yet only mentioned external characteristics, but may now point to certain peculiar spiritual qualities of this part of the Psalter. Listen to the jubilant, sometimes even martial notes, of the psalmists, and observe how completely the old doubts of God's righteousness have died away. *Now* can we find the period? That of the Persian domination is out of the question; the severity of the Persian governors, the excessive taxation, and the passage through Palestine of army after army on its way to Egypt, so depressed the national spirit that any great impulse to civilization from the side of Persia is inconceivable. But who does not know the growing and persistent influence exerted upon the Jews by the Hellenic type of culture? I would not go so far as Mr. Flinders Petrie, who dates this influence from the Jewish migration in Jeremiah's time to the Græco-Egyptian frontier-

---

[1] See Lecture VI. Part I.

city of Tahpanhes or Daphnæ, and then, quoting the fiction by which Josephus[1] tries to save the verbal inspiration of Jeremiah, accounts for the Greek names of musical instruments in Daniel by Nebuchadrezzar's deportation of these partly Hellenized Jews to Babylonia.[2] But we may venture to say that both for the religion and for the civilization of the Jews the foundation of Alexandria, B.C. 331, was an event of the first importance. Whether or no we can trace a vague and indirect Greek influence upon the Book of Ecclesiastes, it is quite certain that Judaism, formerly as inhospitable and exclusive as Egypt itself, had, in the time of Ben Sira, been largely affected by the laxer and softer habits of Greek life.[3] That Greek music was known in Palestine very shortly after his time must be inferred from the Græco-Aramaic names of musical instruments in Daniel, of which Mr. Petrie has, as it would seem, so much exaggerated the antiquity. The date of Ben Sira's Wisdom may be set at about 180 B.C.; but from the picture of Jewish life in Josephus (*Ant.* xii. 5, 1) it is clear that a revolutionary movement in Judæa itself preceded the violent Hellenizing measures of Antiochus Epiphanes. This movement was not exclusively a paganizing one;[d] it was the result of the operation of new and subtle forces, from which there was no escape, and was powerfully aided by the foundation of Hellenistic towns in Palestine itself,[4] and by the friendly relations of the Jews both at home and in Egypt to the three first Ptolemies. The rash attempt of the fourth Antiochus to set up what we may almost call an anti-Messianic kingdom, with Zeus and not Jehovah as the supreme God, collapsed. Jehovah 'arose, like one out of sleep,' and set at nought 'the ungodly that forsook his law.' The desecrated and desolated sanctuary was (in 165 B.C.) purified and restored; and 'with songs and citherns, and harps and cymbals' the faithful Jews kept the feast of the dedication for eight days. This was the achievement of that noble champion, Judas the Maccabee. It was re-

---

[1] Jos., *Ant.* x. 9, 7.
[2] *Tanis*, part ii., pp. 49, 50. (Fourth Memoir of Pal. Explor. Fund.)
[3] Cheyne, *Job and Solomon*, p. 191.
[4] See Schürer, *The Jewish People in the Time of Jesus Christ*, Div. ii., vol. i., pp. 57–149.

served for Simon, the last of the five valiant brethren, to expel (in 142 B.C.) the Syrian garrison from 'the Acra,' that διάβολος πονηρὸς which had so long dominated the sanctuary. He entered it with the same rejoicings as at the dedication of the temple,[1] and 'ordained that that day should be kept every year with gladness' (1 Macc. xiii. 51, 52).

What would we not give for some precise information as to the character of the music at these festivals![e] Wide must have been its discrepancy from the temple-music of Nehemiah's time, just as this too must have differed from that of the pre-Exile period, and we may, nay we must, conjecture that not many years after the second of these festivals, the noble high priest and virtual king, Simon, devoted himself to the reconstitution of the temple psalmody. We know that he did not despise that Greek architecture which had begun to establish itself in Palestine;[f] and can we suppose that he would refuse already familiar 'musical harmonies' (Ecclus. xliv. 5), simply because they had some Greek affinities?

It was a great occasion, an epoch in the outer and inner history of Israel. What more natural than that Simon should follow the example of David his prototype, as described in Chronicles, and make fresh regulations for the liturgical services of the sanctuary? The prosaic narrator, who warms into poetry in telling of the prosperity of Israel under Simon, makes it the climax of his description that he 'made glorious the sanctuary, and multiplied the vessels of the temple' (1 Macc. xiv. 15). Is it likely that he beautified the exterior, and took no thought for the greatest of the spiritual glories of the temple—those 'praises of Israel' which Jehovah was well-pleased to 'inhabit'? If so, he had no feeling for that exquisite psalm which calls the ministers of the temple happy because 'they can be always praising' God (Ps. lxxxiv. 4). No; there cannot be another time so suitable for the editing of the two last books of the Psalter as this period of the Maccabæan history. We have no ancient record of it, and yet perhaps it is more deserving of credence than the story of the completion of the library of

---

[1] Comp. Spencer, *De Legibus Hebræorum*, ii. 1116.

national records by Judas in the untrustworthy second Book of Maccabees (2 Macc. ii. 14).

Our result is that Books IV. and V. of the Psalter received their present form soon after B.C. 142. Egyptian-Jewish pilgrims must quickly have carried it home to their brethren. For the synagogues at Alexandria, one of which rivalled the temple in its splendour,[1] and at least to some extent for the small and little-frequented sectarian temple of Onias at Leontopolis, a manual of sacred song was indispensable.[g] There may indeed have been an earlier version of the Psalter in its incomplete form, but not long after Simon's edition reached 'Israel in Egypt' it was probably put into a permanent Greek form with the title ὕμνοι[2] (=תְּהִלִּים) for the members of the metropolitan community. The date of this event cannot be fixed precisely, but it was at any rate (see p. 83) before the Christian era. Maccabæan psalms in the Septuagint Psalter are referred to both by Philo and by the translator of 1 Maccabees.[3]

NOTE a, p. 4.

'The chaos which at present reigns in Old Testament criticism' (article on 'The Present Desiderata of Theology,' *Expositor*, April 1890). From what point of view are these words written? Not from that of a worker in criticism. Destruction and reconstruction have ever gone side by side. 'The inspiration of the Bible.' In what sense is this phrase used? The Church says, 'I believe in the Holy Ghost . . . who spake by the prophets.'

NOTE b, p. 6.

I shall therefore avoid such arguments as imply the post-Exile origin of the 'priestly code,' though I fully agree with Prof. Robertson Smith that 'a just view of the sequence and dates of the several parts of the Pentateuch is essential to the historical study of Hebrew religion' (*Religion of the Semites*, p. 198).

---

[1] *Succa*, 51b (Wünsche, *Der bab. Talmud*, i. 398). Josephus might well have called this synagogue ἱερὸν, like that at Antioch (*War*, vii. 3, 3).

[2] See Ps. lxxi. 20 Sept., and comp. references to Philo in Hatch, *Essays in Biblical Greek*, p. 174. Josephus, too, describes the Psalms as ὕμνοι εἰς Θεὸν, and the Levites as ὑμνῳδοί (*Ant.* xx. 9, 6).

[3] The references to the Sept. Psalter in the Greek Sirach produced by Ehrt (*Abfassungszeit*, &c., p 128) will not bear examination. See Appendix I.

Note c, p. 7.

As soon, says Carpzov, as an inspired writer composed a psalm, his autograph copy was placed in the 'tabularia' of the temple among the sacred rolls. The frequent recitation of these psalms in the services imprinted them on the memory of the faithful, and, either from memory or from the copies possessed by the Levites, they were written down for the general use. 'Hinc factum est, ut jam Ezechiæ regis tempore psalmorum aliqua prostaret collectio, ut ex 2 Chron. xxix. 30, necnon ex citatis Davidis verbis Jes. xxxviii. 18, Jer. xvii. 7, 8, apparet: quam crediderim privatâ operâ factam, et Ps. lxxii. obsignatam fuisse. Unde clausulâ subjunctâ, "Completæ sunt orationes David, filii Isai:" eæ nimirum, quæ collectori ad manus fuerunt, et quarum sylloge tunc temporis vulgo in populo obtinebat.' But, he thinks, besides these there were other psalms, which were sung, though more rarely, in the church, and that 'the men of Hezekiah' (Prov. xxv. 1) completed the original roll by adding these. This roll, or, it may be, these rolls, were carried to Babylon, and when Ezra restored the temple-worship, and, 'divino nutu,' arranged the Old Testament canon, he edited and finally completed the Psalter by adding some more inspired psalms, including many of David's. He adds, however, the unfortunate suggestion ('nisi forte velis') that the subscription in Ps. lxxii. 19 may refer to the close, not of the book, but of the life of David (cf. 2 Sam. xxiii. 1).

Note d, p. 10.

Freudenthal (*Alexander Polyhistor*, Breslau, 1875, p. 128) puts this very forcibly, but his theory of the date and country of the Jewish writer Eupolemos (accepted by Schürer) has been shaken by the criticisms of Grätz (*Gesch. der Juden*, iii., ed. 4, p. 603).

Note e, p. 11.

Comp. Ecclus. l. 18. I do not deny that the primitive Hebrew music may have survived in some popular religious rites, just as Gobineau assures us that primitive Asiatic music has survived in the ceremonies of the Persian Passion Play.

Note f, p. 11.

Grätz ascribes the erection of the Maccabæan family monument at Modin to John Hyrcanus (*Gesch. der Juden*, iii., ed. 4, p. 81). This, however, is contrary to the positive assertion of the authorities

(1 Macc. xiii. 27-30; Jos., *Ant.* xiii. 6, 5). That the style of the architecture was Greek, is certain, though no traces of the monument have yet been found at Khirbet-el-Mediyeh (the site of Modin). But as early as B.C. 176 we have a monument of naturalized Greek art, erected by a Jewish priest, the colossal remains of which still exist in a trans-Jordanic wâdy ('Arâq-el-Emîr). Grätz's objection that Simon would not have erected a pyramid for himself is answered by a reference to the common practice of Oriental monarchs and grandees.

NOTE g, p. 12.

It may be objected that there is no evidence that psalmody formed part of the public worship in the early synagogues (cf. Gibson, *Expositor*, July 1890, pp. 25-27). But they were at any rate 'prayer-houses' like the temple (Isa. lvi. 7), and I can with difficulty believe that prayer did not include praise (cf. Ps. xlii. 9, Hab. iii. 1): especially as the missionary psalms contain passages specially appropriate to the Diaspora. See further p. 363.

On the history of the temple of Onias (the site of which, as Brugsch and Naville agree, is Tell-el-Yehûdîeh) see Herzfeld, *Gesch. des Volkes Jisrael*, iii. 463; Jost, *Gesch. des Judenthums*, i. 116-120. The temple appealed originally to those who valued the legal sacrifices, but felt a horror at the corruption of the high priestly family just before the Maccabæan times. Philo does not mention it; no wonder, for he was a spiritualizer. 'God,' he said, 'delights in fireless altars.'

PART II.

ANALYSIS OF BOOKS IV. AND V.

LET us now proceed to analyze these two books with a view to determining the date of the groups of psalms which they contain, most of which of course need not be as late as the period of the editors. It is an easy process, because, as Ewald remarks, this collection, being the latest, has undergone fewer changes than the others, and the strata of which it is composed are almost palpably visible. The first question is, Are there any groups of psalms which are most easily explained on the theory of a Maccabæan origin? There are strong reasons for expecting to find such. Consider the greatness of the Maccabæan period, more keenly felt by none than by the writers of the Book of Daniel and the Epistle to the Hebrews.[a] It is indeed morally so great that even if no psalms, probably Maccabæan, had been preserved, we should be compelled to presume that they once *had* existed. If there were psalmists in the age of Pompey (63–48 B.C.), when the stimulus given by Mattathias and his sons was waxing feeble,[b] how should there not have been in the age of these heroes themselves? Prophetic and poetic inspiration being closely connected in primitive times prophetic psalm-writing was a common phenomenon both in the Jewish and in the early Christian Church.[c] If apocalypse the child of prophecy, began so nobly in the Maccabæan Book of Daniel, how can the same spirit of world-subduing faith have failed to find a worthy expression in spiritual song? These considerations, I think, justify the provisional acceptance of a Maccabæan date for those psalms in the fourth and fifth Books which, upon exegetical grounds, seem to require it. The non-exegetical arguments against Maccabæan psalms will be considered in connexion with certain disputed psalms in Books II. and III. What, then, for our present purpose will be the criteria of Maccabæan psalms? I should not lay any great stress on the linguistic criteria, nor can I in this place attempt to indicate them.[d] But this we may and must require—that in typical Maccabæan psalms there should be some fairly distinct allusions to Maccabæan circumstances; I mean expressions which lose half their meaning when interpreted of other times.[e] And, above all, we expect to find an uniquely strong church feeling, an intensity of monotheistic faith, and in the later psalms an ardour of gratitude for some unexampled stepping forth of the one Lord Jehovah into history. We can hardly err in supposing that tests like these were applied by that keenest of the patristic expositors, Theodore of Mopsuestia, in determining his Maccabæan psalms Let me in passing pay a tribute of admiration to the extraordinary genius which at so early an age outstripped all his predecessors.[f]

But we must now seek to apply these criteria for ourselves to one of the more promising psalms—the 118th. The historical background is here singularly definite. Jehovah has interposed; he has avenged the death of his חֲסִידִים; he has put down the idol-gods and their worshippers; friendless Israel has proved too strong for the whole world in arms. The psalm has been written to commemorate this great fact, and to be sung antiphonally in the name of the church by worshippers and by Levites. I know that several great events in the history of the Jewish Church have been thought of—e.g., the erection of the altar of burnt-offering at the feast of Tabernacles in B.C. 536,[1] or the foundation of the second temple in B.C. 535,[2] or the dedication of the same temple when finished in B.C. 515.[3] But neither of the two former can be the occasion, if only because the temple is referred to by the psalmist as completed; nor is the exuberant spirit of independence and martial ardour in the psalm in harmony with the third. But the purification and reconsecration of the temple by Judas the Maccabee in B.C. 165[4] is fully adequate to explain alike the tone and the expressions of this festal song.[g] Read it in the light of this

---

[1] Ezra iii. 1–6; so Ewald. [2] Ezra iii. 8–13; so Hengstenberg.
[3] Ezra vi. 15–18; so Delitzsch. [4] 1 Macc. iv. 37–59, 2 Macc. x. 1–7.

event, and especially *vv.* 10–12, 15–16, 21–22, and 26. Need I show how that thrice repeated refrain, 'In Jehovah's name will I mow them down' (Bruston, 'je les massacre') suits the character of the terrible hero Judas? The rendering 'will I mow them down' supposes an allusion to the 'grass which is cut down and withereth.' If, however, with strict adherence to usage, we were to render 'will I circumcise them,' we should have a very striking paronomasia, closely akin to St. Paul's βλέπετε τὴν κατατομήν (Phil. iii. 2). It is no doubt a meaning too painful to be that intended by the editor, but the original writer may, in Oriental style, have had two meanings in his mind, one for the moment, the other to be brought forth in quieter times. Or need I comment at length on that second triple burden, 'The right hand of Jehovah doeth valiantly, is exalted, doeth valiantly'?[h]—or do more than refer (on *v.* 21) to the prayer of Judas (1 Macc. iv. 30–33) when he saw the Græco-Syrian army at Beth-zur, before that great victory which opened to him the way to Jerusalem?

But I must pause a moment at *v.* 22. Does the 'stone' mean Israel which had, to the surprise of all men, again become conspicuous in the organization of peoples? Or—for this large application of the figure of the building implies too much reflection—may it not have a more special reference to the Asmonæan family, once lightly esteemed, but now to become recognized more and more as the chief corner-stone?[1] Nor can I leave *v.* 27 unexplained; every line of it is significant. 'Jehovah (not Zeus) is God; light hath he given us.' May not this allude to the illumination which gave rise to the second name[j] of the Dedication Festival ('the Lights'), a name which Josephus regards as a symbol of unexpected deliverance[k] (*Ant.* xii. 7, 7)? 'Bind the procession with branches,' the verse, if I understand the obscure words aright, continues, '(step on) to the altar-horns.' True, we cannot tell how the ancient people celebrated its autumn festival; but we do know that solemn processional circuits of the altar were made in the later periods, the priests repeating meanwhile the 25th verse of our psalm. Can we doubt that the same rite was practised in earlier times, and that, as in other cases, the meagre rules in Leviticus should be read by the light of later custom? Ps. cxviii., then (unlike Ps. xxx.), was from the first used as a Dedication hymn. Once more the pipe and the harp were heard in Israel, and this was one of the first strains which reawakened their melody (comp. 1 Macc. iii. 45, iv. 54). I wish that we could at once proceed to study Ps. lxxix., which there is good reason to place in the year before the glorious Dedication. Permit me at least to whet your appetite by quoting from a Jewish poetess who has finely contrasted the scenes in which, as I think, Pss. lxxix. and cxviii. respectively arose:—

> They who had camped within the mountain-pass,
>   Couched on the rock, and tented 'neath the sky,
> Who saw from Mizpah's heights the tangled grass
>   Choke the wide Temple-courts, the altar lie
> Disfigured and polluted—who had flung
>   Their faces on the stones, and mourned aloud,
> And rent their garments, wailing with one tongue,
>   Crushed as a wind-swept bed of reeds is bowed,
>
> Even they, by one voice fired, one heart of flame,
>   Though broken reeds, had risen, and were men;
> They rushed upon the spoiler and o'ercame,
>   Each arm for freedom had the strength of ten.
> Now is their mourning into dancing turned,
>   Their sackcloth doffed for garments of delight;
> Week-long the festive torches shall be burned,
>   Music and revelry wed day with night.[1]

It was with the best of reasons, then, that Ps. cxviii. (as a part of the Hallel,[m] i.e. Pss. cxiii.–cxviii.), though chanted on single days at other festivals, was appointed to be sung on the eight successive days of the Feasts of Tabernacles and of the Dedication.[n] Let us now approach the other members of the second part of the Hallel, and ask, Have they the same historical background as Ps. cxviii.? It cannot be said that either Ps. cxv. or Ps. cxvi., still less that the minute 117th psalm, by itself compels an affirmative answer. But all these come to us from the Church of the Second Temple as members of the same group, or subdivision of a group, as Ps. cxviii., and it is a canon of criticism that when certain psalms,

---

[1] Emma Lazarus, 'The Feast of Lights.'

all of which agree in some leading features, and positively disagree in none, have come to us from ancient times in one group, we are bound to assign them to the same period, though it is only in one instance that we can from internal evidence speak positively as to the date.º And who can deny that the death of the *khasīdīm* ᵖ ('pious ones') spoken of in cxvi. 15 forcibly reminds us of the Syrian persecution? or that the threefold division of the faithful in cxv. 9–13 suggests that the psalm proceeded from the same circle as cxviii. 2–4? ᵍ A truce then to the inconclusive vagueness of De Wette and Hupfeld. Pss. cxv., cxvi., and probably cxvii. (the liturgical introduction to Ps. cxviii.) are Maccabæan, and the historian is justified in using them to give colour to his narrative. Only we may, without violating our canon, assign them to a somewhat later year and a different author. The tone is quieter; the devotional spirit purer and more tender. And yet Ps. cxv., though not the work of a Tyrtæus, may well have been a battle-song of the Ἀσιδαῖοι or *khasīdīm*, just as it was that of the heroic John Sobieski, King of Poland, in 1683, when the tide of Mohammedan invasion was for ever turned back; nor was it perhaps wholly unjustified when Cromwell and his army sang Ps. cxvii. after winning the fight of Dunbar in 1650.¹ 'Not unto us, Jehovah, not unto us,' is surely the very tone of a whole-hearted religious warrior, and the assured conviction of the psalmist in cxvi. 9, 'I shall walk before Jehovah in the lands of the living,' is but another form of the thought expressed in cxviii. 17, 'I shall not die, but live, and declare the works of Jehovah.' For what object could true Israelites have in speeding from land to land but to declare the deeds of the living God, and, in the words of Ps. cxvii., to summon all nations to praise that loving-kindness and truth which are mighty over all, of whatever race, who are 'fearers of Jehovah' (Ps. cxv. 13), and, in the widest sense of the word, proselytes? And before I pass on let me remark that for the Christian Feast of Lights ʳ in all its varied significance, this would be an appropriate group of psalms, if we might interpret the too violent expressions of religious zeal in Ps. cxviii. by the chastened, charitable utterances of Ps. cxvii.

¹ See Harrison, *Oliver Cromwell* (1888), p. 157.

There are two other psalms which have been not less frequently and positively referred to the Maccabæan times—the 110th and the 149th. The difficulty of the former arises from its brevity and obscurity,[1] which are specially remarkable in a temple-song (for such the work is, although in form a mixture of prophetic oracle and encomium). If critical questions could be decided by votes, we should have to allow that at any rate this psalm belonged to the Davidic age.[s] By some strange accident, comparable to that by which the Moabite Stone was only discovered twenty years ago, this Davidic poem waited (it would seem) for a public recognition till (probably) after the Return from the Exile![t] Well, let us admit that this is not absolutely beyond the limits of possibility. When and by whom can it have been written? By a court-poet, it is said, as a glorification of David, who, by transferring the ark to Mount Zion, had become a true successor to the ancient Melchizedek.[u] We are reminded that two striking features of the picture here presented to us recur in 2 Sam. vi. That narrative states that, before fetching the ark to Kirjath-Jearim, 'David gathered together all the chosen men of Israel' (2 Sam. vi. 1; compare Ps. cx. 3), and that he afterwards performed priestly acts, leading in the sacred dance, offering sacrifices, girt with a linen ephod, and blessing the people in the most sacred of names (2 Sam. vi. 13, 14, 17, 18). Believe this who can! Where in the psalm are the ark, the dance, the ephod spoken of? Where is the name Jehovah [Yahveh] Sabaoth (see p. 203)? And where does the historical narrative refer to the tithes which have such a prominent place in the story of Melchizedek? Besides, granting that the establishment of the ark upon Mount Zion strengthened David's hold upon the priesthood,[2] he did not then become a priest for the first time. State and religion being to Orientals identical conceptions, the regal dignity was originally inseparable from the sacerdotal. Saul, David, Solomon, and the kings of Israel and Judah, Sennacherib, Assurbanipal, and Nebuchadrezzar—none of them would have craved the divine permission to assume the title of priest. Why, even David's sons could be styled priests

---

[1] On the obscure second half of *v.* 3 see linguistic appendix.
[2] See Wellhausen, *Prolegomena*, p. 136.

(2 Sam. viii. 18); much more the king himself. If the preceding verses had referred to the erection of the temple, one could understand such an oracle in *v*. 4 as, 'Thou shalt continue my priest for ever;' it is just such a context which introduces the prayer of Tiglath-Pileser I., that Anu and Rammân 'would establish his priesthood for the future like the mountains faithfully.'[1] There would in this case be a reason for the use of the title 'priest,' which is wanting on the hypothesis that David is the hero of the psalm. But no one, I fear, claims the psalm for Solomon.

We must next examine the second view, viz., that Ps. cx. was written in the age of Zerubbabel [v] with reference to the Messiah regarded as priest and king in one. The view is based upon Zech. vi. 9–13. We are there told that three Babylonian Jews had come with a present of silver and gold to the struggling community at Jerusalem. This appeared to Zechariah like a first fulfilment of anticipations such as those of Haggai (ii. 7) that 'the desirable things of all nations should come.' A prophetic impulse stirred him to receive it, and make it into crowns, and to place these (according to the received text) on the head of Joshua the high priest, in order, as St. Cyril long ago explained,[2] to typify Him who as God was king, and as man was high priest. This interpretation is retained even by Delitzsch,[3] except with regard to the divinity of the Messiah, which Zechariah cannot be supposed to have held. Yet, though, following Riehm, I once held this view in a modified form, I must admit that it is critically untenable. The concluding words of Zech. vi. 13, 'and there shall be a priest upon his throne [or, as the Septuagint has, 'at his right hand'], and the counsel of peace shall be between them both,' prove that in the original form of the prophecy two persons were mentioned, each of whom was to be crowned, viz., Joshua with the silver, and Zerubbabel with the gold crown. As Ewald has shown, there can be no doubt that in *v*. 11 we should read, 'upon the head of Zerubbabel and upon the head of Joshua,'[w] and

---

[1] Prism-inscription, col. viii., lines 32–38 (Winckler, in *Keilinschriftliche Bibliothek*, i. 45).

[2] *In Aggæum*, 638 *a*.

[3] *Messianic Prophecy* (1880), p. 98.

with this correction the only proof-passage for the idea of a Messiah-Priest in the Old Testament falls away.[x] Consequently Ps. cx. does not belong to the age of the prophet Zechariah. (Observe in passing that in Zerubbabel's time it was a perfect Davidic king who was looked for—the prophets even thought of Zerubbabel himself;[y] in the Maccabæan times, a trustworthy prophet.[1] In the reign of Hyrcanus, when the Pharisees became unfriendly to the Asmonæan house,[2] it is intelligible enough that the hope of the Davidic Messiah should have revived.[3])

The third view places this strange psalm in the Maccabæan times, which the writer regards as germinally Messianic. The hope of the Messiah may have flourished most in Egypt,[z] but it had not died out (how could it have done so, while the Scriptures were studied?) even in Palestine. The Asmonæan family will, as the psalmist believes, furnish a line of Messianic princes, whose victories will become more and more splendid till they correspond to the grand description in Ps. ii. The accession of one of these had in fact just then awakened all the writer's latent enthusiasm. It seemed as if the 'sure lovingkindnesses of David' (Isa. lv. 3 [aa]) were about to be fulfilled in no scanty measure. Can we be surprised at this, or call it a wild idea that in Judas and his heroic brethren the 'darling of Israel's songs' (2 Sam. xxiii. 1 ?) had come to life again? It has indeed been asserted by a Jewish historian that the leaders of Israel during this period were sober-minded and put a severe restraint on their imagination. He cannnot deny that in the story of the liberation reference is often made to hymns of praise, but supposes that none but old hymns rose to the freedmen's lips! In spite of historical analogies we are asked to believe that there were no Maccabæan psalmists! I do not stand alone in characterizing this view as untenable in the face of the 118th psalm. And even though some parts of this song may seem to favour the Jewish critic's view, yet we have a right to expect that other works will not only in part but altogether point in an opposite direction, and give unqualified witness to a lofty and unmixed enthusiasm.

[1] See 1 Macc. iv. 46, xiv. 41.
[2] Jos., *Ant.* xiii. 10, 5; cf. Targ. Deut. xxxiii. 11.
[3] See Book of Enoch.

Listen, then, to an Israelite who 'has consented to sing in a strange land one of the songs of Zion.'[1] We must not, in our reaction against 'Teste David cum Sibyllâ,' be too severe upon him for assuming the character of a Sibyl. He does but express his belief in that spirit of prophecy which is not confined to the people of Israel, but which cannot anywhere express hopes or ideas at variance with those of God's firstborn son. He is no 'fanatic,' but an 'earnest and courageous missionary.'[bb]

Καὶ τότ᾽ ἀπ᾽ ἠελίοιο[cc] Θεὸς πέμψει βασιλῆα,
Ὅς πᾶσαν γαῖαν παύσει πολέμοιο κακοῖο,
Οὓς μὲν ἄρα κτείνας, οἷς δ᾽ ὅρκια πιστὰ τελέσσας.[dd]
Οὐδέ γε ταῖς ἰδίαις βουλαῖς τάδε πάντα ποιήσει,
Ἀλλὰ Θεοῦ μεγάλοιο πιθήσας δόγμασιν ἐσθλοῖς.[ee]
Λαὸς δ᾽ αὖ μεγάλοιο Θεοῦ περικαλλέϊ πλούτῳ
Βεβριθὼς, χρυσῷ τε καὶ ἀργύρῳ, ἠδέ τε κόσμῳ
Πορφυρέῳ·[2] καὶ γαῖα τελεσφόρος, ἠδὲ θάλασσα
Τῶν ἀγαθῶν πλήθουσα.—*Orac. Sibyll.* iii. 652–660.

And now consider these two points. (1) It has been proved by Hilgenfeld that the quasi-prophetic description which precedes carries us down to the conquest of Greece and the destruction of Carthage by the Romans in 146 B.C., and the seizure of the Syrian throne by the usurper Tryphon in 142 B.C. (2) Just before the latter event Simon the Maccabee succeeded his brother Jonathan. A passage in 1 Macc. xiv., probably derived in part from an old song, shows us how the strange good fortune of his rule stirred the imagination of Judæan writers. Here are some verses from it:—

'And they tilled their ground in peace, and the earth gave her increase, and the trees of the field their fruit. The elders sat in the broad places; they all communed of good things, and the young men put on glorious robes and warlike apparel. He furnished provisions for the cities, and equipped them with means of defence, so that his honourable name was renowned unto the end of the earth. He made peace in the land, and Israel rejoiced with great joy. . . . . . And

---

[1] Drummond, *Philo Judæus*, i. 170.
[2] Comp. 1 Macc. xiv. 9, 43 (Simon's dress; cf. xi. 58).

none was left in the land to fight against them, and the kings were crushed in those days' (*vv.* 8–11, 13).

What more natural than that Egyptian-Jewish writers should follow suit, and that the Sibyl should regard this as the opening of a brief Messianic period, too soon to be followed by the worst troubles which could come upon the human race? It is unimportant to decide whether or no Simon himself is the 'king' referred to.^{ff} If he is, the poetic exaggeration consists, not so much in the use of the title 'king' (see on Pss. xx., xxi.) as in the world-wide influence ascribed to Simon, and it has a superficial resemblance to the idealizing language of Ps. cx. 5–7. If he is not, we may yet suppose, with Dr. Drummond, that the details of the Sibyl's description were suggested by the career of Simon. So that this Egyptian Jew is in any case a witness to the deep impression produced by the last great Maccabee.^{gg}

With still greater confidence, however, can we refer to Ps. cx., as in the fullest sense a glorification of Simon. The poet implies, but does not expressly state, that his hero is about to assume regal authority. Does not this fully correspond to the historical position of Simon? He did not, of course, claim the title of king;[1] but he lacked nothing of the dignity but the name. Syria claimed no authority over him; without asking leave of his nominal overlord he struck coins, and collected armies, and from his accession the Jewish people dated the era of its independence.^{hh} Who else can be meant but Simon? Alexander Jannæus was, no doubt, the first Asmonæan king recognized as such on the coins,ⁱⁱ but he was totally unworthy of a religious poet's encomium. More plausible is the claim (put forward in his first edition by De Wette) in favour of Simon's son, Johanan or John Hyrcanus (B.C. 135–105),^{jj} who may be said to have consolidated the second Israelitish empire. How he struck his contemporaries may be seen from the Book of Enoch, which represents him symbolically as a 'great horn,' his predecessors being smaller horns (xc. 9). Three privileges, says Josephus, were divinely accorded to him, the government of his nation, the dignity of the high priesthood, and prophecy.[2] Those

---

[1] See, however, on Pss. xx., xxi. (Lect. V.).
[2] Jos., *Ant.* xiii. 10, 7, *War*, i. 2, 8.

who would reduce Ps. cx. to the rank of a party pamphlet, might plausibly ascribe it to some Sadducæan writer, who wished to contradict the taunts cast by the Pharisees at Hyrcanus,[kk] by giving a lyric form to one of his master's older prophecies. Against this view, however, it may be urged— (1) that this enmity of the Pharisees towards Hyrcanus arose in the latter part of his rule, whereas this psalm is evidently, like Ps. xlv., addressed to a ruler who has recently come to the throne; (2) that the first part of Hyrcanus's reign was not marked by success; and (3) that the predictions which are ascribed to him were doubtless, like that of Caiaphas (John xi. 51), official oracles, and presupposed the dignity which in Ps. cx. 4 is conferred upon the hero of the psalm. And so we are driven back to the view that the psalm is an encomium upon Simon, who, by the capture of the Acra and the expulsion of its garrison (May 142),[ll] had completed the liberation of Jerusalem, and rendered it possible for a psalmist to say, 'All eagerness are thy people in the day of thy muster upon the sacred mountains' (Ps. cx. 3).

It was a great turning-point of history—the surrender of the Syrian garrison in the Acra. Hitherto, the legend upon Simon's coins, 'Jerusalem the Holy,' had seemed only half-true (for 'holy,' as the corresponding legend on Tyrian coins [mm] proves, signifies 'sacrosanct, inviolable'). But now, the sacred precincts being no longer overlooked by the proud heathen, it seemed like an initial fulfilment of the great prophecy in Joel iii. 17.

The prophetic order was still indeed painfully missed,[nn] but passing gleams of prophecy were not withheld, and the ancient oracles were manifestly receiving a most unthought-of fulfilment (cf. Ecclus. xxxvi. 15, 16).[oo] Jehovah had 'arisen into his resting-place,' had 'clothed his priests with salvation,' and had, at least in a symbolic or typical sense, 'made a horn to shoot forth unto David' (Ps. cxxxii. 8, 16, 17).[pp] Does any one object to my supposition of a symbolic or typical interpretation thus early? But, not to adduce other evidence,[1] did not the psalmist himself interpret 'Melchizedek' typologically, and without adopting such a principle how could the pattern Israelite have 'meditated on God's law day and

---

[1] See the Books of Daniel and Judith.

night' (Ps. i. 2)? 'David' then had become for that generation the type of a righteous and successful king, and a psalmist in quasi-prophetic rapture could thus address the Maccabæan prince, whose symbol was Aaron's rod that budded, 'Thy mighty rod (or sceptre) doth Jehovah stretch forth from Zion, (saying,) Have sway in thine enemies' midst' (Ps. cx. 2).

In truth, it was from Zion that the high priest now began to stretch forth his sceptre. No sooner had the sound of the joyous psalmody[qq] died away, than Simon resolved to raze the Acra and cut away the very steep on which it stood, so that henceforth Zion, instead of the Acra, became the citadel of Jerusalem (Jos., *Ant.* xiii. 6, 7). 'Moreover, the hill of the temple that was by the Acra he made stronger than before, and there he dwelt himself with all his company' (1 Macc. xiii. 52). It was, perhaps, while this great work was in progress that a popular decree was carried in favour of Simon, which throws fresh light on the 110th psalm. It will be found translated with substantial accuracy in 1 Macc. xiv. 27–46.[rr] After detailing the eminent services of Simon, and mentioning that the people had already made him their ruler (ἡγούμενον) and high priest,[ss] it continues thus: 'And it pleased well the Jews and the priests that Simon should be their ruler and high priest for ever (εἰς τὸν αἰῶνα), or at least[tt] until there should arise a trustworthy prophet' (capable of deciding doubtful points, like Elijah). The historian states in conclusion (*v.* 47) that 'Simon accepted this dignity, and was well pleased to be high priest and general (שַׂר) and ethnarch (possibly נָשִׂיא[uu]) of the Jews and priests, and to stand before all.' Can we doubt that the enthusiasm which prompted this decree would further express itself in song? and can we fail to hear an echo of the language of the record in the psalmist's words, 'Thou art a priest for ever'?

And what of the words which follow, 'after the manner of Melchizedek'? Can we illustrate them from the literature of this and the subsequent period? We can. In the so-called letter of Cæsar Augustus in Jos., *Ant.* xvi. 6, 2, Hyrcanus II. is called ἀρχιερεὺς τοῦ ὑψίστου Θεοῦ,[vv] and in the book called 'The Assumption of Moses' (dating from about the beginning of the Christian era), the Maccabæan princes are referred to as 'priests of the most High God' (vi. 17).[ww] This was in fact long the usual title of the ruling prince in letters of divorce and similar legal documents, according to an old Talmudic tradition. Now remember that Melchizedek, 'king of righteousness,'[xx] is called in Gen. xiv. 18, כֹּהֵן לְאֵל עֶלְיוֹן 'priest of God most High,' and can you not see the connexion of ideas? The favourite title of Jehovah in the later period is precisely this — אֵל עֶלְיוֹן,[1] and one of the accounts of the patriarchs [yy] associated this title with the ancient priest-king of Salem. What more natural than to take this righteous and religious personage as the type of another priest-king of Salem, whose conception of God was expressed in the same venerable phrase? It is in fact incredible that Philo should have been the first to reflect on the higher meaning of מַלְכִּי־צֶדֶק and אֵל עֶלְיוֹן.[2]

There was, moreover, a special reason why the thoughts of our psalmist should have been directed to this point. Alcimus, who 'struggled' against Judas for the much-coveted prize of the high priesthood (1 Macc. vii.), had really a far better claim to it, legally, than his rival, being a direct descendant of Zadok; whereas Judas belonged to one of the ordinary priestly families. Accordingly, Alcimus's pretensions were at first favoured by the party of *khasīdīm*, or strict legalists (1 Macc. vii. 14), who were only brought to recognize Judas as not merely a general, but a possible high priest, by the wicked massacre of their too trustful leaders (see on Ps. lxxix.). Our psalmist justifies the popular decree in favour of Simon,[zz] and meets the objections of any still doubtful *khasīdīm*, by showing that Simon, though a 'stone which the builders had refused,' was a high priest of a better order than that of Zadok. Melchizedek himself was his pattern, and that not only outwardly but inwardly. Proudly but truly said the greatest of Babylonian kings,[3] 'I am Nebuchadrezzar, king of righteousness' (*šar mišari*). It remained for Simon to prove that he too deserved this noblest of names. And he

---

[1] See my note on Ps. vii. 18.

[2] *De Leg. Alleg.* iii. 25, 26 (i. 102, 103). Notice in passing how much deeper is the allegory of Melchizedek in Heb. vii. 1-10.

[3] In the opening of the Phillipps Cylinder Inscription (see Ball, in *Proceedings of Soc. of Biblical Archæology*, Feb. 7, 1888).

did deserve it. If his brother Judah was 'the hammer,'[aaa] Simon was more than this—he was in the strictest sense a righteous ruler. If, as *v.* 6 anticipates that he would, he 'shattered heads' of 'lawless and wicked men,' he also 'confirmed all the lowly of his people' (1 Macc. xiv. 14). Did not such an one deserve to be commemorated in the Psalter? and was not his encomium well worthy to be assigned to the golden age of David?

But you will ask me, Can a poet so exuberant in his enthusiasm for Simon really have been inspired? Do not his eulogistic words overshoot their mark? I understand the difficulty, and sympathize with those who are jealous for the honour of canonical Scriptures. My reply is twofold. First, it appears to be certain from many prophetic passages that inspiration was not incompatible with some harmless illusions. Human nature being what it has pleased God to make it, the progress of revelation was not psychologically possible otherwise. The variously gifted Asmonæan princes served God's purposes for a time, but for a time only. It would not have been profitable either to Israel or to humanity that they should have consolidated a great world-empire. Not so could the highest Messianic prophecies be fulfilled. Even the successes of Jonathan and Simon and John Hyrcanus implied a decay of the lofty idealism with which the war began; the good things for which they strove were no longer purely spiritual. But when Aristobulus assumed not only the regal title but the style and manners of an Oriental despot, the old חֶסֶד וֶאֱמֶת ('lovingkindness and truth,' Ps. lxxxv. 11) took flight from the soil of Israel, and the rejoicing of one of the so-called Psalms of Solomon (xvii.) over the fall of the Asmonæan dynasty was but too amply justified.[bbb] All this is true; but could a contemporary of Simon's be expected to know it? Must not a lyric poet, sensitive to all national impulses, have been carried away on the full tide of national enthusiasm? Is there anything in this inconsistent with the facts of inspiration as they are known to us? Secondly, if the psalmist is under an illusion as regards the Asmonæan family, he is not so with reference to the Messianic ideal, of which (as I have said) he considers the successes of Simon to be an initial fulfilment. The indirect Messianic prediction which underlies Ps. cx. has not been belied, nor were the scribes altogether wrong in *applying* the psalm to the expected Messiah.

NOTE ª, p. 15.

See Delitzsch or Rendall on Heb. xi. 34–38. The hints given in this passage were developed at great length by St. Isaac of Antioch (4th and 5th centuries A.D.), who devotes no less than 117 lines of his (Syriac) poem 'On the Bird which sang the Trisagion' to 'Semonitha and her holy sons,' to Mattathias, and to Judas and his brethren.[1] The story of the Maccabees was, in truth, much more thought of by the ancient Church than it is by us, and we might well be led by this to 'consider our ways and be wise.' Both in the East and in the West, August 1 was sanctified as the spiritual 'Birthday of the Maccabees,' by which, however, was meant not the entrance into rest of the five heroic sons of Mattathias, but that of the seven sons of 'Semonitha' (as St. Isaac calls this pious mother), whose death of torture is related (we may hope, truthfully) in 2 Macc. vii. Doubtless this stirring episode laid more hold on the Christian imagination than the rest of the traditional story. 'The seven Maccabees' seems to have been a common phrase, and to the seven brethren, according to St. Augustine, a basilica was dedicated at Antioch, 'ut simul sonet et nomen persecutoris et memoria coronatoris.' How popular the festival ($\pi\alpha\nu\eta\gamma\nu\rho\iota\varsigma$) of 'the Maccabees' was at Antioch we can gather, not only from St. Isaac, but from St. Chrysostom, whose works contain two sermons 'on the holy Maccabees and their mother.'[2] St. Gregory Nazianzen has also left us a fine oration on the same subject.[3] It is largely based, however, on the so-called Fourth Book of Maccabees, which is really, as Freudenthal has shown, a sermon before a Hellenistic Jewish audience on one of the memorial days of the Maccabees (perhaps one of the eight 'Dedication' days) shortly before the fall of Jerusalem. All these eloquent Fathers dwell much on the virtually Christian character of these heroes of faith, but none as forcibly as St. Augustine in his sermons 'on the Maccabees,' whose words are in full accordance with the noble eleventh chapter of the Epistle to the Hebrews.[4]

[1] *Opera*, ed. Bickell, i. 158–163.
[2] *Opera*, ed. 1636, i. 516 &c., 552 &c. ; cf. v. 972 (Serm. lxv.).
[3] *Opera*, ed. 1630, i. 397 &c. (Orat. xxii.).
[4] *Opera*, ed. Ben., v. 1218, 1219. 'Neque enim post passionem suam cœpit habere populum Christus: sed illius populus erat ex Abraham genitus . . . Nondum quidem erat mortuus Christus : sed martyres eos fecit moriturus Christus.'

Note b, p. 15.

It is unreasonable to assert that the Maccabæan age was purely imitative, and to refer in proof to the so-called Psalms of Solomon. These artificial and yet historically interesting works only just fall within our period, and were not completed till after its close (see Drummond, *The Jewish Messiah*, pp. 135–141). They do, however, prove that psalm-composition was not extinct. Remember also the psalms in the Greek Daniel, in Judith and Tobit, in the 'Assumption of Moses' (c. x., Merx), and in the copious Samaritan literature.

Note c, p. 15.

Miriam and Deborah are both called prophetesses (Ex. xv. 20, Judges iv. 4). Notice the use of the verb 'to prophesy,' 1 Sam. x. 5 &c., xix. 20 &c. (see Targ.), Luke i. 67, and cf. 1 Chron. xxv. 1, 3. On the affinity between prophecy and psalm-writing, see 1 Cor. xiv. 26, and cf. Hickes, *The Spirit of Enthusiasm Exorcised* (1709), pp. 31, 32; Weizsäcker, *Das apostolische Zeitalter*, 1886, pp. 577–579; Warfield, in *Expositor*, 1885 (2), pp. 301 &c., 321 &c.

Note d, p. 16.

The argument from the linguistic complexion of the several psalms is generally less cogent than that from the ideas and phraseological affinities, and is therefore seldom referred to in these lectures. The linguistic evidence will, however, be given in the case of certain psalms in the Appendix.

Note e, p. 16.

The writer of the argument to Ps. lv. (lvi.) in Corderius's *Catena* —probably Theodore of Mopsuestia—felt this. He says, Περιπαθέστεροι γάρ πως δοκοῦσιν εἶναι οἱ τοιοῦτοι, σφόδρα ἐπικλασθέντος τοῦ προφήτου πρὸς τὰς συμφορὰς τὰς αὐτῶν. In Corderius, too, we find this comment on lxxviii. (lxxix.) 4, ascribed to Theodore: Πολλαχοῦ δὲ ἐν τοῖς ψαλμοῖς τῶν Μακκαβαίων μέμνηται τῶν γειτόνων ὡς ὀνειδιζόντων εἰκότως.

Note f, p. 16.

The 'Interpreter' *par excellence* of the Syrian Church still waits for an English monograph at once complete and sympathetic. Dr. Swete's article in the *Dict. Christ. Biogr.* is full of learning, but contrasts unfavourably in tone with Bishop Milne's article in the

Church Quarterly Review, vol. i., No. 1. Scant justice moreover is done to the Old Testament work of this great theologian, who, as the Jesuit scholar S. J. Flunk well observes, occupies 'a completely unique position' by his critical talent (*Zeitschr. f. kathol. Theologie*, 1887, p. 181). The fact of which we are assured not only by Leontius but by Theodore himself (see Dr. Swete), that his work on the psalms was the work of a beginner, does but increase our admiration for it. Theodore was not in all respects more competent in later years; the dogmatist could not but impose limitations on the exegete (cf. Harnack, *Dogmengeschichte*, ii. 78, 79, note ¹). His exegesis of the psalms may now be studied with the help of Baethgen's Syriac researches (see articles in Stade's *Zeitschrift*, 1885, p. 53 &c.; 1886, p. 261 &c., often referred to here).

NOTE g, p. 16.

This occasion justifies and explains the use made of the 'Song of Moses' (cf. *v.* 14 with Ex. xv. 2, and perhaps *vv.* 15 and 16 with Ex. xv. 6). As this fine psalm will be several times referred to, let me here (though it does not sensibly affect my argument, but only the general picture of psalm-composition) express my thorough agreement with De Wette, who, in 1807, wrote thus of Ex. xv. 1–18: 'It is too long and too artificial for these times [the Mosaic] and for a popular song.' 'Otmar's conjecture,' he adds, 'is not unplausible, that only *v.* 1 (repeated in *v.* 21) formed the original song' (*Beiträge zur Einleitung ins A. T.* ii. 216). Dillmann himself has the same impression, but thinks that *vv.* 1–3 may have formed the original song of Moses, and that the song as it now stands (except *v.* 17, which is of later date) arose soon after the entrance of the Israelites into Canaan. This early date of the song as a whole is, however, opposed to a truly historical conception of the development of Israelitish religion, and I see no reason for placing the poem earlier than the historical songs in the Psalter. All the arguments against pre-Exile, or at any rate pre-Josian psalms, are applicable to Ex. xv. 1–18. Verses 1–3 may be more ancient than the rest, but what means have we for fixing their date? It is true *v.* 2*a* is copied in Isa. xii. 2*b*. But the snatches of lyric song in Isa. xii. are full of points of contact with post-Exile psalms, and express the joy of the restored exiles in the services of the second temple. This was long ago shown by Ewald, and was confirmed in 1878 by Lagarde (*Semitica*, i. 28). It has been my own view since 1881. I have pointed out similar phenomena elsewhere (see below, p. 214).

Note h, p. 17.

The psalmist speaks like a second Joshua (see Ps. xliv. 4, a Maccabæan passage).

Note i, p. 17.

This is much more natural than the view of Theodore of Mopsuestia that 'the stone' is Zerubbabel. The 'builders' (cf. cxxvii. 1) are possibly those who had reconstituted the Jewish state after the Return, one of whom was Zerubbabel. Remember that the Maccabees were descendants of Aaron, not in the direct line, but in the collateral line of Jojarib (1 Macc. ii. 1). The passage did not much attract the attention of the Jewish doctors. It is only quoted once in the Talmud, and not applied Messianically.

Note j, p. 17.

The first being חֲנֻכָּה = τὰ ἐγκαίνια (John x. 22). In support of Ewald's view on the 'Feast of Lights' cf. Grünbaum, *Zeitschr. der d. morg. Ges.* xxxi. 281.

Note k, p. 17.

The unexpectedness of the liberation was one of the leading ideas suggested by the feast in later times. Hence the selection of Ps. xxx. as one of the psalms for the Hanukka. See *vv.* 6 and 12, and notice (p. 18) Emma Lazarus's fine adaptation of *v.* 12. Of course it does not exclude Ewald's view that the rite of illumination was adopted from heathenism, and was originally connected with the feast of the solstice, i.e. of the new light of the year (*History*, v. 312). Such an origin would account for the reluctance of the Egyptian Jews (who had some special festivals of their own) to adopt this once foreign, though now Palestinian, festival (see 2 Macc. i. 18, where it is the feast τῆς σκηνοπηγίας καὶ τοῦ πυρός). Ewald connects this solstice festival with the Christian Epiphany; comp. J. Réville on the transformation of the Mithriac festival of the renascent sun into Christmas (*La religion à Rome sous les Sévères*, p. 98). Macrobius confounds φῶς and φώς (*Saturn.* i. 7, 31).

Note m, p. 18.

At the passover meal the Hallel was divided into two parts. It is to the second part (Pss. cxv.–cxviii.), sung over the fourth and last cup, that the ὑμνήσαντες of the Gospels refers. Delitzsch's Hebrew N. T. well paraphrases, 'after they had finished the Hallel' (Mark

xiv. 26, Matt. xxvi. 30). It is noteworthy that the only other occasion on which Jesus Christ is reported to have referred to Ps. cxviii. is when He applied one of His parables to those who rejected His Messiahship (see Mark xii. 10, 11, and parallel passages). None of the accounts of His purification of the temple suggest that He thought of Ps. cxviii. and the purification of Judas; the Scripture quotations are from passages of a more spiritual tenor than that vehement psalm.

Note ⁿ, p. 18.

The faithful Jews who rejoiced eight days at the dedication of the new altar in B.C. 165, remembered the miserable Feast of Tabernacles which they had lately kept 'like wild beasts' (2 Macc. x. 6). The new Feast of the Dedication was in fact regarded as a supplement to that of the Tabernacles (2 Macc. i. 9). Thus the old festival was filled with a new meaning, and the new one became the interpreter of the old. (For I can scarcely think, with Geiger, that the Greek translator mistook the meaning of נס !) That the recitation of the Hallel on these occasions goes back to Simon, can hardly be doubted. The Talmud itself (*Pesachim*, 117*a*) states that the Hallel was instituted for a twofold object, to celebrate festival days, and to commemorate deliverance from a great danger (i.e., from the tyranny of Antiochus Epiphanes). See Grätz, *Monatsschrift*, 1879, p. 202.

Note °, p. 19.

It is remarkable, however, that the patristic arguments of the psalms in Corderius's *Catena* say nothing of the possible Maccabæan reference of Ps. cxviii., but explain Ps. cxvi. either of the Return (so also Theodore of Mopsuestia) or of the Maccabees—ἤ, ὡς ἕτερος, τὰ κατ' Ἀντίοχον τὸν Ἐπιφανῆ προθεσπίζει (alluding to Theodoret).

Note ᵖ, p. 19.

On *khasīdīm* see below, p. 56, note ᶜ. It is worth noticing that the word does not by any means occur in all the (probably) Maccabæan psalms, nor yet in the Book of Daniel. It was frequent, however, in the Hebrew Psalms of Solomon, as can be seen even from the Greek version.

Note ᑫ, p. 19.

The reference to proselytes in both these passages is most easily explained if the psalms are of the Greek age.

D

NOTE ʳ, p. 19.

Gregory Nazianzen calls the Epiphany ἡ ἁγία τῶν φώτων ἡμέρα (Orat. xxxix.).

NOTE ˢ, p. 20.

I suspect, however, that the best living scholars would not urge the claims of David as confidently as their predecessors. Graf Baudissin says cautiously that the pre-Exilic kingship is referred to, and probably that of David, if at least the words 'Sit thou at my right hand' refer to David's privilege of setting up his throne beside the ark, the symbol of the divine presence. An Asmonæan prince is not meant, he thinks, because the priestly dignity belonged to this family by inheritance. (Not, however, the high priestly.) See his *Gesch. des alttest. Priesterthums* (1889), pp. 259, 260, and cf. Orelli's explanation in his *Old Testament Prophecy*.

NOTE ᵗ, p. 20.

Even Delitzsch holds this opinion. This is the single Davidic psalm, he says, in which, as in his Last Words (2 Sam. xxiii. 1-7), David looks out into the future of his seed, and has the Messiah objectively before him (*The Psalms*, by Eaton, i. 89). But will Delitzsch's theory of these so-called Last Words stand (see Lect. V.)? and can we, till a parallel is found, bring ourselves to believe in a strictly Messianic psalm (see Lect. VII.)? Elsewhere, if I rightly interpret his implications, Delitzsch suggests that the Asmonæan royalty was regarded by its friends as a fulfilment of the oracles in Ps. cx. (*Messianic Prophecy*, by Curtiss, p. 117). This is a tacit recognition of the plausibility of the Maccabæan theory, and I cannot see what prevents Delitzsch from accepting it as correct, for it is just as easy to hold that a Maccabæan psalm is typically prophetic of Christ as that parts of a Maccabæan prophecy (Dan. xi.) are typically prophetic of Antichrist. For it is noteworthy that, though he has much to say of the New Testament references to Ps. cx. (Matt. xxii. 41 &c., Acts ii. 34-36, 1 Cor. xv. 25, Heb. i. 13, v. 6, vii. 17, 21, x. 13), which he rightly regards as determining the contemporary Jewish exegesis, Delitzsch makes no appeal to the supposed authority of our Lord. He is free, therefore, to give full play to his critical faculty. Let all younger students recognize the admirable fairness of this truly evangelical expositor. He knows full well how inconceivable it is that Jesus Christ should have formed critical decisions upon the date and authorship of the psalms. So at least it appears to me from a not superficial acquaintance with Delitzsch and his works. Some of my readers may be inclined to differ from us both. Let them, however, answer these questions. Did the subject of the authorship of Ps. cx. fall within the range of Christ's teaching, so far as this can be gathered from a historical study of the Gospels? Must not so keen a critic of the Jewish legal tradition have felt the futility of the current Biblical criticism? Is it not clear, then, that Jesus simply assumes the premises of the Pharisees to prove that even thus He is much more than a son of David, that they must carry their Messianic researches into a far higher spiritual region? Later on Jewish controversialists abandoned the strict Messianic interpretation of this psalm. Justin Martyr (*c. Tryph.* 33, 83) and Tertullian (*adv. Marc.* v. 9) mention and refute a view which makes Hezekiah the subject of the psalm. Messianic applications, however, still occur in the Talmud (see Pick, *Hebraica*, April 1886, p. 137).

NOTE ^u, p. 20.

Ewald writes thus: 'Since David took the field in person on this occasion [the campaign against Edom] it may well have been that, as he was previously offering sacrifices and prayers at the holy place, some prophet like Gad or Nathan uttered that wonderfully elevating oracle which supplied a poet of kindred spirit with the starting-point of Ps. cx., and in which the royalty of Israel, combined with the cheerful valour of the people, shone forth with unsurpassable brightness and purity' (*History*, iii. 158).

NOTE ^v, p. 21.

This was still my own view in 1884 (see *The Prophecies of Isaiah*, vol. ii.). The phrase 'an oracle of Jehovah' (Ps. cx. 1) seemed to me out of character with an age which painfully felt the want of prophetic revelations (see 1 Macc. iv. 46, ix. 27, xiv. 41). But I now see that what the age missed was not occasional prophetic oracles, nor even recasts of old prophetic anticipations in a new form (with both of which it was gratified), but true prophets according to its own too narrow conception of the office, men who would never be at a loss, who would have an answer ready for any question, whether it were 'How long?' (Ps. lxxiv. 9), or 'Who is the divinely sanctioned high priest?' or 'What shall be the end of the Syrian tyrant?' or 'What shall be the lot of them that sleep in the dust of the earth?' Some of these questions were answered by the Book of Daniel, but the continuance of apocalyptic writing shows that the thirst for insight into the divine secrets was by no means quenched.

NOTE ʷ, p. 21.

Not improbably (see Hitzig) we should read in v. 13, 'and Joshua shall be a priest upon his throne.' This would imply that Zerubbabel was the personage called 'Shoot' who was to live in perfect harmony with the high priest Joshua. The erasure of the names will then be the record of a pathetic disillusionment: Zerubbabel did not prove the man that Haggai (Hag. ii. 20–23) and Zechariah (Zech. iii. 8, 9, vi. 9–13) took him for; Joshua, too, according to Zerubbabel's (?) words in Ezra ii. 63, Neh. vii. 65, was *not* a perfect priest, because he could not decide by Urim and Thummim.

NOTE ˣ, p. 22.

This was always a distinctively Christian idea (see Stanton, *The Jewish and the Christian Messiah*, pp. 128, 129).

NOTE ʸ, p. 22.

Hag. ii. 20–23, Zech. iii. 8, iv., vi. 9–15. A distorted version of such preaching reached Sanballat (Neh. vi. 6, 7). Chrysostom mentions the view that Zerubbabel was the recipient of the oracles in Ps. cx., and objects that this prince was no more a priest than David.

NOTE ᶻ, p. 22.

Comp. Gen. xlix. 10, Num. xxiv. 7, 17 in Sept., and see Frankel (*Ueb. den Einfluss der palästin. Exegese auf die alexandrin. Exegese*, pp. 50, 182–5). The other passages quoted by Edersheim (*Jesus the Messiah*, i. 72), after Gfrörer, scarcely prove a further development of the doctrine of the Messiah in Alexandria. In Isa. ix. 6 ἄγγελος corresponds to אֵל, and need mean neither more nor less than the Hebrew. A similar remark applies to Ps. lxxii. 5, 7; compare v. 7 with Ps. lxxxv. 11, where no one supposes the Messiah to be referred to. Nor does Sept.'s version of Ps. cx. 3 at all prove (in spite of Rev. xxii. 16) that the translator held a fuller or more definite Messianic doctrine than the psalmist. The version may be Englished thus: 'From the womb, as one more glorious than the morning star, have I begotten thee' (see linguistic appendix). There is nothing in this which, from an Oriental point of view, is inapplicable to a great ruler (comp. Isa. xiv. 12). The pointing יְלִדְתִּיךָ does, no doubt, suggest that the translator regarded Pss. ii. and cx. as parallel; but, however probable it may be, it is not certain that he interpreted Ps. ii. of the Messiah.

Note aa, p. 22.

Besides this famous passage, which is decisive as to the symbolic value of the name 'David,' notice the way in which the narratives of Daniel and Judith (works of unequal value, but in this respect at least parallel) convert Nebuchadrezzar into a symbol of Antiochus Epiphanes. I have spoken above of Judas and his brethren as typified by David. Strictly speaking, however, it is Saul who typifies Judas; while David, and partly Solomon, symbolize the work of Jonathan and Simon. When the two latter buried Judas they adapted the burden of David's lamentation over Saul and his son (see 1 Macc. ix. 19–21).

Note bb, p. 23.

Against Pusey, *Daniel the Prophet*, p. 367, see Ewald, *History*, v. 360. Reuss has called Judas the Maccabee 'the unique fanatic.' This Sibylline poet belongs to the same class.

Note cc, p. 23.

What does this phrase mean? (1) 'From the East'? If so, comp. πρὸς Ἠῶ τ' Ἠέλιόν τε, Hom. *Il.* xii. 239. From the Sibyl's point of view either Simon or any purely ideal king might be described as coming from the east. (It is misleading to compare Isa. xli. 2; Cyrus would be out of place here.) Or (2) 'from heaven,' whence Cyrus (line 286), and honey and fruits, flocks and herds (line 745, &c.), are said to come. The sun may be mentioned here to suggest that, as the Septuagint makes the psalmist say of the priest-king (Ps. cix. 3), the hero spoken of would be 'born more glorious than the morning star' (πρὸ ἑωσφόρου). The Sibylline writer is, moreover, an Egyptian Jew, and to connect a king with the sun is natural in Egypt. Note, too, that in *Orac.* xiii. 151, 164, a Christian Sibyl does not scruple to call Odenathus, priest-king of Palmyra, ἡλιόπεμπτος.

Note dd, p. 23.

The mention of ὅρκια suggests that some historical fact is alluded to (cf. 1 Macc. viii., xii.).

Note ee, p. 23.

Like David the king will be guided by divine oracles, whether those of Scripture or such as that in Ps. cx. 1.

Note ff, p. 24.

Holtzmann thinks that he is (*Judenthum und Christenthum*, 1867, p. 199). Schürer (*The Jewish People in the Time of Jesus Christ*, Div. ii., vol. ii., p. 136) will hear of none but a strictly Messianic interpretation; and similarly Stanton (*The Jewish and the Christian Messiah*, p. 115). Against the latter, see on Pss. xx., xxi. Against the former, note that the true Messianic felicity is certainly placed after the great attack of the nations upon Jerusalem. It is only a foretaste of happiness which the Sibyl describes, and her picture corresponds, as we see, to the poetical idealization of Simon's reign in the old song imbedded in 1 Macc. xiv. Dr. Drummond, with some hesitation, proposes the view which I have adopted (*The Jewish Messiah*, p. 275).

Note gg, p. 24.

It would be a serious objection to this view if the enthusiasm for the Maccabees were limited to Palestine. From the document or documents (of very doubtful genuineness) in 2 Macc. i. 1–36, ii. 1–18, it would seem that in B.C. 143 the Jews of Palestine announced their happy deliverance to those of Egypt, and invited them to celebrate the newly instituted Feast of the Dedication, but that in B.C. 124 they had to write again with the same request. Even if historical, this only proves that the Egyptian Jews, who had special festivals of their own (Ewald, *History*, v. 358), were not inclined to adopt at once what they may have regarded as a local and provincial festival at the bidding of the Judæan authorities. It does not warrant us in assuming that none of the Egyptian Jews sympathized with the great religious champions. There were differences on the subject of the policy of the Maccabees even in Palestine; yet, as 2 Maccabees shows, this did not prevent a full national recognition at any rate of the hero Judas. Add to this, that the allusions to the Alexandrine version of Daniel in the Third Book of the Sibylline Oracles, prove how early the greatest religious monument of the Maccabæan rising found admiring readers among the Jews of Egypt (comp. Sib. iii. 396, 397 with Sept. Dan. vii. 7, and Sib. iii. 613 with Sept. Dan. vii. 23, 24). Prof. Fuller's counter-argument in *Speaker's Comm.* vi. 219, does not appear to me satisfactory. Frankel has good reason to speak of 'eine auf festen Anzeichen u. Facten ruhende Gewissheit, dass zwischen den Bekennern desselben Glaubens in zwei Nachbarländern viele Berührungspunkte obwalteten' (*Ueber den Einfluss der pal. Exegese auf die alexandrin. Hermeneutik*, p. 3). And Jost well remarks, 'Hätten schon die glücklichen Anstrengungen der Religionshelden in allen Gemeinden, wohin die Kunde gelangte, eine lebhafte Spannung unterhalten, so musste die Ernennung Simon's zum Fürsten allgemeine Begeisterung erzeugen' (*Geschichte*, i. 122).

NOTE ^{hh}, p. 24.

1 Macc. xiii. 42 ; cf. Josephus, *Ant.* xiii. 6, 7, who gives the titles of Simon as 'benefactor and ethnarch of the Jews' (on the former, cf. Luke xxii. 25, and on the latter, Jos., *Ant.* xiv. 7, 2—both imply the possession of virtually supreme authority). Several other cities also dated new eras from their declaration of independence about this time (Sidon from 111 B.C.). See also 1 Macc. xiii. 39, and cf. Madden, *Coins of the Jews*, p. 67 (Simon struck coins *before* Antiochus expressly conceded the privilege).

NOTE ⁱⁱ, p. 24.

Josephus (*Ant.* xiii. 11, 1) gives the title to Aristobulus, who reigned but one year ; but on his coins he only calls himself high priest (see Levy, *Gesch. der jüd. Münzen*, p. 54).

NOTE ^{jj}, p. 24.

Helon's Pilgrimage, by Otto Strauss, a historical novel which quickened my own boyish imagination, places its reader in the Judæa of the age of Hyrcanus.

NOTE ^{kk}, p. 25.

Whether or no Hyrcanus was himself originally a Pharisee (see Wellhausen, *Pharisäer und Sadducäer*, pp. 89-91), there is no reason to doubt Josephus's statement that the Pharisees showed violent hostility to him (*Ant.* xiii. 10, 5). This agrees with the anti-Asmonæan spirit of 2 Macc., and the bitter language of *Assumpt. Mosis* (v. 15), and of the *Psalms of Solomon* (xvii.). To prove the legitimacy of the high priesthood of Hyrcanus his friends would, of course, appeal to his supposed prophetic gift—an imperfect substitute for the old oracular responses by Urim and Thummim. What, then, were the oracles of Hyrcanus? If I rightly understand Jos., *Ant.* xiii. 10, 3, they came to him by a Bath Qōl (a 'daughter-voice' or 'echo' of the divine word) in the sanctuary, as he was offering incense (cf. Luke i. 9-11). Even the Talmudic tradition concedes this (Geiger, *Urschrift*, p. 214), and it is no slight admission, as the story in *Sanhedrin* 11a shows. The Sanhedrin was holding its session in the upper chamber of a house in Jericho. Suddenly a

Bath Qōl came from heaven saying, 'There is one here who merits that the Shechina should rest on him, even as on our teacher Moses, but his age is not worthy of him.' Then the wise men turned their eyes on Hillel the elder. Josephus states (*Ant.* iii. 8, 9) that the Urim and Thummim ceased to give oracles 200 years before he wrote his *Antiquities*; comp. Ezra ii. 65, Neh. vii. 65, which suggest that the high priestly lot was in some way restored after the Return, though not immediately. In spite of the Talmudic statement (*Sota*, 48*b*) we must, I think, accept this; but I do not feel bound to take Josephus's calculation quite literally.

NOTE ll, p. 25.

See 1 Macc. xiii. 51. The 23rd of the month Iyyar was kept as a commemorative festival (see the calendar in Grätz, *Geschichte*, iii. ed. 4, p. 562; cf. Derenbourg, *Histoire*, p. 67).

NOTE mm, p. 25.

The Tyrian staters bear the legend Τύρου ἱερᾶς καὶ ἀσύλου. Comp. Jos., *Ant.* xiii. 2, 3, ἱερὰν καὶ ἄσυλον καὶ ἐλευθέραν (of Jerusalem).

NOTE nn, p. 25.

I interpret 1 Macc. iv. 46, xiv. 41, in accordance with ix. 27 (Ps. lxxiv. 9). Derenbourg, however (*Revue des études juives*, 1881, p. 291), thinks that the prophetic herald of the day of Jehovah (Mal. iv. 5, 6) is meant. He reminds us that in the Mishna litigated questions are often said to be postponed till the coming of Elijah. (Comp. *Sota*, 48*b*, with the Baraithâ in Geiger, *Urschrift*, p. 213 note.) May not the two interpretations be combined? Joel ii. 28, 29 pointed to a large outpouring of the spirit of prophecy in the latter days. Others have seen an allusion in 1 Macc. xiv. 41 to Deut. xviii. 18; cf. Num. xii. 7.

NOTE oo, p. 25.

In *v.* 15 the right reading is undoubtedly προφητείας.

NOTE pp, p. 25.

No other religious justification could be offered of the assumption of the Davidic sovereignty by the Asmonæans, which (see *Psalm Sol.* xvii. 6–8) seemed such a heinous offence to the later Pharisaic opponents of that house. One can hardly believe with M. Vernes

NOTE qq, p. 26.

Simon entered into the Acra, says our record, μετὰ αἰνέσεως . . . καὶ ἐν ὕμνοις καὶ ἐν ᾠδαῖς (1 Macc. xiv. 51).

NOTE rr, p. 26.

In defence of the genuineness of the document, see Oscar Holtzmann, *Gesch. des Volkes Israel* (in Oncken's series), ii. 382. In many passages the Greek translator evidently found the Hebrew text difficult.

NOTE ss, p. 26.

In other words he became a high priest who was also a ruler (מָשִׁיחַ נָגִיד, Dan. ix. 25).

NOTE tt, p. 26.

'Or at least.' For the duration of the promised tenure of office differs in the psalm and in the legal document. The psalmist hopes that the Messianic age is beginning; the scribe, more cautiously, that the Asmonæan dynasty will last till the Messianic age.

NOTE uu, p. 26.

שׂר in the above sense was usual at this period (cf. also 2 Chron. xxxii. 21, Sept.); not so נָשִׂיא.

NOTE vv, p. 26.

The old calendar in Megillath Taanith states that the 3rd day of Tisri is a festival, because on it the mention of God in contracts was abolished. A Baraithâ explains that formerly it used to be written: 'In such a year of Johanan, priest of the most High God' (*Rosh ha-Shanah*, 18b). Johanan is here merely a symbol for the reigning high priest (Geiger, *Urschrift*, p. 34; Jost, *Gesch. des Judenthums*, i. 279).

NOTE ww, p. 27.

'Sacerdotes summi Dei,' says the Latin version.

Note ˣˣ, p. 27.

It is perfectly possible that Melchizedek is an old traditional name, meaning (as most think), 'Çedeq is king of heaven;' comp. Adonizedek, the name of a king of Jerusalem (Josh. x. 1; but Sept. reads Adonibezek). But old religious names were constantly reinterpreted; e.g., Yahveh among the Israelites, and Assur (cf. Schrader on Gen. ii. 14) among the Assyrians. Nor is the rendering 'king of righteousness' at all a bad one; 'city of righteousness' was an idealizing title of Jerusalem as early as Isaiah (Isa. i. 25; cf. Isa. xix. 18, in Sept.—a significant parallelism). 'Jerusalem,' too, was probably shortened into 'Salem' to indicate that it was the 'perfect city;' cf. Heb. vii. 3. The same form occurs in Ps. lxxvi. 3 (Persian age; see p. 165). That 'Salem' was an earlier name of Jerusalem (Jerome, *Quæst. in Gen.*) seems disproved by the Tell el-Amarna tablets (see *Academy*, Oct. 25, 1890), which give the name Uruśalim.

Note ʸʸ, p. 27.

Cuneiform researches have not made it really more probable that Gen. xiv. 1-17 is of pre-Exilic origin. But I can afford to leave this on one side. Those who will may argue that the 'uniqueness,' or unparalleled nature, of the contents of the narrative, supported as these are, in some incidental points, by Assyriology, goes far to prove their historical character (so apparently Graf Baudissin, *Gesch. des a. t. Priesterthums*, p. 67). But the appendix to the narrative (*vv.* 18-20) is certainly due to a late, post-Exilic editor, before whose prophetic mind stood a vision of an ideal high priest and civil ruler, and who materialized this fair dream in a corner of the typical biography of Abraham. In the form which his dream or vision took there was nothing extraordinary or against verisimilitude. It is needless to refer to the priest-kings of Arabia. From the close of the Persian period onwards the Jewish high priest acted as προστάτης both in civil and religious matters, and 'judged God's people in righteousness' (Ecclus. xlv. 24, 26; cf. Jos. *Ant.* xi. 4, 8, and see Lect. V., on Pss. xx., xxi.). Philo moreover actually speaks of Ptolemy Philadelphus as sending ambassadors with a view to get the Bible translated πρὸς τὸν τῆς Ἰουδαίας ἀρχιερέα καὶ βασιλέα· ὁ γὰρ αὐτὸς ἦν (*De Vitâ Mosis*, Mangey, ii. 139). The appendix, then, is ideally and prophetically, though not historically, true. If a critic, liberal in many of his convictions, but conservative by nature, like Graf Baudissin, inclines to deny its historicity, one may reasonably assume that many other perhaps over-cautious critics will range themselves ultimately on his side.

Note ᵃᵃ, p. 27.

The need of a justification is shown by the fact that the objections of the strict legalists to the Maccabæan high priesthood revived in the time of John Hyrcanus (see above, p. 39, noteᵏᵏ).

Note ᵃᵃᵃ, p. 28.

This rendering 'Hammer' or 'Hammerer' implies the reading מַקֶּבִי, which Kennicott found in two MSS. of the Megillath Antiochus, and which may fairly be said to be confirmed by the Greek Μακκαβαῖος (κ generally = ק). The Syriac version of the Greek 1 Macc. also took this view (giving Maqbi). Mr. Ball favours the reading with ק, but alters the name to מַקְבָּא (Wace's *Apocrypha*, i. 247, note). Dr. Curtiss, however, in his exhaustive monograph *The Name Machabee* (Leipz. 1876), prefers the more difficult reading מכבי, which is supported by Jerome's Machabæus.

Note ᵇᵇᵇ, p. 28.

Jonathan, Simon, and John Hyrcanus were not, I think, the worldly-minded princes Wellhausen takes them for (*Die Pharisäer und die Sadducäer*, p. 85 &c.). But there certainly is a touch of modernness in their complex characters which marks them off from the unprogressive and, an unfriendly critic might add, fanatical *khasīdīm*.

LECTURE II.

Jehovah! thou hast been our refuge from one generation to another.—Ps. xc. 1.

LECTURE II.

PART I.—The tone of mind proper to this inquiry.—We next consider Pss. cviii. and cix. which form a small group with Ps. cx. Ps. cix., however, may be reserved; it was placed where it is for a purely mechanical reason. Ps. cviii. is a compilation, made presumably under Simon the Maccabee.—The third of the three psalms specially set apart in Lecture I. is Ps. cxlix. This too is Maccabæan, as internal evidence and coincidences with passages in Maccabees prove. A fit psalm for the first 'day of Nicanor.'—And does not this result involve the Maccabæan date of other psalms? How can we separate Pss. cxlviii.–cl. ?— The word *khasīdīm* under certain conditions an evidence of date.—We now ask, Do any psalms in Books IV. and V. require to be dated before the Maccabees (or at any rate before Ezra)? Study the rest of the Hallel and of the Hallelujah psalms. Those groups have points of mutual contact, and were presumably arranged by Simon. But were all the psalms so old? Pss. cxiii. and cxiv. need not be, but post-Exile they must be on the internal and especially phraseological evidence. Pss. cxlvi. and cxlvii. are, at any rate, not older than Nehemiah, but still better suit the age of Simon. The Hallelujah psalms are all certainly either of the Persian or the Greek period. Pss. cxxxv. and cxxxvi. are probably Maccabæan. Pss. cxi. and cxii. go naturally with Ps. cxix. (early Greek ?)—The 'Songs of Ascent,' a collection of psalms for the use of pilgrims. Their date discussed in much detail. They reflect the fluctuating fortunes of the Jews during the Persian and, perhaps, early Greek period.—Israel's third great captivity.— Historical value of the 'minor Psalter.'

PART II.—Consideration of the remaining twenty-five psalms. Pss. ciii. and civ. are clearly contemporaneous with Pss. cv.–cvii. (see Hallelujah psalms). Ps. cix. more difficult. Why not Messianic. Psychological study of the poem. An Exilic date not probable, in spite of the parallels in the Book of Job. Marks of the Persian period (cf. Isa. xxxiv.).—Pss. cxxxviii.–cxlv. ('Davidic'), within which Pss. cxl.–cxliii. form a minor group. Ps. cxli. certainly, Ps. cxxxviii. probably, Maccabæan.—Date of Ps. cxxxix. singularly clear; perhaps early Greek.—We next pause at Ps. ci., which is most intelligible with a Maccabæan background. A companion-piece to Ps. cx.—Why thirteen psalms in Books IV. and V. were assigned to David.—Ps. cxxxvii., why not early post-Exilic, but probably Maccabæan.—Ps. cii., why considerably older than the Maccabees; strikingly illustrates Neh. iv. 3. Historical significance of this.—The 'heptad of new songs' (xciii. and xcv.–c.). Not much later than the Second Isaiah.—Pss. xci., xcii., xciv. are all Persian; Ps. xciv. from the troublous times of Artaxerxes Ochus.—Ps. xc., why not Mosaic.—How to account for the title.—When was the psalm written? Phraseological evidence and the character of the ideas bring it very near the reorganization of the church-people.

PART I.

ANALYSIS OF BOOKS IV. AND V. CONTINUED.

THE 90th psalm is not the starting-point but the goal of my present lecture. Its solemn opening words, however, strike a note to which I fervently hope to be true throughout the course of this inquiry. In my previous lecture I began the analysis of Books IV. and V., which form a small psalter in themselves. I determined the period of Pss. cxv.–cxviii. and cx., our first Maccabæan psalms, and showed that the prince referred to in Ps. cx. was most probably Simon the Maccabee. The question now arises, May we assume, on the analogy of Ps. cxviii., that the psalms which appear to belong to the same small group with Ps. cx. were composed in the Maccabæan period? These psalms are cviii. and cix. The latter psalm may be at once set aside for future consideration. The tone is absolutely opposed to that of the Maccabæan age. A reason for placing it before Ps. cx. was suggested by the catchword in the last verse, 'For he standeth at the right hand of the needy,' which leads on to the שֵׁב לִימִינִי in Ps. cx. 1. But Ps. cviii. (the only Elohistic psalm in the collection) was presumably compiled from the so-called Davidic Psalms, lvii. (*vv.* 8–12) and lx. (*vv.* 7–14), under Simon the Maccabee, and is a fitting introduction to Ps. cx.

Let us pause next at Ps. cxlix., than which no poem in the Psalter is more clearly Maccabæan. This is no hymn of universal benevolence, like Pss. lxxxvi. and cxlv. The members of the great conspiracy against Israel and his God deserve no better fate than that of Midian and of Sisera (*v.* 9, cf. lxxxiii. 10–13). They are the 'peoples that delight in wars' (lxviii. 31); it remains for the 'friends of God,' however averse to it by nature, to seize the two-edged sword, and, lifting a song of praise, to advance to battle (*v.* 6). Is this poetry or history? It is both. Notice the unsought coincidence of *v.* 6 with 2 Macc. xii. 37, 1 Macc. iv. 33, and 2 Macc. xv. 26, 27. Can there be much doubt that the psalm expresses the national rejoicing, not at the return from Babylon, but at the victories of Judas the Maccabee, more especially (cf. p. 178, note ⁸) his last victory over Nicanor at Adasa in March 161? That was a high festival day when the conquerors entered the city and joined the anxious holiday makers in the feast of Purim. Well may this psalm have been sung when the 'day of Nicanor' was first kept in memory of this great salvation (1 Macc. vii. 49, 2 Macc. xv. 36).ᵃ

But does not the Maccabæan date of this psalm carry with it that of others?ᵇ Read Pss. cxlviii. and cxlix. together, and especially compare cxlviii. 14 with cxlix. 1, and you will agree with me that the two psalms cannot be separated in date. And now it is time to say why, although in itself the term *khasīdīm* ('pious ones,' 'friends of God') is not distinctively Maccabæan, yet, taken in connexion with other exegetical phenomena which point to the Maccabæan age, it steps at once into importance as an evidence of the first value. In the Maccabæan rising *khasīdīm* ('Ασιδαῖοιᶜ) was the name given to those 'mighty (or, perhaps, capable) men' who joined the volunteer Church Army under the aged Mattathias, and 'smote sinful men in their anger and lawless men in their wrath' (1 Macc. ii. 44). Judged by a modern standard they may be found wanting. Dean Stanley complains that 'their obstinate foolhardiness vexed the great soul, and their narrow selfishness cost the life of Judas.'[1] But it was a passionate love of the sacred deposit of pure religion which animated them, and if they took umbrage at the treaty between Judas and the Romans, it must be admitted that this alliance was in flagrant contradiction to the traditions of the higher religion. It was not to renew the ideal kingship of David that they had taken the sword, and 'the lofty hymns divine' which were 'in their throat' were inspired far less by the slaughter of God's enemies than by His wondrous and adorable perfections (cxlviii.). They sing for joy, not only upon the field of battle, but in the recovered sanctuary, where Simon, as it would appear, reorganized the service of song in a nobler style.

[1] *Jewish Church*, iii. 333.

There it was that 'Hallelujah' was understood in its full significance as the song of creation's priest to creation's God (Ps. cl.). Consistency requires us to make Ps. cl. contemporaneous in origin with its two predecessors.

And now see how these closing psalms confirm the view which we have taken of Ps. cx. Comparing Ps. cxlix. 7 with Ps. cx. 5, is it not clear that the writers regard the Jewish victories which they have witnessed as the beginning of a world-judgment, the agents in which will be the true Israelites (cf. Dan. vii. 26); in short, that both psalms are germinally Messianic? Next observe that in Ps. cx. 3 we have the remarkable phrase, 'Thy people are self-devotion;' but we do not find anywhere in Ps. cx. that distinctively Maccabæan term (which occurs in Pss. cxlviii. 14, cxlix. 1, 5) *khasīdīm*. That is true; but notice the definition of *khasīdīm* given in 1 Macc. ii. 43, 'every one that freely devoted himself for the law.'[d] Does not this at once explain the concise phrase in Ps. cx. 3, and show that it is really synonymous with 'Thy people are *khasīdīm*'? Is not the case for the contemporaneousness of these psalms reasonably complete? And if one of them be Maccabæan, must not the others be so too?

I now advance a step, and inquire, Are there any psalms in these two books which require to be dated before the Maccabæan period, or at any rate before that promulgation of the Law without which the Maccabæan heroes would have had nothing to fight for? Take the larger groups to which Pss. cxv.–cxviii. and cxlviii.–cl. respectively belong, one of which (Pss. cxiii.–cxviii.) is called the Hallel or the Egyptian Hallel, and the other (Pss. cxlvi.–cl.) the Hallelujah psalms. Both groups[1] present phraseological and other linguistic points of mutual contact. It is highly probable that the arrangement of both goes back to the time of Simon;[2] but of course it does not follow from this that all the psalms were new. Pss. cxiii. and cxiv. have affinities with the great body of literature, partly lyric, partly prophetic, which was called forth by Israel's second wonderful deliverance from foreign bondage.[e] They can hardly be earlier, and may be even later, than Ezra's and Nehemiah's time. Pss. cxlvi. and cxlvii. are at any rate not

---

[1] See Ehrt, *Abfassungszeit und Abschluss des Psalters*, p. 83.
[2] With regard to the Hallel see above, p. 33, note ⁿ.

products of an earlier period; one could easily prove this, granting critical principles, from the literary and linguistic evidence. The only question is whether the fortification of Jerusalem referred to in cxlvii. 2, 13, is that which was celebrated in B.C. 444[f] (Neh. xii. 27), or that in B.C. 142 (see 1 Macc. xiv. 37). It would be delightful to know some of the psalms with which Nehemiah's dedication-feast was celebrated.[g] Still we must not be too confident. The picture in Ps. cxlvii. may possibly be true to the facts of the great governor's time, but it corresponds almost more strikingly with the age of Simon.[h] The reference to the law (*vv.* 19, 20) agrees equally well with both periods. At any rate, it is certain that these psalms received their full meaning when Simon reorganized the arrangements of the temple. Not without some reason did a noble pioneer of modern Jewish scholarship—Nachman Krochmal—call Pss. cxlvi.–cl. the Greek Hallel,[1] because it was collected, if not entirely composed, in the Greek period. At the same time it must be remembered that Pss. cxiii.–cxviii. (of whose title 'the Egyptian Hallel' Krochmal was thinking) have an equal claim to this appellation.

Let us now extend our range of inquiry to the rest of the poems which are in the widest sense Hallelujah psalms. There are altogether seventeen which have a right to this designation, because they all bear on the front the formula *hallelu Jah*, 'praise ye Jehovah.'[j] The remaining psalms of this large group are cv.,[k] cvi., cvii., cxi., cxii., cxxxv., and cxxxvi. The two last are undoubtedly the least original in the whole Psalter, and some perhaps may doubt whether an age so full of inspiration as the Maccabæan could have produced them. But that Pss. cxxxv. and cxxxvi. are dependent upon Maccabæan psalms (the one upon Ps. cxv. and the other on Ps. cxviii.), is certain, and why may not the authorities, even in this stirring period, have had the practical wisdom to employ some less gifted persons to produce a few plain hymns for liturgical use?[1] Pss. cv. and cvi. must have belonged to the temple Psalter at the end of the Persian period, for they contribute to the imaginary psalm in 1 Chron. xvi. 7–36; in other words, are not Maccabæan. But we can go further than this. The trilogy which they form

II. ANALYSIS OF BOOKS IV. AND V. CONTINUED.

with Ps. cvii.[m] is not merely pre-Maccabæan and (see cvii. 2, 3) post-Exilic, but can be determined by the literary allusions (for which see the commentaries) to be not earlier than the latter part of the Persian period. With regard to Ps. cvii. I will only add that it contains (v. 11) the divine name 'Elyōn, which, perhaps from its Phœnician association, was avoided by the pre-Exile prophets and by Ezekiel.[1] Pss. cxi.[n] and cxii. were obviously not written as Hallelujah psalms. They must originally have been without the opening Hallelujah, and have been followed by Ps. cxix. All three belong to the class of alphabetic psalms, in which every verse, or half-verse, or group of verses begins with one of the twenty-two letters of the Hebrew alphabet taken in order. All three are equally appropriate for private and for liturgical use. They are the work of diligent students of the religious classics of Israel (the Torah in the widest sense), who would fain propagate their own peaceable and pious type of character. They might have taken for their motto those fine words in Ps. cxix. (v. 54), 'Thy statutes are the subject of my songs in the house where I am a stranger.' Their post-Exile origin needs no proof. Ps. cxix. in particular contains traces of that internal struggle of growing intensity between the Hellenists and the strict Jehovists which preceded the violent measures of Antiochus Epiphanes. The author is a spiritual ancestor of the Pharisees, as the 'divided ones' (i.e., the religious compromisers) in v. 113 are the forefathers of the Sadducees. The psalm evidently belongs to the pre-Maccabæan portion of the Greek period.[o]

It is natural to refer next to Pss. cxx.–cxxxiv., a little Psalter called 'the Songs of Ascents,' or better 'of Ascent' (compare Ex. xxxiv. 24), which was originally enclosed on both sides by Hallelujah groups.[p] Probably it is a portion of a larger collection of spiritual songs which the pilgrims sang (as the Russian pilgrims in Palestine sing hymns) to enliven their journey to the Holy City. There is great variety in the contents; the pilgrims were not like the narrow-minded and fanatical crowds which swarm from all parts of the Mohammedan world to Mecca. Their religious tone and special interest in Mount Zion prove them to be subsequent

---

[1] See below on Pss. xci.-xcii.

to the centralization of worship in the reign of Josiah.ᑫ We may therefore at once set aside the titles (found in the Hebrew text, but not in the true Septuagint), which assign four of these songs (cxxii., cxxiv., cxxxi., cxxxiii.) to David,ʳ and one (cxxvii.) to Solomon. The only psalm which a modern reader might be tempted (with De Wette, who yet has his doubts) to ascribe to Solomon, is cxxxii. Not only are *vv.* 8–10 put into the mouth of Solomon by the Chronicler (2 Chron. vi. 41, 42), which of course is but a literary fiction, but *vv.* 6 and 8 contain a distinct reference to the ark. This reference, however, is introduced dramatically, nor can the psalm be separated from others of the post-Exile period in which ancient promises are placed in a new setting. Was it written during the governorship of the native prince Zerubbabel, around whose head the Messianic hopes of Haggai and Zechariah played, and who, as the wild growths of later legend prove, was followed with the admiring love of subsequent generations?¹ If so, it is a fresh record of a pathetic moment in Israel's history which has failed to obtain the attention which it deserves. But it seems more in accordance with the comparative principle, which dictates the grouping of parallel psalms with a view to determining their date, to assign it to a somewhat earlier part ˢ of the same period as its twin brother Ps. lxxxix., that is to the last century of the Persian rule. What a fulness of meaning is reflected upon *vv.* 9 and 16 (cf. cx. 4 and cxlix. 5) from the Maccabæan period,ᵗ which, no doubt, is still in the distance, but is being prepared for, alike by the growing corruption of the priesthood, and the closer combination of those faithful worshippers known as *khasīdīm* !ᵘ Troubles enough there were for Israel in this and in the preceding century, though there was a lull when Ps. cxxxii. was written. Not only did satraps and their deputies plunder the land, but a succession of Persian generals on their way to Egypt brought it near famine through the vast supplies of food which they demanded. The defilement of the temple by Bagôses (under 'the other Artaxerxes'), and the 'enslavement' (Jos., *Ant.* xi. 7, 1), took place probably about 383. Disgraceful as the first part of the

¹ See 1 Esdras iii., iv. In Ecclus. xlix. there is already a sign of this admiring love.

story is to the leading family of the Jews, the retribution must have still further embittered the relations between the oppressors and the oppressed. It is not improbable that the Jews joined other nations in revolting in 363, and certain that they did so between 358 and 350. We learn from an early chronologist that captive Jews were settled, 'some in Hyrcania by the Caspian Sea, others in Babylonia.' It was the third of Israel's great captivities.[v]

More than once in the sequel we shall have to call these facts to mind. We do not, I think, sufficiently estimate the manifold and growing unhappiness of the Persian period (see on Ps. lxxxix.). And yet there were moments when Israel, engrossed by its religion and somewhat less tormented by its oppressors than usual, could indite the happy psalms embodied in the pilgrim song-book—such, for instance, as Pss. cxxxiii. and cxxxiv., which, in accordance with the comparative principle, I treat in connexion with Ps. cxxxii. Ps. cxxxiii. (*Ecce quam bonum*) is not a disguised exhortation, whether to Absalom and Amnon (as Castelli, regarding the psalm, against the linguistic evidence, as Davidic), or to the supposed rival chiefs, Zerubbabel and Joshua (as Grätz). It is a pure and lovely encomium on the brotherly love fostered by the Jewish πανηγύρεις. Students of Pentateuch criticism will notice the suggestive reference to the anointing of the high priest. The psalm was placed here by way of illustration; it represents the promises to Zion in Ps. cxxxii. 13–18 as realized, with the exception that there is no reference to the Davidic house. Its author, however, must have lived in an earlier and happier period than the writer of Ps. cxxxii. The case of Ps. cxxxiv. is different. There is no reason why it should not be a late composition, as its place among the Pilgrimage songs suggests. It is one of those plain and unpoetic liturgical compositions of which I spoke before, and upon the analogy of Ps. cxvii. (a still shorter liturgical form), we may assume that it was used as the introduction to some fully developed psalm.[w] From the fact that Ps. cxxxv. in our Bibles actually begins with almost the same form of words,[x] we may be tempted to conjecture that Pss. cxxxv. and cxxxvi. were included in the Pilgrimage Song-book, as the pilgrims' farewell expression of joy and gratitude. But I hesitate to adopt this view, for I can hardly believe that the Songs of Ascent were not completed before the Maccabæan period.

A hint may now be taken from the Chronicler. In 2 Chron. vi. 40-42 there are quotations, more or less complete, from Ps. cxxx. 2, and from Ps. cxxxii. 8-10. This makes it in some degree probable that Pss. cxxx. and cxxxii. (both evidently congregational, though the former is more quietistic in tone) were composed in the same period, though scarcely at the same time. The latter psalm was written, as we have seen, not very long before a grievous desolation of the land and violation of the Temple. And surely no smaller trouble can have occasioned Ps. cxxx.—that unique expression of contrite self-abasement and confidence in God's covenant-love. As historical students, we cannot interpret the *De Profundis* in the manner of Luther and Wesley and of that fine old poet Phineas Fletcher. It is not from the deeps of purely spiritual despondency but from a 'sea of troubles' that the speaker cries to his God.[y] His sense of sin, or rather of sins, has been stimulated by some sore trouble which has befallen the church-nation. The pledge of forgiveness, too, for which the sufferer pleads, is not merely a spiritual but a temporal blessing—a fact of serious import, to which we shall return. In the next psalm[z] (a work of the same circle, if not of the same author, as Ps. cxxx.), Israel has quieted his perturbed mind, and waits patiently for that forgiveness which must, he feels, already be on its way. 'Though it tarry,' says the leader of the choir to his companions, 'wait for it; yea, hope, Israel, in Jehovah from henceforth even for ever' (Ps. cxxxi. 3; cf. cxxx. 7). Not for such an one are the plots of the political party, nor the speculations of the 'wise men' touching the deep things of God's moral government.

But let us pass on to Ps. cxxxiii., the tone of which will lead us to combine it with Pss. cxxi., cxxii., cxxiv.–cxxix. There is no distinct reference to the Return from the Exile even in cxxvi. 1, cxxvii. 1, but who can believe the 'literary miracle' of a pre-Exile origin? Fair-minded students will, I hope, agree that all, even the 127th,[aa] in spite of its title in the Hebrew,[bb] belong to the same period as the other Psalms of Ascent. Ps. cxxv., for instance, expresses the deepest ground of Israel's misery under heathen rule, viz. the fear of being tempted to acts of infidelity (comp. *v.* 3 with Ps. xix. 14, and *v.* 5 with cxix. 113). Ps. cxxix. adds that, submissive as Israel may be, it is hated by its neighbours for its strange exclusiveness. Pss. cxx. and cxxiii. are not included in this little group, being distinctly persecution psalms. Read them in inverse order, and they become a record of deepening misery amidst malicious neighbours and under irresponsible tyrants. They may be referred either to the time preceding the arrival of Nehemiah, or (comparing Pss. lii. and lvii.) to a still later period, not far from that of Ecclesiastes.

And now we can sum up, so far as regards the Songs of Ascent. This little hymn-book is a mirror of the fluctuating fortunes and feelings of Israel during the Persian and perhaps the early part of the Greek period (when the Diaspora became more extensive). It reveals a strong but not stormily-excited feeling for church and nation, and a sweet, childlike spirit of devotion. It shows that we must not judge of the period referred to entirely from the complaints of Ecclesiastes, who is indeed on one side convicted of exaggeration by the portrait painter of the 'virtuous woman' (Prov. xxxi. 10–31).[cc] There was much pure and bright domestic life, based upon the fear and love of God (Pss. cxxvii., cxxviii.), and much spiritual love of the forms of worship (Pss. cxxii., cxxxiii.), though, being true to facts, the picture is not entirely without shadows.

NOTE [a], p. 48.

So Grätz; he disputes, however, the existence of Purim so early. So, too, Zunz, who asks, 'Would the Jews have made a new festival on the 13th (of Adar), if the 14th were recognized as the feast of Purim?' I have ventured to call this hypercriticism (*Enc. Brit.* viii. 561). There is also a Talmudic tradition on the 'day of Nicanor' (Talm. Bab., *Taanith,* 18*b*), with which that in Maccabees should be compared. Nicanor was a Greek eparch, who every day lifted up his hand against Jerusalem and said, 'When will it fall into my hands, so that I can tread it down?' But when the rule of the Asmonæan house had overpowered him, they cut off his thumbs and great toes, and hung them up on the gates of Jerusalem, with the words, 'On the mouth that spoke so proudly, and on the hands which lifted themselves up against Jerusalem, shall vengeance be taken'" (Wünsche, *Der bab. Talmud*, i. 438). Schürer agrees with Grätz as to the date of the victory.

NOTE ᵇ, p. 48.

The alternative is to refer Pss. cxlviii. and cxlix. (as well as cxlvi., cxlvii., cl.) to the circumstances described in Neh. iv. and vi. (see Dillmann, *Jahrbücher f. deutsche Theologie*, 1858, p. 467, &c.), a course which is not equally favoured by the contents of those psalms.

NOTE ᶜ, p. 48.

1. As to the word 'Aσ. employed in 1 and 2 Macc. Its Hebrew connexion is obvious, and in the light of this it is difficult not to regard the *khasīdīm* of those psalms which on other grounds are probably Maccabæan, as mainly at least consisting of the Asidæan party. The Peshitto translator of the Psalms however did not see this; hence the misleading variety in his rendering of *khasīdīm*. The Syriac translator of 1 Macc. is in another way equally blind. He servilely reproduces the Greek term (1 Macc. ii. 42, Lagarde; ii. 42 and vii. 13, Ambrosian MS.), except at vii. 13 (Lagarde), which he mistranslates. The term *khasīdīm* or 'Ασιδαῖοι has been thought to be connected with 'Essenes,' but this is philologically impossible (comp. Lightfoot, *Colossians*, ed. 3, p. 358). 2. As to the statements respecting the 'Aσ. Those who rallied round 'Mattathias and his friends' are described in 1 Macc. ii. 42 as (*a*) συναγωγὴ 'Ασιδαίων (Geiger and Tischendorf however prefer the reading 'Ιουδαίων), (*b*) ἰσχυροὶ δυνάμει ἀπὸ 'Ισραήλ, (*c*) πᾶς ὁ ἑκουσιαζόμενος τῷ νόμῳ. Here (*b*) is clearly limited by (*c*); the 'valiant men' are primarily νομικοί; they have won their spurs in Biblical study (גִּבֹּרֵי חַיִל in the wider sense). This meaning is confirmed by 1 Macc. vii. 12, 13, where the 'Ασιδαῖοι are members of a συναγωγὴ γραμματέων, which gives the exact force of the phrase in (*a*). The context in which this last passage occurs is important historically. When the Syrian king Demetrius sent Bacchides to reinstal Alcimus as high priest, the Asidæans, recognizing the legitimacy of his claims, and trusting his friendly words, made peace with him. The massacre which followed is perhaps referred to in Ps. lxxix. 2 (see p. 93). The third passage, which refers to the 'Aσ. (2 Macc. xiv. 6), represents them as more conspicuous in the war than they really were. The author, who lived in the last century B.C., did not know who the 'Aσ. really were, and confounds them with the personal adherents of the Maccabæan brothers (called in 1 Macc. ix. 26, 28, 'the friends of Judas').

Note d, p. 49.

Notice also that the ideal of righteousness in cx. 4 corresponds with the description of the faithful who joined Mattathias in the mountains as 'many that sought righteousness and judgment' (1 Macc. ii. 29). The same emphasis on 'righteousness,' and the same accidental absence of the word *khasīdīm*, characterize Ps. cxviii. (see *vv.* 15, 19, 20). Hamburger, following out an idea of Geiger's, infers from the occasional reference to 'the righteous' in Maccabæan psalms that there were two religious parties among the Jews (not counting the Hellenizers)—the *Çaddīkīm* and the *Khasīdīm*, the one the more moderate party (= the Sadducees), the other the strict legalists (= the Pharisees)—and supposes the Maccabees to have set on foot a compromise between them (*Realencyclopädie für Bibel und Talmud*, Abth. ii., art. 'Sadd. u. Phar.'). But Σάδδουκ = Zadok (Jos., *Ant.* xviii. 1, 1), and there is no evidence that the name 'Sadducee' was wittily changed into *Çaddīk*. Wellhausen's view of the parties of the time is historically sounder. Against deriving 'Sadducee' from צדק, see also Dr. Taylor's *Jewish Fathers*, p. 4 (top).

Note e, p. 49.

Cf. cxiii. 9 with (2) Isa. liv. 1–3, xlix. 21; and cxiii. 7–9 with 1 Sam. ii. 5, 8. The Song of Hannah ('a very late interpolation,' Kuenen) is certainly, like Ps. xviii., post-Deuteronomic, and probably an early post-Exile work. It has suffered somewhat from editors and scribes, both in the Hebrew text and in the Sept., and two lines (in *v.* 10*b*) were added as a liturgical close to the song. These lines give it a Messianic tinge (cf. p. 207, on Ps. xviii. 51), and perhaps point to the age of Haggai and Zechariah. There was a reason for the interpolation of the song. The fortunes of Sarah and Hannah (both barren, and yet remembered at last by God) were regarded as types of those of Israel; hence the Biblical accounts of them are the New Year's Day lessons in the Synagogue. The Song of Hannah was originally a hymn of praise of the Church-nation, just as its N. T. counterpart, the *Magnificat*, was originally perhaps a hymn of the Israel redeemed by Christ. Independently Smend has defended the national reference of 1 Sam. ii. 1–10 in Stade's *Zt.*, 1888, p. 144: cf. Driver, *Text of Samuel*, 1890, pp. 21, 22.

Note f, p. 50.

Hermann von der Hardt (1713) actually believed that the Hallel was composed by Ezra for this occasion (see Carpzov, *Introd.* ii. 93).

Note g, p. 50.

Sept. gives Ἀλληλούϊα · Ἀγγαίου καὶ Ζαχαρίου as the title of Pss. cxlvi.–cxlviii. (this version divides our Ps. cxlvii. in two parts). I attach no weight to this; the title is clearly the wrong one for Ps. cxlviii. Theodore assigns all this group to the Restoration period, except Ps. cxlviii. But this ignores the points which this and the neighbouring psalms have in common.

Note h, p. 50.

The author of 1 Macc. (ii. 63) quotes Ps. cxlvi. 4 in a shorter form, as if this psalm were very familiar to him. The later the date of Ps. cxlvi.–cxlvii. is, the more intelligible this becomes.

Note i, p. 50.

On the same analogy of the Egyptian Hallel, Krochmal proposes to call Ps. cvii. the Babylonian Hallel.

Note j, p. 50.

'Hallelujah' is the formula with which the liturgies summoned the worshippers to join in praise.

Note k, p. 50.

Pss. cv. and cvi. are so closely connected together, that one seems justified in transferring 'Hallelujah' from the close of Ps. civ. to the beginning of Ps. cv. (see Grätz, *Psalmen*, i. 91).

Note l, p. 50.

H. von der Hardt finds the occasion for Ps. cxxxvi. in Ezra iii. 10, 11. But this psalm is the companion of Ps. cxxxv., which presupposes the completion of the temple (*v.* 2). Ps. cxxxv. was appointed for the first day of the Passover (*Soferim*, 18, 2); its twin brother is sometimes called the 'great Hallel.'

Note m, p. 51.

Hence the justice of Krochmal's designation (see note i above).

Note n, p. 51.

Theodoret refers this psalm to the victory gained by Jehoshaphat, according to 2 Chron. xx., simply because of the reference (see 2

Chron. xx. 21). The same mechanical criticism as Von der Hardt's (see note ¹). See on Ps. lxxxiii.

NOTE º, p. 51.

Jaddua the high priest, whom Josephus brings into connexion with Alexander, was suggested as the author by Hermann von der Hardt. Simon the Righteous would be better. He, like the psalmist, placed love of the Torah first among Israel's defences (see *Pirqe Aboth*, i. 2), and in his own family he saw the first tokens of advancing corruption. But why seek for a name? I do not believe that the psalmist himself fills an important post; he writes, as Chenery well says, 'in the true spirit of an Eastern scholar' (*The Assemblies of Al Hariri*, i. 89). The view, mentioned by Ibn Ezra, that the psalmist is a young captive of high rank in Babylon (such as Daniel), need not be discussed here (see Comm.), though it has been revived by Dr. Forbes (1888).

NOTE ᵖ, p. 51.

I take שִׁיר הַמַּעֲלוֹת as = שִׁירֵי הַמַּעֲלָה; the same idiom as in בֵּית הָאָבוֹת. The title therefore properly belongs to the collection, and not to any particular member of it. Those who in error prefixed it to each psalm must have taken מַעֲלוֹת in the sense of 'pilgrim-caravans;' cf. the title of Ps. cxxi. 1 שִׁיר לַמַּעֲלוֹת, which is grammatically more correct. The traditional Hebrew explanation, however, is that these fifteen songs were so called from as many steps in the temple. This has been lately advocated in a very elaborate form (based of course on Talm. Bab., *Succa*, 51*b*) by Grätz. For six nights, he says, during the Feast of Booths, multitudes thronged the temple-courts in joyful expectation of the bringing of the water from Siloam for the solemn libation which played such a great part in the later ritual. Towards morning their minds were attuned to serious thoughts by the singing of psalms to the accompaniment of musical instruments. The singers were Levites, who stood on the fifteen steps which led from the inner court to the court of the women, and sang the fifteen psalms which, from the place occupied by the Levites, were called the Step-psalms. Grätz also maintains that Pss. cxxxv. and cxxxvi. were sung by the people in response to the song of the Levites. It is an objection to this theory that the Talmud itself does not say either that the Levites sang these fifteen psalms, or that the psalms in question derived their name from the steps. Shortly afterwards, indeed (*Succa*, 53*a*), it does explain their name, but in connexion with a legend upon David and Ahithophel. Nor is it certain that the Sept. title ᾠδὴ τῶν ἀναβαθμῶν is anything more than an uncomprehending literal translation.

NOTE ᵠ, p. 52.

H. von der Hardt ascribed them all to Nehemiah. But Hengstenberg is at least right so far as this—that they are not all from one pen, though, as this critic thinks, they 'fit in well enough to each other.' The Sinaitic Codex of the Sept. Psalms ascribes Pss. cxxii., cxxiv., cxxxi., cxxxiii. to David (for the precise amount of evidence, see Swete). Delitzsch has proved that this, however impossible, is not purely arbitrary.

NOTE ʳ, p. 52.

Ps. cxxii. is ascribed to David simply because the name occurs in *v.* 5. It is, however, post-Exile because of the perfects in *vv.* 4, 5, and, at any rate, not earlier than Nehemiah, because such a bright little psalm on the 'well-knit city' could not have been composed till after that great achievement of Nehemiah—the permanent rebuilding of the walls.

NOTE ˢ, p. 52.

In both psalms Israel longs for the fulfilment of the promise to David (2 Sam. vii.), but in Ps. cxxxii. there is no trace of any recent crushing calamity. Ben Sira, too, in his encomium upon 'mighty men,' alludes to the same prophetic promise (Ecclus. xlvii. 1, 11, 22).

NOTE ᵗ, p. 52.

Hitzig supposes this psalm to have been written for the first celebration of τὰ φῶτα (Jos., *Ant.* xii. 7, 7); comp. נֵר 'a lamp,' *v.* 17. But this assumes that *vv.* 8-10 were adopted from 2 Chron. vi. 41, 42, a view which lacks all probability. That the high priest ('Jehovah's anointed,' *v.* 10; cf. lxxxiv. 10) is προστάτης τοῦ λαοῦ in the writer's time may, however, be taken as certain. Such importance could never have been attached to the priests by a temple-poet of the pre-Exile period. Verse 18 refers probably to the high priestly diadem; comp. יָצִיץ נִזְרוֹ with Ex. xxxix. 30, and see below, p. 199.

NOTE ᵘ, p. 52.

Note the deep earnestness in the psalmist's prayer for the priests and for the *khasīdīm*.

NOTE ᵛ, p. 53.

Syncellus (Dindorf), i. 486. The pseudo-Hecatæus, quoted by Josephus (*c. Ap.* i. 22), tells us of cruel deaths endured by the Jews for their religion in the Persian period. But this is not historical (see Grätz, *Gesch. der Juden*, iii., ed. 4, p. 608).

NOTE ʷ, p. 53.

Ps. cxxxiv. (cf. on Ps. viii.) was probably written for use at the nightly vigils of the priests and Levites (see the nearly contemporary statement of Hecatæus of Abdera in Jos., *c. Ap.* i. 22, and the Talmudic notices in Delitzsch). Grätz boldly connects it (as the complement to which he regards what now forms Pss. cxxxv., cxxxvi.) with the popular rejoicing at the ceremony of the water-libation at the Feast of Booths. He therefore brings it down to the time of Salome Alexandra (between 78 and 69 B.C.). 'In the nights' refers, he thinks, to the six nights of the feast, during which the people remained in the temple-courts and the Levites sang the fifteen 'Step-psalms' (*Monatsschrift*, 1879, p. 241).

NOTE ˣ, p. 53.

More especially if Ps. cxxxiv. 1 be filled out from the Septuagint.

NOTE ʸ, p. 54.

St. Augustine compares the cry of Jonah out of the midst of Sheól (Jon. ii.). Both psalms, in fact, are prayers of the Jewish Church.

NOTE ᶻ, p. 54.

For the title *l'dāvīd*, cf. 2 Sam. vi. 22; 1 Sam. xviii. 18, 23. It is wanting, however, in Sept. (Cod. Al.), Jerome, and Targum. The Peshitto makes the psalm relate to the high priest Joshua (so too Grätz, and Paul Haupt in *Hebraica*, Jan. 1886, p. 105).

NOTE ᵃᵃ, p. 54.

Dean Plumptre has well illustrated cxxvii. 1 by cxviii. 22 and the images drawn from building in Zechariah's prophecies.

NOTE ᵇᵇ, p. 54.

Hengstenberg justifies the Hebrew title 'of Solomon' by the supposed parallelism between *v.* 2 and 1 Kings iii. 5–14 (ידידו

being Solomon; cf. above on Ps. xlv.), and by the coincidence between the ideas of the psalms and those of Proverbs (see especially Prov. x. 22). Against the Solomonic authorship of Proverbs, however, see *Job and Solomon*, pp. 130–133. The title is not found in Sept., which in *v.* 2 reads ἀγαπητοῖς. It was therefore probably inserted subsequently to the time of Simon.

NOTE cc, p. 55.

On this fine alphabetic poem see *Job and Solomon*, pp. 154, 155.

PART II.

CONCLUSION OF THE ANALYSIS.

I RESUME the consideration of the question, Are there any psalms in Books IV. and V. which require to be dated before the Maccabæan period, or at any rate before the promulgation of the Law by Ezra? I may remind you that we have still twenty-five psalms to consider, viz. xc. (which is ascribed to Moses), xci.–c., cii. and cxxxvii. (which are anonymous), ci., ciii. and civ. (these two are properly but one psalm), cix., cxxxviii.–cxlv., which the titles assign to David. It is needless to spend time on proving that the great hymn to Providence (Pss. ciii., civ.) belongs to the same period as Pss. cv.–cvii., viz. the second half of the Persian rule.[a] But what is to be said of Ps. cix., the tone of which differs so widely from that of the neighbouring psalms? It would be too bold to attempt to date it without making sure that we understand it. Is it Messianic? Certainly not, if there be such a science as historical exegesis. I know that our Messiah is reported to have uttered a woe upon His betrayer (Matt. xxvi. 24), but who can compare the restrained passion of those solemn and divinely unselfish words with the refined cruelty of *vv.* 6–20 of the 109th psalm?[b] It is to the honour of Theodore of Mopsuestia, that alone among the Christian fathers he denied that this psalm, under the form of a prayer of Jesus Christ, is a prediction of the treason of Judas.[c] Those who go thus far with Theodore will also, with him, naturally deny that the psalm is of Davidic authorship. Indeed, the burden of proof lies upon those who, contrary to all philological evidence, assert it. Fancy the magnanimous David uttering these laboured imprecations! No: the speaker is not a brave and bold warrior, but a sensitive poet, excited beyond endurance by the sufferings of his people. Believing like Balaam in the power of a curse,[d] he comes forward to execrate this Haman—this arch-enemy of Jehovah's people and religion. In a qualified sense, however, we may accept Chrysostom's explanation of the psalm as προφητεία ἐν εἴδει ἀρᾶς.[1] It expressed, that is, a quasi-prophetic presentiment that the 'curse causeless,' which 'cannot come' (Prov. xxvi. 2) on the good man, will return through the deserved imprecations of the psalmist in the form of punishment on the bad man who uttered it. This presentiment, however, was no genuine intuition but a mere inherited notion, and it was corrupted in the psalmist's mind by the infirmities of human passion. Verses 6–20 are therefore not a prophecy in the truest sense. True prophecy is closely related to prayer.[2] 'Call unto Me, and I will answer thee' (said Jehovah to His prophet), 'and will show thee great things, and secret things which thou knewest not' (Jer. xxxiii. 3). But is there in the opening verses a single tender glance upwards,[3] hallowing the psalmist for his work? No. He does indeed 'pour out his heart' (lxii. 9); but a mere 'pouring out' is not, in the fullest sense, prayer, though it may be, and even in the Psalms often is, the preliminary to true prayer. The element of true prayer in Ps. cix. begins with the appeal to Jehovah's Name in v. 21; all that precedes is but so much clearing away of 'perilous stuff.' We are not bound to defend vv. 6–20 simply because they are found in the Psalter. If I am to love the psalmists, I must sometimes be allowed, I will not say to censure, but to pity them. And have we not in this psalm an occasion for pity quite as great as anywhere in the Book of Job, not so much in the vehemence of the language as in the extremity of the sufferings which led to it?

Some one may object to this comparison that the speeches of Job were not penned by the great sufferer himself. True; but by a sufferer they *were* penned, and by one who, like the psalmist, thought more of the troubles of his people than of his own. The much-tried man who speaks under the mask

---

[1] *Opera* (ed. 1636), iii. 313. He compares Gen. xlix. 37, ix. 25, Matt. xi. 21–23, xxiii. 37, 38.
[2] See Riehm, *Messianische Weissagung*, p. 23 (ed. 1), or p. 38 (ed. 2); comp. Delitzsch, *Messianic Prophecies*, p. 6.
[3] Hab. ii. 1; cf. Ps. v. 4.

of 'Job' is a greater poet than the author of Ps. cix.—that is the chief difference between them. Emotion makes even ordinary natures speak poetically. If, therefore, the author of Ps. cix. does not speak poetically, may we not infer that his passion has already begun to cool, and that he uses language in excess of his feeling? Certainly there is nothing elsewhere in the Psalter (even in Ps. lxix.[e]) quite as startling as *vv.* 6–20. On the other hand, *vv.* 2–5 and 26–31 have a genuine lyric note. They, at least, were written at the inspiration of love. It follows that the original psalm, like so many of the prophecies, was retouched and added to by the author.

The additions are no doubt the least pleasing part of the psalm, but it is from them chiefly that we must determine the date. Some phenomena in them may at first sight seem to favour a Babylonian origin. Thus (1) the awful intensity of the imprecations reminds us of the *mamît* or objectified curse, so prominent in the Babylonian hymns;[1] (2) there are parallels of thought and expression in the Book of Job[f] (a work of the Exile); and (3) the cursing of wicked persecutors meets us again in Isa. lxv. 15—indeed, both Isa. lxv. and lxvi. imply (equally with Ps. cix.) that faithful Israelites were contemned and oppressed by hostile kinsmen (see Isa. lxv. 5, lxvi. 5). Certainly there is nothing in Ps. cix. to suggest a pre-Exile date. But must we therefore assign it to the Exile period? The objectified curse is not peculiar to Babylon.[2] Job was imitated long after the Exile. Isa. lxv. and lxvi. were not written before the Persian period. Then consider (1) the points of contact between our psalm and Ps. cii.,[g] and (2) the stylistic defects of the former, and say if you find any reason for placing Ps. cix. earlier than the time of Nehemiah[h] (in which case the enemy might be Sanballat) or even perhaps than the close of the Persian age.[i] The refined cruelty of *vv.* 6–20 reminds us of an equally artificial chapter in the Book of Isaiah (chap. xxxiv.), which I have elsewhere referred to the same period.

We now pass on to Pss. cxxxviii.–cxlv. (all headed *l'dāvīd*). Ewald separates Pss. cxl.–cxlii., and regards them

---

[1] Sayce, *Hibbert Lectures*, p. 306 &c.; Hommel, *Die semit. Völker*, i. 367.
[2] See Num. v. 11–29; cf. *Koran*, iii. 54, *la'nata-llahi*, 'God's curse.'

F

as pre-Exilic. This appears to me arbitrary. Either the whole group or no part of it is ancient. Surely the general characteristics, religious and stylistic, of the group are post-Exilic, an idea which is already suggested in the headings of Pss. cxxxviii. and cxxxix. in Cod. Alex. of the Septuagint. 'Davidic' these psalms can only be as echoes of earlier so-called Davidic psalms.[j] One may admit, however, that Pss. cxl.–cxliii. form a minor group in themselves,[k] the date of which is approximately determined by the dependence of cxliii. 5 on lxxvii. 6 (Ps. lxxvii. belongs to the close of the Persian period). I do not insist on regarding these four psalms as Maccabæan, in spite of the special appropriateness of some passages to the great persecution and revolt of the second century[1] (see cxl. 8b, cxli. 4–7). Nor can any one be prevented from explaining Ps. cxlv. from the pre-Maccabæan age by the occurrence of the word *khasīdīm* in v. 10, and the parallelism between v. 13 and Dan. iii. 33, iv. 31. The psalm, like most alphabetical ones, is somewhat vague. But the coincidences between Pss. cxlv. and cxlvi. make a Maccabæan origin reasonable for the former as well as the latter psalm.[m] Ps. cxliv. is composite, as Ewald rightly points out. But I cannot, contrary to the stylistic evidence, admit that vv. 12–14 are a pre-Exile fragment.[n] It is, no doubt, Ps. cxli. which misled the great critic—a psalm which is certainly the monument of a bitter persecution, but not of Manasseh's (comp. v. 4 with 2 Macc. vi. 18 and v. 7 with lxxix. 2). Ps. cxliv. consists of two parts, once independent, but united probably by Simon and his priestly helpers. Both are of post-Exile origin,[o] and very possibly of the Greek period; v. 8,

> Whose mouth speaketh deception,
> And their right hand is a right hand of falsehood,

is too strikingly applicable to the Græco-Syrian kings,[p] and the reference to palace architecture in v. 12 may suggest the influence of Greek art. Notice, too, the prayer ascribed to Judas in 1 Macc. iv. 30, 'Blessed art thou, O Saviour of Israel, who didst quell the violence of the mighty man by the hand of thy servant David.' Do not these words throw a light on v. 10 of our psalm?

---

[1] Ps. cxli. 3 may be alluded to in Ecclus. xxii. 27 (see App. I.).

> It is he that giveth salvation to kings,
> That rescueth David his servant from the hurtful sword.

For was not the life of Judas full of parallels to the early life of David? Fitly, then, did this psalmist accommodate to his own times choice phrases from the 18th psalm. It is the distinction of Theodore of Mopsuestia to have first seen that those times were the Maccabæan.[q]

To the close of the Persian, if not to the beginning of the Greek age,[r] we must, upon stylistic and other grounds, refer the composition of the 139th psalm—that profound confession of faith, the spirit of which each Christian student of nature would desire to make his own. The contents agree with this date. The psalm evidently stands in the second half of that long reflective period, the poetic masterpiece of which is the Book of Job, and it may perhaps be grouped with Ps. lxxiii. In *vv.* 19-21 we catch a glimpse of facts such as brought Koheleth so dangerously near to pessimism.

The first psalm of this group (Ps. cxxxviii.) is one of the least original in the Psalter, but it strikes the note characteristic of the post-Exile period. A Maccabæan date is most in harmony with the spirit of daring enterprise claimed by the speaker in *v.* 3, and is directly suggested by the dependence of *v.* 8*a* upon Ps. lvii. 3.[s]

We pause next at that fine sketch of the character of an ideal ruler—the 101st psalm. It was evidently written by a student of Proverbs (or of parts of Proverbs),[t] and since Hezekiah was both a poet and a lover of proverbs (though his 'song' is of disputed genuineness), and also a reformer, Dr. Grätz suggests that he may be the author of this psalm. There is nothing, however, in the style of the psalm, which is vigorous, but unpoetic, to make an early date plausible, and if all the neighbouring psalms are post-Exilic, some strong reason is required for making this one pre-Exilic. With a late historical background Ps. ci. becomes at once intelligible and interesting. The phraseology of *v.* 1 reminds us of Ps. lxxxix. 2, and the ejaculation in *v.* 2*a* (see my note), of Mal. iii. 1. Both these passages, however, belong to the second half of the Persian period, which is too early for a psalm that presupposes the national independence. Now compare Ps. ci. with Ps. cx. They are almost equally short, and serve as the opening and closing psalms of the decade. Ps. cx. is Maccabæan; it sets before us Simon as a 'king of righteousness,' and as sitting at Jehovah's right hand on Mount Zion. Ps. ci. acquires a new distinctness when regarded as a companion to Ps. cx. How forcible is the phrase 'city of Jehovah'[u] (v. 8) as a protest against the Hellenizing party! How real the expression of—shall I say, holy, or fanatical—zeal[v] becomes, if we take it as the programme of one whose achievements are thus described in the history: 'He strengthened all the humble ones of his people; he studied the law to practise it,[1] and every lawless and wicked person he cut off'[2] (1 Macc. xiv. 14). And if a more positive statement be desired to justify us in our reference of Ps. ci. 8 to Simon, take these words of the same narrator: 'so that they also that were in the city of David in Jerusalem, who had made themselves a fortress, out of which they issued, and polluted all about the sanctuary, &c., were cut off'[3] (1 Macc. xiv. 36). There is, I may now add, much reason to suppose that Ps. ci. was written to inaugurate a festival which the Jewish Calendar (*Megillath Ta'anith*, vi. 3) mentions for the 22nd day of Elul, as the celebration of the destruction of the Hellenists.[w]

But I seem to hear some one objecting that, upon this view, Pss. ci. and cx. ought to change places. I reply that the psalms were not arranged on principles of strict chronology. Still Hitzig may possibly be right in supposing the predecessor of Simon to be the subject of Ps. ci.[x] After the death of the hero Judas, we are told, 'The transgressors put forth their heads[4] in all the borders of Israel, and there rose up all such as wrought iniquity,' till Jonathan 'began to judge the people, and extinguished[5] the ungodly (i.e. the Hellenizing party) out of Israel' (1 Macc. ix. 23, 73). It was only after this that the judge became also the high priest, or, as the historian says, 'put on the holy robe' (1 Macc. x. 21), and with this coincides the fact that Ps. ci. contains no reference to the priesthood.

Some one may, perhaps, now ask, why, in the collection

---

[1] ἐξεζήτησε, cf. Sept. civ. (cv.) 45.
[2] ἐξῆρεν, cf. Sept. Deut. xix. 19, Judg. xx. 13 = בָּעַר.
[3] τοῦ ἐξαρθῆναι (see last note).   [4] ἐξέκυψαν.   [5] ἠφάνισε.

CONCLUSION OF THE ANALYSIS.

edited (as I have said) by Simon and his friends, thirteen psalms were ascribed to David, when all the rest but one were left in 'orphanhood' (to use the Jewish phrase), that is, anonymous. Without claiming omniscience, I venture to give my judgment. I believe that these psalms never existed separately as a so-called Davidic hymnbook, and that the collectors provided them with the title *l'dāvīd* in order to give these later books a certain external similarity to the two earliest. The Septuagint translator, or the writer of the Hebrew MS. which he used, sprinkled this title more freely still (see Pss. xc., xcii.–xcviii.): the Greek Psalter even rejoices in an extra psalm entitled ἰδιόγραφος εἰς Δαυίδ. In some cases, even in the Hebrew text, the recipients of this honour seem to have been picked out at random; in others, some excuse for the title is suggested by the contents of the psalms.[y] The ideal description in Ps. ci. seemed suitable enough for the idealized second founder of the monarchy; it reminds us in fact of the idealizing description of David in 2 Sam. xxiii. 2–7 (Josian). Ps. cx. relates, as we have seen, to the heir of the Davidic promises. Pss. cxl.–cxliii. contain numerous allusions to so-called Davidic psalms in earlier books. Lastly, Ps. cxlv., together with the Hallelujah group (cxlvi.–cl.), of which it probably formed the introduction, may have been regarded as a תְּהִלָּה (see the title), as an outburst of jubilant praise, worthy of David himself. So the Jews themselves certainly thought in the time of Mohammed, in one of whose Suras (xxxiv. 10) occur the words, 'And we did give David grace from us, "O ye mountains! echo (God's praises) with him, and ye birds"' (alluding to Ps. cxlviii. 9, 10).

This latter explanation may also justify the title given in the Sept.[z] to Ps. cxxxvii., which, from an æsthetic point of view, is perhaps the most striking in the two last books. In somewhat earlier times, it would, I suppose, have been headed, 'of the sons of Korah.' It is, in fact, in some respects closely analogous to that beautiful lyric which has been divided into Pss. xlii. and xliii., and like it is evidently the work of a temple-musician. When was it written? A post-Exile date is demanded by critical exegesis and favoured by certain grammatical forms.[1] Yet the psalm must not be placed too

---
[1] See Appendix II.

early :[aa] so striking a poem, if composed soon after the Return, would have found a home in the 3rd Book of the Psalms. Let us group it then with Pss. cxxxv. and cxxxvi., and place it in the time of Simon the Maccabee. It is in the fullest sense a 'dramatic lyric.' Just as the author of Ps. xviii. thinks himself into the soul of David, so a later temple-singer identifies himself by sympathy with his exiled predecessors in Babylon.[bb] It was not, however, solely an exercise of the imagination. Edom and Babylon were, even to the prophets, types of the class of Jehovah's enemies.[cc] To a Maccabæan writer (cf. 1 Macc. v. 1, 3) they represented the 'nations' which in his own day had 'come into God's inheritance' (Ps. lxxix. 1), and need I remind you that Rabbinical writers constantly identify Edom and Rome?

The 102nd psalm appears from the heading to have become a popular favourite, and, as such, to have received a partly new interpretation before the close of the Psalter.[dd] No psalm was more clearly written for the collective use of the Church, but sanction was early given by the heading to a secondary individualistic interpretation. It must therefore have been written considerably before the time of the Maccabees. That it is not earlier than the close of the Exile, is evident from its allusions not only to the Book of Job, but to the Second Isaiah.[ee] But it may with good reason be placed, with other kindred elegiac psalms, much later than this. The Restoration was so inadequate a fulfilment of the Second Isaiah's prophecies that a post-Exile psalmist could not but repeat the yearning aspirations of the great prophet, just as other poets went on imitating the Book of Job[1] long after the antitype of Job (Israel) had seen a few gleams of happiness. Our psalmist was one of those moderately gifted writers, whose precise place in the long post-Exile period may sometimes be uncertain. But his own date can surely be fixed without much hesitation. Accompany Nehemiah on his lonely ride around the burned walls of Jerusalem (Neh. ii. 11–20), and listen to Sanballat mocking at the Jews for attempting to 'revive the stones out of the heaps of rubbish' (Neh. iv. 2); you will then recognize the occasion of this psalm, and sympathize with the plaintive words,

---

[1] *Job and Solomon*, pp. 67–70; cf. Hatch, *Essays in Biblical Greek*, p. 244.

For thy servants take pleasure in her stones,
And it pitieth them to see her in the dust.'—(cii. 14.)

We have thus gained a precious source of information for the state of things at Jerusalem during a part of that period (B.C. 457–445) which is undescribed in the Books of Ezra and Nehemiah.[ff] There is good reason to think that it was not Zerubbabel but Ezra who rebuilt the walls; Zechariah in fact anticipates that Jerusalem will remain unfortified, Jehovah being 'a wall of fire unto her round about' (Zech. ii. 4). Great must have been the 'affliction and reproach' of the Jews in 'the province' when, as a consequence, direct or indirect, of the revolt of the great satrap Megabyzos, 'the wall was broken down and the gates thereof burned with fire' (Neh. i. 3).[gg] But I must now ask you to turn back from 'the prayer of the afflicted when he is fainting,' to the glorious 'new song'[hh] (xcvi. 1). It may seem to you an abrupt transition, but it is not really more so than one which occurs in that very 'prayer of the afflicted.' How melancholy is the opening of Ps. cii., but how bright are the subsequent flashes of anticipation which proceed either from that 'new song' or from its inspiring source in prophecy! 'New song' do I call it? It is rather a heptad of new songs (viz. Pss. xciii. and xcv.–c., to which Ps. xlvii. might have been added), all relating to the enthronization upon Zion of the Divine King (Isa. lii. 7)—that 'far off event' to which (see Lect. VII.) the whole previous history of Israel had moved. Or, if you will, we may describe it as a psalm in seven parts, of which Ps. xciii., when disengaged from the fragment attached to it, forms the introduction, and Ps. c. an exactly corresponding conclusion. To what period shall we refer it? Can we study the parallel passages in the two compositions, and doubt that the 'new song' is very little later than the work of the prophet commonly known as the Second Isaiah?[ii] I need not remind you of the strong lyric element in the great Restoration-Prophecy (see e.g. the 'new song' in Isa. xlii. 10–13). The Second Isaiah was almost as much a poet as a prophet, and his work presupposes the existence of a circle of hymnists among the exiles in Babylonia.[1] It is, I believe, a conjecture

---

[1] Comp. *The Prophecies of Isaiah*, iv. 3, ii. 250.

which accounts for all the facts, that one of the younger members of this circle composed this psalm or group of psalms to celebrate the completion of the second temple, B.C. 516. Let the student work out this idea for himself in the light of Ezra vi. 16, and he will be surprised at the fuller meaning which the too familiar phrases acquire. Not without reason did the Templar Knights select the *Venite* as their battle-song, and the Chronicler insert the following psalm in the composite thanksgiving-hymn, sung, as he declares, on the introduction of the ark into the city of David (1 Chron. xvi. 7). And probably not without a basis of tradition did the Septuagint translator give this title to Ps. xcvi., ὅτε ὁ οἶκος οἰκοδομεῖται μετὰ τὴν αἰχμαλωσίαν.[jj]

There still remain three anonymous psalms to date, or, as I may surely say, to understand; these are Pss. xci., xcii., and xciv. How strangely does Ps. xciv. intervene between the two jubilant psalms xciii. and xcv.! Is this due to some sacramental secret, or is it a freak of chance? It is neither the one nor the other. It is not indeed enough to explain it by a regard for phraseological coincidences (comp. xciv. 22, xcv. 1). The true reason seems to be a liturgical one. We know from the Sept. that the arrangement of psalms to be sung on the successive week days which is recorded in the Talmud[kk] was in existence when that version was made. Ps. xcii., e.g., is already marked in the Sept. (as well as in the Hebrew) as the Sabbath-psalm (εἰς τὴν ἡμέραν τοῦ σαββάτου); Ps. xciii. is Friday's psalm (εἰς τὴν ἡμέραν τοῦ προσαββάτου); Ps. xciv. is Wednesday's psalm (τετράδι σαββάτου). The order of Pss. xcii., xciii., and xciv. seems to have arisen out of an attempt (not carried very far) to promote liturgical convenience. Obviously, however, Ps. xciv. must be later than Ps. xciii., from which it differs so much in tone and import. We may safely place it chronologically not far from Ps. cxxxix. Both psalms were written by lovers of Job (that masterpiece of the Exile); both show the same painful interest in the perennial problem of suffering. But trouble pressed more heavily on the author of Ps. xciv., who (if not a contemporary of Judas the Maccabee) may perhaps have seen those terrible days (see on Ps. cxxxii.), when rebellious Judæa was so severely punished by the soldiery of Artaxerxes Ochus.

In Pss. xci. and xcii. we feel that we are in a different

atmosphere. Through the former we become acquainted with another of Job's friends—his later and better friends. Notice in *v.* 1 the two divine names 'Elyōn and Shaddai, which are both marks of a late date,[1] and more especially the latter, which is in a high degree characteristic of the Book of Job. Our psalmist's favourite passage of Job occurs in a speech of Eliphaz (Job v. 17–23); he imitates the picturesque language of the Temanite, but gives it a new and paradoxical sense. Taken literally indeed the psalm would have been most unfit for use in the second temple, but, understood as Gordon understood it, it becomes one of the fairest fruits of the divine education of Israel. To enjoy it we should, I think, read it immediately after Ps. xc., to which it supplies the finest of contrasts. The psalmist, who would fain speak for Israel, 'mourns no more his vanished years;'[1] his outer and inner conflicts have but deepened his sense of the love which has brought him through them, and he 'rejoices in hope of the glory of God.'

The next psalm (xcii.) is a hymn to God's faithfulness. The author is not one who sees δι' ἐσόπτρου ἐν αἰνίγματι. Revelation has made the 'dark speech' or 'enigma' of Ps. xlix. 5 plain to him. God has repeatedly stepped forth in history and justified His ways. The poet looks back upon the fall of two great world-empires, and upon the recent captures of Babylon by Darius Hystaspis (520) and Xerxes (481). He sums up this series of judgments in idealizing language (xcii. 8), which reminds one of a psalm in the First Book (ix. 6, 7). 'Faith cannot be satisfied with weak expressions or imperfect fulfilments.' But the poet, speaking in the name of the more thoughtful members of the Church, cannot yet forget distressful experiences during the blossom-time of ungodliness; he belongs to a somewhat different circle of religious thinkers from the author of Ps. xci. The latter is so absorbed in communion with God that he cannot spare even one stray thought for the days that are past. Yet both writers may be contemporary, and have written in that new sense of security and of energy awakened by Ezra and Nehemiah; and both can add vividness to the picture of the new reformation which, as presented to us in the fragmentary chronicles, is too monotonous in colouring.

[1] Cf. Ps. xc. 9, 10.

We have at length, in our voyage upwards through the last of the Psalters, arrived at port. Can it be called the 'haven where we would be'—this 90th psalm, regarded in the light of historical criticism and exegesis? It is incumbent upon me to give some answer to this question, because in spite of the fact that almost all the ancient and mediæval,[mm] and many of the best modern Christian commentators, deny the psalm to Moses, most English readers are wedded to a belief in the correctness of the title.[nn] I trust to be able to deal frankly and yet considerately with this deeply rooted prejudice. It is true that I find nothing in the language or ideas of this psalm which suggests the fourteenth century B.C. But this is not because I disbelieve in the historical position of Moses, or desire to detract from the great leader's fame.[oo] I should be overjoyed to be shown Mosaic songs similar in psychological truth and linguistic peculiarity to the Gâthic chants of Zoroaster. But I cannot reconcile myself to taking one of its finest monuments from the post-Exile period, and practically rewriting it by an imaginative exegesis to suit the age of Moses. I know that most Bible students regard the question differently, so that what to me is affirmation and discovery, to them is negation and loss. But let such remember that the psalm itself cannot be denied, cannot be lost, and I think that to those who are interested in the divine education of Israel the newer view of Ps. xc., far from belittling it, will invest it with a more pathetic beauty. The case of this song is exactly parallel to that of the poem of Job. Who that has assimilated a more critical view would wish to return to the obsolete theory that it was written by Moses? Putting aside a few half-understood but vaguely edifying passages, what religious help was there in the view of Job as a literally true history written by Moses? But which of us moderns is *not* helped by that almost perfect expression of the conflicting thoughts of an earnest man on the great problem of suffering which criticism reveals to us? And who is most edified by the 90th psalm? He who regards it as a verbally inspired Mosaic work, or he who thankfully accepts ill-connected thoughts, sometimes both right in themselves and grandly expressed, sometimes only half-right and plainly or even awkwardly put, but all proceeding from one who deeply loved his Church, his Bible, and above all his God?

The Mosaic theory of Ps. xc. has passed through several phases. A Rabbi consulted by Origen (Iullos = Hillel) held that its title in the Hebrew and in the Greek determined the Mosaic authorship, not only of that psalm, but of the ten following anonymous psalms; and the same view is found in the Midrash.[pp] The idea was that each psalm corresponded to one of the eleven blessings in Deut. xxxiii. This is an extreme form of the theory. A view suggested by Grotius [qq] is that some later poet may have written the psalm in the character of Moses, analogies for which could doubtless be produced from the Old Testament and from the Psalter itself. But who that approaches our psalm with a fresh mind can accept either this or any other form of the Mosaic theory? If Ps. xc. be an 'imaginary psalm of Moses,' why has the author in *v.* 10 contradicted the statement of Deut. xxxiv. 7 that Moses 'was 120 years old when he died'?[rr] Or if it be really of Mosaic authorship why did the author of that statement (which by the way is in perfect harmony with similar statements respecting Aaron, Joshua, and Caleb) venture to make it in opposition to the psalm? No; the psalm is a precious historical record; it has the ring of genuine passion, but the age of which it is the monument is not the Mosaic.

How, then, shall we account for the title, and when was the psalm written? It was assigned to Moses (as the 110th psalm was to David) partly as a mark of distinction and to ensure for it the respect of future generations. Upon the whole, it must be confessed that the Jewish Church of the Exile and post-Exile period cared but little for its own history. It 'thought upon' the stones of the outward temple, but not much upon those records of the past which are the stones of a temple not made with hands. It was not, however, by a pure caprice that either Moses or David was fixed upon for these important temple psalms. Of the title of the 110th psalm I have spoken already; that of the 90th was suggested by the phraseological parallels between that psalm and the poems in Deut. xxxii. and (perhaps) xxxiii.,[ss] which had long since been ascribed to Moses. The author of the title was not critic enough to see that the contents of both these poems made it impossible that they should really have been written by Moses, and hailed the opportunity of adding another to the laurels of the 'beloved of God and men, whose memorial is blessed' (Ecclus. xlv. 1).

When was the 90th psalm written? Of course later than the main part of the Second Isaiah, the insertion of the Song and Blessing 'of Moses' in Deuteronomy, and the promulgation of the Pentateuch by Ezra, and, as we may presume, not long before, or after, the nearest group of psalms. Some light may be gained by comparing $v.$ 8b with xix. 13b, and $vv.$ 13–17 with xcii. 5–7, 10, 11. The εὐλάβεια of the phrases 'hidden' and 'unknown faults' is characteristic of an age trained to scrupulousness by the strict observance of the Law (see exposition in pp. 356, 357), and the prayer in $vv.$ 13–17 may not improbably be that of which the answer is commemorated in Ps. xcii. If so, 'the work of our hands' (xc. 17) may be fitly illustrated by Ezra vi. 22 and Neh. ii. 18, 20. In short, the psalm may be dated during or just after that reorganization of the Church-people which was completed by Ezra the scribe and Nehemiah the governor.

Note a, p. 63.

I have already remarked on the free, poetic use of the post-Exile cosmogony in Gen. i. Cf. also on Ps. viii.

Note b, p. 63.

Most kindly but decidedly did an Oriel Canon and Bampton Lecturer in 1840 decline to be rebuked for holding that 'even the psalmists may sometimes have been permitted in some of their expressions to fall below the Christian standard of holiness and charity' (Hawkins, *Bampton Lectures*, pp. 306–308). The 109th psalm is an extreme instance of this imperfection. As Grotius says, 'Hoc carmen possumus appellare 'Αράς, sive, ut Virgilius, *Diras*; multum habet hoc de spiritu Legis.'

Note c, p. 63.

It is, however, also to the credit of Theodore's glorious friend St. Chrysostom that, though in deference to the 'prince of the apostles,' he admits that the psalm contains references to Judas, he denies that it is *throughout* prophetic of the great treason. Parts, according to him, refer to some one who plotted against the priesthood after the Return from Babylon ; οἱ φιλοπονώτεροι ἴσασι τοῦτο. 'I shall not cease,' he continues, 'to repeat that though these things seem to be a curse, they are really a prophecy showing how God is irritated by plots against the priesthood.' Contrast Theodore's weak-kneed follower Theodoret ! But though, as a matter of course, we reject the old title *psalmus Iscarioticus*, we must not weaken the force of the poem by taking *vv.* 6–15 as simply a quotation from the curses of the wicked man—the malevolent words with which he sought to blast the poor, helpless god-fearing Israelites. Considering (1) the frequency with which 'we' and 'I' alternate in the psalms, and the probability that in many psalms in which 'I' predominates the speaker is the Church nation ; (2) that in not a few psalms (e.g. xiv., xxxvii., cxl.) the wicked are described now in the 3rd pers. sing. and now in the 3rd pers. plur. ; and (3) that the curses in Ps. cix. are but a little more violent than those in Ps. lxix., which obviously refer to a class of bad men, we can hardly, I think, do otherwise than interpret *vv.* 6–19 as directed against either a class (see the Peshitto) or a class as summed up in their leader (just as the class of pious Israelites is summed up in the psalmist). The individualizing features in the description are so strong that I venture to prefer the latter alternative, which is also nearer to the traditional Church view. It is perhaps surprising that Ps. cix. was not, like Ps. vii., appointed for the Feast of Purim ; יִמַּח שְׁמוֹ (see cix. 13, and comp. Sept.) at any rate became the popular formula for execrating the name of Haman.

Note ^d, p. 64.

Balaam is but a strong instance of the common Semitic belief (cf. Kalisch, *Balaam*, pp. 99–102).

Note ^e, p. 65.

Altogether the nearest parallel is Ps. lxix. Both psalms have been ascribed to Jeremiah (Ps. lxix. by Hitzig, Ps. cix. by Mr. Ball). But Jeremiah, I think, never brooded over his resentment thus.

Note ^f, p. 65.

Dr. C. Taylor suggests the following : *v.* 2 (false charges), cf. Job xiii. 4 ; *v.* 11 ('wander and beg'), cf. Job xv. 23, xviii. 12, xxvii. 14 ; *v.* 13 ('race and name perish'), cf. Job xviii. 17–

19; v. 11 ('strangers spoil his labour'), cf. Job xv. 21 (v. 19, 'stranger'); v. 16 (charge of oppression), contrast Job xxix. 12; v 18 ('he drank cursing like water'), cf. Job xv. 16, xxxiv. 7, xx. 12; v. 23 ('as a shadow'), cf. Job xiv. 2; ib. (נִנְעַרְתִּי), cf. Job xxxviii. 13. Dr. Taylor also agrees with those who compare v. 7b ('Satan' or 'a Satan'?) with Job ii. He thinks that in vv. 6-15 the curses used by the psalmist's enemy are quoted. The wicked man prays that Satan may plead against the good Israelite, as he did against Job. In answer to this the good Israelite, like Job, looks for his vindication to God (vv. 28, 29).

Note g, p. 65.

Comp. cix. 22 with cii. 5 foll.; cix. 23 with cii. 7, 12; cix. 22, 24 with cii. 24; cix. 24 with cii. 5, 6, 10; cix. 28-31 with cii. 25-29. Both psalms, moreover, have affinities to the Book of Job.

Note h, p. 65.

Bunsen actually ascribed the psalm to Nehemiah (cf. Neh. xiii. 25). I could at any rate more easily believe this than that Ezra wrote the poem of 'Job.'

Note i, p. 65.

This is consistent with the dates which I have assigned elsewhere to imprecatory and elegiac psalms (e.g., vii., xxii., xxxv., lv., lxix.). Note that Nehemiah himself was not free from the faults of the psalmist (see Neh. iv. 4, 5, xiii. 25).

Note j, p. 66.

Ps. xlii. will give occasion to return to the question of the date of Ps. cxliii.

Note k, p. 66.

See Ehrt, p. 107 &c. The situation is the same in all, but with slight differences which would be easily explained had we a diary of the period. Even Delitzsch grants that these four psalms are only 'Davidic' in a wide sense. The most strikingly so is Ps. cxl. from its affinities in thought and imagery with 'psalms of David.' The situation is that of Absalom's rebellion (D. compares Pss. lviii. and lxiv.). Ps. cxli. may have been composed by some historian as a lyric illustration of that period. St. Chrysostom also notices its obscurity, and condemns his hearers for repeating their 'evening hymn' so glibly without being stirred up to investigate its difficulties. De Wette confounds this obscurity with originality, and says, 'I consider this and the 10th psalm to be among the most ancient.' He admits, however, that Ps. cxli. refers to the paganizing party among the Jews. Notice יהוה אדני, cxl. 8, cxli. 8 ; certainly not an ancient title of God.

Note ᵐ, p. 66.

Observe especially שָׂבְרוֹ, v. 5, cf. cxlv. 15 ; זֹקֵף כְּפוּפִים v. 8, cf. cxlv. 14. The similarity in the train of thought is equally noteworthy.

Note ⁿ, p. 66.

Verse 15 was added, according to Ewald, by the post-Exile editor who rescued vv. 12–14 (xxxiii. 20 being post-Exile). My own view is that vv. 1, 2, v. 3, and vv. 12–15, are quotations—the two former from comparatively old works, the latter from a more recent psalm, designed to encourage the Church-nation in a troublous time. Verse 4 implies the sad reflection that Jehovah at present does not 'take notice' of Israel (man's chief representative) ; in vv. 5–7, phrases in Ps. xviii. are converted into prayers.

Note º, p. 66.

Comp. cxliv. 9 with xcii. 4, xxxiii. 2 (the ten-stringed *nébhel*), and on vv. 12–14 see Appendix II.

Note ᵖ, p. 66.

See 1 Macc. vi. 62, vii. 10, x. 46, xi. 53, xv. 27, and contrast the emphasis on the Jewish respect for oaths in Jos., *Ant.* xii. 1, 1.

Note ᵠ, p. 67.

Theodoret, however, explains Ps. cxliv. of the troubles of the Jews after the Return ; v. 2b applies, he thinks, to Zerubbabel and Joshua.

Note ʳ, p. 67.

Verse 15 can scarcely refer to the 'pre-existence of souls ;' but vv. 19–22 may perhaps refer to the growth of a Hellenizing religious party. On account of v. 16 the psalm is assigned by Rashi to Adam. The position of Ps. cxxxix. may have been suggested by the occurrence of the catch-word 'thy right hand' (v. 10 ; cf. cxxxviii. 7).

Note ˢ, p. 67.

It is no real argument against this date that the Sept. gives as a duplicate title Ἀγγαίου καὶ Ζαχαρίου. The translator, or his editor, seems to have stumbled at the ascription of the psalm to David, and to have cast about for a more probable author. Just so the preceding psalm is headed Τῷ Δαυὶδ Ἰερεμίου (Cod. Vat.). Haggai and Zechariah are as much a guess in Ps. cxxxviii. as Jeremiah in Ps. cxxxvii. The idea of ascribing certain psalms to prophets is clearly of Egyptian-Jewish origin.

Note ᵗ, p. 67.

An eminent Tamil scholar tells me that many fine Tamil proverbs are of extreme antiquity; why then, he asks, may not 'Solomonic' proverbs be in some form as early as David, and at any rate why may not David's *ēthos* be as advanced as that of the Proverbs? But the Israelitish race developed slowly both in poetry and in morality. Such evidence as we have is against my friend's theory (cf. *Job and Solomon*).

Note ᵘ, p. 68.

The phrase is inconsistent with a pre-Solomonic and most consistent with a post-Exile origin (cf. Pss. xlvi. 15, xlviii. 2, 3, 9, lxxxvii. 3, Isa. lii. 1, lx. 14).

Note ᵛ, p. 68.

'The moralist and the philosopher who reads the words of "the Servant of God, Omar Saleh," may be almost inclined to think that a little dash of his sublime fanaticism would be no bad thing for the civilized world of to-day' (*St. James's Gazette*, Nov. 29, 1889, on the Mahdist Manifesto).

Note ʷ, p. 68.

As to the 'city of David,' see the commentators on 1 Macc. i. 33. Dr. Gatt stands alone in identifying it with the whole city of Jerusalem (*Theolog. Quartalschrift*, 1889, p. 77 &c.). The scholium on the 'Jewish Calendar' tells us that three days' time for repentance was given to the godless ones, after which they were killed. This is against 1 Macc. xiii. 47-50, but 1 Macc. xiv. 14, 36 suggests that a part of the Hellenists was really annihilated (Grätz, *Geschichte*, iii., ed. 4, p. 565; Derenbourg, *Histoire*, p. 69).

Note ˣ, p. 68.

Jonathan the diplomatist may not have been as simple-minded in his religion as the hero Judas (see p. 43), but was not less necessary to the Jewish cause. A psalmist may therefore have written of him.

Note ʸ, p. 69.

Not however, of course, for the latter part of the title of Ps. cxlii., which is as absurd as the Sept.'s addition, πρὸς τὸν Γολιάδ, to the title of Ps. cxliv. (compare Targum on v. 10), and ὅτε ἐμονομάχησε τῷ Γολιάδ in the title of the appended psalm in Sept.

Note ᶻ, p. 69.

Codd. א and B have τῷ Δαυείδ only. Cursive MSS. sometimes add Ἰερεμίου, διὰ Ἰερεμίου (so Complut. and Ald.), διὰ Ἰερ. καὶ Ἐζεκιήλ, διὰ Ζαχαρίου, and ἁγίων φωναὶ τῶν ἐν αἰχμαλωσίᾳ. Mr. Mozley boldly accepts the authorship of Jeremiah, and thinks that he prefixed the psalm to a Davidic collection which he rescued from the king's library (*David in the Psalms*, 1890, pp. 5, 6).

Note ᵃᵃ, p. 70.

Halévy places Ps. cxxxvii. immediately before Cyrus's capture of Babylon (*Revue des études juives*, 1880, i. 22, 23).

Note ᵇᵇ, p. 70.

He forgot the change which had passed over the service of sacred song since the fall of the first temple.

Note ᶜᶜ, p. 70.

The Jews never forgave their old enemy Babylon. In the most ancient part of the Sibylline Oracles (iii. 300–313) woes are announced to Babylon, ὅτι οἱ ναὸν μέγαν ἐξαλάπαξεν.

Note ᵈᵈ, p. 70.

'Partly new,' because the 'afflicted one' referred to in the title is of course one who feels Israel's troubles as his own. Smend, however, thinks that עני is Israel personified, which is possible of course (see, e.g., xxxv. 10, xl. 18), but seems hardly probable here. The psalm presumably had the same heading in a smaller Psalter, intended both for public and for private use.

Note ee, p. 70.

Cf. v. 6 with Job xix. 20; v. 11 with Job xxx. 22; v. 24 with Job xiv. 1; vv. 26-28 with Isa. xlviii. 13, li. 6; v. 28 with Isa. xli. 4 (on which see my note). Delitzsch, with Calvin, places our psalm at the close of the Exile. But this does not allow time for the poets to feel the influence of 2 Isaiah.

Note ff, p. 71.

Comp. also li. 20, 21 (unless this falls a few years earlier), and some of the persecution-psalms in Book I. (xxii. &c.). Ps. cix. (though contrasting in one respect with Ps. cii.) may have been occasioned by the same national trouble. Observe that, although the last echoes of the jubilant 'new song' (xcvi. 1) had died away, the faith of the psalmists still clung to the Messianic promise.

Note gg, p. 71.

The revolt took place (in Syria) B.C. 448; Nehemiah arrived at Jerusalem B.C. 445. The disturbed state of Syria must have encouraged Sanballat to venture on active warlike measures against the Jerusalem community. See further on Pss. xxii., xxxv., lxix.

Note hh, p. 71.

In a synagogue hymn the Song of Moses in Ex. xv., which closes with 'Jehovah shall reign for ever and ever,' is also called a 'new song.' It does in fact probably represent the new sense of Jehovah's world-wide sway which characterized the post-Exile Church. Dr. Muir adduces a parallel from a Vedic hymn, 'Sing (to Indra) without ceasing a new hymn, worthy of him, and unequalled in earth or heaven' (*Rig Veda*, x. 89, 3, in *Sanskrit Texts*, iii. 231). But the idea there is rather that art must seek to outdo itself worthily to praise divine excellences (cf. Ludwig, *Rig Veda*, Introd.), whereas in the Psalms the 'new song' corresponds to the 'new covenant' and the new-born Catholic Church. ἐπεὶ λαὸς εἷς ἦν, καὶ ἔθνος ἐν ἑνὶ τόπῳ καὶ κλίματι καὶ τὸ ᾆσμα καὶ ἡ λατρεία τὸ παλαιὸν περιώριστο (Chrys. in Ps. xcv.).

Note ii, p. 71.

But earlier than Isa. xxiv. 23, Zech. xiv. 9, where Jehovah's kingship is something to be realized in the future (if these are of post-Exilic origin). Contrast also the description of Moses and Aaron as both priests (Ps. xcix. 6) with the phrase 'Aaron the Holy One of Jehovah' (Ps. cvi. 16, more in accordance with the priestly code), and cf. Baudissin, *Gesch. des Priesterthums*, p. 258; Wellhausen, *Prolegomena*, p. 147.

NOTE jj, p. 72.

Sept. adds, however, ᾠδὴ τῷ Δαυείδ.

NOTE kk, p. 72.

See *Rosh hashana*, 31a (Wünsche, *Der bab. Talmud*, i. 336). The explanation of the selection, however, which is there given on the authority of R. Akiba, is as fanciful as the Agadic theory which makes Ps. xcii. to have been composed by Adam on his first Sabbath. Grätz has pointed out that the want of correspondence between the psalms and the works of creation (except perhaps in the case of Ps. xxiv.) shows that the real motive of the selection was the special suitableness of the several psalms to the depressed period when the arrangement was made. Light and shade, reproof and comfort, interchange, with a beautiful regard to the wants of the Jewish Church. The selection, according to Grätz, implies the existence of the entire collection, and, holding that the Sept.'s version of the Psalter was not made till about A.D. 44, he is able to make the arrangement later than the capture of Jerusalem by Pompeius (*Monatsschrift*, 1878, p. 217 &c.). I cannot, however, see how the Sept. version can be brought down so late (see p. 12), nor why the selection implies the complete Psalter. Why should not the arrangement have been made in the last century of the Persian period? The times were certainly gloomy enough to account for the selection. See also on Ps. lxxxi. (Sunday's psalm is Ps. xxiv.; Monday's, Ps. xlviii.; Tuesday's, Ps. lxxxi.; Thursday's, Ps. lxxxi.)

NOTE ll, p. 73.

Pss. xci. and xcii. are, equally with Ps. xcvii., 'Elyōn-psalms, i.e. the divine title 'Elyôn ('most High') occurs in all three (xci. 1, 9, xcii. 2, xcvii. 9). We have found it hitherto only in cvii. 11. It is more frequent in Books II. and III.; the Levitical poets had a special predilection for this great name. (The instances are xlvi. 5, xlvii. 3, l. 14, lvii. 3, lxxiii. 11, lxxvii. 11, lxxviii. 17, 35, 56, lxxxii. 6, lxxxiii. 19, [lxxxvii. 5, lxxxix. 28].) In Book I. we shall find it more rarely (vii. 18, ix. 3, xviii. 14, xxi. 8); in Lam. it occurs twice (iii. 35, 38). Jerome gives 'Elyōn among the ten Jewish names of God; the Jerusalem Talmud, however, expressly includes it among those divine epithets (such as 'gracious,' 'merciful,' 'great,' 'terrible'), which have not an equal degree of sanctity with the most sacred name, and with Elohim, Shaddai, &c. (see Rahmer in Grätz's *Monatsschrift*, 1870, pp. 183–187). Not only the pre-Exile prophets and Ezekiel, but even the pre-Exile narrators, avoid this name, which belonged (if we may base anything on Philo of Byblus) to Phœnician mythology. The reason may be questioned, but not the fact. Num. xxiv. 16 and Deut. xxxii. 8 are the only undoubtedly pre-Exile passages in which 'Elyōn occurs (Gen. xiv. 18–24 being post-Exilic), and these are poetical. The first prophet who uses the name is Exilic (Isa. xiv. 14), and he only uses it in a poetical speech given to the king of Babylon. Post-Exile writers were specially fond of using it, or its Aramaic equivalent (see especially Daniel, Enoch, and Sirach). See further in my comm. on Ps. vii. 18.—Ps. xci. is also a Shaddai-psalm (like Ps. lxviii.). The original pronunciation and meaning of Shaddai are disputed, but it is at least certain that the only undoubtedly pre-Exile passages in which it occurs are Gen. xliii. 14, where no critic will doubt that 'El Shaddai' is due to the hand of the editor, and Num. xxiv. 4, 16 (in the poetical speeches of Balaam). It is clear that this name, like 'Elyōn, was discountenanced by the pre-Exile prophets and narrators (i.e. those who are admitted as such by all critics). It occurs thirty-one times in the Book of Job (where 'Yahveh' is avoided). We also find it in Isa. xiii. 16, Joel i. 15, Ruth i. 20, 21. Also in Ezek. i. 24 (where Cod. B of the Sept., the Hebrew original of which is alone correct, does not contain it), and x. 5 (which Cornill has shown to be an interpolation). It is noteworthy that Ezek. x. 5 is the only passage in which Sept. reproduces the name in Greek letters (Σαδδαι). Nöldeke and G. Hoffmann conjecture that the original pronunciation was שַׂדִי. This would amply account for its rarity in pre-Exile literature. But I do not wonder that Baethgen protests (*Beiträge zur semit. Religionsgeschichte*, p. 293).

Note mm, p. 74.

For a conspectus, see Littledale, *A Commentary on the Psalms from Primitive and Mediæval Writers* (begun by Neale), vol. iii., p. 145, who however does not mention an interesting Jewish theory that Moses uttered the psalm and David placed it in the Psalter, 'for the time of captivity' (see the exposition of Ps. xc. by Maimun ben Joseph, who connects it very acutely with Deut. xxxii., *Jewish Quarterly Review*, ii. 86). This is akin to the view of Theodore of Mopsuestia, as represented by his Syriac epitomator (see Baethgen), that David uttered it 'in the name of the people in Babylon, which entreats that its sufferings may have an end.' Theodoret (see on vv. 16, 17) too expounds in accordance with this theory. As a curiosity, note Saadya's explanation of the title that the singing was entrusted to the children of Moses who were at the king's court (ap. Neubauer, in the Oxford *Studia Biblica*, ii. 12).

NOTE nn, p. 74.

'Man of God'=prophet (1 Sam. ix. 6-9). The same title is given to Moses (comp. Deut. xxxiv. 10) in Deut. xxxiii. 1, Josh. xiv. 6, 1 Chron. xxiii. 14, 2 Chron. xxx. 16, Ezra iii. 2; and to David in 2 Chron. viii. 14, Neh. xii. 24. As we have seen, it was natural to credit a prophet with the gift of sacred song.

NOTE oo, p. 74.

It is not essential that we should wait till the question as to the historical elements in the traditions of the Exodus, &c., has been more thoroughly investigated by home-scholars. Even setting aside these traditions provisionally, 'the internal evidence of the religious evolution itself witnesses most incontrovertibly to the fact and the character of the great beginning under Moses. That Israel never passed through the stage of mythological polytheism, but, so to speak, overleaped it, testifies to his work most conclusively' (Prof. G. F. Moore, *Andover Review*, 1888, p. 549). The case is partly analogous to that of Zoroastrianism (see De Harlez, *Les origines du Zoroastrisme*, 1879, where however the naïve mythic conceptions which descended from the pre-Zoroastrian period seem not sufficiently recognized).

NOTE pp, p. 75.

Grätz, *Monatsschrift*, 1881, pp. 442, 443. The notion that the anonymous psalms are due in each case to the author last named was shared by Jerome (Ep. ad Cyprianum, *Opera*, tom. iv., f. 43b) and many others.

NOTE qq, p. 75.

Grotius even extends the theory to the ten following psalms.

NOTE rr, p. 75.

The only way to turn the point of this argument (already urged by Bellarmine) would be to quote the case of the Book of Job. How little effect has the story of the patriarch had upon the speeches which are the kernel of the work! True; but the heading of Ps. xc. is far from possessing the authority of the titles which introduce these splendid pieces of deeply felt oratory.

NOTE [88], p. 75.

See Appendix II. The allusions in Ps. xc. to these poems (or, to this poem) are not studied, but involuntary. Time must therefore be allowed for them (or, for it) to have gained such a popularity. The date of the Song may be fixed in the reign of Josiah; that of the Blessing, probably, in that of Jeroboam II. (cf. my *Jeremiah* (1888), p. 84).

LECTURE III.

My soul is among lions; if I lay me down, 'tis among firebrands— the sons of men, whose teeth are spears and arrows, and their tongue a sharp sword.—Ps. lvii. 5 (Kay's translation).

LECTURE III.

PART I.—Survey of results of Lects. I. and II.—Two more minor Psalters, Books II. and III.; chiefly Elohistic.—Three groups of Elohistic psalms,—Davidic, Korahite, and Asaphite, besides three anonymous psalms, and a Solomonic one.—Why the majority must be assumed to be pre-Maccabæan.—Yet a study of Pss. xliv., lxxiv., and lxxix. shows that these at least must be Maccabæan.—Reply to *à priori* objections to Maccabæan psalms.—Can these three psalms be the entire lyric record of such a stirring period?—A study of Pss. lx., lxi., lxiii., and lxxxiii. shows that these four psalms are also Maccabæan.—Ps. lxxiii. contrasted with Ps. cix.—Objection to Maccabæan royal psalms; the answer reserved.—Anachronisms in the titles of these psalms (if Maccabæan) accounted for.

PART II.—Are there any psalms of the pre-Maccabæan, Greek, and of the Persian period in Books II. and III. ?—Ps. lxviii. was written either towards the close of the Exile, or in the third century; the latter date is to be preferred.—Pss. xlii. and xliii. (properly one psalm) are also of the Greek period; this follows from the necessity of finding a captivity in the post-Exile period in which captives were carried to the N.E. of Palestine.—Pss. lxxxix. and lxxxviii. discussed in connexion with the Psalm of Hezekiah in Isa. xxxviii. The subject of all three poems is, not Hezekiah, but the Jewish Church of the Persian period, and Ps. lxxxix. in particular was written in the calamitous reign either of the second or of the third Artaxerxes. Date of Pss. lxxxvii.-lxxxiv. discussed. The first, a noble specimen of Jewish catholicity, may be early Greek; so also Ps. lxxxvi. The two last, and so also Pss. lxxxii. and lviii. (strange but interesting works), belong to the Persian period. Pss. lii., liv., lv.–lvii., lix., lxii., and lxiv. form another group of vigorous church-songs. The picture is definite enough; persecution is in progress. But who is the speaker? In particular, is Ps. lv. by Jeremiah? or by Onias III.? Safer to leave this uncertain; the speaker may even be Israel personified. None of these psalms require to be Greek. Thus far Books II. and III. are a collection of church-historical records, chiefly, but not entirely, of the Persian period.

PART I.

MACCABÆAN PSALMS IN BOOKS II. AND III.

LET us now survey the course that we have been taking. These sixty-one psalms—all of them, even Ps. cx., church-hymns—come to us as a collection from the age of Simon the Maccabee. It is not surprising, therefore, that Maccabæan psalm-literature should be represented in it. It is equally certain, however, that the bulk of the collection represents the various stages of the pre-Maccabæan part of the post-Exile period. No single psalm in it is either pre-Exilic or Exilic.[a] Could I enter here into linguistic details,[1] it would be plain that the language of the psalms is, on the whole, favourable to this view. It is true that even the 139th psalm can hardly be said to be written in a 'jargon,' but Aramaisms and peculiar words and forms are characteristically frequent. The relative purity of the Hebrew of these psalms is explained by the sanctity already attaching to the earlier writings, which became literary models to the temple poets. The collection was originally meant as a separate work, and nobly was it introduced by Ps. xc., which seems to cry aloud that 'upon this rock'—the rock of the foundation truths which it sums up—'God will build His Church.' When, however, it was united to Books I.–III. it seemed appropriate to break it in two. In the Law the demands of Jehovah were expressed in a five-fold form; ought not the response of the believing community to have a similar division? Ought there not, in fact, to be a Davidic Pentateuch? The new plan, however, injured the right appreciation of the Psalter. The short book which closes at Ps. cvi. has no right of existence by itself, and the jubilant thanksgiving of the Maccabæan period (Pss.

---

[1] On this subject see Appendix II.

cxlvi.–cl.) is rooted in the grave earnestness and chastened joy of the previous age.

I now pass on to Books II. and III. These minor Psalters contain forty-eight psalms, of which only four are Yahvistic, i.e. evince a predilection for the name Yahveh; the others being Elohistic, i.e. characterized by the predominant use of Elohim.[1] The Elohistic phraseology, however, is at any rate not always due to the authors of the psalms,[b] but sometimes (indeed, in my opinion, often) to an editor, as will be clear from a comparison of Ps. liii. with the recension of the same poem in Ps. xiv., and of Ps. lxx. with the recension of the same passage in Ps. xl. 14–18.[c] The six Yahvistic psalms (lxxxiv.–lxxxix.), of which four (lxxxiv., lxxxv., lxxxvii., lxxxviii.) are traditionally Korahite, one (lxxxvi.) Davidic, and one (lxxxix.) Ethanite, are appended to the Elohistic, proving that the editor who ventured on the alteration only had before him Pss. xlii.–lxxxiii. These psalms, then, formed a great Elohistic collection, and upon examining the titles we are able to analyze the collection into three groups, viz. a Davidic (li.–lxx.), a Korahite[d] (xlii.–xlix.), and an Asaphite (l., lxxiii.–lxxxiii.), besides the three anonymous psalms (lxvi., lxvii., and lxxi., of which the two latter are ascribed to David in the Septuagint), and the Solomonic 72nd psalm. We may assume that the majority at least of these psalms are pre-Maccabæan, for the terms 'Korahite,' 'Asaphite,' and 'Ethanite'[e] had evidently gone out of use when the Fourth and Fifth Books were collected. I say 'the majority,' because there was nothing to prevent a reviser, or 'diaskeuast,' from inserting Elohistic Maccabæan psalms even in Books II. and III., and giving each of them the same title, however anachronistically, as the neighbouring psalms. We know that such a reviser added the Yahvistic Pss. lxxxiv.–lxxxix. as a supplement, and there is no reason why an Elohistic reviser should not have been only a trifle bolder. Can we convert this possibility into a probability? That depends upon our being able to show that none but a Maccabæan date will adequately account for the exegetical phenomena of a group of interesting psalms. Let us take the 44th psalm first, and read *vv.* 18, 19, and 21–23 in Kay's translation—

[1] See Lecture VI., p. 287.

Our heart has not turned backward,
Nor have our steps swerved from Thy path :
That Thou shouldst have bruised us into a haunt of jackals,
And covered us over with death-shade.
Would not God search out that?
For He knows the hidden things of the heart.
Yea, on Thy account are we killed all day long,
We are reckoned as sheep for slaughter.
Rouse Thee :—why sleepest Thou, O Lord?
Wake up, cast not off for ever.

To what period do these words seem to you to point? Pass down the stream of history, beginning with the promulgation of the first Scripture by Josiah.[f] Pause a moment at the mourning of Megiddo. Might the psalm, think you, be the work of one of those pious men who in 608 B.C. were victims of the pathetic illusion that Israel knew and served Jehovah, and had therefore a claim on His protection? No; such a view is inconsistent with the known religious results of that sad tragedy—the defeat and death of Josiah. Well, then, try the Exile period. May the lofty self-consciousness of Ps. xliv. be compared with that of Job? and do the complaints in *vv.* 11–17 fairly answer to the sufferings of the Exile-Church? To both questions you can but answer, Yes; but no fresh mind will admit that the psalm as a whole can be intelligibly expounded as a work of the Exile, and in particular that *vv.* 18 and 19 can be interpreted as they are by Bredenkamp,[1] 'Since our punishment, we have been faithful servants of Jehovah.'

Perhaps you will next think of the latter part of the Persian period, and find allusions in the psalm to the outrages committed by Bagôses, or to the later insurrection (which I have mentioned before) against Artaxerxes Ochus. To the sufferings occasioned by these events Ewald in his youth ascribed this psalm,[g] and I willingly admit that the conscious innocence so characteristic of this psalm appears again in Pss. vii. and xvii., and (with a qualification) in Ps. lxix.,[h] which not improbably belong to the period mentioned. But though this theory may explain some parts of Pss. xliv., lxxiv., and lxxix., it can hardly be said to provide the right historic background for these psalms

---

[1] *Gesetz und Propheten*, pp. 127, 128.

regarded as wholes, much less for the whole group, to which (as we shall see) they belong. Few, for instance, will believe that the sacrilege of Bagôses, caused as it was by the still greater sacrilege of the high priest himself, can be the defilement complained of in the 79th psalm. The Maccabæan period alone remains. Often as it has been repudiated, the minds of critics have constantly returned to it, and the brightest of the early Christian interpreters at once recognized its appropriateness.[1] The objections urged against it do not touch the nerve of the theory, and are partly due to prejudice. I shall return to some of them in the Appendix, but will take them now in the form in which they have been presented by Dillmann.[1] (1) 'Nothing is said in the disputed psalms of the religious differences of the Israelites.' But in the typical 44th psalm it is the Church-nation which speaks. To break the covenant is to cease to be of Israel, and hence in Ps. lxxiii. 1, 'Israel' is defined in the parallel line as 'the pure in heart.' Besides, it is possible that in xliv. 21, 22, the psalmist does cast a glance at the hypocrites. (2) 'Many circumstances of the Maccabæan insurrection are not alluded to.' But the psalmists are not chroniclers, and if in Ps. xliv. there are no appeals to victories already won, remember that it is the wont of the psalmists to base their appeals to God on the wonders of the olden time. Besides, this may be one of the earliest of the Maccabæan psalms. Other writers object—(1) that *vv.* 7 and 8 are inconsistent with the anxiety of Judas the Maccabee to obtain the friendship of the Romans (1 Macc. viii.). But the treaty referred to, which, as a fact, was obnoxious to the *khasîdîm* (they applied the curse in Jer. xvii. 5 to Judas[2]), may perfectly well have been subsequent to the circumstances presupposed by Ps. xliv. (2) 'That there were no defeats of the "armies" of the Maccabees; Judas, Jonathan, and Simon were uniformly victorious.' But this statement is not correct. More than one dark day has found its record in Maccabæan history. Think of the terrible defeat of Beth-Zacharia, transformed in the romantic Second Book of Maccabees into a victory (see 1 Macc. vi.

---

[1] See Dr. Pusey's version, *Lectures on Daniel*, p. 322.
[2] See Grätz, *Geschichte*, ii. 2, pp. 374, 375, and cf. Church and Seeley's admirable chapter 'The Falling Away' in their Maccabæan story, *The Hammer*.

28–54, 2 Macc. xiii. 13–17), and of the still more crushing blow at Eleasa, when the 3000 patriots were hemmed in on either side, 'Judas also was killed, and the remnant fled' (1 Macc. ix. 18). And is it likely that these were the only misfortunes?ʲ (3) 'That Ps. xliv. (and some of the other Maccabæan psalms) do not indicate so lofty a view of the future life as the speeches of the martyrs in 2 Macc. vi., vii.' But the doctrine of the Resurrection was not generally received in the Church so early as B.C. 167. It was to a great extent the Book of Daniel which brought it a more general recognition.

Pardon me if I have taken the longest route. Had I been writing a history of the Old Testament literature I should simply have said that if, as the Nestor of Hebraists (Franz Delitzsch) himself holds, Pss. lxxiv. and lxxix. relate to Maccabæan times,ᵏ it is difficult to resist the impression that Ps. xliv. (which Delitzsch ascribes to David on the false analogy of Ps. lx.) belongs to the same period. Notice the reference to synagogues in lxxiv. 8,ᵐ and remember that a passage from Ps. xliv. was used in a most impressive part of the daily ritual in the Maccabæan period down to the time of John Hyrcanus.[1] It was probably not many years after the death of the same prince that the writer of 1 Macc. vii. 16–17 found in Ps. lxxix. 2 an exact description of the massacre of sixty leading Asidæans by Alcimus.ⁿ This, of course, by itself proves nothing; but when we notice this historian's predilection for post-Exile psalms,[2] and remember that no other post-Exile period described in history but the Maccabæan suits this and the twin psalm (lxxix.), we are entitled to regard the passage referred to as furnishing subsidiary evidence for the Maccabæan theory. Observe too that the same historian in 1 Macc. i. 37 ᵒ indirectly applies Ps. lxxix. 1, 3 to the earlier cruelties of the Syrian Greeks in the time of Mattathias.

Do not think that I am a partizan critic, who fights for theories as other men do for more tangible objects. The only side which I have taken is that of the historical interpretation

---

[1] Talm. Bab., *Sota*, 48a.
[2] Comp. also 1 Macc. ii. 62 with Ps. lxxxiii. 10; 1 Macc. ii. 63 with Ps cxlvi. 4; 1 Macc. ix. 23 with Ps. xcii. 8 (Sept.).

of the psalms; and, unless there be some strange gap in the historical traditions, there is no period which gives the right background for these psalms but the Maccabæan. I am well aware that history repeats itself, and that when the maidens seven sang *Deus, venerunt gentes* in Dante's earthly paradise,

> Beatrice, compassionate and sighing,
> Listened to them with such a countenance
> That scarce more changed was Mary at the cross.[1]

It may be that lovers of the Gospel can, like Dante, feel the apparent defeats of the Gospel as the authors of these psalms felt the blow that had been dealt to the elder form of spiritual religion. But we do not live in such depressing days as Dante, and if we are to realize and vitalize this group of psalms, it can only be by the historic imagination. Either the massacres of Antiochus and Apollonius (1 Macc. i. 24, 30, 2 Macc. v. 11–16, 26), or that of Alcimus[2] (1 Macc. ix. 9–16), seem to be the occasion of Ps. lxxix., and if there be one moment which better than another suits its companion-psalm[p] it is that described in 1 Macc. iii. 46–60.[q] There they stand, those faithful Israelites, gathered as in the first dark days of Babylonian tyranny in the mountain city of Mizpah.[r] From that lofty post of observation they can distinctly see the profaned sanctuary, which supplies the theme of Ps. lxxiv. 3–7, and can imagine that they descry the grand idol-form[s] of 'heaven's lord' ('abomination that maketh desolate' is a punning transformation of this title) on the platform of the altar of Zerubbabel. Clothed in sackcloth, and with ashes on their heads, they spread open a copy of the Law which had escaped the search of the persecutors. What a fulness of meaning is poured into that appeal (*v.* 20), 'Look upon the covenant' (i.e. perhaps, 'the book of the covenant,' cf. 1 Macc. i. 57), from this historical notice! And if you wish to realize the force of the complaint, 'There is no prophet any more' (*v.* 9), recollect that in the next year but one (B.C. 164) some fervently believing Israelite composed the first Hebrew apocalypse, and in the spirit of the wise man Daniel (Ezek. xxviii. 3) answered that pathetic cry, 'O God, how long?' (*v.* 10).[t]

Once more, do not think me the prey of my own fancies.

---

[1] *Purgatory*, xxxiii. –6.   [2] See p. 56.

If you would rather take this psalm as a reflection, not so much of a moment as of a period, I make no objection, provided that you sufficiently realize the moments which make up the period. Indeed I would willingly take it so myself and think of all the details so simply and affectingly related between 1 Macc. ii. 27 (Mattathias crying with a loud voice, 'Follow me, all ye that are zealous for the law') and 1 Macc. iii. 46–60 (the thrilling scene at Mizpah, when they knew that the king had given commandment to abolish the people).

Let me at this point remind you of the non-linguistic criteria of Maccabæan psalms which I ventured to put forward in my first lecture. They were (1) the presence of some fairly definite historical allusions; (2) an uniquely strong church feeling; (3) a special intensity of monotheistic faith; and (4) an ardour of gratitude for a wondrous deliverance. The last criterion, of course, cannot be applied in this form to Pss. xliv., lxxiv., lxxix. Faith, according to these poems, is sorely tried by the unaccountable hiding of Jehovah's face and the 'burning' of his anger against 'the flock that he shepherdeth' (lxxiv. 1, lxxix. 5, 6, 13; cf. xliv. 25). Yet there is no real discrepancy between these and the later Maccabæan psalms. In all there is the same belief in the retribution doctrine, though in the latter God's justice is seen and praised; in the former not seen, and therefore passionately called for. The fourth of our criteria must therefore be modified if it is to be applied to both classes of Maccabæan psalms. But when this has been done, are there no other psalms to be joined to those three earlier Maccabæan works which we have been considering? Surely there must be. The source of inspiration cannot have suddenly dried up. Those who made bold to insert these three Maccabæan psalms in the Third and Fourth Books cannot have had the heart to leave all the rest to dull oblivion.[u]

Well, then, take the other psalms which Dillmann himself accepts as post-Exilic, and admits to be most plausibly viewed as Maccabæan, viz. lx., lxxx., and lxxxiii., and first of all Ps. lx.[v] Can you not see at a glance that *vv.* 3, 12–14 are closely parallel to Ps. xliv. 6, 7, 10? and will you hesitate to infer that these two psalms are related to each other precisely as the 74th is to the 79th — that, in short, they proceeded from the same circle of writers, and were separated by no great interval of time? [w] And does not the reference to a divine oracle in *vv.* 8–10 remind you of the Maccabæan 110th psalm (also headed *l'dāvīd*), and suggest that the person to whom it was given was another of the great Maccabæan brethren? Who, in fact, was so worthy of this particular oracle as the 'lofty Maccabee,' whom Dante so fitly names in Paradise next after Joshua?[1] Some, perchance, will prefer John Hyrcanus, who was doubtless in a fuller measure than Judas the second Joshua of his people. His, indeed, was not the fame of that glorious victory gained almost on the spot where Joshua longed, like Agamemnon, that the friendly sun might for him delay its setting.[x] But it was literally true that he added Galilee, Samaria, the east-Jordan land, and the new Idumæa to the narrow Jewish dominion. Yes, John Hyrcanus, who was like his father a righteous prince, and professed moreover to have received prophetic oracles, might have been the first speaker of the Joshua-like words in Ps. lx. 8–10, if only the psalm did not appear in the Septuagint, and if the depression of the rest of the psalm (St. Cuthbert's 'fit funeral dirge') were in character with his generally prosperous reign. Let us, therefore, try some earlier part of the story of the Maccabees; and why not that which has already furnished us with a very possible occasion for the partly parallel 44th psalm? The expressions in Ps. lx. 3–6 are certainly not too strong for the 'great affliction in Israel' on the death of Judas, 'the like whereof,' according to the Hebrew history, 'had not been since a prophet had not appeared among them' (1 Macc. ix. 27). The crushing defeat at Eleasa, and the grievous famine which followed, might well be likened in poetic language to an earthquake. The reverse of fortune was complete; for the moment the religious patriots were stupefied (cf. Ps. lx. 5*b*), and one of them, I suppose, sadly recalled the words of a somewhat earlier psalm [y] (now lost), and contrasted the promises given to Judas, perhaps in a vision (cf. 2 Macc. xv. 12–16), with the strange blight which had now fallen upon their prospects. 'Who will now be our leader?' said he. 'Under whose generalship will Israel recover the territory wrested

[1] *Paradiso*, xviii. 37–42.

from it by its mortal foes, the Edomites?' It is a psalm, as you see, of the interregnum. The experiences of the long-past time of the Judges are being repeated. There is no leader, and no plan of campaign : the very existence of Jehovah's 'beloved ones' (יְדִידִים) is imperilled (Ps. lx. 7). A Saul is wanted [a] to unite the divided parties into a nation conscious of its unity, and fight the battles of Jehovah with more abiding results.

Ps. lxxx. I make no attempt to claim as Maccabæan. The 'Interpreter' of the Syrian Church is, I am aware, against me, and the too ingenious Hitzig among the moderns. Ewald too (whom Dillmann evidently follows), though he does not make this psalm Maccabæan, regards it as contemporary with the 79th.[1] But the latter, when he eulogizes the mildness of its tone and the refinement of its art, virtually disproves his own critical decision. Very different is the case of Ps. lxxxiii., the tone of which precludes any but a post-Exile, or, let me say at once, a Maccabæan origin.[aa] The author is a student of Scripture,[2] and loves best those early narratives which have a special affinity to Maccabæan circumstances. Like another psalmist (lxxiv. 9), he is fully aware that extermination is the real aim of the enemies of the Jews, and in response to the 'roaring' of the heathen (*v.* 3) he sends a passionate cry for vengeance towards heaven.

When was the psalm written? When did these ten peoples 'conspire against Jehovah's hidden ones' [bb] (*v.* 4)? Well, it seems uncritical to reject the light which falls upon the psalm from the fifth chapter of the First Book of Maccabees. Six of the ten names mentioned by the psalmist occur in this striking narrative. Of the remaining four Gebal is the Gobolitis of Josephus (*Ant.* ii. 1, 2), the Gebalene of Jerome (*ad Obad.* i.) ; [cc] the name was applied illegitimately to a port of the south country of Judah appropriated by the Edomites. The mention of Amalek is half-Haggadic, half-antiquarian, and is parallel to the representation of Haman as a descendant of Agag in the Book of Esther (iii. 1).[dd] The Hagarenes (υἱοὶ Ἀγαρ, Baruch iii. 23) are mentioned in 1 Chron. as dwelling in Gilead, but in the cuneiform inscrip-

---
[1] Cf. Ewald, *History*, v. 98.
[2] Cf. Ewald's remark on the phrase 'sons of Lot,' *History*, i. 312 (note [2]).

tions and in Strabo side by side with the Nabatæans. The name 'Assyria' may as well be given to the Syrian as to the Persian empire,[ee] and Hitzig reminds us that on three several occasions (1 Macc. iii. 41, vii. 39, xi. 60), the δύναμις Συρίας (i.e., the Syrian troops in garrison) plays a subordinate part in the Maccabæan story. Thus the psalm carries us to the year after the re-dedication of the sanctuary, when the nations round about, in their displeasure, 'resolved to destroy the race of Jacob that was among them' (1 Macc. v. 1, 2), but were chastised by Judas in several most remarkable campaigns in B.C. 165 and 164. 'All nations have come about me,' said another psalmist on such an occasion; 'in Jehovah's name will I mow them down' (Ps. cxviii. 10).

Let those blame such language who can. The historical student is not less thrilled by it than by that 'awful sight' which furnishes Ps. lxxxiii. with one of its finest images, 'a spreading forest fire preceded by its wild wind.' There is nothing artificial here as in the 109th psalm. It is all as real as the terrible judgment which Judas executed again and again on those who would have extirpated his people. 'Piety lives in him in whom pity is dead'—these words of Dante[1] might have been adopted by the *khasīdīm* in this their agony. Could it, think you, have been otherwise? The *khasīdīm* were not men of war by nature. '*Anāvīm*, 'humble-minded ones,'[ff] was the term most descriptive of their character. It was from heaven that the 'holy sword' came which was to 'wound the adversaries' (2 Macc. xv. 16). The 149th psalm shows us, indeed, how congenial this work became to those who would once have started back from it with horror; but could we expect the anger of such early saints to be coupled like Christ's with grief at hardness of heart (Mark iii. 5)? Our psalmist, at any rate, has had a glimpse, as I have shown, of a better missionary method. Read *vv.* 17 and 19 together, and you will agree that even the most vehement expressions of Jewish patriotism are not without some permanent religious elements.

But have we exhausted the number of Maccabæan psalms in these books? Granting that Pss. xliv., lx., lxxiv., lxxix.,

---

[1] *Inferno*, xx. 28.

and lxxxiii. are rightly so called, are there no others which may reasonably be joined with them ? Do not the last three of these look like the beginning, the middle, and the concluding psalm of a group ? We must not be too ready to trust appearances. For on closer examination we shall find that Pss. lxxvii.–lxxxi.[gg] have been placed together on the ground of certain similarities of expression, and since Ps. lxxx. is not Maccabæan we have no right to presume that Pss. lxxvii., lxxviii., and lxxxi. are. Nor is there any striking parallelism between these and the three undoubtedly Maccabæan psalms. The same remark is true of Ps. lxxxii., and, in spite of Hitzig, I think we may add Pss. lxxv. and lxxvi.

Pss. lxi. and lxiii.,[hh] however, may well be Maccabæan. Pre-Jeremian such highly spiritual hymns obviously cannot be, and it is only the references to a king which induced Kuenen in 1865 to refer them reluctantly to the reign of one of the last Davidic kings. But we cannot separate them from kindred psalms. It would be not unplausible to make them contemporaneous with Ps. xlii.,[ii] the king being Antiochus the Great; Ps. lxi. 6–9 will then express the gratitude of the psalmist upon his return to Jerusalem from a brief captivity. But it is more natural, especially considering the language of Ps. lxiii. 12, to suppose the king to be Jonathan, or (better) Simon, and then these two psalms will form a natural triad with Ps. lx. There were occasions enough on which faithful Jews at a distance from the sanctuary might entertain the feelings so sweetly expressed in these psalms.[1] The 'liars' are perhaps those calumnious, false-hearted Jews, whom Simon, as described in ci. 7, resolved to put down. I know, of course, the objection that will rise in many minds. Mr. Stanton has already expressed it in discussing a passage in the Sibylline Oracles (see p. 38). 'How should any of these (Jonathan or Simon or John Hyrcanus) be even called a king?'[2] I will reply to this when we come to Pss. xx. and xxi., between which and Pss. lxi. and lxiii. there is some degree of parallelism.[jj] Suffice it to remind you here of the significant use of the name Melchizedek in Ps. cx. 4.

---

[1] See my study on Ps. lxiii., *Expositor*, April 1890.
[2] *The Jewish and the Christian Messiah*, p. 115.

But here let us pause a moment. Our object has been attained. The extent of the latest editorial additions to the Second and Third Books has been approximately made out. There are seven psalms which present clear traces of a Maccabæan origin. The Maccabæan editor (whether he lived in the time of Judas or of Simon need not here be determined) threw himself into the spirit of the original collector, and made his additions Elohistic to correspond to the earlier psalms of the Korahite, the Asaphite, and the second Davidic collections. He was no doubt guilty of an anachronism, not indeed in his substitution of 'Elohim' for 'Yahveh,' which must still have commended itself to a certain class of religious minds, but at any rate in his adoption of the headings 'of the sons of Korah,' 'of Asaph,' 'of David.' The heading *l'dāvīd* is of course not a worse anachronism in the case of the 60th than of any other psalm; but the other two headings do appear to need a special excuse, because the division of singers which they imply had already been modified in the time of the Chronicler,[kk] and had passed away when the Fourth and Fifth Books were collected. Do they indicate a wish of the Maccabæan editor to infuse a leaven of contemporary thought and feeling into hymnals which otherwise might not have been sufficiently valued? Yes; but we can say more than this. It can be rendered probable that among the psalms described as Korahite there are some which are of the Greek period, though pre-Maccabæan. Consequently the heads of the Hemanite guild which had taken the place of the Korahite had already set the example of adding psalms to the Korahite collection which did not really belong to the Korahite period (see note [e]).

NOTE [a], p. 89.

One may remark that though neither in Books IV. and V. nor in the earlier books can we venture to find Exilic psalms, we have not only fragments of spiritual song in the Second Isaiah, but a collection of lamentations on the sad estate of Israel, both belonging to the Exile. On the date of the latter I have spoken at length in the *Pulpit Commentary*; cf. *Jeremiah, his Life and Times*, pp. 177–181.

Note ^b, p. 90.

No one will care to defend 'O God, my God' in xliii. 5, and similar impossible readings in xlv. 8, lxiii. 2, lxvii. 7, lxviii. 9, nor the equally impossible 'Elohim Çebāōth' in lxxx. 8, 15 (cf. lix. 6, lxxx. 5, 20, lxxxiv. 9).

Note ^c, p. 90.

In Ps. liii. 'Yahveh' is throughout changed into 'Elohim;' in Ps. lxx. the same change is made three times (for in Ps. xl. 18 we should certainly with Ewald read יהוה), but, as a compensation, in *v.* 6 יהוה is substituted for אלהי.

Note ^d, p. 90.

Dean Plumptre thinks that the Korahite psalms were all composed in the reign of Hezekiah (*Biblical Studies*, p. 147 &c.). But how improbable that psalms with so many dissimilarities should be contemporaneous! The truth is that Hezekiah's age presents the first distinct germs of the religion of the post-Exile period, to one or another part of which all these Church-songs must belong.

Note ^e, p. 90.

The title 'of the sons of Korah' must originally have stood at the head of the collection, and only by a later editor have been prefixed to each psalm. And who were the 'sons of Korah'? That the phrase *may* mean descendants of an ancient Levite named Korah is admitted. But it is indubitable that it may also mean members of a society or guild (like בְּנֵי אֵלִים, Ps. xxix. 1, and the parallels cited in my *Psalms*, p. 379). To adopt the former view on the unsupported authority of the Chronicler, a saintly man but a prejudiced historian, seems to me uncritical. Why 'Asaph' is used as a title for the guild of Asaphites, instead of 'sons of Asaph,' I do not know. The two expressions may be synonymous, as 'Aaron'= 'the house of Aaron' (1 Chron. xii. 27 &c.). Or possibly the collector of the Asaphite songs meant to assign them to the ideal founder of the Asaphite guild, just as another collector ascribed the early Davidic songs to the traditional founder of psalmody. The same explanation may be given of the expression 'of Ethan the Ezrahite' (Ps. lxxxix. 1), where 'Ethan' (as we shall see) is equivalent to the 'Jeduthun' of Pss. xxxix., lxii., lxxvii. Ethan is, in fact, the ideal founder of a guild of Ethanites which takes rank in the Chronicler's time beside Ḥeman (the substitute for Korah, see title of Ps. lxxxviii.) and Asaph. Observe that the Chronicler understood 1 Kings v. 11 (iv. 31 Auth. V.) to mean that both Ethan and Heman were sons of Mahol, whereas the tradition in Kings states that Ethan was 'an Ezrahite' (or Zarhite). Doubtless he followed a tradition of modern origin, which was guided in its choice of the two new names of singers by the mention of Heman (as was thought) and Ethan as 'sons of Mahol' i.e. of the dance, see Ps. xxx. 12, and elsewhere).

Note f, p. 91.

Lagarde's attempt to bring Ps. xliv. into the age of Hezekiah is desperate. He takes the 'reproacher and reviler' of v. 17 to be the Rab-shakeh, and thinks that in B.C. 701 Judah could justly boast of its fidelity to Jehovah (*Mittheilungen*, ii. 376, 377). So too Dean Plumptre (*Biblical Studies*, p. 194).

Note g, p. 91.

See *Dichter des A. B.* (1835), ii. 353 &c. ; cf. *History*, v. 120, note. His later view was that Pss. xliv., lxxiv., lxxix., lxxx., cxxxii., and lxxxix., lx., and lxxxv., belong to the end of the sixth or the early part of the fifth century. Professor Robertson Smith inclines to Ewald's first view (*Enc. Britann.* xx. 31), which De Jong too peremptorily rejects (*Disquisitio de psalmis Maccabaicis*, p. 10). I have hesitated myself, on the ground that, just as history has almost failed to record the destruction of Jerusalem's walls in Ezra's time, so it may possibly have lost the memory of a burning of the temple at a later period. It is also possible that the Jews may have furnished a contingent to the army of the Syrian revolters in the time of Artaxerxes Ochus, and that this is referred to in Ps. xliv. 10 (cf. lx. 12). But can it be called probable? Josephus has heard of the 'defilement' of the temple by Bagôses. He is not given to minimizing; surely some echo of a still greater blow to his religion would have reached him, if the blow ever took place. And would a 'contingent' have been described by a poet as 'our armies'? Even if we refer Pss. xliv., lxxiv., lxxix. to this troublous time, we must at any rate assume that literal accuracy has been departed from in Ps. lxxiv. 7 (see on that psalm).

Note h, p. 91.

The hatred which the Jews experienced had a religious ground (lxix. 8, 10), but Israel knows that God can discern his hidden 'guiltinesses' (v. 6), on which cf. Lect. VII. Part II.

NOTE ^{i}, p. 92.

Bar-Hebræus, who represents Theodore's views, entitles Ps. xliv. 'a prayer of the Maccabees, when compelled by Antiochus to sacrifice to idols' (Baethgen in *Zeitschr. f. d. alttest. Wissenschaft*, 1886, p. 273). Theodoret, who insinuates a suspicion that Theodore was sometimes more anxious to have the Jews on his side than 'the nurslings of the faith' (*Præfat. in Psalmos*), and Chrysostom, who cares more for simple exegesis than for criticism, both adopt the same view without any hesitation.

NOTE ^{j}, p. 93.

I admit that the First Book of Maccabees is veracious, but not that it is complete. It is not impossible that the occasion of Ps. xliv. may be some earlier defeat than either of the above, which occurred (as Theodore of Mopsuestia appears to have held) in the lifetime of the great 'reviler' (see Ps. xliv. 17) Antiochus Epiphanes. So Grätz argues, *Gesch. der Juden*, ii. (2), p. 446. Prof. J. P. Peters, in his *Scriptures Hebrew and Christian* (ii. 410), heads this psalm 'Prayer of Judas Maccabæus.'

NOTE ^{k}, p. 93.

Delitzsch, however, candidly points out certain phrases in Ps. lxxiv. which appear to him to suit the Chaldæan better than the Maccabæan period—viz. 'everlasting ruins' (*v.* 3*a*), and 'they set on fire thy sanctuary' (*v.* 7*a*). I feel with him, but is it not probable that Ps. lxxiv. was partly remodelled after the great deliverance so as to serve as a memorial of *two great troubles*? We may compare the combination of features from the Scythians and the Chaldæans in certain prophecies of Jeremiah, and, as I venture to think, the reference to the (Chaldæan) burning of the temple in Isa. lxiv. 11, which probably belongs (see note ^{s}, p. 130) to the period of Artaxerxes Ochus. Let me add that the theory that Ps. lxxiv. was retouched perhaps by the author himself is not a wilful one ; *vv.* 12–17 were certainly not placed where they now stand by the deeply moved writer of the rest of the psalm. Also that a Maccabæan date is permitted (for Pss. xliv. and lxxiv.) by the translators of our Geneva Bible, and virtually given to Ps. lxxiv. by Dean Jackson (17th cent.), who appeals to 'best interpreters' (*Works*, viii. 62). Lastly, the same view is taken both of Ps. lxxiv. and of Ps. lxxix. by Theodore, and of Ps. lxxix. by Theodoret and Eusebius (*Dem. Ev.* x. 1). Theodoret's argument to Ps. lxxix. I quote as characteristic of a class :

Ἀντιόχου, τοῦ ἐπίκλην Ἐπιφανοῦς, τὴν κατὰ τοῦ λαοῦ τῶν Ἰουδαίων μανίαν ὁ προφητικὸς προθεσπίζει λόγος. τὴν δὲ χρησμολογίαν εἰς εὐχὴν σχηματίζει, ὡς ὑπὸ τῶν εὐσεβῶν τῶν ἐσομένων τηνικαῦτα προσφερομένην· οὐδέπω μὲν νενικηκότων, ἔτι δὲ περικλυζομένων ταῖς συμφοραῖς.

Note ᵐ, p. 93.

See my note on this verse, and cf. De Jong, *Disquisitio*, pp. 21–23, 26–28. For the early use of the term συναγωγὴ for a place of prayer and instruction by Greek-writing Jews, cf. Jos., *War*, vii. 3, 3 ; *Psalms of Sol.* xvii. 18. Israel Sack (*Die altjüd. Religion*, 1889, pp. 277, 278) revives Gesenius's view that Ps. lxxiv. 8 (written during the Exile) refers to the *bāmōth*, which is only possible if the psalm be pre-Josian.

Note ⁿ, p. 93.

The quotation is introduced by the words κατὰ τὸν λόγον ὃν ἔγραψε. Understand ὁ γράψας (i.e. Asaph). The Syriac inserts 'the prophet,' which may imply that the psalmist spoke, according to the translator, in the character of the Jews of the Maccabæan age. If so, his impression doubtless was that this is a Maccabæan psalm, though prejudice compelled him, as it constantly compelled Theodore, to throw the psalm back nominally to pre-Exile times. It has been asked whether or no (following the Greek text) the historian quotes the passage as a Scripture. Ehrt (p. 23) decides in the affirmative, and infers that Ps. lxxix. is pre-Maccabæan. Of course, the psalm had already been included in the temple-hymnbook ; but what has this to do with its date? Taking Ps. lxxix. as Maccabæan, it is interesting to notice that two of the ideas of that psalm are brought together in the confession of Daniel (cf. Dan. ix. 16*b* with Ps. lxxix. 4, 8*b*).

Note ᵒ, p. 93.

Καὶ ἐξέχεαν αἷμα ἀθῷον κύκλῳ τοῦ ἁγιάσματος, καὶ ἐμόλυναν τὸ ἁγίασμα (1 Macc. i. 37).

Note ᵖ, p. 94.

For other indications of a Maccabæan date, see my notes on lxxiv. 9, 20.

Note ᵍ, p. 94.

See the lines quoted from Emma Lazarus (p. 18). A less probable occasion is the moment before Judas joined battle with Gorgias at Emmaus (1 Macc. iv. 6–11). 'Remember how our fathers were delivered in the Red Sea,' says Judas (compare these words with Ps. lxxiv. 14). 'And now let us cry unto heaven, if peradventure it will have mercy upon us, and remember the covenant of our fathers' (cf. Ps. lxxiv. 20). Then, we are told, 'the strangers (ἀλλόφυλοι) saw their coming, and went out of the camp to battle.' Now read the last verse of Ps. lxxiv. May not this abrupt close be a proof of the highest art, and indicate that the psalm was meant as the war-song of the Jewish army, and found its sequel in the onset and the 'confused noise' of the *mêlée* and the swiftly won victory? Yes; but the psalmist's tone of discouragement accords but ill with the general tone of the speech of Judas.

Note r, p. 94.

The Greek has Massēpha (cf. Judges xx. 1, Sept.). In 1 Macc. v. 35 the Gileadite Mizpah is referred to as Maspha (cf. Josh. xiii. 26, Sept., ed. Lagarde).

Note s, p. 94.

Dr. Pusey (*Daniel the Prophet*, p. 442) denies this; but see Talm. Bab., *Taanith*, 28*b*, 29*a*. That an idol is meant by שִׁקּוּץ שֹׁמֵם (Dan. xii. 11; cf. xi. 31, ix. 27), is now certain. The phrase is an intentional alteration of בעל שמם *Baal-šamem* (i.e. Zeus). The first Phœnician inscription of Umm el-'awâmîd (B.C. 132) begins לאדן לבעלשמם, i.e. to Zeus; the Phœnicians were more complaisant than the Jews to the patron-god of the Seleucidæ. According to the Syriac version of 2 Macc. vi. 2 the temple at Jerusalem was called by Antiochus's emissary 'the temple of heaven's lord.' See Nestle's cogent exposition in Stade's *Zeitschrift*, 1884, p. 248; cf. G. Hofmann, *Ueb. ein. Phön. Inschr.*, 1889, p. 29.

Note t, p. 94.

The solution of the problems of the Book of Daniel is probably almost as complete as we can hope to see it made, both on the side of language and on that of subject-matter, and those who most dislike deviating from tradition will at the very least concede that in its present form the book is of Maccabæan origin. I say 'in its present form,' because there are some who think that narratives of earlier origin were worked up with the visions. In my opinion, this view has not yet been made plausible. I admit that the writer of the narratives is not wholly dominated by the thought of making Nebuchadrezzar a type of Antiochus (cf. p. 37); he carries with him other more friendly ideas respecting non-Israelites. Still the wish for a type of the present persecution is foremost in his mind, and there is an essential unity underlying the book, in spite of its inconsistencies in detail. There is as yet no complete treatise on Daniel representing the present state of the question, but it can hardly be long delayed. My revered friend (for the last twenty years of his life) Franz Delitzsch is in this, as in some other points, a mirror of his time. In 1858 he published an article on Daniel in Herzog's *Realencyclopädie*, written from the point of view of Hävernick. In the second edition of that work, however, he printed another article which differed materially from the first, inasmuch as it made that least possible concession referred to above. This was in 1878. In the same year I endeavoured to summarize the actual state of the question for English readers in the art. 'Daniel' in the *Encyclopædia Britannica*, but without entering (as it is now my privilege to do in official teaching) into the relation of the results of Daniel-criticism to apologetics. This *lacuna* does not exist in the article of Delitzsch. His apologetics will not indeed satisfy all; there must for a long time be various solutions of apological problems. But his contribution is of importance for all who approach this subject from a theological point of view. The critical solution, I may add, is becoming almost every year more clear and definite. I will only here notice Nestle's explanation of the phrase rendered βδέλυγμα ἐρημώσεως (just referred to), and Cornill's researches on the 'seventy weeks' (Königsberg, 1889). The hint given above will, I hope, assist the reader in realizing the object of the Book. Men complained of the disappearance of God's interpreters the prophets. True, replied a 'fervently believing' Israelite, they have disappeared. But, God helping me, I will bring back one of them, viz. Daniel, from Hades, and question him concerning the ways of Jehovah. Some old seer *must* have prophesied of these days, for 'the Lord Jehovah doeth nothing but he revealeth his secret unto his servants the prophets' (Am. iii. 7). The present problem therefore was to recover this seer's words, not without prayer and fasting. But why Daniel's words? Did this pious writer infer from the circumstance that Daniel was only mentioned in Ezek. xiv. 14, xxviii. 3, that he must have been a contemporary of Ezekiel's (whereas Ezekiel would have placed him in long past primitive times), or was there really a tradition that Daniel was one of the exiles in Babylon? The former view seems the more probable. There can hardly have been two such widely different traditions about the age of Daniel. In either case, 'Daniel' is an enigmatical name. It occurs only once again, viz. in 1 Chron. iii. 1; but the Mas. text there probably needs correction (see the variants in the Sept. of 1 Chron. iii. 1; 2 Sam. iii. 3, and Klostermann on 2 Sam. *l.c.*). It is barely possible that

'Daniel' may have been coined out of the Zend *dânu*, 'wise' or 'wisdom' (see, for this word, Darmesteter, *Ormazd et Ahriman*, p. 29), an appropriate title for a revealer of the divine secrets like Zoroaster (cf. Ezek. xxviii. 3). If the bareçma (the bundle of sacred twigs held by the Magian priests) found its way to Jerusalem in Ezekiel's time (Ezek. viii. 17), may not this highly receptive prophet have heard of Zoroaster in Babylonia? 'Zarathustra' itself would have been extremely difficult to Hebraize. It is more than probable that the Iranian sage was already glorified by legend, and assigned to a too early age. Plutarch found it stated that 'Zoroaster the Magian lived 5000 years before the Trojan war' (*De Is. et Osir.*, c. 46). Hyde naïvely enough brought him into contact with Abraham; Ezekiel may have placed him between Noah and Job.

NOTE u, p. 95.

It is possible (see above, on Ps. cx., p. 23) that the parallelistic structure and the poetical phrases which here and there strike us in 1 Maccabees arise from lost Maccabæan psalms. The suggestion is due to Reuss.

NOTE v, p. 95.

The heading of Ps. lx. may be explained like that of Ps. lii. and the companion-psalms. The Hebrew enables us to correct the text of 2 Sam. viii. 12, 13 (see Klostermann on 2 Sam.).

NOTE w, p. 96.

Theodoret misses this parallelism, and explains Ps. lx. of the Captivity. Theodore is wiser. His views are thus expressed in the argument in Corderius's *Catena* (ii. 185): 'When the land was being held by the aliens, whether the neighbouring nations or the generals of Antiochus, I will drive away the enemies,' he says, 'and recover the land from them, and give it back to you, dividing it out.' The tendency of a fair though cautious criticism is well expressed in these words of Nowack: 'If we think of the pre-Exile period for our psalm, *v.* 8 limits us at any rate to the last century; but I do not see how we can find a place for the psalm in it. If we admit a post-Exile date, there is most to be said for the time of the Maccabees; at least *v.* 12 will not, I think, suit an earlier period.' Delitzsch, however, still maintains the Davidic authorship because of the Hebrew heading. This he supposes to be derived from a history of David's time which contained poetical illustrations such as this psalm and Ps. xviii. I too hold the same theory of the heading.

But it does not follow that David wrote the poem which the historian communicated. The tone of Ps. lx. and the phraseological coincidences between it and decidedly late writings, render this most improbable. The only question can be whether *vv.* 8–11 (or the main part of these verses) are an old Davidic fragment, as Ewald, Renan, and (apparently) Klostermann believe. If they are, the heading must originally have referred to them and not to the whole of our present psalm. But the view of the psalm given above seems to me easier. It will be observed that I base no argument on *v.* 6*b*, which both A.V. and R.V. render, 'that it may be displayed *because of the truth*' (i.e. in defence of the true religion), because, with most critics, I think this version grammatically and exegetically improbable. How Delitzsch can render *v.* 6*b* thus, and yet admit this psalm to be Davidic, I cannot see. To me, this version would at once prove Ps. lx. to be post-Exilic.

NOTE ˣ, p. 96.

Josh. x. 12, 13*a*; comp. *Il.* ii. 412–418, and see below on Ps. xix. 1–7. Just so, in a popular song, the Syrian fellahîn cry to the sun to hasten his going down that they may rest; and so Milton supposes the sun to delay ('suspense in heav'n') to hear the angel tell his (the sun's) generation (*Paradise Lost*, vii. 99 &c.). The second half of Josh. x. 13 is due to a misunderstanding of the prosaic commentator. But surely the victory (יְשׁוּעָה) of Joshua is scarcely rendered more wonderful by an 'abnormal prolongation of daylight.' Nor was the second victory of Beth-horon less important to revealed religion.

NOTE ʸ, p. 96.

A psalm of David according to Ewald and Renan. But the expressions of the oracle cannot without violence be applied to the campaigns of the great king, as Ewald against his will acknowledges. It is not decisive against the above view that the first person is employed in *v.* 11 as well as in *vv.* 8–10. Of course, the psalmist would interpret *vv.* 8–10 as spoken for the community of Israel. After the death of Judas, Israel assumed more fully those hopes and fears which Judas had cherished in its name. Yet I have no wish to quarrel with any one who can get on without my theory, explaining *vv.* 8–10 on the analogy of xliv. 7, 8, 16, where 'I' clearly = 'we.'

NOTE ᶻ, p. 97.

The dirge in 1 Macc. ix. 21 is just such as might have been sung over Gideon or Jephthah.

Note aa, p. 97.

(Other views of Ps. lxxxiii.) Delitzsch and Lagarde explain from 2 Chron. xx. 1, 2. Freudenthal points out that the Hellenistic Jewish writer Eupolemos represents not only Suron (Huram) king of Tyre, but the Edomites, Ammonites, Moabites, Ituræans, Nabatæans, and Nabdæans, and the Assyrians and Phœnicians in Gilead, as sending presents to Solomon, which he supposes to be based on Ps. lxxxiii. (*Alexander Polyhistor*, p. 115). But a writer of this school needed no *point d'appui* in a psalm. Freudenthal himself remarks on the imaginative character of the history of Eupolemos. And Ps. lxxxiii. says nothing of presents to a Jewish king.

Note bb, p. 97.

De Wette and Hupfeld take the catalogue of names to be a poetic way of saying that all the enemies whom Israel has ever had have risen up against him. This altogether blurs the historic outlines, and is contrary to analogy. The psalm is a *Gelegenheitsgedicht*. Ewald would rather find a reference to the attacks on the new Jerusalem described in Neh. iv. and vi. But, as he admits (in his 2nd, not 3rd, edition), this was a comparatively 'small danger.' No attempt was then made to extinguish the name of Israel. The object of the enemy (with which many of the Jewish nobles sympathized) was simply to abate the seemingly excessive religious pretensions of the advocates of legal 'holiness.' And though 'Asshur' (*v.* 9) may mean Persia, represented by the satrap (see Ezra vi. 22), it is more natural (Babylon being out of the question) to take it as equivalent to Syria.

Note cc, p. 97.

Josephus reckons Marissa to Idumæa (*Ant.* xiii. 9, 1 ; 19, 4) ; comp. 2 Macc. xii. 35. Marissa = Mareshah, 2 Chron. xi. 8.

Note dd, p. 97.

'Half-Haggadic ;' comp. the ancient Midrash, *Mechilta*, 63a, where Amalek is the type of the class of God's enemies. 'Half-antiquarian ;' note that Mordecai is represented as descended from Kish, the father of the conqueror of the Amalekites (see on title of Ps. vii.). In illustration of this, observe that the 'Second Targum' on Esther traces the ancestry of Haman to Esau, and that of Mordecai to Jacob, while the Targum of Jerusalem comments thus on Num. xvii. 16 ; 'The first king who will sit upon the throne of the kingdom of the sons of Israel, Shaul the son of Kish, will set the battle in array against the house of Amalek, and will slay them ; and those of them that remain will Mardekai and Esther destroy.'

Note ee, p. 98.

See on Ps. lxxxiii. 9, and add a reference to Jer. xlii. 11, Ezek. xxxii. 29 (both Sept.) ; Jos., *Ant.* xiii. 6, 7 ; Eupolemos, in Euseb. *Præp. Ev.* ix. 30 (τοὺς ἐν Γαλαδηνῇ Ἀσσυρίους καὶ Φοίνικας). Hitzig's interpretation of the Sept. headings of Pss. lxxvi. and lxxx. ('Assyrian' = 'Syrian') is plausible but not probable. Theodore and Rashi both explain Ps. lxxvi. of Sennacherib's invasion (because of *vv.* 3, 4) ; Sept. will have done the same. Observe that in both psalms Cod. Sin. omits the reference to the 'Assyrian.'

Note ff, p. 98.

In the post-Exile period, '*anāvīm* and '*aniyyīm* became standing designations of the true Israel, as opposed to the indifferent, the selfish, the proud, and the paganizers. See my note on Ps. ix. 13 (where also Dr. Grätz's theory of the 'Anāvitic Levites' is referred to).

Note gg, p. 99.

It may be asked why Pss. lxxvii. and lxxxii. follow Pss. lxxvi. and lxxxi. respectively. The answer is that Pss. lxxvi. and lxxvii. both refer to a theophany, and Pss. lxxxi. and lxxxii. both introduce God speaking as a Judge.

Note hh, p. 99.

Ps. lxii. will be treated in connexion with Pss. iv. and xxxix. ; all three must belong to the same period, viz. the Persian. The position of Ps. lxii. in the Psalter was perhaps suggested by the parallelism between lxii. 8*b*, 9*b*, and lxi. 4.

Note ii, p. 99.

That Ps. xlii. has affinities with Pss. lxi., lxiii. is obvious. The general idea of the fainting, longing heart of the believer is common to all. De Wette's rendering 'from the end of the land' in lxi. 3*a* would suggest a parallelism with xlii. 7. It is safer to compare xlii. 9, xliii. 3, with lxi. 8*b* ; xlii. 9*b* with lxiii. 7 ; and the use of מִן in lxi. 9, lxiii. 5. In lxi. 3, 'Lead me upon the rock' reminds one of 'God my rock' in xlii. 10, as well as of the fine title of Jehovah in lxxiii. 20, 'the rock of my heart.' The painful transition in *v.* 10 suggests the similar one in lxxiii. 27. Notice also the affinity between lxi. 1-9 and xxvii. 1-6 (a far finer lyric utterance).

Note ⁱⁱ, p. 99.

Comp. especially lxi. 6-8 with xxi. 2, 3, 5, 7; lxi. 6*b* may be corrected from xxi. 3*b*. A less satisfactory view is that of Giesebrecht, who maintains that lxi. 7, 8, and וְהַמֶּלֶךְ יִשְׂמַח in lxiii. 12 were inserted in the time of the Asmonæan kings (in which case the original psalms may belong to the time of Zerubbabel), unless both psalms are altogether Maccabæan (in which case lxi. 6*b*, reading אֲרֶשֶׁת, may refer to the desire of Aristobulus 'to change the government into a kingdom,' Jos., *Ant.* xiii. 11, 1; but see below on Ps. xx.). Stade's *Zeitschr.*, 1881, p. 326.

Note ᵏᵏ, p. 100.

By the beginning of the Greek period the two guilds of singers had, as we have seen, developed into three; for evidently in 1 Chron. xxv., as elsewhere, the Chronicler antedates the temple arrangements of his own day.

PART II.

PSALMS OF THE PRE-MACCABÆAN GREEK AND OF THE PERSIAN PERIOD IN BOOKS II. AND III.

IN the history of psalm-composition the Maccabæan age cannot be separated by any hard and fast line from that which precedes it. We shall presently see that to the pre-Maccabæan Greek age not only Korahite but Asaphite and Davidic psalms most probably belong. Take for instance Ps. lxviii.,[a] once called the most difficult in the Psalter, but now, thanks to the exegesis of the last half-century, easier than many which may appear far simpler—easier, that is, to understand as a historical product, not easier to interpret in all its peculiarities of phrase. I will not pause to develop the argument from the names of God,[b] but will assert that two periods, and two only, can now be defended for its composition. It was written either towards the close of the Exile, or during one of the dynastic wars between Egypt and Syria, for the possession of Palestine; either in the sixth century (more precisely, a little before the defeat of Crœsus at Sardis, B.C. 549), or in the third (probably between 220 and 217, or between 203 and 198 B.C.). It is the work of a poet who is not less learned than patriotic, and delights to refer to the Restoration-prophecy, and to various popular as well as cultured lyric poems of various dates.[c] Its literary reminiscences, however, whether allusive or in the way of quotation, reveal no contemptible degree of art, and are vivified with a true lyric sentiment. The psalm as a whole has a wonderful power and range, and is in this, as in other respects, easier to understand in the Greek than at the dawn of the Persian period.[d] Time was needed for the Second Isaiah to become a mine of learned suggestion. All the other psalms which are dependent on the Restoration-pro phecy are subsequent to the Return; why should this be an exception? Above all; read *vv.* 20–28 consecutively, and tell me if you think it reasonable to take *vv.* 20–24 and 25–28 as referring to different periods. No; if, as I have said, the psalm divides at *v.* 20—if, 'strengthened in his faith by the foregoing pictures of the past, the poet [now] throws himself into the interests and prospects of the present' —why should we burden him with a gratuitous inconsistency in *vv.* 25–28, as if he all at once glanced backward at the religious usages of the first temple? Indeed, how *can* we do so, considering that the four tribes mentioned are precisely those which correspond to the two orthodox post-Exile provinces, Judæa and Galilee? Pre-Exilic the poem cannot be; and, I may add, Maccabæan it cannot be.[e] Not yet has Israel been faithful unto death for his religion; not yet has he been driven to take up arms in self-defence; his modest part as yet is to recall God's ancient wonders, and to intone the chant of waiting faith,—

> Lord, in our cause make sure and strong
>   Thy word and gracious will,
> Thou Watcher of Jerusalem,
>   From Thy most holy hill.—(*vv.* 28*b*, 29*a*, Keble.)

But when Keble introduces into the closing verse the words,

> 'Tis Israel's God who gives
>   Might to His own, and deeds of war,—

he plainly violates the spirit of his author. The divine gift which Israel implores—what is it? Not the ability to 'bind their kings in chains, and their nobles with links of iron,' for the psalmist himself will presently utter the prayer,

> Rebuke him that bemires himself for gain of money,
> Scatter the peoples that delight in wars.—(*v.* 31.)

Not 'deeds of war,' exploits Davidic or Maccabæan, but that bulwark of inviolable peace which Jehovah unaided can produce for His waiting people.

In spite of its literary indebtedness, there is no greater ode in Hebrew literature than the 68th psalm. Now, can we believe that it stands alone in the period to which we have referred it? The psalm which I have been led to couple with it is the

I

42nd, of which the 43rd is the conclusion, tastelessly separated by the latest editor from the body of the poem.[f] Not because both psalms (the 68th and the 42nd) express a passionate love of the temple; psalms not belonging to the Greek period have this characteristic, and the language of the 42nd psalm has a deeper spirituality than that of the 68th. But for two reasons—(1) that only in the Greek period can I find circumstances like those presupposed by the 42nd psalm; and (2) that according to a probable view of *v. 7*,[g] there is a striking allusion in Ps. xlii. to Ps. lxviii. That the 42nd psalm is post-Exile, must be clear to all who are accustomed as critics to range freely over the Old Testament, and to be ever giving more definiteness of outline to their picture of Israel's history. I need not therefore discuss the theory of Ewald that Ps. xlii. is the melodious farewell of the royal exile Jehoiachin, as in 597 B.C. he was being carried away beyond the ridge of Hermon.[h] The writer is no king but a temple-musician (cf. xlii. 5, 9), and the problem before us is to find out a captivity either of the nation or of a part of the nation in the post-Exile period of Jewish history, the scene of which was the north-east of Palestine, on the border of Syria. Now the particular moment which (following Hitzig in all but his dogmatism) I am about to select, may or may not be right, but it is difficult to resist the impression that this captivity is subsequent to the division of Alexander's empire, by which Syria fell to the Seleucidæ and Egypt to the Ptolemies.[i] Is there a time when Jerusalem was taken, and its inhabitants ill-treated by a foreign foe? Certainly; but neither of the two occupations of the Holy City by Ptolemy Lagi is the occasion of which we are in search.

It was not until B.C. 199–198 that an event took place, the sequel of which will account for the 42nd psalm (see Jos., *Ant.* xii. 3, 3). The enemy this time was the Ætolian mercenary Scopas, who, in the enforced absence of Antiochus the Great, sought to reattach Syria to Egypt, and among other cities captured those of Judæa. The Book of Daniel seems to refer to this, when it states that a party of 'young high-minded' Jews, who had risen against the 'king of the south,' should meet with a fall (Dan. xi. 14). Probably this means that Scopas punished the Seleucid party severely, after which is it not fair to presume that he carried away some Jewish captives? It was in the winter-time, as Josephus tells us, and it was to the northern highlands that the conqueror bent his way. But Antiochus, returning from Asia Minor, was at hand. Not long afterwards, amidst the scenes so vividly described in the 42nd psalm, the two warriors met 'at the sources of the Jordan.' It must have been at Bāniās, from the hill above which so glorious, but to a captive, so melancholy, a prospect is visible. The Ætolian was defeated, and nearly all his army destroyed. Thus the Jewish captives were delivered; they returned of course with Antiochus to Jerusalem, where the supreme council,[j] to make up for its recent compulsory defection, gave a splendid reception to the Syrian king. Do we not now understand the complaints of the psalmist better? He does but hint at the severity of the rain-storms of the Hermon district in winter (xlii. 8). It is from the 'oppression' of the 'loveless nation' (the unscrupulous Egyptian mercenaries), and bitter heathen railleries, that he prays so earnestly to be delivered, and swiftly and surely was the prayer answered. The bringing back of Jewish captives was one of Antiochus's chief cares,[k] though of course the captive psalmist looks behind 'second causes,' and trusts, not in princes, but in his faithful God. We need not, however, suppose that this beautiful poem is a literal transcript of the thoughts of the captive at Bāniās. It is more probable, comparing the phenomena of Ps. lxxvii., that it received its present form after the psalmist's happy return to Jerusalem.

And what of the allusion to Ps. lxviii.? I have not forgotten it. Ps. xlii. 7 is variously explained, but unless we too boldly omit the two last words מֵהַר מִצְעָר altogether, there must, I think, be a contrast between the lofty Hermon-summits ('the Hermonim') and 'the mount of insignificance' (cf. Gen. xix. 20, where Zoar is מצער, and therefore not worth destroying); hence Jerome's rendering 'de monte minimo' is a good one. This consideration is not affected by the reported discovery of a high mountain in West Jordan-land, called Miç'ar; is not this name merely κατ' ἀντίφρασιν, according to an usage more Arabic than Hebrew? At any rate in this context a poet would hardly single out a mountain with this particular name. Now, if such a contrast is intended, it is difficult not to suspect an allusion to Ps. lxviii. 15, 16. In other words, הר מצער is probably Mount Zion, and מ (as Hitzig suggests) was prefixed in error, owing to the closing letter of the previous word (on the analogy of Jer. xxix. 8).ᵐ The verse thus obtains a rich meaning, which will be of service to us later on (see Lecture VII.).

Such is the historical setting in which I would fain place this gem of sacred song. It is pleasant and not contrary to analogy to suppose that, though corruption had infected the degenerate descendants of the righteous Simon, the less exalted temple-ministrants still cultivated the sweet ancestral piety. What they felt most in that unhappy time when the Jews, as Josephus says, 'were very like to a ship in a storm which is tossed by the waves on both sides' (*Ant.* xii. 3, 3), was the enforced removal of some of them to a distance from the temple, a lot which they of course shared with others of their nation. It is in the name of their brethren, as well as in their own, that these unselfish minstrels frame their heart-felt songs.

I pause for a moment to remark that there is nothing in these results at which we need be surprised. They are in a very true sense conservative; that is, they prove the continuity of the succession of 'spiritual men' (Hos. ix. 7) and of highly gifted religious poets in ancient Israel. By their help we can distinguish far more clearly than of old that

> chime of rolling rivers
> Through the forest of the psalms,

of which a poet-preacher dear to many in Oxford has told us.[1] We must not, however, assume that all the psalms in Books II. and III. are of the Greek period; we may confidently expect that earlier periods will be also represented in the collection. In the remainder of our survey of Books II. and III. we will keep in view the possibility that there are yet more psalms of the Greek period, but will aim chiefly at discovering the lyric utterances of the preceding age. Certainly the 89th psalm must, if my own exegesis be correct, belong to the Persian age, when there was no native ruler of the Davidic line.

---

[1] Bishop Alexander of Derry.

However much the concluding verses may sound like the personal complaint of a Davidic king (see especially *v*. 48), the 19th verse, as Tholuck remarks, proves that the psalm had not a regal author even in poetic fiction. Nor is the psalmist really desirous (like the author of the companion-psalm, the 132nd) to bind Jehovah to the letter of his promises to David in 2 Sam. vii.;[n] it is the fate of Israel in which (like Ben Sira in his encomium,[o] where, as I think, he twice alludes to our psalm) he is absorbed—of Israel who, as prophets and psalmists agree, has become the heir of 'the sure mercies of David.'[p] How the old promises are to be fulfilled, and through whom as His organ Jehovah will in future govern His people, does not cause this poet a moment's anxiety. He has not even an idealistic regard for royalty; he is one of the *Soferim* (students of Scripture), or, if his partiality for the word *khésed*, 'love' or 'lovingkindness,' justifies this specializing use of the term,[q] of the *khasīdīm*— those who responded to God's covenant-love of Israel by obeying His commands at all cost and believing the promises of His *tōrāh*. Like the author of the 86th psalm, he could truthfully have said, 'Preserve thou my soul, for (although neither great nor strong) I am duteous in love' (*khāsīd*, lxxxvi. 2).

Still it is not, I think, surprising that Eichhorn, the father of recent criticism, should have been tempted to ascribe Ps. lxxxix. to Hezekiah.[1] For who more fitly than this king, especially as he is described in 2 Chron.,[2] could claim the epithet *khāsīd*? or on whose lips would the complaints in *vv*. 46 and 48 be more natural than on those of him who became 'sick unto death' in the midst of an Assyrian invasion? Yes; if Hezekiah really composed that sweet and plaintive 'writing' which bears his name, it is plausible to conjecture that he also wrote the 88th,[r] and was in the mind of the writer of the 89th psalm (*v*. 46*a*). But if, as for the last ten years I have maintained, the so-called Song of Hezekiah is a post-Exile work, it will be clear that those who share Eichhorn's impression respecting Ps. lxxxix., ought

---

[1] *Einleitung in das alte Test.*, v. 24 (ed. 4, 1824). Manasseh, Josiah, and Jehoiachin have also been thought to be referred to.

[2] Note the phrasing of 2 Chron. xxxii. 32.

logically to become converts to the critical theory expounded in this lecture. The subject of this 'strange psalm' (as Dr. Grätz calls the 89th), and not less so of Ps. lxxxviii., as well as of the song in Isa. xxxviii., is no longer Hezekiah, nor any other individual sufferer, but the post-Exile Jewish Church; and the period to which Ps. lxxxix. at any rate is best assigned, is that of the terrible calamities which befell Judæa under the second and third Artaxerxes, and which very possibly called forth that wonderful psalm-like meditation, so parallel in some respects to Ps. lxxxix., Isa. lxiii. 7–lxiv.[8]

In fact, no psalm, perhaps, contains such abundant evidence of its date as the 89th, and even those passages which may seem like 'purple patches' are eloquent of contemporary thought and feeling. We cannot say as much of Ps. lxxxviii., which is eloquent enough, no doubt, in its own sad way (cf. Ps. vi.), but of which historical criticism cannot venture to fix the date too precisely. The reference to v. 4 in Ecclus. li. 6 shows, however, that it was written before the appendix to Ecclesiasticus. Doubtless it describes some gloomy portion of the pre-Maccabæan post-Exile period. This is confirmed by its resemblances to other psalms of lamentation, and by its author's predilection for the most melancholy portion of the Book of Job, the hero of which he evidently regards as a symbol of the Jewish people. May we not say that even the limitations of this 'spiritual man' (Hos. ix. 7) have a pathetic interest? The darkness is ever deepest before the dawn. Israel is on the eve (as we shall see in a subsequent lecture) of the discovery—or revelation—of immortality.

The 87th psalm lifts us up again, just as at an earlier point the 68th stirred and refreshed us after the 69th. Clearly the editors of the Psalter appreciated the effect of strong contrasts. How tantalizingly incomplete but how suggestive this psalm is! Its author is a temple-singer who, devoted as he must be to his own class, looks forward with joy to the enlargement of the sacred choir by the admission of foreigners. This, however, is not the main subject of the psalm. The idea which fills this holy minstrel with enthusiasm is the expansion of the Church of Israel into the Church universal. And though direct references to historical facts are wanting, the grand universalism of the psalm, and the choice of the national types of worldly success, leave us in no doubt as to its period.ᵗ The prophecies of both Isaiahs have had at least an initial fulfilment. Worship has been fully centralized by the rebuilding of the temple and the firm establishment of the Levitical system, and an influx of proselytes has suggested that great new metaphor, now so old, of the second birth of conversion.ᵘ

Ps. lxxxvii. transports us, as it would seem, into the early Greek age. To the same period we may perhaps assign Ps. lxxxvi., also (see *v.* 9) a missionary psalm. Very unlike, however, are the respective psalmists in literary talent; they belong to different circles and own different principles of composition. Even the early collectors must have been struck by this, for while Ps. lxxxvii. is Korahite, Ps. lxxxvi. bears the very unusual title—'prayer of David' (cf. Ps. xvii.). Another such piece of mosaic work scarcely exists in the earlier books: Ps. cxliii. is its only parallel in the Psalter. Not that these two psalms breathe exactly the same spirit. In lxxxvi. 2 the speaker pleads for preservation on the ground of his piety, but in cxliii. 2 he deprecates judgment because 'before God no man living is righteous.' Is not this difference significant? If the 143rd psalm is of the Persian period, may not the 86th belong to the succeeding age, when the anti-Hellenistic reaction so greatly intensified the self-consciousness of the *khasīdīm* or strict Jehovists? Yes; and we can perhaps also *prove* that it does so; for it contains undeniable allusions to Pss. liv. and cxvi.ᵛ—both productions of the Greek period.[1] It belongs, I suppose, to a comparatively peaceful portion of the early Maccabæan age, when the *khasīdīm* had gladly exchanged the sword for the pen, and the battlefield for the student's chamber.

In Ps. lxxxv. we meet with the *khasīdīm* again; 'his people' and 'his *khasīdīm*' are synonymous terms in *v.* 9. There is, however, in the true text no reference to an idolatrous party, and the Hasidæan tendency certainly began before the Greek period. Nor is there anything to suggest a later period than the Persian for Ps. lxxxiv., for the 'anointed' in *v.* 10 is probably (note the context) the high priest.ʷ

[1] Cf. *Jeremiah, his Life and Times*, p. 105.

This beautiful lyric reminds us somewhat of Ps. xlii., but (with all deference to Ewald) the historic background is altogether different. A poem over which sweet peace so calmly broods cannot be the complaint of an exile. The only pains which the speaker knows are those inseparable from the pilgrim's life; they are now past, for he is on the point of appearing before his God in Zion [x] (*v.* 8). Neither he nor his nation has anything to fear at present from the great heathen power; he casts but one side-glance at the 'tents of ungodliness' (lxxxiv. 11). Would that we had this psalm in as complete and original a form as the 42nd! In the more connected portion of it (*vv.* 2-8), several indispensable words have fallen out of the text, while the concluding part has very possibly been altered for liturgical purposes by the Elohistic editor.[y] In spite of its title, the song may, I think, once have belonged to the book of the Songs of Ascent.[z]

We next cross over into the Asaphite Psalter, pausing at Ps. lxxxii., with which the 'Davidic' 58th psalm is closely connected. The former is a fine poetic commentary on the phrase 'who only hath immortality.' The 'Elohim' and the 'sons of 'Elyōn' are the prince-angels of the nations, so that the psalmist is a witness to that renascence of mythology which characterizes some of the later books. The strange threat in *v.* 7, like the parallel passage Isa. xxiv. 21-23, can only be explained by the light of apocalyptic eschatology. To the illustrative references given elsewhere, I may add the Targum on Judg. v. 13, which makes one of the deliverers or patron angels of Israel descend and break the power of the *gibbōrīm* of the nations. Who are these *gibbōrīm*? We can answer by referring to Joel iii. (iv.) 11, where Jehovah's *gibbōrīm* are certainly the angels. So then the putting down of injustice is imagined as a war between the angelic powers. We know how prevalent this mode of thought was in the Greek period (Dan. x. 13, 20, 21). But we need not bring down Pss. lviii. and lxxxii. so late.[aa] The yearning for a fuller theocracy and the belief in a coming war of Jehovah are characteristic of Joel, of the close of Zechariah, of Isa. xxiv.-xxvii., and of Isa. xxxiv.,[bb] all of which writings belong to the Persian period, and some, perhaps, to those dark days when even a wise man 'commended death rather than life'

(Eccles. iv. 1-3). The psalmists are not of the spirit of Ecclesiastes. The closing verse of Ps. lxxxii. is parallel to that of the next psalm, written probably later, which assures us that now at length 'Jehovah, and he alone, is most high ('*Elyōn*; cf. Ps. lxxxii. 6) over all the earth' (Ps. lxxxiii. 19).

Let us turn next to Pss. lii.–lix., which stand between an Exile or early post-Exile psalm and one of the Maccabæan period.[cc] As we might expect, not a single psalm written either before or even during the Exile has found its way among them. We are assured of this (in spite of the heading *l'dāvid*) by an examination of the phraseological allusions to other psalms or Old Testament books. To which period shall we refer these psalms? or have more periods than one contributed to the group? The latter question I at least must answer in the negative, feeling bound to regard all members of a group which have common characteristics as belonging to the same period. In the present instance there is a group within the group. Ps. liii. is but a more corrupt form of Ps. xiv. (notice the incoherence of *v.* 6), which must be considered later; and Ps. lviii. requires, as we have seen, to be coupled with Ps. lxxxii. There remain Pss. lii., liv.,[dd] lv.–lvii., and lix., with which Pss. lxii. and lxiv. should (see my commentary) be connected, though now, for obvious reasons,[ee] placed elsewhere. All these are animated by a strong church-sentiment. The speaker is either a leading Israelite, who has suffered indeed with his nation, but who draws some of his details from personal experience; or Israel personified; or perhaps we may say that he is sometimes one and sometimes the other. He is oppressed by foes both native and foreign, who, without actually drawing the sword, wage deadly war against the true religion, and who (especially the disloyal Israelites) watch for opportunities of manifesting their hatred of those for whom the psalmist speaks. 'Swords are in their lips' (lix. 8; cf. lv. 22), and worldly power is in their hands. Faithful Israel is pressed beyond endurance, and bitter, vindictive words force themselves from his lips (see especially lv. 16, lviii. 7-10, lix. 12).

One tyrant is specially mentioned (lii. 3), whom we may identify with the false friend in lv. 13-15, unless, indeed, we feel compelled by an excessive regard for consistency to convert not only 'thou tyrant,' but 'my companion and my familiar friend,' into a collective term.^{ff} Theoretically, this is, of course, allowable; but lovers of literature will probably be unwilling in this and in similar instances[1] to use the licence.

To appeal to the literary instinct may perchance be stigmatized by some as uncritical. This need not disturb us; it is one of our objects to enjoy the psalms as works of literature, and were they not sometimes enlivened by personal references, their poetical charm would be very seriously impaired. And yet we must not, in quest of biographical touches, follow the acute and original Hitzig (not to mention an earlier writer, Dean Jackson) in ascribing a number of psalms, and among them the 55th, to Jeremiah, simply because his is the richest character, and the most fully recorded life, of the introductory period of the Jewish Church.^{gg} This would be only a less error than ascribing the psalms in question to David, a theory which merely rests upon an early misunderstanding. All that we can safely admit is, I believe, this—that certain psalmists, who had partly formed their ideals of life upon Jeremiah, expressed the spirit of that noble prophet even more strikingly than he had done himself.^{hh} Not that they wrote imaginary psalms of Jeremiah,ⁱⁱ just as a great prose-writer imagined the last discourses of Moses,^{jj} but periods came when the life of Jeremiah was a true parable of the fortunes of the Church. Now in which period can it have been seen to be so to such an extent as to explain Ps. lv.? It must have been a period in which the 'love of many' for the true religion had 'waxed cold,' and when the faithful few were deserted by their natural leaders, and opposed by a great world-power.^{kk} I do not say that this is an accurate description of the circumstances of Jeremiah, but it was near enough for those who studied that prophet for edification, and it corresponds to the picture presented in these psalms.

Was the age of Nehemiah such a period as we are in search of? Surely not. To mention only one objection: there was no great coalition of the heathen world against Israel in the times of Nehemiah. But to the psalmist or

---

[1] Cf. Ps. xxxv. and Lam. iii., and see below (Lect. VI.).

psalmists the present calamities of Israel are great enough to be the first stage in that uprising of the heathen world so vividly described in Joel and in the Second Zechariah. This is why Jehovah 'laughs' at them (lix. 9 ; cf. ii. 4) and will send 'his army' (the angels) to overthrow them (lix. 12 ; cf. Joel iii. 11). It is not the petty tribes of the neighbourhood who are arrayed against the Jews, but one of the great powers of the East. Is it Persia, or is it the Græco-Syrian kingdom? Theodore of Mopsuestia,[1] with an acuteness worthy of Hitzig, supports the latter view with regard to Pss. lv.–lix. (and lxii.). In Ps. lv., for instance, he makes David assume the character (πρόσωπον) of the pious high priest Onias III., who is filled with horror at the wickedness of the citizens, and, knowing that there are designs upon his life, meditates flight. This view of the contents is based upon a tradition, found also in two passages of Josephus,[ll] according to which Onias III. was not murdered in the sacred grove at Daphnæ (as 2 Macc. iv. 34, 35 asserts ; cf. Dan. ix. 26), but fled into Egypt, and there built the temple at Leontopolis. In other respects Theodore agrees with the narrative in 2 Maccabees. The treacherous friend in Ps. lv. 13–15 he takes to be that προστάτης τοῦ ἱεροῦ, called Simon,[mm] who fell out with the high priest Onias, and gave information to the court which led to the sacrilege of Heliodorus (2 Macc. iii. 4-7). In this last identification Theodore certainly goes too far. The psalm is not spoken in the name of a high priest, for the speaker calls his faithless friend 'a man of his own rank' (v. 13) ; nor is it any isolated act of treachery which is referred to, but the hostility of a party-leader.[nn] Nor can I anywhere else in this group of psalms discover a clear reference to the Hellenistic movement in Judah. The tyrant who glories in mischief (lii. 1) is no more the ungodly high priest Alcimus[2] than Doeg the Edomite ; he is only in practice, not in theory, an apostate. The moral scenery of these psalms reminds us of that of Pss. xciv. and cxxxix. as well as of Isa. lix.[oo] and the Book of Ecclesiastes, none of which have been proved to be later than the close of the Persian period. But here I must pause. Some of the most interesting psalms of Books II. and III.

---

[1] See Baethgen in Stade's *Zeitschrift*, 1885, p. 88 ; 1886, p. 276 &c.
[2] Cf. 1 Macc. vii. 9, and see above, p. 56.

still remain for another lecture. Suffice it to have shown that thus far these books, like the fourth and fifth, are a collection of precious church-historical records mainly of the Persian, but to some extent also of the Greek period.[pp] Our conception of the range of Bible-history and of the extent and methods of inspiration has already, I trust, begun to widen. The opening words of Heb. i. 1 ($\pi o \lambda u \mu \epsilon \rho \hat{\omega}s\ \kappa a \grave{\iota}\ \pi o \lambda u \tau \rho \acute{o} \pi \omega s$) should already be acquiring a richer and a more satisfying significance.

Note a, p. 112.

Ps. lxviii. closes a small group of four psalms, all provided with titles containing the words מִזְמוֹר and שִׁיר. If even one of them is post-Exile, the presumption is that all are. Nothing however indicates that they are absolutely contemporary. Why were they grouped? For some musical reason? Because of a common universalistic element? At any rate, Pss. lxvii. and lxviii. are parallel in their openings (comp. the one with Num. vi. 24, 25, and the other with Num. x. 35).

Note b, p. 112.

There is a tendency sometimes visible in writings which on other grounds are post-Exile to accumulate names for God (cf. the epithet πολυώνυμος given to Greek divinities, and see on Ps. l.). Ps. lxviii. and the Song in Exod. xv. are instances of this. Both poems have יהוה, אלהים, אל, and אדני. The psalm also has שַׁדַּי (v. 15), which first appears in authoritative religious literature at the close of the Exile (see on Ps. xci.). יָהּ occurs perhaps in v. 5 of the psalm, and certainly in v. 19; also in Ex. xv. 2, xvii. 16 (the first of which may be, and the second must be, pre-Exilic), and in Cant. viii. 6 (which may be pre-Exilic); but also forty-two times in Biblical passages which on various other grounds are all most probably (I speak within bounds) either Exilic or post-Exilic. (Of these forty-two passages, thirty-nine are in the Psalter; the other three are Isa. xii. 2, xxvi. 4, xxxviii. 11.) I base no argument on the infrequency of יהוה in Ps. lxviii. (only vv. 17, 21) as compared with אדני (six times), as such phenomena may be due, or partly due, to the editor and the scribes.

Note c, p. 112.

Cf. v. 4 with Isa. xxxv. 10, li. 10, 11; v. 5 with Isa. xl. 3; v. 7 with Isa. xlii. 7, xlix. 9, lxi. 1; vv. 30–32 with Isa. xlv. 14; v. 21

with Isa. xxvi. 29 (idea). Among the lyric poems referred to are the ancient song in Judg. v., Moses' marching prayer in Num. x. 35 (priestly code), the Song and Blessing of Moses (cf. my *Jeremiah*), and the grand Exilic, or more probably post-Exilic, Ode in Hab. iii. (Grill compares *v.* 8 with Hab. iii. 12, 13 ; *v.* 11 with Hab. iii. 14 ; *v.* 12 with Hab. iii. 9 ; *vv.* 18, 20 with Hab. iii. 8 ; *v.* 21 with Hab. iii. 13 ; *v.* 22 with Hab. iii. 13, 14 ; *v.* 25 with Hab. iii. 6, 7, 10 ; *v.* 29 with Hab. iii. 2 ; *v.* 34 with Hab. iii. 6. But the points of contact are not all equally clear.)

NOTE ^d, p. 112.

Among other points favouring a very late date, note the development of the heavenly host into 'many myriads' (*v.* 18). The best defence of the earlier date will be found in J. Grill, *Der achtundsechzigste Psalm* (Tübingen, 1883) ; cf. Kautzsch's review, *Theol. Litztg.*, 1884, cols. 129-131. For a fuller development of my own view (assuming the later date), see my Study in *Expositor*, Sept. 1890. Nowack's conclusion is similar ; he is much impressed by the phraseological coincidences between Ps. lxviii. and Isa. xl., &c. (he would add, following Grill, Isa. xxiv.–xxvii.). J. W. Pont may also be quoted on this side. His monograph (specially valuable for its critical survey of the theories of previous commentators) is entitled, *Ps. lxviii., eine exegetisch-kritische Studie* (Leiden, 1887). It is no step in advance when two eminent Jewish scholars, Grätz and Halévy, agree in dating our psalm at or near the close of the Jewish state. The existence of the temple being presupposed, the psalms must, as they strangely think, be pre-Exilic. The antithesis of the 'righteous' and the 'wicked' (*vv.* 3, 4) points to the recent introduction of the Deuteronomic Law, which was not as effectual as its promoters wished. So at least Grätz, who adds that the psalmist dreads Pharaoh Neco. Halévy, however, denies this. The 'wild beast of the reeds' (*v.* 31) is Babylonia. To Egypt the psalmist is friendly, he says, because an Egyptian army was Judah's one hope in Zedekiah's reign (Jer. xxxvii. 5). שַׁי, *v.* 22, is emended into שָׁנָי, and the verse-groups are partly rearranged to produce a better whole. Halévy is independent to a fault. It is not wise to disdain one's predecessors. See *Revue des études juives*, xix. 1–16.

NOTE ^e, p. 113.

Some one has, however, explained the psalm of Judas's victory at Bethhoron and the re-dedication of the temple (see Grimm on 1 Macc. iii. 24).

NOTE ᶠ, p. 114.

Ps. xliii. has no title in the Hebrew. Sept. calls it a psalm of David, and Mr. Mozley takes this literally, offering various exegetical arguments, e.g. (see *v.* 4) that the first person sing. is never used in the direct ascription of thanks and praise in the Levitical psalms, whereas 'David' often uses it. David, he thinks, completed the work of a Levite (*David in the Psalms*, pp. 38–42). But an untitled psalm is abhorrent to Sept., and David was the typical psalmist. Cod. Alex. adds words to the title ascribing Ps. xliii. to the sons of Korah.

NOTE ᵍ, p. 114.

This verse almost determines the date of the poem. It probably refers to the mercenary troops of Egypt and Syria (cf. the story of Heliodorus). See however Hupfeld (*Psalmen*) and Land (*Theologisch Tijdschrift*, 1872, pp. 564, 565), who limit the reference to Syria.

NOTE ʰ, p. 114.

Dean Stanley is reminded of the 'last sigh of the Moor'—the name of the spot from which Boabdil bade farewell to his beautiful Granada. Against Ewald, cf. my *Jeremiah, his Life and Times*, p. 163. I need simply chronicle the undoubting belief of Delitzsch that our psalm is the work of a Korahite Levite in the train of David, when he was in exile beyond Jordan (at Mahanaim in Gilead). The ideas, he thinks, come from David's works, but are reproduced with a freshness due entirely to the author. He refers for the Davidic ideas to Pss. xxiii., xxvi., lv., lxiii. Theodore and Theodoret both place the psalm in the Exile. Cornill, while of course rejecting Ewald's theory that Jehoiachin himself is the author, still thinks that this psalm (with lxxxiv. and lxxxv.) may have been composed by one of Jehoiachin's fellow-exiles (Luthardt's *Zeitschrift*, 1881, p. 337 &c.). Halévy prefers to date the psalm at the very close of the Exile (*Revue des études juives*, i. 27). To all these theories a critical commentary will at once suggest numerous objections, to which may be added the use made of Ps. xlii. in Jon. ii. 2–9 (see note ⁱ), and (for those who follow my arguments) the parallelisms between our psalm and psalms of post-Exile origin (e.g. comp. xlii. 2 with lxiii. 2; xlii. 9, xliii. 3, with lvii. 4; xlii. 9, 'my Rock,' with lxxvii. 7; xlii. 4 with lxxx. 6, lxxix. 10, cxv. 2).

NOTE ⁱ, p. 114.

The only objection I see to this is the use made of Ps. xlii. in the psalm of Jonah. But this psalm is not really more connected with the story of Jonah than the psalm of Hannah is with that of Hannah (see above, on Ps. cxiii.), and may have been inserted in Jonah subsequently to B.C. 198. It is a composite work, in the style of Ps. cxlii., like which (see Jon. ii. 2, A.V. 1) it probably once bore the heading תְּפִלָּה 'a prayer,' and describes how afflicted Israel wrestled with its despondency. Its familiar symbols were transparent to the editor, who placed it where it now stands, and who knew that the Jonah of the Book was, like Job, a מָשָׁל or similitude for the people of Israel (cf. Jer. li. 34). I have assigned the psalm of Hannah to the early post-Exile period. The psalm of Jonah, a greatly inferior work, was not improbably written about the same time as the תְּפִלָּה in the appendix to Ecclesiasticus (li. 1–12). In fact, the two last-mentioned lyrics are as much a pair as Pss. xxvi. and xxviii., and the latter alludes to (cf. Ecclus. li. 5, 'belly of hell,' with Jon. ii. 3) and throws light upon the former. Israel's sore peril arose from 'an accusation to the king by an untruthful tongue' (Ecclus. li. 6), i.e. a charge of meditated rebellion. Now can we doubt that Onias II.'s non-payment of taxes to Ptolemy Euergetes, shortly after that king became lord of Judæa, had a political cause (Jos., *Ant.* xii. 4, 1 as explained by Herzfeld and Edersheim)? The threat of colonizing Judæa with Egyptian soldiers was surely quite dangerous enough to occasion both these Hebrew lyrics. See further, Smend, Stade's *Zt.*, 1888, p. 145; my views however owe but little to his article. The purpose and date of the Book of Jonah are treated of in my two articles, *Theological Review*, 1877, p. 211 &c., *Encyclop. Britannica*, and in Dr. Wright's *Biblical Essays*, and the text-criticism in Böhme's article, Stade's *Zt.*, 1887, p. 224 &c. Renan's view (*Histoire*, tom. ii., and *Journal des Savans*, Dec. 1888) that the book is a 'pamphlet against prophetism' is a caricature of the truth. You might as well say that it, like Isa. lviii., is a pamphlet against the legal fasting.

Note j, p. 115.

This council preceded and was distinct from the Sanhedrin. It is mentioned in this connexion in a letter of Antiochus III. for the first time (see note k), and is probably the חבר היהודים attested by the early Maccabæan coins. Josephus traces the supreme council under the high priest to the return from Babylon (*Ant.* xi. 4, 8). Probably, however, it was adopted from the Hellenic aristocracies, as it corresponds to the increased power of the high priest in the Greek period.

Note k, p. 115.

Antiochus, in his letter to Ptolemy, speaks of the general poverty and depopulation of Jerusalem at this time, and expresses his resolve to remedy the former by the remission of taxes and liberal gifts to the temple, and to bring back those who have been scattered abroad (Jos., *Ant.* xii. 3, 3).

Note m, p. 116.

Thus Ps. cxxxvii. 5 becomes partly parallel. The objection to Hitzig's view is that in *v.* 8 the psalmist addresses God (not Zion). But this is hardly as important as I once thought. From the temple the transition is easy to the temple's God. And observe that in *v.* 5 the psalmist 'remembers' or 'thinks upon' the joyous processions to the temple. The connecting link is suggested by Ps. xliii. 3, 'Send forth thy light,' &c. At any rate, the text must be wrong, and Hitzig may be right.

Note n, p. 117.

Written in the time of Hezekiah or (much more probably) Josiah (see *Jeremiah, his Life and Times,* p. 88). As Wellhausen remarks its comparatively late date is as obvious as that of 1 Sam. ii. 27–36, to which it is parallel (Bleek's *Einleitung,* ed. 4, p. 223). This result has satisfied such a sober critic as C. H. Cornill ('Die Quellen der BB. Samuelis,' in *Königsberger Studien,* Bd. i.). I do not of course deny that this idea of the perpetuity of David's royal house is older than the time of Josiah (see Am. ix. 11, Hos. iii. 5, Isa. ix. 7, xi. 1). But the psalmist undoubtedly refers to the later expression of this idea.

Note o, p. 117.

There is only a vague Messianic hope in Ecclus. xliv.–l. (see *Job and Solomon,* p. 188). Ben Sira's real interest is in the perpetuity of the people of Israel, which at present is identified for him with the continuance of the high priesthood (Ecclus. xlv. 26, l. 24 Pesh.). The latter passage (in which, with Grätz and Edersheim, I prefer the Syriac text, but without their emendations) runs thus: 'And with Simon (the high priest) let lovingkindness be established, and with his seed as the days of heaven.' There is no sufficient objection to the text-reading ܢܣܒܼ. The Hebraizing sense 'lovingkindness' is above suspicion (see Pesh., Ecclus. i. 13), and the absence of a suffix may be explained by a reference to Ps. lxxxix. 3 (חסד יבנה). The concluding figure is from Ps. lxxxix. 30 (cf. Deut. xi. 21).

NOTE P, p. 117.

Comp. *v.* 18*b* with *v.* 25*b*, and see Isa. lv. 3 (cf. 2 Sam. xxiii. 5). Verse 19 assumes the point of view of Nathan's prophecy. ' It was promised that we should have kings whom God Himself would protect.' But the essential point with the writer is the lot of the nation (hence '*our* horn').

NOTE q, p. 117.

One can hardly suppose that *khasīdīm* was as yet used as a party name. A stronger reaction against Hellenizing manners was needed before the 'straitest sect' of legalists assumed a special right to this fair name. 'Koheleth' only advises his disciples not to be 'righteous overmuch' nor to be 'overwise' (Eccles. vii. 16).

NOTE r, p. 117.

Dean Plumptre is half disposed to assign Ps. lxxxviii. to Hezekiah (*Biblical Studies*, p. 172). Eichhorn simply says, 'Written long after David's time, perhaps under Hezekiah, or even as late as the Exile.' Venema thought of Jeremiah (because of the pit in *v.* 7), but as an alternative suggested that the psalmist writes in the character of Job in his leprosy (so too Delitzsch and Klostermann). The Targum and the Rabbis (except Ibn Ezra) interpret the psalm of the still present dispersion of the Jews. The unreason of this was seen by Theodore of Mopsuestia and Theodoret, who (followed by De Wette) regard it as a lamentation of the exiles in Babylon. The title of our psalm has suggested to Delitzsch and Klostermann the view that 'Heman the Ezrahite' was the author of the Book of Job, parts of which the psalm so much resembles. But the first of the two 'conflate' titles deserves the preference over the second. In spite of 1 Chron. ii. 6, Heman was not a Zarhite, but a son of Mahol (1 Kings iv. 31). It is only a later student who represented the Korahite 88th psalm to be a 'Maschil of Heman the Ezrahite' to provide a companion for the 'Maschil of Ethan the Ezrahite' (Ps. lxxxix.). That Pss. lxxxviii. and lxxxix. have no strong affinity is clear; 'both in poetical character and in situation the two psalms are different' (Delitzsch). Nor are there any incidental ideas or expressions common to both which justify their being grouped together. On the other hand, between Pss. lxxxvi. and lxxxviii. there are several points of contact; cf. lxxxvi. 1, lxxxviii. 3, 16, lxxxvi. 10, lxxxviii. 11; and especially lxxxvi. 13, lxxxviii. 7. These psalms may once have stood side by side, though it is true that Ps.

K

lxxxvii. is not exactly misplaced. It is in fact a poetic sketch of the happy results of the conversion of the nations anticipated in lxxxvi. 9.

NOTE ˢ, p. 118.

See my review of G. A. Smith's *Isaiah*, in *Expositor*, Feb. 1891. In 1881 I placed this evidently liturgical composition early in the Exile. This was preferable to assigning it to the same period as Isa. xl. &c., and could be supported on exegetical grounds. Still this is not a likely date for a writing which stands between late Exile and post-Exile works. The view adopted above suits all the requirements of the case much better. The references to the Divine Spirit suggest a date not very far from Nehemiah (and Ps. li.). Notice too that according to Isa. lxiii. 18 Jehovah's servants have had but a short possession of His holy mountain. Isa. lxiv. 10 reminds us of Ps. lxxxix. 41, and the heroic insistence on thanksgiving in Isa. lxiii. 7 of Ps. lxxxix. 2, 3. But I confess that I cannot believe in a burning of the temple at this period (see p. 102). Was the description in Isa. lxiv. 11 inserted by the author himself (see note ᵏ, p. 103, for an analogy) to make this section available as a liturgical commemoration of the earlier catastrophe under Nebuchadrezzar? That the proposed date suits both Ps. lxxxix. and Isa. lxiii. 7 &c., is sufficiently clear. In such troubles it might well seem as if nothing short of a theophany (Isa. lxiii. 19; cf. lviii. 2, post-Exile) would meet the needs of Israel, and Israel himself might complain of having grown old before his time (Ps. lxxxix. 46), and of 'fading as a leaf' (Isa. lxiv. 5). For how else can we explain these passages? Can it be Rehoboam whose 'days' have been 'shortened' by disgrace? So thinks Delitzsch. But as Dr. Forbes remarks, 'whatever may have been the original occasion of the psalm, its present position and connexion . . . point distinctly to the cessation of the outward visible kingdom' (*Studies*, p. 96). And why should we deny that not only these but the expressions of the psalm point either to the Exile (as Grotius, with the Peshitto) or the post-Exile period, though not necessarily to the Maccabæan age, to which Rudinger and Hitzig refer it? Notice the doctrine of God and of the angels implied in *vv.* 6–9, and the parallelism between *vv.* 10, 11 and Isa. li. 9, 10. Also the representation of the 'kings of the earth' as 'sons of God,' whose chief was the king of Israel (*v.* 28). The pre-Exile writers do not describe even the Messianic king as God's son; that title belongs to the people of Israel, Ex. iv. 22, Hos. xi. 1; cf. Deut. xiv. 1. After the Exile the ordinary Oriental title for kings was adopted in connexion with the view, now sanctioned by the psalmists, that the earthly kingdoms had heavenly patrons (see on Ps. lxxxii. 1, 6).

Note ᵗ, p. 119.

Hengstenberg and Delitzsch (with whom Dean Plumptre agrees) place Ps. lxxxvii. in the reign of Hezekiah, remarking that the prophets had already beheld the king of Babylon in the foreground of the future, and represented him to themselves as the heir of Assyria, to prove which they refer to Isa. xxxix. 6, 7, Mic. iv. 10. But it has been shown (see my notes) that these passages, either entirely or in part, have been inserted by later editors, who were so full of the great deliverance from Babylon that they made references to it where none originally existed. Besides, the author knows the Book of Isaiah as a whole; comp. Isa. xxx. 7, li. 9 (Rahab); xviii. 7, xlv. 14 (conversion of Cush); xix. 18-25, xlv. 14 (conversion of Egypt); xx. (Philistia); xxiii. (Tyre). It is possible, indeed, that one of these passages (Isa. xix. 18-25) was inserted in the Greek period; but it would not follow that Ps. lxxxvii. was equally late. Post-Exile, however, the psalm must be. The ideas (as Calvin clearly saw) are those which Isa. xl. &c. made familiar to the Jewish Church (cf. Isa. xliv. 5, Zech. viii. 22, 23); and the statement respecting Babylon shows that the embitterment caused by Babylonian oppression had long since passed away.

Note ᵘ, p. 119.

See my Study on Ps. lxxxvii., *Expositor*, 1889 (2), p. 360 &c. The historical situation of the psalm would be unimaginable if we did not assume an initial fulfilment of the prophecies of conversion. Stade may be right in seeing in 2 Chron. xv. 9, xxx. 6-11, a reflection of conversions of the descendants of the ancient Israelites in the early Greek period (*Gesch. des Volkes Israel*, ii. 198, 199). But this will not go very far towards explaining the situation. There must have been conversions from heathenism not only at home but abroad, news of which had reached the psalmist. Cf. the reference to 'fearers of Jehovah' in Pss. cxv., cxviii.

Note ᵛ, p. 119.

Comp. lxxxvi. 14 with liv. 5; *v*. 16 with cxvi. 16. That liv. 5 is quoted in its Elohistic form, proves that the Elohistic redaction of the Korahite and Asaphite *fasciculi* preceded the composition of Ps. lxxxvi.

Note ʷ, p. 119.

See p. 60 (note ᵗ), and cf. pp. 119, 339, and notice that, side by side with the revived archaism Yahvè Çebáoth (*v*. 9, see next note), we have the stately and solemn combination 'Yahvè Elohim,' which characterizes the widened theological outlook of the Persian period.

NOTE ˣ, p. 120.

David's authorship is irreconcilable with the language used of the sanctuary. Clearly the erection of the temple is an event of the past. Baudissin cautiously remarks, 'One may suppose that it is of the regal age' (*Gesch. des Priesterthums*, p. 260). If so, the latter half of the reign of Josiah is the only period which can be thought of (see my *Jeremiah*, p. 105). But we must not, without some special reason, isolate this psalm from its companions. And, as remarked already, can we imagine pure and spiritual church-psalms existing thus early?

NOTE ʸ, p. 120.

Can we avoid supposing that Ps. lxxxiv. 9, 10 has at least been touched by the editor of Pss. lix. (see *v.* 6) and lxxx. (see *vv.* 5, 8, 15, 20, and cf. my commentary)? 'El, Elohim, Yahveh' (l. 1) is unpoetic enough, but 'Yahveh Elohim Çebáoth' is still more so. A frigid accumulation of these divine names is intelligible in Ps. l. 1 (written by a wise man who had turned poet), but hardly in such deeply felt lyrics as Pss. lix., lxxx., lxxxiv. I therefore take Ps. lxxxiv. 9, 10, to be a late liturgical insertion which took the place of verses more suitable for pilgrims than for the Church at large. The phrase 'our shield' was perhaps suggested by *v.* 12*a*.

NOTE ᶻ, p. 120.

Herder long since claimed Ps. lxxxiv. as a pilgrim-song. Olshausen agrees with this. So also Derenbourg in his Study on this psalm (*Revue des études juives*, avril–juin 1883, p. 162).

NOTE ᵃᵃ, p. 120.

Observe that Ps. lxxxii. is one of the proper psalms for the successive days of the week (see on Ps. xciii.). It is probable that this arrangement is not as late as the Greek period.

NOTE ᵇᵇ, p. 120.

On the dates of these books, or portions of books, see articles in *Encycl. Britannica*. My own article on Isaiah, the latter part of which developed some neglected results of Ewald in a form which seemed to me in fuller accordance with the exegetical facts, was published in 1881; I could now give it much greater precision. Other critics too are tending in the same direction. With regard to Isa. xxiv.–xxvii. it has lately been well said by Kuenen that there are few left who doubt that the prophecy belongs to the Persian period. Ewald in 1841 referred it to the reign of Cambyses; but most will feel that this is too early. Dillmann (1890) takes a somewhat wider range; Isa. xxiv. 4–13 may, he thinks, point to the wars and disturbances under Cambyses and Darius. Vatke in his posthumous *Einleitung* (1886) preferred the reign of the tyrant Artaxerxes Ochus, when Sidon, as a punishment for its large share in the revolt, was destroyed (B.C. 351). Hilgenfeld (1885) thinks the prophecy to be occasioned by Alexander's conquest of Tyre, and long before him Vitringa had even brought it down as late as Antiochus Epiphanes. In 1884 Smend thus summed up his own conclusions: 'We have the choice either to place the events which are here presupposed in the 60 years between Zechariah and Ezra, or in the 200 years between Nehemiah and Hyrcanus the farmer of the taxes. The latter view has the most probability' (Stade's *Zeitschrift*, 1884, p. 210). For Joel even Prof. A. B. Davidson has committed himself to a post-Exile date (*Expositor*, March 1888); for a fuller discussion see Matthes, *Theologisch Tijdschrift*, 1885, pp. 34 &c., 129 &c. On 2 Zechariah I can refer to my own article, written in 1879 (before Stade's articles appeared) on the publication of Dr. Wright's *Bampton Lectures*, and published without alteration in the *Jewish Quarterly* for Oct. 1888. Dr. Kuenen's conclusions in the new edition of his *Onderzoek* are very similar to my own.

NOTE cc, p. 121.

The mutual points of contact of these psalms and their connexions with other writings are worth noticing, as they have a bearing on criticism. I select a few of them:—

Ps. lii. 4, cf. lv. 12 (lvii. 2).
,, ,, 10, ,, xcii. 14.
,, ,, 11*b*, cf. liv. 8*b*.
,, liv. 5, cf. lxxxvi. 14.
,, ,, 6, ,, cxviii. 7.
,, ,, 9, ,, lix. 11, xcii. 12.
,, lv. 11, ,, lix. 7, 15.
,, ,, 12, ,, Isa. lix. 14 (post-Exile).
,, ,, 13–15, cf. xli. 10.
,, ,, 22, cf. lvii. 5, lix. 8.

Ps. lvi. 2, cf. lvii. 4.
,, ,, 5, 10, 12, cf. cxviii. 6.
,, ,, 7, cf. x. 8, 9.
,, lix. 4, ,, x. 8, 9.
,, lvi. 8, ,, lix. 6 ('the nations,' in antithesis to 'my people,' *v.* 12; cf. 'ruler in Jacob' *v.* 14).
,, lix. 5, ,, vii. 7.
,, ,, 8, ,, xciv. 4.

Pss. lvi. and lvii. are closely connected; lv. and lix.; (liii.) lviii.

and xiv. Comp. also several phenomena in Pss. vii., ix., x. In fact, the persecution-psalms have not a few striking features in common (comp. Delitzsch on Ps. lvii.). There are also affinities between Pss. lviii. and lxxxii., and (as Dr. Kay points out) between Ps. lviii. and Isa. lix. (see above, on lv. 12). Observe, too, that in the Hebrew Pss. lii.–lv. are each headed *maskil*, and Pss. lvi.–lx. *miktam*. The two groups are mechanically linked by the 'dove' in lv. 7, lvi. 1. In each group one psalm seems inserted by an afterthought. Ps. liii. gives a theoretic justification of the special case described in Ps. lii.; Ps. lviii. performs the same office for Pss. lvii. and lix.

Note dd, p. 121.

Theodore of Mopsuestia (according to Baethgen's Syriac text) explains Pss. lii., liv., and, of course, liii. (see on xiv.), of Hezekiah's times. So too the anonymous arguments in Corderius (ii. 1). Rabshakeh, says the writer (Theodore?), was a renegade Hebrew captive. Theodoret (on Pss. lii., liii.) also follows Theodore, but saves his respect for the title of Ps. lii. by means of a prophetic theory. Ps. lxii. he explains as if Maccabæan (cf. Theodore, p. 123).

Note ee, p. 121.

The closing verse, lxiv. 11, resembles lxiii. 12. Ps. lxiii. is itself of the Greek period. Ps. lxii. is placed after Ps. lxi. because the titles 'rock' and 'refuge' for God occur in both (lxi. 3, 4, lxii. 3, 7, 8, 9). It has, however, also a close connexion with Ps. xxxix. Both poems have a touch of the Hebrew reflectiveness (see on Ps. xxxix.).

Note ff, p. 122.

My spoken words were that such a criticism can rob the rose of its perfume. The phrase might pass as representing the mood of the moment, but it were unfair to adhere to it. The sufferings of a nation have a still subtler fragrance than those even of the noblest of its members. The collective theory must be applied in cxx. 6, 'Full long has my soul had her dwelling beside him who hates peace' (Kay's version). It may be applied in Ps. lv. 13–15, and still more easily in Ps. xli. 10 (comp. Obad. 7). At any rate, the treacherous friend was not alone in his treachery, if we may trust psychological verisimilitudes. Comp. Job xix. 19, Prov. xix. 7.

Note gg, p. 122.

Hitzig originally (in 1835–1836) referred as many as twenty-seven psalms to Jeremiah, viz. v., vi., xxii.–xli., lii.–liv., lxix., lxxi. In his later commentary (1863-1865) he is content with specifying twelve or fourteen, viz. v. (?), vi., xxii., xxx., xxxi., xxxv., xxxviii., xxxix. (?), xl., liii. (= xiv.), lv., lxix., lxx. (= xl. 14-18), lxxi., though in his introduction he seems inclined to add more ; and Mr. Ball, claiming his authority, is inclined to refer Pss. xxiii., xxvi.-xxviii. to the prophet's pen (*Expositor's Bible: Jeremiah*, 1890, p. 10). The exegetical and historical combinations by which Hitzig supports his theory are interesting and suggestive. It would be delightful to be able to modify our view of Jeremiah by his own lyric disclosures of his inner life ; delightful, too, to learn something definite about the impression produced in Judah by the wave of ruin which swept along Palestine early in Josiah's reign (see my small *Jeremiah*, p. 30). It was Ewald's opinion that Ps. lix., and Hitzig's that Pss. xiv. (= liii.) and lv. refer to the Scythian invasion, but this is hardly a good specimen of the critical tact of these eminent scholars. It is the exegetical arguments of Hitzig on which the acceptance of his theory of Jeremiah's authorship depends. To some they will probably appear plausible ; both Ewald and Delitzsch do in fact, as we shall see, agree with Hitzig in one or two instances. I am not surprised that Mr. Ball is even more moved by the great Zurich professor. If these psalms are neither Davidic nor Exilic and post-Exilic, what age is so fit for them as that of Jeremiah? It is true that the age of Jeremiah is at first sight equally fit for other writings, and will by degrees become somewhat too full of literature, especially considering the troubles of the time ; but while we look at each critical problem separately, this circumstance is likely to escape us. I fear I must at various points go on objecting to Hitzig's view (see e.g. Lect. V., Part II., note P). At present, however, I need only repeat the criticism which I offered in 1883, that though the parallelism between certain psalms and Jeremiah's life and works is to some extent a real one, the explanation provided is too easy. 'We have to deal with the fact that there is a large body of Biblical literature impregnated with the spirit, and consequently [presenting] many of the expressions, of Jeremiah. The Books of Kings, the Book of Job, the second part of Isaiah, the Lamentations, are, with the psalms [in question], the chief items of this literature ; and while, on the one hand, no one would dream of assigning all these to Jeremiah, there seems, on the other, to be no sufficient reason for giving one of them to the great prophet rather than the other. With regard to the circumstantial parallels in [certain] psalms to passages in the life of Jeremiah, it may be observed (1) that other pious Israelites had a similar lot of persecution to Jeremiah (cf. Mic. vii. 2, Isa. lvii. 1) ; (2) that figurative expressions like 'sinking in the mire and in the deep water' (Ps. lxix. 2, 14) require no groundwork of literal biographical fact (not to remind realistic critics that there was no water in Jeremiah's prison, ch. xxxviii. 6); and (3) that none of the psalms ascribed to Jeremiah allude to his prophetic office, or to the conflict with the 'false prophets,' which must have occupied so much of his thoughts (*Pulpit Commentary: Jeremiah*, vol. i., p. xii.). Dean Jackson's form of the theory requires no criticism; it was a resting-place for faint-hearted critics, who did not wish to reject the time-honoured headings. This is that a number of 'Davidic' psalms (including Ps. xl.) 'were penned, or paraphrased upon, by Jeremiah for the people's use in the Babylonish captivity' (*Works*, viii. 84). And what shall we say of the headings of these psalms? I think that we can easily account for them in the case of Pss. lii., liv., lvi., lvii., lix. The historical notes attached to them suggest that these psalms had once been inserted as illustrations in the history of David, or, better perhaps, that they were conventionally used by teachers to illustrate David's life. It was a small step further in those days to say that David was the author of those psalms.

Note hh, p. 122.

Jeremiah, his Life and Times, p. 110, cf. p. 126. Jeremiah being the most Christlike of prophets, it was natural that a psalm, like Ps. lv. inspired by him, should be thought a prophecy of Jesus Christ, σκιαγραφίαν τινὰ ἔχων τῶν δεσποτικῶν παθημάτων (Theodoret).

Note ii, p. 122.

Stade, I observe, thinks that the author of Lam. iii. poetizes in the character of Jeremiah (*Geschichte*, p. 701).

Note jj, p. 122.

I might add, just as another psalmist 'thought himself,' however imperfectly, into the person of David (Ps. xviii.).

Note kk, p. 122.

I do not, with Olshausen, press the reference to 'evening, morning, and noon' as times of prayer (Ps. lv. 18). Even if a post-Exile writer, the psalmist is not thinking of the obligation of praying thrice in the day, but of his constant need of free prayer to the God of his life.

Note ll, p. 123.

War, i. 1, 1, vii. 10, 2-4; cf. Talm. Bab., *Menachoth*, 109a; *Yoma* (Jer.), 6, 3. In *Ant.* xii. 9, 7, xiii. 3, 1-3, xiii. 10, 4, xx. 10, however, it is more correctly Onias IV. who builds the Egyptian temple. Nowhere does Josephus refer to the murder of Onias III. at Daphnæ, and Theodore appears to desert 2 Maccabees deliberately at this point. Both Baethgen and Wernsdorf (not Schürer) regard the story of the murder as one of the fictions of 2 Maccabees. But why? The narrative of Josephus is certainly not complete (see *Ant.* xii. 5, 1), and Theodore had an object in deserting 2 Macc. (viz. to illustrate Ps. lv. 7–9).

NOTE mm, p. 123.

In the *Catena* of Corderius (ii. 61, on Ps. lv. 14) Theodore comments thus upon ἡγεμών μου (Sept's. read. of אַלּוּפִי)—ὡς πρὸς τὸν Σίμωνα· ἐπειδὴ τοῦ μακαρίου Ὀνίου ἀρχιερατεύοντος προστασίαν τινὰ ἐγκεχείριστο. He goes on to say that the subordinate officers of kings are called their captains.

NOTE nn, p. 123.

Hitzig's theory is not open to this objection. Pashur, whom he takes to be the false friend of the psalmist, was but one of many בְּעָרְבּוֹ; cf. Jer. xii. 6, xxvi. 8, 11.

NOTE oo, p. 123.

Notice in Isa. lix. the points of contact both with Ps. lviii. and with Jeremiah's prophecies. This was a time in which psalmists and prophets alike saw a striking resemblance to the age of Jeremiah.

NOTE pp, p. 124.

Vatke, in his posthumous *Einleitung*, remarks of Books II. and III., 'Many, especially Korahite, psalms were evidently written under the Diadochi' (p. 529).

LECTURE IV.

Be his name [blessed] for ever;
While shines the sun, may his name have increase;
May [all tribes of the earth] bless themselves by him,
May [all] nations call him happy.—(Ps. lxxii. 17.)

LECTURE IV.

PART I.—Psalm lxxii. Must this psalm be either in the narrowest sense Messianic or a piece of bombast? Coleridge thought so.—Another question—Is it spoken dramatically of Solomon? or of Hezekiah? or of one of the Asmonæan princes? Conclusive objections to each theory.—Is the psalmist carried ἐν πνεύματι into the age of the Messiah? Objections.—The only remaining theory.—The psalm not being pre-Exile, may not the king be a foreigner? Two kings are possible—Darius and Ptolemy Philadelphus. Reasons for preferring the latter, who was not only a magnificent and fortunate prince, but a special friend of the Jews. Hitzig's theory criticized.—The poem probably written soon after the accession of Philadelphus (B.C. 284), who is called in v. 1 'the king's son,' because his royal father was still alive. Objections answered.—The Joseph-psalms, a monument of Israelitish patriotism in the Persian period.—Pss. lxxiii. and xlix. both on the same subject, and reaching the same conclusion. The former about contemporary with Ecclesiastes; the latter somewhat older.—Ps. l. not a mere didactic poem, but a quasi-prophetic utterance with a definite historic background. Argument for a post-Exile origin (Persian period) both for Ps. l. and for Ps. xl. 1-12.

PART II.—Ps. li. why not Davidic. Written probably after the Return, but before the great rebuilding of the walls by Nehemiah. Nor do any of the remaining psalms of Books II. and III. (among which note especially Ps. xlviii., a festival psalm, specially designed for pilgrims) belong to the Greek period, except Ps. xlv. What is the date of this 'song of lovely things'? Does it refer to Ahab? or to Jeroboam II.? Objections to each. Analogousness of this psalm to the 72nd. It was not, indeed, written as a church-hymn, but is not without Messianic features and by its fine moral and religious spirit contrasts with the 17th Idyll of Theocritus addressed (like Ps. xlv.?) to Philadelphus. Objections to this view of Ps. xlv. answered. Meaning of 'Jehovah thy God.' Conjecture as to the origin of the poem.—Reason for the fulness of detail in the preceding argument; such hypotheses must be set forth tentatively, and are unimportant unless they account for a large number of phenomena.—Historical and phraseological allusions in favour of this hypothesis.—How came Ps. xlv. to be admitted into the Psalter? Theory of its reference to Solomon. Its profoundly Christian moral sentiment.

PART I.

PSALMS LXXII., LXXIII., XLIX., L., ETC.

THE times are past when even Samuel Taylor Coleridge could say that 'in any other than the Christian sense Ps. lxxii. would be a specimen of more than Persian or Mogul hyperbole and bombast.' Against such words the young sciences of language and religion enter a protest, which all who share in the intellectual life of our time must eagerly endorse. The poetic glorifications of Egyptian and Babylonian kings which have been disinterred from the dust of ages glisten to us of this generation with a strange and pathetic beauty. The high hopes attached to Rameses, to Nebuchadrezzar, to the early Ptolemies, may have been bathed in illusion, but were 'too fair to turn out' wholly 'false.' The names, in the ancient sense of the word, of these righteous kings may have passed away, but their 'souls are in the hand of God,' and, may be, their hopes are fulfilled in the 'land of the silver sky.'[a] And so far as their aspirations passed the bounds of what is permitted to man, they are true of Him of whom all worthy kings are types, of Him who, more completely than Nebuchadrezzar (Ezek. xxvi. 7), is 'king of kings and lord of lords.'[b]

Permit me now to resume the thread of my inquiry, linking two sections together in Hebrew fashion by a catchword. The question has been raised whether there are any 'imaginary psalms of Jeremiah.' This is a plausible view doubtless, and may to some suggest the idea that the author of Ps. lxxii. assumes the character of a contemporary of Solomon. That the poem can at most have only a dramatic reference to that king, is clear. The social state of Israel was radically unsound in the time of Solomon, nor did he resemble the 'prince of peace' portrayed by the psalmist (1 Kings xi. 14-25, xii. 4, 18).[c] Even supposing that a temple hymn-book existed in

Solomon's days, how can one suppose that a psalm which would read like bitter irony would find or at least keep a place within it? On the other hand, if it be true that we have not only several 'imaginary psalms' of Jeremiah, but also at least one (see Ps. xviii.) of David, written long after the great king's time, why may not this be a similar imaginary psalm or dramatic idealization of Solomon? The view is confirmed, to some slight extent, by the heading of Ps. lxxii., εἰς Σαλωμών, i.e. 'with reference to Solomon,'[d] but is to be rejected on these two grounds: (1) that underneath the ideal glory of the picture we fail to trace the lineaments of the historical Solomon, and (2) that the tone of supplication requires a reference either to a contemporary or to a future king.

Dr. Grätz proposes another view. The psalmist is, he thinks, the spokesman of devout Levitical singers and musicians (according to him, the ʿanāvīm, or 'meek and lowly' ones, so often spoken of), who send up their loyal and religious aspirations for the new king Hezekiah. I will not say that such a reference is plainly impossible. If, as a late Regius Professor of Hebrew thought,[1] the subject of Isa. ix. 6, 7, is this youthful prince, 'whose nascent virtues qualified him in a peculiar manner to be the object of the nation's hope,' Ps. lxxii. may plausibly be viewed as a lyric expansion of that great prophecy. The anticipations were, no doubt, too high, but there would be no such moral incongruity in keeping a record of them as if they related to a despot like Solomon. It must be objected, however, that Professor Nicoll's interpretation is very doubtful, and that upon the phraseological evidence we cannot put the psalm earlier than the seventh century (v. 17b being dependent on Gen. xxii. 18, xxvi. 4), or, more precisely, than the Exile (v. 12 resting on Job xxix. 12, and v. 16b on Job v. 25).[e] It is even a question with some whether, simply on the ground of the allusion which they find in v. 8 to Zech. ix. 10,[f] the psalm must not be brought down as late as the conquests of Alexander. In this case we might follow Professor Church,[2] who seems inclined to apply Ps. lxxii. to Judas the Maccabee. Verses

---

[1] See Prof. Nicoll's *Sermons* (Oxford, 1830), p. 57. The Memoir prefixed to this volume should not be overlooked.

[2] Church (and Seeley), *The Hammer*, p. 370.

12–14 do in fact accurately describe the public character of Judas, and *v.* 11 might perhaps express the aspirations of the chieftain's friends. But 'the Hammer' was rather a Judge (in the old sense) than a king of Israel. Hyrcanus I. and Hyrcanus II. might both, in different senses, be called 'kings' and 'kings' sons.'[g] But the other conditions of the problem are not satisfied by either of them (comp. on Ps. cx.), least of all by the second—that feeble son of a queenly mother.

Shall we then explain the psalm, with Coleridge and so many others, of a king future to the psalmist? Most of the older writers (whose view does not stand or fall with the heading) suppose the psalmist to have been carried by the spirit of prophecy into the age of the Messiah. The Targum for instance paraphrases *v.* 1, 'O God, give the course of thy judgments to the king Messiah, and thy righteousness to the son of King David.'[h] This is not, indeed, absolutely impossible. The strict Messianic idea emerges now and then in the post-Exile literature. The words 'Behold, thy king cometh unto thee' (Zech. ix. 9) may conceivably have stirred up some poetic writer to prepare a hymn suitable for the accession of the 'desired king.' It is strange, however, that he does not display a more rapturous joy at such a delightful vision—strange, too, that he describes the king, not as 'the son of David,' but simply as 'the (or, a) king's son.' I can think of no way to remove these difficulties. The idealisms of the psalm seem to me to be gathered about a kernel of solid fact. The hero who is celebrated is not only a king, but a scion of a royal stem (*v.* 1), and the psalmist's prayer is that he may redeem his youthful promise, and deserve the blessings and intercessions of the grateful people of Jehovah (*v.* 15*b*; cf. *v.* 2*a*). Imagine this being said of the Messiah, or even of any idealized Israelitish king![1] Was it not the glory of the latter to be Jehovah's son (Ps. ii. 7, lxxxix. 27, 28), and his special privilege to intercede for and to bless his people (1 Kings viii. 22, 55)? Yet Ps. lxxii. is no mere court-poem; it is a seriously meant expression of the church-nation's homage to a king reigning (though a foreigner) by the grace of God. But must we stop here? May we not, with due modesty, seek to determine the age, and even, if possible, the name of this favourite ruler? The search will at any rate be profitable ; until we are better acquainted with the history of the Jewish Church, and apply it to the illustration of the Scriptures, we shall miss much of the pleasure, and some at least of the lessons, which the Bible was intended to yield us. Probably we shall think first of all of the Restoration period, from B.C. 515 onwards. Darius was personally well worthy of such an eulogium as Ps. lxxii., and it is not inconceivable that the good deeds of Cyrus (especially the liberation) were credited to his successor. I could wish to explain Ps. lxxii. of this noble believer in Ahura Mazda. But it appears to me that the Persian king was too far away from Judæa (cf. Eccles. v. 7) to be represented as ruling there in person, and certainly the psalmists of the Restoration rose to sublimer strains (see Ps. xciii. &c.).

But was there no prince less remote but not less powerful than Darius, for whom the Jews had the strongest feelings of loyalty and gratitude? Yes, there was one—Ptolemy Philadelphus,[j] who 'to the Jews became (as) a Jew, that he might gain the Jews,' and who, almost better in some respects than Cyrus and Darius, deserved a Hebrew poet's encomium.[k] He was in fact the second Cyrus of Israel, not only because he continued the privileges granted by his father to the Jews, but because he redeemed at his own cost a multitude of Jewish captives.[l] It is a misfortune that we have no contemporary authority for this fact, but there is no sufficient reason for rejecting the statements of 'Aristeas' where they are credible,[m] and it is in a high degree credible that the captives *were* released, and that on hearing the glad news and receiving the rich presents intended for the temple the Jews at once offered sacrifices and public prayer for the gracious monarch.[n] I do not assert that Ps. lxxii. 14 either describes or predicts (as a *vaticinium post eventum*) the release of the captives. The poem was most probably composed in Jerusalem before this event—not long after the accession of Philadelphus in his father's lifetime, B.C. 285, an allusion to which may be traced in the expression, 'the king's son,' in *v.* 1. But I must admit that Hitzig's theory (that much of the psalm is but disguised history) is, from an external and realistic point of view, plausible enough when we consider how literal in some cases was the fulfilment. How forcibly Theocritus's description of the conquests of Philadelphus (*Id.* xvii. 86–89) reminds us of *vv.* 8–11 of our psalm, closing as it does with the words—

θάλασσα δὲ πᾶσα καὶ αἶα
καὶ ποταμοὶ κελάδοντες ἀνάσσονται Πτολεμαίῳ.º

The Syracusan poet, however, omits what the psalmist, in his anticipations, records for all time—that, prosperous as this Ptolemy was in war through policy and the skill of his generals, his most durable glories were those of peace.ᵖ The dominant note of the psalm is righteousness. How earnest a spirit breathes in these words :—

> May he give doom to thy people in righteousness,
> And to thine afflicted ones according to right.
> Before him let foemen bow,
> And let his enemies lick the dust, . . .
> *Because* he delivers the needy when he cries,
> The afflicted also who has no helper (*vv.* 2, 9, 12).

Surely it is possible enough that the reputation of this popular Ptolemy justified such anticipations. It was too soon for the faults of the young prince to have cast a shadow upon his name. Fortunate then will Israel be under such a humane ruler. And yet, as the phrase 'thy (i.e. God's) people' implies, this post-Exile writer will not permit even the kindest of sovereigns to take the place of Jehovah.

A Ptolemy can only be the deputy of Israel's true King. But could even a second David be more? And it is as a second David, or a second Cyrus, that the poet praises the young Ptolemy :—

> His name shall last for ever ;
> While the sun shines, his name shall be perpetuated ;
> And men shall bless themselves in him,
> All nations shall tell of his felicity (*v.* 17, Kay).

That is, May the Messianic promises be visibly fulfilled in and through this kind and equitable ruler!

Does any one assert that no pious Jew could have written thus of a non-Jewish king, and remind me of Israel's self-concentration upon the Law and the faithfulness unto death of the Maccabees? I reply that I have shown already how deeply I respect these great qualities, but that, as the Books of Ruth, Jonah, and 'Malachi' prove, neither the work of Ezra and of the Maccabees, nor frequent heathen oppression, prevented the rise of a new charity on Israel's part towards the 'nations.' Under the Ptolemies, as Ewald has pointed out,[1] the union or association of Israelites and Greeks could not but appear both easy and desirable. There was in this a strong element of illusion, and a reaction followed. To the author of the apocalypse of Daniel such an object appeared in a very different light. Least of all could he have ventured to attach a quasi-Messianic character to a king of Hellenic stock; he could not have idealized even an Alexander. And he was doubtless right. The religious tendency of the Macedonian conquests was the opposite of that of the Persian.[2] But this did not at once become clear. It was the frantic Antiochus who revealed the wide difference between his Olympian Zeus and Ahura Mazda. But Ptolemy Philadelphus acted in another spirit, and a psalmist in the century before 'Daniel' could not but regard him as a friend both of the Jews and of their religion. Why should he not have expressed his gratitude? Rebuke him for his lofty words, and he will reply, like those Jews in the Gospel, 'That he was worthy for whom he should do this, for he loveth our nation.' And long afterwards the Jewish philosopher of Alexandria embalms the great Ptolemy's memory in this splendid eulogy: 'He was, in all virtues which can be displayed in government, the most excellent sovereign not only of all those of his time, but of all those that ever lived. . . . All the other Ptolemies put together scarcely did as many glorious and praiseworthy actions as this one king did by himself, being, as it were, the leader of the herd, and in a manner the head of all the kings.'[3]

The dark places of history must sometimes be illumined by the torch of conjecture. A hypothesis which meets all the conditions of the case has at least the value of a symbol (see p. 171). Philadelphus, or some foreign king like Philadelphus, is most probably the hero of the psalm, if we would read it, not as the

---

[1] *History*, v. 225; cf. Stade, *Zeitschr. f. d. A. T. Wiss.*, 1882, p. 289.
[2] See Ranke, *Weltgeschichte*, Band i.
[3] Philo, *De vitâ Mosis* (Mangey, ii. 138, 139).

early Christian Church, nor yet as Simon the Maccabee read it,[1] but as the original poet intended it to be read. It is an expression of early Jewish catholicity, and as such forms no unworthy close of the Second Book of the Psalter. Other psalms may be finer specimens of Hebrew poetry, but this one has a 'tone of large magnificence' which delights the ear, and suggests the widest applications.

The three psalms between lxviii. and lxxii. are manifestly not of the Greek period,q and will be most conveniently treated in Lecture V.[2] We may therefore proceed to ask, Are there any productions of the Greek period among the Joseph-psalms (those which are marked by the use of the term 'Joseph,' viz., lxxvii., lxxviii., lxxx., lxxxi.)? Ps. lxxvii. may conceivably be one. It opens with a kind of colloquy between the higher and the lower self, such as we have already met with in Ps. xlii., and a fine phrase in v. 7 may seem to be an imitation of Ps. xlii. 9. Still we are not forced to make this psalm as late as the 42nd. The wonderful psalm-like meditation in Isa. lxiii. is almost as completely parallel, and this, though post-Exilic, cannot be later than the Persian age (see p. 130), while the phrase in v. 7 ('Let me call to mind my song in the night') may be based on Job xxxv. 10, an Elihu-passage which must have been well known before the Greek period. Besides, the last four verses of our psalm, which are a fragment joined on by an editor, are a poetical sketch in the manner of, and probably imitated from, the ode in Hab. iii., which is one of the lyric passages inserted in the prophecies in the Persian period.r Ps. lxxviii. (with which Ps. lxxxi. 6b–17 must be grouped[s]) contains nothing suggestive of the Hellenistic age.[3] It presupposes, however, the general currency of the Yahvistic and similar narratives (note in passing the allusion in v. 13 to Ex. xv. 8), and its view of the Davidic kingdom resembles that of the Chronicler.t It would be foolish therefore to separate it from Pss. cv.–cvii.; judging from v. 49, it may, like Ps. lxxvii., be nearly contemporary

---

[1] For the sense in which Simon probably understood this psalm, see on Ps. xlv. (p. 173).

[2] On Pss. lxix.–lxxi. see pp. 230–233.

[3] The same remark is of course true of the fragment, Ps. lxxxi. 2–6a. Olshausen produces no distinct evidence in favour of a Maccabæan date for Ps. lxxxi.

with the speeches of Elihu (cf. Job xxxiii. 22). Ps. lxxx., a beautiful specimen of parallelism, tampered with by the Elohistic editor,[1] is also most naturally referred to the Persian period; v. 13 reminds us strongly of lxxxix. 41, 42, and the mention of Ephraim, Benjamin, and Manasseh in v. 2 can hardly be explained except on this theory. For if this psalm were of the Greek age, to which Hitzig refers it, should we not have had, instead of Ephraim and Manasseh, Zebulon and Naphtali (i.e. Galilee) as in lxviii. 28?

These four psalms are in fact a fine monument of the Pan-Israelitish sentiment of the Persian period. Wherever the term 'Joseph' occurs (even in lxxxi. 6) it is a symbolic archaizing expression[u] for the northern tribes—archaizing, one may fairly say, since M. Groff's discovery (see on lxxvii. 16), in a fuller sense than of old. The psalmists are evidently preoccupied with the thought that Judah alone cannot properly represent all Israel.[v] North and south had an equal right in the great passover-festival (lxxxi. 6), and equally belonged to the flock of Jehovah. These religious patriots delighted in the old story of Joseph the hero of the north, and select for imitation that part of the blessing of Jacob which belongs to Joseph.[w] One phrase above others in that section seems to have delighted them: Jehovah was the 'shepherd of Israel,' and Israel's highest honour was to be 'the sheep of his pasture.'[x]

Pss. lxxv. and lxxvi. will be best treated in connexion with Pss. xlvi. and xlviii.; but Ps. lxxiii., a psalm of the Church within the Church, claims immediate attention.[y] It reminds us of Koheleth in that it deals with a grave moral problem, but whereas the wise man leaves the difficulty almost where he found it, the psalmist discovers for it a deep religious solution. The poem doubtless belongs, like Koheleth, either to the last part of the Persian or to the beginning of the Greek period. As its position suggests, it stands in close historical connexion with the two Maccabæan psalms, lxxiv. and lxxv. You know the course of the psalmist's thought. Many Jews had given way to the seductions of a sceptical view of life. They had thrown off the restraints of Jehovah's religion (cf. cxxxix. 19, 20). They had become rich, and

---

[1] See above, note b, p. 101 (top).

oppressed their poorer brethren, and it seemed as if Providence were on their side (cf. Mal. iii. 15). The Hebrew Pascal broods over these things till he can bear it no longer. He knows the Book of Job, but he cannot rest in another man's imperfect solution of the perennial problem of suffering. He recovers his mental balance in the sanctuary. There he realizes that the punishment of these bold, bad men is but postponed, and as for himself, he needs no other reward than the sense of nearness to God, and the prospect of being taken to His glory (vv. 23, 24, 28).[z] And now see the contrasts which the editor suggests to us. One of the peculiar words of Ps. lxxiii. is משאות 'ruins;' 'thou castest the ungodly down,' we read, 'into ruins' (Ps. lxxiii. 18). In Ps. lxxiv. 'everlasting ruins' (v. 3) are actually visible to the psalmist; but alas! they are those of that very temple in which the author of Ps. lxxiii. won back his faith.

The problem then recurs, 'Has God after all forgotten the righteous?' 'No,' we seem to hear another psalmist answer us in Ps. lxxv.; 'ye did wrong to be envious at the boasters, at the ungodly' (lxxiii. 3). Grievous indeed was their tyranny, but now 'unto the boasters,' saith Jehovah, 'Be not so boastful,' and to the ungodly, 'Set not up your horn' (lxxv. 5). So varied are the moods of the psalmists, and so cunningly, to judge from a few glimpses, has the order of the psalms been devised to stimulate devout study of Israel's history.[aa]

It is natural to connect Ps. lxxiii. with Ps. xlix.[bb] The problem in both is the same, viz., how to justify the ways of God to the suffering righteous man. Both writers in treating this rise for a time to the heights of mystic devotion (cf. xlix. 16b with lxxiii. 23b), but relapse into the same didactic tone in which they began. From both the problem receives the same solution, though the expression of this is clearer in Ps. lxxiii.[1] Both writers agree moreover (see the two passages last referred to) in alluding to the story of Enoch in the priestly narrative (Gen. v. 24), and the author of Ps. xlix. probably refers besides to the account of man's origin in Gen. i. (see Ps. xlix. 13, 21). Both, too, have points of contact with Job and Ecclesiastes. It seems to me, how-

---

[1] See Lecture VIII.

ever, that the difficult plural *behémoth* in Ps. lxxiii. 22 may be best explained as an allusion, not to Job xl. 15, but to Ps. xlix. 13, 21. Considering also that the historical circumstances presupposed in Ps. lxxiii. are more overwhelmingly painful than those in Ps. xlix., and at the same time that the treatment of the problem in the former is more skilful, I think that we may reasonably place the 49th psalm somewhat before the close of the Persian period. More on this point later.[cc]

Ps. l. differs both in its tone and in its historical setting from the other Asaphite psalms; its isolated position in the Psalter is thus sufficiently accounted for. There is no indication that a part of the Israelites have fallen away from their faith, nor that Israel is languishing under foreign oppression. *Khasīdīm* in v. 5 has not the well-defined party acceptation which it obtained in Hellenistic times; it designates the entire body of nominal Israelites, good and bad alike, who, as the psalmist says, are to assemble (viz., from the lands of the Dispersion, cf. Ps. cvii. 3) that Jehovah may set before them His claims, and sever the good, though imperfectly instructed, Israelites from their unworthy fellows. The former are plainly told that animal sacrifices, though tolerated by God, are childishly absurd.[1] The latter are convicted of having 'omitted the weightier'—nay, this poet would say, the only weighty, 'matters of the law' (cf. Matt. xxiii. 23 [dd]). Their punishment will be that of all the nations who are forgetful of God (ix. 18)—some terrible form of death. On the other hand, the reward of the acceptable worshipper will be a delighted gaze on that great expected blessing of which even in one of the darkest parts of the post-Exile period another poet can say—

> My soul pines away for thy salvation;
> For thy word have I waited.
> Mine eyes pine away for thy promise,
> Saying, 'When wilt thou comfort me?'
>
> (Ps. cxix. 81, 82, Kay.)

The psalm is throughout grammatically easy; and some critics have mistakenly described it as a mere didactic psalm. That, however, is a grand mistake. It is, as Ewald has said,

---

[1] See below, Lecture VIII.

more akin to a prophetic discourse than to a song, and prophetic discourses, as we know, are not merely didactic, but have a definite historic background.

The view of that great critic himself, tenable enough in 1835, I only mention as a starting-point. He connects this psalm with Josiah's thorough-going reformation of the national life on the basis of the Deuteronomic law, and regards it as a warning of a disciple of the prophets (cf. Jer. vii. 22, 23, viii. 8) against the spiritual drawbacks incident to a book-religion. The ceremonialism and hypocrisy spoken of in the psalm were no vague abstractions, but had taken shape before the psalmist's eyes. In favour of this view is the constant reference of the psalmist to the contents of Deuteronomy and the affinity of his ideas with those of the prophet Jeremiah. Against it is the strong improbability (1) that the ideas of Jeremiah should be so fully grasped and so distinctly expressed thus early; and (2) that this alone among the Asaphite psalms should be of pre-Exile origin. With regard to the first point, it may be observed that even Jeremiah is not entirely consistent with himself in his utterances on sacrifice;[1] and with regard to the second, that without some very strong reason all the psalms in one well-defined group ought to be assigned to the same period,[ee] ought at any rate to be reckoned uniformly as either pre-Exilic or post-Exilic.

I may now advance a step further. Not only does nothing speak against, but there is much positively in favour of, placing this psalm in the post-Exile period. That was the time when poets delighted in descriptions of theophanies,[ff] and when the thought of the Divine Judgeship dominated every mind. That was the time when the national canonization of Jeremiah led to the composition of a group of literary works which we may call Jeremianic. That was the time when the people as a whole could be called *khāsīd*, 'pious,' and when formalism and hypocrisy became so general as to stir 'the indignation' not merely of prophets but of temple-poets. That was the time, as we shall see later,[2] when there

---

[1] See *Jeremiah, his Life and Times* (1888), p. 157; on Ewald's hypothesis cf. p. 105.
[2] See Lecture VI., p. 287.

was much anxious speculation on the names of God, some men preferring to cease using the name Jehovah, and others to substitute or to add other names, such as Eloah (see Ps. l. 22), Elohim, or Adonai. I do not scruple to affirm that such an accumulation of divine names or titles as 'El, Elohim, Yahveh' (or, less probably, 'the God of divinities, Yahveh') is only intelligible after the return from the Exile. We find the same accumulation in Josh. xxii. 22.[88] The document to which this passage belongs is by very many critics assigned to a post-Exile writer or writers. And even if some of us reject this theory, yet no one can help admitting that Josh. xxii., or some part of it (including *v.* 22), proceeds from the school of religious thinkers to which I have referred. So that, in any case, Ps. l. 1 confirms the view that the great work of 'Ezra the scribe' lies behind and not before the psalmist.

This result may not be plausible from a mechanical evolutionary point of view. Anti-ceremonial utterances like those of Ps. l. would, it may be said, most naturally precede the promulgation of the Law. It is difficult to believe that Ezra and Nehemiah had opponents among the temple-poets as well as among unprogressive prophets and priests (cf. Neh. vi. 14, xiii. 29, Mal. i. 6). Perhaps; but history does not follow the course prescribed by theory. We must allow for the varieties of religious sentiment. Ezra at any rate (as the Books of Ruth and Jonah prove) was not an autocrat, and the author of Ps. l. may have belonged to a somewhat different school than that of the great reformer. I shall have more to say on this subject later. Suffice it to remark that while the psalmist admits the temporary validity of the established legal system, he looks forward to the realization of nobler visions than those of Ezra. He has in his mind the deeply spiritual intuitions of one of the later prophets:—

'Thus saith Jehovah, The heavens are my throne, and the earth is my footstool; what manner of house would ye build for me? and what manner of place for my rest? For all these things did my hand make; [I spake] and the world arose; but this is the man whom I regard, the man who is afflicted and contrite in spirit, and trembleth on account of my word' (Isa. lxvi. 1, 2).

And not only these, but also the bold ideas expressed in the following sentence (*v.* 3), which declares (or seems to declare) that the sacrifices of the Jews have no essential superiority to the heathenish cults still practised in obscure corners of Palestine.

Some will at once divine the inference which I venture to draw, but would by no means press upon every one. If Isa. lxv. and lxvi. form the second of two appendices to the Restoration-prophecy, and were written subsequently to the completion of the second temple,[hh] we may safely make not only Ps. l. but that fine psalm or psalm-fragment Ps. xl. 1-12, nearly contemporaneous with them.

Note [a], p. 141.

An Assyrian phrase for heaven. 'Silver' means 'sunlit;' so Hariri speaks of 'white day' as opposed to 'black night;' cf. Delitzsch, *Iris*, p. 30.

Note [b], p. 141.

In 1 Tim. vi. 15 this is a title of the invisible God; but in Rev. xvii. 14, xix. 16 it seems to denote the Messianic world-wide empire, agreeably to the Hebrew usage.

Note [c], p. 141.

The picture in Chronicles is no doubt more reconcilable with the psalms than that in Kings (note that in 2 Chron. ix. 23 'all the earth' has become 'all the kings of the earth'); and, later on, popular legend exaggerated Solomon's empire to the full extent of the psalm (see *Orac. Sibyll.* iii. 167-170; cf. xi. 79-92). But nothing is said in the psalm of the king's surpassing wisdom (that favourite subject of later ages, cf. Ecclus. xlvii. 14-17). Justin Martyr remarks, καὶ ὅτι μὲν βασιλεὺς ἐγένετο ἐπιφανὴς καὶ μέγας ὁ Σολομῶν, . . . ἐπίσταμαι, ὅτι δὲ οὐδὲν τῶν ἐν τῷ ψαλμῷ εἰρημένων, συνέβη αὐτῷ φαίνεται (*Dial. c. Tryph.*, c. 34, cf. c. 64). Justin, however, is a prejudiced critic, and seeks to extol the Christian Messiah at the expense of Solomon. So also Tertullian (*adv. Marc.*, v. 9), whereas Theodore of Mopsuestia (see Baethgen, in Stade's *Zeitschrift*, 1885, p. 65) takes an opposite line. St. Jerome adopts a typical Messianic theory. 'Ex parte autem et quasi in umbrâ et imagine veritatis in

Salomone præmissa sunt, ut in Domino Salvatore perfectius implerentur' (Comm. in Dan. xi. 24). This at least recognizes the rights of history.

NOTE d, p. 142.

That this is an incorrect interpretation must, I think, be admitted. If *l'dāvīd* means 'written by David,' *lish'lōmōh* can only mean 'written by Solomon.' The author of the heading either meant that Solomon prayed this prayer for himself (cf. 1 Kings iii.), or that he wrote it, not for himself, but for the congregation to pray on his behalf. Of course, this is as impossible as the statement in the headings of Ps. cxxvii., Prov. i. 1, x. 1, xxv. 1. Calvin's view, however, that Solomon versified David's last prayer for his successor (see Ps. lxxii. 20) is scarcely more critical; in a cruder form this theory was held by the Jews in Justin Martyr's time.

NOTE e, p. 142.

I do not include the supposed allusion in *v.* 8 to Zech. (see above). The phrasing may, after all, *not* be borrowed; it sounds conventional enough.

NOTE f, p. 142.

On the date of Zech. ix.–xiv., see my art. in *Jewish Quarterly Review*, Oct. 1888 (written in 1879), and cf. Stade's articles in his *Zeitschrift*, beginning 1881 (Heft 1), and Wellhausen's art. 'Zechariah' in *Encyclopædia Britannica*. The choice of date lies between the Persian and the Greek period.

NOTE g, p. 143.

S. Weissmann even finds an allusion to the Jewish name of Hyrcanus (II.) in the ἅπ. λεγ. ינון, *v.* 17 (*Jüd. Literaturblatt*, May 13, 1886).

NOTE h, p. 143.

So also the Midrash on the Psalms, referring to Isa. xi. 1, 5. Verse 17 supplied Talmudic Judaism with one of the seven names of the Messiah (*Yinnōn*); see e.g. *Nedarim* 39*b* (Wünsche, *Der bab. Talmud*, 209, also Midrash on Prov. xix. 21).

NOTE i, p. 143.

An occasional special prayer for a Jewish sovereign (see Pss. xx., xxi.) can be understood, but scarcely that constant repetition of prayer and blessing (Ps. lxxii. 15), except for a foreign ruler of whom much spiritual good might be hoped, but little as yet could be known. Let me add that התפלל בעד (*v.* 15) occurs thirteen times elsewhere, and that the act thus described is always that of a prophet or priest (Job in Job xlii. 10 is virtually a prophet). See especially Gen. xx. 7, 'for he (Abraham) is a prophet, and he shall intercede for thee, so that thou livest,' and remember that Israel in the later period more and more regarded itself as the prophet and the priest of the rest of humanity.

NOTE j, p. 144.

Compare what follows with the discussion of Ps. xlv. My view is that of Hitzig and Reuss; Olshausen too agrees that some non-Jewish post-Exile king is meant. As will be seen presently, I do not interpret *vv.* 8–14 in Hitzig's matter-of-fact style. The poet gives us well-grounded aspirations or anticipations—neither more nor less. Nor, though the reference to rain (*v.* 6) and to the mountains of Palestine (*v.* 16) does not settle the point, do I think it at all probable that the psalm was written in Egypt.

NOTE k, p. 144.

See the striking passage in Droysen, *Hellenismus*, ii. 51, 52. Cyrus restored the Jews to obtain a secure advanced post for an attack upon Egypt. Egypt equally needed this *Brückenland* (Judæa) for its commercial enterprises. The second Ptolemy from the first planned to win and hold at least the south of Syria. Hence his ceaseless efforts to make friends with the Jews.

NOTE l, p. 144.

Josephus, in lieu of any direct encomium, says of this Ptolemy that he 'caused the Jewish law to be interpreted, and set free 120,000 natives of Jerusalem who were in slavery in Egypt' (*Ant.* xii. 2, 1).

NOTE m, p. 144.

Mahaffy (*Greek Life and Thought*, &c., p. 472) agrees; cf. Oort, *De laatste eeuwen van Israel's volksbestaan*, i. 34. The release and sacrifices are described in pp. 20–22 of the letter (cf. Jos., *Ant.* xii. 2).

Note ⁿ, p. 144.

Cf. Ezra vi. 10, 1 Macc. vii. 33, Baruch i. 11. Josephus represents the refusal to offer sacrifices for foreigners, and notably for Cæsar, as the true beginning of the war with the Romans (*War*, ii. 17, 2).

Note °, p. 145.

If, in speaking of this psalm and Ps. xlv., I refer so often to Theocritus, it is of course with no wish to lower the psalmists to his level. The author of Ps. xlv., especially, is much liker in spirit to the devout Pindar. The above lines of Theocritus were written subsequently to the marriage of Ptolemy and Arsinoe II. (which took place in or before B.C. 273). The inscription of Pithom discovered by M. Naville, by its references to the wars of Philadelphus, confirms this. See Wiedemann, 'Die Ehe des Ptol. Philad. mit Arsinoe II.,' in *Philologus*, N. F., i. 81–91. The Hebrew psalmist's picture must therefore be anticipative, the Greek poet's historical.

Note ᵖ, p. 145.

Droysen, *Hellenismus*, ii. 236. Comp. Thirlwall on the tendency of Alexander's measures and institutions (*History*, vol. vii.).

Note ᑫ, p. 147.

Ps. lxxi. precedes our Ps. lxxii. partly on account of the catchword 'thy-righteousness,' which occurs both in lxxi. 24 and in lxxii. 1. This psalm drew with itself two other 'Jeremianic' elegies—lxix. and lxx.

Note ʳ, p. 147.

The earliest possible date is, I am sure, the Exile period. But the strong expressions can hardly be accounted for by an Exilic background, unless we are content to regard this church-ode as more or less of an academic exercise. The most natural position for it is in the Persian period. It was doubtless appended to Habakkuk for the same reason for which Isa. lxiii. 7–lxiv. was attached to the great prophecy of Restoration, viz. that the earlier national troubles seemed to the Jewish Church to be typical of its own sore troubles after the Return. The writers of this period seem to have delighted much in descriptions of theophanies (cf. Ps. l. 1, the Accession-psalms, and the Book of Daniel). The lovely closing verses of Hab. iii. are also in a tone congenial to the later religion. How imitative and artificial, in a word, how late (in spite of its affectations of archaic roughness) the style of the ode is, need not be shown here. Like the so-called Song of Hezekiah, it once evidently formed part of a liturgical collection (cf. Hab. iii. 19, Isa. xxxviii. 20). On the whole question cf. Stade (*Zeitschr. f. d. alttest. Wissenschaft*, 1884, p. 157)—who, however, damages his cause by urging some doubtful arguments—and, I can now add, Kuenen, *Onderzoek*, ed. 2, ii. 394, 395.

NOTE ˢ, p. 147.

This part of Ps. lxxxi. is, like Ps. xix. 2–7, a fragment of a separate psalm (so Olshausen and Bickell). From its hortatory use of ancient history it is presumably contemporary with Ps. lxxviii. It was the psalm appointed for Thursday in the weekly liturgy (see on Ps. xciii.); the tinge of hope in its closing verses prepared the way for the more cheerful psalms for Friday and for the Sabbath.

NOTE ᵗ, p. 147.

An able Zend scholar, M. de Harlez, concludes from the glorification of David and the non-mention of the temple of Solomon that the author of Ps. lxxviii. wrote under David, whence it follows that 'the belief in demons was much anterior to the period of the first possible relations between Judæa and the Iranian lands' (*Proceedings of Soc. of Bibl. Arch.*, ix. 372). The latter deduction is wrongly formulated. Not demons (cf. Sept.) but 'hurtful angels' are referred to in *v.* 49, and even if we hold the belief in a *plurality* of such angels to be post-Exile, we need not derive it from Persia. And the conclusion as to the date of the psalm is uncritical. Even Calvin sees that the psalm must have been written long after the death of David, and, indeed, after the schism of the tribes, though he does not notice that the didactic use of past history is of itself decisive against a pre-Exile date (see on Pss. cv., cvi.).

NOTE ᵘ, p. 148.

Comp. Zech. x. 6, and notice in passing the friendly attitude of 2 Zechariah to Ephraim, and his anticipation of its joining with Judah in a war against Javan (Zech. ix. 13).

NOTE ᵛ, p. 148.

Ps. lxxviii. cannot properly be urged against this view. Ephraim may have sinned grievously, and the temple of Shiloh have been rejected. But Jeremiah fully admits this, and yet prophesies the repentance and return of Ephraim. So too might the psalmist.

NOTE ʷ, p. 148.

Comp. Ps. lxxx. 16 with Gen. xlix. 22, and the passages referred to in the next note with Gen. xlix. 24, xlviii. 15. One can easily believe, moreover, that the Joseph-story, with its perfect justification of the dealings of Providence, specially commended itself to an age which longed in vain to see righteousness adequately rewarded. Comp. Ps. cv. 16–22.

NOTE ˣ, p. 148.

See lxxvii. 21, lxxviii. 52, lxxx. 2; cf. lxxiv. 1, lxxix. 13, xxiii. 1, xcv. 7, c. 3, and note Sept.'s rendering of יְנַהֲגֵנוּ ποιμανεῖ αὐτοὺς xlvii. (xlviii.) 14. The Second Isaiah, too, had said, 'He will feed his flock as a shepherd' (Isa. xl. 11); comp. Jer. xiii. 17, xxxi. 10 l. 19, Ezek. xxxiv. 11–16. The idea, of course, is an old one. An ancient king was a 'shepherd of the peoples,' cf. 1 Kings xxii. 17, Zech. xi. 8, and Ass. *ri'u*, 1. herdsman, 2. sovereign.

NOTE ʸ, p. 148.

Ewald groups Ps. lxxiii. with Pss. lxxvii. and xciv., and too boldly assigns them to the writer who, later on, produced Pss. xcii., xciii., and xcv.–c.

NOTE ᶻ, p. 149.

See Lecture VIII., and cf. the late Prof. Elmslie's exposition, *Memoir and Sermons* (1890), pp. 175–191.

NOTE ᵃᵃ, p. 149.

Here is another instance of the suggestiveness of this order. How comes it that a single Asaphite poem—Ps. l.—should have been interposed between a group of Korahite and a group of so-called Davidic psalms? For the answer, see my Commentary, p. 144.

NOTE ᵇᵇ, p. 149.

A similarity in the opening words is all that connects Pss. xlix. and xlvii. There is a more real affinity between the former and Ps. xxxix., but the conclusions of these psalms are very different.

NOTE ᶜᶜ, p. 150.

Delitzsch illustrates the large didactic claims of *vv.* 2–5 by the oratorical promises of the eager Elihu (Job xxxii. 17 &c., xxxiv. 2–4,

xxxvi. 2-4), whose discourses he regards as pre-Exilic, and, indeed, of the age next to the Solomonic. Plumptre comes near this view when he assigns Ps. xlix. to the reign of Hezekiah, connecting *vv.* 8-12 with the Shebna of Isa. xxii. 15 &c. If Job and the proem of Proverbs are late, such early dates become impossible. The earliest defensible date is the post-Deuteronomic part of the reign of Josiah (i.e. after his 18th year), because this is the earliest possible date for the proem of Proverbs. But even if the address to 'all nations,' the large conception of wisdom, and the startling social contrasts implied in the psalm, correspond to the circumstances of that period, the solution of the moral problem with its eschatological reference, points very decidedly to a later age even than that of the Exile, to which in some respects (consider the facilities for growing rich in Babylon, and the deepening ethical reflection) it might be plausible, with Prof. Grätz, to assign it. I shall return to this in Lecture VIII., Part II.

NOTE ^{dd}, p. 150.

Can βαρύτερα here mean 'harder,' as Prof. B. Weiss supposes?

NOTE ^{ee}, p. 151.

The conception of Jehovah as Judge in Ps. l. is characteristic of the Asaphite psalms (cf. King, *The 'Asaph'-psalms*, Hulsean Lectures for 1889). Notice also that parallels to passages in Deut. and Jer. occur not only in Ps. l. but in the Asaphite fragment Ps. lxxxi. 6*b*-17; one of them consists of the clause 'I am Yahveh thy God' (lxxxi. 11, cf. l. 7). Comp. further עם=חסידים, l. 4, 5, lxxxv. 9; and זיז שדי, l. 11, lxxx. 14.

NOTE ^{ff}, p. 151.

Note הוֹפִיעַ, *v.* 2, as in lxxx. 2 (prayer for a theophany). Comp. Deut. xxxiii. 2. I do not forget Ps. xviii. 8-16, the prototype of similar passages. See also Lecture VII., Part II.

NOTE ^{gg}, p. 152.

May we compare 'Yahveh Elohim Çebaoth' in Ps. lxxxiv. 10 (Massoretic text)?

NOTE ^{hh}, p. 153.

See art. 'Isaiah,' *Encycl. Britannica* (1881) and art. in *Expositor*, Feb. 1891, and cf. Kuenen, *Hist. krit. Onderzoek*, ed. 2, part 2 (1889), pp. 140, 141. How far down this appendix (Isa. lxv., lxvi.) must be brought depends mainly on the date given to the somewhat earlier one, Isa. lxiii. 7–lxiv., which I incline (see p. 118) to make later than Prof. Kuenen, and to explain of a still greater calamity than that referred to in Neh. i. 3 (see on Ps. xxii.). It will be admitted that the recrudescence of superstitious cults alluded to in Isa. lxv. 3–5, lxvi. 3, 17 will suit the times of Artaxerxes Ochus as well as any earlier period of national disaster, and that lxvi. 24 suits the embitterment of these fearful times much better. Lastly, the description of the judgment in Isa. lxvi. strongly reminds us of Joel iii. and Zech. xiv. ; comp. also Isa. lxvi. 21 with the equally wide-hearted promise in Zech. xiv. 21 (second half of Persian period). I see how necessary it is to return to this subject elsewhere from the inadequate though learned and most interesting treatment of Isa. lxiii.-lxvi. by that eminent scholar, Dillmann (1890).

PART II.

PSALMS LI., LXV.–LXVII., XLV., ETC.

WE now pass to a psalm which, though akin in spirit to its predecessor, must rank still higher in our estimation. For surely there is no passage in the Old Testament at once more inspiring and inspired than the 51st psalm. Must we not, then, be eager to throw what light upon it we can from the circumstances of its origin? True, it will be answered, but this has already been done. In the matter of the psalm-headings, or at any rate of an arbitrary selection from them, we most of us still stand where our forefathers stood in the seventeenth century.[a] The vowel-points, indeed, are no longer held to be inspired, but the titles, or at least some of them, virtually are. A full account of the occasion of Ps. li. is given in the heading. To this I must object that hitherto the titles of the psalms have not yielded a single trustworthy biographical reference, and that a faithful exegesis proves that the title of Ps. li. is no exception. I do not say that it is valueless. It suggests thus much, that when the editor of this psalm lived, the ordinary tone of the Jewish Church was less penitential than it was sometimes—less so, for instance, than when church-writers penned the confessions in Ezra ix. and Dan. ix., and especially in Isa. lix. and lxiv. The original writer, if I may build upon the printed results of my own exegesis, spoke in the name of the Church.[b] The editor, however, did not perhaps feel the appropriateness of a 'general confession to be said of the whole congregation,' no provision for which is made even in the deepest part of Leviticus—the law of the Day of Atonement. He owned the touching beauty of the psalm, but set it on one side, as it were, for great sinners like David, justifying this, no doubt, by the superficial resemblance between *v. 6a* (hastily read) and 2 Sam. xii. 13*a*. That the title implied this, may have been felt by our prince of poets, when he made King John say:—

> But in the spirit I cry unto my God,
> As did the kingly prophet David cry,
> Whose hands as mine with murder were attaint.

This great psalm is in every sense the crown of the second 'Davidic' collection. If you cannot enjoy it without imagining that you know its author, then you might not unreasonably, upon exegetical grounds, give your voice for the poet-prophet whom we now call the Second Isaiah. It is a proof of the desultoriness of ancient criticism that the Septuagint translator, who assigns several of the psalms to prophetic writers, left this obvious conjecture for Hitzig. But, for my own part, I think it safer to ascribe our psalm, not to the Second Isaiah, but to one of those lyric poets (see p. 71) who were subject to the spell of his genius. May we presume that the psalmist lived during the Babylonian Exile? Both Theodore of Mopsuestia and Ewald held this theory, which is pleasing enough to the imagination. The sacred singers, according to Ps. cxxxvii., hung their harps upon the willows; here we see the harps taken down and used. The view is not precluded by the reference to the priestly rite of purification (*v.* 9; cf. Appendix), nor by *vv.* 20, 21, an epilogue which may, or must, have been added in the time of Nehemiah (cf. on Ps. cxlvii.).[c] Nor does the view of sacrifices in *vv.* 18, 19, of itself prove that Ps. li. is quite contemporaneous with Ps. l. Still we must remember that the other Deutero-Isaianic psalms are post-Exilic, and that Isa. lix. and lxiii. 7–lxiv., of which this church-psalm in parts so strongly reminds us, are also at earliest works of the age of Nehemiah.[d] We may reasonably consider, then, that Ps. li. was written during the Restoration period, before the great rebuilding of the walls by Nehemiah (see *v.* 20).

Let us now turn to Pss. lxv., lxvi., and lxvii., of which the first is called Davidic; the other two are nameless. When were they written? Ewald finds a great resemblance between Ps. lxv. (*Te decet hymnus*) and Pss. xlvi. and xlviii., which he brings close up to Judah's great deliverance in Hezekiah's reign. The parallelism, however, is really confined to a single verse (*v.* 8; cf. Ps. xlvi. 3, 4, 7), nor is it urged by Delitzsch, though he agrees with Ewald as to the date of the psalm. My own grounds for differing from both are derived from the phraseological affinities of the poem[e] and from the history of Biblical theology.[f] It is the second temple which engrosses the church's affection, and which Israel longs to see the spiritual centre of the world, and it is deliverance from one of the troubles that befell Judah, say, under Artaxerxes I. (465–425), which calls forth the song of grateful praise.[g] The same period will suit the somewhat similar 67th psalm (*Deus misereatur*), which is a psalmist's commentary on the priestly blessing, Num. vi. 24–26. We now come to Ps. lxvi. (*Jubilate Deo*), which one modern critic (Tholuck), under the glamour of the Isaianic period, actually refers to king Hezekiah. But must we—may we—on these four slender grounds, (1) that an individual gives thanks for the nation; (2) that he and they have been delivered from a crushing burden and a furnace of affliction; (3) that his prayers are the expression of an honest and believing heart; and (4) that Hezekiah was, according to the common opinion, a poet, ascribe the psalms to that pious king? The acute Theodore of Mopsuestia gives a much more reasonable explanation of this and the preceding psalm. In accordance with his theory of prophecy, he thinks that David was transported into distant times, and prophesied the return from the Exile. His Biblical theology may be at fault, but the critical view which he implies is here again almost equal to the best.[h] The 66th psalm does not belong to the Solomonic temple, and though post-Exile, is not, on the ground of a single expression (cf. *v.* 7 with lxviii. 19), to be brought down as late as the Greek period.

We are now approaching another station in our route. Ps. xlvii. has only an artificial connexion with Pss. xlvi. and xlviii. It struck a later editor as the lyrical expansion of the idea of Ps. xlvi. 11, that Jehovah is both *de jure* and *de facto* the governor of the nations. But it interrupts the far closer as well as more obvious connexion of Pss. xlvi. and xlviii. It was not amiss to group these three psalms for the temple-service, but, considering the clear affinities between Ps. xlvii. and the 'new song' in celebration of the second temple (viz. Pss. xciii. and xcv.–c.), we are bound to regard it as properly a misplaced fragment or perhaps a *replica* of that 'new song.'[i] Pss. xlvi.

and xlviii., however, have a family connexion. They agree in presenting remarkable coincidences both of thought and of expression with Assyrian prophecies of Isaiah. Nowhere can these be found so fully set forth as in the commentary of Dr. Perowne, to which I may refer the reader. My own opinion has varied. In 1870 I thought with Hitzig that the prophet Isaiah might have been also a psalmist, and have written these psalms on the great deliverance from Sennacherib. I no longer think so.[j] The Jewish Church in Isaiah's time was far too germinal to have sung these expressions of daring monotheism and impassioned love of the temple; and the word '*Elyōn* (xlvi. 5; cf. xlvii. 3) as a title for Jehovah never occurs in Isaiah, but frequently in the (probably) later psalms. Of what *later* age,[k] then, are these fine psalms the records?

Well, Isaiah soon became a favourite prophet—Jeremiah for instance abounds in allusions to him, and in any part of the post-Exile period the temple-poets may have resorted to him for stimulus. The divine name, Jehovah Sabáoth, and the title '*Elyōn*, were in use both in the Persian and in the Greek period (see for the former, Pss. lxxxiv. 9, lix. 6), and the admiration expressed for the beauty of Jerusalem in Ps. xlviii. 3 reminds us of the loving encomium in Ps. l. 3, and points to a period subsequent to the completion of the second temple. Then indeed it was true in a far larger sense than ever before, that Jerusalem was 'the joy of the whole earth.'[1] Then it was, that at the great feasts Jerusalem became too small for the thronging Jewish pilgrims from every land, all familiar with the leading parts of the Scriptures, and eager to realize the scenes of the sacred story. To whom so fully as to a pilgrim of the Diaspora do these words apply?—

> According to thy name, Elohim,[m] so is thy praise
> Unto the ends of the earth:
> Thy right hand is full of righteousness.
> Walk about Zion, and make the round of her,
> Reckon up the towers thereof.
> Mark well her rampart,
> Study her palaces,
> That ye may tell the next generation.—(Ps. xlviii. 11, 13, 14.)

[1] An allusion to Lam. ii. 15.

Yes; Ps. xlviii. at any rate is, I think, a festival psalm, inspired by the idea, now becoming a practical reality, of the Catholic Church. It presupposes a knowledge of the Scriptures, and may be grouped with the well-known historical psalms, from which it differs only in its more poetic character. Thus and thus only can we account for the exaggeration in *v.* 5,

> For, behold, the kings [n] assembled,
> They passed on together.

Not thus would a contemporary of Isaiah have written. But after the Return it was perfectly natural to use this seeming exaggeration. For the overthrow of Sennacherib, like that of Pharaoh, became then typical of the great future overthrow of the assembled hostile nations predicted by the later prophets.[1]

The use of historical motives in Ps. xlvi. is more delicate than in Ps. xlviii., though not less certain. You have one parallel for it close by in Ps. xlvii. 4, 5, which is a retrospect of the subjugation of the Canaanites and the conquest of Canaan. You have another in a psalm to which I would next invite your attention—Ps. lxxvi., which, together with Ps. lxxv., Ewald places immediately after Pss. xlvi. and xlviii. and considers to have been occasioned by Sennacherib's overthrow.[o] You will observe at once that Ps. lxxvi. begins, like Ps. xlviii., with a reference to Jerusalem, and that lxxvi. 9 and lxxv. 4 are parallel in part to xlvi. 7. Affinities to Isaiah are not wanting [p] in either of these psalms, though they are much less striking than those in the former pair. The Septuagint, moreover, prefixes to Ps. lxxvi. the title ᾠδὴ πρὸς τὸν Ἀσσύριον.[q] But if Pss. lxxvi. and lxxviii. are post-Exilic, much more are Pss. lxxv. and lxxvi. Observe, for instance, the use of 'Salem' for 'Jerusalem' in Ps. lxxvi. 3 (as in the post-Exilic passage, Gen. xiv. 18–20; see p. 42), and the legal tone of 'Make vows and pay them' in Ps. lxxvi. 12. Notice also the pervading antithesis in both psalms between the 'ungodly' and the 'evil-doers' on the one hand, and the 'righteous' and the 'afflicted' or 'humble-minded' on the other. This last feature may even suggest to some the

---

[1] Comp. Ezek. xxxviii., xxxix., Isa. lxvi. 6–24, Joel iii. 2, Zech. xiv. 2.

possibility of a Maccabæan reference. It does not of course necessitate this, but it would be quite in harmony with it. And so, too, is the keynote which is struck in Ps. lxxv. 1 :—

> We give thanks unto thee, Elohim, we give thanks unto thee ;
> And they that call upon thy name rehearse thy wonders.

These answers to prayer and these wonders of Elohim— can they be limited to the 'old lovingkindnesses'? Then read these words in *vv.* 5 and 6 :—

> I say unto the boasters, Be not so boastful,
> And to the ungodly, Do not exalt your horn ;
> Do not exalt your horn towards heaven,
> Nor speak arrogantly of the Rock.[r]

Ask yourselves now, to whom do these disparaging titles and statements more fitly belong than to the pagans and paganizers, Antiochus Epiphanes and his myrmidons, the ὑπερηφανία of whose speech is expressly imputed to them as a crime both in Daniel (vii. 8, 11) and in 1 and 2 Macc. (1 Macc. i. 24, vii. 34, 2 Macc. ix. 4)? And then look at Ps. lxxvi. No Asaphite psalm is equally vivid and vigorous ; it is 'keen as swordblades flashing down upon Syrian helms.' Yes ; the psalms may be Maccabæan,[s] as Hitzig would have them, but we cannot claim for this view the highest degree of probability, especially as neither psalm refers to any warlike deeds of Israelites. It is safer, I think, to connect these twin-psalms with Pss. xlvi. and xlviii., and assign them, at the earliest, to one of the happier parts of the Persian age.

The only remaining psalm of Book II. is the prelude to the Song of Songs—the 45th. Let it be understood that I speak, not of the virtually re-written psalm of the old Catholic Church, but of the Hebrew 'song' in its original meaning. For both I need not say that I have the utmost reverence, but as I am endeavouring to throw myself back into the period when the psalms were written, I must not allow myself to be influenced by the ideas of later interpreters. I need not, therefore, stay to show that the opening words attribute to the author a real but not a prophetic inspiration.[t] Nor yet that the royal subject of the 'song' is by no means 'King Messiah,' as the Targum and most Jewish and early Christian interpreters supposed,[u] but some contemporary monarch. The most conservative views which seem to me tenable are those of Hitzig and of Ewald.[1] Of the two I prefer Ewald's.[v] The life of Ahab gains no doubt in melancholy interest, if *he* be the king referred to. One thinks of that young man who was untrue to his vocation, but whom Jesus beholding loved. But it is easier to understand the psalm of that great king, Jeroboam II., who to the devout historian seemed Israel's divinely sent deliverer (2 Kings xiii. 5). We may be sure that the political revival of Ephraim was not without effect upon its literature. Indeed, there may be a hint of this in a discourse of Amos, probably composed in the second half of Jeroboam's reign. It occurs in a description of the luxurious practices of the nobles of Samaria and Jerusalem, which included 'singing idle songs to the sound of the viol,' and 'devising for themselves instruments of music like David'[w] (Am. vi. 4, 5, R.V.). And we may infer from it, not only that there was no deep gulf in David's time between religious and non-religious music, but above all that there was a class of court-poets in northern Israel who sang the praises of the king and his nobles, of wine and love, and the achievements of heroes. Alfred von Kremer has drawn a vivid picture of such a class under the Caliphs; it would not be surprising if the increase of luxury produced a similar current of song in ancient Palestine. Of course, this may have been the case as early as the reign of Ahab, but it is still easier to understand it in the following century, of which we have somewhat more complete historical information.[x] The developed art of Ps. xlv., and of an analogous production—the Song of Songs [y]—is also more in harmony with the theory of Ewald, who points out that 'though lofty, sometimes bold, and throughout elegant, the poem (Ps. xlv.) lacks the pure fire within,' that 'it is a mere work of art, and not of elemental, primitive force.'

But from possibility to probability is a long step. Remembering our critical results hitherto, I judge it more reasonable to seek a home at any rate for the courtier's love-poem (Ps. xlv.) in the post-Exile period;[z] the linguistic affinities of certain words can at least as readily be accounted for on this

---

[1] See my *Psalms*, p. 123. Delitzsch thinks of Joram, but fails to account satisfactorily for xlv. 13. And could Athaliah, a native Israelitish princess, be called שֵׁגַל ?

hypothesis as on any other. If you ask: In which part of the post-Exile period? I reply, Most naturally in the part to which we have already referred Ps. lxxii., the only other direct eulogy of a king in the Psalter. And if Ps. xlv. belongs to the age of Philadelphus, surely that friend and patron of the Jews may (or must) be also its subject. Striking themes are generally taken up in the Psalter a second time. If the author of Ps. lxxii. could pray that in this 'king's son' the Messianic promise might be visibly fulfilled, may not the religious court-poet who wrote Ps. xlv. have addressed his work, which is not without Messianic features, to the same favourite prince? [aa]

My own instinct would here again have led me to prefer Darius. But historically there is nothing in Ps. xlv. which is plainly unsuitable [bb] to Ptolemy Philadelphus (see p. 144 &c.). It was, no doubt, of himself and his Hellenic brothers that Theocritus thought when he said:—

> None entered e'er the sacred lists of song,
> Whose lips could breathe sweet music, but he gained
> Fair guerdon at the hand of Ptolemy; [cc]

but the partiality of Philadelphus for the Jews is an undoubted fact, nor was Philomêtor the first Ptolemy who was interested in Jewish writers.[dd] To whom so well as to the most condescending, generous, and literary of the Ptolemies do the first two verses of this Hebrew song apply? And can we think of any ruler of the Jews between Solomon and Ptolemy Philadelphus to whom the words would be more fitly addressed—'Grace' (a Greek would have said, Peitho) 'hath been shed upon thy lips'?

It is too true that Philadelphus violated the highest ideal of marriage more conspicuously than some of the better Oriental monarchs.[1] The elevated strains of Ps. lxxii. do not refer to this, but we may justifiably trace an allusion to it in Ps. xlv. 10. The writer is certainly no friend of polygamy, but, though as devout as Pindar himself, he cannot turn a court-poem into a sermon. Still, to those who can read between the lines, he forbids the king to sink below the standard of the Solomon of poetry, 'Sexaginta sunt reginæ

---

[1] Droysen, *Hellenismus*, ii. 237.

. . . . ; una est columba mea, perfecta mea' (Song of Sol. vi. 7, 8). One further advice, or rather request, he has to urge, for Ptolemy himself most wholesome, for Israel the 'righteous' and the 'lowly,' who is already scattered in many lands, a matter of life and death. As a divine hero, the king is to gird on his sword and fight, not merely for empire, but for righteousness and lowliness (*v.* 5). See how far our poet surpasses Theocritus, and how delicately he refers to the expected patronage of his own people (cf. lxxii. 2)! And though *v.* 17 has been thought [ee] to show that a Persian king must have been meant, the Rosetta stone (where the Ptolemy is styled κύριος βασιλειῶν) shows that this is a very hasty conclusion. Palestinian writers knew the character of their Egyptian rulers, and interpreted by the Messianic promise, a loyal Jewish subject might well accept the Ptolemy's title, and paraphrase it in the words of *v.* 17 (comp. lxxii. 8). Yes; it is no unworthy enthusiasm which animates the Hebrew poet, even in *vv.* 7, 8. He idealizes his king, not in the (to a Jew) blasphemous deifying style of Egyptian court-poets and scribes,[ff] but precisely as Cyrus was idealized by the Babylonian Isaiah. The words 'Jehovah thy God' can hardly mean as little as 'Jehovah' means when a Hebrew writer describes the thoughts of Potiphar (Gen. xxxix. 3). They imply certainly that the king stood in a special relation to Jehovah,[gg] and possibly an expectation that he will before long acknowledge that 'the God who hath no form and whose name is a mystery' (Egyptian expressions) is Jehovah. For although there is an innocent and genuinely Hebraic sense in which Jehovah and Zeus are one (cf. Mal. i. 11 and Ps. lxv. 3 ?), yet the highest hope of a prophet who is perhaps quoted by our poet is that Yahveh's name may be one (Zech. xiv. 9). Already there are some favoured non-Israelites, whom the true God gently leads to a fuller knowledge of Himself. That one of these was Cyrus, might be inferred (2 Chron. xxxvi. 22, 23) from these words of the prophet, 'that thou mayest know that I am Jehovah, I that call thee by thy name, the God of Israel' (Isa. xlv. 3). That Alexander was another, must have been believed by some, though the Aggadic form of the belief may not be earlier than Josephus.[hh] And why should not the young Ptolemy, as an heir of the noble schemes of Alexander, have been a third? If the first Greek sovereign of Asia adored the most sacred name, why not also another of his race?

Do not make the personal character of Philadelphus an objection; time could not as yet have revealed its darker aspects.[ii] But even had the poem been written later, remember how highly an earnest Jew like Philo esteemed this Ptolemy. In this he does but carry on the tradition of the prophets. It was, of course, no regal virtue, as Jeremiah said, to 'vie with Ahab'[1] in magnificence; but to 'judge the cause of the poor and needy' was a quality so noble that the prophet can even describe it as 'knowing Jehovah' (Jer. xxii. 16). 'Philanthropy towards all men, especially towards Jewish citizens,'[2] was a note of the character of Philadelphus; was not this a reflection of the philanthropy of Jehovah? And if the king seemed at the top of human happiness, must it not be 'Jehovah his God' who had thus 'anointed him with the oil of joy' above the other Hellenic kings?

I will venture upon a further conjecture, which is not bolder than many which pass current among us. If Onias, the founder of the rival Egyptian temple, could believe that Isa. xix. 18 referred to his own circumstances,[3] may not another Jew have conceived the delightful idea that *vv.* 23–25[jj] of the same chapter would be fulfilled by the conquests of the Ptolemies: and why should not this Jew be, like Onias, a member of the high priestly family, who offered this encomium in return for his advancement to the civil and religious headship of his people? And what opportunity could be so favourable for this as a nuptial feast? I conjecture, then, that the author of Ps. xlv. may have been that Eleazar or (if Eleazar be a fiction) Manasseh who upon the death of Simon I. succeeded to the προστασία instead of the legitimate heir Onias.[kk] This event may be dated in B.C. 287. Two years later Ptolemy Soter abdicated in favour of his son, afterwards called Philadelphus. It is probable[4] that the brilliant and world-famous coronation-festival was soon followed by the marriage of the young king to Arsinoe, daughter of Lysimachus, king of Thrace, and that Eleazar or

---

[1] Jer. xxii. 15, following Sept. (Cod. Alex.).   [2] 'Aristeas,' Merx, i. 260.
[3] Jos., *Ant.* xiii. 3, 1.   [4] Droysen, *Hellenismus*, i. 632.

Manasseh sent his panegyric on this occasion—sent it in all good faith, believing the new Ptolemy to be in reality, what his father was, for the first time in history, called, 'a saviour.'[11] He wrote it, of course, in Jerusalem, in surroundings happily very different from those in which Theocritus in Alexandria was inditing idylls to a Jew necessarily so profane.

The reader will excuse the length to which the preceding exposition of a so-called 'mere conjecture' has gone. Identifications of this kind must be set forth tentatively, and their value is largely symbolic (see p. 146, foot). The more phenomena they take account of, the greater their importance to the student. Of course in a history of the Jews or of Jewish religion such a conjecture as the present would occupy a very subordinate place. Ps. xlv. would there be referred to simply as post-Exilic. The first half of these lectures however is critical, and some fulness of detail is necessary to avoid the charge of rashness.—But are there any historical or phraseological allusions in favour of this view (with or without the preceding conjecture)? Surely the tone of large magnificence harmonizes admirably with it. Among the details (which may once have been more numerous, if the poem has been edited for church-use) note the allusion to Tyre in v. 13a ('daughter of Tyre' and 'king's daughter' are not the same), which reminds us that Phœnicia equally with Judæa formed part of the province of Cœle Syria, and that though Ptolemy Soter had in 312 'impoverished' the island-city (Zech. ix. 4), it recovered, at least commercially, from the effects of the siege. The harvest of literary allusions is less abundant than in Ps. lxxii., but this is because our poem is less distinctly religious. Still in v. 2 the phrase 'a ready scribe' cannot but remind us of the description of Ezra (Ezra vii. 6), and v. 4b is illustrated by Ps. xxi. 6 (post-Exilic). And if vv. 7 and 8a are suggestive of Isa. xvi. 5, v. 8b is equally so of Isa. lxi. 3 (Exilic), while v. 10b ('gold of Ophir') reminds us of Job xxii. 24, xxviii. 16, Isa. xiii. 12 (all Exilic). We may also compare Ps. lxxii. itself, where the same prominence is given to 'righteousness' and 'humility.' And as in Ps. lxxii. 8 there is probably an allusion to Zech. ix. 10, so in Ps. xlv. 6 there may be a melancholy, distant echo of Zech. ix. 9,

'Behold, thy king cometh unto thee, righteous is he and helped (viz. by the God of battles), humble,' or perhaps, comparing Ps. xviii. 36, 'condescending.' I say, 'a melancholy echo;' for I am well aware of the haze of illusion which encompassed our poet, and from which Philo himself, long afterwards, was not free. Bard and wise man alike overrated this Ptolemy, the former because he took too external a view of the Messianic promise, and both because they were flattered by a Hellenic king's partiality for their people. Philo, moreover, exaggerated the significance of the royal desire for the translation of the Pentateuch, which appeared to him 'zeal and longing for the laws of Israel,' but which is amply accounted for by a literary and political interest. Our poet wrote, I suppose, before this translation had been thought of, but not before that peaceful interaction of Jewish and Hellenic ideas had begun, which was violently stopped by the madness of Epiphanes. He was a student of the prophets, and, remembering what they had said of Cyrus and Nebuchadrezzar, he made a bold venture of faith, and trusted God to fulfil His promises, and 'make Himself known to Egypt' in the person of its king (Isa. xix. 21). Blame him, if you will, for taking up the singing-robes of a court-poet, but acknowledge that it was a good way, not only of expressing gratitude, but of insinuating a pure religious morality. There can have been no difficulty in getting his poem rendered into Greek; some of our psalms may already have been translated in some shape for private use among the Egyptian Jews. It is another question whether such a Greek version can have charmed the royal ears.[1]

But I lay no stress on this conjecture. The Septuagint version of Ps. xlv. was at any rate not prepared from the autograph Hebrew copy. It is more important to explain the admission of such a poem into the Psalter. One of Philadelphus's chief titles to fame (the origination of the Septuagint) is said to have been regarded with much disfavour in Palestine. How, then, came these very Jews to canonize Ptolemy's encomium?[mm] Well, the Talmudic tradition may have some basis of fact,[nn] but is valueless as a testimony to Jewish opinion in the age of Philadelphus.

[1] Comp. Ebers's story, *The Sisters*, E.T. ii. 97, 102.

Whether or no Palestinian rabbis in Alexandria had a share (it can only have been a small one) in the work of translation, the first Greek version of the Pentateuch cannot all at once have aroused such hostility in Palestine. Time was needed for its deadly errors to be discovered; St. Paul, at any rate, failed to discover them. I grant, however, that an eulogy of Ptolemy would not as such have been adopted into the permanent Psalter by Simon the Maccabee. Doubtless in his time the original occasion of the psalm had been forgotten; we can hardly overrate the carelessness of tradition on such points. But Simon at least must have formed some theory respecting this psalm. Did he explain it as referring to the personal Messiah? Scarcely. The Messianic interpretation of psalms (in the stricter sense) originated as a protest against the later Asmonæans. It is far more probable that Ps. xlv., like Ps. lxxii., was explained by Simon (uncritically, no doubt) of Solomon. This view is perhaps confirmed by the latter part of the title, which runs thus in the Septuagint, ᾠδὴ ὑπὲρ τοῦ ἀγαπητοῦ [oo] (some manuscripts insert after ᾠδὴ, τοῦ Δαυίδ). The translator either read שיר ידיד and took ידיד as short for ידידו (ידידיה) 'his beloved,' in cxxvii. 2, was interpreted by an editor—see the Hebrew title—of Solomon [pp]), or else vocalized יְדִידָת (not יְדִילֹת), and explained this, as Kimchi did afterwards, but in a different sense, as short for יְדִידָת יָהּ (cf. יְדִידָת נַפְשִׁי, Jer. xi. 15). In either case, the ἀγαπητός of the Greek title may be Solomon, who is called יְדִידְיָה in 2 Sam. xii. 25. It is true, the Solomonic reference of Ps. xlv. harmonizes neither with the Book of Kings nor with that of Chronicles. According to the first, Solomon was neither specially pious nor eminently warlike; according to the second he was pious enough, but by no means warlike; and according to neither was he a champion of the poor and oppressed.[qq] But the theory was plausible enough for Simon (or the collector), who may have compared the description of the 'king's daughters' in Ps. xlv. 10 and the 'virgins' in xlv. 15 with the passage to which I have already referred in Song of Sol. vi. 8. It was uncritical, as I have said, but surely not more so than the ascription of the spiritual and churchly sentiments of Ps. li. to David. And may not Simon in his heart have prized the psalm (as we, I hope, still prize it) as an expression of moral, and I may almost say, Christian optimism? You might have thought from Ecclesiastes that Israel was rapidly sinking into an abyss of pessimism. Not so; a little sunshine of prosperity rekindled its faith in the ultimate predominance of righteousness. Persia had fallen, like Nineveh and Babylon, but a better kingdom had arisen,[π] which, while it obeyed the law of justice and mercy, could mock at change. With this thought I take leave of this psalm.[ss] A philosopher [1] has called the Jews the most optimistic race in history. Elastic, indeed, was their optimism; it adjusted itself to disillusionments without number, and it rested on the truth that righteousness tendeth to life, and is the only secure basis of an empire. And is not this truth a profoundly Christian one? and, as we read the 'goodly words' of the 45th psalm, may we not join hands with the author across the centuries, and acknowledge a still present power in his words to delight and to instruct? Lovers of the psalms cannot admit that chivalry is a purely Christian conception. Long ages before Arthur, 'truth, meekness, and righteousness' formed the Hebrew ideal of kingship, and for that grand fifth verse of our psalm I know no better parallel than the song of Arthur's knights :—

> Blow trumpet! he will lift us from the dust.
> Blow trumpet! live the strength, and die the lust!
> Clang battle-axe and clash brand! Let the King reign.

NOTE ª, p. 161.

Hildersam, a Puritan divine, in his *CLII. Lectures upon Psalm LI.* (Lond. 1642), says that the titles of the psalms 'are a part of the holy Scripture given by Divine inspiration,' and infers that 'it is a sin and matter of great danger to neglect and slight them.' Very different is the attitude of that great expository preacher, St. Chrysostom, who, like his friend Theodore of Mopsuestia (see note at beginning of Lect. V.), accepts the Davidic authorship of the psalm, but is enabled by his theory of prophecy to interpret it as having a non-Davidic as well as a Davidic reference. His theory of Ps. li. is that David, who foresaw the falling away and captivity of the Jewish

[1] Schopenhauer.

people, wrote this psalm as a medicine both for his own wounds and for those of his people. In a word, the psalmist is to some extent like a tragic poet (ἐτραγῴδησεν), who throws himself into the misfortunes of other men. The latest German commentator (F. W. Schultz) assigns the psalm to the Exile. So, too, Nowack in his edition of Hupfeld, but adding that a still later date is more probable. In our own land Dr. Stanley Leathes and Mr. Mozley adhere to the Davidic authorship, remarking that David had much building work to do at Jerusalem. But Henry V. on his deathbed took a truer view of the meaning of *v.* 20.

NOTE ᵇ, p. 161.

So Theodore, who explains *v.* 6*a*, 'against thee, thee only,' by an implied antithesis, 'not against the Babylonians' (cf. Hab. iii. 13). (The editor of Ps. li. overlooked 'thee only,' when he explained the psalm of David's sin with Bathsheba.) On the church-reference of this and other psalms, see Lect. VI., p. 262 &c.

NOTE ᶜ, p. 162.

Smend, indeed, maintains that *vv.* 20, 21 form an integral part of the psalm, but this hangs together with his theory that they relate to the Messianic age (cf. Mal. iii. 3), which is at any rate unnecessary. Delitzsch, who regards *vv.* 3–19 as Davidic, is inclined to admit that *vv.* 20, 21 are 'a liturgical addition of the Church of the Exile.' So virtually Theodoret, and after him 'one of the wise men of Spain' referred to by Ibn Ezra. This acute commentator has himself no objection ; 'we may say that they were uttered in the spirit of prophecy' (ברוח הקודש). So, too, Kimchi. This is merely to save the current orthodox theory.

NOTE ᵈ, p. 162.

It is not improbable, however (see p. 118, on Ps. lxxxix.), that the prophecy in Isa. lxiii. 7–lxiv. was written during the troubles under Artaxerxes Ochus. Ps. li. can easily find a home in the same period, like Ps. cxxx. ; *vv.* 19, 20 may allude to the breaking down of the walls which was probably a part of the cruel punishment inflicted upon the Jews for their revolt. The date here proposed seems to me clearly the best for Isa. lxiii. 7 &c., but I hesitate somewhat with regard to Ps. li.

NOTE ᵉ, p. 163.

See my commentary. Note also that if דּוּמִיָּה in lxv. 2 be correct, it suggests connecting this psalm with the neighbouring 62nd psalm (in *v.* 2 of which 'ר may have, as here, an ethical meaning— see Delitzsch).

NOTE ᶠ, p. 163.

The views of spiritual religion are developed beyond the average pre-Exile standard (cf. Isa. lvii. 7 and Mal. i. 11, both post-Exile). Note also the parallelism between *vv.* 2, 3 and Ps. l. 14, 15. Tholuck remarks, 'David names the two sacrifices of the pious which are demanded in Ps. l.'

NOTE ᵍ, p. 163.

(Ps. lxv. not pre-Exile.) Many MSS. of Sept. (with Complut. and Ald. editions) prefix ᾠδὴ Ἱερεμίου καὶ Ἰεζεκιὴλ τοῦ λαοῦ τῆς παροικίας, ὅτε ἔμελλον ἐκπορεύεσθαι. This shows us how to explain the use of prophets' names elsewhere in the Greek headings; they are chiefly symbols of a period. Kimchi also interprets this psalm of the Return. Comp. the Greek heading of Ps. lxxi.

NOTE ʰ, p. 163.

Post-Exile characteristics in Ps. lxvi. are in *vv.* 1–4, 8, the invitation to the nations to praise Jehovah; in *v.* 6, the didactic view of history; in *vv.* 10–12, the retrospect of the Exile (cf. Pss. cxxiv. and cxxix.); in *vv.* 13–15, 18, 19, legalism.

NOTE ⁱ, p. 163.

It is strange that Theodore did not notice this; he explains Ps. xlvii. as if Maccabæan. Eichhorn goes to the other extreme. According to him, the psalm celebrates the bringing up of the ark to the city of David. But the 'going up' of the ark is, in fact, in Ps. xlvii. 6 a symbolic expression for the 'return of Jehovah' to the (second) temple. Notice the phrase 'Abraham's God' in Ps. xlvii. 10. There is no sure reference to Abraham in the whole of the pre-Exile poetry and prophecy.

NOTE ʲ, p. 164.

Ewald and Lagarde long ago convinced me that Isa. xii., which is evidently a fragment of a psalm (and that by no means an original psalm), was not written by Isaiah. The latter critic, as we have seen (p. 31), refers it to the time of the completion of the second temple. Of course, Pss. xlvi. and xlviii. might, nevertheless, be of the period mentioned above, to which Ewald refers them. Yet I venture to reject this view for the reasons given in the text. It should be added that Perowne extends the Sennacherib reference to all the three psalms, and that Lagarde admits it for Ps. xlvi. (he thinks that Immanuel=Hezekiah, cf. Ps. xlvi. 8, 12).

Note ᵏ, p. 164.

'Later age.' For Hitzig's theory that these two psalms were occasioned by the ill success of the Syro-Israelitish assault upon Jerusalem (2 Kings vi. 5) is inconsistent with the mixed character of the Immanuel-prophecy, for which the circumstances of the time amply account. The Jehoshaphat theory (comp. note ᵃᵃ, p. 109) mentioned by Calvin, once favoured by De Wette, and adopted (for Pss. xlvii. and xlviii.) by Hengstenberg and (for all three psalms) by Delitzsch, has against it, (1) that it leans solely on the Chronicler (2 Chron. xx.); (2) that even according to Chron. the allied forces did not actually threaten Jerusalem; and, (3) that these psalms have striking points of contact with Isaiah. To the last objection Delitzsch replies that Ps. xlvi. is not an echo but a prelude of Isa. xxxiii. But when two writings are parallel, the one a prophecy and the other a poem, the presumption is very strong that the former is the original.

Note ᵐ, p. 164.

Probably the editor has substituted 'Elohim' for 'Yahveh:' see Ps. cxiii. 3.

Note ⁿ, p. 165.

Comp. Ps. ii. 2, 'the kings of the earth' (at least, if the psalm be held to refer imaginatively to the Hezekian age).

Note ᵒ, p. 165.

So Hengstenberg and Delitzsch. It is against this view, in my own judgment, that Ps. lxxv. alludes (see note ʳ) to the Song of Hannah, and Ps. lxxvi. to the Song in Ex. xv., the former of which is (see p. 57, note ᵉ) probably, and the latter almost certainly (see p. 31) post-Exile. (I doubt whether Dillmann's view of Ex. xv. 1–18 can be justified—that an old song from the Mosaic age was developed subsequently, but not so late as the times of David and Solomon, into a great festal ode.)

Note ᵖ, p. 165.

Ps. lxxv. 2 (?),	cf. Isa. xxx. 27,
,, ,, 4a,	,, ,, xiv. 31,
,, ,, 8,	,, ,, xxxiii. 22,

Ps. lxxvi. 12 (מורא), cf. Isa. viii. 13,
„ „ 13 (יבצר), „ „ xviii. 5,
„ „ „ (רוּחַ), „ „ xxxiii. 11.

The description in lxxvi. 4–7 suggests the overthrow of Sennacherib (as described in Isaiah's prophecies), though a touch is borrowed from the account of the catastrophe of Pharaoh (Ex. xv. 19). But these overthrows were regarded as typical specimens of the working of Him who 'alone doeth great wonders' (Ps. cxxxvi. 4, 10–18, Isa. xliii. 17).

NOTE q, p. 165.

Theodoret states that he found this heading 'in some copies,' though not in the Hexapla. It is, in fact, omitted in Cod. Sin., as also the similar one of Ps. lxxx. That 'the Assyrian' is to be taken literally (in spite of Hitzig) must be presumed from the fact that no other titles in Sept. point as late as the Syrian-Greek period, and that Theodore and Theodoret (like Rashi afterwards) explain this psalm of Sennacherib's invasion (because of vv. 3, 4). Observe in passing that while Theodore takes a similar view of Ps. lxxv., Theodoret regards this psalm as spoken in the person of the captives at Babylon.

NOTE r, p. 166.

Reading בְּצוּר (see my crit. note, and cf. Baethgen, *Jahrb. f. prot. Theol.*, 1882; Lagarde, *Mittheilungen*, ii. 378). Comp. Ps. lxxv. 6b (thus corrected) with 1 Sam. ii. 2b, 3a.

NOTE s, p. 166.

We might compare, for Ps. lxxvi., the prayer ascribed, with great psychological fitness, to Judas before the great battle of Adasa ('on the Judæan watershed, four miles north of Jerusalem') in 1 Macc. vii. 40–43 (cf. 2 Macc. xv. 22), which refers to 2 Kings xix. 35 (=Isa. xxxvii. 36).

NOTE t, p. 166.

Hebrew as well as Greek antiquity regarded poetry as a direct divine gift. Cf. Pind., *Pyth.* iv. (end), εὗρε παγὰν ἀμβροσίων ἐπέων. An encomium like Ps. xlv. may far more fitly be compared in its spirit with Pindar's odes than with Theocritus's idylls. Its subject is not merely the king's prosperity, but the love of God to him; and this poet, like Pindar, means what he says.

Note ᵘ, p. 166.

Apart from the other difficulties of the old Messianic interpretation, it was contrary to the ideal of an Israelitish king to ride upon a horse. See Zech. ix. 9; Psalms of Sol. xvii. 37. Dr. Westcott says that Ps. xlv. is not quoted in the N. T., except in Heb. i. 7, 8. But Rev. vi. 2, at any rate, alludes to Ps. xlv. 5, 6. Theodore is one of those who adopt the Messianic explanation.

Note ᵛ, p. 167.

In the first and second editions of his work on the Psalms, Ewald only ventured to maintain that some king of N. Israel must be meant; in the third, he selected Jeroboam II. Upon Hitzig's view see further my Commentary, p. 123, and note that no member of the house of Ahab bears a name compounded with Baal. His son is *Yeho*ram; his daughter Athal*yah* or Athal*yahu*.

Note ʷ, p. 167.

Cf. 1 Chron. xxiii. 5, 'the instruments which I made (said David) to praise therewith;' Neh. xii. 36. Remembering this, perhaps, our old dramatist, George Peele, gives David an ivory lute !

Note ˣ, p. 167.

Notice that the custom of adorning the houses of the rich with ivory had become general in the time of Jeroboam II. (Am. iii. 5, vi. 4, and comp. Ps. xlv. 9, Cant. vii. 5). Ahab's ivory palace (1 Kings xxii. 39) was doubtless unique.

Note ʸ, p. 167.

'An analogous production.' Read both poems again, and then judge if the phrase be inappropriate. But even the comparison of single passages will help much. Thus compare *v.* 3 of the psalm with chap. v. 13; *v.* 4 with iii. 8; *v.* 8 with viii. 13; *v.* 9 with iv. 14, vii. 5; *v.* 14 with iv. 7, v. 16; *v.* 16 with 1, 4, &c. An additional argument is based on the Aramaic colouring of both poems (but see appendix). Kuenen (*Hist. krit. Onderzoek*, iii. 386, cf. *Religion of Israel*, i. 373) thought that both may have come from one author— must have come from the same age (that of Jeroboam II.). Why should not Ps. xlv. have been written on occasion of Jeroboam's marriage? Why not, if we approach Ps. xlv. with the preconceived opinion that the Song of Songs *in its present form* is a pre-Exilic work? But is it such? I have long hoped to discuss this question in a fitting place, and so to redeem the promise made in *Job and Solomon* in 1887.

NOTE ᶻ, p. 167.

Giesebrecht thinks that Ps. xlv. is a 'dramatic lyric' by a post-Exile poet, who was caught by the romantic tendency of his time (attested by the Song of Songs) to idealize Solomon and his court (Stade's *Zeitschrift*, 1881, p. 318). I could almost as soon believe that Theocritus's 17th idyll was the work of a Greek contemporary of Horace. But I welcome Giesebrecht's adhesion to a post-Exile date.

NOTE ᵃᵃ, p. 168.

The idealisms of Ps. xlv. 3-8 remind us indeed of Isaiah, but the Messianic world-empire is not so prominent in Ps. xlv. as in Ps. lxxii. 'Thy fellows' in *v.* 8 are independent kings, though less mighty ones than Ptolemy. The psalm begins and ends as an encomium. Verse 18 corresponds to *v.* 2; it is the natural close of such a poem (contrast Ps. xviii. 50, and cf. Pindar, end of third and fourth Pythians). The writer hopes by his 'work' ($\pi o i \eta \mu a$) to hand down the memory of the king to distant ages. (I cannot see with Smend that the speaker is the Jewish Church.)

NOTE ᵇᵇ, p. 168.

It may be urged that Ptolemy Philadelphus did not descend from a long line of kings (see *v.* 17). But if Theocritus in his panegyric can speak of that king's fathers, so can the Hebrew poet.

NOTE ᶜᶜ, p. 168.

Id. xvii. 112-114 (cf. *Id.* xiv. 60 &c.), Calverley's version, which in *l.* 1 omits 'of Dionysos.' The whole of this idyll of Theocritus deserves to be read both for its parallels and for its contrasts to the psalm. See also the close of Callimachus's hymn to Zeus, who, says the poet, gives to all kings, but to none so much as 'to our ruler' (cf. Ps. xlv. 8, 'above thy fellows').

NOTE ᵈᵈ, p. 168.

Grätz thinks that Philomêtor (B.C. 181-146), not Philadelphus (B.C. 285-247), was the patron of the Greek translation of the Pentateuch (cf. *Jewish Quarterly Review*, Oct. 1890, p. 196). But the statement in the text seems to me probable enough.

NOTE ee, p. 169.

At first, for instance, by De Wette. He followed Augusti, who thought of Mordecai as the author and Xerxes (Ahasuerus) as the royal hero of the poem. Comp. *v.* 10*a* with Esth. ii. 9, 17. It is possible, too, that 'lord of kings' in the Phœnician inscription of Eshmunazar (line 18) refers, not to any Persian king, but to one of the early Ptolemies, and certain that this is the case in Cyprian inscriptions and in that of Ma'sūb (cf. Ganneau, *Revue archéol.*, 1885 (1), p. 384, and Berger, *R. a.*, 1887 (2), pp. 6-8).

NOTE ff, p. 169.

The apotheosis of the king of Egypt began at his coronation. As Synesius says, he was 'a god who was raised after death to the rank of a superior god' (*De Prov.* i. 5, quoted by Wiedemann). Theocritus's 17th Idyll may be artificial as a Greek poem, but it accurately reflects *Egyptian* sentiment. On the stele of Pithom we read, 'The living Horus, the victorious child . . . . the son of Ra, the lord of diadems, Ptolemy, living like Ra eternally.' Arsinoe, too, is dressed as a goddess, and identified with 'the mighty Isis, the great Hathor' (Naville, *The Store City of Pithom*, pp. 16, 17). Elsewhere, too, we find references to 'the god' (Philadelphus) and 'the gods Adelphoi' (*Records of the Past*, iv. 71, x. 76). No Jew could have tolerated, much less adopted, such phraseology (see Isa. xiv. 12-15, with my commentary); the Phœnicians were less particular (Inscr. of Ma'sūb, lines 7, 8). Even the Hellenized Judaism of 'Aristeas' recognizes 'one only true God,' and Philo, speaking of a king, says that he is human in his οὐσία, though in his rank '*like* the supreme God' (Mangey, ii. 673, top). The author of Wisdom (xiv. 16-20) expressly reprobates the evil Egyptian custom, and we know the storm evoked by the self-deification of Caligula. I admit that, from a purely historical point of view, Dr. Westcott's censure of the language of Theocritus may be too severe (*The Epistles of St. John*, p. 256). What Josephus says of Demetrius might fairly be applied to any Egyptian king, τιμῶν ἰσοθέων ἔτυχε παρὰ τοῖς εὖ παθοῦσι. If the Nile river might be divinized, why not also he upon whom devolved the maintenance of a just system of irrigation? And Philadelphus was, as we know, in a special sense an εὐεργέτης. But from the severely monotheistic Jewish point of view, to represent this king, or any king, as God, was impossible (Zech. xii. 8 is no proof to the contrary). And even orthodox Christian expositors, while rendering כסאך אלהים 'thy throne, O God' (*v.* 7), felt the difficulty of the expression as interpreters though not as dogmatic theologians. Theodoret, for instance, noticed how thoroughly human the whole picture in Ps. xlv. was, and had nothing better to say on *v.* 7*a* than this : 'Inasmuch as the earlier description was too lowly for the divine dignity [of Christ], he fitly teaches us by these words that He is God and an everlasting King, and neither had a beginning nor shall have an end.' Dr. Westcott, too (on Heb. i. 8), feels the same difficulty, and actually insists on going back to Döderlein (1779), and rendering 'Thy throne is God.' I have read the Cambridge professor's note and also the privately circulated tract by Dr. Hort, which advocates the same view, with surprise and regret. This rendering of the Hebrew words and of the Greek version is inadmissible (cf. Driver, *Hebrew Tenses*, ed. 2, p. 286). None of the instances quoted to justify it are in point ; exegesis condemns it unhesitatingly. 'Thy throne is God's throne' is, of course, a possible sentence, though, as the style of our poet is so simple, we should have expected 'Thou sittest beside Yahveh on his throne,' or the like. But 'Thy throne is God' (i.e. belongs to the class of divine beings) is not possible ; it would contradict the great doctrine of the psalmists that, not the temple, not Jerusalem, not any created object, was the true safeguard of Israel, but the Lord Jehovah (cf. Jer. xvii. 12, 13, where the true sanctuary is stated to be Jehovah). The Rev. Vers. of Heb. i. 8 is therefore more correct than Dr. Westcott's version ; the Sept., like the Targum, supposes a transition in *v.* 7 from the king to Jehovah. But the critical editor of the Hebrew text is bound either to read יהיה for אלהים (יהיה had, it is conjectured, been misread יהוה), with Giesebrecht and others, or to follow Bickell, as I have done in my commentary. Giesebrecht's proposition is ingenious, but his Hebrew does not please my ear ; it is bald, and exhausts an important detail too soon. But the sense either way is the same.

Note gg, p. 169.

It is a remarkable fact that both Persian and Greek sovereigns are described in Babylonian inscriptions as grateful worshippers of Marduk. An inscription of Antiochus Soter, dated B.C. 259, is quoted in Hommel's *Gesch. Babyloniens und Assyriens*, pp. 792-794, and, what is more interesting for us, a terra-cotta cylinder is extant which contains a description of the capture of Babylon in 538 and in general of the policy of Cyrus (see Sir H. Rawlinson, *Journal of R. A. S.*, Jan. 1880, pp. 70-97). I have already entered into this subject, and will only now say that it appears unsafe to maintain, on the ground of this inscription, either that Cyrus was a polytheist, or that, if a Mazdayasnian, his religion was to him a purely national matter, so that he could afford a disdainful tolerance for the gods of inferior nations. I think that he was in some sense a grateful worshipper of Marduk, or rather of the 'god of heaven,' whose highest name was Ahura Mazda, but who might also be called either Marduk or Jehovah. Prof. Sayce regards the religious eulogy of Cyrus in the cylinder-inscription as 'the flattery exacted by a successful conqueror' (*Hibbert Lectures*, p. 86). I think myself that the inscription truthfully represents Babylonian sentiment, and enables us, comparing well-known passages in the Second Isaiah, to understand the attitude of Cyrus. In order to do justice to the Babylonian and the Hebrew references to Cyrus, and, I ask permission to add, to Ps. xlv., we must remember that, not only in the religion of Jehovah but in those of Marduk and of Zeus, there was a nearly contemporary tendency to universalize the conception of the Deity. Now if Cyrus was a Mazdayasnian he would have a special interest in the religions of Israel and the Chaldæans, and in the restoration of their temples. And again, if Ptolemy appreciated the width of Jewish theism, we are no longer forced to account for his kindness to the Jews solely from political motives. In this connexion the views of 'Aristeas' may deserve attention (ed. M. Schmidt, Merx's *Archiv*, i. 255, 256).

NOTE hh, p. 169.

Jos., *Ant.* xi. 8, 5, cf. the Talmudic story in *Yoma*, 69a (Wünsche, *Der bab. Talmud*, i. 374). We also read in Talmudic legends of a Cæsar Antoninus who was a proselyte. Pre-Maccabæan Judaism can hardly have been less ready to believe the best of worthy rulers.

NOTE ii, p. 170.

Persian seriousness was conspicuously wanting in Philadelphus. But one of those moral errors with which he is most often reproached —his second marriage with his sister—would not be recognized as such from a Persian any more than from an Egyptian or from an ancient Semitic point of view (see Spiegel, *Eran. Alterthumskunde*, iii. 678; Ebers, *Durch Gosen zum Sinai*, ed. 1, p. 83; Robertson Smith, *Kinship and Marriage in Arabia*, p. 162 : cf. Gen. xi. 29). The pseudo-Aristeas (about 200 B.C.) tacitly condones the act, while the pseudo-Phocylides (first century A.D.) forbids such a marriage. This variety of view is intelligible enough. The former, who lived under a Ptolemy, knew the Egyptian theory that such marriages preserved the purity of the divine royal race; the latter, who lived probably under Tiberius, felt the necessity of a vigorous moral protest against heathen corruption. We are not called upon to dogmatize as to the line which the psalmist would have taken had he written a little later. At any rate, he would have severely reprehended the murder of Nicocles and the execution of the nephew of Antigonus.

Note jj, p. 170.

It would be not unnatural in the Greek age to use 'Asshur' as an equivalent for 'Syria' (cf. note on Ps. lxxxiii. 9). In the above conjecture I assume that Isa. xix. 18–25 was written in the time of Ptolemy Lagi, and request readers of *The Prophecies of Isaiah* to record this as my present conclusion. If the passage is (as I have admitted) a subsequent addition to the prophecy, and later prophetic writing delights in the circumstantial style, why should we hesitate to refer the verses to the Greek age?

Note kk, p. 170.

Jos., *Ant.* xii. 2, 5 ; cf. 4, 1. Grätz (*Geschichte*, ii. 2, p. 242) rejects Eleazar, because derived from the letter of 'Aristeas,' which, however, he seems to bring down too late.

Note ll, p. 171.

Vatke explained the psalm of Demetrius Poliorcetes (the least likely of all persons to be idealized by a Jew). He also discovers imitations of Homeric phrases (see his Life by Benecke, pp. 551, 552), precisely as Grätz finds Theocritean phrases and images in the Song of Songs. I cannot, for my part, believe in a Hebrew parallel to Latin Alexandrinism (cf. Mommsen, *Rome*, iv. 609). The psalm is thoroughly Oriental in phrase and imagery.

Note mm, p. 172.

This objection has been raised by S. Weissmann in connexion with a similar theory of Ps. lxxii.

Note nn, p. 172.

See *Soferim*, i. 8, with Joel Müller's note ; and comp. Grätz, *Geschichte der Juden*, iii., ed. 4, p. 578 ; Frankel, *Vorstudien zu der Septuaginta*, p. 61. The notice in *Soferim, l.c.*, describes the 'day' of the Greek translation as 'a hard day for Israel, like that on which Israel made the calf.' In *Meg. Taanith* (last chapter) the 8th day of Tebeth is indicated as a fast-day for this calamity. It was probably appointed out of opposition to the Alexandrian festival day spoken of by Philo (*Vit. Mosis*, ii. 140, Mangey).

Note ᵒᵒ, p. 173.

So Symmachus, ᾆσμα εἰς τὸν ἀγαπητόν. Jerome, 'canticum amantissimi.' Eusebius of Cæsarea (*Eclog. Proph.* iv. 12) compares Ps. lxvii. 12 (Sept.), ὁ βασιλεὺς τῶν δυνάμεων τοῦ ἀγαπητοῦ (where ὁ ἀγαπ. = Israel, cf. Jer. xi. 15), explaining both passages of Christ. Aquila, however, has ᾆσμα προσφιλίας; and so Ewald, Hitzig, and Dyserinck ('love-song').

Note ᵖᵖ, p. 173.

ידיד is also a title of Solomon in the Talmud (*Menakhoth*, 53).

Note ᑫᑫ, p. 173.

There are reasons enough for not following Simon or the collector in his view of Ps. xlv. Two more may be added, viz., (1) that in the traditional songs of David (Ps. xviii., 2 Sam. xxii. 1, xxiii. 7) the idealized hero speaks in his own person, and (2) that this psalm, according to its natural meaning, refers to a contemporary king, whom, together with his consort, the poet desires to propitiate (comp. on Ps. lxxii.).

Note ʳʳ, p. 174.

'It may be truly asserted that his (Alexander's) was the first of the great monarchies founded in Asia that opened a prospect of progressive improvement, and not of continual degradation to its subjects; it was the first that contained any element of moral and intellectual progress.' Thirlwall, *History of Greece*, vii. 111.

Note ˢˢ, p. 174.

One small point remains. It may be asked, Why was Ps. xlv. placed where it now stands? Partly, it would seem, because of the external similarity between xliv. 5*a* and xlv. 7*a*. Such a reason does not appeal at all to modern minds, but the truth in criticism is sometimes most unmodern. Delitzsch and Cornill may have sought to prove too much with regard to catchwords, but they have at least shown that ancient editors and arrangers were often partly influenced by such external minutiæ. I will add that it is likely that *v.* 7 was already mutilated when the 2nd Book was collected.

LECTURE V.

I call upon him who is to be praised, upon Jehovah; so am I saved from mine enemies.—Ps. xviii. 4.
But thou art the Holy One, enthroned upon the praises of Israel.—Ps. xxii. 4.

LECTURE V.

PART I.—The earliest of the minor Psalters.—Necessity of testing the headings even here by their compatibility with history.—Ewald's conclusion that fourteen psalms and psalm-fragments are Davidic.—Criticism of this theory. Ewald's imperfect grasp of the historical principle of development. Church-hymns not possible in the time of David or even of Isaiah. David a gifted musician and poet, but best known in the age of Amos by his secular poetry. That he may have composed religious songs, though not in the style of our psalms, need not therefore be denied. And it is barely possible (especially considering that one genuine fragment of Solomonic poetry has survived) that phrases or whole verses of Davidic origin may have passed into some of our psalms, or at least have exerted some influence on the psalmists. Of course, this can only have been very occasional; the favourite 'old songs' would naturally be those inspired by the teaching of the higher prophets.—Another possibility. The authors of these older songs may have been influenced by a great poet whom we may call a second David, and the assumption of whose existence makes various phenomena more intelligible. Gifted he must have been, but when composing psalms for the first temple, he was bound to consider the low spiritual average and the rough singing of the worshippers.—The ground being thus cleared, we can proceed to break up Book I. into groups. We start from Ps. xxxiii., the one nameless psalm among those headed *l'dāvīd*. Is it an early post-Exilic or a Maccabæan psalm? The latter alternative is preferable; and since this is not the only Maccabæan psalm in Book I., *l'dāvīd* should probably be restored, for which there is some Greek authority.—And which are the other Maccabæan psalms? There is a plausible case for reckoning as such Pss. vii., xiv., xvi., xx., and xxi. An examination of these seems to show that, while all may be, two (viz. xx. and xxi.) must be Maccabæan, so that Ps. xxxiii. is probably a rightful member of the first 'Davidic' psalm-book. Among the points of detail in the preceding examination, note the discussion of the use of 'king' for Maccabæan prince (hence a fresh illustration of 'Malki-çedeq').—For convenience sake we next consider the three fine nature-psalms (viii., xix. 1–7, and xxix.) which occur at regular intervals in Book I. The second and third of these are specially connected by their mythic imagery, and we naturally pass from these to Pss. xviii. and xxiv. 7–10, which have also more or less mythic colouring. Of all these, the most interesting historically is Ps. xviii. Is this, like Pss. xix. and xxiv., a composite psalm? If so, may it contain a Davidic element? Renan is of this opinion; but no sufficient reason exists for separating the two parts (if two parts there be) of the psalm by any long interval. Applying the comparative method, we can only hesitate between the reign of Josiah and some part of the Persian period. The former is here preferred, but with the admission that the song, thus dated, cannot have been originally intended for use in the temple-services (*v.* 51 is probably a later addition).—Ps. xxxvi. is considered next in order, because of the similarity of its title to that of Ps. xviii.

Nothing however in its contents reminds us of Ps. xviii. The psalms with which it may rightly be compared belong to the Persian period.

PART II.—We pass to the first large group of cognate psalms (Pss. iii.-vii., ix.-xiv., xvii.). Criticism leads to the result that no member of this group can be much earlier than the close of the Persian period. Those in which the tone is most depressed or agitated may refer either to the tyranny of Bagôses, or to the troubles under Artaxerxes Ochus. A confirmation of this view arises from the title of Ps. vii.—The second group of persecution-psalms may be analyzed into two minor groups. Pss. xxii., xxxi., xxxv., and xl. 13–18 (=lxx.), with which we may connect Pss. lxix. and lxxi., have very similar characteristics, and belong (with the possible exception of the imitative psalms xxxi., xl. 13–18, and lxxi.) to the same period, viz. that which preceded Nehemiah's first journey to Jerusalem. The second minor group contains Pss. xxvi., xxvii. 7–14, xxviii., xxxviii., xxxix., xli. These all belong to the later persecution-period referred to above. From Ps. xli. (the last in Book I.) we have to make our way backward to Ps. i., which, from a critical point of view, is the last of the temple-songs. A discussion of various psalms, all (as it appears) of the Persian age, follows. First, Ps. xl. 1-12 (another 'new song,' cf. Isa. xlii. 10); next, Ps. xxx. (which is partly parallel), Ps. xxxvii. (an alphabetic psalm, like Pss. xxv. and xxxiv.), and Pss. xxv., xxxiv., xxxii. (a triad of 'songs of deliverance'). Then by an easy transition we pass to the 'Guest-psalms' (xv., xxiv. 1–6, xxvii. 1–6, xxiii. cf. *v.* 5 and lxi. 5). The didactic fragment, Ps. xix. 8–15, is the only Davidic psalm which remains. How vividly it describes the devout churchmen of the Persian and the Greek age! Pss. i. and ii. are without a heading; they are the double gate of the Psalter. Internal evidence shows that Ps. ii. is of the post-Exilic and most probably of the (pre-Maccabæan) Greek period. It may be viewed as an idealized historical picture with a strong eschatological tinge. The writer throws himself back into the age of David or Solomon. He is more of a prophet than an historian, but also a great lyric poet. Ps. i. is often said to be pre-Jeremian, on account of a parallelism between *v.* 3 and Jer. xvii. 8. Objections to this view. The psalm is at any rate pre-Maccabæan. It has some points in common with Ps. ii., but the two psalms are not on this account organically connected. Probably they are nearly contemporaneous, and certainly both are introductory psalms. Even if not written as such, they were well adapted to fulfil this function, Ps. ii. for the first 'Davidic' hymn-book, Ps. i. for a large pre-Maccabæan Book of Psalms.

PRINCIPAL NOTES.—PART I.: Lists of Davidic psalms.—Criticism of Kuenen. —Was David a prophet?—Solomonic fragment in Kings.—Temple-hymns before the Exile.

PART II.: Date of Isa. xxxii. and xxxiii.

PART I.

THE EARLIEST OF THE MINOR PSALTERS.

IN our voyage up the stream of song our last station must be made at Book I., in some respects the most interesting as it is certainly the earliest of the minor Psalters. All the psalms which it contains, except i., ii., and xxxiii. (I do not include x. because of its close connexion with ix.), are directly ascribed in the titles to David. I need not stay to prove that these titles are no more authoritative than those which assign the collection of sayings in the centre of Proverbs (x.–xxii. 16) to David's keen-witted successor. They do, indeed, represent an early tradition respecting the origin of the first Psalter, but it is probable that they also represent an early misunderstanding of that tradition; I mean that (like *Shīr hamma-'alōth*) the title *l'dāvīd* may have been originally prefixed, not to the separate psalms, but only to the collection, which may therefore have contained some hymns which the first collector himself would not have had us ascribe to David.[a] At any rate, the traditional titles form no part of the authentic text,[b] and must in each case be tested by their compatibility with the much more secure historical tradition of the life of David. Ewald, who would willingly strain a point to do honour to the poet-king, himself admits this, though not as distinctly as one could wish. He professes to have gained a clear view of the character and poetic genius of his hero from the narrative of his life, and finds that there are fourteen psalms and fragments of psalms which are so fine that none but David can have written them, and which can without violence be attached to episodes or periods in David's career.[c] 'None but David.' 'Can without violence.' Do you not see the inherent weakness of such arguing? The man of whom we are speaking was not an isolated student-poet. A child of the people, he cannot (if at least we can trust historical analogy) have had an absolutely unique talent of song. The divine fire must have passed from others to him, and again from him to others. Why may not successors of David have been his equals in natural and his superiors in spiritual capacities? Admit this, and you at once disengage the criticism of the psalms from a crowd of illusions. You have no longer any interest in proving (contrary to all reasonable exegesis) that the circumstances of David's life are the most natural historical setting of the 'Davidic' psalms, nor that this 'man of war' (1 Chron. xxviii. 3) was on a higher spiritual level than is assigned to him in the Books of Samuel. You will not, I am sure, mistake me. I have said enough elsewhere of the good side of Ewald's exegesis and critical rearrangement of the Psalms. Ewald is my oldest teacher in criticism, but since the publication, twenty years ago, of the *Godsdienst van Israel*, I have owed an equal debt to Kuenen.[d] That the latter, in spite of his extraordinary modesty, is in some respects the greater historian, can scarcely be questioned. Not to him can those words of Dorner, spoken of Heinrich Ewald, be applied, ' He fails to perceive the connexion of the internal and external history of Old Testament religion, and has not grasped the principle of historical development.'[1] It is one of the tasks of critical theology to show that neither David himself nor the psalms lose even in religious interest when studied on sounder principles than Ewald's.

But I speak to-day neither in the name of Ewald nor in that of Kuenen, but for myself, without inquiring who may chance to agree with me. Let dictionaries give an exhaustive catalogue of critical theories; it is for the lecturer to elucidate the process of research by frankly explaining how he came to his results, and so enabling the student to see with his teacher's eyes. Let this lecturer then say for himself that he cannot divide sharply between the age of David and that, say, of Isaiah. The latter is no Christian, nor is the former a heathen. It is possible, that if we had a sufficient number of the more religious songs of David, we might detect in them some real affinities to the religion of Isaiah. But it may be questioned whether these affinities would have struck

---

[1] *History of Protestant Theology*, E.T., ii. 437.

an uncritical observer, and above all whether either David (who was not a church-leader like Zoroaster) or even Isaiah could have dreamed of church-hymns such as those contained in the Psalter.[e] That David was a gifted musician, is indeed attested, not only by the prophet Amos (vi. 5, but not according to Septuagint), but by one of the very earliest historical traditions[1] (1 Sam. xvi. 14-23), and we may assume that he could also, like the Arab prince-poet Imra al-Kais, as a 'sweet song-maker' (2 Sam. xxiii. 1), fascinate his half-primitive people. His poetry would, of course, be chiefly occasional in its character. The early races quickly fell into the moods of joy and grief, both of which required the services of the poet; but, strange to say, passionately as the Israelites loved dancing (cf. 1 Sam. xx. 11, Jer. xxx. 19, xxxi. 4), the only two indubitably Davidic compositions are in the elegiac style. You know them full well—one is in 2 Sam. i. 19-27, the other in 2 Sam. iii. 33, 34.[f] The latter may be a fragment of an impromptu; the former is a fine specimen of the simple but exquisite art of early poesy. How soon they were written down, we cannot at present conjecture,[g] but both were probably preserved in a pre-Exilic song-book called 'The Book of the Upright' (i.e. of Israel).[h] But though these may be the only authentic specimens of David's work, and his posthumous fame rested chiefly upon his secular poetry (Am. vi. 5), we need not assume that all his compositions had a non-religious character. It is not an unreasonable conjecture that when 'David and all the house of Israel played before Jehovah with all their might, and with songs and with (divers musical instruments),'[2] some of these songs had been made for the purpose by the poet-king. Only, as critics, we cannot consistently suppose that the religious songs of David (if there were any) were as much above the spiritual capacities of the people as the psalms which, I will not say the later Jews, but which Ewald or Hitzig or Delitzsch would assign to him. It would be only a step further to accept the Christianization of David in Browning's well-known masterpiece (*Saul*). Consider, moreover, the strict conventionalism by which early religious art is controlled. From the point of view of the history of

---

[1] Bleek's *Einleitung*, ed. Wellhausen (1878), p. 216.
[2] 2 Sam. vi. 5 (correcting, with Klostermann, after 1 Chron. xiii. 8).

art, not less than from that of the history of religion, the supposition that we have Davidic psalms presents insuperable difficulties. Even the 18th psalm must, in spite of the contrary opinion of Ewald, be transferred to a later poet than David. This can, I believe, be positively decided by the internal evidence. To objectors who point me to the admission of the poem into the appendix to Samuel[1] (see 2 Sam. xxii.), I reply that this only proves that the poem was conjecturally ascribed to the idealized David not long before the Exile, just as Ps. lxxii. was assigned by a still later student to the idealized Solomon.

Our result fully justifies what I said in my first lecture, that the most productive and spiritually the richest of the ages of psalmody cannot have been the earliest. The only question is whether, considering how fond the psalmists are of quotations, they may not have preserved phrases or even whole verses of Davidic hymns, and whether the editors of the psalms may not in the same conservative spirit have combined old Davidic with new and very un-Davidic material. It was Wilhelm Vatke who first suggested this in 1835. 'Single songs,' he says, 'may have survived in the mouth of the people, and in an altered shape have passed into our Book of Psalms, or at least have exerted an influence as ancient models.'[1] This is barely possible, no doubt. A fragment of an old religious song which, though not Davidic, may perhaps really be Solomonic, is quoted by an Exilic writer from the songbook called the 'Book of the Upright.' It runs thus:—

> The sun hath Yahveh set up in heaven;
> But he said he would (himself) dwell in darkness:
> I have built a high mansion for thee,
> A place for thee to dwell in for all ages.

To this particular passage there is no allusion in the Psalter; even the two so-called Solomonic psalms present no points of contact with it. Of course, this does not decide the question. Other genuine relics of the Davidic and Solomonic poetry might conceivably have influenced the psalmists, and it is not unnatural to imagine a Davidic element in Pss. xviii.

---

[1] *Die Religion des A.T.*, i. 291-293. Against Vatke, see De Wette's famous article in *Theol. Studien und Kritiken* for 1837.

and lx.¹ Only we must be on our guard against pleasant illusions. No concession can be made which a conservative of the old school would think worth accepting. The religious reorganization of the people in Ezra's time was too complete to allow any considerable influence to archaic liturgical formulæ. In spite of the analogies from the Chaldæan, the Vedic, and the Zoroastrian hymns,[k] it is not possible to hold that there is any large admixture of old and new in the Hebrew Psalter; almost every psalm might be appropriately styled 'a new song.' And even if any relatively old songs *were* used as models by the temple-poets, the preference would surely be given to those inspired by the teaching of the higher prophets, such as Ps. xviii. (if this be not post-Exilic) and the lyric fragments incorporated into the Second Isaiah.

I do not, however, deny that the authors of these older songs may themselves have been influenced by some still earlier gifted hymnist. Indeed, I feel bound to assume the existence of a 'David' (using the name in a symbolic sense [m]) subsequently to the poet-king, to account for the literary character of the Book of Amos. He cannot indeed have been alone; he must have had able followers, by whose help he influenced his age, and left a deeper impress than the historical David, not only upon Amos, but after Amos upon the authors of the earliest extant psalms (Deut. xxxii., Ps. xviii. ?). The grand fault of the elder orthodoxy is that it identifies these two Davids—the one the hero of the transition from rudeness to culture, the other of a more cunning art and a more spiritual religion—the herald of greater glories to come. Let us be thankful for both Davids, but not rank even the second of them too high, at least as the author of psalms intended for the first temple. For all the evidence goes to show that throughout the pre-Exile period the service of religious song was not committed to any special class,[n] but was the privilege of the congregation at large (2 Sam. vi. 5, Am. v. 21-23, Isa. xxx. 29), and as late as the fall of Jerusalem the noise of the Chaldæan soldiery in the temple is likened to that made by the worshippers on a feast-day (Lam. ii. 7). When the singing was so rough, recalling the humble origin of the Hebrew *t'hillah*,² the psalms themselves cannot

---

¹ See pp. 108, 203.   ² See Appendix I., part ii. (on תְּהִלָּה).

have been too polished in style. We might even infer from Am. v. 21–23 that they were as formal and unspiritual as the sacrifices which they accompanied. At any rate, we require more than the individual efforts of an eminent psalmist to account for the beauty and perfection of the hymns of the earliest collection.º

I cannot, however, linger on this interesting theme. What we have to do is, if possible, to break up the first Psalter into groups, and apply the same comparative method as before. The groups indeed are somewhat less easy to distinguish than in Books III.–V., but they exist notwithstanding. We shall do well to start from Ps. xxxiii., the one nameless psalm (according to the Hebrew text) which interrupts the 'Davidic' series.ᴾ It is a smooth and easy, alphabetizing,ᑫ liturgical psalm in praise of Jehovah as He was conceived of subsequently to the Second Isaiah.ʳ Not long since, a heathen nation had oppressed Israel, but the Creator had interposed in behalf of the 'righteous ones' (v. 1; cf. cxviii. 15, 20, Maccabæan)ˢ who trusted not in the equipments of war, but in the protection of a loving God (v. 20; cf. cxv. 9–11, Maccabæan). A 'new song' was demanded by these new proofs of the divine fidelity; but to which divine deliverance does the phrase refer? To the overthrow of Babylon and the resettlement of Israel in its own landᵗ (as in Isa. xlii. 10, Ps. xcvi. 1, xcviii. 1), or to the early victories of the Maccabees leading up to the re-dedication of the temple (as probably in cxliv. 9, cxlix. 1, Judith xii. 2, 13)? The fact that there are other points of contact between Ps. xxxiii. and the Maccabæan songs which close the Psalter justifies us in preferring the latter reference. It is no objection to this, that the speaker disclaims trust in armies (cf. xliv. 7), for he contrasts his own scanty numbers with the well-equipped infantry and cavalry of Syria. The *khasīdīm* had in fact only been nerved to fight by religious enthusiasm, and returned with joy to their old peaceful habits of life and thought. The great Maccabee himself could have sung *vv.* 16 and 17, for, as has been well said, ' he possessed a simple and constant faith in the divine power to give the victory to those who were not strong, and the race to those who were not swift.'[1]

[1] Conder, *Judas Maccabæus* (1879), p. 159.

But is this correctly viewed as a nameless psalm? May not certain Greek translations be right in prefixing τῷ Δαυιδ,[u] a mere accident having perhaps caused the omission of the title in the standard Hebrew manuscript from which our text seems to be derived? This is possible if there is good reason to suppose that any of the psalms in Book I., which are headed *l'dāvīd*, are of Maccabæan origin. To decide this question we must examine Pss. vii., xiv., xvi., xx., and xxi., for which Maccabæan circumstances may with most plausibility be assumed as a background.

The 7th psalm is one of those in which the divine title 'Elyōn occurs, which, as experience has shown, is specially post-Exilic.[1] The context proves that it sums up and symbolizes the great truth, so slowly reached, of monotheism. As in the post-Exile Asaphite psalms, the God whom Israel worships, is also the Judge of the nations. As in the post-Exile 139th psalm (see *vv.* 1, 23) and the Maccabæan 44th (see *v.* 22), He is the καρδιογνώστης—'the trier of the hearts and reins.' The oppressors of Israel are the 'ungodly,' or 'unrighteous;' Israel on the other hand is both outwardly and inwardly righteous (comp. xliv. 18, 19, Maccabæan). And yet the psalmist, speaking for the 'upright in heart,' cherishes a bitterness towards his enemies which (see Lev. xix. 17) proves that they were not Israelites, but heathen (though, of course, degenerate Israelites may have swelled their number). That faithful Israel, and not any individual as such, is the speaker, is manifest from the sequence of thought in *v.* 9, 'Jehovah judgeth the peoples; (therefore) give sentence for me, Jehovah.' There are some points of contact with Jeremiah; comp. with *vv.* 10 and 11, Jer. xi. 20, xvii. 10, xx. 12, and with *v.* 15, Jer. xviii. 20, 22.[v] But a church-psalm in the proper sense of the word is to me inconceivable as early as Jeremiah;[w] and since during the Exile the tone of faithful Israel was penitential (see Lamentations), the psalm must be brought down below the legislation of Ezra. It need not, however, be Maccabæan but may be placed with other psalms of persecution in the last gloomy days of the Persian period. The abruptness of the style is no objection to this view (cf. Ps. lix.), of which I hope presently to produce a somewhat novel confirmation.

[1] See my note on *v.* 18.

The 14th psalm,[1] too, is clearly post-Exile, some may even think Maccabæan; comp. v. 1 with Ps. lii. 3, a comparison all the more attractive, because the psalm *Dixit insipiens* occurs again in a less correct (Elohistic) form as Ps. liii.[x] If, then, the 'foolish' atheist in v. 1 is meant to be an individual, may he be Antiochus Epiphanes, or one of the Syrian generals, Nicanor for instance (1 Macc. vii. 26), whom we might also identify with the 'tyrant' of lii. 3? If, moreover, with Hitzig and Hupfeld, we find a historical perfect in v. 5, may the defeat spoken of be one of those mentioned in 1 Maccabees (see e.g. 1 Macc. vii. 40–44)? This is at any rate more probable than the reference to Sennacherib and the Rab-shakeh, suggested by Theodore the Interpreter,[y] which is opposed by the similarity of Ps. xiv. not only to Ps. xii. (a later work) but also to passages in Jeremiah certainly not influenced by our psalm.[2] It is, however, not favoured by a sober exegesis of the psalm as a whole. 'The fool' is not here an individual, but a collective term. Still, we must not give it the sense of 'the foolish people' who 'contemn Jehovah's name' (Ps. lxxiv. 18, Maccabæan), but rather illustrate it by the description in Ps. x. 13 of those bad Israelites who 'contemn God, *saying in their heart*, Thou wilt not punish' (רָשָׁע is admittedly collective). Nor is the perfect in v. 5 historical; in such a context it cannot but be prophetic. The close of the Persian period meets all the requirements of this psalm and of the group to which it belongs (see below). In v. 3 some may excusably find a touch of the pessimism of Koheleth (Eccles. vii. 28, 29), and in the liturgical ἐπιφώνημα (v. 7) they may be reminded of Zech. xiv. 3, Isa. lxvi. 6, all which passages were written at the close of the Persian period.

The 16th psalm I did myself for a time regard as Maccabæan. Certainly no one who thinks that, upon the whole, history is marked by progress rather than by degeneration can, without inconsistency, affirm this psalm to be Davidic.[z] It cannot even be pre-Exilic at all, but is the fruit of that long weaning from the world, begun in Babylonia and perfected under another foreign yoke in Israel's recovered

---

[1] On Pss. xiv., xv., xvi., and xix., cf. Delitzsch, 'Der Dekalog in Exodus und Deuteronomium,' in Luthardt's *Zeitschrift*, 1882, p. 290.

[2] See especially Jer. v. 1, 23, x. 21, 25.

home. It is in fact one of the finest church-songs. The 'excellent' and the 'holy ones' in *v.* 3 (in the received text) can be no other than the priests, who, as represented by the 'high (literally, great) priest,' were more and more found to be Israel's firmest support against heathen aggression;[1] it is the period of what Ewald calls the 'hagiocracy' to which *v.* 3 clearly points. Its highly spiritual view of life and death forcibly reminds us of Pss. xlix. and lxxiii. The reference to religious dissensions points either to a paganizing movement in the Persian period (cf. *v.* 4*a* with Isa. lxv. 11), or somewhat more probably to the early Hellenistic one described by Josephus (*Ant.* xii. 5, 1). Need I remind any one of the prominence of libations apart from other sacrifices in the daily life of Greeks and Romans? More especially were they common before and after meals (see e.g. Hom., *Il.* vii. 480), and it is to such libations that I suppose our psalmist to refer (cf. Ps. cxli. 4*b*, and the abhorrence of later Jewish writers for heathen wine יֵין נֶסֶךְ, *Aboda zara*, 55*a*). At any rate, it is evident that true believers are tightening the bands of religious association (comp. *v.* 3 with Ps. cxli. 4, 5); there seem to be at least the germs of the Asidæan movement.[aa] We can therefore thank that early editor who styled this psalm *miktām*, thus connecting it with the other psalms bearing this title[2] (lvi.–lx.), which are best viewed as monuments of the Persian and Greek periods.

Two of our test-psalms still remain—the 20th and the 21st. May we consider the king who is the object of such religious loyalty to be one of the Asmonæan princes?[bb] This will only be possible if a post-Exile origin should upon the whole appear probable. Are there any indications of such a date? We must not insist too much upon the clear, flowing, and often elegant style, at least if we refer the Book of the Praise of Wisdom (Prov. i.–ix.) to the happier part of the reign of Josiah.[cc] It is conceivable that when the usual sacrifices were offered before the campaign which cost Josiah his life, the 20th psalm was sung, and that it had been recently composed by some gifted friend of the king, while Ps. xxi.,

---

[1] Ewald, *History*, v. 204.

[2] On the external features common to the Miktām-psalms, see Delitzsch's introd. to Ps. xvi.

the style of which is less smooth, may have been written for Hezekiah. I have myself held this view,[dd] which seemed plausible until I began to apply the comparative method more consistently. I now feel that there are various opposing considerations of great cumulative force. It is impossible to separate these psalms from Pss. lxi. and lxiii., which, as wholes, scarcely admit of a pre-Exile date. Next, looking at the tone of this pair of liturgical poems, we are almost driven to refer them to the post-Exile period, when poets and wise men so frequently adopted an oracular style; and we are equally struck by the transition from 'we' to 'I' in *v*. 7 (cf. lxxxv. 9), and the reference to 'Zion' as the centre of Jehovah's sovereignty and the starting-point of His judgments (comp. xiv. 7, lxviii. 36). Nor are these the only indications of a late date. The phrase 'Be thou exalted' (xxi. 14), i.e. 'exercise Thy supernatural power as El 'Elyōn,' is found again in lvii. 6, 12, comp. xlvi. 11. A disciple of the prophets might of course have used it before the Exile, but this psalm expresses the mind, not of a small circle, but of the church-nation. Ps. xx. 8 is closely akin to Pss. xxxiii. 17, cxlvii. 10 (both probably Maccabæan passages), and Ps. xxi. 5 to Pss. xlv. 3, lxi. 7[ee] (probably of the Greek period). Lastly, the peculiar word rendered '(we) stand upright' (xx. 8) virtually occurs again in Pss. cxlvi. 9, cxlvii. 6, and there only. Can we hesitate to draw the natural inferences? First, the psalms are post-Exilic. Next, a Persian or Græco-Egyptian king being out of the question, must not the king (who has no chariots and horses) be one of the early Maccabæan princes, who so mightily stirred the popular enthusiasm? Most probably he is Simon; in Ps. xxi. 7, 8 (cf. xx. 8, xxxiii. 16, 17, cxlvii. 10) there may be a backward glance at the victories of Judas over the Syrian cavalry (at Emmaus and Beth-zur). The 'crown of pure gold'[ff] (Ps. xxi. 4) will be the 'sacred crown' (נֵזֶר) of pure gold on the high priestly tiara (Ex. xxix. 6, xxxix. 30, cf. Ecclus. xlv. 12), while the phrase 'his anointed,' Ps. xx. 7, is parallel to 'thine anointed,' Pss. lxxxiv. 10, cxxxii. 10 (of a high priest in Persian times); see pp. 60, 119, 339).

And now read these psalms in connexion with 1 Macc. xiii. 42–47. Do they not seem twice as fresh as before, and can you not more easily account for the passionate vehemence which, from a Christian point of view, deforms Ps. xxi. (*vv.* 10, 11)? Then place side by side the 110th and the 21st psalms. Is it not probable that the one is the pendant to the other? The former says, 'Thou art a priest for ever;' the latter virtually adds, 'Thou art a king for ever' (I explain xxi. 5 by lxi. 7, and compare 1 Macc. xiv. 41).[1] Are we surprised that this psalmist, unlike the other, should directly claim for his hero the title of 'king' (cf. lxi. 7, lxiii. 12)? But we must remember that, although parties were not yet sharply divided, there were already some Jews who felt much more keenly than others the indispensableness of the temporal power of the pontificate, and who proportionately emphasized the more secular side of the Melchizedek prophecy. Long after this Philo quite innocently calls even the pre-Maccabæan high priest βασιλεύς,[gg] as being not only a spiritual but in some degree a temporal sovereign. Still more natural was it to apply the name, poetically or rhetorically, to Simon the Maccabee, who, like David, had 'taken away the yoke of the heathen from Israel,' and been freely chosen by the people to be their 'captain and leader' (1 Macc. xiii. 41, 42). And I think that any other expression for a legal Jewish prince than מֶלֶךְ would have been intolerable in a psalm framed on the Davidic model. Rightly or wrongly it was believed that a portion of the psalms came from David or his age. Such a title as נָשִׂיא or נָגִיד would not have been in keeping with the style of the Psalter, and would also have suggested an idea which was hardly in the writer's mind.[hh] Nor can it be objected that the belief in a Davidic Messiah must have prevented the poetic designation of Simon as a king. The hope of a personal Messiah had not indeed died out, but it was not strong at this time in Palestine; it is markedly absent from Daniel.[ii] On the other hand, I willingly admit that as soon as the Asmonæan princes themselves publicly assumed the regal title, and entered the fellowship of Oriental βασιλεῖς, it must have become impossible for a psalmist to give it to them. The authors of Pss. xx., xxi., lxi., lxiii. had used the word מֶלֶךְ in the good old Semitic sense well expressed by the Latin 'consul,'[2] but the royalty of

---

[1] Cf. also xxi. 7*b* with cx. 1*a*. [2] See appendix (linguistic affinities).

Judas Aristobulus (surnamed Φιλέλλην) and his descendants was too clearly akin to the selfish and oppressive tyranny of the Græco-Syrian kings.[jj] In the days of the former it would be natural enough that psalms like xx. and xxi. should assume a new meaning—the Messianic.

I hope that I have kept well within the bounds of the probable, and that I shall not be thought to have taken up an arbitrary and unreasonable hypothesis. It seems, then, that there are at any rate two Maccabæan psalms in the group which both the Hebrew and the Greek texts assign to David. We may therefore follow those Greek versions and include Ps. xxxiii. in the first Davidic hymn-book. The editor wished, as it were, to convert Book I. (as well as Books II.–V.) into a 'new song' by infusing a Maccabæan element. It would be delightful could we ascertain that not only the latest but the earliest age of developed spiritual religion was represented in this treasure-house. We have failed to find records of this period in the other minor Psalters; we could wish to be compensated here. Well, there is no harm in the wish; compensated, we are sure to be, for 'he that seeketh, findeth;' only we must not dictate the form that our compensation is to take.

Let us first of all seek historical homes for the three beautiful nature-psalms (viii., xix. 1–7, xxix.) which occur at regular intervals in the first book. Ps. viii., as the Song of the Moon and Stars, is the pendant to Ps. xix. 1–7; as the hymn of creation it is still more fitly compared with Ps. civ.[kk] The wide sweep of thought in both suggests of itself the beneficial influences of the Exile. Many students will go still further, and admit that if the priestly code is post-Exile, those psalms which (as the author of Hebrews may already have held with regard to Ps. viii.[ll]) allude to the first chapter of Genesis, must be post-Exile too.[mm] This date agrees with the moral indignation at successful wickedness which the psalmist cannot wholly suppress. The phrase in Ps. viii. 3, 'to still the enemy and the revengeful' (imitated perhaps in Ps. xliv. 17[nn]), implies that when the psalm was written, Israel had put forward some assertion of superiority which its neighbours felt as an injury to themselves. Can we doubt what this was? It was that claim on behalf of the religion and people of Jehovah which found its sharpest expression in the isolating policy of Ezra and Nehemiah.°° The one objection to a post-Exile date is the apparent allusion to Ps. viii. 5 in Job vii. 17. A single parallelism like this has, however, an uncertain value. The psalmist may, contrary to the general opinion of interpreters, imitate the wise man; or, unwillingly I say it, the Book of Job may, as a whole, be post-Exile.^{pp}

Pss. xix. 1–7 and xxix. must be studied together. Both belong to that literary revival of Hebrew mythology during and after the Exile of which the Books of Job and to some extent Jonah are monuments. With fearless step these kings of sacred song—the psalmists—venture into the recesses of popular imaginative symbolism, and reclaim them from superstition to the service of the Most High. The swift-running hero Shemesh, the caste or guild of the Elohim, the crashing voice of the Thunder-god, fine myths debased by unholy associations, were by them transfigured into poetic symbols of 'the throne and equipage of God's almightiness.'^{qq} Once, indeed, this might have been dangerous; but now that the true Jehovah (for the name Jehovah had itself needed transfiguration) reigned in Israelitish hearts, His worshippers might innocently delight themselves in the fancies of their forefathers.^{rr} Both psalms were, however, in a sense, criticized by later writers. The Song of the Sun (Ps. xix. 1–7) was provided with a new conclusion more in harmony with the intense Scripturism of the later post-Exile period, and probably contemporaneous with the 119th psalm (Greek period). The Song of the Storm (Ps. xxix.) was known to the author of the 96th psalm, for he repeats *vv.* 1 and 2 of the Song in a slightly modified and expanded form, caring more for correctness of doctrine than for poetry of phrase. Ps. xcvi. need not, however, have been composed very much later than Ps. xxix.; 'the glory of his name' and 'Jehovah is enthroned as king for ever' (Ps. xxix. 2, 10) are the two watchwords of the Return.^{ss}

There are two other psalms in Book I. which, though not in a full sense nature-psalms, have yet more or less mythic colouring—these are the 18th and the 24th. Let us take the latter first, because, like Ps. xix., it is composed (as Ewald pointed out and Delitzsch all but admits) of two fragments of psalms joined together. The mythic element centres in *vv.* 7-10, a fragment of a simple and yet sublime triumphal song. What is its date? Can it be one of those Davidic passages in which Wilhelm Vatke was half inclined to believe? I do not mind admitting that when David 'danced before Jehovah with all his might,' and again when he offered sacrifices before Jehovah, to celebrate the entrance of the ark into David's city (2 Sam. vi. 14, 17), the voice of song must have accompanied these ancient rites. But who can believe that either Ps. cx. or Ps. xxiv. 7-10 (very dissimilar psalms, by the way) represents the tone of David on this occasion? That would indeed be a reconstruction of history as bold as anything in the most reckless recent criticism.^{tt} Let it not be urged in reply that the titles given to Jehovah in Ps. xxiv. 8, 10, were specially appropriate to the age of David, and that the king is expressly said (2 Sam. vi. 18) to have blessed 'the people in the name' of 'Jehovah [Yahveh] Sabaoth.'^{uu} None of these divine titles have an exclusive fitness for David's age; the grandest of them all occurs virtually fifteen times in psalms probably of the Persian and the Greek periods.^{vv} Read the psalm-fragment with a fresh mind, and you will see that it simply refers to the return of Jehovah to His sanctuary after fighting for and delivering His people. The only question can be, whether the earthly sanctuary is meant (as lxviii. 19, 25) or the heavenly (as perhaps xlvii. 6, cf. Isa. xxxi. 4). Most probably (as in xlvii. 6) both are intended; the psalmist, like a true Semite, rises from the symbol to the thing symbolized, and idealizes the former in the light of the latter. The 'ancient' or 'everlasting doors' are chiefly, at any rate, those of the temple ^{ww} which Isaiah saw in vision (Isa. vi.), and of which another psalmist tells us (alluding to Isa. vi. 3) that 'every part of it saith, Glory' (Ps. xxix. 9). But they are also those 'gates of righteousness' on Mount Zion which, being 'the gate of Jehovah' (Ps. cxviii. 19, 20), cannot be overcome by the 'gates of Hades.' It is a processional hymn in the post-Exile manner,[1] and reminds us forcibly of that splendid post-Exile fragment, Isa. lxiii. 1-6, to which, indeed, it might almost be added as a not less grand finale.

And now suffer me to ask, What have we lost by substi-

[1] Comp. Pss. cxviii., cxxxii.

tuting a positive critical result for a time-honoured but irrational tradition? Has the psalm which we have last considered become, I will not say less interesting (for on that side the critic is safe), but less rich in religious suggestiveness? Mr. Aubrey de Vere has finely applied *vv.* 7-10 to the manifestation of the 'entering God—Flashing from star to star,' which is the recompense of the devout astronomer.[1] This he could not have done, had he been content to rest in the still prevalent explanation of the 24th psalm. But it is the old church application about which most of my readers will be chiefly anxious. If they follow Delitzsch, they may well be anxious. If, however, they accept the view which has been here maintained, they will find that the familiar poetry of faith can without effort be grafted upon it,[xx] and that for them too those noble lines were written—

> Bright portals of the sky
> Emboss'd with sparkling stars;
> Doors of eternity,
> With diamantine bars,
> Your arras rich uphold;
> Loose all your bolts and springs,
> Ope wide your leaves of gold;
> That in your roofs may come the King of kings.[2]

And seeing the 'high priest of our profession' seated in royal glory at God's right hand, they ask themselves, not with shrinking awe, but with faith in the indwelling Presence, 'Who shall ascend (like my Lord) into Jehovah's mount, and who shall rise up in his holy place?' And the answer is echoed from within, 'He in whose heart Christ dwelleth by faith, and who seeketh those things which are above—he shall be kept by the power of God through faith unto salvation.'[3]

Instead of discussing at present the first part of this composite psalm, I would ask leave to pass on to Ps. xviii. This poem, too, or at least the first half of it, is rich in mythic elements, and is therefore presumably, other things being equal, either very early or rather late. A very early date,[yy]

---

[1] See 'The Death of Copernicus,' a poem by Aubrey de Vere, *Contemporary Review*, Sept. 1889.
[2] Drummond of Hawthornden.
[3] See Study on Ps. xxiv., *Expositor*, Dec. 1889.

however, is excluded by the wide religious and political outlook in *vv.* 32, 44, 50, by the Deuteronomic view of the covenant in *vv.* 21–28 and the Deuteronomic expressions in *vv.* 22–24, by the reference to the heavenly temple which presupposes the existence of an earthly one [zz] in *v.* 7, and by the points of contact between the psalm and the so-called Song and Blessing of Moses (Deut. xxxii.).[1] It has been suggested that the psalm may contain, as M. Renan says, ' some verses either David's, or like those which David must often have made.' But though I am myself tempted to believe that an earlier poem, containing the theophany, was adopted and completed by a later writer,[aaa] I think that the conception that Jehovah dwells in a 'temple' or 'palace' (*v.* 7, cf. xi. 4) is inconsistent with Davidic authorship. Pre-Exilic the passage may well be (observe the *non-Babylonian* conception of the cherub as a flying animal [bbb]), but what is there in it that suggests the history of David? If we compare Ps. xviii. 8–20 with the lyric in Hab. iii., we may be inclined to think that the former poem refers, not to any event in the past, but to a great divine interposition hoped for in the near future. This points us either to the Assyrian or far more probably to the Babylonian period. Thus, even if the psalm be of dual authorship, neither part has any claim to a Davidic origin; indeed, for our present purpose the unity of the poem may be assumed. Now, can we hesitate as to its period? Surely, unless we think that Hezekiah and his circle had attained to views of truth not unlike those of Deuteronomy, we are driven to place the psalm subsequently to the second royal reformation—that of Josiah. Applying the comparative method consistently, it is most reasonable to assign it to that blossoming of the church-historical spirit which relieved the dulness of the Exile, but which began as early as the age of Deuteronomy. Just as several great prose writers and poets busied themselves with reproducing what must have been the last words of Moses, or what would have been his last words, if he had lived in their own time, so at least two great poets endeavoured, so to speak, to think themselves back into the soul of David.

---

[1] Cf. *v.* 4 ('Rock,' used of God) with Deut. xxxii. 4, 15, 18, 30, 31, 37; *v.* 11 with Deut. xxxii. 11; *v.* 32 ('Elōah') with Deut. xxxii. 15, 17; and same verse (idea) with Deut. xxxii. 39*a*. Cf. also *vv.* 10, 11, 32, with Deut. xxxiii. 26.

One of these poets is the author of the striking poem in 2 Sam. xxiii. 1–7; the other is the author of the 18th psalm.[1] I do not say that either poet has, from an objective historical point of view, succeeded. Ps. xviii. 21–46 describes David (an unfriendly critic might assert) as copying the proud self-assertion of Assyrian kings, or, as a more sympathetic student would say, as having inherited the promises, such for instance as Gen. xv. 18, xxviii. 13, 14, Deut. xi. 24. Upon neither interpretation can *vv.* 21–46 correspond to the historical reality. It is not the true David but an interpreter of prophecy who speaks, and who in the language of faith represents a promise as a virtual possession. To one who can pierce below the surface he prophesies of future sons of David who shall raise their kingdom to a height never attained by the historical David. This is perhaps the view expressed in the liturgical appendix (*v.* 51).[ccc]

And can we fix the date of this interpreter of prophecy more precisely? I think that we can, using with due caution his points of contact with other writers. He would appear to have lived before the authors of Pss. lxxxix., cxvi., cxliv.,[ddd] and the composite psalm in Jon. ii., and before the great prophet of Israel's restoration,[eee] but not before the invention or revival of the divine names 'Elyōn and Elōah,[fff] and, in spite of Mic. vii. 17 (comp. *v.* 46), not before the publication of Deuteronomy.[ggg] The facts point, so far as one can see, to the happy period, free from what the psalmist calls 'the strifes of peoples,'[hhh] between 621 and 608. This at any rate is the earliest possible date. I accept it not without much hesitation, and cannot complain if some prefer to regard the psalm as an imaginative work of the Exile.[iii] As a temple-poem it can hardly have been written in Josiah's reign; its advanced ideas and polished style would not be suitable for the services of the first temple. May it not have been intended as a literary illustration of some current life of David? Its noble and almost epic[jjj] style well fitted it to serve this purpose. May it not be a Paralipomenon by the author of 2 Sam. vii.? (compare the title of Ps. xviii. with 2 Sam. vii. 1). It was at any rate adopted into the later liturgical service as in some sense a

---

[1] See my *Jeremiah, his Life and Times*, pp. 87, 88.

prophecy of a great future Davidic ruler or line of rulers (see the appended verse).

Next in order let us take Ps. xxxvi., because, though its contents are not very like those of Ps. xviii., it has the same short but striking title which originally introduced Ps. xviii.,[kkk] and the form of which may have been suggested by Jer. xxxiii. 21. If titles have any critical value, these two psalms should be the earliest in the book. One can understand that as long as only a few psalms were recognized as Davidic the scribes found leisure to write 'Of the servant of Jehovah, of David,' but that afterwards a plain *l'dāvīd* seemed enough. And yet neither of the parts of Ps. xxxvi. (for like Pss. xix. and xxiv. it is composite) can be Davidic, or even of the later years of the pre-Exile period. The first part (*vv.* 2-4) must be grouped with Pss. xii., xiv., lviii.; the second (*vv.* 6-13) with Ps. lvii., and other later psalms of the divine lovingkindness.[lll] The psalm was only thought to be Davidic because of a single phrase in *v.* 12;[mmm] it may have been written in more than one part of the Persian period.

NOTE [a], p. 190.

So Robertson Smith, Bickell, and others. We cannot even be quite sure that it was the first editor who prefixed *l'dāvīd* to the collection. The title may conceivably have been added later to distinguish this collection from others.

NOTE [b], p. 190.

Theodore of Mopsuestia, though no rationalist, rejected the authority of the titles of the psalms. It is to him that Theodoret alludes in the words, τὰς ἐπιγραφὰς τῶν ψαλμῶν τινες ἀπεκάλεσαν (*Præf. ad Psalmos*). I must admit, however, that Theodore swallows the Davidic origin of the Book of Psalms as a whole. It is only the compulsory reference of all Davidic psalms to events in the history of David that he rejects. David often spoke, he thinks, prophetically, and assumed the character of men yet unborn. This will not satisfy the Bishop of Cyrus. The Seventy, he says, were inspired to translate the titles. Τολμηρὸν οἶμαι καὶ λίαν θρασὺ ψευδεῖς ταύτας προσαγορεύειν, καὶ τοὺς οἰκείους λογισμοὺς τῆς τοῦ Πνεύματος ἐνεργείας σοφωτέρους ὑπολαμβάνειν. The freedom with which the Septuagint translator dealt with the Hebrew titles is unknown to him. On the ascription of psalms to authors, see further Appendix I., p. 459.

NOTE ^c, p. 190.

These two criteria are embodied in Gustav Baur's canon, as quoted by Schrader (De Wette's *Einleitung*, § 332). Ewald's fourteen Davidic psalms or psalm-fragments are xi., vii., xxiv. 7–10, xxiv. 1–6, ci., xxix., xix., viii., lx. 8–11, xviii., xxxii., iii., iv., lxviii. 14–19 (place undetermined). Between xxiv. 1–6 and ci. he inserts xv. (as an early imitation of xxiv. 1–6), and between viii. and lx. 8–11 he places cx. (as belonging to David's age), and after iv., ii., and cxliv. 12–15 (as proceeding from the first half of the Solomonic period). Hitzig also assigns fourteen psalms to David, but makes a somewhat different selection (comp. my *Book of Psalms*, Introd., p. xvi.). He remarks (and Ewald evidently agreed with him) that, though many psalms might be mistaken for David's, no really Davidic psalm could possibly be ascribed to a weaker hand. It will be noticed that all but five of the eighteen Davidic and early Solomonic psalms specified by Ewald belong to Book I. A few other psalms (e.g., xxiii., xxvii., lxii., lxiv., cxxxviii.), according to this critic, might seem to be Davidic, but upon a closer examination they do not come up to the Davidic loftiness of spirit. Let us pass now to the conservative school. Delitzsch is not always clear in his own mind, and hence the amount of the Davidic element allowed by him is slightly uncertain. Strack, however, calculates that he admits 44 psalms as Davidic, partly on the ground of the headings, partly because of 'their creative originality, their impassioned and predominantly elegiac strain, their graceful flow of movement, their language antique yet clear' (*The Psalms*, by Eaton, i. 11). These are, iii.–xix., xxii.–xxiv., xxvi., xxviii.–xxx., xxxii., xxxiv., xxxvi.–xxxix., xli., li., lii., liv., lvi.–lxiii., ci., cx. He expresses himself doubtfully with regard to xxv., xxvii. (1–6), xxxi., lv., lxiv., ciii., cix. The remaining $23\frac{1}{2}$ of the so-called Davidic psalms are, according to Delitzsch, not David's work. The latest orthodox commentator (F. W. Schultz, in Strack and Zöckler's series) occupies a position midway between that of Ewald and Hitzig on the one hand and that of Delitzsch on the other. Only 17 of the so-called 'Davidic' psalms must, he thinks, be ascribed to David for historical reasons, viz., iii., iv., vii., xi., xv.–xviii., xxiii., xxiv., xxvii., xxx., xxxii., xxxvi., lxii., ci., cx. But there are 17 others which there is no sufficient reason to deny to the poet-king, viz., v., vi., viii., xii., xiii., xix.–xxii., xxix., xli., lii., liv., lvi., lvii., lxi., lxiii. Pss. ix., x. may also be defended as Davidic.

NOTE ᵈ, p. 191.

The importance of Kuenen's *Religion of Israel* (a new and revised edition of which is greatly needed) is that it enables one to see how this eminent scholar's later critical results fall of themselves into an intelligible picture of Israel's history. I am, of course, far from undervaluing his *Historisch-kritisch Onderzoek*, to which (in spite of its repellent form) some of the best scholars are under manifold obligations. And I am equally far from being satisfied with the cold and unsympathetic religious tone of the *Religion of Israel*. Yet I must venture to say that the book is in its way a masterpiece, and that in its method of proceeding from the well known to the less known it is severely scientific. It is not, in my opinion, justly censured on the ground of its 'naturalistic' tendency. Surely a true historian cannot help being a 'naturalist' or rather a 'psychologist,' *so far as the case admits*. He need not, however, deny the existence of 'wonders.' 'Every day wonders, easily verifiable, do take place in the spiritual life; wonders with which the historian is not concerned, but which, to a reverent mind, attest the supernatural in nature. Wonders are reported to have also taken place within the sphere of external nature, wonders which are not so easily verifiable as the others, because they [for the most part] depend on the testimony of men of long past ages. It belongs to the historical critic to study the periods from which these testimonies come, and to sift the reports which convey them. When he has approached the facts as nearly as he can, he has to interpret the facts, or his image of the facts, in accordance with the commonly recognized laws or principles of nature, if this be possible; and if it be not possible, to leave them unexplained.' This, as it appears to me, is what Kuenen has in general done. He is a psychologist, not merely, as all scholars of Lightfoot and Westcott, Bruce and Davidson, are in exegesis, but in criticism. If he rejects this or that tradition of a wonderful occurrence, it is first because the tradition is not sufficiently ancient, and next, because he has a bias in favour of psychology. The objection urged against F. C. Baur does not meet Kuenen's case. It does not really meet the case of his eminent predecessor Vatke, the Hegelianism of whose *Religion des Alten Testaments* is skin-deep; still less does it meet that either of Kuenen or of his brilliant junior Wellhausen. (See further my article, 'Reform in Teaching the Old Testament,' *Contemp. Review*, August 1889.)

NOTE ᵉ, p. 192.

We may regard Isaiah as in a certain sense the founder of the Jewish Church; at least, the allusions in his discourses to a kind of guild of disciples (see Isa. viii. 12, 16), combined with his remarkable prophecy of the 'remnant,' show that the idea of a spiritual society had loomed before his mind. The profoundly spiritual Jeremiah succeeded to Isaiah's ideas, and developed them. In quite another sense the author of Deuteronomy may deserve the title of founder of the Church, imperfectly as he can have defined the idea; after him Ezra and his colleagues, and not the least the psalmists. But church-hymns, like our psalms, cannot be imagined even in the age of Deuteronomy. I know that Kuenen has said that the origin both of temple-song and temple-poetry may go back to the time of Josiah, though song and poetry took a higher flight after the Exile (*Religion of Israel*, iii. 23). But this can hardly be meant to justify putting any considerable part of the Psalter before the Exile. The style of the temple-singing and the spiritual state of the nation, as revealed to us in Jeremiah and Habakkuk, forbid such a view. (It has been already pointed out that Hab. iii. as well as Isa. xxxviii. 10–20, is post-Exile.) I remember too that Delitzsch has called the prophet Samuel the father of psalm-poetry (Introd. to Ps. l.). But the 'great word' in 1 Sam. xv. 22 (to which Delitzsch refers) is as inconsistent with the primitive story of Samuel as the 'Davidic' psalms are with the traditional narrative of the life of David.

Note f, p. 192.

Duncker stands almost alone in denying the Davidic authorship of both these elegies (*Hist. of Antiquity*, ii. 144, 148); Vernes, however, is equally sceptical with regard to the former (*Revue de l'histoire des religions*, jan.-févr. 1889, p. 69). I cannot follow them, least of all Vernes, whose attempt to *bouleverser* Old Testament criticism bodes ill for French study of the Scriptures. See Kuenen's review in the *Theologisch Tijdschrift* for 1889, and Piepenbring's in the *Rev. de l'hist. des rel.* for 1890.

Note g, p. 192.

The Vedic and the Gâthic hymns, which were metrical, were also preserved by oral tradition. So too was the ancient (secular) Arabic poetry. Every poet had his *râwî* or 'vates,' who learned each poem as it was composed, and transmitted it to others (cf. R. V. of 2 Sam. i. 18). Solomon, too, *spoke* his moralizing similitudes (1 Kings iv. 32, 33). But I leave the question of the antiquity of written Hebrew poetry open.

Note h, p. 192.

Alluding perhaps to a popular etymology of 'Israel' as יְשַׁר אֵל 'God's upright one' something like that of Asur (Asshur) as 'the good or righteous (god).' In an early poem, proceeding from a disciple of the prophets, we find the Israelites referred to as 'upright ones' (Num. xxiii. 10; cf. Ps. cxi. 1), i.e., 'doing that which is right in the eyes of Jehovah;' and somewhat later the artificial synonym for Israel—'Jeshurun' εὐθύς, Aq., Symm., Theod.), Deut. xxxii. 15, xxxiii. 5, 26, cf. Isa. xliv. 2. The 'Book of the Upright' is mentioned again in Josh. x. 12, 13, and probably in 1 Kings viii. 12, 13 (τῆς ᾠδῆς in Sept. translates הַשִּׁיר, which must be a corruption of הַיָּשָׁר; for the quotation, see p. 212). It is likely that the songs in this collection were accompanied by prose narratives, in which the 'upright' acts glorified in the songs were set forth in detail. This is at any rate in harmony with later usage.

Note 1, p. 193.

Observe that the psalm in 2 Sam. xxii. stands outside the historical framework of the Books or rather Book of Samuel. The same remark applies to the so-called 'Last Words of David' in 2 Sam. xxiii. 1–7. That Ewald should have regarded even this 'dramatic lyric' as David's work shows how true Dorner's judgment respecting him was (see p. 191). How strange that one who has written so much and so well on the idealizing or transfiguring tendency of later Hebrew writers on Elijah, should have overlooked this tendency with regard to David! He really appears to have thought that the versatile condottiere, chieftain, and king (whose truly noble qualites I would not for a moment disparage) became in his advanced age a prophet (*Dichter des A. B.* i. *a*, 145). Would it not be simpler to suppose that all through his life the 'faculty divine' of prophecy as well as of poesy had been David's—the theory so well expressed by Delitzsch (Introd. to Ps. cx.)? If we reject this theory, which is solely based on the tradition current subsequently to the completion of the O. T. literature, so far as it relates to by far the larger part of David's career, must we not hesitate to apply it to the closing scene of the mighty warrior? Thankfully will we accept the later idealistic view of David as expressing that secret prophetic meaning which we who come after can see in his life-work, but we have no right to use it to the prejudice of the critical study of history. The case of these last words is parallel to that of the last words of Moses. We have both a psalm and a prophetic utterance of the legislator, and we find a similar pair of compositions ascribed to the aged king. In each case the prophetic utterance is the harder; can we be surprised at this? The hardness does not prove that it has a better claim than the psalm to be ascribed to the hero whose name it bears; it is of the essence of a prophetic oracle, when undiluted by the prophet's subsequent reflection, to be hard. As long as Hebrew was written, it was perfectly possible to write in a hard style ; Ps. cx. is hard enough. The introductory formula נְאֻם דָוִד וגו׳ is evidently based upon Num. xxiv. 3, 4, 15, 16. The description of the covenant in *v.* 5 points back to 2 Sam. vii. The gnomic or mashalic style of *vv.* 6, 7 shows the influence of the early prophetic anthologies. To the age of Hezekiah or (better) Josiah a critic may soberly refer this beautiful though difficult poem, as well as the prophecy dramatically put into the mouth of Nathan. Certainly it is in Josiah alone that the opening words of the poem were fully realized, and we may fairly say that the writer idealizes the earlier in the light of his experience of the later king.

NOTE J, p, 193.

It is to Wellhausen that we are indebted for the virtual discovery of this song-fragment (see Bleek's *Einleitung*, ed. 4, p. 236, and cf. Klostermann's notes on 1 Kings viii. 12). The passage may have run thus—

שֶׁמֶשׁ הֵכִין בַּשָּׁמַיִם יַהוֶה
אָמַר לִשְׁכֹּן בָּעֲרָפֶל
בָּנֹה בָנִיתִי בֵּית זְבֻל לָךְ
מָכוֹן לְשִׁבְתְּךָ עוֹלָמִים :

Lines *b*, *c*, *d* are given in 1 Kings viii. 12, 13 as a speech of Solomon's before his benediction. It is clear, however, that *v.* 14 ought to follow *v.* 12, and in Sept. we find *vv.* 12, 13 in a more complete form (i.e. with the addition of line *a*), with an introductory and a closing formula after *v.* 33—Τότε ἐλάλησε Σολομὼν ὑπὲρ τοῦ οἴκου ὡς συνετέλεσε τοῦ οἰκοδομῆσαι αὐτόν, Ἥλιον ἔστησεν ἐν οὐρανῷ κύριος, καὶ εἶπε τοῦ κατοικεῖν ἐν γνόφῳ Οἰκοδόμησον οἶκόν μου, εὐπρεπῆ σεαυτῷ, τοῦ κατοικεῖν ἐπὶ καινότητος. Οὐκ ἰδοὺ αὕτη γέγραπται ἐπὶ βιβλίου τῆς ᾠδῆς ; I have here followed Lucian, who reads ἔστησεν for ἐγνώρισεν. In the Hebrew of *b*, *c*, and *d*, however, I have not tried to correct the text by the Septuagint, feeling with Klostermann that the received text gives a finer meaning than the Greek (which in any case requires some emendation). The contrast in *a* and *b* is between the sun in his glorious heavenly mansion and the cloud-inhabiting Creator. Then in *c* and *d* Solomon exclaims that he has built a lofty house for Yahveh (that men might no longer worship the sun instead of the Creator), a house eternal as those heavens in which the sun is fixed (cf. Ps. lxxviii. 69*a*). καινότητος of Sept. (in *d*) implies that עוֹלָמִים was misread עֲלוּמִים (cf. the opposite mistake Ps. lxxxix. 8, Isa. liv. 4, Sept.), and τῆς ᾠδῆς=הַשִּׁיר for הַיָּשָׁר. The heading of the fragment in Sept. reminds us that Ps. cxxvii. was also

v. THE EARLIEST OF THE MINOR PSALTERS. 213

(apparently) interpreted as a speech of Solomon's at the building of the temple. If this psalm was wrongly so explained, have we any certainty that the origin given to the fragment by the writer of 1 Kings viii. 14–66 is correct? When the 'Book of the Upright' was compiled we do not know; nor can we be sure that it ascribed the fragment to Solomon. Still, I venture to hope that the fragment *is* Solomonic, just as the elegy on Saul and Jonathan (preserved in the same song-book) is believed to be Davidic. On the date of 1 Kings viii., see Wellhausen, *loc. cit.*

Note ᵏ, p. 194.

On the ancient Chaldæan hymns preserved by later editors, see Sayce, *Hibbert Lectures*, p. 342. Passages from the Veda, in which a distinction is drawn between old and new hymns, are quoted by Muir, *Ancient Sanskrit Texts*, iii. 224–232. The old hymns had the prestige of age, the new of greater elaborateness and refinement. According to Holzman private hymns were sometimes adapted by editors to their own theological conceptions, and old hymns were worked up to suit the taste of a later generation (Steinthal's *Zeitschrift*, 1884, p. 17). On the Zoroastrian hymns, see De Harlez, introd. to his translation of the Avesta, p. lxxiii., and especially Mills, introd. to the Gâthâs, *Oxford Zendavesta*, part iii.

Note ᵐ, p. 194.

Why not? David was the type of a psalmist, Solomon of a wise man (Targ. on Jer. ix. 22). If Neubauer's translation of *Baba bathra*, 14*b* ('David wrote the Book of Praises with the help of ten ancients, Adam, Melchizedek, Abraham, Moses, Heman, Jeduthun, Asaph, and the three sons of Korah') is correct, the tradition implies that each of these persons had the same poetic and religious inspiration as David. Dalman, however, renders עַל יְדֵי 'for,' i.e. 'in the name of,' comparing Mishna, *Baba mez.* vii. 9, and Gemara, *Gittin*, 67*b* (*Der Gottesname Adonaj*, p. 79, note).

Note ⁿ, p. 194.

Ordinary singers were not much thought of; Neh. vii. 67 classes them with slaves. Even the temple singers were not quite equal to the Levites in Zerubbabel's time (Ezra ii. 40–42, Neh. vii. 43–45).

Note ᵒ, p. 195.

It would be absurd to maintain that there were no psalms before the Exile. But it is not absurd to question whether temple-hymns can have greatly resembled those in the Psalter. There must indeed have been a common element in them; and though Jer. xxxiii. has been touched by more than one editor (see Hitzig), I am disposed to infer from *v.* 11 the early existence of the rhythmical thanksgiving formula which we find in Ps. cxxxvi. 1, and would remind doubters that the pilgrim's song called the *Talbīya*, which tradition declares to be pre-Islamic, contains an analogous formula (see Hughes, *Dict. of Islam*, s. v.). A further inference can be drawn from Lamentations, viz. that penitential songs were known before the Exile, though we cannot be sure that these songs much resembled our Lamentations. That Isaiah and Jeremiah contributed liturgical hymns is not only in itself improbable, but has been, as I think, disproved. It is true, however, that the latter prophet was among the first moulders of the later 'dialect of stated prayer.' His priestly soul delighted to plead with God in the name of the people (see e.g. Jer. x. 23-25, xiv. 7-9, 19-22). Passages in the later eucharistic style also occur sometimes embedded in prophecies not post-Exilic (see Isa. xii., xxxviii. 10-20, Hab. iii., Isa. xlii. 10-12, xliv. 23, xlv. 8). It is probable, however, that the first three of these passages were inserted subsequently in a psalm-loving age, like the psalms in the Books of Samuel.

NOTE P, p. 195.

The absence of a title to Ps. xxxiii. and the affinity between xxxii. 11 and xxxiii. 1 have led some to conjecture that Pss. xxxii. and xxxiii. either form one poem (Venema) or are at any rate twin psalms (Hengstenberg). Their difference in form and in contents is however too marked to justify this view. All that we can say is that xxxii. 10 would naturally suggest placing Ps. xxxiii. next to Ps. xxxii. (Grätz however makes xxxii. 11 the first verse of Ps. xxxiii.)

NOTE q, p. 195.

Not earlier therefore than the close of the Assyrian period (see below, on Pss. ix., x.).

NOTE r, p. 195.

The reference to Jehovah's goodness and wide-reaching Providential care (see on *v.* 5) points to that deeper conception of the divine nature which, though it began perhaps in Jeremiah's circle, yet became much more general during and after the Exile. So, too, the way in which the ideas of creation and of Israel's preservation are brought into connexion reminds us strongly of the 'Great Unknown' who glorified the close of the Captivity. As Hengstenberg says, 'The fundamental note of the psalm is, Fear not, thou worm Jacob, and thou small people of Israel;' but the national element in the psalm is raised and ennobled by a deepened intuition of that which Israel has in its God.

NOTE ˢ, p. 195.

If the pointing of Ps. xxxiii. 7 be correct there is yet another parallelism between this psalm and the Maccabæan group referred to in the text. 'Like a heap' would be an allusion to Ex. xv. 8 (cf. the allusion to Moses' Song in Ps. cxviii. 14).

NOTE ᵗ, p. 195.

Notice in this connexion the parallels between Ps. xxxiii. and Pss. cxlvii., cxlviii. Comp. xxxiii. 1 with cxlvii. 1, xxxiii. 9 with cxlviii. 5, xxxiii. 12 with cxlvii. 19, 20, xxxiii. 16–18 with cxlvii. 10, 11, and remember that Pss. cxlvi.–cxlviii. are assigned in Sept. to the prophets Haggai and Zechariah.

NOTE ᵘ, p. 196.

The Hexapla Septuagint title is τῷ Δαυίδ (and so the Cambridge Sept., following Cod. Vat.). But Origen remarks that the psalm is ἀνεπίγραφος in the Hebrew and in Sept., Aq., and Theod. Similarly Eusebius. But Quinta and Sexta do give the title. Who can dogmatize here?

NOTE ᵛ, p. 196.

Among other phraseological affinities note that between v. 15 and Job xv. 35, and between v. 11 (God, a 'shield') and Ps. iii. 4, xviii. 3, 31, xxviii. 7, xxxiii. 20, lix. 12, cxix. 114, cxliv. 2 &c.

NOTE ʷ, p. 196.

'A church psalm in the proper sense of the word.' See note ⁿ, p. 213. From a pardonable conservative impulse I assigned this psalm in my Commentary to the latter part of the reign of Josiah, supposing the occasion to be the danger from Neco. But comparing this with kindred psalms, I see now how improbable this is. The author is a devout post-Exile poet who, like the writer of Ps. vi., loved and copied the prophecies of Jeremiah.

NOTE ˣ, p. 197.

'Less correct.' The only doubt is with regard to Pss. xiv. 5, 6, liii. 6. There are three possible views, (a) that in xiv. 5, 6 we have the original text which was retouched (liii. 6) to make it refer to the plague in Sennacherib's army, (*b*) that liii. 6 had this or a similar reference, but not through any interference with the original text, which in fact it represents, xiv. 5, 6 having arisen from an attempt to make sense out of a partly illegible MS., (*c*) that xiv. 5, 6 gives the original text, liii. 6 being accounted for by ordinary mistakes in transcription. The third view is advocated in my Commentary.

NOTE ʸ, p. 197.

So on the verge of this century Paulus, who assigned Ps. xiv. to Isaiah. This would agree with the view (*a*) in note ʷ. (I assume that 'they feared' is the 'prophetic' perfect. Hitzig, however, who ascribes this psalm to Jeremiah, explains it as a historical backward glance at Sennacherib.)

NOTE ᶻ, p. 197.

Hitzig and Delitzsch both defend the Davidic authorship of the psalm on the ground of the strikingly poetic (Delitzsch adds, the somewhat archaic) phraseology. The former also finds an occasion for the psalm in the life of David; *v.* 3*a*, rightly translated, indicates that the psalm accompanied the present which David sent from Ziklag to the elders of Judah (1 Sam. xxx. 26). A weak hypothesis indeed (see linguistic appendix)! Delitzsch rejects it, but can himself only offer the conjecture that David had fallen sick, and, as the title of the partly parallel (?) 30th psalm suggests, was thereby hindered from entering his new cedar palace (2 Sam. v. 11, 12). He also refers to the points of contact between Ps. xvi. and Pss. iv., xi., xvii., and early portions of the Pentateuch (Ex. xxiii. 13, xix. 6, Gen. xlix. 6); but from my point of view these are not inconsistent with a post-Exile date for the psalm. Delitzsch's linguistic evidence will be noticed in its proper place in the appendix. A pre-Exile date is, I think, only possible if we confine our view to *v.* 4, and connect the 'libations of blood' (*v.* 4) with the human sacrifices put an end to by Josiah (2 Kings xxiii. 10). But is not this connexion very far-fetched? If I had to defend a pre-Exile date, I would sooner take נָסַךְ as = Ar. *nasîka* 'a sacrifice,' prop. 'a pouring out,' and suppose that some Jews had fallen away to a primitive type of sacrificial worship preserved in Arabia (on which see W. R. Smith, *The Religion of the Semites*, pp. 320, 321, and cf. Nilus quoted in Wellhausen, *Skizzen und Vorarbeiten*, iii. 57). But there is another and a better view. The religious and literary affinities of the psalm seem to me post-Exilic. A post-Exilic

V. THE EARLIEST OF THE MINOR PSALTERS.

prophet describes his abhorrence of the sacrifices, both animal and cereal, of formal Jehovah-worshippers by treating them as equivalent to human sacrifices and libations of swine's blood respectively (Isa. lxvi. 3)—'He that slaughtereth an ox is a man-slayer,' . . . 'he that bringeth a *minkhah*, it is swine's blood.' This prophet refers, I suspect, to a revival of Syrian idolatries, but his form of expression would be equally suitable for a writer in the Hellenistic period. Ewald strangely infers from *v.* 3*a* that the writer is one of the exiles. Baethgen takes the same view of the date of the psalm, but infers from *v.* 3 that a part of the exiles had already returned home. He traces points of contact between *v.* 3 (corrected by the help of Sept.) and Isa. xlii. 21, lxii. 4; comp. also *v.* 3 (אָחֵר) with Isa. xlii. 8, xlviii. 11; *v.* 4 with Isa. lxv. 14. At any rate the psalmist has read 2 Isaiah; but is he therefore a contemporary? Moreover, Isa. lxv. is probably post-Exile.

NOTE aa, p. 198.

The representative of faithful Israel, who is the speaker, describes himself (*v.* 10) as חָסִיד, like the author of Ps. lxxxvi., who belongs, as we have seen, to the early part of the anti-Hellenistic movement.

NOTE bb, p. 198.

The Targum and some Rabbis (and among the moderns, Lengerke and Forbes, but not Hengstenberg nor Delitzsch) regard Ps. xxi. as strictly Messianic (chiefly on account of the grandeur of the wishes for the king). But Ps. xxi. belongs to the same category as Pss. xlv., lxxii., cx., nor can it be separated from Ps. xx. (which Forbes, indeed, with bold consistency, interprets of the Messiah). Theodore of Mopsuestia, followed by Theodoret, explains Ps. xx. by 2 Kings xix. 14. David, he thinks, foresees the danger from Sennacherib, and shows us the Jewish people joining its prayers with those of the king. Ps. xxi. he considers to have been written in the name of the people as its thanksgiving for Hezekiah's restoration to health.

NOTE cc, p. 198.

Prov. i.–ix. is admittedly later than the main part of our Book of Proverbs. It is not earlier therefore than the last half century of the Davidic kingdom. This fits in with the most probable date of the Book of Job (Exilic). The stage of intellectual development in 'Job' is more advanced than that in the 'Praise of Wisdom.' In Prov. viii., moreover, Wisdom offers herself to men, and religion is but the first part of her teaching; but in Job xxviii. the divine plan of the world is beyond human study, and religion is all the wisdom possible to man. Dillmann, although a pupil of Ewald, takes the same view, and so Hitzig, Kuenen (?), and Hooykaas. Ewald, Delitzsch, Riehm, and (in a monograph, 1889) Seyring, reverse the order of composition; but they also place Job before the Exile, which is scarcely a tenable view. It is also, I admit, possible that both Job and Prov. i.–ix. are post-Exile (see Lect. VIII., p. 365). This is the view of Stade, who in the personification of Wisdom (Prov. viii.) detects the influence of Hellenism. But I am now arguing for the post-Exile date of Pss. xx., xxi. on relatively conservative grounds.

NOTE dd, p. 199.

Jeremiah, his Life and Times, p. 95 (cf. Theodoret, above). An earlier king than Hezekiah is at any rate most improbable, if the comparative principle has any validity in the criticism of the psalms. Hitzig, who is inclined to explain Pss. xx. and xxi. of Hezekiah, does not disguise the philological objections to this view (see appendix).

NOTE ee, p. 199.

Ps. lxi. 6 should probably be corrected from Ps. xxi. 3 (see my Commentary), the parallelism elsewhere in this psalm being so very complete.

NOTE ff, p. 199.

The עטרה is not confined to the king, any more than the נֵזֶר is to the high priest. Comp. Zech. ix. 16 with Isa. lxii. 3, and Ex. xxix. 6 with 2 Sam. i. 10. Notice also that in Zech. vi. 11 the word for the 'crowns' on the head of Joshua (and of Zerubbabel?) is the plural of that used in Ps. xxi. 4 (עטרות).

NOTE gg, p. 200.

See the quotation in p. 42. I need hardly quote instances of the wide classical use of βασιλεύς. Comp. however another passage from Philo's *De Vitâ Mosis* (Mangey, ii. 152), Πρὸς δὲ καὶ κίδαρις κατεσκευάζετο. κιδάρεις γὰρ οἱ τῶν ἑῴων βασιλεῖς ἀντὶ διαδήματος εἰώθασι χρῆσθαι, and this from *De Profugis* (i. 562), Καὶ ὅτι τὴν κεφαλὴν οὐδέποτε ἀπομιτρώσει, τὸ βασίλειον οὐκ ἀποθήσεται διάδημα, τὸ σύμβολον τοῦ οὐκ αὐτοκράτορος μὲν, ὑπάρχου δὲ καὶ θαυμαστῆς ἡγεμονίας. According to this last passage the high priest occupies a position such as Mordecai's (Esth. viii. 15); he is the king's *alter ego*. It is perfectly true that it was only at the close of the Persian

V. THE EARLIEST OF THE MINOR PSALTERS.

or the beginning of the Greek period that the high priesthood became an object of ambition as a temporal as well as a spiritual dignity. But Wellhausen appears to me to have shown that the union of spiritual and temporal power, so noteworthy in the Greek period, was in full accordance with the theory of the priestly code (*Prolegomena*, pp. 155–157). The argument from the colours of the high priestly vestments in Delitzsch, *Pentateuch-kritische Studien*, No. v., is, I fear, of no weight.

NOTE hh, p. 200.

נָשִׂיא was the official title of the head of the Sanhedrin. As used in the O.T., it suggests that the personage referred to has but moderate importance or authority (see 1 Kings xi. 34, Ezek. xii 10, and other passages in that book). It is no objection to this that Ezekiel calls the future Davidic king נָשִׂיא (Ezek. xxxiv. 24, xxxvii. 25), for this prophet fears to magnify even the Messiah too much, nor that Abraham is called נשיא אלהים (Gen. xxiii. 6), for the Hittites are skilled in compliments. נָגִיד is a term of fuller contents. This title is given to Saul, David, and Solomon in Sam. and Kings, but still with an implication of humility, which would be out of place in expressions of the church-nation's loyalty. Hezekiah in his weakness is also spoken of as a נָגִיד (Isa. xx. 5), and the king of Tyre, with a depreciating reference, in Ezek. xxviii. 2. In Dan xi. 22 the high priest (Onias III.) is called נְגִיד בְּרִית.

NOTE ii, p. 200.

It seems bold in Dr. Grätz to say, 'Only a descendant of David, who would at the same time be the expected Messiah, could, as the people at that time viewed matters, be a true king' (*Gesch. der Juden*, iii., ed. 4, p. 59).

NOTE jj, p. 201.

The Jews complained to Pompeius that Hyrcanus II. and Aristobulus II. (the rival Asmonæan claimants of the kingdom) 'sought to change the government of their nation to another form in order to enslave them' (Jos., *Ant.* xiv. 3, 2). Comp. Mommsen's description of the motives which led Cæsar to avoid the title of king, one of which was the association of the name with Oriental despotism (*Hist. of Rome*, iv. 499). It was the bitter experience of Herodian and subsequently of Roman oppression which led to the frequent introduction of the divine title 'our king,' 'king of the world,' into the Jewish liturgy.

Note kk, p. 201.

It was probably inserted by an afterthought, for Pss. vii. and ix. are connected, not only by similarity of theme, but by the parallelism between vii. 18*b* and ix. 3*b*.

Note ll, p. 201.

See Heb. ii. 6–8. The connexion cannot have escaped any student even in those primitive times. On which side the priority lay, according to the Christian writer, seems clear from the fact 'that all his representations of salvation in the early chapters rest on the accounts of man's primary history contained in Genesis' (Bruce on Hebrews, *Expositor*, 1888, part ii., p. 364).

Note mm, p. 201.

But pre-Maccabæan (cf. *v.* 4*a* with cxliv. 5*a*; *v.* 5 with cxliv. 3). Hitzig and Delitzsch offer but a weak defence of the Davidic authorship. The former explains Ps. viii. by 1 Sam. xxx. 1, 2. But see Commentary and linguistic appendix.

Note nn, p. 201.

I follow Grätz in reading מִפִּי for מִפְּנֵי (cf. Delitzsch on Prov. xv. 14). Thus Ps. xliv. 17*b* may be indebted to both members of Ps. viii. 3.

Note oo, p. 202.

This is confirmed by a small point of phraseology. The psalm begins יְהוָה אֲדֹנֵינוּ. This is a phrase of Nehemiah's, Neh. x. 30; 'our Lord' is also a synonym for Yahveh in Neh. viii. 10, Ps. cxxxv. 5, cxlvii. 5. The universal Lordship of Yahveh is a specially post-Exile belief.

Note pp, p. 202.

Prof. Robertson Smith connects Ps. viii. with Ps. cxxxiv. as regards its original liturgical use. Both were, he thinks, psalms of the night-vigils in the temple (see p. 61). Theophrastus (4th century B.C.), whose attention was attracted by the music of the temple, speaks (ap. Porphyry, *De Abst.* ii. 26) of the worshippers as passing the night in gazing at the stars and calling on God in prayer. Prof. R. Smith only quotes this, however, as possessing a general illustrative value, and not as an authority for a detail of the later ritual (art.

'Psalms,' *Enc. Br.* xx. 34). I would rather view Ps. viii. as one of the night-hymns of faithful worshippers at home (see xlii. 9, cxix. 55, 62).

NOTE qq, p. 202.

The phrase is Milton's. Comp. his use of Ps. xix. 6 in *Parad. Lost*, vii. 371-375, a sonorous passage, but less antiquely natural than George Peele's noble lines (1599),—

> As when the sun, attir'd in glistering robes,
> Comes dancing from his oriental gate,
> And bridegroom-like hurls through the gloomy air
> His radiant beams.

If our own poets revel in myths, we may pardon the first readers of the psalms for not understanding that the life-giving sun could itself be as lifeless as a clod, and those who adopted the popular language in Gen. i. 16, xxxvii. 9, and especially Josh. x. 12, where Joshua speaks almost as if he had Ps. xix. 6 in his mind. Even the latest of the wise men speaks as if the sun were conscious of human doings (cf. 'under the sun,' 26 times in Ecclesiastes, with 'before the sun,' 2 Sam. xii. 12), a view which we find expressed in Ps. Sol. ii. 13, 14, Enoch c. 10, civ. 8. As an early instance of mythic symbolism, observe Isaiah's use of the seraphim (Isa. vi. 2). Hezekiah had doubtless put down the worship of the brazen serpent, so that such symbolism was now possible (see my note).

NOTE rr, p. 202.

Dr. Kay adopts 'ye kindreds of the peoples' (xcvi. 7) as a correct paraphrase of בְּנֵי אֵלִים (which he renders 'sons of the mighty ones' = 'worshippers of the false gods'). This spoils the poetry of xxix. 1, 2. Still the later psalmist does give a part of the earlier one's meaning. According to a popular Israelitish mode of thought, there was a close connexion between the protective angels ('sons of Elim,' or 'of Elohim') and the lands or peoples entrusted to them (see on Ps. lxxxii.). Comp. Ps. xcvii. 7.

NOTE ss, p. 202.

Naturally enough this glorious psalm (xxix.), with its final assertion of Jehovah's sovereignty, was appointed for festival use. On the different traditions, and especially on that embodied in the Septuagint heading, see Delitzsch, whose explanation is confirmed by a Syrian exegetical tradition.

NOTE ᵗᵗ, p. 203.

Cf. Vatke, *Biblische Theologie* (1835), pp. 317, 318. In his posthumous *Einleitung* (1886), this acute scholar explains Ps. xxiv. as an aspiration after the rebuilding of the temple, written probably by the Second Isaiah.

NOTE ᵘᵘ, p. 203.

'Jehovah [Yahveh] Sabaoth' seems to have been the old name of the God worshipped at Shiloh (1 Sam. i. 3). By blessing the people in this name, David intimated that he had succeeded to all that was most important in the office of Eli.

NOTE ᵛᵛ, p. 203.

This includes two passages in so-called Davidic psalms (lix. 6, lxix. 7). But few will defend the Davidic authorship of Ps. lxix. Notice too that Jehovah is called 'hero' (*gibbōr*) in lxxviii. 65, and 'a man of war' in Ex. xv. 3 (both post-Exile passages), and that עִזּוּז 'strong' occurs again in Isa. xliii. 17, and there only.

NOTE ʷʷ, p. 203.

So the Haggada referred to by Justin (*Dial. c. Tryph.*, c. 36 ; cf. *Shabbath* 30a, ap. Wünsche, *Talm.* i. 124). Nothing in the context suggests that the gates intended are those of the old Jebusite citadel.

NOTE ˣˣ, p. 204.

I have developed this in the latter part of a Study on Ps. xxiv. in the *Expositor*, Dec. 1889. It is true that (as I hope to show further on) the names 'Jehovah' and 'Adonai' cannot legitimately be applied to Christ. But if St. Paul can call Jesus Christ τὸν κύριον τῆς δόξης (1 Cor. ii. 8), and an evangelist can say that Isaiah saw the glory of Jesus, and spake of Him (John xii. 41), it is surely not too bold at Ascension-tide to apply the phrase 'Lord [not Jehovah] of Hosts' in this truly inspired psalm to the glorified Messiah. By so doing the Church affirms the moral significance of a phrase which in our own poet Wordsworth is still too much connected with human passions (Ode for Jan. 18, 1816). The deliverance of the weak and oppressed Jewish Church becomes a type of the deliverance of redeemed humanity, and the phrase itself is interpreted by Matt. xxviii. 18. The early Jewish application of Ps. xxiv. equally deserves attention. In the liturgy of the second temple this was the psalm for Sunday. Probably *vv.* 7–10 were interpreted as prophetic of the coming of

Jehovah to judgment (comp. i. 5), which might naturally be assigned to the first day of the week. Theodoret, as naturally (from his point of view), explains the Greek heading (τῆς μιᾶς τῶν σαββάτων, found, as he says, 'in some copies, but not in the Hexapla'), of the Lord's Resurrection. The highly dramatic use of *v.* 7 in the apocryphal *Descensus Christi* can scarcely be viewed as more than a poetical licence.

NOTE yy, p. 204.

I do not argue against the Davidic authorship of Ps. xviii. on the ground of the mention of David in *v.* 51. It is true, the Hebrew poets do not, like the mediæval Germans, name themselves at the end of their poems. But *v.* 51 is probably a later liturgical addition. My arguments are exegetical and phraseological. To reply to these by urging the existence of a second recension of the psalm in 2 Sam. xxii. is useless (see above, p. 193).

NOTE zz, p. 205.

It will hardly be contended that the temple of Shiloh was grand enough to be referred to. Indeed, another psalmist hesitates to call this sanctuary a temple at all (lxxviii. 60).

NOTE aaa, p. 205.

I willingly admit that the (supposed) second psalmist has connected the two parts of the psalm fairly enough by the four central distichs in *vv.* 25-28 ; probably, too, the immediately preceding verses belong to him. And if any one prefers to suppose that one versatile poet wrote the whole, I shall not quarrel with him, provided that he recognizes the dissimilarity of the parts. The first part is very fine ; the colouring is vivid, the expression energetic and apparently original. These epithets are by no means applicable to the second part, the form of which is by comparison prosaic. On the other hand, the course of thought in the less poetical portion is sublime in its absolute idealism. Hupfeld inclines to the theory of a twofold authorship—i.e., 'the author perhaps expanded the psalm from a Davidic basis in part i.' This is surely too vague.

NOTE bbb, p. 205.

It is in Greece that the winged genii, derived from Assyria, first became actually flying. But I presume that no one would assign Ps. xviii. to the Greek period. Whether the flying character of the cherub is a token of Egyptian affinities (see my note at end of *Isaiah*, vol. ii.), or of native Palestinian development, we need not inquire.

Note ccc, p. 206.

'To David and to his seed for ever' implies, 1, that the subject is not so much David as his family, and, 2, that the deliverances will continue to increase in grandeur.

Note ddd, p. 206.

The despondent cry in Ps. lxxxix. 50 probably alludes not merely to Nathan's prophecy but to Ps. xviii. Ps. cxvi. 3 is based on Ps. xviii. 5, 6. Lastly, Ps. cxliv. imitates Ps. xviii. 3, 10, 15, 17, 35, 44–49. I may add that Prov. xxx. 5 (post-Exile) copies *v*. 31, and Hab. iii. 19 echoes *v*. 34.

Note eee, p. 206.

Isa. xliv. 8 copies *v*. 32, and Isa. lv. 5 (see note) alludes to *v*. 45.

Note fff, p. 206.

The former occurs in *v*. 14; the latter in *v*. 32. See linguistic appendix.

Note ggg, p. 206.

The consistent application of literary tests compels us to admit, not only that Mic. vi. and vii. 1–13 belong to a prophet of the reign of Manasseh (see *Micah*, in Cambridge Bible, p. 14), but that Mic. vii. 14–20 consists of two post-Deuteronomic additions (observe the phraseological affinities).

Note hhh, p. 206.

In *v*. 44, read עַמִּים ; 2 Sam. xxii. has עַמִּי.

Note iii, p. 206.

Among other grounds for some hesitation as to the date of Ps. xviii. is the use of the term עֲנָוָה with reference to Jehovah (*v*. 36). It is true, the word occurs again in Ps. xlv. 5 (Mas. text, עֲנָוָה), Prov. xv. 33, xviii. 12, xxii. 4, Zeph. ii. 3 ; but the conception of Jehovah's lowliness, or sympathy with the lowly, is more strikingly post-Exilic than pre-Exilic. The difficulty would be removed if in

v. THE EARLIEST OF THE MINOR PSALTERS. 225

Ps. xviii. 36 we might read, with the second recension (2 Sam. xxii. 36) וַעֲנֹתְךָ, 'and thine answering' (i.e. 'thy help,' cf. Ps. lxv. 6).

Note jjj, p. 206.

Epic, alike in its wide view of the subject and in its adoption of mythological elements (comp. Ewald, *History*, i. 37).—It may be asked whether the closing verse forms an integral part of the psalm. It is not, like the rest of the poem, in trimeters, and was evidently added for liturgical purposes. But the psalm need not have waited till post-Exile times for liturgical recognition (notice the reference in v. 51 to the king).

Note kkk, p. 207.

The collector of the 'Davidic' psalms in Book I. *extended* the title of Ps. xviii. by the help of 2 Sam. xxii. It is worth noticing that Ps. xix. follows Ps. xviii. because of the phrase 'thy servant' (xix. 14), just as Ps. xxxv. precedes Ps. xxxvi. because of the parallelism between 'his servant' (v. 27) and 'Jehovah's servant' in the title of the next psalm. The editor therefore found the titles already in existence; he was not the inventor of them.

Note lll, p. 207.

Notice that the expression 'mountains of God' (xxxvi. 7) recurs in l. 10. A trifle perhaps, and yet not to be neglected as an illustration.

Note mmm, p. 207.

The phrase אל־תנדני has been supposed to allude to David's wanderings (cf. נודו xi. 1).

PART II.

LARGER GROUPS OF PSALMS IN BOOK I.

MY course to-day has been seemingly irregular, but a little thought will prove to you that there has been method in the irregularity. I now turn to the first great group of psalms with common emotional and phraseological characteristics; they are the heart-utterances of the Church amidst some bitter persecution. The group consists of Pss. iii.-vii., ix.-xiv.,[1] xvii., though Ps. v. might also be grouped with the Guest-psalms (which will come before us later). Alike exquisite are its beginning and its ending. Mark the tone of calm superiority to fear and danger in Pss. iii. and iv., and then observe how in Ps. xvii. the poet rises from the harassing troubles of earth to a 'faint foreshadowing of the Beatific Vision' (Kay). Need I pause to discuss the misleading theory of the Davidic authorship of the two former psalms?[a] All that acuteness can do, has been done by Hitzig, who rightly felt that if the theory be correct, there should be some direct or indirect allusions to David's circumstances. But even Hitzig abandons the theory for Pss. v. and vi., and explains Pss. iii. and iv. not (as the title of Ps. iii. suggests)[b] by the flight from Absalom, but by that striking scene after the capture of Ziklag, when 'David was greatly distressed, for the people spake of stoning him, but David strengthened himself in Jehovah his God' (1 Sam. xxx. 6). Search the story of David's life from end to end, and you will find no situation which corresponds to these psalms, and for the very good reason that the Jewish Church, in whose name the psalmist speaks, did not yet exist. The sources of danger to the spiritual kernel of the nation are, first, an Israelitish faction openly opposed to the *khasīdīm* iii. 2, 3, 7, iv. 3-6), and, secondly, the many desponding

---

[1] Ps. xiv. has been already considered.

friends of the cause of truth, who are discontented at the prosperity of the strict Jehovists (*v.* 7). The comparative method leaves no doubt as to the period of the psalm. The myriads of foes that have started up against Israel (iii. 1, 2, 7) correspond to the hostile multitudes of whom, as we have seen, the unwarlike Church complains in lv. 19, lvi. 3. The love of prayer, and the 'joy and peace in believing' which are expressed in iii. 5, iv. 1, 4, 8, 9, form the very atmosphere of Ps. lxii., where we also find traces of a personage (comp. 'my glory,' iv. 2; 'his dignity,' lxii. 5) who is the Church's bulwark, and seeks to lead rather by persuasion than by authority.[c] Add to this that both in Ps. iv. and in Ps. lxii. the speaker appeals to his enemies (who are a 'loveless nation,' xliii. 1) on the ground of humanity, and to susceptible Israelites on that of the union between Jehovah and his people which needs to be vitalized by trust. Lastly, the 'vanity' and 'lying' and the longing for earthly prosperity which characterize, the one the psalmist's enemies, the other his despondent friends in iv. 3, 7, correspond exactly to the description in lxii. 5, 11. Notice, too, how passages in the psalm which we have just studied illustrate an obscure verse in Ps. iv.[d] (cf. iv. 5, xxxvi. 2, 5). Can we hesitate to refer Pss. iii. and iv. to the period to which we have already assigned Pss. vii. and xiv., and many later psalms—the period when faithful Israelites were so sorely oppressed both by traitors in their midst and by their Persian tyrants?

Psalms iii. and iv., however, express the heroic faith of the few, or that of the Church at large at a time of less grievous affliction. The prospect soon became darker. The character and conduct of Israel's enemies are described in Ps. v. not more favourably than in Pss. xii. and xiv. The Church's last and best hope is in prayer. The answer for which she 'looks out' (Ps. v. 4) is recorded in Ps. xii. 6. The context of that passage does not tell us where the revelation came to the psalmist, but Ps. v. 8 informs us—it was in the sanctuary (cf. lxxiii. 17). Ps. vi. (with which compare Ps. lxxxviii.) is in a much more depressed tone; death seemed the only prospect for Israel and for its members; Ps. xxx. is its complement (see xxx. 10). The acute Ibn Ezra thought that David spoke prophetically of Israel in exile, which he compared to a sick man; he saw that the words did not suit the circumstances of David.[e] Taking these psalms by themselves, we might place them just before the arrival of Nehemiah, B.C. 445. 'What do these feeble (sapless) Jews,' says Sanballat (Neh. iii. 34 = A.V. iv. 1); 'Pity me, Jehovah, for I am enfeebled (become sapless),' says righteous but despondent Israel in Ps. vi. 3.[f] But it is safer and, as I think, more critical to date them like the other members of the group.

Pss. ix. and x., like Pss. xlii. and xliii., must be treated as one poem, or, if you will, as one poem in two parts. In its original form there was no bifurcation; it was of simple alphabetic structure. According to Ewald, it may have referred to the fall of Nineveh (B.C. 607), which the prophet Nahum so jubilantly anticipated (B.C. 660). Considering that alphabetic composition is perhaps traceable in Nah. i. 2–10, this view might be admissible, if the tone of the Jewish nation in 607 corresponded to that of the psalm. History shows, however, if I read it aright,[1] that this was not the case; the year 607 was the worst possible time for the composition of church-hymns. When was the psalm written, then?[g] The expressions used of Jehovah (ix. 3, where note עֶלְיוֹן, 5, 6, 8, 9, x. 16) and of Israel (seven times עֲנִיִּים or עֲנָוִים) on the one hand, and of the nations on the other (ix. 6, 16, 18, 21, x. 16), are parallel to those used elsewhere by post-Exile poets. Notice, too, on the one hand, the command to 'publish God's exploits among the peoples' (v. 12; cf. xcvi. 3, 10, cv. 1, Isa. xii. 4), which indicates that a time of national good fortune (the Restoration) is past, and on the other, the many references to misery such as we know to have existed in ever deepening degree in the Persian period. The editorial changes, of which I have spoken elsewhere, may be summed up thus.[h] First, the Daleth and Kaf stanzas were omitted, but, with this exception, the first part of the original psalm (Alef to Yod) was kept unaltered, and formed by the addition of a concluding quatrain (in place of the Kaf stanza) into an independent psalm. Then the stanzas from Mem to Çade were omitted, and replaced by six non-alphabetic stanzas (in our Bibles, x. 3–11). Thus a second

---

[1] See *Jeremiah, his Life and Times*. p. 131.

psalm was produced, adapted to the circumstances of the editor, in whose time the oppressors of Israel were, to judge from the inserted stanzas, degenerate Israelites as well as foreigners. (Notice the suggestive parallel between x. 8, 9, and lvi. 7.) No part of Pss. ix. and x. therefore can be removed very far chronologically from the neighbouring psalms.

As to the date of Pss. xi.–xiii. and Ps. xvii., the exegetical phenomena collected elsewhere seem to me conclusive. Ps. xvii. in particular not only has affinities with the other psalms of this group and with some other late persecution-psalms (see my note on *vv.* 9–12), but with the Praise of the Law[1] (Ps. xix. 8–15) and with Pss. xvi. and xlix., and (see on *v.* 14) the Books of Job and Ecclesiastes.

To sum up. No member of this group can be much earlier than the close of the Persian period. The psalms in which depression, agitation, or embitterment is most visible (vi., vii., x. 2–11, and xvii.) may refer either to the slavery (to use Josephus's word, *Ant.* xi. 7, 1) into which the Jews were brought for seven years by Bagôses, or to that other outburst of Persian fury under Artaxerxes Ochus (see pp. 53, 61) when Jewish captives were carried away to Egypt, Babylonia, and even Hyrcania. It is no objection to this that in some of these psalms (vii. and xvii.) a strong consciousness of legal righteousness is expressed. The high priestly family might at this time be capable of awful crimes (Jos., *Ant.* xi. 7, 1), but the mass of the Jews were doubtless faithful to their principles (see on Ps. cxxxii.). The 7th psalm indeed, if I am not much mistaken, gives a hint of its origin in its title which should probably run thus, 'A Shiggaion of David, which he sang to Jehovah because of (Mordecai) the son of Kish,[1] a Benjamite'[j] (see Esther ii. 5). We know from a Talmudic treatise[2] that the psalm was used at the feast of Purim, and from 2 Macc. xv. 36 that one name of this festival was ἡ Μαρδοχαϊκὴ ἡμέρα. The editor who prefixed the title seems to mean that David, as a prophet, assumed the character of Mordecai; this is at least an attestation that the psalm was very early regarded as a work of the Persian age.

---

[1] There is no root בּוּשׁ in classical Heb.; in the Talm. 'ב = spindle.
[2] *Massechet Soferim*, xviii. 2 (ed. J. Müller).

It was probably the tyranny of Ochus which won admission for Purim into Judea;[k] if so, it was but natural to take a psalm occasioned by that tyranny as the Purim-psalm.[m]

Let us now take up the second group of persecution-psalms (viz., xxii., xxvi., xxvii. 7-13, xxviii., xxxi., xxxv., xxxviii., xxxix., xl. 13-18, xli.), and among them let us give the precedence to Pss. xxii., xxxi., xxxv., and xl. 13-18[n] (= lxx.), with the last of which we may connect Pss. lxix. and lxxi. These form a group within the group, and most certainly belong to the same period and the same circle, with the possible exception of Pss. xxxi., xl. 13-18 (= lxx.), and lxxi., which have a specially imitative character, and may therefore be of later date. We will begin with Ps. lxxi., which Ewald regards as a work of the old age of the author of Ps. li. Nothing is gained, I think, by this imaginative conjecture, but it records the perfectly just impression that the school which modelled itself upon Jeremiah represents a decline as compared with that which formed itself upon the Second Isaiah. Turning to the Septuagint, we find as the second part of a 'conflate' title, 'Of the sons ($\tau\hat{\omega}\nu$ $\upsilon\hat{\iota}\hat{\omega}\nu$) of Jonadab, and of the first captives.'[o] This is not less fanciful than Ewald's view. The Rechabites and the first captives both receive more or less praise from Jeremiah (see Jer. xxiv., xxxv.), and it seems to be hinted that the psalm was written by Jeremiah in the reign of Zedekiah, and preserved by his most faithful adherents. Hitzig and Delitzsch are bolder. They plainly assert this prophet to be the author of Ps. lxxi., to which Hitzig adds Pss. lxix. and lxx. (the latter, a fragment of Ps. xl., which the same critic ascribes in its entirety to Jeremiah). Some critics also refer other members of the group to the weeping prophet; Hitzig, for instance, as early as 1831, pronounced the Jeremian authorship of Ps. xxxi. to be 'certain.'[p] This fancy for giving authors' names to the nameless psalms is a mark of weakness and not of strength. Noticing how much Ps. xxxi. in particular has in common with so-called Davidic psalms of post-Exile origin, we ought to hesitate to argue from Jeremian affinities to Jeremian authorship, more especially when the theory of Jeremian authorship has not satisfied our tests in other cases.

None of these so-called 'doubtful' psalms has, I submit,

so clear a historical background as Pss. xxii., xxxv., and lxix.,[q] which I call primary members of the group, and which, being representative or typical psalms, were probably often imitated. The most original and striking of the three is Ps. xxii. If I am somewhat brief upon it now, it is that I may return later to so tempting a theme. Was the psalm written, as Ewald supposed, during the first of Judah's two captivities? This might account for the keen edge of the sufferings described, and for the expressions in *vv.* 4*b*, 23, 26, which imply the continuance of the temple-services. To me, however, this view seems scarcely more plausible than the ascription of Ps. xlii. to Jehoiachin going into exile. Such ripe fruits of spiritual religion could not, methinks, have been produced in the miseries and anxieties of that period. Besides, the author of Ps. xxii. stands in a close relation, not only to Job, but, as Calvin already saw, to the Second Isaiah,[r] and can we doubt which is the more original? No; the earliest possible date either for this or for any of the parallel psalms is that which has been proposed for Ps. cii.—the period which preceded Nehemiah's first journey to Jerusalem, when, as Hanani told him in Shushan, 'The remnant of the Golah there in the province are in great affliction and reproach' (Neh. i. 3), a sad piece of news indeed after all that Zerubbabel and his successors had done, and only half explained (see p. 71) by the mysterious statement that 'the wall of Jerusalem is broken down, and the gates thereof are burned with fire.' I have mentioned one of the periods in which the life and fortunes of Jeremiah seemed to be a parable of the life and fortunes of the Church, and in which the temple-poets, feeling this, wrote almost like Jeremiah's biographers. The time which I have just referred to was another such period. Not indeed to an equal extent. There is no evidence that any great world-power was actively hostile to the Jews at this period. The Persian court had given full authority to Ezra to regulate the civil and religious concerns of his people, and the policy of religious isolation (that is, of holiness, in the ritual sense) adopted by the great reformer made it imperative to set aside prophetic idealisms (Zech. ii. 4, 5) and fortify the Holy City. It was no Persian satrap (the revolt of Megabyzus in Syria absorbed the whole attention of Persia), but probably Sanballat the Horonite, Tobiah the Ammonite, Geshem the Arabian, and with them the 'army of Samaria' (Neh. ii. 10, iv. 1–8), who broke down Ezra's walls, just as upon Nehemiah's arrival they united to oppose the rebuilding of them. There is indeed no reference to the walls in Ps. xxii., but there may be at least an allusion to them in lxix. 36, and possibly (see below) xxxi. 22. And may we not compare the famous 'Roll it on Jehovah' (Kay's rendering of xxii. 8) with Neh. iv. 2 (iii. 34 in Heb.), 'What do these feeble Jews? will they leave the matter to God?'[3] It is as if the author of Ps. xxii. had been present when Sanballat 'laughed the Jews to scorn, and despised them' (Neh. ii. 19), and recorded the scene in his deathless poem. There are the 'many bulls,' the 'strong ones of Bashan' (v. 13), i.e. the Ammonites (who had occupied Gad, Zeph. ii. 8, Jer. xlix. 1). There are the 'lions' (v. 14), i.e. the Arabian tribes who had displaced the Edomites, and the wild pariah-'dogs' (vv. 17, 18), i.e. those whom Ben Sira calls the 'foolish folk that dwelleth in Shechem' (Ecclus. l. 26). The explanation, which is that of Lagarde,[1] though not certain, is plausible; it is in the manner of the prophets,[2] and I cannot help adding, of that great student of Scripture, Dante. How much more poetic are these natural symbols than the symbolic cypher which an unwise editor has thrust into Jer. xxv. 25, 26! The precise equivalent of the symbols might be forgotten, without their eternal significance being at all impaired. The Church in its various troubles can put its own interpretation upon them, and if any one prefers to think that the psalmist himself simply meant by a threefold symbol to emphasize the bitterness of his enemies, he may refer to another sketch of (probably) the same scene :—

> Aliens whom I know not gather together against me,
> And cry out unceasingly (Ps. xxxv. 15).

It is interesting also to find in Ps. xxxv. 11 a figurative description of the false accusation of rebellion, which added fresh point to Sanballat's taunts (Neh. ii. 19, end), and in vv. 12–15a of the false Israelites who had formed the closest of ties with strangers (Neh. vi. 18).[t] Nor is the 69th psalm

---

[1] *Orientalia*, ii. 63, 64.   [2] See my commentary on Jer. v. 6.

deficient in references to the divisions of the Jews at this time and the religious ground of the hatred which they encountered (lxix. 8, 9, 13, 21); and in *v*. 26 the writer may even allude to the tent-dwellers among Israel's enemies. And lastly, is it not possible [u] that the frustration of Sanballat's underhand practices and the final completion of the wall are recorded, not only in the 6th chapter of Nehemiah, but in these words of Ps. xxxi.,

Thou hidest them in the covert of thy face from slanderers among men :
Thou treasurest them in a bower against the accusing of tongues.
Blessed be Jehovah !
For he hath made passing great his lovingkindness unto me in a fenced city.

Six members of the larger group still remain (Pss. xxvi., xxvii. 7–14, xxviii., xxxviii., xxxix., xli.); they all belong to the later persecution-period to which certain psalms have already been assigned. Pss. xxvi. and xxviii. may be taken together with Ps. v., the leading petitions of which are similar. The 'anointed' in xxviii. 8 is the high priest, as in lxxxiv. 10. The petition in the next verse, 'shepherd them' ($\pi o i \mu a \nu o \nu$ $a \dot{\upsilon} \tau o \grave{\upsilon} s$, Sept.) connects Ps. xxviii. with the Asaphite psalms. Ps. xxvii. 7–13 and Ps. xxxviii. connect themselves, not only with Pss. v. and vi.[1] but with Ps. xxxv. (note the false witnesses) and Ps. xxxi. (note the friends who stand aloof) respectively. In other words, both the preceding groups have influenced these psalms.

The exquisite 39th psalm has strong affinities with the Book of Job, but also with Ps. lxii.,[v] as you will see by comparing *v*. 3 with lxii. 2 (דּוּמִיָּה), and *vv*. 5–7 with lxii. 10, 11. Notice too the fondness in both psalms for the particle which introduces the conclusions of victorious faith—אַךְ, and the double title 'of Jeduthun' ('to the charge of Jeduthun') and of 'David' prefixed to both in the Hebrew. Comp. also *v*. 5*b* with lxxxix. 48.[w] Ps. xxxix. looks more original than Ps. lxii., but need not have been written long previously. It is clearly a persecution-psalm (see *vv*. 9–12), and so too is Ps. xli. (putting aside the introductory verses), with which compare Pss. vi., xxxv., and xxxviii., and, for *v*. 10, Ps. lv. 13–15.[x]

---
[1] See my Commentary.

We have now to strike inland and make for the ordinary starting-point of voyagers, viz., the first, which, from our point of view, is the last of the songs of the Psalter. 'How beautiful upon the mountains are the feet of him that bringeth good tidings, that publisheth peace.' Such were the thoughts of the framer of David's song-book when he included Ps. xl. 1–12—one of the 'new songs' of the 'bringers of good tidings' (see *vv.* 4, 10).[y] The 'righteousness' of which he loves to discourse is the series of national mercies which culminated in the rebuilding of the temple.[z] He loves the Bible within the Bible—that which speaks of God's free love to Israel, and of what St. James afterwards called 'the perfect law of liberty.' There may be, even after the Return, 'arrogant' men who fall away to the idolatries of Canaan (Ps. xl. 5 ; cf. Isa. lxv. and lxvi., also lix. 13 ; all post-Exile passages); but the psalmist will not (like those described in Mal. iii. 15) call such men happy. He is one of those *khasīdīm* who are worthy of the name, and in his views of sacrifice he reminds us strongly of the authors of Pss. l. and li.[1] To some extent parallel (cf. *vv.* 2–4 with xxx. 3–5) is Ps. xxx., a song perhaps (see above, p. 227) of the afflicted ones who had prayed Ps. vi. on their unexpected deliverance. In spite of its title, which connects it with the 'dedication festival,'[aa] and in spite of the parallelism between Pss. xxx. 4 and cxviii. 18, and between Pss. xxx. 6, 12 and cxviii. 27*a*, it is not a Maccabæan psalm. The descriptions are too general, nor is the tone at all in harmony with the martial spirit of the *khasīdīm* in the time of Judas the Maccabee.[bb] No; we can spare the 118th psalm for the Maccabee and the Huguenots, but Hannington's psalm came from heroes of another mould. Its very phraseology points us to the pre-Maccabæan part of the post-Exile period.[cc] (Cf. *v.* 4 with Ps. xxviii. 1, *v.* 10 with Ps. vi. 6, *v.* 13, 'my glory,' with Ps. vii. 6, and *v.* 6 with Ps. cxxvi. 5, Isa. liv. 7, 8.)

We next come to Ps. xxxvii., a didactic poem, with affinities to various post-Exile psalms. Cf. especially *v.* 1 with lxxiii. 3, *v.* 7 with xxii. 9, *v.* 21 with cxii. 5. The psalmist also well knew the Book of Job.[dd] Like the author of Ps. xci. he was specially drawn to the first speech of Eliphaz. Recent

Cf. Lect. IV., p. 153.

national mercies seem to have revived the old-fashioned doctrine of adequate temporal retribution. For in spite of v. 25 this is a church psalm; it is the fortunes of righteous Israel (Jeshurun) which preoccupy the psalmist. Need I say which those national mercies must be?

The 37th is an alphabetic psalm, and thus connects itself with Pss. xxv. and xxxiv.[ee] It lacks however the curious irregularity of structure which distinguishes those two psalms, and its tone, which is throughout didactic, is different. The Israel of Ps. xxv. is a self-condemned though not despairing sinner. Members of the nation have 'broken their faith' to Jehovah (v. 3); and it is only too plain from Israel's present dangers and distresses that God remembers sins which His people has partly forgotten (v. 7). Still Jehovah remains 'good and upright;' He is the great teacher[1] and redeemer; and unto Him the eyes of friendless Israel are directed (vv. 15, 16). Ps. xxxiv. agrees in its leading ideas, but was evidently written after an improvement in Israel's circumstances (comp. vv. 5–7, 23, with xxv. 15–22). The phraseology of xxxiv. 8 (cf. xxxv. 5, 6) is fully consistent with a reference to the age of Nehemiah,[ff] and the proper names in Ezra and Nehemiah seem to suggest that the phraseology of Ps. xxv. was frequently on Jewish lips in that period[gg] (cf. v. 15 with Elyoenai or Elyehoenai, Ezra viii. 4, the name of one of Ezra's companions, and v. 22 with Pedaiah, Neh. iii. 25, the name of one of the builders of the wall). And now, to make up a triad of 'songs of deliverance,' add Ps. xxxii., which is more spiritual in tone than Ps. xxxiv., and in so far is a better counterpart to Ps. xxv. Luther, who loved to call it a Pauline psalm, grouped it with the 51st, and a recent German critic, following in the steps of Luther and Delitzsch, ventures on this comment, that 'one of the commonest of sins with Oriental despots so shocked David's conscience that he expressed his penitence as no saint has ever done.'[2] I do not yield to Orelli in admiration of this brightest of penitential lyrics. But I cannot, at the bidding of a late and uncritical tradition, convert a David into a Paul.[hh] No; certain features in the description may indeed be drawn

---

[1] Comp. Ps. xxxii., and see Lect. VII.
[2] Orelli, art. 'David' in Herzog-Plitt, *Realencyclopädie*, iii. 519.

from private experience, as in some other psalms in which
'the speaker's personality leaps up as it were into his song.'[1]
Even if so, however, the individual is not a self-seeking
monarch, but a believer, who walks by the soft guidance of
Jehovah's Eye (*v.* 8). A believer? Permit me rather to use
his own word *khāsīd*, i.e., a man of love (cf. Prov. xi. 17 Heb.),
to whom Jehovah's lovingkindness is 'better than life itself'
(Ps. lxiii. 3), and whose chief claim to distinction is that he
can express that which thousands feel. Like Daniel, he can
say that he 'confesses his own sin and the sin of his people
Israel' (Dan. ix. 20). He is indeed in some sense, like Daniel,
a prophet, as being a representative of the Church, which is the
inheritor of the prophetic spirit.[ii] It is a church-psalm,
and has some affinities not merely with Ps. xxv., but also
with Pss. xxii. and lxix., the date of which we have already
fixed.[2] The tone and ideas of the psalm are in harmony
with this view.[jj]

The transition is an easy one from Ps. xxxii. to what I
may call the Guest-psalms,[3] viz., xv., xxiv. 1–6, xxvii. 1–6,
and xxiii. (to which two psalms in a more subdued tone may
be added, which at least allude to the security of Jehovah's
guests, viz., Ps. v. on account of *v.* 5*b*, and Ps. lxi. on account
of *v.* 5*a*). Why is forgiven Israel so joyful? Because it is
delivered from earthly trouble? Yes; but chiefly because it
can once more fearlessly enter Jehovah's house. When were
these church-psalms written? Most who have followed me
thus far will readily admit that they imply the existence of
the second temple. The requirement of moral rightness in
Jehovah's temple-guests is found again in one of the later
persecution-psalms (see Ps. v. 5–8). The use of 'generation'
for 'class' (xxiv. 6) reminds us of Ps. xii. 9, xiv. 5, lxxiii. 15,
cxii. 12, Prov. xxx. 11–14, Deut. xxxii. 5. This is, at any
rate, against a very early date, while the special sense of
'righteousness' in Ps. xxiv. 5 is Deutero-Isaianic. There is
also an allusion in Ps. xv. 4 to the Priestly Code, which
became the law of the church-nation through Ezra the scribe.[kk]

---

[1] Ker, *The Psalms in History and Biography*, p. 3.

[2] Comp. *vv.* 3*b*, 4*b* with xxii. 2*b*, 16*a*, lxix. 4; *v.* 5*a* with lxix. 6, and *v.* 6*a* with lxix. 2, 3.

[3] See Lect. VIII.

It is, of course, no objection to this view that Pss. xv. and xxiv. 1–6 are parallel to a fine description of the righteous citizen in Isa. xxxiii. 15, 16. Isa. xxxiii. has long been regarded as only in a secondary degree Isaianic, and it has lately been argued with great force that its composition or compilation belongs to the post-Exile age[ll]—to the period of the final editing of the prophetic writings. If this be correct (as I believe that it is), the date proposed for these psalms is strongly confirmed; but, in any case, church-psalms like these cannot, as we have seen, be pre-Exilic. Ps. xxvii. 1–6 reminds us of passages in Pss. lxi. and lxiii., which probably belong to the early Maccabæan period. The originality, however, lies with Ps. xxvii. 1–6, which obviously describes the feelings of the Church[mm] (see *v.* 6) amid some of the troubles of the Persian age; *v.* 3 reminds us of iii. 2, 7, iv. 9, and *v.* 5 of xxxi. 21. Its companion-psalm is the 23rd (comp. *v.* 6 with xxvii. 4), that sweet expression of resting faith, which surely belongs to one of the most gifted of the 'Davids' of the Psalter. How unlike it is to a last meditation of the historical David—how unlike even to those 'last words' which tradition assigns to him! But how like those two characteristic psalms of the age of Nehemiah, cxxvii. (see *vv.* 1, 2), and cxxxiii. (see *v.* 2), when, too, as we know from psalms in Books III. and IV., the figure of the divine Shepherd became specially dear to the church-nation![nn]

The didactic fragment attached to the Song of the Sun in Ps. xix. alone remains. How delightful, could we vindicate its pre-Exile origin! Davidic, indeed, it cannot be; fancy the worldly-minded, even though religious, David inditing a hymn in praise of a rich and varied handbook of spiritual religion.[oo] Must one really spend precious moments in dispelling this illusion? Read the Decalogue (Ex. xx. 1–17) and the Book of the Covenant[pp] (Ex. xx. 23–xxiii.), part of which at least may, if not must, have been known to David, and then try to sing:

The law of Jehovah is perfect, restoring the soul,
The testimony of Jehovah is faithful, giving wisdom to the simple,
More to be desired are they than gold, yea, than much fine gold,
Sweeter also than honey, or the honey-comb (xix. 8–11).

But, even if not Davidic, may not this fragment belong to

the Josian age—to those halcyon days which followed the publication of the first Scripture ? This is at least plausible. If a Josian poet wrote Ps. xviii. 21-24 and 31,^{qq} why should he not have written Ps. xix. 8-11 ? Certainly, Deuteronomy is a 'rich and varied handbook,' not perhaps unworthy even of such a glowing eulogy. 'It sought to place the whole moral and spiritual life upon a new basis.'[1] Moreover, there is a passage in Deut. iv. 28 which is but a slightly less fervent eulogy of the new Law-book. The objection is twofold, (1) that the original Law-book of Josiah did not include the first four chapters of the later book of Deuteronomy, and no consistent historical critic can place these chapters before the Exile; and (2) that the tremulous conscientiousness which expresses itself in *vv.* 13 and 14^{rr} is specially characteristic (read the 119th psalm) of the Persian and the Greek age. The author was in fact one of the *khasīdīm*, who lived under heathen rule, and who were tempted to the 'great transgression' of apostasy.

The Davidic collection now lies behind us; indeed, we have passed the entire Psalter in review, except Psalms i. and ii., which form as it were the double gate of the temple. As I have already said, I do not think that the second psalm has a contemporary historical reference. No period can be found in which even by a poetic exaggeration an Israelitish king could be described as ruler of the world. If we ask when the writer lived, all the internal evidence points us to the post-Exile period. Like Pss. lxxxix. and cxxxii., our psalm presupposes the promises to David in 2 Sam. vii.,^{ss} and, like the former psalm, it adopts a mode of speaking of the king which harmonizes better with Egyptian and Babylonian than with the early Biblical phraseology.^{tt} Its tone of lofty confidence renders it possible that the troubles of the Persian age may lie behind the writer. Shall we place it before or after the Maccabæan insurrection ?^{uu} It certainly presents some points of contact with Pss. lxxxiii. and cx., which are Maccabæan.^{vv} Indeed, if we might connect both *v.* 2 and *v.* 3 with the first oracle in Ps. cx., and *v.* 5 as well as *v.* 4 with the second, and might follow the Septuagint rendering of Ps. cx. 3*b*,[2] the resemblance between these oracles and that in Ps. ii. 7-9 would be remarkably great. I do not, however,

---

[1] *Jeremiah, his Life and Times*, p. 63.   [2] Vocalizing יְלִדְתִּיךָ

think that the really certain affinities between Ps. ii. and those Maccabæan psalms are decisive, and the picture presented in the former is evidently different. In Ps. lxxxiii. the neighbouring nations have imperilled the very existence of Israel; in Ps. cx. a large but not necessarily world-wide empire is *anticipated* for the hero. But in Ps. ii. there is no real danger to Israel; [ww] contrast the feverish anxiety of Ps. lxxxiii. The king already has a world-wide sovereignty, though the vassal kings of the earth have risen in revolt. The picture in this psalm is largely influenced by Jewish eschatology, and has parallels in Joel and 2 Zechariah,[xx] both of which are post-Exile but pre-Maccabæan works. But the psalm is not simply eschatological. Being a lyric poem, the circumstances which it describes must have a certain quasi-historical basis. In other words, the writer throws himself back into a distant age—shall we say into that of Hezekiah, or into that of David (or Solomon)? There is something to be said for the former. Isaiah's apostrophe to the 'far nations' in Isa. viii. 9, and the picture of an attack on Zion in Pss. xlvi. and xlviii. have a general resemblance to Ps. ii.; indeed, some expressions in this pair of lyrics are somewhat parallel to phrases in our psalm.[yy] But none of these affinities are decisive. A vivid poem like Ps. ii. could not but resemble others of its class; and the manifest allusion in *v.* 7 to 2 Sam. vii. 14*a* (which, however, is used freely),[zz] combined with the analogy of Ps. xviii., compel us to pronounce in favour of the Davidic or the Solomonic as the assumed age of the writer. In Ps. xviii. the idealizing poet speaks in the name of David as if the world's dominion were already his. It was only a step further for another poet to speak, in the name of the king (see Ps. ii. 7-9), as if that dominion not only had been won, but was now being disputed by rebel-kings. Ps. ii. is therefore the complement of Ps. xviii., but written from a later point of view. Like that psalm, it prophesies of the Messiah, but only to one who can 'pierce below the surface,' and recognize that spirit or tendency which carries a poet beyond himself, and makes his words symbolically prophetic.[aaa]

And why was Psalm ii. placed where it now stands? Because the collectors loved to give a prominent position to psalms of a lofty idealism, and because this psalm in particular seemed to illustrate the contents of the following 'Davidic' psalms, in which a leading Israelite complains of his numerous enemies. Ps. ii. was not, however, called 'Davidic,' because it was composed after the Davidic hymn-book was complete, and very possibly as an introduction to it.

We now pass to Ps. i., which, according to a Jewish fancy, referred to Josiah, as the only king who avoided sinners and followed the law.[bbb] More plausibly Hengstenberg and Delitzsch regard it as an early psalm because imitated, as they assert, by Jeremiah (cf. v. 3 with Jer. xvii. 8). We must not put this argument aside on the ground of the difficulty of deciding which of two parallel passages is the original. No one, I think, will accuse me of underrating the delicacy of such a critical process, for it is to my own essay on the subject that English conservative critics must refer their readers.[1] There are cases in which a dogmatically expressed decision is inexpedient, but sure I am that the case before us is not one of these. It may seem a slight thing to say that there is nothing in the psalm corresponding to Jer. xvii. 6, and that the two pictures in Jer. xvii. 5–8 are much better contrasted than those in Ps. i. 3, 4. But when we consider further that the psalmist has added a feature to the description of the happy man which is not found in Jer. xvii. 5–8, and that this feature is specially characteristic of the post-Exile period, ought any critic to doubt that Jeremiah is the source from which a post-Exile psalmist has drawn? It were easy to strengthen my argument by referring to the critical analysis of the Book of Joshua;[ccc] but I forbear. The comparative principle suggests grouping this psalm with Ps. xix. 8–15 and cxix. (cf. also Pss. cxi. and cxii.); and I am content with having shown that the parallelism referred to by conservatives does not hinder us from following the suggestion.

The combination of elements in the character of the psalmist favours a late date. It is true that the moral class-names which he employs ('ungodly,' 'righteous,' 'scoffers'[ddd]) are common even in the earlier portions of the Book of Proverbs. But the authority which he ascribes to the written Law or Revelation distinguishes him from the older writers on morality who make no reference to a Scripture,[eee] and

[1] *The Prophecies of Isaiah*, ed. 3, vol. ii. p. 241, &c.; cf. p. 234.

points to a time when the 'wise men' as a class had accepted the form of religion established by Ezra. The author of Ps. i. belonged to a school from which afterwards the wise son of Sirach proceeded.[fff] His submission to the law was no feigned or forced one, but that of a child to a parent, and a disciple to an all-wise teacher. Writing, however, as he does, not for Rabbis but for ordinary believers ('day and night' is surely a 'counsel of perfection,' as in Josh. i. 8), he lays more stress on the practical importance of study of the Scriptures than upon those intellectual results which Ben Sira dwells upon in Ecclus. xiv. 20, 21, xxxix. 1–11.

Whether the psalm was written during the early Hellenistic movement, cannot be positively determined. It is at any rate pre-Maccabæan, nor need it have been composed long after Ps. ii. The parallelism between these two psalms is obvious (note the catchwords common to both—'Happy,' 'meditate,' 'the way,' 'perish,' and the common idea of the judgment), and combined with the circumstance that Ps. ii. has no title, led many ancient theologians, both Jewish and Christian, to regard Ps. ii. as the second part of Ps. i.[ggg] This is clearly a mistake. Nothing in Ps. i. corresponds to the vivid scene-painting in Ps. ii., and the divine judgment in Ps. i.[hhh] is less of a convulsion than in Ps. ii. We cannot therefore even suppose (with Hengstenberg and Hitzig) that they are separate works by the same author. But both may nevertheless be not only of the same period, but of the same class—that of introductory psalms. If Ps. ii. was the preface to the 'Davidic' Psalter, Ps. i. may well have been the introduction to a large pre-Maccabæan Book of Psalms which included that smaller hymnal. Though not necessarily composed (any more than Ps. ii. was composed) to be a preface, it was admirably adapted to become one, both from the simplicity with which it inculcates fundamental truths of the psalmists' religion, and from the parallelisms between it and the second psalm which brings out another aspect of the cardinal Messianic doctrine. The final Maccabæan editor had obviously no reason for displacing this noble pair of psalms, which by their beatitudes seek to allure disciples to the purest and best theology of the Jewish Church.

NOTE ᵃ, p. 226.

See a singular argument in favour of the headings by Delitzsch (Luthardt's *Zeitschrift*, 1882, p. 118), who thinks that Ps. iv. 7*b* is an echo of Num. vi. 25, 26. But see on Ps. lxvii.

NOTE ᵇ, p. 226.

The Ambrosian MS. of the Peshitto supplements the Hebrew heading of Ps. iv. thus, 'when Saul sent out to slay him in his house' (1 Sam. xix. 11).

NOTE ᶜ, p. 227.

Does not this view do more justice to one's natural impression on reading Ps. lxii. than the theory that the Church alone is the speaker? Indeed, how could the spiritual Israel have held its ground without leaders, especially when the high priests were unworthy of their high position?

NOTE ᵈ, p. 227.

Ps. iv. 5, 'Tremble and sin no more;' for hitherto no 'dread of Elohim' has been 'before your eyes.' And 'form (good) resolves upon your bed,' where hitherto ye have 'devised mischief.' Bredenkamp takes 'say in your hearts' to mean 'pray silently' (cf. 1 Sam. i. 13). But see Ps. x. 6, 11, 13, xiv. 1.

NOTE ᵉ, p. 228.

Delitzsch endeavours to show that both בית and היכל in Ps. v. 8 can mean the Tabernacle; see however my note. If the rest of the psalm were Davidic in tone, we might conjecture that *v.* 8 was a later insertion. The only possible pre-Exile date for Pss. v. and vi. is the age of Jeremiah, to which prophet Hitzig would assign both psalms (Ps. v. not without some hesitation). Cf. Ps. vi. 1 (xxxviii. 1) with Jer. x. 24, and *v.* 6*a* with Jer. xlv. 3; also Ps. v. 9 (line 3) with Jer. v. 16, and the imprecations in Ps. v. 10 with those in Jer. xii. 3. Hitzig's theory has been dealt with elsewhere. Suffice it to say that Ps. vi. at any rate belongs to the school of Job. Cf. Ps. vi. 8*a* with Job xvii. 7; Ps. vi. 8*b* (עתק 'senescere') with Job xxi. 7; and Ps. vi. 6 (in its dread of Sheól) with Job vii. 7–10, x. 20–22, and (for 'Death' as equivalent to 'Sheól') Job xxviii. 22. The case of Ps. vi. is in fact precisely similar to that of the 'Song of Hezekiah' (also uttered by a representative pious man. note the alternation of 'I' and 'we' in Isa. xxxviii. 20'.

Note f, p. 228.

Ps. vi. 2 (see my note) expresses a sense of guilt. But the guilt is inferred from the misfortunes of Israel. As v. 9 shows, the Church is no more conscious of deliberate transgression than in Pss. vii. and xvii.

Note g, p. 228.

Delitzsch places our psalm (ix., x.) in the period which followed the transference of the ark to Mount Zion; 'to determine the situation more precisely is impossible.' He argues with much ability for the early origin of Hebrew alphabetic composition, but, as I think, disregards the evidence of facts. Hengstenberg thinks that there was no historical occasion for the psalm, and that David composed it to be used by the Church in a possible contingency. Forbes, too, sees that the psalm is altogether a liturgical one (*Studies*, p. 235). St. Chrysostom's commentary seems to me a complete though unconscious refutation of the Davidic theory; see e.g. his remarks on David's consummate 'philosophy' in v. 10 (A.V. 9); he compares xl. 18. Venema, alone among critics, refers the psalm to the Maccabæan period; the 'son' in the heading, he thinks, is Judas Maccabæus.

Note h, p. 228.

Prof. Abbott of Dublin has made a fresh attempt to restore the alphabetic arrangement where it is defective in the present text (see *Hermathena*, 1889, pp. 21–28).

Note i, p. 229.

Note the striking expression 'the word of thy lips' (xvii. 4) for the Law. Comp. the whole verse with Ps. cxix. 101, 104.

Note j, p. 229.

The Targum concludes the heading of Ps. vii. thus, 'concerning the destruction of Saul, the son of Kish, a Benjamite.' Hence Krochmal's correction as above. The liturgy for Purim contains this sentence on Haman, 'He was proud of his riches, and *digged a pit for himself*' (comp. Ps. vii. 16).

Note k, p. 230.

The introduction of the feast of Purim was opposed (Talm. Jer., *Megilla*, 70d). In the time of Josephus (*Ant.* xi. 6, 13) it was already generally observed even in the Diaspora. According to Grätz (*Geschichte*, iii. 1, p. 171) it was adopted in the interval between the composition of the two books of Maccabees (see above, p. 55).

NOTE ᵐ, p. 230.

'The enemy' (Ps. vii. 6) and the man who 'does not turn' (*v.* 13) were interpreted of 'Haman' (cf. Esther vii. 4, 6), whose just fate seemed to be alluded to in *vv.* 16, 17. Theodore of Mopsuestia did not venture to think of Haman, but made the best choice possible on the assumption of the Davidic authorship. The psalm, he says, according to his Syriac epitomator, was 'spoken by David when he heard that Ahithophel had hanged himself' (Baethgen, in Stade's *Zeitschrift*, 1885, p. 92). The writer must, however, really have meant the Persians and their leader, whose fate he anticipates. David, who 'played with lions as with kids' (Ecclus. xlvii. 3), is not the man to have written *v.* 3, and of course his mental horizon was as unlike as possible to that of our psalmist.

NOTE ⁿ, p. 230.

It was a custom of Oriental editors to join together hymns or fragments of hymns (see on Ps. xix.). Verse 13 is perhaps a link-verse to the two originally separate passages united in Ps. xl., introduced by the editor. This conjecture may or may not be accepted, but even Delitzsch admits that the composite origin of Ps. xl. is an obvious hypothesis, and will not venture to reject it.

NOTE º, p. 230.

Delitzsch argues from the singularity of this title that it must be based on tradition. Grätz thinks it worth while to hunt up a variant 'Ηναδὰβ, and correct 'Jonadab' into 'Henadad.' The 'sons of Henadad' were among the Levites who superintended the rebuilding of the temple (Ezra iii. 9, Neh. iii. 18). Thus he thinks that he gains an evidence for the exilic date of the psalm. Both critics assume that the Septuagint translator's Hebrew Psalter really gave a title for Ps. lxxi. The first part of the Greek heading ascribes the psalm to David—the aged David (*v.* 18), who will presently indite Ps. lxxii. as his dying prayer for Solomon !

NOTE ᵖ, p. 230.

Hitzig, *Begriff der Kritik* (1831), p. 71 ; cf. above, note ᵍᵍ, p. 134. Kuenen (*Onderzoek*, ed. 1, iii. 298) and Robertson Smith

(*The Old Testament in the Jewish Church*, p. 202) seem nearly convinced. Ewald agrees with Hitzig as to Ps. xxxi., but remarks with regard to xxxiv., xxxv., xl., li., lxix., lxxi., and others, 'These songs have a certain resemblance to Ps. xxxi., and something might be said for ascribing them also to Jeremiah. But this resemblance does not continue throughout. Besides, the opening of Ps. lxxi. is clearly an adaptation of Ps. xxxi.' Theodore of Mopsuestia virtually ascribes Ps. xxxv. to Jeremiah, in whose name he says that it was spoken by David (Baethgen, in Stade's *Zeitschrift*, 1885, p. 99).

NOTE q, p. 231.

Of these psalms the first is explained by Theodore of David's flight from Absalom, the second of the sufferings of Jeremiah, and the third of the troubles which led to the Maccabæan rising. Calvin gives up the hope of finding any particular occasion in David's life, at any rate, for the first and third. Dean Jackson (17th century) goes further, and doubts the Davidic authorship of Ps. xxii. (*Works*, viii. 138). And justly so, for if no scene in the life of this brave and bold king justifies such terrors and such complaints, how can we suppose, with any psychological propriety, that David was the author of the psalm? Against Hitzig's view, which assigns Ps. xxii. to Jeremiah, and Orelli's somewhat similar theory, see my Commentary, and cf. above, pp. 135, 136.

NOTE r, p. 231.

In the argument to this psalm Calvin says, 'Ita Psalmus duobus membris illud vaticinium explicat, *E carcere* &c.' He refers to Isa. liii. 8; cf. also Isa. xli. 14, xlix. 7, lii. 14, liii. 2, 3, and see the commentaries.

NOTE s, p. 232.

Of course, the psalmist's phraseology is modelled on Jer. xi. 20; in their deepest trouble, both he and Nehemiah would remember their Scriptures. In interpreting the difficult passage of Nehemiah, one may either follow Ryssel, who quotes עָלֶיךָ יַעֲזֹב (Ps. x. 14), 'on thee (the helpless) leaves all,' as Kay renders, or better Stade, who corrects לָהֶם (on the analogy of 2 Sam. iii. 13, Hos. xiii. 2). Sanballat in Neh. iv. 2 continues, 'Will they sacrifice? Will they make an end in a day?' As if the Jews thought that by trusting in Jehovah and propitiating Him by sacrifices they could expect to make the work fly.

NOTE ᵗ, p. 232.

Among the phraseological indications of date in Ps. xxxv., note the parallelism between *v.* 10 (copied in lxxi. 19) and lxxxvi. 8. 'Who is like God' (Michael) is the great thought of the Church-nation; and the proof of the uniqueness of Jehovah is the deliverance of 'the poor' (i.e., Israel: Heb. *'ānī*) from 'a stronger than he' (i.e., a foreign oppressor); cf. Ps. lxviii. 5–7, cxlvi. 5–9.

NOTE ᵘ, p. 233.

Ps. xxxi. can only be used with reserve, for the reason mentioned above.

NOTE ᵛ, p. 233.

Ps. lxii. 12, 13 reminds us of an Elihu-passage (Job xxxiii. 14–16). That the Elihu-speeches are a late, and indeed a post-Exile addition to the poem of Job, will by more and more critics be regarded as certain.

NOTE ʷ, p. 233.

Ps. lxxxix. ('Ethanite') belongs to the same guild of singers as Ps. xxxix., 'Jeduthun' being an incorrect substitute for 'Ethan,' cf. 1 Chron. ix. 16, xxv. 1, 6, 2 Chron. v. 12, xxxv. 15, Neh. xi. 17. The third 'Jeduthunite' psalm is lxxvii.

NOTE ˣ, p. 233.

(Ps. xli.) How untenable the theory of Davidic authorship is upon the exegetical data! 'Oh that his name might perish,' say the enemies of the speaker (xli. 6) i.e., 'Oh that his posterity might be cut off' (see cix. 13). Who were the malicious friends and neighbours of David who entertained this wish? But of course the date of this psalm depends on that of others, especially of Ps. lv. The opening verses (*vv.* 2–4) seem to have been added by the framer of the collection to adapt the poem to the use of the Church in his own time. The original opening must have been different.

NOTE ʸ, p. 234.

בשׂר εὐαγγελίζεσθαι (Sept.) only occurs thrice in the Psalter (xl. 10, lxviii. 12, and xcvi. 2); in 2 Isaiah, it occurs seven times.

Note ᶻ, p. 234.

On 'thy marvels' (xl. 6), Apollinarius compares Isa. xxv. 1 (a striking parallel to those who can see the late date of the prophecy).

Note ᵃᵃ, p. 234.

There is a doubt whether the heading indicates the original occasion of the psalm or simply the liturgical use which was made of it. I prefer the latter view (cf. the heading of Ps. xcii.); 'house'= 'temple.' That Ps. xxx. was anciently the proper psalm for the Hanukka festival is certain (see *Soferim*, xviii. 2, with Joel Müller's note). Delitzsch on the other hand (following Ibn Ezra) gives as the occasion of this psalm and Ps. xvi. a supposed illness of David, which threatened to postpone the 'dedication of the house' (=palace). I have already been forced to reject this theory (see above, p. 216, note ᶻ), which equally with that of Calvin (that the psalm refers to David's re-dedication of his palace after the death of Absalom) obscures the true exegesis of the contents. Indeed, it is only to save the accuracy of the *second* title, *l'dāvīd*, that such theories are put forward.

Note ᵇᵇ, p. 234.

This argument, I know, is not conclusive. The *khasīdīm* were only accidentally warriors, and gladly withdrew from the tumult of the field. But it has a subsidiary value.

Note ᶜᶜ, p. 234.

Lagarde, on the ground of the title, holds Ps. xxx. to have been written for the original dedication of the second temple under Darius I. (*Mittheilungen*, ii. 378). Hitzig, as might be expected, maintains Jeremiah's authorship, interpreting the imagery realistically (comp. Jer. xxxvii., xxxviii.), and also indicating points of contact in expression between our psalm and Jeremiah (*v*. 3*b*, cf. Jer. xvii. 14; *v*. 12*a*, cf. Jer. xxxi. 13; these are the best). More useful is his remark that Ps. xxxi. seems to allude to Ps. xxx. (*v*. 7*a*, cf. xxxi. 23; Delitzsch adds *v*. 5*a*, cf. xxxi. 24*a*). Kuenen in 1865 dated our psalm within 100 years after Hezekiah's death, on account of the similarity of the last half to the Song of Hezekiah (*Hist.-krit. Onderzoek*, iii. 298). But it is the Song which imitates (see *Isaiah*, i. 228, 229). The Song is probably post-Exile, as Ps. vi.

Note dd, p. 234.

See for the parallelisms, *Job and Solomon*, p. 88. G. H. B. Wright remarks (*Book of Job*, 1883, pp. 239–240),—'Thus the author of Job selects the main threads from the complete treatise of Ps. xxxvii., and interweaves them into the highly poetical discourse of Eliphaz.'

Note ee, p. 235.

The position of Ps. xxv. was probably suggested by the phrase in *v.* 1 (with which comp. xxiv. 4*b*); that of Ps. xxxiv. in relation to Ps. xxxiii. needs no comment.

Note ff, p. 235.

'Those who fear him' are the Jewish Church, as ciii. 11, 13, 17. Round about them Jehovah encamps (cf. Zech. ix. 8); his representative is the 'angel of Jehovah,' i.e., either the 'prince of Jehovah's host' (Josh. v. 14, a late passage, see Kuenen), 'the angel of his face' (Isa. lxiii. 9), or any one of the angelic host whom God may send. 'This poor man,' however, is not Israel personified (cf. Ps. xxii. 25), but each faithful Israelite. The heading may be explained like that of Ps. lii. and its fellows.

Note gg, p. 235.

I have refrained above from quoting Pedahel and Pedahzur, which occur in the priestly code (Num. i. 10, ii. 20, xxxiv. 28), because it is obvious that such names would, if genuine, be highly appropriate for the age of Exodus. But I may observe that they are equally appropriate for the post-Exile period, to which the priestly code most probably belongs, and that El and Zur (*çūr* 'rock') occur as divine appellations in psalms which we have recognized as post-Exile.—For an ingenious but too bold conjecture of Lagarde's, see my Commentary, p. 71 (on Ps. xxv.). It would be strange, as Perowne remarks, that the only two names of psalmists which have (*ex hyp.*) in such a very singular way been preserved, should both be compounds of *pādāh*.

Note hh, p. 235.

Theodore of Mopsuestia explained Ps. xxxii. of the pious Hezekiah. That is at least plausible; *v.* 6 might allude to the Assyrian invasion (cf. Isa. viii. 7, 8). Pss. xxviii. and xli. are explained by Theodore of the same period. The heading in Pesh. (Walton) makes David speak of the sin of Adam. That too might pass, if Adam be a symbolic representative of mankind.

NOTE ii, p. 236.

Comp. below. It is splendid audacity to infer from such psalms as this the gradual appearance of a prophetic spirit in David (Ewald, *History*, iii. 197).

NOTE jj, p. 236.

Notice especially the contrite tone and the idea of God as an educator, both of which are characteristic of the post-Exile author of the speeches of Elihu (Job xxxiii. 14-30).

NOTE kk, p. 236.

I lay no stress on this fact. Ewald and Delitzsch admit the reference to Lev. v. 4, but are not hindered by this from ascribing the psalm to David, and represent Isa. xxxiii. 13-16 as a variation upon the same theme. How improbable both views are need hardly be said. David's poetic style was not didactic, and Isaiah is not likely to have copied from a work so much below his own poetical standard. At all ages the ideas of the psalm needed to be enforced, and not least after the Return (see Zech. vii. 9, 10, viii. 16, 17, and cf. Ps. ci.). Hitzig, who ascribes Ps. xv. to David, makes no such claim for Ps. xxiv. 1-6. I wonder that he did not ascribe the former to Ezra; that would have been at least plausible.

NOTE ll, p. 237.

See Stade, *Zeitschr. f. d. alttest. Wiss.*, 1884, pp. 256-271; Guthe, *Das Zukunftsbild des Jesaia* (1885), p. 44; Kuenen, *Hist. krit. Onderzoek*, ed. 2, part ii. (1889), pp. 84-88; and cf. my own commentary. Kuenen differs from his predecessors in attaching all the three sections, Isa. xxxii. 1-8, xxxii. 9-20, and xxxiii. to the late pre-Exile period (reign of Josiah). I should myself refer at any rate the first and third to the period when Pss. ii., xlvi., and xlviii. were written. The points of contact are obvious. The subject well deserves renewed investigation. [Dillmann's treatment of Isa. xxxii., xxxiii., in his recent commentary deserves careful attention. He has made some progress, but hardly enough, beyond Ewald. Perhaps, if I may speak freely of the greatest member of the school of Ewald, he is kept back by his conservatism on other points, e.g. on the dates of the psalms.]

NOTE mm, p. 237.

Or, if this be preferred, of some leader of the Church. Only it must be remembered that the whole Church is to sing it. Jeremiah, therefore, to whom Hitzig seems half inclined to ascribe Ps. xxvii., will not do, even if we were to allow that one or another psalm might conceivably have proceeded from his pen. Cf., however, Ball, *Jeremiah*, p. 11.

NOTE ⁿⁿ, p. 237.

I have not pressed the argument against the Davidic authorship derived from the reference to the 'house of Jehovah' (Ps. xxiii. 6), though I do not myself see how 'dwelling in the house of Jehovah' can mean merely 'being once more (spiritually) at home in the tabernacle' (see Delitzsch's introduction to this psalm). For it must be granted that 'house' (בַּיִת) might conceivably denote the so-called tabernacle, just as *bait* in Arabic may be used of a tent. The argument from ideas and from phraseology seems to me however absolutely decisive; comp., among other parallels, *vv.* 2*b*, 3*b* with xxxi. 4, and *v.* 5 with xvi. 5, xxii. 26, xxxi. 20. Hitzig thinks that the plain style and transparence of expression force us to bring down the psalm to the seventh century, and that it may therefore possibly proceed from Jeremiah, to whose spiritual character it corresponds, and who, he thinks, when cast out by his family, found refuge in the temple (cf. Pss. xxiii. 6, xxvii. 5, Jer. xii. 6, xxxvi. 26). I confess that Jeremiah does not strike me as having been endowed with such a happy nature as every line of this psalm reveals. Mr. Ball, however, adopts Hitzig's suggestion (*Jeremiah*, vol. i., p. 10).

NOTE ᵒᵒ, p. 237.

I agree with Delitzsch (article in Luthardt's *Zeitschrift*, 1882, p. 118, cf. *Genesis*, 1887, p. 8) against Kautzsch (*Studien und Kritiken*, 1889, p. 383) that the expressions of Ps. xix. 8-15 are too lofty to refer merely to the Decalogue.

NOTE ᵖᵖ, p. 237.

Note that Ex. xxi. begins, 'And these are the *judgments*;' cf. Ps. xix. 10*b*, but also Deut. v. 1, 28, vi. 1 &c.

NOTE ᵠᵠ, p. 238.

Note 'Jehovah's ordinances' in xviii. 33; and xix. 10, and His 'well-tried promise' in *v.* 31, cf. xix. 10*a*. Probably the collector of the temple Songbook noticed these coincidences, and by them, and by the parallelism between 'thy servant' (xix. 14) and 'the Servant of Jehovah' in xviii. 1 (title), was led to place these two psalms side by side.

Note rr, p. 238.

It is difficult to see how these verses can be a lamentation over 'the obscurity of the light and want of life-inspiring energy to be found in the law' (Forbes, *Studies in the Book of Psalms*, p. 254).

Note ss, p. 238.

The horizon of the poet is different indeed from that of the historical David, to whom Dr. Perowne (comparing 2 Sam. x. 6, referred to already by Delitzsch) assigns it. It is not less arbitrary to make Solomon in his early days the author of the psalm (so Ewald, rendering in *v.* 6 'I have anointed my king'). Grätz prefers Hezekiah (cf. 2 Kings xviii. 8). This is at any rate more plausible. 'My holy mountain' implies that the temple had long been the centre of worship. The other Zion-psalms are all later than Hezekiah, and Ps. ii. is based upon 2 Sam. vii., which cannot be pre-Hezekian, and was written probably, like Ps. xviii., in the last happy days of the reign of Josiah (see p. 128). Kuenen, I am glad to find, accepts this date for 2 Sam. vii. See his *Onderzoek*, ed. 2, i. 377.

Note tt, p. 238.

For the Egyptian and Assyrian analogies, see my note on Ps. ii. 7. To these analogies add Nebuchadrezzar's phrase for Marduk, *ilu bāniya*, 'the God my begetter (creator),' and the Phœnician and Aramæan names in W. R. Smith, *The Religion of the Semites*, pp. 45, 46. The Homeric Greek analogies are well known.

Note uu, p. 238.

Rudinger assigns Ps. ii. to the age of the Seleucidæ; Hitzig makes even later (see on Ps. i.).

Note vv, p. 238.

Comp. *v.* 1 with lxxxiii. 3,
   v. 2 ,, ,, 4, 6*a*,
   v. 5 ,, ,, 18*a*.
Also *vv.* 1, 2 (nations, kings) with cx. 5,
   v. 7 with cx. 1*a* (see note),
   v. 9 with cx. 5, 6.

Note ww, p. 239.

Both in Ps. ii. 3 and Ps. lxxxiii. 5 the enemies of Israel express the objects of their enterprize in impassioned words. But the difference in the respective objects is significant.

Note xx, p. 339.

See my commentary, and as a parallel to Ps. ii. 5a add Zech. ix. 10, 'he shall speak peace to the (hostile) nations.' The Talmud makes the psalm refer to the destructive war to be waged by the nations Gog and Magog in the time of the Messiah. See the acute contrast drawn between Pss. ii. and iii. in *Talm. Bab., Berachoth,* 7b (Wünsche, *Der bab. Talmud,* i. 21), and cf. *Aboda zara,* 5a.

Note yy, p. 239.

Cf. מלכי ארץ . . . נוסדו; xlvi. 7; המו גוים, with ii. 2, רגשו גוים (Sept., Targ. נועדו) ii. 2, with המלכים נועדו, xlviii. 5; יבהלמו, ii. 5, with נבהלו, xlviii. 6.

Note zz, p. 239.

In the prophecy of Nathan the divine fatherhood is referred to in connexion with Solomon; in Ps. ii. (possibly) in connexion with David. In the former, the phrase 'to be a son to Jehovah' is used metaphorically of the beneficent moral discipline which the king will receive from Jehovah; in the latter, the words 'Thou art my son' are the formula by which the person addressed is inducted into the office of God's viceroy. In the former, divine sonship is a special privilege of Solomon; in the latter, if we compare Ps. lxxxix. 28, it is common to the king spoken of with all the other kings of the earth.

Note aaa, p. 239.

There is therefore substantial truth in the application, which is as old as the Psalms of Solomon (xvii. 26), of Ps. ii. to the Messiah. Mark i. 11 implies the combination of Ps. ii. 7 with Isa. xlii. 1. On the other New Testament references, see Delitzsch's introduction (*The Psalms,* by Eaton, i. 118, 119). On the similar later Jewish applications see Pick, *Hebraica,* Apr. 1886, p. 129, and add to his references *Succa,* 52a (Wünsche, *Der bab. Talmud,* i. 400).

Note bbb, p. 240.

Breviar. 3, quoted by Lagarde (*Novæ Psalt. Græc. Ed. Spec.*, p. 11). The ancient Celtic expositor Columbanus mentions a theory that the 'happy man' was Jehoash, king of Judah, but only to refute it (see Prof. Stokes in *Expositor*, 1889 (2), pp. 142-3). Nicolaus de Lyra (†1340) ascribed Ps. i. to Ezra, while Hermann von der Hardt, according to Carpzov, found some following for his opinion that *vv.* 1-3 referred to the family of Zerubbabel, and *vv.* 4, 5 to that of Joshua the high priest. Perowne goes even further, and names the author, viz. Solomon, who, 'as appears probable, made a collection of his father's poetry for the service of the temple.' The somewhat proverbial style of the psalm and its general doctrine (compared with that of the 'Solomonic' proverbs) seem to him to confirm this view. Hengstenberg assigns both Ps. i. and Ps. ii. to David; Hitzig to Alexander Jannæus.

Note ccc, p. 240.

The psalmist has expressed the new detail (see *v.* 2, and cf. Josh. i. 8) in language borrowed from a portion of the Book of Joshua (chaps. i.-xii.), which critical analysis has proved to belong to the closing years of the kingdom of Judah.

Note ddd, p. 240.

לֵצִים 'scoffers' occurs nowhere else in the Psalter (cf. *Job and Solomon*, p. 120, note ³). Sept. gives λοιμοί (cf. Sept. Prov. xix. 25, xxi. 24, xxii. 10, xxiv. 9), a class-name which still survives in 1 Macc. x. 61 (parallel to παράνομοι), xv. 3, 21.

Note eee, p. 240.

Wherever *tōrāh* occurs (Prov. xiii. 14, xxviii. 4, 7, 9, xxix. 18), it simply means moral or religious precept or direction.

Note fff, p. 241.

Ecclus. xiv. 20, 21 is evidently based on Ps. i. 2.

Note ggg, p. 241.

One result of uniting the two psalms was to make the total number of the psalms that of the years of the patriarch Jacob (147). To the references for the combination of the psalms in *Comm.*, p. 1, add *Megilla*, 17*b* (Wünsche, *Der bab. Talmud*, i. 531), where the position of the ninth of the eighteen Benedictions is explained by a reference to Ps. x. (*v.* 15), which 'David spoke in the ninth place.' See also the exhaustive collection of ancient evidence in Lagarde *Novæ Psalterii Græci Editionis Specimen* (1887), pp. 16–18, noticing the corrected form of some lines of Apollinarius,

Ἐπιγραφῆς ὁ ψαλμὸς εὑρέθη δίχα,
Ἡνώμενος δὲ τοῖς παρ' Ἑβραίοις στίχοις·
Ἄλλως δ' ἐδευτέρευσε Δαβίδου κρότους,
Ἐπεὶ παρ' αὐτοῖς ἔννατος τμᾶται δίχα.

NOTE hhh, p. 241.

It is, I believe, the great future Messianic judgment (using the word 'Messianic' in a general sense) which is meant in Ps. i. 5.

LECTURE VI.

Where is he that put his holy spirit in the midst of them?—
Isa. lxiii. 11 (R.V.).

LECTURE VI.

PART I.—Transition to the theological part of these lectures. Reply to modern Gregories of Nyssa. The critical result from which we start—that the Psalter is a religious monument of the Jewish Church - is confirmed by a sound exegesis. The personification theory in the Psalter. Early Jewish and Christian anticipations of it. The Church felt that it ministered to one of her most sacred instincts. An insecure theological basis. The objection, 'But did not the psalmists prophesy of Christ?' considered, and the latest form of the old Messianic theory (that of Delitzsch) criticized. True significance of the New Testament quotations from the Psalter. Psychology of the life of Jesus. Superficial treatment of the personification theory deprecated. Its application illustrated from the Greek choruses and the Old Testament. The difficulties of applying it in the Psalter cannot be greater than in the Second Isaiah. The 'Servant' passages; necessity of a consistent interpretation. The analogy which Isa. liii. furnishes for the explanation of Ps. xxii. Happy result of recognizing the voice of the community both here and elsewhere in the Psalter. The theory must not, however, be pressed to the extent of denying all personal references. Special characteristics of Books IV. and V. as compared with Books I.-III. The Christian doctrine of the Church anticipated.—But, granting that the Psalter is a Church record, can we still look up to it as a religious classic? Does its religion possess originality? for all the psalms, except the 18th, are post-Exile, and during both the Exile and the post-Exile period the Jews were in contact with highly-developed religions. Discussion of the probable extent of Babylonian and Persian religious influence upon the Jews (excluding for the present the Resurrection belief). There was a precedent for a cautiously-liberal policy in the Yahvistic story. That this policy was continued we see from the later literature (Gen. xiv., the Priestly Narrative, and the Book of Job). No important novel beliefs were borrowed (in pre-Maccabæan post-Exile times). But where the same or analogous beliefs existed in Israel and among the Babylonians or the Persians, the development of these must have been helped forward in Israel by its contact with born adherents of the other religion. The lofty mysticism of the Psalms, however, is neither of Persian nor of Babylonian origin (cf. Lect. VIII.).

PART II.—The 'theology' of the Psalter. Anthropomorphisms of the psalmists no proof of barbarism. Childlike symbols, not even yet fully outgrown, but not all equally admirable. John Hyrcanus's criticism of Ps. xliv. 24. Evidences in the Levitical psalms as edited, and in Job and other books, of a disinclination to use the divine name Yahveh. How far should we endorse these criticisms? Certainly not so far as to give up the name which we commonly pronounce Jehovah. It seems that we use the substituted name 'the Lord' too frequently. 'Jehovah,' rightly interpreted, is a creed in a nutshell, and contains the answer to our question, Who is the God of the psalmists? True, the psalmists did not all rise to the highest conception of Jehovah, especially with regard to

His relation to the heathen. Their works present two mutually exclusive ideals of the Servant of Jehovah, the one supported by the only pre-Exile psalm (the 18th), the other by the Second Isaiah (who recasts a passage of Ps. xviii. in a new spirit). The inconsistency, however, is not complete, and, so far as it is real, can be psychologically explained, and paralleled from the Iranian Scriptures. Dr. Drummond quoted in excuse of the harshness of later Jewish writers towards the heathen. But can we exonerate the Jews for having made so little effort to warn the nations of their danger? How far has Israel recognized its function as the prophet-people? At first sight not at all. But as we look more closely we see indications in Isa. lvi. 1-8, in the Book of Jonah, and in Ps. xxii. 24, that even in the Persian period there were some Jewish preachers of true religion and some who gave ear to them among the nations. In the Hellenistic period there are clear evidences of a turning of the heart of the Jew to that of the Gentile. References to Sirach, to Daniel, to the psalms of this period (including even the Maccabæan psalms), and to the Maccabæan history. The 'duality' of later Judaism already conspicuously marked.

PRINCIPAL NOTES.—PART I.: Modifications of view on the 'Servant of Jehovah,' and on the apologetic use of the Psalms.—Babylonian influence on the Jehovist (Yahvist).—Nebuchadrezzar, Cyrus, and Darius compared.—Persian influence on Jewish beliefs.—Views of critics on Zoroastrian theism.

PART II.: The meaning of the divine name Adonai, and the growing preference of the Jews for it.—The divine fatherhood.

PART I.

THE RELIGIOUS IDEAS OF THE PSALTER NOT BORROWED.

IN the preceding lectures I have attempted by the use of the comparative method to throw some fresh light on the dates of the psalms. It is more than possible, however, that some hearers have inwardly uttered the judgment of Gregory of Nyssa,[1] that 'He who by means of them (the Psalms) "fashioneth our hearts," careth not for these things.' To me this appears a dangerous misunderstanding of the historical character of our religion, and of the tender regard which the Divine Spirit ever pays to the laws of mental development. And to the authority of Gregory I may oppose that of two vastly greater interpreters, Theodore of Mopsuestia and his friend Chrysostom, who were the first to set an example— though but on a small scale—of the hallowing of criticism. Should any one still ask, What has the historical origin of the Psalter to do with the defence of Christian truth? I need only reply, How could we possibly use the Book of Psalms as a record of Church theology until we had critically proved that it belonged to the period of the Jewish Church? Now that this proof has been given (the 18th being, as it would seem, the only possible pre-Exile psalm—and even this late enough to be called in a certain sense a Church composition), we can venture to say that it is the consciousness of the Church, or of some leading members of the Church, which finds a voice in every part of the Psalter.

This dictum is, in my opinion, confirmed by a sound critical exegesis. It can be shown that in most cases, even when the psalmist uses the first person singular, the speaker is really either the Church or a typical pious Israelite. This

---

[1] *Commentarius duplex in Psalmos* (Ingolstadt, 1600), p. 196.

is sometimes represented as a very modern theory; it was not, however, by any means unknown to the ancient interpreters. Among the rabbis, Rashi, the exponent of tradition, is its chief supporter; but the germs of it are to be found in the Targum and even in the Septuagint.[a] From the Synagogue it passed to the Christian Church, where it found a congenial home. The Old Testament Scriptures, being at first the only religious authority besides the words of Christ, and even afterwards retaining an equal importance with the purely Christian Scriptures, had to be Christianized, both for the purpose of edification and for that of the defence of the faith. Hence the Saviour of the world was regarded as not only the goal but the centre of the Hebrew Scriptures, and since the union of Christ and the Church was a leading Christian idea, to say that a psalm was spoken by Christ was equivalent to declaring it to be, at least in parts, a prayer of the Church. St. Augustine, who so long reigned supreme in the exegesis of the psalms, says that 'Christ is the whole Body of Christ; and whatsoever good Christians that now are, and that have been before us, and that after us are to be, are an whole Christ.' And again: 'Scarce is it possible in the Psalms to find any voices but those of Christ and the Church, or of Christ only, or of the Church only.'[b] It was only indirectly and unconsciously, however, that the personification theory was for the most part applied. Bound by the titles of the psalms in the Hebrew and Greek Bibles, the Church expositors, following the earliest writers, were compelled to assume the Davidic authorship of more than half the psalms. How then could the Christian instinct be justified and David be proved to have spoken of Christ and His Church? Only by the consistent application of the principle that the psalmists spoke 'by the Spirit,' i.e. were prophets or foretellers. He 'on whose head are many crowns' (Rev. xix. 12) must have this glory among the rest, that before His coming He, as it were, absorbed the personalities of the psalmists into His own. Hence all that is too extravagant in expression for himself the prophet David wrote, or was bidden to write, for his unseen Lord, and for that Church in which the incarnation of the Word was to be, so to speak, prolonged.

I am bound in honesty to say that the theological doctrine of the union of Christ and His Church is a very insecure basis for the personification theory. If the psalmists did not, in the strictest sense of the word, prophesy of Christ, how can they have prophesied of the Church? But did they not prophesy of Christ? Has not the greatest of living interpreters, of whom the present lecturer has repeatedly expressed his admiration,[1] arrived at the conclusion that they did? To postpone my answer to the question, Did not the psalmists prophesy of Christ? would hamper the subsequent course of these lectures. Let me then, with all gentleness, touch on the logical inconsistency from which even this father of the modern Church has not escaped. No one has more distinctly accepted the psychological method of exegesis than Franz Delitzsch; but has he been faithful to it in dealing with the so-called Messianic psalms? Can we be satisfied with his slight modernization of the typical theory of the Bishop of Mopsuestia? Listen to this sentence: 'David is aware in all his psalms that his destiny, and that of his enemies, stand, according to the divine decree, in causal connexion with the final result of human history, and prophesies concerning the Messiah, not as an objective person of the future, but as represented by himself, since he regards himself *sub specie Christi.*'[2] No less a man than Hengstenberg long ago pronounced similar views unpsychological. How does Delitzsch meet the objection? He thinks it enough to identify the mystery of the consciousness of David with the mystery of all poetry. 'The genuine lyric poet does not,' he says, 'give a mere copy of the impressions of his empirical Ego.'[3] Most true. It is the mystery of human life, recognized not less by Browning the poet than by Kant the philosopher—

> God be thanked, the meanest of His creatures
> Boasts two soul-sides.

But, we may ask, would not the two soul-sides be seen to be related if we knew them? And, granting that David, like other poets, might idealize himself, how could he work into

---

[1] Last of all in my *In Memoriam* sketch in *The Guardian*, April 9, 1890.
[2] *Messianic Prophecy*, by Curtiss, p. 47; cf. Hengstenberg, *The Psalms*, i. 363.
[3] *The Psalms*, by Eaton, i. 93.

his poetry thoughts and experiences which had no root in his own inner and outer life?

Could Delitzsch only have seen his way to assign more of his Messianic psalms to Jeremiah, he might have somewhat strengthened his position; for the inner and outer life of Jeremiah has obviously more affinity to that of our Lord than David's has. Of course I do not blame Delitzsch, whose poetic taste rebelled against the realistic interpretations of Hitzig. Nor do I, in rejecting the old Messianic theory even in its latest form, mean in the least to disparage the quotations from the Psalter in the New Testament. We are all conscious sometimes of moods when the past is nearer to us than the present, and when such quotations, imaginatively viewed, suggest a 'pre-established harmony' between sacred poetry and not less sacred facts.[c] The New Testament applications of the Psalter may not indeed be proofs either of doctrine or of facts, but they do prove the transforming power of the Gospel, which could turn the valley of Baca into a place of fountains, and they suggest deep speculative trains of thought. And in following up these suggestions, we shall find out another and still closer connexion between Christ and the Psalter. If, as we may justifiably hold, the history of Israel is a preparation for the Advent, its religious literature, which is so closely related to that history, must partake of this character. The devout musings and anticipations of the noblest Israelites embodied in the psalms must have helped to produce the spiritual atmosphere in which alone the Messiah could draw His breath. The Scriptures, and not least the Psalter, must have contributed to form His chosen ones for the Christ, and the Christ for His chosen.

But I must forbear to dilate on this high theme, which belongs, if I may say so, to the psychology of the life of Jesus. There *is* a connexion between the true Messiah and the Psalter, but it is not one that explains the seeming extravagances of the psalmists. And if my readers persist in seeking an explanation of such expressions, they need ask for no better one than this, that the psalmists speak in general, not as individuals but in the name of the Church-nation. We are, in short, driven by the necessities of scientific exegesis to a large extension of the personification theory.

I venture to lay so much stress on this theory because it has hitherto received a somewhat superficial consideration. I am myself not free from blame, for it is only within the last ten years that I have at all adequately recognized its claims. Strange that it should be so uncongenial to English students, whose road to Jerusalem begins at Athens, and who know alike their Sophocles and their Isaiah. Take almost any of those choruses, snatches of which soothed the last moments of that noble type of the old Oxford theologian Bishop Moberly —that fine one, for instance, in the 'Œdipus at Colonus,' which contains the words—

> I know not, but my mind
> Presageth me that soon
> The spoiler shall give back
> The maiden sorely tried, sorely by kinsman vexed.
> To-day, to-day, some great thing Zeus shall do :
> I prophesy the triumph of the right.
> Oh that I were a dove, that I might wing the wind
> With pinion swift and strong,
> And from some airy pinnacle of cloud
> Content mine eyes with gazing on the fray.[d]

Can there be any doubt as to the best explanation of this passage? Is it not the chorus personified which is the speaker? And then turn to the work of the great poet-prophet, called the Second Isaiah. What theological student questions that the 'Servant of Jehovah,' who again and again here speaks or is spoken of, is in some sense the people of Israel? For what right have we to apply different theories in the explanation of closely related passages? It is frequently obvious at first sight that the reference is either to the people of Israel or to the Church within the people.[1] How, then, can we doubt that somehow or other the meaning is the same in the other passages? I admit that it is often found difficult to satisfy the student that this is the case. There is a felt want of a connecting link between the two classes of passages derived from the spiritual furniture of Jewish minds. True ; but has not the missing link been discovered? Have we not by this time learned that the Jews, equally with their neighbours, believed in the supersensible existence of ideals (see

---

[1] *The Prophecies of Isaiah*, ed. 3, ii. 214.

Dan. vii. 13), such as Wisdom, Israel, Jerusalem, which could from time to time become visible? If so, it becomes at once plain that even in that strikingly individualistic description, Isa. lii. 13–liii. 12, the writer may refer to the people of Israel, the heavenly ideal of which, 'formed' (Isa. xliv. 21) from eternity by Jehovah, is personalized by vivid imagination.[e]

Now, if the difficulties in the application of this theory have been overcome in the Second Isaiah, why should they much longer prove obstinate in the Psalter? Let us then courageously face them. In those parts of the Psalter which sound most distinctly individualistic let us recognize the voice sometimes of the suffering and sin-conscious or jubilant and forgiven people of Israel, sometimes of the self-forgetting poet, who accepts his share of the experiences of his people. And as for that difficult psalm, the 22nd, let us place it beside Isa. liii., and explain it accordingly of the Genius of Israel as embodied either in those prophetic teachers in whom, to the eye of faith, it preached and suffered and, in spite of appearances, overcame, or in an individual Israelite, the flower of his race, whom the writer conceives so vividly that he anticipates the future and represents as a historical personage. Which of these alternatives is to be preferred for Ps. xxii.? The second is naturally delightful to a Christian, but is there any analogy for it in the Psalter? The answer is Yes, at least to a certain extent, if in Ps. ii. the poet projects himself into the still future Messianic age; but No, if you agree with me that the psalm *Quare fremuerunt* is rather an idealization of the long-past Davidic age.[f] In the latter case, this is the position which you must, I think, take up. The complaints of Ps. xxii. are uttered by the faithful of Jerusalem, who are the kernel of the restored nation, and in whom the Genius of Israel is most adequately represented. They are not indeed perfect (comp. Ps. lxix.), but the Genius which inspires them *is* perfect, and it is in virtue of this that they will prevail; ἐν τούτῳ νίκα. For a time they are persecuted, and Israel, as Jehovah's Servant, seems at death's door. Their sufferings are intensified by the thought that Israel was created to make known God's name to the nations, and that His work therefore is cut short and His kingdom delayed. But while the speaker prays the assurance comes to him (*v.* 22) that salvation is at hand, and that his wonderful deliverance will supply him with a potent argument in his missionary preaching. In *vv.* 23 and 26 the personality of the psalmist is for a moment visible; but elsewhere it is the personalized Genius of Israel who speaks, or more precisely the followers of Nehemiah, including the large-hearted psalmist. For no mere genius in the modern sense can possibly be meant. The Jewish Church worshipped abstractions no more than the Christian. She could not indeed quite have said, 'I believe in Abraham,'[g] as the Christian says, 'I believe in Jesus Christ,' but the lives of spiritual heroes like Abraham, Moses, Jeremiah, had the effect of making the Genius of Israel objectively real to Israelitish hearts.

Many of my readers will, I think, notice how strongly the resemblance between Ps. xxii. 7 and Isa. xlix. 7, liii. 3, confirms the view that in Isa. liii. likewise it is the Genius of Israel as personified, not in one historic personage alone, but in the Israel κατὰ πνεῦμα which speaks. And they will perhaps readily accept the conjecture that to the author of Ps. xxii. the condition of the Jewish Church in his own time was partly foreshadowed in Isa. liii. 2–9, and that that passage with its context was the sacramental sign used by God for the revival of his faith.[h] Nor will it be denied that Pss. lxix. and cii., which are akin to Ps. xxii., are to be explained analogously, though the features of Israel's Genius are here less perfectly reproduced in the imagined speaker.[i]

To apply the nation-theory to the 22nd psalm is a severe test. In most cases we need not have recourse to the Genius of Israel: it is the actual struggling and sinning church-nation which is the speaker. But even in the case of Ps. xxii. I ask confidently, Has the interest of the psalm been lessened in the process? Surely not. Both here and everywhere the Psalter becomes more and not less human when regarded as the utterance of the nation.[k] We may perhaps have to confess with Bishop Alexander, that English church-poetry is 'fair, angel-fair, but frozen;'[1] but we cannot truthfully say so of Jewish, and we know the reason. The religious poetry of Israel was fervent, just because its writers spoke for the community, having absorbed that passionate love of God and

---

[1] *Poems*, p. 67.

country which glowed in each of its members. The Psalter (at any rate Books I.–III.) reminds one of that mystic eagle in Paradise, composed of interwoven ruby-souls, glowing with the rays of the divine sun, whose beak Dante heard 'utter with its voice both *I* and *My*, when in conception it was *We* and *Our.*'[1] Never were there such prayers and praises as those of Israel, precisely because in the psalmists as such the individual consciousness was all but lost in the corporate.[m] I say 'all but lost,' because it ought not to be denied that the personality of a psalmist does now and then start into view[n] (see p. 319). Indeed, I see no objection to recognizing in some psalms both a personal and a national reference; this appears to me to heighten the poetry and enrich the meaning, where the two references can be combined. But that there are many passages in which the person who speaks or is spoken of is simply and solely the nation,[o] is becoming evident, and if we read the rest of the Old Testament with this in our mind, we shall perhaps be surprised at the number of parallels which it presents.[p]

The Psalter then is a monument of Church-consciousness; exegesis fully confirms the voice of criticism. If this can be shown even from Books I.–III., still more easily can it from Books IV. and V., most of the psalms in which are self-evidently congregational utterances.[q] One might illustrate the combination of 'I-' and 'We-' psalms by parallels from the Greek choruses. But the phenomena of Books IV. and V. are perhaps best explained thus. The instinctive personification of the Church-people in the 'I'-psalms was a survival—an inheritance from antiquity. It was natural that later religious poets should begin to look upon their nation in a more modern light as an organization of individualities. They did not indeed go so far as those modern hymnists who have half filled the popular hymnals with lyrics of a strongly personal tone.[r] Rarely do the Hebrew psalmists disclose their personality. They had, indeed, their private joys and sorrows, but they did not make these the theme of song. The individual consciousness was not sufficiently developed for this, and so an unselfish religion was easier for them than it is for us. But the later 'We'-psalms, though not less national than

[1] *Paradise*, xix. 11, 12 (Longfellow).

the others, indicate a perception that, as Kingsley has said, 'communities are for the divine sake of individual life, for the sake of the love and truth that is in each heart, and is not cumulative—cannot be in two as one result.' And surely here is another anticipation of Christianity, if at least I rightly interpret Eph. iv. 12–16 as an exposition of the true doctrine of the Christian Church, which is personified in this passage as a constantly growing man ('the Israel of God,' Gal. vi. 16), not as a mere collective, but as the organic unity of the individual believing members. So that the highest doctrine of the Church in both Testaments gives us the reconciliation of the opposing theories of individualism and socialism.

I now pass on. Do not regard the preceding inquiry as a digression. Without it I could not have justified the use of the Psalter as a handbook of Church theology. To have shown that as a rule the psalms were written in the name of the church-nation, makes the Psalter equal in value to the great church-prophecy of the Second Isaiah. But we have now to ask, If, as we have seen, all the psalms except the 18th are post-Exile, can we still look up to the Psalter as not only a poetic, but a religious classic? Can we still depend upon the purity and originality of its ideas? For the so-called Captivity was no seclusion. It brought the exiles face to face with a higher and yet a kindred civilization, and a kindred and not in all respects a lower religion. Jeremiah himself had bidden his brethren in Babylon acclimatize themselves (Jer. xxix. 4–7), and it is certain that some departments of their life must have been profoundly affected by their new surroundings. If even Ezekiel received such a strong imaginative stimulus from Babylonian art, how much more must younger and more inquisitive minds have felt that inspiriting shock of strangeness, by which elsewhere such wondrous intellectual results have been produced. From one of these minds we have received the original part of the Book of Job—a poem too broadly human in its scope to owe much to any single teacher, but which has several mythic descriptions reminding us of Babylonia.[1] To others it has been sometimes held that we are indebted for those parts of the Genesis-narratives which approach most nearly to the parallel cuneiform

---

[1] See *Job and Solomon*, pp. 76–78.

narratives.¹ And if we admit that Chaldæan mythic stories have influenced the form of the Hebrew narratives, can we think it impossible that new forms of religious belief may have been adopted into the Jewish system on Babylonian soil?²

This is not a point to be decided offhand. The reception of the view to which I have just referred would involve some grave consequences. For even granting that the exiles thoroughly assimilated the new elements, what in this case becomes of the originality which has been thought to give a normative value to the religious teaching of the Old Testament? Can we still speak of the Israelites as in a special sense the chosen people? Does not their religion become somewhat dangerously composite, and if we still accept it as the basis of our own, must we not admit the Babylonians, and presently perhaps the Persians, to an absolute religious equality with the Israelites? I do not say that this result would be fatal to Christianity, but only that it would be serious for Christian theology. And yet we must not refuse to weigh certain facts and considerations which may seem to lead on to this very result. From of old Israel was a receptive nation. That Abraham learned from Accadian and Moses from Egyptian hymns, is, I presume, an uncritical fancy, but this question seems fair enough, Why, if the Canaanites could poison Israelitish religion, should not the Chaldæans have contributed to purify it? That there is an affinity between the later Hebrew and the best later Chaldæan religion is certain; and there may be a dim perception of this in that fine confession imaginatively ascribed to Nebuchadrezzar (Dan. iv. 31–33), which offended the narrow orthodoxy of a Talmudic doctor.³ I know that some have represented the Babylonian hymns as 'colourless, declamatory, and unspiritual,'⁴ and I suppose that Nebuchadrezzar's prayers would not be judged too favourably. But we must not let ourselves be carried away by Christian prejudice. Half the sympathy which we bring to the Psalter would reveal un-

---

¹ Friedr. Delitzsch, *Wo lag das Paradies?* p. 94; Haupt, *Der keilinschriftliche Sintfluthbericht*, p. 20; Sayce, *Theological Review*, 1873, pp. 375–377; cf. Goldziher, *Hebrew Mythology*, pp. 317–326.

² See Goldziher, *l.c.*; Sayce, *Hibbert Lectures*, pp. 39, 40.

suspected beauties in the much older sacred songs of Chaldæa. Nor can these beauties be explained as mere survivals from a primitive revelation, forms of speech from which all spiritual life has departed. 'What stirs us in these hymns is no reminiscence of ancient truths. . . . There were men behind those psalms who remembered—no things, but God, and when any man remembers God in the vital Biblical sense, God Himself is at hand.'[u] If the lost psalms of pre-Exile Hebrew poetry were equal in depth of feeling to the early Babylonian hymns, the psalmists had no cause to blush for their predecessors. These later poets, who shine like stars in the firmament, had entered into the labours of God's noblest interpreters. Had the teaching and purifying agency of the 'goodly fellowship of the prophets' been granted to Babylon, it is conceivable that its later hymns might have rivalled those of the Hebrew Psalter.

There was a time when everything Babylonian was overrated. We heard much of a Chaldæan Genesis, and of a divine personage Ilu, 'the god par excellence, the absolute god, who crowns the ladder of the divine hierarchy.' It is no disrespect to François Lenormant if we now take a somewhat more moderate view of Babylonian attainments. Certainly that lamented scholar seems to have exaggerated the monotheistic tendency in Babylon under Nebuchadrezzar.[1] An eminent authority assures us that it was never so strong in Babylonia as in Assyria;[2] it is, at any rate, certain that it was not less clearly marked in the latter. The god Assur was supreme among the gods, as his royal vicegerent was supreme among men. We even find an Assyrian name, Mannu-ki-ilu-rabu,[3] 'Who is like the great God?'—which reminds us of the monotheistic Hebrew name Michael. In the neo-Babylonian empire the priestly class had such an all-pervading influence that the supreme divine power was divided between two gods, Marduk (whose attributes marked him out as specially the royal god) and Nabû (who, as the god of revealed knowledge, was closely allied to the priestly order). But, as

---

[1] *La divination*, &c., pp. 214–216.
[2] Sayce, 'Polytheism in Primitive Israel,' *Jewish Quarterly Review*, ii. 32; cf. *Hibbert Lectures*, p. 122.
[3] Schrader, *Die ass.-bab. Keilinschriften*, p. 147.

these gods were father and son, it might be reasonably maintained that in the highest sense the unity of the supreme Godhead was unbroken. Hence Nebuchadrezzar, whose name placed him under the direct protection of Nabû, felt it no detriment to the divine monarchy to devote himself chiefly to the service of Marduk. Under this name especially the divine power and goodness were eulogized by him with a purity and depth of feeling which even Tiele finds worthy of the Hebrew psalmists.[v] It is, however, to the hymns that we must turn for a full account of the religious conceptions of the age of Nebuchadrezzar, for though mostly of very ancient date, they received the sanction of the later priests, by whom they were edited (p. 213), if necessary, in such a way as to suit a more advanced period. Do we find in these hymns any near approach to a moral conception of God as the ruler of the universe, all-powerful and all-wise, just and yet compassionate, to a moral view of sin, to a belief in the 'life everlasting'? We do; all these ideas are genuinely Babylonian. But it is also certain that the two former are characteristic of Jewish religion from the Exile onwards; the only doubt can be as to the time of the appearance of the third. Were they borrowed by the Jews from Babylon? There are some difficulties, distinct from those which I have mentioned already, in the way of an affirmative answer. For although these ideas are for the most part very clearly expressed by the Second Isaiah, yet this same prophet exults[w] over the expected fall of the very god who is specifically the god of resurrection (Isa. xlvi.), and utters a protest against Babylonian dualism (Isa. xlv. 7). And if we turn to the hymns of the post-Exile Church, we observe that when a kind reference is made to Babylon it is on the assumption that she steps from her throne and enters the federation of the new Israel (Ps. lxxxvii.). Can we suppose that the exiles themselves were more inclined to accept any vitally important religious novelties from Babylon?

The view that I am criticizing seems to me to ignore the principle of historical development. We ought never to assume that ideas of an advanced religion have been altogether borrowed, until we have done our best to discover any germs of them in the native religious literature. It has been shown by critical exegesis that the chief ideas of the later religion are germinally present in the earlier Hebrew writings. The only question is whether the germs are sufficient to account altogether for the later developments. In my opinion they are not; we may and must make some concessions to the new view. The Old Testament religion, unlike Islam, but like Christianity, is a religion of historical development. To a certain extent the authorities of the Jewish Church were not unwilling that their religion should be influenced from without. A precedent had been already set by one of the undoubtedly pre-Exile Hexateuchal writers :—I allude to the fact that the Yahvistic story, as we now have it, has been enriched from Babylonian traditions.[1] It was no small proof of moral stability, and of a higher spiritual guidance, that a wise and pious man, whose 'name is written in heaven,' could effect this without detriment to religion, and it must have encouraged the later church-authorities to continue the same cautiously liberal policy. The proof of this is apparent in the later Hebrew literature. Not only did the author of the Priestly Code (whom I venture at this point to refer to the early post-Exilic period) work up fresh material derived from Babylonian sources, while another learned writer did the same in that remarkable and unique passage Gen. xiv., but thinkers and poets (see the Book of Job) deliberately threw themselves into what may quite innocently be called a mythic revival. The leaders of the Church permitted this; they were content to moderate and turn to wholesome uses a tendency which they could not extinguish. Only where the fundamentals of religion were concerned they stood firm, and if we notice a parallelism even in these between Israel's religion and Babylon's, the coincidence proves, not that Israel borrowed from Babylon, but that the same Spirit of holiness had been training His disciples on the banks of the Euphrates and of the Jordan. But when fellow-disciples come together, may they not confirm each other in the truths which they hold in common? May we not reverently think that Israel was brought to Babylon partly at least to strengthen its hold on lately acquired truths, just as 'Magi from the East,' according to a Jewish-Christian tradition, were led by a star to Bethlehem to do willing homage to the infant Christ? And may I not add that Nebuchadrezzar and Darius, and their wise men, were not only, like Epimenides (Tit. i. 12), prophets relatively to heathendom, but also in some degree at least relatively to the central people of revelation?[1]

For you will readily admit that whatever 'excellent things are spoken' of Nebuchadrezzar belong also to Jehovah's other 'servants,' Cyrus the Great [y] and Darius—noble representatives of an ἔνθεον ἔθνος,[z] which could not, under favourable circumstances, help attracting the attention of the Israelites. A Magian rite is probably referred to in Ezek. viii. 17, though only as a superstitious usage adopted by heathenish Jews. Such evidence proves nothing as to the influence of genuine Mazdeism upon the higher Israelitish religion, and though the Second Isaiah betrays his sympathy with the religion of Cyrus, yet, as Babylon was not yet actually overthrown, we cannot suppose the religious influence of Persia upon Israel to have been thus far considerable.[aa] Sublime indeed are the confessions of faith in the inscriptions of the Achæmenian kings, and a description of the 'Lord Omniscient' (Ahura Mazda), the founder of the 'Righteous Order' (Asha), compiled from the Avesta, would be found to differ but little from those given of Jehovah by the Hebrew prophets and psalmists.[bb] And yet not even from Zarathustra and his nameless successors did the Second Isaiah derive his faith in the creatorship and all-wisdom of the Most High God. Nor can it be shown that that poetic masterpiece of the Exile, the Book of Job, presents any undoubtedly Iranian affinities. If anything there has been borrowed, it has been so Hebraized as to be undistinguishable from genuine Hebrew material.

Let us pass, then, to the period of the Return. Here we may expect to find traces of Persian influence, but also to find the Church-leaders refusing any belief which would affect the purity of Israelitish religion. Otherwise they would be less earnest than Zarathustra himself, by whom, as Mills remarks, 'no trifling with any form of evil, least of all with a foreign creed, was to be tolerated.' One of the earliest of the Jewish Benedictions, probably of pre-Maccabæan origin, contradicts a fundamental Persian doctrine, viz. the antithesis of the kingdoms of light and darkness, and whether or not we hold that the cosmo-

---

[1] The hostility of 2 Isaiah towards Babylon on the eve of restoration is not conclusive against this view.

gony in Gen. i. has been partly modelled on the Persian,[cc] we may agree that its tendency is opposed to all forms of dualism. It is only on such secondary points as the time of the first prayer,[dd] the number and personality of angels, and the existence of demons or evil spirits that we can imagine Jewish believers to have been directly and absolutely indebted to their new lords. To say that the lofty mysticism of the psalms is of Persian origin is only a few degrees less rash than to derive it from Babylonia.[ee] They may indeed present affinities to the most spiritual parts of Zoroastrianism (see Lect. VIII.), and even allude here and there to popular beliefs of partly Persian origin. But the spirit of the Psalter is as pure and original as that of the Gâthâs. The other Scriptures of the post-Exile period may not be all equally lofty, but in none of them does the purity of Israel's religion suffer any serious obscuration. That the guides of the Church-nation watched over this, and in the performance of their task looked up to Him who had 'placed his holy spirit within' his people,[1] cannot be doubted. And it is because the psalmists evidently claim to rank among these spiritual guides that they speak at times in the authoritative language of the prophets[ff] as the appointed representatives of the prophetically gifted 'Servant of Jehovah.'

NOTE [a], p. 259.

See the titles of Pss. xxxviii. and lvi., and the text of Pss. xxiii., lxix., lxxxviii. (which last, however, is given rather as a prayer *for* Israel than *of* Israel), as paraphrased in the Targum. Notice how 'the Lord is my shepherd' (xxiii. 1) becomes 'the Lord fed His people in the wilderness.' Also the Septuagint titles of Pss. v., lv., and (in many MSS.) lxiv. A Talmudic passage records a difference (at the end of the 1st century A.D.) between two rabbis. 'R. Eliezer said, David said all the psalms on his account; R. Joshua said, On account of the congregation. The wise men (i.e. the majority of the school) made a compromise, saying, "Some of them are said on his own account, and others on account of the congregation"' (*Pesachim*, 117*a*, *ap*. Neubauer, *Studia Biblica*, ii. 7). But the grounds of the compromise were very weak. See also *Pesachim*, 118*b*, where Raba explains Ps. cxvi. as spoken by Israel.

[1] Isa. lxiii. 11.

NOTE b, p. 259.

St. Augustine on Ps. lix. 2 and title of Ps. lx. (Oxford translation, 1849). Cf. Tertullian, *Adv. Prax.*, 'Omnes pæne psalmi Christi personam sustinent' (*Opera*, ed. 1634, p. 642). As specimens of an incomplete and unconscious application of the nationalistic theory, take Eusebius's description of Ps. xlii. as a 'supplication of the prophets over the rejection of the Jewish people,' and of Ps. cxxx. as the 'prayer of the martyrs.' The latter psalm is the *De Profundis*, which, with the other six penitential psalms, the Church has constantly interpreted of its own spiritual wants. St. Chrysostom, too, remarks on Ps. li. 1 (*v.* 3 in the Hebrew) that the words are equally applicable to David, and to the captive people of Israel, and also to Christians under a sense of guilt. See also Theodoret on Ps. lxxvii. and some other psalms.

NOTE c, p. 261.

Comp. my *Prophecies of Isaiah*, ii. 194-198. The views there expressed differ from those of Theodore of Mopsuestia (ap. Swete, *Dict. of Christian Biography*, iv. 946), in that they leave room for the action of the natural law of development; and also from those of Delitzsch's friend Hofmann of Erlangen, in that no attempt is made to sketch out a system of typical Old Testament history, the basis of the theory being that pious faith in early foreshadowings described in my quotation from Stanley. Obviously, the traditional account of ancient Israel being only in part historical, we cannot go beyond quasi-poetical speculations, which have their own justification, but which must not form part of the ἀπολογία recommended in 1 Pet. iii. 15.

NOTE d, p. 262.

Soph. *Œd. Col.* 1076-1084, in Whitelaw's translation. Smend refers with the same object to Soph. *Œd. Rex*, 1086, 1095; *Electra*, 479, 492; Horat. *Carm. Sec.* 72, and to the odes of Pindar (Stade's *Zeitschrift*, 1888, p. 60). Let me add that, just as in the Greek choruses, though for a different reason, the later Israelites sometimes personified their people as a woman. So in Rev. xii. 4, where the woman is the heavenly Israel (Spitta); so, too, Shulamith in the Song of Songs was interpreted in the Targum and Midrash of the כנסת ישראל, and the greatest of the 'Servant' passages in 2 Isaiah is enclosed by sections which describe the Jewish people as a handmaid (Isa. lii., liv.). Cf. Ps. lxxxvii. 16, cxvi. 16, 'the son of thy handmaid.'

T

NOTE ᵉ, p. 263.

'We Aryans of the West are accustomed to draw a hard and fast line between the ideal and the real; but the unphilosophical Israelite made no such distinction. The kingdom of God he regarded as really in heaven, waiting to be revealed; and so the ideal of Israel was to an Israelite really in heaven, in the super-sensible world, waiting for its manifestation.' It would carry us too far away to collect all the ancient parallels for such a belief (both Egypt, Babylonia, and Persia supply them in abundance). Let me only refer to the wonderful personification of Wisdom in the Wisdom of Solomon and to the more recent parallels in the works of Boethius and Dante. This imperious craving for personification has abated in modern times, but poets like Wordsworth remind us that it is not dead. So that the Second Isaiah did nothing strange in personifying, not merely as a fiction but as the representation of a fact, the ideal of Israel. In order to be real, this ideal had to be personal. But when it took flesh could it retain its ideal purity? Looking at the noblest representatives of the ideal from a little distance it might seem that this was possible (see Ps. xxii., Isa. xlii. 1–7, xlix. 1–9, l. 4–9, lii. 13– liii. 12). But more often, when a psalmist becomes the mouthpiece of the Church-nation, he admits the power of the real world to obscure the ideal by introducing into his description features alien to the true Genius of Israel (see Ps. lxix.). Let me add that the Second Isaiah gives an objective existence, not merely to the ideal Israel but to the ideal Jerusalem (Isa. xl. 9, xlix. 14–19, lii. 7–9, lxii. 6), and that in the New Testament and in the Talmud (see p. 450) we also find these ideal or heavenly figures (see for the one Rev. xii. 4, and for the other Rev. iii. 12, xxi. 2, 10 ; cf. Gal. iv. 26, Phil. iii. 20, Heb. xi. 10, xii. 22, xiii. 4), which evidently belong to the same circle of images as the Platonic ἰδέαι and their Egyptian and Iranian analogues. But into how lofty a service have these conceptions been pressed by the Jewish writers!

NOTE ᶠ, p. 263.

I must therefore modify my statement in *Isaiah* (ed. 3), ii. 202–204, and in my Commentary, reasonable as I still consider it to be. Those who prefer a more nearly orthodox view will at any rate agree with Theodore of Mopsuestia, Calvin, and Hofmann (*Schriftbeweis*), that the psalmist's experiences do not accord in all points with those of Jesus Christ. St. Augustine's view of the predictive character of Ps. xxii. (see his comment on the title of Ps. lxxxv.) is of course impossible.

NOTE g, p. 264.

The well-known late Jewish belief in the merits of 'the fathers' (cf. Targum on Pss. lx. 6, 7, lxxxiv. 11) might, it is true, almost have justified the phrase. Cf. Ex. ix. 6, Deut. iv. 37, x. 15, Rom. xi. 28. And who should this leader—this *root* of the new Israel—be but He who was also the *flower* of the old?

NOTE h, p. 264.

I have returned, as the reader will see, to the view expressed in *The Book of Isaiah Chronologically Arranged* (1870), pp. 191-193, cf. 155. The individualizing features of Isa. liii. are no doubt unusually strong,[1] but not more so than those of the poetic portrait of Job, who is a symbol of humanity, and especially of Israel. I have also been impressed by the fact that the Messianic interpretation of the 'Servant' passages cannot be traced earlier than the Psalter of Solomon (B.C. 63-48), if it can be traced even in this book (cf. *Ps. Sol.* xvii. 30 with Isa. xlix. 6, and xvii. 42, 43 with Isa. xlii. 4*a*), while Dan. vii. 13, 14, cf. 22, 27, looks like an early interpretation of Isa. lii. 13-15, liii. 12 (first clause). Need I add that I have also been greatly moved by my renewed study of the phenomena of the psalms? This 'return' does not, of course, mean that I renounce the Christian application of Isa. liii.; for is not Jesus Christ the flower of the old and the root of the new Israel?—nor that I disparage those who are still contented with the interpretation given by Delitzsch. In any case, it must be admitted that the theory of the adaptation by the Second Isaiah of an older prophetic fragment (see my *Isaiah*, ii. 39) is not unplausible. Was not Job himself an individual before he became a symbol? It also supplies an additional justification for the application of Isa. liii. to the Christian Messiah. If an individual prophet, Jeremiah for instance, by his faithfulness unto death so largely realized the ideal of the Servant of Jehovah that a prophetic dirge upon him could be utilized in a portrait of the personalized Genius of Israel, much more may we apply that touching description to Him whom we regard as our perfect Teacher and Example.

NOTE i, p. 264.

In other words, these psalmists think less of the ideal and more of the actual Israel; or we may say that they speak for the handful

[1] Chap. liv., referred to by Giesebrecht (*Beiträge zur Jesaiakritik*, p. 184), is not a complete parallel, for here the allegoric intention is apparent. The adaptation-theory (see above) seems to me to lighten the difficulty of the ordinary reader.

of earnest Israelites, whose number we may hope that they underestimate.

NOTE ᵏ, p. 264.

The psalms lose nothing in interest through being assigned in the main to the Church-nation. What is necessary to preserve for them the affections of Christendom is a historical background. Whether we seek this in the life of David and his successors, or in the larger life of the Church-nation, seems, from the point of view of mere dramatic interest, unimportant. But let no one give up the one background unless he is prepared to adopt the other. The eighteenth-century critics could not appreciate *Samson Agonistes* because they judged it by a purely artistic standard; those of the nineteenth century, reading it as a contemporary record, as the expression of a heroic soul, can admire it. It would be sad to enjoy Milton's tragedy more than those lyrics which to our forefathers seemed more intense than any others because of the story which underlay them. As mere academical exercises by not merely unnamed but unknown individuals, the psalms will neither greatly edify the Church nor charm the literary student. But if we can show that in losing one David we have gained a succession of still sweeter psalmists, and that though we know not their names we partly know their history, and can follow them in their changing moods and experiences, we shall more than compensate the educated reader for the temporary and unintentional pain to which our criticism may have subjected him.

NOTE ᵐ, p. 265.

Compare the saying of Abaje, 'In prayer a man should always unite himself with the community' (*Berachoth*, 29*b*). Especially in festival prayers the wants of the individual (צרכי יחיד) were to be forgotten, said the teachers, in view of common blessings.

NOTE ⁿ, p. 265.

Even then, however, except in Ps. xlv. and perhaps in Ps. cvi. 4, 5, the psalmist does not speak merely as an individual; he represents either a class within the Church-nation or the whole of the faithful community. See e.g. (besides Ps. xxii.) Pss. xix. 12–15, xxxii., xxxix., xlii. and xliii., lv., lxi., lxvi., lxxiii., lxxvii., cxxi., cxxii., cxxix.–cxxxi. On Ps. cvi. 4, 5, comp. Binnie, *The Psalms, their History*, &c., p. 291. Of course, it is possible that if we knew more of the post-Exile developments of Hebrew poetry and 'wisdom,' we might find that here too there was an individualistic reaction against the Church-movement of Ezra.

Note º, p. 265.

'There are not many [of the seemingly personal] psalms,' says Hoekstra, 'in which you cannot imagine the collective servant of God as the subject throughout' (*Theol. Tijdschrift*, 1871, p. 4). Similarly, Smend, in his essay 'Ueber das Ich der Psalmen' (Stade's *Zeitschrift*, 1888, pp. 49–147); cf. his review of Nowack in *Theol. Lit.-zeitung*, Nov. 2, 1889, which is, I fear, less conciliatory than the essay. Both writers exaggerate, but have done good service, notably Smend, by forcing attention to a neglected principle. Stekhoven, in his reply to Smend (Stade's *Zt.*, 1889, pp. 131–134), admits that a number of psalms (e.g. liv., lx., lxxix., cxxix.) are unintelligible upon the individualistic theory. His own theory is that not a few songs which originally expressed the feelings of an individual have been converted into Church-hymns by the addition of some couplets, by fusion with other songs, or by other editorial processes. To me this seems only admissible within very narrow limits. At any rate we are bound to dispense with it as often as we can. In most cases the supposition that the original psalmist sometimes speaks as any pious Israelite, who shares the joys and sorrows of his nation, would speak, is sufficient. To say that Pss. vi., cii., cxxx., cxxxix. must have been materially altered from their original form, seems to me an arbitrary and needless hypothesis. In justice to myself I should add that the views on this subject expressed here and in my commentary have been formed independently of Smend, but that I have been helped much by Olshausen.

Note ᵖ, p. 265.

See e.g. the priestly blessing (Num. vi. 23–26), the Decalogue, many parts of the exhortations in Deuteronomy, the fine monologue of the true Israel in Micah vii., Hos. iv. 4, 5 (the priestly caste), vii. 8, 9, Isa. xii. 1, 2, xxv., xxvi., parts of 2 Isaiah, and Lam. i., iii. (see my Introd. to Lamentations in the *Pulpit Commentary*, p. iii.). Comp. also some of the so-called Psalms of Solomon (see esp. *Ps. Sol.* i., where Israel speaks, not however *Ps. Sol.* xvi., which is the utterance of an individual), and a beautiful hymn in the Atonement Day Service (*Festival Prayers*, by De Sola, iv. 250).

Note ᵠ, p. 265.

This observation has also been made by Mr. Lock in one of his excellent contributions to a volume of *Keble College Sermons* (1889). It appears to him that a thoughtful even if not critical study of the structure of the Psalter will promote the growth of a less purely individualistic and in a good sense more churchly religious sentiment. 'The psalms,' he says, 'are the hymnbook of the Jewish Church, and they are a hymnbook composed by putting together several previous hymnbooks;' and 'in the main you will find that throughout the whole there is a gradual growth of the thought which seems to take a new departure with each book.' Thus in Book I. the psalms, we are told, are nearly all individual, personal. In Books II. and III., side by side with some of the most personal psalms, there are many with a strongly national element. In Book IV., the tone is predominantly national; indeed, sometimes more than national. In Book V., there are still many national and historical psalms, and yet there is also a deep personal tone (e.g. Pss. cxix. and cxxxix.); 'but at last we come to that wonderful closing group, where all that is personal passes away,' and 'the very words "I" and "mine" are nowhere found'—it is the great Hallelujah group. This theory has the merit of presupposing no critical knowledge in the student. It may, I hope, prepare some students for a not less edifying but perhaps more critical and therefore more satisfying view of the Psalter.

NOTE r, p. 265.

It is not enough to reply with Dr. Binnie that Christian hymn-books, the Olney collection for instance, contain a number of lyrics which were originally composed simply for the comfort and edification of the writers (*The Psalms, their History, Teaching, and Use*, p. 11); for who would dream of including one of our hymnbooks among the primary sources of Christian theology?

NOTE s, p. 267.

Rab imputes to the Babylonian king the arrogant intention of surpassing all the psalms and hymns composed by David, and states that an angel cut the heathen king short by giving him a violent blow on the mouth. Daniel himself took too favourable a view of Nebuchadrezzar in Dan. iv. 24 (27), according to *Baba bathra*, 4a, a criticism which accounts for the divergent view of the text in the Septuagint.

NOTE t, p. 267.

Edersheim, *Prophecy and History*, p. 26; E. Meyer and Zimmern also take an unfavourable view of these hymns, but unjustly. They are not of course monotheistic; other gods are mentioned besides that one who is invoked as the highest. True; but such gods only appear as mediators, and these hymns were written long before Nebuchadrezzar. Zimmern himself admits the Biblical turn of the phraseology in parts of the Chaldæan hymns. Comp. my commentary on Pss. lxxxvi. and cxlv., which, even if of post-Exile origin, may yet carry on a movement begun during the Exile. That the Chaldæan hymns were sometimes used as spells, need not surprise us; so too were the Vedic hymns and even the Hebrew psalms (the *shimmūsh t'hillīm* describes the various magic uses of the latter).

NOTE u, p. 268.

Prof. Francis Brown, *Presbyterian Review*, Jan. 1888, p. 85; cf. Ragozin, *Story of Chaldæa*, pp. 333, 334. There is a suggestive Assyrian word for prayer—*'iḳribu*, 'a drawing near' (קרב).

NOTE v, p. 269.

See the India House Inscription, especially the passages quoted by Sayce, *Hibbert Lectures*, p. 97, with whom Tiele agrees, *Bab.-ass. Gesch.*, p. 553. The same pure note, however, is struck in the words of that Assyrian prefect who, about 707, attempted to introduce into Assyria the worship of Nabû as the highest if not the only god—'Place thy confidence in Nabû, and thou wilt give it to no other god' (Tiele, *Bab.-ass. Gesch.*, pp. 207, 212).

NOTE w, p. 269.

Cyrus, however, did not realize the Second Isaiah's expectation (see the Cyrus cylinder-inscription). Such liberality as his was from a prophet's point of view dangerous. Nor did his theism develope as Isa. xli. 25 may be intended to suggest.

NOTE x, p. 270.

It is not a tenable view that the early Yahvistic narratives are independent of the Babylonian. The old view of Sayce, Friedrich Delitzsch, and Haupt, that they were compiled from cuneiform sources by a Jewish monotheist during the Exile, is inconsistent with the surest results of Hexateuchal criticism. It is also unnecessary, since from the time of Ahaz there were opportunities enough of communication between Palestine and Babylon. The embassy of Merodach-Baladan to Hezekiah is well attested (Isa. xxxix., 2 Kings xx. 13–19), and if Schrader is correct in accepting the fact of the Babylonian captivity of Manasseh (2 Chron. xxxiii. 11–13), this event too may have facilitated the introduction of Jewish scholars to the Chaldæan traditions. Budde has well pointed out that this does not involve bringing down the original Yahvist as late as Ahaz, Hezekiah, or Manasseh, and Kuenen now thinks that the early Yahvistic narratives received additions from a Babylonian source in the reign of Manasseh or even later (*Theol. Tijdschrift*, 1884, p. 168; *Hexateuch*, p. 248; cf. Budde, *Urgeschichte*, pp. 515-518). These additions of course are thoroughly Hebraized in their religious tendency. The same remark may be made of the cosmogony in Gen. i. 1-ii. 4*a*. The Chaldæan myth of Creation was never harmonized with the noble religion of Nebuchadrezzar; the Creator was not the younger but the elder Bel, and the story is full of polytheism. The corresponding Hebrew story, however, is in complete accordance with the purest prophetic religion.

NOTE ʸ, p. 271.

Nebuchadrezzar—Cyrus—Darius. It would be difficult to find greater men in the ancient world than these—great, for what they were in themselves, and not merely for what they were enabled to effect. It was Nebuchadrezzar's to reorganize a kingdom which had been reduced by constant wars with Assyria to a state almost of desolation. The hero felt this; he tells us in his inscriptions, not of his successful wars, but of the honour that he paid to religion and of the grandeur of his buildings. With regard to Cyrus, the Persians, the Jews, and the Greeks vie with one another in extolling the nobility of his character. Nöldeke, alone among recent critics (*Aufsätze*, 1887), disputes this view, and considers Cyrus to be only a wild conqueror. But the permanence of the empire which Cyrus founded and the details of his cylinder-inscription seem to me, as well as to E. Meyer, to be strongly opposed to such an estimate. This great conqueror was also, like Nebuchadrezzar, an able organizer, and what is more, the spring of his energy was a religious enthusiasm, which shines with a gentler glow in him than in any Semitic conqueror. Cyrus was a pious Mazdayasnian (this is the secret of his great character), and being such, it was no effort to him to spare the religious feelings of his subjects. Whatever be the date of those passages of the Avesta which commemorate the pious men of all countries, the principle is not too refined for any of the earlier stages of Mazdeism. Nor can we give inferior praise to Darius Hystaspis, faithful alike to the 'Great God' and to his people, eminent alike in war and in peace, and in his friendly consideration for the religious feelings of his subjects, the true successor of Cyrus. If Cyrus liberated the Jews, Darius caused their temple to be rebuilt, and if he also built a temple to Amen the Egyptian sun-god, we need not question that he justified this step on religious as well as political grounds. (See Wiedemann, *Gesch. Aegyptens*, &c., 1880, p. 239, &c.; Birch, *Egypt*, pp. 177, 178.) It was the Sassanian kings who entered upon the fatal course of religious exclusivism.

NOTE ᶻ, p. 271.

So Celsus calls the Persians (Orig. *c. Cels*. vi. 80). Hyde, one of the glories of old Oxford, remarks on the 'peculiar love of God for the Persian people,' shown especially in His revelation of Christ to the Magi, and caused by the survival of so large a part of the primæval knowledge of God in Persia (*Hist. relig. vet. Persarum*, 1700, p. 379). In this sentence, however, he overlooks the fact that the narrative in Matt. ii. 1-12 does honour not less to Babylon than to Persia. I should add that, according to Hyde, the first lawgiver of the Persians was Abraham !

NOTE ᵃᵃ, p. 271.

A popular French writer comes to this conclusion—'that Judaism essaying in the Achæmenid epoch to speak of a law, a prophet, an Exodus, and one only God, in the very countries in which Mazdeism developed, must have found in Mazdeism a powerful helper,' and adds that we must regard Judaism as a religion 'constamment imitatrice de la persane' (Bellangé, *Le judaisme et l'histoire du peuple juif*, 1889, pp. 281, 282). This is a manifest exaggeration. We must not attach too much weight even to really striking coincidences, if the phenomenon to be illustrated can be sufficiently accounted for in the natural course of development. I have myself mentioned some such coincidences, but do not regard all of them as proving the historical indebtedness either of Israel to Persia or of Persia to Israel. Persian influence upon Jewish belief was, I admit, most real, and it evidently increased as time went on (read the Apocalypse from this point of view, not to mention the Talmudic literature). But during a great part of the Persian period the relations between Israel in Palestine and the satraps were not such as to predispose the former to become the conscious imitator of Persia. Indirectly Persia must have influenced the Jews throughout her vast empire, but directly not so much the Jews in Palestine as the large Israelitish colonies on the east of the Euphrates and the Tigris, which, however, must have transmitted the results to the Jews in Palestine. We may thus account for any Iranian elements which criticism can allow in the historico-legislative work known as the 'priestly code' and in the other Hebrew books presumably of the Persian period. And may not this be the real meaning or implication of the Talmudic saying, 'The angels came up with the Jews from Babylon'? At any rate the mention of 'Babylon' does not forbid us to think likewise of the vast spirit-world of Iran (for even if the Iranian belief in spirits be to some extent historically connected with the Babylonian, it came before the

Jews as an independent doctrine). It is true that the Babylonian God Marduk is described as the 'lord of the angel-hosts of heaven and earth' (Sayce, *Hibbert Lectures*, p. 99), and this is no isolated expression. But how much more stress is laid in the later Avesta on the fravashis (to whom we shall return) by whose countless and irresistible hosts Ahura Mazda Himself is in some sense helped, and through whose brightness He maintains the sky (*Farvardin Yast*, § 1)! Whether the Satan-belief in Job, or even in Chronicles, is materially affected by Iranian doctrine, is a matter for argument. But who can fail to see that the Satan of the Book of Revelation is the fellow of Ahriman? Later Jews even adopted the name Ahriman in the corrupt form of Armîlos[1] (see *Isaiah*, ii. 218) for that רשיעא κατ' ἐξοχὴν who was to be the last and greatest oppressor of the faithful, and a synonym of Ahriman (Aeshma-dêva, 'the raving fiend') in the form of Asmôdai. And whether or no Lagarde's particular explanation of Purim be correct, it is very probable that the festival has really a Persian origin (*Encycl. Brit.*, art. 'Esther'). Several other traces of direct or indirect Persian influence will be pointed out later. On these questions compare, besides commentators on the Avesta, Spiegel, *Eranische Alterthumskunde*, Bd. ii. (1873); Darmesteter, *Ormazd et Ahriman* (1877); Kuenen, *Religion of Israel*, ii. 156, iii. 32–34; Ewald, *Old and New Test. Theology*, pp. 72–78; Grätz, *Gesch. der Juden*, ii. 2, pp. 409–419; Goldziher, *Hebrew Mythology*, pp. 326–329; Kohut, 'The Zendavesta and Gen. i.–xi.,' *Jewish Quarterly Review*, April 1890 (Kohut's articles are learned but somewhat uncritical), his *Antiparsische Aussprüche im Deuterojesaias*, *Morgenländ. Zeitschr.*, part xxx., and his *Ueb. d. jüd. Angelologie u. Demonologie in ihrer Abhängigkeit vom Parsismus*; Fuller, *On Angelology*, &c. (*Speaker's Comm. on O. T.* vi. 348, &c., and *On Apocrypha*, i. 171 &c.); C. de Harlez, *Proc. of Soc. of Bibl. Archæology*, ix. 368; Cheyne, *Job and Solomon*, pp. 79, 80; Lagarde, *Purim*, &c. (1887).

NOTE bb, p. 271.

An uncritical reader of the Avesta may question the spirituality of the God of Zoroastrianism, just as an uncritical reader of the Bible may question the spirituality of the God of the Bible. Dr. Murray Mitchell, formerly of Bombay, denies that Ahura Mazda is a purely spiritual being (*The Zendavesta*, &c., Rel. Tract Soc., p. 13). M. de Harlez however remarks, 'Tel qu'il paraît généralement dans l'Avesta, il est le Dieu unique, spirituel, tout puissant, omniscient, créateur ; ses caractères principaux sont l'activité, l'intelligence, la sainteté' (Introd. to Avesta, p. lxxviii.). Prof. De la Saussaye more cautiously affirms,

---

[1] As a Persian name, however, Ahriman becomes אֲהוּרְמִין, corresponding to הוֹרְמִיז, *Sanhedrin*, 39a.

'No people ever came nearer to monotheism than the Persians.' '(Ahura Mazda) was not only the highest god; he has some [? the principal] features which belong to the one God' (*Lehrbuch der Religionsgeschichte*, ii. 32). These differences of statement are caused by the inconsistencies of the Avesta, which are greater even than those of the Bible. The resemblance of Ahura to the Jehovah of the most advanced Hebrew writers is greatest in the Gâthâs, in which dualism is not so prominent as in the Vendîdâd, while polytheism which is prominent in the rest of the Avesta is here almost if not altogether absent. From the parallelism between Ahura and Jehovah the veteran Zend scholar Spiegel infers that the conception of the former (=Sanskr. Asura, 'he who is') has been influenced by that of Yahveh (*Eran. Alt.* ii. 26). Biblical criticism, however, in its present advanced stage negatives this, and in his latest essay, though he still dwells much on foreign influences on Iranian ideas, Spiegel admits that 'in the principal points the Iranian ideas came forth of themselves from the ancient Aryan ideas' (*Le Muséon*, Nov. 1887, p. 623). Certainly the title or name Ahura, (which means (1) spirit, (2) God, (3) lord, divine or human) stands in no historical relation either to Yahveh or to Adonai. Nor can a prophet like Zarathustra, whichever of the current dates we accept, have borrowed a name for God from a people so inconspicuous and religiously so backward as the pre-Exile Israelites.

Note ^{cc}, p. 272.

Lagarde, *Gött. gel. Anzeigen*, 1870, p. 1551, &c.; *Purim*, 1887, p. 44; D'Eichthal, *Mém. sur le texte primitif du 1er récit de la Création*, 1875, pp. 26–31. But though Dr. Caland has improved the statement of the case for an Iranian original of Gen. i.–ii. 4a (*Theol. Tijdschrift*, March 1889), can it be denied that the affinities of this document are primarily with the Babylonian cosmogonies in Berosus and in G. Smith's tablets? See my art. 'Cosmogony,' *Encyc. Brit.*, 1876.

Note ^{dd}, p. 272.

The Sh'ma and the blessing יוצר אור were to be said at dawn in the temple (see Grätz, *Geschichte*, ii. 2, p. 419). This was not improbably suggested by the Zoroastrian usage of praying at daybreak, which is of course much more ancient than the forms of prayer given in the Khorda Avesta. We shall return to the subject in connexion with the Essenes.

Note ^{ee}, p. 272.

A Persian origin is claimed for the mysticism of the psalms by Réville, *Revue des deux mondes*, 1 mars 1872, and by Gustave d'Eichthal, *Mémoire sur le texte primitif*, &c. (1875), p. 55 ; a Babylonian, as it seems, by Goldziher, *Hebrew Mythology*, pp. 318, 319.

Note ff, p. 272.

The adoption of prophetic language by the psalmists can be paralleled from the Gâthâs. It was Zarathustra's belief that through prayer the right words were revealed to him for the liturgical chants (Yasna, xxviii. 7, xlviii. 8). The Iranian poet-prophet, however, lays more stress upon this than the Hebrew psalmists. He has to form or re-form a Church ; the psalmists do but take up the work begun by prophets and scribes. Zarathustra's confident belief that his hymns were in some not altogether unspiritual sense revealed to him helped to produce the later practice of invoking the sacred ' Gâthâs,' which acquired (see p. 396) a sacrificial character. In course of time even the truly spiritual Hebrew psalms were converted into spells ('carmina'). This was in the sad period of Jewish ignorance, and had no official sanction. But the predictive character of the psalms was no doubt recognized by high authority, and at the rise of Christianity was practically unquestioned. In Matt. xiii. 35 (xxvii. 35) 'psalmist'='prophet;' see also Tertullian, *Resurr. Carnis*, c. 20, and cf. Neubauer, *Studia Biblica*, ii. 7, 8. Compare also the growth of the belief in the inspiration of the Vedic hymns (Max Müller, *Hibbert Lectures*, p. 137 ; Muir, *Ancient Sanskrit Texts*, iii. 232–238).

PART II.

WHO IS THE GOD OF THE PSALTER?

LET us now with fitting reverence approach the religious ideas of these children of the prophets, or, in other words, the theology of the Psalter—a phrase which I only use on the express condition that we do not confound the religious kernel with its theological integument. Accurate and systematic thinking is no characteristic of the ancient Semites, and least of all of the psalmists. But though we may decline to regard Korah or Asaph any more than Zarathustra as a scientific theologian, we may well take the holy psalmists as guides in religion, and long to repeat some at least of those deep experiences which psalm-theology embodies. No man can communicate these to another, but it is possible to help one's neighbour by showing him where they are most vividly described. 'What men most of all need,' says Hengstenberg, 'is that the blanched image of God should again be freshened up in them. The more closely we connect ourselves with the psalms, the more will God cease to be to us a shadowy form, which can neither hear, nor help, nor judge us, and to which we can present no supplication.'[1]

Who, then, is the God of the Psalter, regarding the book in the light of the preceding researches? Mistaken inferences have often been drawn from its anthropomorphisms. From the time of the first Deists onwards it has been asserted that the religion of the psalmists was still half-barbarous. And doubtless the expressions referred to *are* akin to those which anthropology indicates as characteristic of savage tribes. Rightly viewed, however, they are no proof of barbarism, but rather of Israel's complete emergence from barbarism. The freedom with which the psalmists use anthropomorphic, or

[1] Quoted in Ker, *The Psalms in History and Biography*, p. 188.

let us say at once mythic expressions, is a consequence of the sense of religious security which animates them. They have no expectation of being taken literally; they know that each member of the Church has the key to their meaning. Israel in Babylon has put away its childish religion, but retains a childlike love of mythic phrases.[a] Now that these have been emptied of their superstition they may do good service as religious symbols. And why should they not? Can we find better ones ourselves? How vivid they are! How near they bring God to the heart, and God's children in all ages and of all religions to each other! From the earliest psalm—the epic of the Davidic family (the 18th)—to that most striking, theologically, of the latest psalms (the 139th), how ineffaceable are the traces of the mythic element! What was it that made the psalms, and the Scriptures in general, the classics of the Jewish Church? The inspiration of their authors? Yes, partly, but also this, that, as the Talmud says of the Torah, they spoke 'the tongue of the children of men.'[b]

> Thy wisdom plays with us as with a child;
> Who playing learns his Father, loves him well.

But shall we, in our reaction against the Deists, praise all the mythic symbols that we find, and set them down as equally classical in the theology of the psalms? Surely not. Herder did not live in vain; the key which ancient Israel possessed has been recovered by Christian scholarship. The Scriptures are the annals of a society more familiar with the extremes of woe than any other. Illusions born of sorrow impaired the purity of the idea of God. Instead of growing in all points into God's likeness, the psalmists did sometimes as it were transform God into their own.

The first express criticism of a psalmist's idea of God proceeded from John Hyrcanus. With reference to the passage, 'Awake, why sleepest thou, Jehovah' (Ps. xliv. 24), he said, 'Doth God then sleep? Hath not the Scripture said, Behold, the keeper of Israel neither slumbereth nor sleepeth?'—and he forbade the liturgical recitation of those too thrilling, too passionate words.[1] But even before his time the frequent change of Yahveh (Jehovah) into Elohim

---

[1] *Sota*, 48a (cf. iii. p. 8).

in the Levitical psalms (see above, pp. 90, 101), and notice a similar phenomenon in Prov. xxx. 5, cf. Ps. xviii. 31, and in Hab. iii. 3, cf. Deut. xxxiii. 2), and the fact that the writers of certain books [c] (Job, Koheleth, Esther, Daniel) almost or altogether avoid the word 'Jehovah,' prove the sense of the inadequacy of any personal name for Him who is 'far above every name that is named.' Possibly, too, the same feeling dictated that obscure question of Agur, who will not even call God 'Elohim' (he prefers 'Qedōshim,' i.e. 'the All-Holy'), and asks, 'What is his name, and what is his son's name, if thou knowest?' (Prov. xxx. 4). I inquire now, Must we not partly sympathize with Hyrcanus and his predecessors? The agonized cry, 'Why sleepest thou,' can of course be excused, not indeed on the ground of a 'sacred εἰρωνεία,' but of a too limited conception of God; and yet to Christian readers it needs correction in the spirit of 'Not as I will, but as thou wilt.' [d] The theory which underlies the prayers of the Psalter is, that men should pour out their whole complaint to Jehovah (Ps. cxlii. 3, cf. lxii. 9), but should not rest content till they have emerged from the 'straits' of anguish into the 'wealthy place' of full trust in God (Ps. cxviii. 5). Then they can 'look out' (Ps. v. 4) in the full assurance of faith, and the divine Spirit conveys to them an answer of peace (Ps. lxxxv. 9). This theory has the force of a law, and on the rare occasions when (as in Pss. xliv. and lxxxviii.) it is broken, the devout worshipper cannot but feel with Hyrcanus that criticism and correction are called for—that criticism and correction which would have been silently applied by the writer himself, had he completed his psalm in a more trustful spirit.[e] Next, with regard to the early dissatisfaction with the name 'Jehovah.' Though declining to regard this name as a mere badge of particularism, inconsistent with a Catholic ideal of the Church, one may heartily admit that it should only be used by those who habitually interpret it in the spirit of the Second Isaiah and the 102nd psalm.[f]

Perhaps this may appear to some to require explanation. It is our duty to enter into the feelings of those who in certain passages changed 'Yahveh' (Jehovah) into 'Elohim' (God), and of those who afterwards by degrees substituted 'Adonai' (the Lord) for 'Yahveh.' Considering the probable mythic origin of the name 'Yahveh,' and the difficulty and importance of holding up the standard of spiritual monotheism, the good effects of these measures (upon the latter of which I must hope to speak at length elsewhere)ᵍ might be fairly held to preponderate over the evil.[1] I ask, however, Do these considerations retain their force, and is it well, now that circumstances have changed, to restrict ourselves to 'God' and to 'Lord' in addressing Him in whom we 'live and move and have our being'?

Let me not be thought to depreciate the title 'Lord' which we have received from the later Jewish Church. To a thoughtful believer it suggests much more than it expresses, for with the true God sovereign power cannot be dissociated from wisdom and love. The Zoroastrian Church felt this when it said,[2] 'We worship Him for His sovereign power and His greatness, beneficent (as they are),' and again, 'We worship Him under His name as Lord, to Mazda dear, the most beneficent (of names).' And the Jewish Church expresses the same idea in the words, 'I say (i.e. confess) unto Jehovah, Thou art Adonai ; my welfare is nought without Thee' (Ps. xvi. 2), i.e. to be Thy servant is perfect happiness. We cannot indeed identify the feeling with which the restored exiles pronounced the name Adonai with that with which the Christian Church remembers that it was 'bought (by the Lord Jesus) with a price;' and yet there is a real affinity between the cases. The virgin daughter of Babylon has none to redeem her, but 'as for our Goel,' cries the prophet, 'Jehovah Sabaoth is his name' (Isa. xlvii. 4). To be the servant of such a Lord was equivalent to being His son (Mal. iii. 17); only the humility of the Jewish Church was content with the lower title. All this may be granted, and yet from a Western point of view it may be inexpedient to use the term 'Lord' too constantly. To Gentile Christians those words of St. Paul have an especial force, 'Ye did not receive the spirit of bondage (leading) back unto fear, but the Spirit of adoption, wherein we cry, Abba, Father' (Rom. viii. 15). The conception of God as Lord is therefore not to

---

[1] Upon the evil effects, see Ewald, *History*, v. 199.
[2] *Oxford Zendavesta*, iii. 286. In the Gâthâs Mazda (omniscient) seems to be preferred to Ahura (Lord). See note ˣ, p. 435.

be the fundamental one in our religion. Philo, too, from his Greek point of view, remarks that the name Κύριος does not of itself convey more than the idea of supreme authority and power, which does not satisfy all the legitimate cravings of the religious nature.[h] These hints however produced no effect on too many Western theologians, by whom the idea of the divine Lordship was so grasped as to obscure the proportions of truth, and to provoke an irreligious reaction.[i] That sad time is nearly over, but we still need all available helps in deepening our conception of God, and one of these is the intelligent use of the hallowed name Jehovah. I have nothing to do here with the primitive meaning of the word Yahveh[j] (as the Israelites doubtless pronounced it). The distance between Yahveh the storm-god and Yahveh the Holy One of Israel is as great as that between the less developed sky-gods of the Veda and the Ahura Mazda of the Avesta.[1] The name Jehovah is a relatively complete symbol of truth, summing up all the ideas and intuitions of the Jewish Church respecting its God. It signifies not only (in Palestine) the Eternal and (in Alexandria) the Self-existent, but still more the God who in His lovingkindness stepped out of His unchangeable repose, and revealed Himself to men; it is in fact the seal of a covenant made with Israel for the sake of humanity, 'ordered,' as a poet says, 'in all things, and sure' (2 Sam. xxiii. 5). And this is why so much is said about the name of Jehovah from the earliest to the latest psalms. The writers do not indeed mean primarily the word 'Jehovah,' but that 'wonderful' name (Judg. xiii. 18), which represents at once the known and the unknown, the actual and the possible manifestations of the divine nature. They tell us respecting this name, sometimes that it is 'holy and reverend' (cxi. 9, cf. xcix. 3), sometimes that it is 'good' (liv. 8) and 'pleasant' (cxxxv. 3), and that God's saints 'love' it (v. 12, lxix. 37). Never do they dream that it can be shut up in a single word or formula. The doctrine of the divine namelessness may be specially Alexandrine,[k] but it is not contrary to the spirit of the religion of Palestine, for it presupposes, not at all the unreality, but merely the imperfec-

[1] The 'holy' deity Varuna (see p. 357) might have developed into Ahura Mazda. Such however was not the actual course of history.

tion of the believer's knowledge of God. As a Hebrew poet who avoids the name Jehovah says,

> Lo, these are the ends of his ways;
> But what a mere murmur we hear,
> And the roar of his great strength who knows?[1]

Still a fervent Theist cannot wholly dispense with a name for the Being to whom he prays. A name is a creed in a nutshell; by addressing God as Jehovah the Jewish Church 'held fast the confession' of its faith. Imperfect as every human name for God must be, the psalmists will not, cannot give up the covenant-name. They love to pronounce it, not 'with bated breath and whispering humbleness'[m]—for that were heathenish—nor yet with the light-hearted freedom of antiquity, but with the manly reverence due to a spiritual Deity. And why should not we too pronounce it in this spirit, and confess that we have met together to-day to worship Jehovah? Why should we not give this practical expression to the truth expressed in John iv. 22—that 'salvation is of the Jews,' in fact, that our religion has a history, and a right noble one? More especially in reading the psalms, why should we not substitute, either orally or mentally, the old covenant-name for that conventional symbol ('the Lord'), which, even in Moslem theology,[2] is but an *ismu ṣifah* or attribute, not the 'exalted name' itself? Philosophy can offer no objection to this. It is of the nature-gods and their changing names that our own philosophic historian of religion says that 'they vanish by one thought like the mist of the morning.'[3] Christian orthodoxy is equally unaggrieved. The 'Jehovah' of prophetic religion represents to some extent the truths summed up in the Nicene doctrine of the Father and the Son, and praying to Jehovah may be taken as an expression of the belief that the Father and the Son are one.[n] Nor can a really sound Jewish theology object, if at least I am right in preferring the warm and living practical theology of the Book of Job to the cold, sceptical philosophy of Ecclesiastes.

---

[1] Job xxvi. 14 in Gilbert's version (1886), which seeks to reproduce the original rhythm.
[2] See Hughes, *Dictionary of Islam*, pp. 141, 142.
[3] Max Müller, *Hibbert Lectures*, p. 234.

The author of the latter refuses to name God, but the profound thinker who has sketched the phases of his inner history in Job comes back to the name 'Jehovah,' and the philosophic singer of Ps. cxxxix. has never abandoned it. One of those noble writers who refutes the saying that there is no nature-poetry in the Old Testament, expressly adopts the compound title 'Yahveh Adōnēnū' (Jehovah our Lord) to describe the God of all the families of the earth (Ps. viii. 2). Yes; the Jehovah of the psalms *is* 'the God' (1 Kings xviii. 39), in the full sense of the word, as the self-revealer, the just but loving Father,° not only of Israel but of the world, not only of Hezekiah and Josiah but of Nebuchadrezzar and (if I may venture to say so) the foreign king of Pss. xlv. and lxxii.

True, the universal love of God (that is, His will that all nations should be brought by persuasion into His flock) was not understood by all, nor adequately realized by any of the psalmists. Essential as this characteristic is to a thoroughly satisfactory conception of Jehovah, it was beyond the mental range of some religious poets. Turn to the 18th psalm, written perhaps in Josiah's reign, while as yet there were but a few hearty converts to the spiritual religion of Deuteronomy. The writer has no doubt a high moral conception of the Deity (*vv*. 21–32), and as a consequence believes in monotheism. He pictures with delight the great future Davidic empire of the world in which he believes as if it were present. But how is this empire won? Listen to the words of the imaginary David :—

> I pursued mine enemies and overtook them,
>   And turned not again till I had consumed them (*v*. 38);
> They cried, but there was none to save,
>   Unto Jehovah, but he answered them not (*v*. 42);
> Thou didst set me to be head of the nations,
>   People whom I knew not served me.
> As soon as they heard, they were obsequious unto me;
>   Aliens came cringing unto me (*vv*. 44, 45).

Now contrast the brief recast of this section in a book which powerfully impressed many of the psalmists—the Second Isaiah. The prophet is speaking of David, and alludes to this psalm: 'Behold, for a witness to the peoples I appointed him, a ruler and commander of the peoples.

Behold, people that thou knowest not 'shalt thou call, and people that have not known thee shall run unto thee, because of Jehovah thy God, and for the Holy One of Israel, inasmuch as he hath glorified thee' (Isa. lv. 4, 5). What does the poet-prophet mean? This—that David's appointed work of bringing together the peoples into a single righteous kingdom could only be effected by a witness or preacher of the truth, and that this witness or preacher was to be Jehovah's Servant, the regenerate people of Israel. Need I repeat that well-known passage (Isa. xlii. 1–4) in which the same truth is so nobly set forth? But it is not only here that we find it. The Psalter itself contains recognitions enough of Israel's missionary function. Is it not clearly implied in Ps. xxii., in which the deliverance of the sufferer is brought into such close connexion with the setting up of God's kingdom in the world? There are also other psalms, of less massive ore, but equally precious as the lyric utterances of the newly organized Church. Israel, as it would seem from these,[1] has but to 'rehearse God's glory among the nations,' to call forth their liveliest joy at having Jehovah for their king, somewhat as St. Augustine longed to recite the psalms in all lands to subdue the pride of the human race. The force of truth, then, is the motive relied upon for the spiritual subjugation of the world. And this is equally implied in Pss. lxv. and lxvii. (of the Persian age), the second of which might be correctly headed, 'Veni, redemptor gentium!' They are the psalms which contain these fine verses:—

> Let the peoples rejoice and shout for joy:
> Because thou wilt judge the nations rightly,
> And wilt guide the peoples upon earth (Ps. lxvii. 5).
> O thou that hearest prayer,
> Unto thee may all flesh come (Ps. lxv. 3).

Already had the same noble thought been expressed by Zarathustra, and a later writer in the Avesta (but not later probably than our psalmist) had declared in the spirit of Mal. i. 11 that there were holy men in all countries.P But alas! this great hope did not always shine thus brightly, and Persia herself is responsible for its obscuration among the Jews. Under the second and third Artaxerxes (reactionary kings,

---

[1] See Pss. xcvi. 3, 4, 13, xcvii. 1, 2, xcviii. 9, xcix. 1–3, c. 1, xlvii. 2, 3, 10.

who compromised the purity of Mazda-worship) Israel seemed almost crushed by oppression ; again and again he speaks as if his very name will soon be blotted out. He knows indeed that he can call himself the great Jehovah's servant (lxxxix. 51), but he takes no delight in recalling the Second Isaiah's noble promise. His ideal has been 'not to fail or be discouraged till he shall have set' true religion 'in the earth' (Isa. xlii. 4). His present practice is to complain, 'How many are the days of thy servant? when wilt thou execute judgment on my persecutors?' (cxix. 84, cf. lxxxix. 46, 48). He thinks, too often at least, not of the new but of the old ideal, of an ever-fortunate king, and shattered enemies. And even later than this, in spite of the teachings of Providence, the same worn-out ideal of Josiah's reign attracted the prophetic author of the 2nd psalm (see *vv.* 8, 9).

The two forms of representation are obviously contradictory. The Church is in a period of transition. The old ideal of the servant of Jehovah was that of the warlike king, the new is that of the teaching prophet. The Church cannot all at once reject the old language, and sometimes falls into vehement expressions which warn us that the Christ has yet to come. Still the contradiction is not as complete as it may seem. If the psalmists could theorize on the state of the non-Jewish world, they would probably say that it was composed of two classes—those who were 'forgetful of God' (Ps. ix. 18),[q] and those who, as the Second Isaiah said, were 'waiting for his law' (Isa. xlii. 4, comp. li. 5). That the former should be most in the minds of the psalmists, is but natural. They were the larger class, and were more dangerous than words could describe. In spite of the nobler elements in Persian religion, there was abundant superstition to counterbalance these, and the nations more immediately in contact with Palestine were immoral polytheists. The Jews honestly believed that the deposit of true religion was with them, and that to crush Israel was equivalent to the darkening of the world. It is not therefore a mere grasping nationalism which leads so many of the psalmists to identify the righteous with Israel and the unrighteous with the Gentiles.[1]

---

[1] See my note on Ps. iii. 8, and comp. St. Paul in Gal. ii. 8, 'We being Jews by nature and not ἁμαρτωλοί of the nations.'

As Dr. Drummond says,[1] 'the actual coincidences between the presumed election of God and the ethical appearances of the world,' go far to account for such a mental attitude. Similar phenomena moreover are not wanting in the Gâthâs of Zarathustra, whose vehemence towards the members of the Daêva-party does not prevent him from praying for their conversion.[2]

Still the question must arise within us, and may with unfeigned reverence for the psalmists be uttered, Are these doomed nations wholly responsible for their ungodliness? What friend has warned them of their danger, and adjured them to feel after God if haply they may find him? To Israel of old Jehovah sent 'all his servants the prophets, rising up early and sending them' (Jer. xxv. 4), filling up a long day, like the householder in the parable, with calling his labourers. But where have been the prophets to the heathen? A call has indeed been sent to the prophet-people. But what has been its reception? Something no doubt has been done. A profession of God's unity has been made, and a nation has been built up on what may with some truth be called a theocratic basis. This is at once a claim and a prophecy of gigantic magnitude. In addition to this, the glory of the true God, that is, His wonderful guidance of His people Israel, has to some extent been 'rehearsed' as the psalmist bade, 'among the nations' (Ps. xcvi. 3). So much we cannot help assuming, if we would not reduce a statement of frequent occurrence in the Psalter to a mere barren formula. And I think that the assumption is to some extent confirmed by two Old Testament documents.

The first is a short discourse complete in itself (Isa. lvi. 1-8), directed against the Jewish pride of race, and although imbedded in the Babylonian Isaiah, most probably composed in the legalistic age of Nehemiah. It refers apparently to certain foreign converts and (Israelitish) eunuchs at Babylon who desired to join the community at Jerusalem, but feared an unfriendly reception.[3] The second is the exquisite Book of Jonah, which, though seemingly a pre-Exile history, is

---

[1] *Philo Judæus*, i. 208.
[2] See, in the *Oxf. Zendavesta*, Yasna xxxiii. 2, liii. 5 (cf. Mills' commentary).
[3] See my art. 'Isaiah,' *Encyc. Brit.*; and cf. art. in *Expositor*, Feb. 1891.

really a sermon to the next generation after Ezra.⁸ The author belongs to that freer and more catholic school, which protested against a too legalistic spirit, and he fully recognizes (see Jonah iv. 2) that the doctrine of Joel ii. 12 applies not merely to Israel but to all nations. He is aware too that Israel (typified by Jonah 'the dove') cannot evade its missionary duty, and that its preaching should be alike of mercy and of justice. I do not indeed think that the Israelites can often have secured an audience for their preaching in the Persian period. It is but in a figure that Jonah penetrated to the court of the Assyrian king, and a psalmist can only declare that he (i.e. Israel) would gladly speak of God's admonitions before kings, if he might be visited with a fresh salvation (Ps. cxix. 41–46), while another, in his revulsion against heathen ungodliness, would rather be the humblest of the guests of Jehovah than dwell in heathendom (Ps. lxxxiv. 11). Once, and only once, do we find a reference to proselytes in the psalms of this period. 'Ye that fear Jehovah, praise him' (Ps. xxii. 24) is an expression which certainly includes the spiritual as well as the natural seed of Israel (see note on Ps. cxv. 12). But how few proselytes can there have been when Ps. xxii. was indited amidst the bitter taunts of Sanballat! Hence it is a part of a contemporary poet's plea for God's help in the rebuilding of the walls of Jerusalem that this great mercy to 'destitute' Israel will attract the nations to fear Jehovah's name (Ps. cii. 16–18).

So then, without any fault of Israel, the mission of the Servant of Jehovah is still unfulfilled.ᵗ This cannot justify the harsh expressions of the psalmists, but it does help to account for them. Israel could neither love the heathen nor be a missionary to them so long as they imperilled its very existence. A persuasive presentation of true religion only became possible in the Hellenistic age. It was the 'heaven-sent reconciler and pacificator of the world' (such was Alexander's view of his function [1]) who turned the heart of the Jew to the Gentile, and the heart of the Gentile to the Jew. We have seen how natural it was at this period that the Jews should dream of an approaching union of nations. Even

---

[1] Stanley, *Jewish Church*, iii. 213 (cf. Plutarch, *Alex. Fort.* i. 6).

the somewhat unprogressive son of Sirach makes wisdom personified declare,

> In the waves of the sea, and in all the earth,
> And in every people and nation, I got a possession.
> (Ecclus. xxiv. 6.)

And still more definite are the visions of the psalmists. It is in psalms not improbably of the early Greek period that we find those pure expressions of catholicity—Ps. lxxxvi. 5, 9, 10, and above all Ps. lxxxvii., and if I may venture to assume no improbable hypothesis, the admission of a righteous foreign king among the number of the friends of Jehovah (Pss. xlv. and lxxii.).

Turn lastly to the Book of Daniel and to the psalms which are probably almost contemporary with that wonderful book. The former, though written in the heat of the Maccabæan struggle, is not without signs, at any rate in the pictures of Nebuchadrezzar and Darius, of a hopeful disposition towards non-Israelites. In the latter it must of course be admitted that violent expressions are not wanting. We may excuse them as modern Rabbis excuse the fierce self-isolation of the Jews of a later age,[u] and we can add that neither Syrian nor Roman oppression could extinguish the spirit of friendliness, not indeed towards polytheism, but towards polytheists.[1] Already we can say that there is a wonderful 'duality' in Judaism, exclusiveness and liberality coexisting in the same church and people—a phenomenon which constantly strikes us in later history. It is in a Maccabæan psalm that the object of Israel's restored life is thus defined,—

> I shall not die, but live,
> And tell out the works of Jehovah [v] (Ps. cxviii. 17);

and that 'those that fear Jehovah' are called upon to confess Jehovah's lovingkindness and to continue to put their trust in him (Ps. cxv. 11, cxviii. 4), which suggests that an influx of proselytes had taken place in the early Greek period (see on Ps. lxxxvii.); while in another passage Jehovah is described as 'righteous in all his ways, and loving (φιλάνθρωπος) in all his works' (Ps. cxlv. 17, cf. 8, 9). And

---

[1] Cf. Joel, *Blicke in die Religionsgeschichte,* i. (1880), p. vi.

the recorded facts of history fully bear out the natural inferences from these passages. Think of the Maccabees allying themselves with Rome and Sparta [1] (some historical basis there must surely be for the precise narratives in 1 Macc. viii., xii.), and above all of the great effort to reconcile Judaism with the highest ethnic philosophy which opens so important a chapter in Jewish history.

NOTE ª, p. 286.

(Israel's spiritual change in Babylon.) I do not deny that the old heathenish tendencies may for a time have reappeared among the restored exiles (see Isa. lxv. 3-5, 11, and cf. Neh. vi. 17-19). But they must have been checked and extinguished by the vigour of the reformers.—For 'mythic' conservative theologians may substitute 'metaphorical;' cf. Jeremy Taylor, *Ductor Dubitantium*, p. 256. I have defended the accuracy of the former phrase in *Expositor*, 1888 (1), p. 60, &c.

NOTE ᵇ, p. 286.

Berachoth, 31*b*. Hermann Schultz in 1869 described the anthropomorphic passages of the O. T. as 'the noblest part of its utterances upon God' (*Alttest. Theologie*, ed. 1, i. 276). The view of the divine nature which they presuppose is certainly nobler than that of more abstract forms of Theism, and it is far more vividly represented by these popular expressions than it could be by a mere list of divine attributes. Even 'Onkelos,' who is sometimes said to have objected to anthropomorphism on principle, leaves expressions like the 'eye' and the 'hand' of God unaltered. No theological theorizing could extinguish the anthropomorphic tendency. Read the fine 'Hymn of Glory,' which closes the daily prayerbook of the Synagogue (Vallentine's ed., pp. 344-345).

NOTE ᶜ, p. 287.

יהוה' only occurs twice in in the speeches of Job and his friends (Job xii. 9, xxviii. 28). We must remember that these monuments of Jewish wisdom were written during the Exile, and represent the 'thoughts of many hearts' at a time when God seemed to have cast off His people, and consequently, according to an old popular belief, ' it was forbidden to make mention of the name of Jehovah' (Am. vi. 10). The poet himself however had fought his way to a recon-

[1] Note the phrase ἀδελφότητα καὶ φιλίαν ἀνανεώσασθαι, 1 Macc. xii. 10.

ciling faith, and in token of this employs the much-loved name, not only in the prose narrative (if that be his work), but twice in the speeches. The author of Koheleth is less happy in his Theism. He has lost the sense of the love of God; how then should he venture to use His name? The Book of Esther is a greater puzzle. Is it from reverence, or because the book was originally meant merely for recreation, that the writer avoids even the use of אלהים? (Cf. my art. 'Esther,' *Encycl. Britannica*.) In this extreme reserve he reminds us of the author of 1 Maccabees, who out of pure reverence suppresses all divine names, substituting either 'heaven' or a simple pronoun. In Canticles we have a popular cantata, brought into its present shape perhaps after the Exile. We need not therefore be surprised that the name יהוה has not been allowed to enter; we do however find שלהבתיה 'a divinely sent flame' (Cant. viii. 6). Partly reverence, partly a sense of dramatic propriety, will account for the fact that the sacred name occurs but seven times in Daniel, and that in a single chapter (Dan. ix.). It may be added that the compiler of Chronicles, though he frequently uses יהוה, shows a tendency to prefer אלהים (cf. 2 Chron. x. 15 with 1 Kings xii. 15; for other passages, see Driver, *Sunday School Lessons*, 1887, p. 82 note).

NOTE d, p. 287.

We must not, with some eminent churchmen, explain Ps. xliv. and Job ii. as specimens of irony. The 'holy men' who 'speak as if God were hard and unjust upon them' do not 'all the while feel the fullest and most penetrating conviction of His goodness,' as a writer quoted with approval by Dr. Hannah (*Bampton Lectures*, 1863, p. 313) supposes. The author of Ps. xxii. may no doubt have had such a conviction (see vv. 22–32), but Ps. xliv. contains nothing to justify the hypothesis. Is not the striking Church-hymn, 'Come, Lord, and tarry not,' also somewhat too impatient in tone?

NOTE e, p. 287.

Of course, however, we cannot account in this way for all the cases of questionable anthropomorphism in the Psalms.

NOTE f, p. 287.

See note on Ps. cii. 26–28. That there are other instructive names of God in the Psalter, is not denied. We have, e.g., Shaddai, Elyōn, El Elyōn, Yahvè Elyōn, Yahvè Çebaoth, Adonai Yahvè, Yahvè Elohim, and even El Elohim Yahvè (l. 1.), and perhaps we may add Qādōsh (xxii. 4, xcix. 3, 5). On these names comp-

Schultz, *Alttestamentliche Theologie,* and Ewald, *Old and New Test. Theology,* chap. vii. For the later Jewish names of God see Talm. Bab., *Soferim,* c. 4, and Dukes, *Rabbinische Blumenlese,* p. 228.

NOTE ^g, p. 288.

The object of this change is to draw away men's minds from any special divine manifestation to the Deity Himself. In a Phœnician inscription found at the Piræus (line 6) we find אלם בעלצדן 'the divinity Baal-Sidon,' where, as Renan has pointed out, *'ĕlīm* is used as a singular, precisely as the Hebrew *'elōhīm* (*Revue archéologique,* 1881, p. 7; cf. G. Hoffmann, *Ueber einige phönik. Inschriften,* 1889, p. 17, where other instances are given).

That 'Adonai' is not a shortened form of 'Adonainu,' as Ewald thought (*Die Lehre der Bibel von Gott,* § 230; or, *Old and New Testament Theology,* p. 98), seems to be clear from the passages in which its natural meaning is neither 'our Lord' nor 'the Lord,' but 'my Lord' (Pss. xvi. 2, xxxv. 23, and probably xliv. 23, lxxvii. 8, Isa. xlix. 14, Gen. xviii. 3 if in this last passage we should not rather read אֲדֹנִי). אֲדֹנָי must therefore have been equivalent originally to אֲדֹנַי 'my lords,' which is the 'plural of majesty,' and so an appropriate title for the great King (cf. אֲדֹנִי 'my lord'=the king, Ps. cx. i.). To guide the reader when the heavenly King and not any earthly lord, however great, is meant, the points give ־ָי, and not ־ַי, in the final syllable of 'Adonai.' The alternative offered by Lagarde (*Uebersicht über die Bildung der Nomina,* 1889, p. 188)—to consider אֲדֹנָי as an Aramaism of late introduction, meaning 'lordly' (like Syr. *malkóy* 'regal')—seems to require some further explanation. At any rate, the name or title 'Adonai' has no direct connexion with 'Adonis,' the termination of which is probably Greek; cf. Βααλτ-ίς and Herodotus's Κάδυτ-ις, i.e. קְדֵשֶׁת. We have now to ask, How far can the substitution of 'Adonai' for 'Yahveh' be traced? From the fact that the Sept. (the beginnings of which may go back to 250 B.C.) gives Κύριος for the Hebrew 'Yahveh,' Dalman infers, but with some hesitation, that this substitution became the usage at some point in the period between Ezra and Ptolemy Philadelphus. I think that he does well to hesitate, though he might have given a better reason for his hesitation than the fact that, according to Origen (on Ps. ii.) and Jerome (Ep. 136 ad Marcellam), the older copies of the Sept. had not Κύριος, but the Tetragrammaton itself.[1] For surely it is not probable that, if יהוה had ever been pronounced in the Greek Scriptures,

---

[1] Dalman, *Der Gottesname Adonaj und seine Geschichte,* p. 42 (cf. p. 36); Ewald, *Old and New Testament Theology,* p. 100.

Philo would not have given some obscure hint of this. So far from doing this, he distinctly asserts that, not as a mere modern innovation, but as a part of the Mosaic law, none might either speak or hear the most sacred name save in the holy places with ears and tongue purified by wisdom,[1] i.e. he ascribes to Moses the well-known traditional precept that the Tetragrammaton was never to be used 'in the borders' (i.e. outside the sanctuary), and in the temple to be used only by the priests in the daily benediction, and by the high priest ten times on the Day of Atonement.[2] He is wrong no doubt, but could he have fallen into such an error if יהוה had ever been pronounced in Egypt in the Greek period? Even if the earliest Greek copies reproduced the Tetragrammaton in some form it was not pronounced, but read as Κύριος. There is however clearly a difference between the substitution of Κύριος for יהוה in a Greek version of the Scriptures, and consequently also in Hellenistic Jewish society, and that of אדני for יהוה in the Hebrew original and in Palestinian-Jewish society. The former was a far less arbitrary act than the latter, and likely to be ventured upon at a much earlier period. Dalman might therefore more reasonably have hesitated on this ground to propose so early a date as 300 B.C. for the substitution of 'Adonai' for 'Yahveh.'

There are also some facts, partly disputed (I believe), partly misinterpreted by Dalman, which cannot be reconciled with the date which he proposes. There is first a passage in Sirach which implies that the name 'Yahveh' might still with due reverence be pronounced.[3] It was doubtless inexpedient to 'name the Holy One' frequently in conversation; substitutes like 'heaven,' or 'the name,' or 'the Holy One,' would generally meet every need.[4] But there

---

[1] Philo, *De Vitâ Mosis*, Bk. iii. (Mangey, vi. 152), χρυσοῦν δὲ πέταλον ὡσανεὶ στέφανος ἐδημιουργεῖτο, τέτταρας ἔχον γλυφὰς ὀνόματος, ὃ μόνοις τοῖς ὦτα καὶ γλῶτταν σοφίᾳ κεκαθαρμένοις θέμις ἀκούειν καὶ λέγειν ἐν ἁγίοις, ἄλλῳ δὲ οὐδενὶ τὸ παράπαν οὐδαμοῦ.

[2] *Sifre* on Num. vi. 23-27; *Yoma*, 39b.

[3] Ecclus. xxiii. 9, Ὅρκῳ μὴ ἐθίσῃς τὸ στόμα σου, καὶ ὀνομασίᾳ τοῦ ἁγίου μὴ συνεθισθῇς. According to Dalman, the wise man dissuades from causelessly referring to God by any name. I would rather interpret him in accordance with Lev. xxiv. 16 (Sept.).

[4] The Laudian professor of Arabic (Mr. Margoliouth), in his essays towards the retranslation of Sirach into Hebrew, makes use of the names יה and יהוה. This has called forth some criticism, but may, it would seem, be defended by a reference to Proverbs, which must to a great extent (greater than this writer is disposed to admit) have been Sirach's model. Of the substitutes mentioned above, the first is frequent in 1 Maccabees. The second occurs in the present Hebrew text of Lev. xxiv. 11. A later scribe (surely not the original writer) sought by substituting הַשֵּׁם for יהוה to avoid an unpleasant collocation. Possibly, too, he is responsible for the insertion of שֵׁם before יהוה in v. 16. Bickell's supposed

were times which the reverent mind would determine—reading the Scriptures would be one of these—when it was natural and right to utter the word 'Yahveh.' The wise man grants this, but exhorts to caution. Secondly, there is the occurrence of יהוה or יה in the Maccabæan psalms (see especially Pss. cx. and cxviii.[1]), which, to many students at least, refutes the view that even in the temple the Tetragrammaton was only pronounced in the cases mentioned by later tradition. And if the existence of Maccabæan psalms should be disputed, yet few will now deny that the Book of Daniel is a work of the early Maccabæan period, and when we examine that remarkable chapter which contains Daniel's prayer and confession (Dan. ix.) we find that the name 'Yahveh' occurs no less than seven times. It is true that 'Adonai' occurs eleven times, which is not the proportion we should have expected from a study of the Psalms. But it is not possible to give any reason for the relative frequency of 'Yahveh' and 'Adonai' either here or in the different parts of the Psalter.[2]

Next, how can this striking inclination to use 'Adonai' be accounted for? Ezekiel (in whose book אדני יהוה[3] occurs 227 times, and אדני alone 5 times) with his intense supernaturalism prepared the way, and Ezekiel did but give a purified expression to the common feeling of the Jews after the recent catastrophe. 'Jehovah' became, to adopt a phrase interpolated into a passage of Deuteronomy after the Return,[4] a 'glorious and fearful name,' too 'glorious and fearful' to be pronounced with the frank simplicity of earlier days. Later on, the manifold oppression, culminating in a fresh captivity, which saddened the last century of the Persian rule, may have indisposed many of the Jews to pronounce the dear old familiar name of their God (cf. Am. vi. 10). There is a passage of a psalm, in which

---

discovery of הַשֵּׁם in Ps. xiv. (which he thinks an acrostic psalm) has been well criticized by Delitzsch. The third occurs four times in Sirach.

[1] On the absorption of יה (Jah) implied in Sept.'s rend. of Ps. cxviii. 5, and (for the pre-Massoretic text) by the absence of the suffix in זמרת, Ps. cxviii. 14, see *Church Quarterly Rev.*, April 1889, p. 131. This singular expedient of reverence may have arisen in the second part of the Maccabæan period.

[2] There are 55 instances of אדני in the Psalter, including 4 of אדני יהוה and 4 of יהוה אדני. Of these, 46 are in Pss. i.–lxxxix, and 9 in Pss. xc.–cl. This is difficult to account for on any purely chronological theory. Probably the difference in the tone of Books IV. and V. will account for the rarity of אדני. National and missionary psalms are here specially frequent, and fresh themes of praise are constantly sought for. It is remarkable, too, that 29 of the instances of אדני occur in the Elohistic psalms. This riddle, however, seems to me to baffle conjecture. How far, I wonder, is its existence due to the scribes?

[3] On this name of God in Ezekiel, see Cornill's excursus in his *Ezekiel*, pp. 172–175.

[4] Deut. xxviii. 58 (see Dillmann); cf. Pss. xcix. 3, cxi. 9.

one might almost think that the original reading had been changed by a later editor, so much more smoothly does it run if we read אֲדֹנָי for יהוה,

> 'Behold, as the eyes of servants are upon the hand of their lord,
> As the eyes of a handmaid are upon the hand of her mistress,
> So our eyes are upon the Lord our God
> Until he have pity upon us.
> Have pity upon us, O Lord, have pity upon us,
> For we are full enough of contempt.'[1]

The conjecture would however be mistaken.[2] We may indeed read between the lines of the passage that a strong current is carrying men away from the old name of God. But must we not also read that the psalmist seeks to moderate this tendency, and by the introduction of a title which destroys the parallelism reminds believers that their God is no mere despot but (cf. Eph. iii. 15) a personal friend with a personal, family name? He cannot however have hoped, nor (being himself a child of his age) have wished to turn the current back. He would have had against him the growing class of teachers and expositors of the Law, among whom a literalistic principle of interpretation had long been gaining ground. Now there were three passages of the Pentateuch[3] which certainly discouraged a thoughtless use of the sacred name, and might be so interpreted as almost to forbid its being used at all, viz.,

> 'Thou shalt not pronounce the name of Jehovah (Yahveh) thy God for vanity' (Ex. xx. 7).
> 'Ye shall not profane my holy name' (Lev. xxii. 32).
> 'So shall they put my name upon the children of Israel; and I will bless them' (Num. vi. 27).

---

[1] Ps. cxxiii. 2, 3. In Isa. xxvi. 13 we might be tempted to make the same substitution; cf. Ps. lxxxvi. 15, 16 (where 'Adonai' naturally introduces 'thy servant'). But love for the name Jehovah is too marked in Isa. xxvi. to justify this.

[2] The probability that an editor or a scribe would alter יהוה into אדני is almost infinitely greater than that he would take the reverse course. The Targums, it is true, may seem to take this course. But the truth is that (except in cases like Pss. xvi. 2, xxxv. 23, where the suffix in אֲדֹנָי has its proper force) they recognize no distinction between יהוה and אדני. Both words in the Aramaic text are represented by יהוה, which, however, was undoubtedly read אדני.

[3] Some would add Lev. xxiv. 16 (see Kalisch), but Dalman has shown (pp. 44-49) that the entire Jewish tradition is in favour of interpreting נֹקֵב 'he that blasphemeth.' The readings of Sept. and Targ. Onk. have been misunderstood. It is not merely uttering the name of God, but uttering it in a curse, which the translators understood to be referred to. Comp. Prov. xxx. 9, 'Lest I become poor and steal, and grasp at the name of my God' (cursing Him as the author of my misfortune; see Delitzsch).

How was any one to be quite sure in ordinary life that he had sufficient cause to use the most sacred name, especially as the only instance in which the Law gave an express sanction for its use was the case of the priests reciting the daily blessing? How natural it was in that age of growing scrupulosity, when the Pharisees first come before us as the trusted guides of the people, to 'make a hedge around the Law,' and forbid the pronunciation of 'Jehovah' altogether!

It is worth noticing (1) that even in the earlier period there are perhaps signs of a scrupulousness in the pronunciation of the divine name. I allude to such shortened forms of theophoric personal names as Ahaz for Jehoahaz, Nathan for Jehonathan, with which compare Abdi for Abdijah after the Return, the Egyptian abbreviation Petu for Petuosor 'the gift of Osiris' (Révillout), and the Moslem name Abduh 'his servant' for Abdullah 'servant of Allah' (observe that the name of Allah itself is not thought to be profaned by frequent repetition). And (2) that Adonai itself, in the religious syncretisms of the East and especially of Egypt, acquired some of the sanctity of the Tetragrammaton. This we see from the so-called Abrasax-gems (used as amulets), and from Egyptian magical papyri, on one of which (found by M. Groff) storms are said to be calmed by pronouncing the name Adonai.

[Compare the lucid statement of a writer in the *Church Quarterly Review*, April 1889, pp. 123-125. I am glad to find that he is equally opposed with myself to the surrender of the name 'Jehovah.' Compare also Geiger's learned and acute researches in his *Urschrift* (pp. 261-278), and the more sober and cautious treatise of Dalman referred to above.]

NOTE h, 289.

See e.g. *Quis Rer. Div. Heres*, Mangey, i. 476; Κύριος παρὰ τὸ κῦρος is Philo's phrase. Note also his fine saying, Παρρησία δὲ φιλίας συγγενίς· ἐπεὶ πρὸς τίνα ἄν τις ἢ πρὸς τὸν ἑαυτοῦ φίλον παρρησιάσαιτο; Philo does not indeed retain the traditional Hebrew name of God, nor was this either possible or expedient then; but his saying justifies us in doing so. See also *De Sacrificantibus*, Mangey, ii. 258 (as beneficent, the Self-Existent One is called Θεός; as punitive, Κύριος); cf. *De Abr.* (ii.19). I know of course that '*abd* ('servant,' 'slave') in Hebrew, Phoenician, and Arabic, when compounded with the name of God or of a god, can be used as a title of honour. It is a very subtle idiom in Arabic, by which one of the plurals of '*abd* ('*ibâd* in '*ibâd Allah*) describes faithful Moslems, and another ('*abîd*) all mankind, as the creatures of God. Even non-Moslems are not *mamālīk* or 'bondslaves' of Allah; while Moslems, though His servants, are not, as such, worse off than sons. The argument in the text assumes, not the Semitic but conventional Western ideas of lordship and servitude, and is directed against a too exclusive use of the phrase 'the Lord' for the God of Revelation. Even interpreted from a Semitic point of view, this title, too exclusively used, would be open to exception. It favours a too supernaturalistic view of God, like that which Mohammed borrowed from the Judaism of his time, and which in borrowing he exaggerated.

NOTE i, p. 289.

Cf. Briggs, *Messianic Prophecy*, Preface, p. xi.; Boyd Carpenter, *Bampton Lectures* for 1887, p. 309. Dalman surely forgets this when he commits himself so unreservedly to the title 'the Lord' as opposed to 'Jehovah' (*Studien*, p. 81), and equally so does a far less reverent scholar, Renan, when he speaks of Yahveh or Jehovah as 'le nom d'un dieu barbare et étranger,' 'un dieu particulier, le dieu d'une famille humaine et d'un pays' (*Histoire d'Israel*, i. 86), against which we may quote the statement from the same author's *Hibbert Lectures* (p. 16), that 'the worship which Rome has spread abroad in the world is the worship of Jehovah.'

NOTE j, p. 289.

See Prof. Driver's paper *Studia Biblica*, i. 1–20. The objections to 'Jehovah' already urged by Genebrard (16th century) are—(1) that it is an impossible form of modern origin, and (2) that it suggests comparison with 'Jove' (see Delitzsch, *Isaiah*, E. T., 1890, i. 51). There was some cause for Genebrard's opposition. 'Jehovah' was sometimes Latinized as 'Jova,' and in a 'Psalme of Sion' (1593) we have 'Jehova's throne on hie,' and also 'To Jove, the God of love.' But to English ears Jehovah is more euphonious and now more familiar than Yahveh, and 'Jove' (for 'Jupiter') is not now much in use. I do not defend the use of Jehovah in altogether technical, philological books.

NOTE k, p. 289.

See Drummond, *Philo Judæus*, ii. 20–22, cf. p. 63. Thinkers in all ages have taught this doctrine. Not to quote Lâo-tze, the great Egyptian hymn to Amen-Ra says, 'Whose name is hidden from his creatures; in his name which is Amen' (i.e., hidden). *Records of the Past*, ii. 132. Ewald calls the teaching of Philo a 'fundamental error' (*Geschichte*, vi. 256). But Hooker nobly says, 'Whom although to know be life, and joy to make mention of his name, yet . . . our safest eloquence concerning him is our silence' (*Eccl. Pol.* i. 2, 3).

NOTE ᵐ, p. 290.

A mysterious and fatal power was attributed by the Babylonians to the names of their gods (cf. Laurie, *Bibliotheca Sacra*, July 1888). Even in the (later) Avesta the recitation of the twenty names of Ahura is represented as the surest protection against evil and the evil one (*Oxford Z. A.* ii. 21). Mohammed, too, according to tradition, opened Paradise to those who should recite the 99 'excellent names' of God.

NOTE ⁿ, p. 290.

This does not justify popular writers in speaking of the Lord Jesus Christ as Jehovah, which no Jewish Christian could ever have done. Bishop Pearson indeed appeals to *Midrash Tillim* on Ps. xxi. and *Echa rabati* on Lam. i. 6 (*Exposition of the Creed*, 1676, p. 148); very poor authorities! 'El gibbor' in Isa. ix. 5 (6) is not a synonym for Jehovah, and κύριος in Luke ii. 11, Phil. ii. 11 is הָאָדוֹן (Delitzsch), not אֲדֹנָי, if we should not in the former passage rather read κυρίου (as in Luke ii. 26, ix. 26); cf. Lam. iv. 20 (Sept.), Psalm. Sol. xvii. 36, where the same correction is required.

NOTE º, p. 291.

This expression may be criticized. Only once are believers in general called Jehovah's 'sons' (Ps. lxxiii. 15), and only once is Jehovah compared to a father (Ps. ciii. 13). Twice the privilege of divine sonship is accorded to the king (Pss. ii. 7, lxxxix. 27, 28). But the conception at any rate pervades the tender and more universalistic passages of the Psalter. When one of the psalmists says, 'Thou wilt lead the nations upon earth' (lxvii. 5), and another describes Jehovah as 'He that nurtureth the nations' (xciv. 10), they implicitly recognize the divine fatherhood. That the word 'father' is so seldom applied to God by the Biblical writers (see Jer. iii. 4, Isa. lxiii. 16, Mal. i. 6, ii. 10), is significant. Like another divine title—'Sun' (which the three versions Sept., Pesh., and Targ. carefully avoid translating at Ps. lxxxiv. 12)—it may have had too strong a flavour of nature-religion. Yet Hosea had long since accepted it, in the spirit of the 'Our Father,' as the symbol of moral affinity between the true God and His worshippers (see my note on Hos. i. 10).

NOTE ᵖ, p. 292.

See Yasna xxxi. 3, and Farvardîn Yast, § 143 (Spiegel and De Harlez agree with the Oxford translators). That the priority in the utterance of this universalism belongs to Zoroastrianism, need not surprise us. The truth that God is the God of the individual, and not of this or that people, was recognized in the Iranian before it became the common property of the Jewish Church. Later Parsism anticipated not merely conversion as the result of missionary effort, but universal restoration by an inherent cosmic necessity. That the germ of this doctrine lay in the mind of Zarathustra, can hardly perhaps be affirmed.

NOTE q, p. 293.

So in Ps. xxii. 28 'turning to Jehovah' is represented as a 'remembering.' Both expressions imply that Jehovah speaks even to the Gentiles through the conscience (cf. Rom. i. 19–21). Comp. the phrase 'He that admonishes the nations' (Ps. xciv. 10). There may, however, also be an allusion to the covenant with Noah (Gen. ix. 1–17), as in Isa. xxiv. 5, where the 'commandments' and 'statutes' broken by the inhabitants of the earth must be more than the 'dictates of conscience.' Later Judaism taught that the heathen deliberately rejected even the 'seven commandments of Noah,' and consequently neither had the knowledge of God nor were subject to the influence of His Spirit. See a singular passage in *Aboda zara*, 2, 3 (cf. Wünsche, *Der bab. Talmud*, ii. 2, pp. 300, 301).

NOTE r, p. 294.

The reply of later Judaism was unfavourable to the *gōyīm*, but was based on the figment of the rejection of the Torah by the heathen world.

NOTE s, p. 295.

The Book of Ruth, too, which is post-Deuteronomic, because it presupposes the need of an explanation of the 'levirate,' is most easily explained on the analogy of Jonah, which, as Delitzsch remarks, is 'a justification of the God of Israel against the misapprehension that He is exclusively the national God of the Jews.' Cf. Bleek's *Einleitung*, ed. Wellhausen (1878), pp. 204, 205; Kuenen, *Religion of Israel*, ii. 242–244.

NOTE t, p. 295.

Long afterwards we find St. Paul, in an early Christian record, representing himself and Barnabas as the first preachers of spiritual Theism to 'the nations,' whom in time past God had 'suffered to walk in their own ways' (i.e. in self-chosen forms of religion), Acts xiv. 15, 16, cf. xvii. 30.

NOTE ᵘ, p. 296.

Among these we ought hardly to include Ps. lxxix. 6, 7, which is certainly a quotation, and possibly an interpolation (see my note). The idea is that Israel's calamities imply a degree of anger on Jehovah's part which would more naturally be called forth by the heathen.

NOTE ᵛ, p. 296.

Ps. cxviii. 17 reminds us of the psalm-like passage in Tob. xiii. (written perhaps somewhat later), which contains the words, 'Confess him before the nations, ye sons of Israel, for he hath scattered us among them. There declare his greatness, extol him before all that lives' (*vv.* 3, 4 ; cf. *v.* 6). The Book of Tobit, says Ewald, 'is an energetic summons to glorify the true God among the heathen.' This critic dates the book in the age of Ezra; it can, however, hardly be earlier than the Maccabæan period, if only because of its doctrinal teaching. (Jewish opinion inclines to makes it even post-Christian. See Neubauer's *Book of Tobit.*) The Jews of the Dispersion formed a natural bridge between the mother-Church and the heathen nations (cf. H. Schultz, *A. T. Theologie,* ed. 4, p. 386).

LECTURE VII.

Give ear, O Shepherd of Israel, thou that leadest Joseph like a flock; thou that sittest upon the cherubim, shine forth.—Ps. lxxx. 1 (R. V.)

LECTURE VII

PART I.—Reassertion of the purity of the religious ideas of the Psalter, which are also the germ-ideas of Christianity. Later on, Greek thought may have contributed to their development, but not in the psalmists' period. 'Germ-ideas' they were; but not in the sense that they must necessarily have developed into Christianity. A new fertilizing principle was needed, and as a fact such a principle entered the world with Jesus Christ. Instances of its working. Resuming the subject of the last lecture, it is asked, I. Within what sphere does the Lord Jehovah work? The mythic view. Moderation of the psalmists' concessions to it. The conception of heaven begins to be spiritualized. The range of Jehovah's working is universal; but in a more special sense Israel is 'his dominion.' But the relation between Israel and its God is no longer a purely natural one. How the connexion between them was constantly renewed. The sacramentalism of the post-Exile Church studied both from the outside and from the inside. Help derived from the psalmists. Explanation of Pss. xlii. 7, xlviii. 3. Ps. xlviii. valuable (especially if a pilgrim song) as proving the enthusiasm of the Jewish Church for the temple. But is it only within the nation that Jehovah's working is manifest? No; the Psalter itself proves this. The individual can look up to Jehovah as his God, though he turns towards the temple in doing so.—II. By what agency does Jehovah work? Change produced in Jewish Theism by the Exile. Ezekiel's supernaturalism. Emergence of a new problem, how to reconcile the transcendence and the immanence of God. Practical, imaginative solutions of the psalmists. The divine agents, such as the word, or words, of God; his Spirit; the divine Wisdom (and the like); the 'hosts' or 'ministers' of God, whether quasi-personal, or (as we should say) impersonal. Why angels are so rarely mentioned, and why mentioned at all. Even those names of heavenly beings which are of mythic origin are turned to noble account. Contrast between the policy of the psalmists and that of modern missionaries. Misplaced repugnance to finding mythology in the Bible. Permanent value of mythic symbols.

PART II.—One of the agencies by which Jehovah works still remains—the Messianic. Need of a wider explanation of the term 'Messiah.' It is applied (either expressly or virtually) to six persons and classes in the Psalter. The Messianic psalms, and the idea which underlies them, reduced to its simplest form.—III. How does Jehovah work, and with what results? 1. By ruling. His reign over Israel (the centre in some sense of His dominion) goes back to the conquest of Canaan. A new accession however dated from Israel's second Exodus (that from Egypt), and the conception of the theocracy became correspondingly deeper. But the jubilant tone of Ps. xciii. &c. could not be maintained. The keynote of the later age was, 'Jehovah shall become king.' What, then, must Jehovah's royal policy in Israel be? He must reveal His perfect sympathy and educate His people in His ways. Figure of the Shepherd, which corresponds to the deeper conception of God formed in post-Exile times. Explanation of 'thy lowliness,' Ps. xviii. 36. It was a part of Jehovah's 'glory' to abide at once in the highest heaven and in the individual souls. Literal theophanies were no longer expected; those writers who do introduce appearances of Jehovah use the language symbolically. Israel is learning the spiritual presence of God, and the moral purpose of its election.— The idea of the covenant, spiritualized by Jeremiah, and presupposed in the Psalter. Pss. xviii., xxv., xxxii. considered. The last-mentioned reveals a pathetic imperfection in the psalmists' theology but also gives fresh testimony to the view of Jehovah as an educator. And how does He educate His people? By drawing out the spiritual contents of the Scriptures. Schools and teachers were necessary instruments, but their efficacy came from a higher Teacher. Difference between the *sōferīm* (represented by Ps. cxix.) and the 'wise men' (represented by the kernel of the Book of Proverbs). The true symbol of the covenant not so much the temple as the Scripture. No absolute distinction between the Law and the other Scriptures. The Law has become much more than a collection of ordinances. It is educational, and works by moral means. It is Jehovah's best gift to Israel.

PRINCPAL NOTES.—PART I.: On Jehovah's holiness.—On angelology.
PART II. : On Ps. xc.—On the psalmists' conception of sin.

PART I.

JEHOVAH'S SPHERE OF WORKING AND HIS AGENCIES.

WE are warned by these intensely Palestinian words[1] to resist the fascinations which at the close of the last Lecture Alexandria presented to our view. It was not in the time of the psalmists that Hellenic thought knocked for admittance into the Jewish Church. In replying to the question, Who is the God of the Psalter?—illustrations may be drawn from Babylon and from Persia, but not from Hellas. The substitution of the Greek for the Persian rule promoted the ends of the Spirit of revelation, but not at first to any appreciable extent through the infiltration of Greek ideas. It is to Palestine, let me rather say to Jerusalem, aided in some respects by Babylon and Persia, that we are, historically speaking, indebted for the anticipations of Christianity in the Psalter. Those deep conceptions of the meaning of Jehovah's name, of His 'coming to judge the earth' and to 'lead the nations,' and of that Catholic Church in which there is neither Egypt, nor Babylon, nor even Israel,[2] belong to pure Palestinian theology. I do not say either that they were all equally recognized by the Jewish Church, or that they must necessarily have developed into Christianity. Certainly the last of them is but a lightning-flash which illumines the distant summits—the intuition of an individual or at most of a school—of that school which has imbibed Job's universalism, but harmonized it with churchly feeling. And even those conceptions which were the common property of the later writers are by no means as prominent in Talmudic Judaism as on evolutionary grounds we might expect.[a] It would seem as if a new fertilizing principle was required to develop

---

[1] See the text (Ps. lxxx. 1, R.V.).   [2] See above, p. 118.

adequately the germs of spiritual religion. And whence, if not from the East, nor yet from the West, could this new life-giving element come? Is it not a fact that it is due to the creative originality of Jesus Christ, who gave a development to those germ-ideas which amounts sometimes to transfiguration?

Take for instance the great foundation-truths to which I have already referred. The personal responsive God may have ceased to be called Jehovah, but in lieu of this another name or title, avoided by the psalmists [1] from its naturalistic associations, has been restored to use with enriched meaning. '*O Father* . . . I have manifested thy name unto the men which thou gavest me'[b] (John xvii. 5, 6). The name of 'Father' henceforth symbolizes in their application both to humanity and to the individual all those truths which hitherto have had too predominant a reference to Israel.[c] So too the conceptions of the divine 'holiness' and of the kingly rule and final judgment of Jehovah have been deepened in the Gospels till we hardly perhaps recognize their Old Testament ancestry. And lastly, St. Paul has taken up the obscure hints of the Hebrew prophet and psalmist, and developed them into a theory of Catholicity which is startling to a large section of the Church of his time. I will simply quote that noble saying, which illustrates several fine psalm-passages, 'There is no distinction between the Jew and the Greek; for they all have one Lord, who is rich (in goodness) unto all that call upon him' (Rom. x. 12).

I will not excuse myself for reasserting from a critical point of view the intimate relation between the two parts of our Bible. 'The Old Testament religion is not simply one of the great religions of the world; it is the one out of which Christianity was born—the only one out of which it could have come;' and one of our best warrants for accepting the authority of the New Testament is the capacity of its writers for apprehending and developing the highest religious elements in the Old.[d] The connexion between the germ-ideas and the Christian developments is a study which urgently calls for candid labourers. When will some English adherent of critical views first map out the field with more science than

---

[1] See p. 305, note º.

Ewald, and then claim the honour of beginning some part of the work? Returning from this digression, I have to ask, first, Within what sphere does the Lord Jehovah act, according to the psalms; next, through what organs; and lastly, how, and with what results?

1. Within what sphere? The mythic view was that God literally dwelt in heaven (hence the title El Elyon, God Most High), and its influence upon popular speech can be traced throughout the Psalter (see e.g. Pss. ii. 4, xi. 4, xiv. 2, xviii. 7, xx. 7, xxix. 9, cii. 20, civ. 3, cxxiii. 1, cl. 1 °). Still we never find the psalmists condescending to popular weakness by descriptions of heaven, such as we find in Enoch xiv. 9-23 (a fine passage, however, in its own style, which of course is not the liturgical). The tendency of the psalmists, somewhat like that of Zarathustra in his hymns, is to spiritualize the conception of heaven, just as we shall see that they are being led to spiritualize the conception of the temple. In the Maccabæan age a psalmist writes, 'As for our God, he is in heaven; all that he pleaseth, he worketh out;' the second statement is the corollary of the first (Ps. cxv. 3, cf. cxxxv. 6, 2 Chron. xx. 6). The word 'heaven' is becoming a symbol for the reservoir of divine powers, or, more shortly, the beyond, the spiritual world. 'Exalt thyself above the heavens' (the physical heavens), says a somewhat earlier psalmist (lvii. 6, 12); that is, rectify the moral balance by a fresh display of almighty righteousness. In fact, being the unexhausted source of life, and the incalculable Disposer of events, Jehovah must be in some sense 'a God that hideth himself' (Isa. xlv. 15), yet, being the Creator[1] and Preserver of the world, He must fill it with His presence and operation. 'Do not I fill heaven and earth, saith Jehovah' (Jer. xxiii. 24)?

Within what sphere doth Jehovah not work? is therefore the question which the devout reason sanctions. He even 'bringeth down to Sheól and bringeth up,' according to a psalm not included in the Psalter (1 Sam. ii. 6; cf. Deut. xxxii. 39, Ps. lxviii. 21). How then can any part of the 'land ᶠ of the living' (Ps. cxvi. 9) be excepted from His direct and constant supervision? He is $\pi\alpha\mu\beta\alpha\sigma\iota\lambda\varepsilon\grave{\upsilon}s$ in the Greek Sirach (Ecclus. l. 15), and whatever the popular belief or the later Rabbinic

---

[1] On Jehovah as the Creator, see p. 322.

doctrine may have been, the greater psalmists undoubtedly held that all nations were under Jehovah's hand.¹ Still there was a special sense in which Israel was the sphere of His working. Upon this people His 'name had been called'ᵍ— a phrase which signifies that Jehovah had claimed Israel as His property, and guaranteed to it His protection. Freely and unconditionally? No. The post-Exile Church did not believe that it had a natural and indefeasible right to Jehovah's patronage. The figures of sonship and wifeship were no longer adequate to express Israel's relation to its Lord. The church-nation had constantly to renew its connexion with Jehovah in the place which He had 'chosen to place his name there'ʰ by right and acceptable acts of worship (cf. Ps. li. 21, and perhaps iv. 6). And correspondingly it was one of the highest privileges of the priest to lift up his hands over the congregation, and lay the name of Jehovah upon it (Num. vii. 22–27, cf. Lev. ix. 22, 23, Deut. x. 8, xxi. 5).

This solemn rite was not of a magical but of a sacramental nature. A more or less conscious sacramentalism followed necessarily from the loss of that temple within the temple— that בֵּית אֵל or 'house of God' in the strictest sense of the phrase, the ark. Need I justify this description of the ark? Not only to the Philistines (1 Sam. iv. 7), but according to Num. x. 35 to Moses himself the ark was clothed with divinity, because inherent in it was the wondrous power (the *numen*) of 'the God of the armies of Israel' (1 Sam. xvii. 45), and hence in the narrative books the name 'Jehovah Sabáoth' can be accurately paraphrased 'the God of the ark.'¹ Jeremiah indeed had higher intuitions. He looked forward to a worship which would be independent not only of the ark but of any 'house of God' in an exclusive sense; the whole of Jerusalem would become Jehovah's throne (Jer. iii. 16, 17). He evidently felt that the name of God could not be shut up either in a word or in a building. Even to use the old language and the old forms of thought in a sacramental sense was to fall short of the ideal of spiritual religion. If he still recognized the sanctity of Jerusalem, it was because this city was to be, according to the old prophecy (Isa. ii. 2, 3), the centre of missionary activity and religious instruction. But

¹ See e.g. Pss. xxii. 29, xlvii. 9.

the evangelical prophet (as Jeremiah has the best claim to be entitled) was far in advance both of his own [j] and of the next generation. The idealism of which he was the first exponent was beyond the horizon both of Ezekiel and of Ezra, who felt that the new Jewish Church had educational functions to discharge, and conceived that a ritual system centred in a material sanctuary could not in their time be dispensed with.

And yet how different in all respects was the theory of the temple realized in the post-Exile Church from that against which Jeremiah preached! Let us first regard this theory from the outside. In the earlier period, the land of Canaan was Jehovah's house in a primary, and the temple at Jerusalem only in a secondary sense.[k] In the later the relative positions were reversed.[m] This change may be attributed to the deep impression produced upon the most religious minds by two great events—the retreat of the army of Sennacherib and the Babylonian Exile. The local worships made a stout resistance, but their power was waning long before Jehovah, as it was thought, deserted His land ; and no serious attempt was ever made to revive them,[n] the restored exiles being pronounced adherents of the Deuteronomic law. Henceforth that mystic union with God, which was the original object of sacrifices, could only be obtained by bodily or mental presence in the one temple at Jerusalem. Some of the psalmists, no doubt, reached the confines of a higher region of thought.[1] We marvel at their attainments, but recognize their limitations. They could not know 'the liberty wherewith Christ hath made us free.'

And now let us consider the post-Exile theory of the temple from the inside. In doing so we shall rely entirely on the authority of the psalmists. These temple-poets retain the old mythic language. 'Make melody to Jehovah who dwelleth in Zion' (Ps. ix. 12), says a psalm of the early Persian period, while a psalm of the Greek age speaks of 'the mount which God hath desired to dwell in' (Ps. lxviii. 17). Other mountains may be grander. The Bashan range may in a Semitic nature-religion be regarded as a 'mountain of Elohim' (Ps. lxviii. 16). But to the God who is spirit (for do not the psalmists virtually confess this truth?) a humbler elevation

[1] See Lecture VIII., p. 387.

supplies a more fitting sanctuary. Therefore, 'when my soul droopeth within (lit., upon) me, from the land of mighty Hermon, I think upon thee, thou little mountain;' such, according to Hitzig's striking explanation, was the thought of a captive psalmist in the Greek period[1] (Ps. xlii. 7). He drew comfort from the thought that, just because Jehovah's mountain was naturally so insignificant, its God might be trusted to interpose in supernatural majesty. In Ps. xlviii. 3, if the text be right, there is a still more remarkable use of mythic phraseology. In commenting upon the words rendered in the Revised Version—

> Beautiful in elevation, the joy of the whole earth,
> Is mount Zion, (on) the sides of the north,
> The city of the great King,

the conservative critic, Hengstenberg, makes this remark, 'The only legitimate exposition is that which is derived from a comparison of Isa. xiv. 13, 14.' You remember the passage. The King of Babylon looks forward to as proud a pre-eminence after death as he has enjoyed in life. He will become like the most High, and enthrone himself above the stars on the sacred mountain, on whose summit the divine beings dwell.[o] The psalmist may be thinking of the same myth, and says, 'We have a better Olympus than that of any of the nations; it is Mount Zion, the dwelling-place of Jehovah.' Those who object to emending the text cannot help accepting this view. But even if we take another course, it is certain that the psalmists regarded Mount Zion as a symbol of 'heaven's high steep,' the invisible 'mountain of Elohim' spoken of by Ezekiel (xxviii. 14).[p] It is once (if I understand Ps. lxxxvii. 5 aright) actually called עֶלְיוֹן, a word which is often applied to God Himself;[q] the expression was probably suggested by 1 Kings viii. 8, where we should supply אֲשֶׁר הָיָה עָלָיו from 2 Chron. vii. 21. We can understand therefore that sometimes there is a doubt whether the earthly or the heavenly dwelling-place of Jehovah is intended (e.g. Pss. vii. 8, xlvii. 6, lxviii. 6, 19). Also that the permanence of the earthly should seem guaranteed by that of the heavenly sanctuary (Pss. lxviii. 17, lxxviii. 69, cxxxii. 14, cf. xciii.

---

[1] See Lecture III., p. 115.

2, 4, 5). The second temple is in fact in a certain sense that which the ark was of old to the Israelites.

> They that trust in Jehovah are like Mount Zion,
> Which cannot be shaken, but is seated for ever.
> Jerusalem—mountains are round about her;
> Jehovah too is round about his people
> From henceforth even for ever (Ps. cxxv. 1, 2).

I say, in a certain sense, for we must remember the symbolizing, sacramental tendency of the Jewish Church. Israel's true protector is Jehovah Himself. This intuition, which before the Exile was confined to the great prophets and their disciples (see Isa. xxviii. 16, Jer. xvii. 13—much misunderstood passages[r]), is now the common property of the Church. Her teachers may speak of Zion, as they also speak of heaven, as Jehovah's dwelling-place, but what they more or less consciously mean by both words is the store of those hidden spiritual forces, the manifestation of which constitutes the 'glory of Jehovah.' At any moment the Church can appeal to the God 'who dwelleth in Zion' to uncover this latent glory (Pss. iv. 7, lxxx. 4). The answer may be delayed, but the pain of suspense is balanced by the pleasure of trust. Even in the darkness faithful Israel can say—

> Our soul waiteth for Jehovah :
> He is our help and our shield.
> For our heart shall rejoice in him,
> Because we have trusted in his holy name.
> (Ps. xxxiii. 20, 21.)

And looking back at a time of peace upon the national history, a psalmist can exclaim,

> There is a river, whose streams make glad the city of God,
> The holy place of the dwelling of the most High.
> God is in the midst of her ; she cannot be moved ;
> God doth help her, and that right early (Ps. xlvi. 5, 6).

Thus Jehovah—the true Jehovah—was sacramentally present in the temple to all faithful worshippers,[1] and the sense of security which this presence gave was the characteristic blessing of Zion,

---

[1] Supplement the above by the statements in Lect. VIII. on the Guest-psalms.

> For there Jehovah appointed the blessing,
> Even life for evermore (Ps. cxxxiii. 3),

which has to be explained by Ps. cii. 29—

> The children of thy servants shall abide,
> And their seed shall be established before thee.

Can we wonder that so precious a possession as the temple excited such enthusiasm in the Jewish community, both at home and abroad? Upon some of the expressions of this I shall have to comment later; suffice it now to refer to Ps. xlviii., a pilgrim song, if I am not mistaken, and parallel therefore to Ps. cxxii.

> Walk about Zion and encompass her,
> Number her towers ;
> Mark ye well her rampart,
> Note thoughtfully her fortresses ;
> That ye may tell the generation following,
> That this God is our God for ever and alway ;
> It is he that will guide us evermore.
> (Ps. xlviii. 13–15, De Witt.)

But is it only within the sphere of the nation, whose spiritual centre is the temple, that Jehovah works? Is there not a divine plan for the individual's as well as for the nation's life? Cannot each and every Israelite pour out his own private griefs and joys before Him who 'fashioneth hearts' (xxxiii. 15)? And does not Jehovah reward such confidence, and, directly or indirectly, punish the want of it? Certainly if the individual had been left to himself so far as sensible proofs of Jehovah's interest in him personally were concerned, he would have sought in magic the satisfaction of his irrepressible cravings. But such was not the case, as even the Psalter sufficiently shows. It is not the Church but an individual who tells us in the 139th psalm that sleeping or waking he is ever busy with the thought of God (*v.* 18), and an individual who in the 73rd so trustfully alludes to the plan by which his God leads him (*v.* 24). Nor can the lovely 23rd psalm have merely a national reference, as some theorists have persuaded themselves,[3] unless indeed the allegory in John x. can have a similarly restricted meaning. Which of us, even if we be critics, can believe that the writers of these psalms do not pray in their own behalf? Yet we must with all emphasis affirm that the individual never felt himself standing alone—instinctively he connected his personal joys and griefs with those of the Church-nation. A sign of this (necessary to those who had not attained to the exalted idealism of Jeremiah [t]) was the custom of turning in the act of prayer to the holy mount, which was as it were the starting-point of the desired answer to his supplication (see Pss. iii. 5, v. 8, xxviii. 2, cxxxviii. 2, and cf. 1 Kings viii. 29, 30, Dan. vi. 11). And hence the blessing pronounced on the God-fearing man runs thus, the most unselfish boon being placed first,

> Jehovah bless thee out of Zion!
> Behold thou the prosperity of Jerusalem
> All the days of thy life;
> Yea, behold thou thy children's children.
> Peace be upon Israel.   (Ps. cxxviii. 5, 6, De Witt.)

2. We have next to inquire by what agency Jehovah works, according to the psalmists. A great change has passed in their time upon Israelitish Theism, which expresses itself with singular clearness in certain forms of language. Notice for instance the fondness of Palestinian Jewish writers for the divine title El Elyōn[u] (or its Aramaic equivalent, see Dan. iii. 26, &c.), and in connexion with this a strange reluctance in some quarters to employ the venerable name Jehovah. The God who, as antiquity delighted to believe, had once appeared to men in bodily form, now seemed to have retired to an infinite distance from created things.[v] This was the first result of prophetic thought upon the recent national judgments.

> How shall I behold the face
> Henceforth of God or angel, erst with joy
> And rapture so oft beheld?

Nowhere is this intensified supernaturalism (the beginnings of which can be traced in Isaiah) more strikingly exhibited than in Ezekiel—one of the greatest of those reformers who have recognized the importance to popular religion of the transcendental element in the conception of God, or, in Hebrew phrase, of God's 'holiness' and 'glory.'[w] There were those however in the post-Exile period who misused this supernatural Theism. Some of them extracted from it an argument for immorality (like the 'fool' who said in his heart, 'There is no God,'[1] i.e., none but an inactive Deity), others (like the author of Ecclesiastes) for a low-toned estimate of human life. Others again may have recoiled from it into a critical agnosticism (Prov. xxx. 1–4), and others, though they did not 'restrain devotion' (Job xv. 4), yet could fall into the complaint that God had 'hidden his face' (Pss. xliv. 25, lxxxviii. 15). No doubt there were also wise men in Israel who sought to correct these evils and (if I may employ modern terms) to solve the problem of reconciling God's transcendence with His immanence. Ezekiel was the first of these, but Ezekiel was not the man to devise sufficiently sympathetic modes of meeting the difficulty.

Did the psalmists succeed better? A practical, imaginative solution of the problem is of course all that we can expect from them; logic and metaphysics were not the natural domain of the Jewish intellect. They appear to have conceived of God in a way at once profound and popular as surrounded by a number of ideas and ideals, of plans for the race, for the nation, and even for individuals, and of forces both natural and spiritual, some of which they personalized, not arbitrarily, but on the basis of primitive beliefs, and some they did not. God's words, for instance, they imagined as standing near Him, ready to express and carry out His thoughts or ideas (see Pss. xxxiii. 6, cvii. 20, cxlvii. 15, 18, and cf. Isa. lv. 11, Wisd. xviii. 15).[x] Or we may quite correctly say that His words are at once His spoken and His as yet unspoken thoughts; a דָּבָר may be that which God says in (more strictly, to) His heart or mind.[2] To think or plan is with God to create, but His thoughts need outward expression. His 'word' is said to come to a prophet (Jer. ii. 1), and to alight upon a nation (Isa. ix. 8).[y] This divine, supernatural word may also be translated into human speech, and handed down to succeeding generations. In this case, however, an 'uncovering of the eyes,' or, as we may also say, an 'opening' of the divine words themselves, is indispensable for him who would comprehend them (Ps. cxix. 18, 130). This idea of the 'word' of God gave a light and comfort to

[1] Pss. xiv. 1; cf. x. 4, 11, 13, lxxiii. 11, Job xxii. 13, 14.
[2] Gen. viii. 21 (cf. xxiv. 45, xxvii. 41).

believers which no merely supernatural God could convey.
'Of God do I boast, even of his word,'[z] says Israel in the
midst of sore trouble (Ps. lvi. 5, 11), for of the preservation
of Israel not less than of the creation and preservation of the
world, it is true to say 'He spake, and it was done' (Ps.
xxxiii. 9, cf. 10 and 11).

The conception of Jehovah's word is closely connected
(as is plain from Gen. i. 2, 3) with that of His spirit,—a connexion which is specially characteristic of the Old Testament.[aa]
It was no blind force inherent in nature which produced this
beautiful world, but a divine Thinker. The spirit represents
the universal life-giving principle which is communicated by
a 'word,' or, as Ps. xxxiii. 6 says, 'by the breath of God's
mouth.' A mythic origin is here too obvious to be disputed.
It was this that invested the term with the popularity which
commended it to religious writers, though less to the psalmists
than to others. 'Spirit of Jehovah,' or a similar phrase, occurs
four times in the Psalter, viz., in li. 13, civ. 30, cxxxix. 7,
cxliii. 10. Of these passages, the first represents the Spirit
as the energizing principle of 'holiness' (i.e. in this context,
of devotion to the covenant between Israel and Jehovah)[bb];
the second, of creation or re-creation; the third, of the divine
action in its totality; and the fourth, of providential guidance.
The third is doctrinally the most interesting, because it suggests more distinctly than the rest the personality of the
Divine Spirit.[cc]

Twice only do we find a certain half-independence ascribed
to the divine creative wisdom or understanding (civ. 24,
cxxxvi. 5),[dd], and we may ascribe this to the influence of
Prov. viii. 22–31, at least if we accept the pre-Exile date of
this noblest of cosmogonies [ee] (cf. note [cc], p. 217). Thrice, too,
is a quasi-personal existence given to God's 'truth' or 'truth-
fulness' (xliii. 3, lvii. 4, lxi. 8), twice to His 'lovingkindness'
(lvii. 4, lxi. 8), and once to His 'light' (xliii. 3) as the agencies
or agents of deliverance. All these expressions are suggested
by the unconscious idealistic philosophy of early ages, and
find their parallels both in Zoroastrian and in Talmudic
theology.[ff] Nor are these the only ἰδέαι (if I may apply the
term) which encircle the Creator's throne. There are cosmic
as well as ethical δυνάμεις through which the God of nature

works. The 'hosts' and 'ministers' (Sept. δυνάμεις, λειτουργοί) in Ps. ciii. 21 include, not only personal or partly personalized, but even altogether impersonal agents, such as the storm-wind (mythicized sometimes as the cherub),[gg] and the lightning-flame (civ. 4), and the sun, the moon, and the stars, which are still regarded as not wholly inanimate (see on Ps. xxiv. 6). And hence the phrase 'Jehovah Sabáoth,' i.e. 'Jehovah the God of hosts,' means in the psalms (except perhaps in Ps. xxiv.) not merely the God of the armies of Israel, but more especially (somewhat as the similar Babylonian title [1]) the God of the manifold spiritual and physical powers which He can employ for His people.[2] 'Angels' is a term which can be applied to any of these 'hosts' of God; twice (xxxiv. 8, xxxv. 5) we even find 'the angel of Jehovah,' who may be either a direct embodiment of Jehovah Himself, as in the early narratives, or the particular angel who has been selected from the myriad members of his class either, as in xxxv. 5, to punish, or, as in xxxiv. 8, to protect. In xci. 11 'angels' in general are spoken of as defending the believer; the sense, however, is the same as in the two former passages. No recognition is given either to the existence of a personal evil principle (though Sin, or Apostasy, is once personified as a quasi-divine power in xxxvi. 2, comp. Zech. v. 8 [3]), or to the names of evil angels, or to the attaching of a special angel or angels to an individual.[hh] And delightful as the psalmists' references to angels are, they are comparatively so few in number as to suggest[ii] that a doctrine of angels lay as yet outside the programme of the leaders of Jewish thought.[jj]

What, then, may be presumed to have been the psalmists' object in their occasional mention of angels? The same as that of the great narrators who adopt certain popular myths and legends, not with a historical object (for what we call history was not yet born), but to fill them with a new and purer spirit. The psalmists' object was, not merely to regu-

---

[1]. See Schrader, *Cuneiform Inscriptions*, ii. 105; Sayce, *Hibbert Lectures*, p. 217.

[2] So even in Ps. lix. 6; cf. Isa. xxix. 6.

[3] Cf. Enoch xlii. 1–3 (where Wisdom and Unrighteousness are opposed, as in Proverbs Wisdom and Folly).

late, but so far as possible to render subservient to edification a dangerous popular tendency which had been strengthened by Babylonian and Persian influences. Much reference to the spirit-world would have been worse than useless. The people understood well enough who the angels were, and what they did, though probably they preferred to call them by other names. Some of these the psalmists themselves have now and then employed for the sake of variety. Thus we see from lxxxix. 6, 8,[1] that the angels were also called the 'holy,' i.e. the superhuman, supersensible ones, while in ciii. 20[2] they are mentioned as the 'heroes,' and in lxxviii. 25 [kk] as the 'mighty.' Who can help admiring the beautiful tact with which the two latter titles are introduced? 'To the nation whose romantic history it enriched,' the phrase, 'the bread of the mighty,' became, as Dr. Martineau observes, 'the favourite emblem of the providing care of God.'[3] And if the angels, with whose worship the Church associates her own, are 'heroic in strength,' it is only, according to the psalmist, that they may 'perform His word'—the word of Him who has said, 'Upon all their host do I lay commands' (Isa. xlv. 12). Thus their glory lies in their emptiness of self-hood. To all who would exalt the angels above measure, the psalmists, like the first great Christian commentator on their words, would reprovingly exclaim, 'Are they not all ministering spirits, sent forth to do service?' (Heb. i. 14 R.V.)

There were also other names of angels of more doubtful sound, because associated with myths uncongenial to the higher religion. I refer to the phrases 'the gods' (*ēlīm*[4] or *elōhīm*[5]), 'the sons of the gods' (*b'nē ēlīm*,[6] *b'nē elōhīm*, or *b'nē hā-elōhīm*[7]), and the sons of the most High[8] (*b'nē 'elyōn*), which describe certain 'principalities and powers' of which a secondary divinity is predicated, and which together form the 'council' of Jehovah.[ll] I have said so much elsewhere on these mythic phrases [mm] that I must be brief now. Suffice it to say that, in spite of their avoidance of the divine name

---

[1] Cf. Job v. 1, xv. 15, Zech. xiv. 5.   [2] Cf. Joel iv. 11, and see Targum
[3] *Hours of Thought*, i. 164.   [4] Ps. lviii. 2.
[5] Ps. lxxxii. 1, 6.   [6] Pss. xxix. 1, lxxxix. 7.
[7] Gen. vi. 2, 4, Job i. 6, ii. 1, xxxviii. 7.   [8] Ps. lxxxii. 6.

'Father,' the psalmists have not refused to employ these, as we cannot help thinking, strange titles. But to what noble purpose have they turned them! Nothing, for instance, will more heighten our respect for the Hebrew Scriptures than a careful study of Psalms xxix., lviii., and lxxxii. in connexion with the Prologue of Job, and, to take a still wider range, with those narratives of Genesis which have sometimes been so unwisely ridiculed. We at least can see that, though they scorned not to pick the wayside flowers of mythic imagery, the Old Testament writers have most deftly interwoven them with blooms of another clime, that they have in short pressed popular imagination into the service of religion.

But is this in accordance with modern analogies? Do we not find in our foreign mission fields—in Japan, for instance —that translators of the Bible are obliged to adopt terms of pronounced mythic origin to express Christian conceptions? And yet the well-instructed Christian convert has no thought, as he reads his Bible, of the old mythic affinities of the terms. May not the mythic terms in the Hebrew Scriptures have had their meaning as absolutely transformed as those in the Japanese Bible? No; the cases of ancient Judah and modern Japan are different. Christianity has interrupted the natural development of Japanese religion. The prophets of Israel, however, historically regarded, aimed not at interrupting but at guiding and spiritualizing the inherited religion of their people. It is not possible to interpret the Old Testament critically upon the same theory as the Japanese Bible, nor can Biblical exegesis leave out of account the original meaning of mythic phrases.

Pardon me for insisting upon so obvious a truth. It appears to me that exegesis is in danger of being led astray by a misplaced modern repugnance to mythology. For instance, the view that both in Ps. lxxxii. and in Heb. ii. 5 prince-angels are referred to, is sometimes rejected because it is opposed to conventional modes of 'thought.[nn] I venture to regret this, and sympathize with one of the Oxford missionaries in Calcutta, who finds comfort in the thought that 'the Angel of India and his host are more than they that are with them.' Why should I fear to recognize mythic forms of speech in the New Testament? There, or anywhere else, if of the nobler kind, they delight, they edify me. The yearning after God which they imply touches me somewhat as the author of *Religio Medici* was touched by the music of the streets. Nor can I see that anything is gained by rejecting them. You may call them myths, and declare, with Max Piccolomini in Coleridge's version of *Wallenstein*, that 'they live no longer in the faith of reason.' But myths are not necessarily fables, and are wholly exempt from the criticism of the lower reason. Some myths at least were regarded in the early Church as symbols of truths which could not otherwise be expressed. And can it be shown that the capacity of man for apprehending supersensible facts has been materially widened? Cannot poetry still enter where dogmatic theology stands without?

Permit me, then, to hope that some whose lot it is to speak of the Old Testament will join me in the path which Herder long since indicated. Thus and thus only can some of those misconceptions be removed which keep doubters from us. Thus and thus only will Christian students win the key to many of their own dearest symbols, and be enabled to draw honey from the neglected myths of Hebrew antiquity. Truly said Max Piccolomini, expressing Schiller's own protest against the vulgar rationalism,

> . . . . a deeper import
> Lurks in the legend told my infant years
> Than lies upon that truth, we live to learn.

A localized Olympus is useless to us, but the Christian heart has still its 'mount of God;'[∞] and since the Church is a '*royal* priesthood,' each member thereof may in a true sense adopt the language even of the King of Babylon.[1] Our angelic visitants have indeed no material mountain to descend, and when we dream, it is of no ladder like Jacob's; and yet, whenever the Christian poet speaks of heaven and of angels, he uses the imaginative material inherited from the days when the world was young. How else, truly, can he express his sense that nature is not a lifeless machine, but 'full,' as some one has said, 'of eyes which are always gazing into ours'? Those 'eyes' must be friendly human eyes; do we not all prefer the conception of the angel in the patriarchal

---

[1] Isa. xiv. 13, 14.

stories to that of the cherub? And yet the latter, on which Jehovah was thought to ride from heaven to earth (Ezek. i., x.), is too striking a symbol to be cast aside. The God of the Christian as well as the Jewish Church is 'high above all nations' (Ps. cxiii. 4), but the Spirit-taught utterances of believing hearts can at any moment bring Him nigh. For, as the elder Church sings, 'Thou, the Holy One, on whom our fathers trusted, art enthroned (not upon the cherubim of fancy, but) upon the praises of Israel (Ps. xxii. 4).[1]

Note a, p. 312.

Weber, *Altsyn. Theol.*, p. 150 (view of name Jehovah); Cremer, *Bibl. Theol. Lex.*, p. 662 (on 'kingdom of heaven,' or 'of God'); cf. Edersheim, *Prophecy and History*, pp. 350, 351. In comparing Israel's religion with those of other nations, we must therefore not look too exclusively at its latest phases, as is done by Asmus (*Die indogerman. Religion*, ii. 330, &c.).

Note b, p. 313.

The passage has, however, a wider meaning. Comp. also Matt. xi. 27, where a very ancient reading (Origen) is: 'No one knew (ἔγνω) the Father save the Son,' illustrating this by John i. 18.

Note c, p. 313.

One of the finest examples is in Matt. xi. 25, with which cf. Eph. iii. 15. Ben Sira makes a fine individualizing use of the term in Ecclus. xxiii. 1–4; li. 10 (see Edersheim) is not in point, the Church being here the speaker. Philo often uses it of God in His relation both to the world and mankind. In a noble description of the Divine Kingship (*Opera*, Mangey, ii. 634, 635), he remarks that God is no tyrant but a king who uses a gentle and legal sovereignty, βασιλεῖ δὲ οὐκ ἔστι πρόσρησις οἰκειοτέρα Πατρός. In its reference to the nation, it is common in the Jewish liturgies (see the fifth and sixth of the Eighteen Benedictions and the prayer called *Abīnū Malkěnū*, 'our Father, our King'). The learned nonjuror Hickes admits this, but adds that the old Jews, being under a servile dispensation, never presumed to address themselves unto God by

---

[1] Cf. *Expositor*, Jan. 1888, p. 29; *The Hallowing of Criticism*, pp. 109, 110.

that familiar appellation before the times of Christianity, 'when they saw that the Christians, who reproached them as bondmen to the Law, came with such freedom to the throne of grace' (*The Spirit of Enthusiasm Exorcised*, 1709, p. 35).

NOTE d, p. 313.

Compare Ritschl's almost too bold expression of this truth in *Die christliche Lehre von der Rechtfertigung*, ii. 15–17 (ed. 1874). In the next sentence but one, the reference is to Ewald's last great work on Biblical Theology (*Die Lehre der Bibel von Gott*, &c.).

NOTE e, p. 314.

Note also the characteristic phrase 'the God of heaven' (Ps. cxxxvi. 26), and compare the use of שָׁמַיִם as a kind of ideograph for God (cf. p. 298, and see Landau, *Die dem Raume entnommene Synonyma für Gott in der neuhebr. Literatur*, 1888).

NOTE f, p. 314.

If we should not, in Ps. cxvi. 9, rather read 'paths' with Dr. Weir (see crit. note in my commentary).

NOTE g, p. 315.

See Deut. xxviii. 10, Isa. lxiii. 19, Jer. xiv. 9, vii. 10, 11, xv. 16, Am. ix. 12, 1 Kings viii. 43, and cf. Isa. iv. 1, 2 Sam. xii. 28. See also Kautzsch, *Zeitschr. f. die alttest. Wiss.*, 1886, pp. 18, 19.

NOTE h, p. 315.

See Deut. xii. 5, and cf. Isa. xviii. 7, 1 Kings viii. 17, Tobit xiii. 11. Originally 'the name' in 'the place of the name' and similar phrases must have meant the ark (cf. the language used of the temple at Shiloh, Jer. vii. 12, and see next note). But in the higher religion it meant as certainly 'the God who answers prayer,' 'the God of revelation' (cf. Isa. lvi. 7, 'my house shall be called the house of prayer').

NOTE i, p. 315.

Comp. the Phœnician inscription of Eshmunazar, lines 16, 17, where it is the 'very lofty name' of Astarte or Esmun which dwells in the god's temple. Spencer (*De Legibus Hebræorum*, ii. 892, &c.)

fully grasps the original meaning of the ark, quoting the Targum on Jer. iii. 16 (which adds to the prophet's words, 'neither with it shall they go to battle'), and Prudentius' description of the ark as 'Deum circumvagum.' It is unnecessary to read with Klostermann in 2 Sam. vi. 2, 'the ark of God, the name of which was called Yahveh Çebáoth.'

Note J, p. 316.

See Jer. vii. 4. But all Jeremiah's contemporaries were not formalists. 1 Kings viii. 27–30 is clearly a compromise between the exalted idealism of Jeremiah and the sweet old religion of holy places; and similar conceptions are implied in Pss. v. 8, xxviii. 2 (cf. my Study in *Expositor*, Jan. 1890). The Prayer of Solomon was probably written (as Kuenen has shown) not long before the first captivity. How M. Vernes can think that the view of the temple which it expresses points rather to the Greek period (*Les résultats de l'exégèse biblique*, p. 210), is difficult to understand.

Note k, p. 316.

'The trumpet to thy mouth!' says Jehovah to His prophet Hosea; 'as an eagle he cometh against the house of Jehovah, because they have transgressed my covenant, and trespassed against my law' (Hos. viii. 1; the opening words of the passage seem incomplete). The 'house' is the land of N. Israel, as in Hos. ix. 15.

Note m, p. 316.

The superiority of Jerusalem to the other 'dwellings of Jacob' is recognized in Ps. lxxxvii. 2. A post-Exile prophet, noticing the unworthy pride which this superiority nourished at Jerusalem, foretells the time when such self-exaltation shall cease, Judah and Jerusalem being equally holy (Zech. xii. 7, xiv. 21). See further Wellhausen, *Prolegomena*, p. 22, note.

Note n, p. 316.

This statement is correct, whatever be the date of Isa. lxv., lxvi. (see pp. 153, 159).

Note o, p. 317.

In my note on Isa. xiv. 13 I have remarked that, tempting as it is to identify the 'mountain of (the divine) assembly' with the mythic Babylonian 'mountain of the lands,' we are not bound to follow the Assyriologists in this point, since the Jews themselves believed in a 'holy mountain of Elohim,' on the slopes of which lay the 'garden' (or park) of Eden (Ezek. xxviii. 13, 14). It now appears somewhat doubtful whether the 'mountain of the lands' was localized anywhere upon earth. Jensen (*Die Kosmologie der Babylonier*, pp. 203–209) thinks that the name belonged to the earth itself, which was regarded as a mountain. He thinks further (p. 23) that the prophet's הר מועד, if it corresponds to a Babylonian belief, may mean the heaven, regarded as a mountain, for which view he finds points of contact in the cuneiform texts. He does not however deny that the Iranian mountain Harā-berezaiti, on which the divinities Mithra and Rashnu dwelt, and Meru, the Indian mountain of the gods, were localized on the earth.

Note P, p. 317.

We find the same symbolical view of a temple at Babylon and Nineveh. At the former place the great temple was called 'the palace (*êkal*) of heaven and earth;' at the latter, 'the house of the great mountain of the lands.' 'So far as I know,' says Tiele, 'the name *êkal* is only given to such metropolitan temples.'

Note q, p. 317.

The ordinary rendering of Ps. lxxxvii. 5 according to which עֶלְיוֹן=הוּא, is usually supported by a reference to 1 Sam. xx. 29, where however the Sept. appears to have read otherwise, and some correction is indispensable (see Klostermann and Wellhausen). In Ps. *l.c.* I take עֶלְיוֹן adverbially, with Geiger (*Urschrift*, p. 34).

Note r, p. 318.

In the former, the 'stone' referred to is the whole of Mount Zion (cf. Isa. iv. 5), including especially the temple, but the object of Israel's faith is not the rock, but He who founds it, viz., Jehovah. In the latter, Jeremiah addresses God as 'Thou throne of glory . . . . thou hope of Israel, Jehovah.' He means to say that Jehovah who needs no temple is alone the fitting hope of Israel (contrast the language of the Jews, Jer. vii. 4).

Note s, p. 319.

Philo gives the psalm not merely a national but a cosmic reference, and yet even he says that it may also be said by the individual (*De Agric.*, Mangey, i. 308).

Note ᵗ, p. 320.

After the fall of the temple opinions became divided as to the necessity of turning towards Jerusalem in prayer. The doctrine of the omnipresence of the Shekina seemed to many Rabbis to render this unnecessary (*Baba bathra*, 25, ap. Wünsche, *Talm.* ii. 2, p. 158, &c.). It was in fact a remnant of externalism which we too, from the highest prophetic point of view, may justly criticize. But in doing so, we must give full credit to pious Israelites for having to so great an extent thrown off the fair but dangerous religion of local and material sanctity. For it is clear that the psalm-passages which I have referred to above presuppose a compromise between the teaching of Jeremiah and an unenlightened antiquity. Comp. Study on Psalms xxvi. and xxviii., *Expositor*, Jan. 1890.

Note ᵘ, p. 320.

Ὕψιστος, as a name of God, which is found so often in the Greek version of Sirach, occurs, however, but twice in Wisdom (v. 15, vi. 3), and Dr. Drummond does not enter it among the divine epithets in Philo. Yet no Jewish teacher ever felt the 'transcendence' of God more strongly than Philo.

Note ᵛ, p. 320.

As a Midrash pointedly expresses it, the last of the ten descents (ירידות) of God will take place in the age to come (*Pirqe de Rabbi Eliezer*, c. 14, ap. Delitzsch).

Note ʷ, p. 320.

Jehovah's holiness and His glory are correlative ideas. In Himself, as compared with man, He is 'holy,' and His appearance is glorious. This illustrates Isa. vi. 3 as compared with Ps. xxix. 9. Both terms have a suggestion of fearfulness, especially in the moral stage of Jewish religion. Those who are not altogether at peace with God may well fear one who is raised so high above nature, and whose vesture is of fiery light. But to those who are friends of Jehovah, His 'glory' is a synonym for His 'pleasantness' (see my note on Ps. xxvii. 4), and His 'holiness' for His fidelity to His covenant (Ps. xxii. 4). And so, when in the passage last referred to the psalmist addresses Jehovah as 'Holy One,' he uses the term not in the sense of 'One infinitely above the human race,' but 'One who cares for Israel' (cf. the Isaianic phrase, 'the Holy One of

Israel,' which occurs but thrice in the Psalter, lxxi. 22, lxxviii. 41, lxxxix. 19). In Ps. xcix. 3 Israel is exhorted to give thanks to Jehovah as 'the Holy One;' His name is no doubt also called 'great and terrible,' but, as I have shown on Ps. lxv. 6, cxxxix. 14, 'terrible' is a word of double meaning. And in Ps. xcviii. 1, the help which Israel has experienced is traced to Jehovah's 'holy arm.' Evidently the object of Israel's most spiritual teachers at the opening of the later period was to make the thought of God's 'holiness' a source of inspiration and not of overpowering dread. We shall return to this in Part II. How the sense of the term 'holiness' was modified in the N.T. has been well shown by Issel, *Der Begriff der Heiligkeit im N.T.* (Leiden, 1887).

NOTE ˣ, p. 321.

This fine symbolism developed in an unlooked-for direction. The מֵימְרָא, or 'Word,' for which in the Palestinian Targum we also find the synonym דִּבּוּרָא or דַּבְּרָא, and the שְׁכִינָא, or 'glorious divine presence,' have a manifest tendency to become quasi-independent organs of the Most High. Both titles are based upon Biblical passages, somewhat unduly pressed (see, e.g., for Memra, the above passages, and for Shekina, Num. ix. 17–22 and Ps. lxxxv. 10). Both too have a long history. The Shekina is the later word; it was coined, as Landau thinks, by R. Akiba. And while the conception of the Memra, so far as I can at present see, is independent of foreign influences, that of the Shekina, which is connected with that of the light as in some sense the body or the garment of the Lord, must apparently have been helped forward by the precisely similar Zoroastrian belief. The symbolism of light was indeed native to Hebraism, but was immensely more developed after the Return. Into the development of the Shekina-belief in Talmudic and Sufic theology I cannot enter.

NOTE ʸ, p. 321.

Comp. Dan. iv. 31, 'there fell a voice from heaven.' It may be objected that this is an involuntary allusion to the 'Bath Qol' (see note ᵁ p. 39) of later Jewish religion. True; but this 'oracular echo' is itself a revival of an earlier belief (see 1 Sam. iii. 3, 4, and on the interpretation put upon unexpected sounds by the ancient Arabs see Wellhausen, *Skizzen*, iii. 139).

NOTE ᶻ, p. 322.

My *Book of Psalms* (1888) gives the ordinary rendering of Ps. lvi. 5, 11, 'Through God can I praise his word' (reading, of course,

דְּבָרוֹ in both verses). But it now appears to me that the passages are not parallel to Ps. lx. 14, 'Through God (באלהים) we shall do valiantly,' but rather to Isa. xxvi. 13, 'in thee alone can we glory, even in thy name.' That this *is* the required meaning in the latter passage, seems to me required by the context (see Lect. VIII.), and since the preparation of these lectures this rendering has been adopted by Dillmann, whose grammatical instinct is keen. The context favours a similar interpretation in Ps. lvi. Glorying in God's promise is synonymous with 'trusting without fear.' For the continued action of the preposition, see Isa. xxviii. 6, and other passages cited by Ewald, *Lehrbuch*, § 351 *a*.

Note aa, p. 322.

Mohammed called our Lord not only 'God's Word' (*kalima*) but 'a spirit from Himself' (*Korán*, Sur. iv. 169). His followers call Jesus *rûḥu 'llah*, 'Spirit of God.' The uses of *ruḥ* in the Korán betray Jewish influence, which was strong in Arabia.

Note bb, p. 322.

See above, note w, and cf. on Ps. li. 13. Hitzig, who gives the phrase 'holy spirit' a simple ethical meaning, regards רוח קדש as the translation of the Zend *çpento-mainyus* (the holy Spirit, as opposed to *angro-mainyus*, or the evil spirit). This, however, is as groundless as Hitzig's connexion of Yahveh with Ahura ; nor is *çpento* etymologically parallel to קדוש (see Spiegel, *Avesta*, Bd. iii., Einleit. pp. iv., v.). To the later Jews 'holy spirit' meant especially 'spirit of prophecy.' Hence Targ. Jerus. paraphrases Gen. xxx. 25, 'Jacob said by the holy spirit concerning the house of Joseph, They are to be as a flame to consume the house of Esau'). More correctly, 'a spirit of Elohim,' in Gen. xli. 38, is interpreted by Onkelos (and also Targ. Jerus.), 'the spirit of prophecy from the Lord.'

Note cc, p. 322.

On Ps. cxliii. 10, see my Commentary, and cf. notes on Isa. xl. 13, lxiii. 10. In the oldest part of the Avesta (the Gâthâs) the *çpento-mainyus* (see note bb) is spoken of as having personal existence.

Note dd, p. 322.

Cf. Jer. x. 12 (Jer. x. 1–16 was written by one of the many admirers and scholars of the Second Isaiah).

Note ee, p. 322.

Cf. *Job and Solomon*, pp. 160, 161. The striking personification in Enoch xlii. 1, 2 reminds us strongly of Prov. viii., Job xxviii., and Ecclus. xxiv., and the Prologue of the Fourth Gospel (John i. 11). In the Zoroastrian Gâthâs, the personified understanding of Ahura is synonymous with His Spirit, and in the later Yasna we find the 'heavenly wisdom, Mazda-made,' which in the very late book called Mînôkhired is described like σοφία in the Book of Wisdom.

Note ff, p. 322.

The personification of divine attributes and gifts pervades the Gâthâs. But it is not a mere poetic figure. Zarathustra did not indeed regard Asha, Sraosha, Aramaiti, as literally persons, but he probably did assign to them an objective existence. Even Complete Welfare (Haurvatât) and Immortality (Ameretatât) may, consistently with primitive philosophy, have been thus objectified. So too in Talmudic theology God's righteousness, His mercy, His goodness, His condescension, and even His will or good pleasure (cf. εὐδοκία, Luke ii. 14) appear as quasi-independent beings (see Joel, *Blicke in die Religionsgeschichte*, i. 114, 115). In this light we can better understand how the angels can be represented as 'springing forth new every morning' (Hymn Akdāmūth, sung at Pentecost, *Festival Prayers*, ii. 152) ; cf. Lam. iii. 22, 23.

Note gg, p. 323.

Cf. the phrase, 'that is enthroned on the cherubim' (Pss. lxxx. 2, xcix. 1, cf. xxii. 4, and my notes on these passages).

Note hh, p. 323.

Evil angels. The primitive Israelites doubtless classified the divine powers, not as good and evil, but as helpful and hurtful. There would have been little harm in this, if they had recognized, or had always recognized, the dependence of both classes of Elohim upon the supreme God. But they were too prone to worship the spirits of nature, which had no moral character, and which were called *shēdīm* (cf. Assyrian *šidu*) ; see Deut. xxxii. 17, Ps. cvi. 37. Probably with many Jews in the Persian period these δαιμόνια (as Sept. calls them) took the place of the 'demons' of Ahriman's kingdom in Zoroastrianism ; cf. the later Jewish belief as described by Weber (*System*, p. 245). The psalmists, however, would have reckoned even hurtful angels among the 'angels of service,' and even the author of Ecclesiastes (close of Persian period) represents the destroying angel as the minister of God (Eccles. v. 6 ; see *Job and Solomon*, p. 216). For the psalmist's view, see Ps. lxxviii. 49*b* (R. V.), 'a band of angels of evil' (Sept., ἀγγέλων πονηρῶν, i.e. 'hurtful angels,' cf. θηρία πονηρὰ, Ezek. xiv. 15 ; Symm. ἀγγέλων κακούντων ; Targ. אִזְגַּדִּין בִּישִׁין). The writer carefully excludes the popular notion by the word מִשְׁלַחַת 'a mission' or 'commissioned band (of),' and insists that the many destroying angels (the מַזִּיקִין of later Judaism ; see Targ. on Ps. cvi. 37) are but personifications of God's 'hot anger, fury, and fervent ire.' The Talmud, however, will have it that 'anger' and 'wrath' are really two angels (Jer., *Taanith*, ii. 65*b* in Weber, p. 149). Observe that 'Satan,' as a more or less independent evil spirit, is not once referred to in the Psalms (even in Ps. cix. 6) ; he is also studiously ignored in Ecclesiasticus (see *Job and Solomon*, pp. 79, 188).—*Naming of angels.* The angels Gabriel and Michael in the Book of Daniel are probably two of the 'seven holy angels' referred to in Tobit xii. 15, cf. Rev. i. 4, a detail of angelology which is clearly of Zoroastrian origin, though modified Hebraistically, Jehovah not being one of the seven (see Kohut on Angelology, and Mills, *Zendavesta*, part iii., p. 145 ; and cf. Ewald, *Old and New Test. Theology*, p. 76). Later on, other angels were named, as we see both from the Book of Enoch and from the Talmud. The Essenes carefully guarded the names of the angels, doubtless with a view to supernatural revelations (Jos., *War*, ii. 8, 7). The early teachers of the Jewish Church may have been shocked at the invocation of the fravashis in the contemporary Zoroastrianism, and on this account have hesitated to give names to angels.—*Patron-angels.* If there were patron-angels of nations (see on Ps. lxxxii.), why should there not be such of individuals? So the later Jews thought, passing beyond Ps. xci. 11, where a general charge is given to God's angels to watch over the righteous man (for their interpretation of Ps. *l.c.*, see Weber, *System*, p. 166). Their inference was, however, probably helped forward by the elaborate Zoroastrian theory of fravashis (see next Lecture). That there is great religious depth in this conception, which (as Daya in Lessing's *Nathan* says) 'Christian, Jew, Mussulman, agree to own,' and which symbolizes the individuality of the relation between God and the soul, cannot be denied. See Matt. xviii. 10, and cf. Acts xii. 15, also Korán, l. 16.

NOTE [ii], p. 323.

Especially in connexion with the fact that the Priestly Code does not once refer to the angels. The Gâthâs of Zarathustra, it should be noticed, refer to the Amshaspands (who suggested the archangels), but mainly as personified abstractions, and not at all to the Fravashis or the Yazatas.

NOTE ʲʲ, p. 323.

It was otherwise in the subsequent period. In the Book of Daniel (which, as we have seen, cannot be an Exilic work) there are already clear tokens of change. Later on, the Scribes, developing Biblical germs, produced an angelology which is in its main outlines presupposed both by Jesus and by the New Testament writers. It was felt that men were not worthy to be the only intelligent and moral subjects of the divine kingdom, and that the voluntary self-surrender of the angels to the moral aims of the kingdom was a most helpful example for poor frail man. Thus the actual reign of God over the angels became a prophecy of His perfect rule over men in the day when there shall be no more any partition-wall between heaven and earth, when the angels shall go in and out among men, and men shall become ἰσάγγελοι (Matt. xxii. 30, cf. xvi. 27, Enoch xxxix. 1). And since that which actually is in heaven cannot strictly speaking arise, and the day towards which history moves is even now with Jehovah (Isa. ii. 12, 'Jehovah hath a day' &c.), the disciples are taught to pray, 'Thy kingdom come.' But though an angelology is undoubtedly presupposed in the N.T., it is used popularly and with poetic freedom, precisely as the later Jewish doctrine is used by R. Yehuda Hallévi in his noble hymn (*keaūshāh*) for the Day of Atonement. And it is an important fact that neither in Christianity nor in Judaism is the doctrine of angels a fundamental article of faith as it is in Islám.

NOTE ᵏᵏ, p. 324.

Jerome renders in Ps. lxxviii. 25 'panem fortium;' Sept., ἄρτον ἀγγέλων.

NOTE ˡˡ, p. 324.

Pss. lxxxii. 1, lxxxix. 8. Let no one take offence at the above. 'With whom took he counsel?' are the words of the Second Isaiah (xl. 14). 'He stood in no need of the holy council,' says the supposed Enoch (xiv. 22), recognizing the mythic form of speech but cautioning the reader against misconception. The psalmists evidently agree with both. The Book of Daniel, too, though it ventures on naming two archangels, expresses in the name of one of them the incommensurableness of Jehovah and any angel (Michael='who is like God,' cf. Ps. lxxxix. 7, 8). This might be a protest against the inclusion of Ahura Mazda among the seven 'immortal holy ones' (the Amshaspands), an inconsistency found in some passages of the Avesta.

NOTE mm, p. 324.

See my Commentary, and *Job and Solomon*, pp. 81, 82. I may add here that 2 Chron. xxviii. 23 furnishes a good illustration of Ps. lxxxii. It implies that there really were secondary Elohim, but that they had no jurisdiction over Israel (comp. Deut. xxxii. 8, 9 Sept.), and for an Israelite to worship them would be to his own ruin. Later on, speculation produced a שר העולם or 'prince-patron of the world,' who is to be distinguished from the heads of the Satans and of the *shēdīm* respectively. He would, of course, be one of the principal *elōhīm*. See *Chullin*, 60a; *Sanhedrin*, 94a (quoted by Wünsche, *Erläuterungen*, on John xii. 31).

NOTE nn, p. 325.

See Dean Perowne's introd. to Ps. lxxxii., Dr. Edersheim's note on Ecclus. xvii. 17, and Dr. Bruce on Heb. ii. 5 in *Expositor*, 1882 (2), p. 362, &c. Certainly there is nothing in a reference to 'prince-angels' to surprise the student of Jewish theology (see Weber, *Alt-synagog. Pal. Theologie*, p. 165). In a yet larger sense, the world was conceived, by both Jews and Christians, to be subject to 'ministerial spirits.' On the angels of the elements, and even of human impulses, see Weber, p. 167; and on the Pagan and Gentile-Christian doctrine of δαίμονες, see Baur, *Church History*, ii. 162; Bigg, *The Christian Platonists*, pp. 258, 259; Réville, *La Religion à Rome sous les Sévères*, p. 40, &c.

NOTE oo, p. 326.

See Heb. xii. 18, 22. In a lovely *terzina* of Dante we find the phrase 'nell' alto Olimpo' (*Purg.* xxiv. 15).

PART II.

HOW JEHOVAH WORKS, AND WITH WHAT RESULTS.

We have not yet completely answered the question, By what agency does the Lord Jehovah work? One special agency will have long since suggested itself to the reader, and must now in the last place be considered—the Messianic.[1] The hope to which it appeals has assumed various forms in the Old Testament, but common to them all is the idea that God's permanent presence among His people is the supreme bliss of the future. The belief in a great coming descendant of David, of ideal character and fortunes, is the form which ultimately asserted itself most strongly in religious minds (see, even before the Gospels, the Similitudes of Enoch), but it is far from being the only one. It is necessary therefore to expand the narrow conventional sense of the word Messiah. The term 'Anointed One' is either applied or applicable to any one who has received from God some unique commission of a directly or indirectly religious character. Thus David and each of David's successors were, theoretically rather than in fact, Messiahs (Ps. xviii.), and a descendant of David, of ideal character and fortunes, was to be, both in theory and in fact, a Messiah (see Isa. ix., xi.; it is implied too of course in the idealization of David in Ps. xviii.). A non-Israelitish prince is called 'Jehovah's Anointed' in Isa. xlv. 1 (cf. Ps. xlv. 8), and the Jewish high priest 'the Anointed' in Lev. iv. 3, 5 (cf. Ps. lxxxiv. 10).[a] So too (virtually) is the mysterious Servant of Jehovah, who stands in such close relation to Israel, in Isa. lxi. 1 (and is not the same idea implied in Ps. xxii.?). Lastly, the actual people of Israel was a

---

[1] Pages 338-340 are not of course meant as a summary of results on the Messianic idea in the Psalter. They give only what the argument at this stage requires—an explanation of the term 'Messiah,' and a fundamental idea common to all the Messianic psalms.

Messiah, both theoretically and to some extent in fact (Ps. lxxxix. 39, 52, virtually).[b]

To each of these six Messianic persons and classes references expressed or implied occur in the Psalter, and if on some points of detail students are divided,[c] need we be surprised? In 1881, in an essay addressed to students of apologetics, I expressed views on Pss. ii., lxxii., and cx., which seem to me now inexact. They were and still are tenable, however, because they are based, not on mere tradition, but on criticism. It is a fact that, even after the royalistic form of the Messianic conception had become antiquated, sporadic references to a hoped-for Messiah do occur in the post-Exile Scriptures, so that there was no *à priori* absurdity in supposing that a few such might be found in the Psalter.[d] For the psalmists were deep students of the earlier Scriptures. It was also more reasonable to hold that there were three such psalms[e] than, with Delitzsch, that there was only one (the 110th); for how should a single writer, without the support of fellow psalmists, have ventured on so new a path? Delitzsch himself, too, admits that no recorded events in history account for the expressions of the 2nd, and he might well have added, for those of the 72nd psalm. But I have sufficiently explained the grounds of my present opinion, which rests perhaps on a firmer and more consistent application of the comparative method. Messianic, both the 2nd and the 110th psalms of course remain. The idealization of historical persons which they present presupposes the belief in an ideal Messianic monarchy, now or at some later time to be granted to Israel. The same remark applies to the 18th, the 45th, the 72nd, the 89th, and the 132nd, and in a less degree to the 20th, 21st, and 101st. If in some cases the ideal kingship has been ascribed to a non-Davidic Israelite, and in others even to a foreign prince, this does not alter its close connexion with the personal Messianic hope; 'David' was undoubtedly becoming a type or symbol.[1] I need not say anything here of the other class of Messianic psalms—those which refer to the persecuted church-nation—my change of opinion being less important here than in the former case.[2]

---

[1] See pp. 22, 25, 37, and comp. *The Prophecies of Isaiah*, ed. 3, p. 201.
[2] See pp. 263, 292.

All these psalms are (let me say it again, for it concerns modern apologists to be frank) only Messianic in a sense which is psychologically justifiable. They are, as I have shown, neither typically, nor in the ordinary sense prophetically Messianic. What is the fundamental idea of the Messianic psalms? Simply this—that the people of Israel is to work out the divine purposes in the earth, and to do this with such utter self-forgetfulness that each of its own successes shall but add a fresh jewel to Jehovah's crown. Whether a king (past, present, or future), or the people of Israel, is referred to, makes no difference. The Messianic king is primarily the representative of the Messianic people. Special gifts are only granted to him that he may the better lead the people to the conquest of the nations. And the final aim is that with or against their will all mankind may be united under the righteous sway of Jehovah. Even in that grandest of the more strictly Messianic psalms, in which the king enthroned on Zion is called the 'son of Jehovah' Himself (Ps. ii. 7), the concluding verses point us to the heavenly King as the true Lord of the nations, and pronounce those alone happy who take refuge in Him.[f]

3. How does Jehovah work, and what results flow from His working? He works, firstly, by ruling wisely, irresistibly, and for moral ends. Rule, He must; for how should there be peace, even in 'His high places' (Job xxv. 2), if He did not keep the created 'principalities' within bounds? So at least it seemed to those who, like the poet of Job and one or two of the psalmists, admitted the temporary quasi-independence of the 'sons of Elohim.' And how should there be peace on earth, if the 'King of the nations'[1] never uttered His royal judgments upon transgressors?

> He ruleth by his might for ever;
> His eyes observe the nations:
> Let not the rebellious exalt themselves (Ps. lxvi. 7, R.V.)

But one favoured region there is in which Jehovah's rule is more manifest than elsewhere. As the prologue of the Blessing of Moses tells us, 'He became King in Jeshurun when the heads of the people were gathered, all the tribes of Israel

---

[1] Jer. x. 7 (not earlier than the close of the Exile); cf. Rev. xv. 3.

together' (Deut. xxxiii. 5); that is to say, the theophany and the legislation of Sinai led up to the accession of King Jehovah (cf. Isa. vi. 5, but not Ps. xx. 10) in the land of the people of Israel.[g] The prophets and psalmists, however, were not satisfied [1] with what I may call the early part of the reign of Jehovah, during which the divine rights over Israel were so often infringed by upstart and idolatrous tyrants (cf. Isa. xxvi. 13, lxiii. 19), not to speak of the obscuration of the theocracy (I adopt the later or Church-point of view) by the institution of the native royalty (1 Sam. viii. 7, cf. 2 Chron. xxxv. 18). Hence, when the events of history seemed like a repetition of the Exodus, and of the thunder and lightning of Sinai, and when, as the crowning mercy, the symbolic dwelling-place of God had been rebuilt, they burst into those fine songs of praise, the accession-psalms (see above, p. 71). Once more, 'Jehovah had become king.' And what a King! How the old conception had become purified, deepened, and enriched! All the neighbouring peoples had their theocracies;[h] but compare even the noblest of them with the theocracy conceived by the Jewish Church. The Zoroastrian Church alone, as we partly know and partly divine from the Gâthâs, can claim to meet the Jewish on something like equal terms. Still there is a historical continuity in the records of the Jewish Church which is wanting in those of the Zoroastrian. We can, by means of historical criticism, follow the movement of this grand idea even in the single Book of Psalms. That first impassioned outburst of praise was half based upon illusion. The perfected theocracy turned out to be still future. A psalmist, in his festival mood, had bidden the 'vain gods' prove their claim to be alive by recognizing their own defeat.

> Shamed are all they that serve graven images,
> That make their boast of vain gods;
> Worship him, all ye gods (xcvii. 7).

But alas! the so-called 'vain gods' still seemed to mock Jehovah, and to divide the theocracy among themselves. The worshippers of Ahura Mazda had deserted the pure moral precepts of their religion, and become as cruel to Jehovah's

---

[1] See the touching words in which Jehovah Himself complains, Ps. lxxxi. 12-17.

people as the idolaters.¹ Many of them, indeed, with an innovating king (Artaxerxes II.) at their head, had (like some of the Parsees in India) themselves made concessions to idolatry. Add to this that not a few Israelites had avowedly or virtually fallen away, and become godless oppressors of their people (see commentary on Pss. ix., x., xiv., lv.), and we cannot be surprised that it sometimes appeared to a psalmist as if 'the whole (race of man) had turned aside' (Ps. xiv. 3, cf. xi¹. 1, 2)—a fresh illusion, which afterwards became crystallized in the general Talmudic doctrine of the conscious hostility of the heathen world to God.¹ It was at any rate a stern, hard fact that in their relations with the Jews the heathen were too often a גוֹי לֹא חָסִיד (xliii. 1), a people without that φιλανθρωπία which, though often overlaid with less lovely elements, had become an essential part of the Israelitish character.ʲ

> They crush thy people, Jehovah,
> And afflict thine heritage;
> They slay the widow and the sojourner,
> And put the orphans to death (xciv. 6).

And so the author of Ps. lxxxii. has not the heart to take up the burden of the accession-psalms, lest some doubting philosopher, like 'Ecclesiastes,' should hurl back the denial,—

> Jehovah reigneth not; he hath put off his majesty;
> The world is not stablished, but moveth to and fro.²

But, though not jubilant, he will not be disloyal to Jehovah. Never shall Satan or Ahriman dispossess the true king. In his closing words he expresses this with a force which explains the popularity of the psalm in later times.ᵏ Jehovah is but waiting till his hour shall strike (cf. Ps. lxxv. 3). He will yet 'arise' out of his seeming inactivity (v. 8), or, in other words, will 'become king'ᵐ (Zech. xiv. 9), though at present 'all the foundations of the earth are out of course' (Ps. lxxxii. 5), and though, in spite of synagogues and schools, it can already be seen that 'not all are Israel that are *of* Israel' (Rom. ix. 6).ⁿ

And now can we not see what direction Jehovah's royal policy in Israel is bound to take? For king He assuredly is; He has but veiled, not put off, His majesty. How should

---

¹ See Weber, *Altsyn. Theol.*, p. 65.   ² Comp. Ps. xciii. 1.

struggling believers persevere amidst the breaking of their illusions, if their God did not train them in His providential purposes and reveal His perfect sympathy? Let us then regard Jehovah as the sympathetic Friend and all-wise Teacher, or, to use a term of large compass suggested by the Asaphite psalms,[1] as the Shepherd of Israel. What this figure meant in Israel's later period, we may learn equally well from Ps. xxiii. and from John x.º In the olden times it might have been simply a synonym for 'king,' or even for 'captain' or 'commander' (cf. ναῶν ποιμένες, Æsch., *Suppl.* 767). But now, plainly enough, all that one can imagine of strong, patient, watchful, and considerate helpfulness is being gathered up in the thought of the Shepherd. This half-Christian transfiguration of the image is one out of many tokens of a deeper and gentler conception of the divine character. And parallel to it is the frequent reference, direct or indirect, of the post-Exile poets to the divine condescension. I am well aware that there is a direct mention of this attribute (ענוה) in Ps. xviii. 36, and for this among other reasons I have doubted (see p. 206) whether this fine poem may not really be a monument of the Babylonian Exile. But at any rate in the Persian period it first became a vital Church-belief that Jehovah dwelt not only 'in the high and holy place,' but 'with him also that was contrite and humble in spirit, to revive the spirit of the humble, and to revive the heart of the contrite ones' (Isa. lvii. 15). The conception of God formed by the Jews during the Exile was oppressive in its awful grandeur till in their deep depression they ventured to dream that the same greatness and goodness which filled the world might by a miracle of love contract itself within a human heart, or, to speak more accurately, within the hearts of all those who belonged to the true Israel. And so a new and peculiar element became visible in the divine glory,[2] viz., that 'though Jehovah be high, yet hath he respect unto the lowly' (Ps. cxxxviii. 6; cf. cxiii. 6). Finely and with deep insight did Rabbi Johanan say, 'Wherever thou findest the greatness of the Holy One expressed, there wilt thou also find His lowliness' ᵖ(or, condescension), and the passages which he

---

[1] See p. 148, and note ᶻ, p. 158.
[2] Cf. note on 'holiness' and 'glory,' p. 331.

quotes (Deut. x. 17, 18, Isa. lvii. 15, Ps. lxviii. 5, 6) all belong to the time when idealized poverty had become an Israelitish characteristic. To lowly Israel Jehovah revealed Himself anew as in some sense a lowly God. The divine '*anāvāh*,' referred to in such a strange connexion in Ps. xviii. 36, is more than 'gentleness;' it is that blessed sympathy which pleases itself not less with the smallest objects than with the greatest, not less with poor, weak, ignorant man than with the cedars of Lebanon or the morning-stars. It is a condescension which forgets that it has condescended ; say rather, which neither 'descends' nor 'condescends,' but raises up.q 'Thy humility made me great.'

Do not think that I am digressing. The essential part of deity as well of royalty, such was the Israelitish not less than the Moabitish belief,[1] was ability to help or save. Not only in the more naïve pre-Exile period, but even after the Church had been formed, a sign-loving people required this proof of Jehovah's divinity. But Israel in the later period was well aware of the magnitude of its demand. Help from such a great and high King was not the same as the help of the Jehovah of antiquity, who had been popularly supposed to be in an exclusive sense the God of Israel. It is nothing short of a divine 'self-emptying,' to use St. Paul's bold phrase (Phil. ii. 7), for which the Jewish Church craves. Strange that the Jews could combine so deep an insight into God's 'holiness,' or supernatural greatness, with so firm a faith in His perpetual nearness to His people. They looked of course for no literal theophanies. Without laying any stress on their non-occurrence in the 'priestly code,' it is clear from the theophanies of the psalms (see e.g. Pss. xviii., l., xcvii., and cxliv.r) that the old statements of Jehovah's visible appearance have but a symbolic value. And yet the truth behind the symbol was never more believed in than now. Faith had its own miracles, saw angels with the inner eye, and filled the dry vale of Baca with fountains (Ps. lxxxiv. 7). Kimchi may be astonished that there is no miracle of bringing water out of the rock in the Book of Ezra, and Josephus may have to seek a parallel to the greatest miracle of the Exodus in a legend of Alexander. The Pharisaic writer of

---

[1] Cf. l. 4 in Mesha's inscription.

2 Maccabees may scatter angel appearances and surprising wonders over his romantic work. But the pious contemporaries both of Ezra and of the Maccabean brethren were content with the providential wonders of history. Their cry was not for a literal repetition of the wonders of antiquity, but for Him who 'alone doeth great wonders' (Ps. cxxxvi. 4). 'Then Israel remembered the days of old,' says one of the later prophecies in 'Isaiah;' 'where is he that brought them up out of the sea? . . . . . where is he that placed his holy spirit within him' (Isa. lxiii. 11)? Israel was in fact being educated in God's ways. It was learning the doctrine of the spiritual presence of God, and the moral purpose of its selection to be Jehovah's people.

And now we are brought face to face with an important conception which lies at the root of the psalmists' ideas respecting Israel's relation to Jehovah. The word בְּרִית indeed is only used fifteen times in the Psalter of this relation;[1] but the idea of a covenant between Jehovah and Israel (unlike that supposed one between Chemósh and Moab, in that it implies a moral and not a merely natural relation) pervades the Book of Psalms. It was Jeremiah and the author of Deuteronomy who first succeeded in impressing it on the national conscience; and we find it in a simple, untechnical form in Ps. xviii., that is, probably, in Josiah's reign. We there learn that Jehovah's action towards His servants is conditioned by a regard to character. To those who are frankly and earnestly obedient God on his side will be frankly and earnestly helpful. The poet has no doubt that his king and people are thus perfect in obedience, and therefore only alludes in a single line to the possibility of God's changing towards them;—'with the wayward,' he says, 'thou showest thyself wayward' (v. 27b). But pass on to Ps. xxv.—the first psalm in which the word בְּרִית occurs. Israel, reflecting on its spiritual position, is a prey to mingled hope and fear. Whence comes this new self-distrust? From the religious influence of Babylon? No; from the troubles of the nation (p. 235). Misfortune and punishment are to the Israelite synonymous—a mode of thought to which a fatal stability

---

[1] See Pss. xxv. 10, 14, xliv. 18, l. 5, 16, lxxiv. 20, lxxviii. 10, 37, ciii. 18, cv. 8, 10, cvi. 45, cxi. 5, 9, cxxxii. 12.

has been given by his native idiom (see on Pss. xxxi. 11, cxxx. 8). Let us next study Ps. xxxii., which, though it does not contain the word 'covenant,' presents the conception in a very full form. It tells us that God rewards the righteous and punishes the wicked, but that the 'transgressions' of the imperfectly righteous will be 'taken away' upon their sincere confession.ˢ It also lets us into one of the psalmists' most pathetic limitations. Even those best of Israelites could not conceive of trouble as sent to test and purify their love of God, and so, when trouble came, they often leaped to the conclusion that God was angry with them.

But the problem of suffering was too complex to be thus solved, and the half-truth was not without injurious effects. One of these was the occasional lapse of the psalmists into those less worthy anthropomorphisms which we have already noticed. Another was an excessive readiness on the part of the Church-nation to accuse itself, or else (an evil effect of the old doctrine of national solidarity) to suppose that God was remembering the sins of its ancestors.ᵗ This subject, I know, calls for tender handling, for Christianity has ever regarded a deep sense of sin as a condition of its best blessings. But is there not in Ps. xxxii. 1–5 and elsewhere a feeling akin to that of Job that the all-seeing God is looking out for 'secret faults,' being determined not to hold His people innocent?[1] The compensating beauty of these passages is that the writers are not, like Job, embittered by such thoughts, because they know that God will not bring Israel 'into the dust of death,' or at any rate will not keep it there. I refrain with regret from supporting this idea by an exposition of some verses of the 90th psalm.ᵘ Suffice it for the present to quote a verse from the prophet Jeremiah, which seems to have become a favourite with the psalmists,—

> Correct me, Jehovah, but with justice,
> Not in thine anger, lest thou bring me to nothing.[2]

Nor have we yet exhausted the lessons of the 32nd psalm. It supplies a fresh confirmation of that lovely view of Jehovah as an educator which we lately gained. Generally the

---

[1] See Pss. xix. 13, xc. 8, and cf. Job ix. 28, 29, x. 6.
[2] Jer. x. 23 ; cf. Pss. vi. 2, xxxviii. 2.

psalmist speaks as if all that he desired were forgiveness, i.e. the removal of his temporal distress and the restoration of his communion with God. But there is one verse, not logically connected with the rest, which contains a special word of promise revealed to the psalmist. (The psalmists, as we have seen, felt themselves to be half-prophets.)

> I will instruct thee, and show thee[v] the way thou art to go;
> I will counsel thee, with mine eye upon thee (v. 8, Kay).

Observe, now that he has been forgiven, the speaker no longer fears that keen but tender glance. 'The eyes of servants look upon the hand of their lord,' but friends look in each other's eyes. And still more prominent is the craving for trustworthy moral guidance in the 25th psalm which I referred to before.

> Direct me in thy truthfulness, and teach me,
> For thou art my saviour-God.
> Good and upright is Jehovah,
> Therefore will he instruct sinners in the way.
> The lowly will he direct in that which is right,
> Yea, the lowly will he teach his way (Ps. xxv. 5, 8, 9).

And more strikingly still,

> The secret (or, intimacy) of Jehovah is for them that fear him,
> And his covenant for their instruction (Ps. xxv. 14).

And is not this one of the lessons of the 51st psalm, that the covenant of the great King with His people includes, not merely judging them by providential discipline proportioned to their character, but purifying and deepening their views of moral and spiritual truth, and giving them, together with a new conception of sin, which I cannot here pause to examine,[w] a more delicate tact in moral practice?

> Behold, thou desirest truth in the inmost parts,
> Therefore deep within make me to know wisdom.
> Cast me not away from thy presence,
> And take not thy holy spirit from me (li. 8, 13),

with which last line compare these words from the great national confession in Neh. ix., 'Thou gavest also thy good spirit to instruct them,' and this from Ps. cxliii. 10:—

> Teach me to do thy will, for thou art my God;
> Let thy good spirit lead me in an even path.

We see, then, that in post-Exile times God revealed Himself specially as an educator. The conception was not indeed new; the older prophecy could not help developing this aspect of Jehovah's pastoral character.[x] But it certainly became deepened, as the meaning of the pastoral figure itself became deepened, after the Exile. And how does Jehovah guide or educate His flock? How does He purify their views of truth, and refine their moral perceptions? Listen to a writer in one of the darker parts of the Persian period.

> Happy is the man whom thou nurturest, Jehovah,
> And teachest out of thy law (Ps. xciv. 12).

The religion of Israel could never have risen so high, had it been always under the tutelage even of prophets like Isaiah (cf. Isa. xxviii. 9, 10, xxx. 21). Unique as it was, Hebrew prophecy could not last for ever, nor could the class of humanists or 'wise men' undertake the anxious charge which the prophets relinquished. The transition had to be made from a bookless to a book-religion, but how hard this would be, the abortive attempt in the reign of Josiah had already shown. It was felt in the post-Exile period that the higher truths must be transfused from the written book into the hearts of the people. Hence the necessity of schools and of an army of 'teachers' such as those spoken of in the Book of Daniel (xi. 33, 35, xii. 3, R.V. marg.), the subject of whose instruction was to be not moral wisdom in general, but, to use a phrase in Ezra, 'the wisdom of God that was in their hand'[y] (Ezra vii. 25). In what spirit did these teachers work? Did they recognize Jehovah as the true educator? The model *sōfēr*, or scribe, of the early Greek period, who speaks in the 119th psalm, will answer us. 'Teach me, Jehovah,' is the burden of the whole psalm, and though the writer does not boast like the Talmudists, we soon discover that his prayer has been heard, and that he is ever learning more and more of the infinite meaning of the golden book (cf. *v.* 18). And so, though some of the *sōferīm* may adopt the literary style of the 'wise men,' the class as a whole is separated from them by profound differences. The 'lamp' of the *sōfēr* is not the 'spirit of man' (Prov. xx. 27), divine as this too may be, but that brighter 'light' (Ps. cxix. 105), which includes the ancient 'wisdom,' as a part of an already varied and comprehensive Bible.[z] Of this treasure-house of divine truth one of the psalm-editors, without any tinge of the later superstition (see note [w]), virtually declares that it is like the sun in the firmament (see Ps. xix.). Can we wonder that as the symbol of the covenant κατ' ἐξοχὴν even the glorious second temple should early have found serious competitors in the sacred classics? 'Happy are they that dwell in thy house' (Ps. lxxxiv. 5) expressed no doubt the highest ideal, but 'Happy is the man who meditates on the law of Jehovah' (Ps. i. 1, 2), was a more practical one, because alone universally applicable. The temple was the spiritual centre of the scattered communities, but the flag for which all good Jews were ready to die was that of the Scripture. The Maccabæan rising proved this; but all pointed in this direction even in pre-Maccabæan times. As a Jewish historian says, 'the foundations of the temple were undermined by the schools before it had been trampled upon by enemies from without and desecrated by bloody feuds from within.'[1]

But it may be asked, Have we a right to speak of the Scripture as a whole as a means by which Jehovah educated His people? Ought we not to have referred to one part of it, viz. the 'Mosaic' Law, at an earlier point as an expression of the will of the divine *Governor* of Israel? No; the Jewish conception of Law has become transformed. To the early Israelites a law was an ordinance and nothing more, but to restored Israel it formed part of a rule of life, divine in its origin, but human in its exquisite adaptation to the circumstances of the people. Penalties might give this rule a frowning aspect, but only to those who saw not that 'righteousness' was the one condition both of Israel's continuance and of the Messianic salvation. It was from the consciousness of this that more and more the Israelites regarded the Law as the crowning proof of Jehovah's love.

> He declared his word unto Jacob,
> His statutes and ordinances unto Israel (Ps. cxlvii. 19),

is the climax of thanksgiving to a contemporary of Simon the Maccabee; and one of the oldest prayers in the Jewish

---

[1] Jost, *Geschichte des Judenthums*, i. 291.

liturgy calls upon 'our Father' and 'our King' to 'teach us as thou didst teach our fathers statutes of life.' aa

---

NOTE a, p. 338.

In Ps. xxviii. 8, and cxxxii. 10, the 'anointed' is also very probably the high priest. Cf. Lev. iv. 3, 5, Dan. ix. 26 (of Onias III.).

NOTE b, p. 339.

The term 'Jehovah's anointed' is here applied to the people of Israel as the heir of the promises made to David. That is, the psalmist speaks as if a rightful Davidic king still existed, though, as *vv.* 41, 42, 46, 52*a* show, the people of Israel is the real sufferer, and absorbs all the psalmist's thoughts. So in Ps. xxviii. 8 'his anointed' may possibly mean not the high priest, but the church-nation; at least, this view seems favoured by Hab. iii. 13 (in a great post-Exilic ode).

NOTE c, p. 339.

Rudolf Smend, for instance, who regards the Psalter as a post-Exilic work, finds as large a Messianic element in it as any of the older interpreters—a much larger one than I can at present admit. The effect of this is perhaps a weakening of the poetic effect of the psalms. To interpret such psalms as xxiv. and xlvii. as merely prophetic of the final Messianic sovereignty and judgment seems to me extremely hazardous.

NOTE d, p. 339.

The strictly Messianic psalms, or portions of psalms, in the Targum are seven in number, viz. ii., xviii. (second half), xxi. (*vv.* 2 and 8), xlv., lxi. (*vv.* 7, 8), lxxii., lxxx. (at least, בן in *v.* 16 is the Messiah).

NOTE e, p. 339.

According to Leontius of Byzantium, Theodore only 'referred three psalms to the Lord.' But from Cosmas Indicopleustes, and from the Syriac commentary based on Theodore it would appear that four psalms were referred by Theodore directly to Christ, viz. ii., viii., xliv. (xlv.), and cix. (cx.). Kihn thinks that Leontius omitted Ps. viii. because the fifth Œcumenical Council had censured Theodore's explanation of this psalm. Theodore also interpreted Pss. xv. (xvi.),

xxi. (xxii.), lxviii. (lxix.) as typically Messianic in his commentary on the Minor Prophets, a view which the same Council censured. In his work on the psalms, however, if we may judge from the Syriac work described by Baethgen, the two typical Messianic psalms are lxxxix. and cxvii. (cxviii.). See Kihn, *Theodor von Mopsuestia* (1880), p. 454; Baethgen, in Stade's *Zeitschrift*, 1885, pp. 67, 81.

Note f, p. 340.

The harmony of the closing strophe of the psalm is greatly improved by correcting נשקו בר (*v.* 12) either as proposed in my critical note, or, with Lagarde into מוֹסְרוֹ or נַשְׂקוּ מוֹסְרוֹ (the plural form of the suffix would also be possible). 'Put on (again) his bonds' makes a parallel to *v.* 3. With Kamphausen (review of Nowack's *Psalmen* in the *Studien und Kritiken*, 1888) I would now accept this brilliant conjecture, which Lagarde fortifies by a palæographical reference to the Palmyrene characters (*Novæ Psalterii Græci Editionis Specimen*, 1887, p. 24). Sept. and Targ. both certainly read מוסר (cf. Grätz).

Note g, p. 341.

The 'gathering' referred to took place, not in Sinai, but in Canaan. As Ps. lxviii. 18 puts it, Jehovah transferred his throne from Sinai (originally His central sanctuary, cf. Ex. iii. 1, xviii. 5) to the holy hill of Zion, i.e. He led His people to the land which He had destined for them. Without the gift of a land, the Sinaitic legislation would have been inoperative. As another psalm says, Jehovah 'gave (Israel) the lands of the nations . . . that they might keep his statutes and observe his laws' (Ps. cv. 44, 45). In post-Biblical times, however, the Jews did not feel that the land of Israel was essential to Jehovah's sovereignty; the great dispersion had destroyed this ancient sentiment. Hence *Mechilta* 73*b* says that Israel at Mount Sinai resolved to take upon itself 'the kingdom of heaven.'

Note h, p. 341.

Cf. Baethgen, *Beiträge zur semit. Religionsgeschichte* (1888); Tiele, *Vergelijkende Geschiedenis der oude Godsdiensten* (1869); W. R. Smith, *The Religion of the Semites*, p. 66, &c. The expression 'theocracy' is due to Josephus (*c. Ap.* ii. 17), who coins it to describe the form of government ordained, as he says, by 'our legislator.' He apologizes for it with the words, ὡς ἄν τις εἴποι βιασάμενος τὸν λόγον. Cf. Wellhausen, *Prolegomena*, chap. xi. (beginning).

NOTE ⁱ, p. 342.

See p. 292. From our present point of view, the ideal Mazda-worshipper is Cyrus. The persecution of heresy advocated in parts of the Avesta, which is contrary to the spirit of Cyrus, may be due to the dangerous multiplication of sects in Persia in the Sassanid period (see De Harlez on *Vendîdâd* iv. 142, 149). The Gâthâs only inveigh against doctrines which lead to vicious thoughts, words, and deeds; the Daêva-worshippers were on moral grounds bitterly hated by Zarathustra (see *Yasna* xxxii. 3–5). Cf. however Wilhelm, 'Priester und Ketzer im alten Erân,' *Z.D.M.G.*, 1890, p. 142, &c.

NOTE ʲ, p. 342.

Cf. Wisd. xii. 19, Ὅτι δεῖ τὸν δίκαιον εἶναι φιλάνθρωπον. Josephus eulogizes Agrippa as τοῖς ἀλλοεθνέσι φιλάνθρωπος, but τοῖς ὁμοφύλοις συμπαθὴς μᾶλλον (*Ant.* xix. 7, 3)—a fair description of a Jewish philanthropist. See note on Ps. xliii. 1.

NOTE ᵏ, p. 342.

Ps. lxxxii. was selected as the psalm for Tuesday (see pp. 72, 83).

NOTE ᵐ, p. 342.

Zech. xiv. 9 can hardly be earlier than the latter part of the Persian rule. 'Jehovah shall reign' occurs again in Ps. cxlvi. 10, but there it means 'shall go on reigning,' as the following words show. A Maccabæan psalmist doubtless believed that Jehovah had once more 'become king,' i.e. had revealed His sovereignty.

NOTE ⁿ, p. 342.

The same distinction between a true and a false Israel is implied in Pss. xii. 8, xiv. 5, xxiv. 6, lxxiii. 1, 15, cxii. 2.

NOTE ᵒ, p. 343.

The shepherd's office, in the interpretation of the figure, includes teaching; 'hear my voice' (John x. 16) means 'hearing a word, saying, This is the way, walk ye in it' (Isa. xxx. 21). In Eccles. xii. 11 'shepherd' is even a synonym for 'teacher' (cf. Prov. x. 21), and Ps. xxiii. is interpreted accordingly of Jehovah as a Teacher by Sept. and Targ. This may account for ὁδηγήσει εἰς πᾶσαν τὴν ἀλήθειαν, John xvi. 13 (cf. ὁδηγῶν ὡσεὶ πρόβατα, Ps. lxxix. 1, Sept.). The figure of the shepherd occurs again in Heb. xiii. 20, 1 Pet. ii. 25 (where ποιμήν is explained by ἐπίσκοπος; cf. *Orac. Sib.*, 'Proem.' 3), v. 4 (ἀρχιποίμην). In the 17th of the Psalms of Solomon the Messiah, as the leader of the perfected theocracy, is described as ποιμαίνων τὸ ποιμνίον κυρίου ἐν πίστει καὶ δικαιοσύνῃ. A similar train of thought suggested the traditional saying of Mohammed that every prophet must have been for a long time a shepherd.

NOTE p, p. 343.

The quotation is from *Megilla*, 31a, and forms part of the evening service for the conclusion of Sabbath. See Wünsche, *Der bab. Talmud*, i. 546.

NOTE q, p. 344.

Comp. St. Augustine, *Conf.* VII. 18. 'Condescending' is too equivocal a phrase to be applied either to Jehovah or to Christ and His disciples. He of whom Isa. lvii. is spoken cannot strictly be said even to 'descend.' Sympathy makes Jehovah, as, according to Hebrews, it made the Messiah, like unto common men in their lowliness. St. Paul, too, never meant to say, 'Condescend to things that are lowly' (Rom. xii. 16 in R. V.), but rather תִּתְנַהֲגוּ אֶת־הַשְּׁפָלִים, 'familiarize yourselves with the lowly' (συναπαγόμενοι is to be explained by Semitic rather than by Greek idiom; נָהַג = to be accustomed to). See *Expositor*, Dec. 1883, pp. 469-472.

NOTE r, p. 344.

It may be objected that the description in Ps. xviii. 9-13 is so frankly mythological that it may well represent a belief in the possibility of a literal theophany. But the expressions in *v*. 17 are inconsistent with any but a symbolic view of their meaning. It will be noticed that in all the passages quoted fire plays a very prominent part. The pillar of fire is the favourite symbol of the divine presence in the priestly narrative (see Lev. ix. 4, 6, 23, xvi. 2; Num. ix. 15, 16, xii. 5, xiv. 10).

NOTE s, p. 346.

Theodoret actually sees here a prophecy of the grace of baptism.

NOTE t, p. 346.

See Pss. xxv. 7, xxxviii. 5, lxix. 6, lxxix. 8, 9, cvi. 6, and cf. Ezra ix. 6, 10-15, Neh. ix. 33, 34. Ezekiel had protested against this notion, which we find also in hymns to Varuna (Max Müller, *Ancient Sanskr. Lit.*, p. 540; *Hibbert Lectures*, p. 285).

NOTE ᵘ, p. 346.

The central part of Ps. xc. contrasts strikingly with the opening and with the closing verses. Verses 1–4 are in the fullest sense a classic utterance. In *vv.* 5, 6 the poet's wings begin to droop, and in *vv.* 7–12 his thoughts are ill-connected and from a Christian point of view sorely in need of correction. As far as *v.* 7 the psalmist speaks in the name of the human race, for even *v.* 1 applies to non-Jewish as well as Jewish believers. But now he pleads with the Lord (Adonai, *v.* 1) for Israel. 'For we are consumed,' he says, 'by thine anger;' 'all our days have vanished in thy displeasure.' Such is frequently the language of the psalmists; when describing the calamities of their people, they employ the figures of sickness and death. But this is not the only peculiarity common to our psalmist with other temple-poets. In his tenderness of conscience, he accounts for the national calamities by assuming the existence of great national sins, and even of sins which no self-examination can discover (*v.* 8 ; cf. xix. 13, lxix. 6, and on these passages see pp. 76, 102). Does he not in this respect remind us of the sweet singer of Ps. xxxii. (*vv.* 3–5)? Calamity presses heavily upon God's people. The happy years of the national life have passed as quickly as a sigh. What remains is but the dregs of life, the 'sere and yellow leaf,' dry summer herbage which will soon have withered away (comp. cii. 12). And this is because, with all its exertions in the service of Jehovah, Israel has not obtained the assurance of the forgiveness of his sins (cf. Heb. x. 1, 2). Jehovah has not 'cast their sins behind his back' for ever, but gazes upon them, yes, even upon 'unobserved sins' in the bright 'light of his countenance' (*v.* 8).

In *v.* 10 one of those abrupt transitions occurs, with which we are familiar in the psalms. The psalmist speaks, as in *vv.* 5 and 6, of the lot of humanity—not of the many Israelites who must have died before his eyes of a broken heart or of the miseries incident to the time, but of those who in all countries go down to the grave in a full age. It cannot, however, be said that the description in *v.* 10 is all that one could wish either in thought or in expression. Certainly it cannot rank with the opening of Job xiv. or with the fourth verse of this very psalm. In expression, as a literal translation shows, it falls far below them, and it contains one clause which to the modern Christian reader is at most a half-truth—I mean the clause, 'and their pride (or, their boasting) is (but) labour and sorrow.' It is only in one of the darker periods of Israel's history that such an estimate either of youth and mature age or of old age could be given, and the psalmist's form of expression reminds us painfully of the author of Ecclesiastes, who, as Eccles. xii. 1 shows, took an even more pessimistic view of the latter than of the earlier years of life. Shall we blame the pious psalmist? No; he seems to repeat the pleading entreaty of Job, 'Have pity upon me, O ye my friends' (Job xix. 21). But how can we pity him till we duly realize his circumstances? Briefly, then, his case is this. He holds in his mind two inconsistent ideas—one an old idea, that calamity is a proof of God's displeasure, and another a comparatively new one, that God is eternal and unchangeable (see *vv.* 1–4), and such is the bitterness of Israel's present calamity that for the moment he forgets that the new idea was specially revealed to the later Jewish Church, nay more, he even allows his estimate of the human lot to be coloured by his despondent view of the national fortunes. He speaks amiss, and yet not wholly amiss. For it *is* perfectly true that what in 1 John ii. 16 is called 'the pride of life' is by its very nature transitory, and that whether or no there is any other human possession which endures, the longest human life is but a drop compared to God's eternity. Holding so much truth as our psalmist does, it is impossible that he should not at last escape from his morbid mood. But the time is not yet. He is still at a low spiritual level. All that he can say at present is,

> Who knoweth the power of thine anger,
> And thy wrath according to thy fear? (*v.* 11.)

Taken by themselves, the words may seem wisely and truly said. But in the context, they must, I fear, be interpreted otherwise. Is it really all that the psalmist can infer from the troubles of the time that God is visiting Israel's offences with the rod? Has he not heard that 'whom Jehovah loveth, he chasteneth'?

The twelfth verse connects itself with the tenth; the psalmist has no skill in linking thought to thought. This verse has no special reference to the fortunes of Israel, but applies to all men, whether prosperous or not. There is no better practical wisdom than a strict performance of duty, for on the one hand God 'hateth all workers of iniquity,' and on the other, 'There is no work, nor device, nor knowledge, nor wisdom in Sheól whither thou goest.' In the closing verses the psalmist recovers his equanimity, but to expound them lies somewhat aside from my present purpose.

Note ^v, p. 347.

The Hebrew is אוֹרְךָ, which suggests the true meaning of תּוֹרָה. The Torah, whether legal or prophetic, gave direction in the difficult journey of life (cf. Isa. xxx. 21). See below, p. 357 (note).

NOTE ʷ, p. 347.

In studying the conception of sin distinctive of the Psalter we naturally turn first of all to the technical words for sin. In Ps. xxxii. 1, 2, for instance, we have three such words, פֶּשַׁע, חֲטָאָה, עָוֹן, the first of which describes sin as a breaking loose, the second as a missing of the right aim, and the third as perversion or distortion. It will be seen that all these terms (cf. עָבַר, p. 466) imply the idea of law; but what sort of law is meant, depends upon the stage of religious development reached by the writer who uses the terms. The rule from which, according to the original usage, the sinner deviated, was mainly the unwritten one of divinely sanctioned custom (see Gen. xx. 9, xxxiv. 7, with Dillmann's notes). The gradual growth of written collections of laws, and finally the promulgation first of Deuteronomy and subsequently of the priestly code as the basis of the national life, profoundly modified the conception of sin. The transition is visible in Jeremiah (comp. *Jeremiah, his Life and Times,* p. 39); it is already past in the time of the psalmists. To them a word like חֲטָאוֹת suggested, not a mere national even though consecrated custom, but the 'delicate outline' of that virtue which is required by an 'exceeding broad' commandment (Ps. cxix. 96), the manifoldness of whose precepts sharpened the moral perceptions.

Had the psalmists what may be called a definite theory of sin? The reader of these Lectures will not easily believe that they had. They had indeed made various moral observations, but they had no complete theory to account for them. Sometimes they take the gloomiest possible view both of Israel and of the world (see Pss. xii., xiv.), in which, as in Sodom, it would almost appear that there were not ten righteous men; sometimes Israel at least is acquitted of any serious transgression (see e.g. Ps. xliv.). But the general tone of the circles in which the psalmists moved is that of watchfulness (see e.g. Pss. xxxiv. 14, xxxix. 2, cxli. 3). There is even in the pious the possibility that doubting thoughts may arise which may even lead to open apostasy (see Ps. lxxiii. 2). These must be striven against, best of all in the sanctuary (*ib. v.* 17). Weak as human nature is, it is not impossible to reject evil and choose good (cf. Ps. lxxxi. 9-11, 14 with Deut. xxx. 15-20), at least as long as Jehovah's *tōrāh* (the precepts enshrined in the Scriptures) is within the heart, moulding the character, and giving the man moral insight and an impulse towards goodness (cf. Pss. xix. 12, xl. 9, li. 8, 14, Deut. vi. 6, Jer. xxxi. 33). But no watchfulness can prevent those sins of infirmity, which in many cases no human eye can discern, and which are therefore called 'errors' (=lapses) and 'secret things' (see p. 354). Even these Jehovah in

His severity may sometimes punish; earnestly therefore does the Church supplicate Him, in the name of His goodness, not to take notice of them by a judicial sentence (Ps. xix. 13). One who is formed of dust cannot always maintain the highest standard (Ps. ciii. 10, 14), especially in the passionate season of youth (cf. Ps. xxv. 7), or when placed, as Israel has so often been, by divine appointment, in difficult circumstances (Ps. li. 6 ; cf. Isa. lxiii. 17). The origin of sin, equally with that of death, the psalmists leave unexplained ; neither Ps. li. 7 nor Ps. xc. 8 refers to human nature in general. And now, what are the peculiar merits of the psalmists' treatment of sin, as compared with that of the Vedic and Gâthic hymn-writers? First they lay much less stress than the former (see Rig Veda, vii. 86, 3) on the excuses of sin. They do not even once refer to Satan or to 'the Satan,' and only once do we find such a plea as that in Ps. li. 6. In general the post-Exile writers love to magnify human responsibility, nor is this denied by the agonized writer of Ps. li. Another point in which the psalmists' treatment of sin differs widely from that of the Vedic poets is that they do not put the non-offering of libations on a level with moral offences.

Christian students must not however underrate the morality of Vedic religion. In other sections it may be ritualistic, but 'with Varuna it goes down into the depths of the conscience, and realizes the idea of holiness' (Barth, *Religions of India*, p. 17). And still more respect is due to Mazdeism. The priestly writers of the Avesta have not indeed completely disengaged the idea of moral from that of ceremonial purity. But we remember on the one hand the ceremonialism of Leviticus and on the other passages in the Gâthâs which are in perfect accord with Pss. xv. and xxiv. Ahura Mazda is the God of purity and truth; how then can it be correct to say that Mazdeism only knows physical defilement? No psalmist can detest evil more than Zarathustra and his successors, and the threefold division of sins into those of thought, word, and deed in Ps. xvii. 3–5 is thoroughly Zarathustrian (see e.g. *Vendîdâd* viii. 100). For essays on the Vedic and on the Babylonian conceptions of sin respectively, see M. Holzman in Steinthal's *Zeitschrift*, 1884, Heft 1; G. Evans, *Christian Reformer*, 1887, pp. 122–128.

Note [x], p. 348.

It is disputable whether מוֹרֶיךָ in Isa. xxx. 20 is singular or plural. At any rate, since the *tōrāh* of priests and prophets comes from Jehovah, He might justly be called 'Teacher' (strictly, 'director'). 'Teaching' is indeed ascribed to Jehovah in Isa. ii. 3 (Mic. iv. 2), xxviii. 26. Cf. p. 352, note º.

NOTE ʸ, p. 348.

Comp. also the Jerus. Targ. on Gen. i. 1, 'By wisdom the Lord created,' where 'wisdom' means the Tōrāh or Law, which was in the period of this Targum considered one of the seven antemundane things. Precisely so the Zoroastrian Dîn or Daêna, the impersonation of the Zoroastrian Law, is said to have come from the heavenly dwelling, and to be created by Mazda (see the Dîn-Yast, *Oxford Z. A.* ii. 264–269). But there is no historical connexion between the beliefs. They are natural inferences of the idealistic philosophy which lies at the root of the ancient Oriental religions.

NOTE ᶻ, p. 349.

That other books besides the Law and the Prophets (e.g. especially Job) early acquired the position of religious classics, could be easily shown.

NOTE ᵃᵃ, p. 350.

Much has been said (see e.g. Siegfried, *Theol. Literaturzeitung*, Oct. 5, 1889 ; W. R. Smith, *The Religion of the Semites*, p. 418) of the reactionary character of the Jewish ceremonial system. If there be a danger that the reformed churches may fall back into a system in which rites have an inherent value, it is not amiss to speak severely of Ezra's work. But from a historical point of view, it appears to me that a milder judgment upon Jewish ceremonialism is called for. Could the principles of Jeremiah and the Second Isaiah have been carried out? Was it not all-important to organize the restored people on a strongly religious basis ? and how could Ezra, under his circumstances, have acted otherwise than he did, building upon the sacerdotal traditions with which as a priest he was familiar? Happily he was not the only educator granted by Providence to his people. If Ezra was a *sōfēr* of the Law (see Ezra vii. 11 Sept.), other men were equally devoted *sōferīm* of the writings of Jeremiah. And even the Law, side by side with its traditional 'survivals,' contains passages enough which are full of inspiring and inspired moral earnestness. In short, Jewish legalism was not without a truly spiritual and even an evangelical element. The misfortune was that after Christianity in one way, as Buddhism in another, had taken up what M. Réville, in his *Prolegomena of the History of Religions*, calls the 'principle of redemption,' a fatal logical necessity drove Judaism to identify itself more and more with a strict and unspiritual legalism. Jewish readers will understand, however, that I am not so blind as to assert that this identification has ever been complete. Cf. my article on 'The Jews and the Gospel,' *Expositor*, 1885 (1), pp. 401–418.

LECTURE VIII.

God hath spoken once, twice have I heard this; that power belongeth unto God. Also unto thee, O Lord, belongeth mercy [American revision, *lovingkindness*]; *for thou renderest to every man according to his work.*—Ps. lxii. 12, 13 (R. V.).

LECTURE VIII.

PART I.—But if the Law is Jehovah's best gift to Israel, how is it that the ritual system is so seldom referred to by the psalmists? Two explanations can be given, one partial, the other more complete; (1) the framers of the Psalter took thought for the needs of distant brethren, and (2) the phrase 'the Law' meant more to the later Church than it seems to have done to Ezra.—The growth of schools or sects, a consequence of accepting a 'Law' of such varied contents. The two extremes, represented by the promoters and editors of the priestly legislation (cf. Ps. li. 20, 21) and by Isa. xliii. 23, lxvi. 3, Pss. xl. 2–12, l., li. 3–19; the middle school by Pss. i. and cxix., and by the Books of Joel and Jonah, but scarcely by Prov. i.–ix. (pre-Exilic), nor by Ps. xix. 8–15 (too legalistic in spirit). We might, however, perhaps include the Hallelujah psalms in the third group. Was, then, the great idea of spiritual sacrifices the monopoly of a single school? No; but some Churchmen welcomed it more heartily than others. They found a Bible within the Bible, from which the spiritual meaning of sacrifice dawned upon them. Not to ritual sacrifices but to the self-oblation of Jehovah's Servant do they (like 2 Isaiah) ascribe the full regeneration of Israel. Thus they anticipate Christian truth (Heb. x. 1–10). Reply to objections.—How is it, then, that the benefits derived by Israel at large from Jehovah's Servant (the phrase is explained elsewhere) are not more clearly referred to by the psalmists? Perhaps they were afraid of too much efficacy being ascribed to the merits of the righteous. The Servant might indeed prepare the way for Israel's return to its God. But obedience was still the only acceptable sacrifice.—But how could turning from evil ways make up for past sins? An important question, for even those who were symbolized by the 'Servant of Jehovah' were sadly imperfect. Of this the psalmists are for the most part well aware. A keen self-distrust has come upon the Church-nation. It is felt that obedience can in the first instance only take the form of repentance. Application of Ps. li. 13, 17, 19. Explanation of the professions of innocence in Ps. xliv. 18, 19, &c.—And what is it that makes repentance possible? The thought of the divine lovingkindness. Explanation of *khésed*. It is the characteristic attribute of the two parties to a covenant, such as that which bound each Israelite to his people, and the people of Israel to its God. Jehovah's *khésed* is the one safeguard of erring Israel. Distinction between 'lovingkindness' and 'mercy,' between historic faith and devotional philosophy. —But will the lovingkindness of the divine Shepherd never attain its end? Must Israel perpetually alternate between sinning and repenting, suffering oppression, and receiving deliverance? No; the Judgment Day is coming. But we cannot frame a consistent picture either of the judgment or of the succeeding age. On this as on other subjects, a study of the Psalter reveals somewhat different schools of thought. Manifold contrasts (of which specimens are given) and underlying unity. The psalmists, like the prophets, suppose the Day of Jehovah to be nearer than it really is. Occupation of the waiting Church.

PART II.—A further question of importance arises. Had the psalmists a real though vague presentiment of a judgment of individuals after death? The author of Ecclesiastes had none, but he was thoroughly out of sympathy with the psalmists. Considering the variety of views in the post-Exile Church, is it not probable that opinions like his would provoke a reaction in the opposite direction? Can we not understand a bold venture of faith issuing in the presentiment referred to? May not Ps. xlix. 15, 16 be such a venture?—We must start from a general view of Ps. xlix. as a protest against the old Hebrew notion of Sheól, and must explain *vv.* 15, 16 in accordance with the ideas of the writer's age. The surmises of an earlier age on the possibility of escaping death, or at least of escaping out of the realm of death. Can the post-Exile Church have failed to meditate on these? Was it possible that in these latter days Enoch's and Elijah's happy lot might be that of many pious Israelites? Or, putting this aside, and accepting Sheól as their portion after death, what was the nature of the life in Sheól? Might there be a worshipping Church even there? To judge from the Psalter there was no unanimity on this subject. On the one hand we have Pss. vi. 5, 6, xxx. 10, lxxxviii. 11-13, lxxxix. 49, and on the other, Pss. xvi., xvii., xlix., lxxiii. The latter belong to the class of mystic psalms, which are closely connected with the 'Puritan' psalms already referred to. Characteristics of the former, especially of the 'guest-psalms.' Note especially the attitudes of the writers towards the temple; they seem on the point of dispensing with the visible temple altogether. Exegetical problems of Ps. xvii. 13-15. Is the writer, who reminds us of Johannine mysticism, and who represents a class, indifferent to such external matters as death and the hereafter?—Reasons why some critics reply in the affirmative. Pfleiderer's interpretation of Ps. lxxiii. 25 criticized. The author's conclusion—that Pss. xvii. and lxxiii., and probably xvi., recognize the principle of, at any rate, moral compensation of the righteous after death. The enigma of Ps. xlix. 15, 16 too has at any rate been half solved.—We must now devote ourselves to the unexplained part of this enigma. It is only permissible to find in it a reference to retribution after death, if external evidence warrants us in ascribing such an idea to the psalmist. Might the Jews have been led to the belief in Babylon? Scarcely. Escape from the gloomy Underworld was no doubt possible, according to the Babylonians, but only for kings, and not as the reward of exceptional goodness. Resurrection, too, was not an unknown idea. Marduk would not be Marduk if he could not 'make the dead to live.' The stress which Babylonian religion laid on these conceptions may, or even must, have stimulated Jewish thinkers to work out their own religious problems more earnestly and hopefully, but more than this could not be expected.—Let us now turn to Persia. Is the idea in question a Persian one? Importance of the study of Zoroastrianism. What are the spiritual elements in this religion, by which it must have attracted the most spiritual Jews? We must seek them in the Gâthic hymns, which are the utterances of the founder of the Zoroastrian Church, though supplementary information may be gained from the later Avesta, and even from the Bundahis. Study of the Zoroastrian theory of sacrifice and of morality. The former must be viewed in its highest form; we may then compare it with the theory of the Puritan psalmists. Defence of the Zoroastrian morality. Still greater interest of Zarathustra's conception of the rewards of righteousness. Heaven and hell, primarily states of the soul; vision of God after death; ἀποκατάστασις. These ideas not less prominent in the later Zoroastrianism.—Can the Jewish Church have been uninfluenced by this congenial religion? Surely not. Iran and Israel were predestined fellow-workers in the cause of religion. Not all Israel's religious writers were prepared to co-operate with Iran; only some, both prophets and psalmists, were able to select precisely what was needed to fill up the Church's theology. Not all selected the same elements. We must re-read certain Biblical passages in a Persian light to give to each writer the credit which is his due, and remember that assimilation of Persian ideas is not at all inconsistent with vagueness and variety of statement. Dogmatic phrases are of course still in the far distance. The passages are, (*a*) Isa. xxv. 8, xxvi. 19, (*b*) Isa. lxv. 17-22, lxvi. 22, (*c*) Dan. xii. 2, (*d*) Ps. xlix. 15, 16, (*e*) Ps. xvii. 15, (*f*) Ps. xvi. 10, 11, (*g*) Ps. lxxiii. 24-27, (*h*) Ps. xxi. 5, (*i*) Ps. xlv. 3, (*k*) Ps. lxxii. 5, (*l*) Ps. lxiii. 9, 10, (*m*) Ps. xi. 7; cf. cxl. 14, (*n*) Ps. xli. 13*b*, (*o*) Ps. xxxvi. 10.—A turning-point has now been reached, and the importance of the result justifies the lecturer in seeking for some external confirmation of its soundness. If the Books of Proverbs and Job, which are in the main earlier than the period of the Psalter, contained either or both of the ideas in question (immortality and resurrection), the object would be gained; for we should certainly have a right in this case to expect references to the ideas in the Psalter. But neither of these books can be shown to contain these ideas. We must therefore look further, and perhaps from the records of the following periods we shall gain the confirmation which we desire.—Reply to an objection. Let us turn first to the so-called Psalms of Solomon and the Book of Enoch. Further illustrations from Justin Martyr, the Fourth Book of Maccabees, the New Testament, and the Mishna. Last of all, we must consult the Targum and Midrash, and critically study Josephus's account of the three Jewish 'sects.' Result—that the later developments of Jewish thought favour the view that the idea of eternal life may be traced in the Psalter. Immortality, then, is no mere evolution out of the old Semitic belief in Sheól; the fostering influence of a more advanced system of thought was needed for its development. But may not this system have been Greek philosophy rather than Zoroastrianism? Reply to this inquiry. Zoroastrian preceded Hellenic influences, and made the success of these possible. Views of Dr. Grätz and M. Montet rejected. Conclusion.

PRINCIPAL NOTES.—PART I.: On the anti-sacrificial tendency of later Jewish religion.—On the meaning of *khésed* or 'covenant-love.'

PART II.: Meaning of phrase 'guest of Jehovah.'—Can the Avesta be safely used by a critical historian?—Age and mission of Zarathustra.—Is the hope of immortality traceable in the Wisdom-literature?—The intermediate state in the Apocalypse.—The Targum on the Psalms.—The accounts of the Essenes in Josephus; present position of moderate conservative criticism.—M. Montet's views on the history of the doctrine of immortality.

PART I.

HUMAN OBEDIENCE AND DIVINE LOVINGKINDNESS.

IF the giving of the Law was Jehovah's crowning lovingkindness, the question arises, How is it that the psalmists allude so seldom to the details of the ritual system, and in particular to sacrifices? To some extent this may be accounted for by the destination of the Psalter. Had the various collections of Hebrew psalms been intended only for the temple, we can guess from the other ancient Oriental hymnals (the respective dates of which do not here concern us) what a difference it would have made in the contents. But the authorities well knew that the great mass of Israelites frequented, not the temple, but the synagogues, and would not have enjoyed hymns full of references to the temple sacrifices. For instance, Paul and Silas at Philippi would hardly have been so ready with their prayers and praises (Acts xvi. 25) if the appointed prayer-book and hymn-book had been tinged on every page with the sacrificial spirit. That I am not assuming in the framers of the Psalter too strong a regard for synagogue worshippers, will be clear, not only from their inclusion of Ps. xlviii. (see above, p. 164), but from the prominence which many of the other included psalms give to the duty of praising God among the nations (see, even in Book I., Ps. ix. 12). And I think that this sympathy was noticed by the authors of the *Shemoneh Esreh* (or Eighteen Benedictions), which were evidently designed, not for the temple, but for the synagogues, and which appear to be largely suggested by passages in the psalms.[1] Still we may reasonably ask for a more complete explanation than this. May we not, then, say that the meagre reference of the Psalter to the sacrificial system is to be accounted for by something like a reaction against the

---

[1] See Isidore Loeb, *Revue des études juives*, xix. (1889) p. 17, &c.

spirit of Ezra? Great as the authority of this noble reformer was, he could not mould the Church entirely as, if Ezra vii. 10, 11 describes him correctly, he must have wished. And so he, or at any rate his successors, were led by circumstances to accept a compromise. It was not possible to erect the 'Mosaic' Law into an absolute standard of religious truth. The growing regard in the Church for the records of the old prophecy protested against it. How could Jeremiah and (the Second) Isaiah be said to be on a lower level than Moses? Hence 'Moses and the prophets' together were honoured as the Tōrāh in the wider sense (see on Ps. i. 2), and were fully recognized as such in the Sabbath-lessons of the synagogues.

The inevitable result of the variety in the contents of the Tōrāh was the growth, first of all, of schools of thought, and then, other circumstances helping, of societies and sects or parties. Of the former alone can we find any sure traces in the Psalter. When the author of Ps. cxix. declares that he is a חָבֵר or 'associate' of faithful observers of the Law he makes no allusion to the חֶבֶר or 'association' of the Pharisees. Nor can we venture to infer from the predilection of many psalmists for the word חֲסִידִים or 'pious ones' that this had already become altogether a party name; the apparent parallelism between קְהַל חֲסִידִים (Ps. cxlix. 1) and a disputed phrase in 1 Macc. ii. 42 (see above, p. 56) is no proof to the contrary. But schools of thought, or definite tendencies which could not but issue in schools of thought, we cannot fail to observe in the psalms. And we are warned of their existence by the different attitude of particular psalmists towards sacrifices.[a] For instance, the *sōfēr* who wrote Ps. cxix. does not under-estimate the 'Mosaic' Law, and yet even he (v. 108) beseeches God to 'accept the freewill offerings of his mouth' (i.e. prayer and praise). Nowhere does he make mention of any other sacrifice. Still more remarkable are the expressions of certain psalms (Pss. xl. 2-12, l., li. 3-19),[b] the work, as it would seem, of an advanced Puritan section within the Jewish Church, to which 'Malachi' among others was inclined (see Mal. iii. 4, and cf. i. 10, 11,[1] R. V.), and some of whose members in post-Maccabæan times boldly denounced both temple and sacrifices as 'unclean.'[c] The early Jewish

---

[1] See on Ps. lxv. 3. I do not venture to add Hag. ii. 14.

Church seems in fact to have set an example of comprehensiveness. It had its two extreme schools of thought (I cannot say 'parties,' for there was no definite practical antithesis), viz., the promoters and editors of the priestly legislation (not indeed mere formalists, but somewhat too near to formalism) on the one hand (cf. Ps. li. 20, 21) and students of Jeremiah, like the writers of those three psalms and of passages like Isa. xliii. 23, lxvi. 3, on the other.[d] Midway between the two stood devout students of Scripture like the writers of Pss. i. and cxix., and, may I not add? the authors of the Books of Joel and Jonah.[e] Gladly would I mention other decided adherents of the respective schools, if there were sufficient undeniable evidence. Could it be shown, for instance, that the whole Book of Proverbs was, like the Psalter, the gradual product of the post-Exile period, I should be able to point to some striking statements of the all-sufficiency of the fear of Jehovah (Prov. i. 7, cf. xxviii. 14), and of the superiority of prayer and obedience to a ceremonial system (Prov. xv. 8, xvi. 6, xxi. 3, 27). To this critical theory, however, I am still opposed. The greater part of the first collection seems to me almost necessarily pre-Exilic, and I do not see sufficient grounds for disintegration. My only strong doubt is whether Prov. i.–ix. should not be included among those parts of the Book which really are post-Exilic (see above, p. 218). There is much less objection to the view that great outbursts of praise, such as the Hallelujah psalms, belong to the intermediate school to which I have referred; of these I shall have to speak again presently. But I do not venture to include the Praise of the Law (Ps. xix. 8–15) among the records of this school, because its author's εὐλάβεια reveals a legalism which has passed the bounds of moderation.[f] The 'yoke of ordinances' may indeed be mitigated to him by a spiritual love. Still it *is* a 'yoke,' and the ταλαίπωρὸς ἐγὼ ἄνθρωπος of St. Paul and the tears of the dying Johanan 'the light of Israel' are not so very far off. There is a more serene temper in the three distinctly Puritan psalms. Their authors prize the temple much (see Ps. l. 2), both for its associations and as the most sacred house of prayer, but not less the 'roll of the book' (Ps. xl. 8); and there is a Bible within this Bible from which the spiritual meaning of sacrifice—the only symbolism which can any longer satisfy the soul—has dawned upon them. They evidently think that sacrificial rites were only permitted and in some sense enjoined because of the dulness of men's spiritual sensibilities, and that the essential parts of the Law are those everlasting 'statutes' which, as summed up in the 'tables of the covenant,' are probably already recited in the daily prayers.[g] To them, statements like 'Jehovah spake unto Moses, This is the law of the burnt offering' (Lev. vi. 8, 9), appear less accurate than the authoritative assurances of Jehovah in Jeremiah, 'I spake not unto your fathers . . . concerning burnt offerings or sacrifices,' 'How can ye say, We are wise, and Jehovah's law (tōrāh, 'direction') is with us! but behold, into a lie the lying pen of the scribes hath made it,' and 'This was the thing that I commanded them, Hearken unto my voice, and I will be your God, and ye shall be my people' (Jer. vii. 22, viii. 8, vii. 23).[h] Yes; these psalmists are the true sons of Jeremiah and forerunners of Christ. The 'right sacrifice' is obedience in those 'weightier matters' which formalists are tempted to 'omit' (see p. 150). Or if there be a second sacrifice, it is like unto the first; 'open lips' are the fitting companions of 'open ears.'[1] Obedience and thanksgiving are the true divine service ($\theta\rho\eta\sigma\kappa\epsilon\acute{\iota}\alpha$, James i. 26), and in the abeyance of such cultus from 'the nations' Jehovah looks for it to the members of the great spiritual corporation. Israel is the priest of the peoples as man is, or should be, the priest of creation.[1]

This great truth was of course not the monopoly of a school, though the adherents of a certain school of thought may have been the first to welcome it. We can see it in psalms which became in the highest degree utterances of the worshipping Church. Passages like 'Bless thou Jehovah' (thou, at least, in double measure), 'O my soul' (Ps. ciii. 22), almost justify the strong statement of Philo that 'by an excess of fellowship and goodwill to all men everywhere the Jewish nation performs prayers and other rites both for itself and for those who have escaped from the due acts of worship.'[2] For remember that thanksgiving is the second and nobler half of prayer.[3] Some-

---

[1] See Isa. lxi. 6, and cf. Deut. ii. 24.
[2] *Philonea*, ed. Tischendorf, p. 53; cf. *De Mon.* ii. 6 (Mangey, ii. 227).
[3] See my note on Ps. xlii. 9.

times the psalmists even speak as if Jehovah could not endure to be without praise (Ps. vi. 6, Isa. xxxviii. 18). Not that He is stained with self-love, but being rich in lovingkindness, He longs for the response of grateful hearts. Moreover, the declaration of Jehovah's praises is one appointed means of bringing in the nations to the fold.[1]

To thinkers of the school of Ezra the views of what I have called the Puritan school appeared, I will not say erroneous, but liable to misinterpretation. They were themselves far enough removed from the old naïve view of sacrifices, but they still gave too prominent a place in their theory to the ritual system. One of their number was apparently the first editor of Ps. li., who added *vv.* 20 and 21 to the original poem. I have elsewhere protested against a sweeping disparagement of the Levitical Law,[2] which was, teleologically speaking, the providential instrument for preserving the deposit of spiritual religion. Still, the sympathies of a Christian must be chiefly drawn to the prophetically minded authors of the Puritan psalms. They are in fact more than half Christian in the points referred to, if at least we follow that New Testament writer who assures us (quoting from a kindred psalm) that the only efficacious sacrifice is the representative self-oblation of the perfect Man (Heb. x. 1–10). Does any one object to my statement, on the ground that the author of Hebrews does not use such directly anti-sacrificial language as I have represented these psalmists to have used? But this early theologian has a carefully constructed theory, and the temple poets do but give us the germs of theories. Every good lyric, according to Goethe, was suggested by an occasion, and this is emphatically true of the psalms referred to. In other circumstances, and with leisure for reflection, the writer of Ps. l. might have said that the present will of God was for the maintenance of sacrifices, and that therefore all honour ought to be shown to them. He might also for himself and his school have drawn healthful meanings from the sacrifices, regarding them, as the Second Isaiah may have regarded the sin-offering (Isa. liii. 10), as acted parables. So that this objection at least falls to the ground. Another

---

[1] Comp. Isa. xliii. 21 with 1 Pet. ii. 9.
[2] See above, p. 358; *Job and Solomon*, pp. 3, 4.

objection, from a different point of view, will perhaps be that the author of Hebrews exaggerates the Gospel element in psalms like the 40th. To some extent he does, but not so much as was thought by the elder rationalism. The complex conception of the Servant of Jehovah includes the idea of the capacity of the better Israelites to benefit their less advanced brethren. Not only in the Second Isaiah, but in some of the noblest psalms,ʲ it is the self-oblation of Jehovah's Servant to which are either expressly or by implication ascribed the full regeneration of Israel and the spiritual conquest of the world.

Let me not be thought to speak too dogmatically. The benefits derived by the Church-nation at large from the more perfect representatives of Israel's Genius [1] are not so clearly referred to by the psalmists as by their favourite prophet the Second Isaiah. It is possible that the former were apprehensive of the appearance of some such theory to account for these benefits as was actually put forward by the later Rabbis. They may have vaguely dreaded that doctrine of the atoning efficacy of the merits of the righteous in their generation [2] which has contributed to weaken the idea of sin in Talmudic Judaism. At any rate there can be no doubt as to the intuitions of the nobler psalmists. All that the Servant of Jehovah could do, whether for Israel at large or for humanity, was to prepare the way for a spontaneous movement of sinful souls towards their God. The Servant might, by teaching, and by exhibiting the graces of a godlike character, enlighten, soften, stimulate. But obedience was still the only acceptable sacrifice, alike for the righteous and for the sinner.

But how could the forsaking of wicked ways (Isa. lv. 7) make up for a long course of transgression? The psalmists provided for this case. Indeed, they drew no hard and fast line between the righteous and the sinners. They felt (putting aside Ps. xliv., which needs some excuse) that the actual Servant of Jehovah was at the best sadly imperfect, that the Genius of Israel never had been perfectly embodied, so that not even for themselves could the righteous Israelites render a complete obedience. The very psalmist who says in the name of Israel that he is *khāsīd*, or pious, appeals, as the Septuagint finely interprets him, to the divine ἐπιείκεια ᵏ

---

[1] See Lect. VI., p. 263.   [2] See Weber, *Altsyn. Theologie*, p. 285, &c.

(lxxxvi. 5), without which he can neither please God nor carry on His work in the world. A keen distrust of himself has come upon Israel, caused, as we have seen, partly by the long series of national troubles, and partly by the extreme minuteness of the legal requirements. This is why, with a spirituality far in advance of the Law,[m] the true Israelites are introduced in certain psalms voluntarily assuming the place of the 'chief of sinners,' to whom obedience can only take the form of repentance, or, as Sirach perhaps already expressed it, *t'shūbāh*, 'returning.'[n] 'I blot out as a mist thy transgressions, and as a cloud thy sins; return unto me, for I redeem thee' (Isa. xliv. 22). 'In the time of sins show repentance' (Ecclus. xviii. 21). 'Thou didst make thy sons to be of good hope because thou givest repentance when men have sinned' (Wisd. xii. 19). And long afterwards, a sweet singer of Israel thus exhorts his people,

> The altar of repentance (*t'shūbāh*) arise and make,
> Bind also upon it thy lusts.[1]

A very imperfect sacrifice, doubtless; but—'a broken and a crushed heart, O God, thou canst not despise' (Ps. li. 19). To return to thee (such is Israel's meaning) is the only obedience which I can yet render. Thou hast thyself called me; cast me not away. Open my lips by forgiving me, and my tongue shall show thy praise. Take not thy holy spirit from me; for without it how can I return, and having returned how without it can I obey? And so from its very falls the spiritual Israel has gained a deeper notion of obedience, and a fuller consciousness of redeeming love.

Do not suppose me to imply that the psalmists, or the Church for which they speak, always remained at this high spiritual level. Long after the period at which we have ventured to place Ps. xviii. we find professions of innocence,[o] which are at variance with the normal Christian sentiment (cf. 1 John i. 8). But even if the writers of Pss. vii. 9, 10, xvii. 3–5, xxvi. 1–5, xliv. 18, 19, seem to claim too much for themselves or for Israel, it is only fair to remember that their standard is not the external one of religious or social custom (see note [w], p. 356), but the inward judgment of the unseen

[1] R. Yehuda Hallévi.

God (cf. Ps. vii. 9, cxxxix. 23). Their professions are, moreover, historically significant. The language of Ps. xxvi. 6*a* is not to be attenuated by the remark that the sins disclaimed by the psalmist are those of oppressors, and not of an oppressed people. They had • once been characteristic of Israel. Not only its greatest king but its most prominent and religious citizens had been guilty of the sin of murder (see on Isa. i. 15, lix. 3), which to pious Israelites seemed to pollute their land with an indelible stain. The Church in the 51st psalm prays (*v.* 16):

> Deliver us from blood-guiltiness, Jehovah my Saviour-God.
> And my tongue shall sing of thy righteousness.

It was no small thing that Israel had now purged itself from this awful guilt, and could describe its religious ideal in the words of Pss. xv. and xxiv 3–6 (cf. lxxiii. 1). Shall I add that the above views of certain psalms are not really opposed to Dean Church's finely expressed argument in favour of the divine guidance of the Israelites? At least it is with the letter and not with the spirit of his argument that they conflict. The psalms may belong to different periods, and the national character of Israel may have passed through various phases, and yet they may be of the highest value to the Christian apologist.

The passages referred to above are at any rate exceptional. It is upon the whole true that the Jewish Church is deeply conscious of its imperfections, and that nothing but the thought of the divine lovingkindness makes repentance sweetly possible to its members. 'A heavenly psalm of mercy' is Sir Philip Sidney's name for Ps. li., and most appropriate it is, at least if 'mercy' may be taken as a synonym for 'lovingkindness.' And what is this 'quality of mercy' to the Jewish Church? It is a 'bond of perfectness,' a 'religio,' according to St. Augustine's derivation of the word, binding fast both the Israelite to his fellow, and Israel to his God. The *khasīdīm*, of whom we have had to speak so much, are those who love Jehovah because He first loved Israel (Deut. iv. 37, vii. 8, x. 15), and who show forth their love in action. חֶסֶד (*khésed*), it is true, is not simply love. God first had a sympathy with the righteous Abraham, and then entered into a close moral relation with him (Gen. xviii. 19); and for the sake of Abraham 'my lover' (אֹהֲבִי, Isa. xli. 8) He first loved,[p] and then formed a moral compact with Israel. The primal love of Jehovah (אַהֲבָה), regulated by this moral compact, and manifested in act, became חֶסֶד.[q] This is Israel's safeguard; for from the first it has fallen far below the standard of its great ancestor (Isa. xlviii. 8). Israel's God is righteous, and yet can love the imperfectly righteous, because, by the ways which we have studied, the Good Shepherd can bring back His own sheep to the fold. As the psalmists look back, this is their view of the mutual relation between Jehovah and His people, —

> Their heart was not steadfast towards him,
> Neither were they faithful unto his covenant.
> But he is full of compassion,
> Forgives iniquity and destroys not;
> Yea, many a time takes he back his anger,
> And arouses not all his wrath.
> So he bethought him that they were but flesh,
> And wind that passes away, and comes not again.
> (Ps. lxxviii. 37–39.)

Inexhaustible are they in praise of this gracious quality,[r] without which prayer itself, in the highest sense of the word, could not exist. What is it that glorifies one of the least poetical of the later psalms (Ps. cxxxvi.), and justifies its liturgical title, the great Hallel? Simply its exquisite refrain, 'For his lovingkindness endureth for ever.' How should the faithful worshipper enter the temple save in his God's 'abundant lovingkindness' (Ps. v. 8)? If God were only 'wise in heart and mighty in strength' (Job ix. 4), who could plead with Him? But God is not simply the Lord but Jehovah; not simply the Most High but the lowly; not simply the merciful but He who is full of lovingkindness to His covenant-people.

Can you wonder that some scholars regret that the levelling hand of King James's translators (following those of Alexandria) has so greatly weakened the distinction between חֶסֶד, 'lovingkindness,' and רַחֲמִים 'tender mercies'?[s] It is more than a pedantry of scholarship which is concerned; it is the balance of revealed truth. There are no doubt moods in which even the Christian is almost weighed down by the thought of the divine omnipotence, and then by a strong reaction of faith extracts comfort from it, and exclaims, 'O God, who showest Thine almighty power most chiefly in showing mercy and pity.'[t] This is what I may call the highest devotional philosophy, nor can we dispense with it. Still an ordinary work-day religion must base itself not upon theory, but upon facts ; we must approach God as those whom He has led out of Egypt, and with whom He has definitely entered into covenant. A gifted Israelite of Alexandria says that God, who is a δεσπότης, 'despotizes over his own strength' for moral ends.[1] But how do we know that God is a moral God ? By a historic revelation in the past, which, accepted by us, has become a not less historic revelation in the present. The psalmists, as the interpreters of Moses and the prophets, undoubtedly take this ground. They postpone that devotional philosophy which they too more and more hold, to the good old historic faith, viz. that God is Jehovah (Ps. cxviii. 27), and that it is righteous for Him to love and to guide His covenant people. And the weakness of the psalmists is simply this, that they have not thoroughly fused the new devotional philosophy with the old historic faith of the covenant-God.[u] Let not this hinder us from restoring mentally to our Psalter that fine symbolic phrase, of which the Gospel has taught us the full significance, 'O let Israel say, that his lovingkindness endureth for ever' (Ps. cxviii. 2).

But must the lovingkindness of the Good Shepherd always take the same form ? Will the divine education of Israel never be complete ? Must there be a perpetual alternation of sinning and repenting, wandering and returning ? And this 'deep sighing of the poor,' and this straining look for the morning, must the one always be met by a call to patience, and the other by the watchman's neutral report, 'The morning cometh, and also the night' ? Oh, no ; the Hebrew not less than the Iranian hymns[v] are the bearers of good tidings. The day is at hand which shall close the school-time of God's people, a day of burning anger and burning love, anger against all whether within or without Israel who oppose God's gracious purpose, and of a love which 'reacheth unto the heavens' to

---

[1] Wisd. xii. 18, cf. 16.

the upright and to the pure in heart. It would not be safe, however, to combine the various elements in the Psalter which may be called Messianic into a single picture either of the judgment or of the succeeding age. Though the psalmists all (or all but one) belonged to the post-Exile Church, they were not without considerable differences, which reflect themselves, not only in their estimate of the ritual, but even more distinctly in their hopes for the Church's future.

To select but a few of the manifold contrasts which suggest themselves. How different are Pss. i. and l. from Pss. lxxii. and cx.! In the two former the Messianic judgment stands apparently out of relation to ordinary history; in the two latter, it seems, as it were, to grow out of the events happening before the psalmists' eyes. How different again is Ps. ii., in which (as also in Ps. lxxxii.[w]) there are distinct traces of apocalyptic influences! And how unlike to all these is the glorious 22nd psalm! Speaking generally, it is from a Christian point of view a weakness in the Messianic parts of the Psalter that so little stress is laid on the moral preparation of mankind for the final judgment. And yet who can be surprised at this? It is only incidentally that we can expect the psalmists to refer to the mysterious future. The 22nd psalm is an exception to their general style; it is a dramatic monologue somewhat in the manner of the Second Isaiah, and presupposing his advanced teaching on the missionary functions of the Church. The object of the temple-poets as a class was not to paint the future—that they left to the prophets and the apocalyptic writers—but to brighten the present. Of course they imply the same general view of the Day of Jehovah, which, like the prophets, they continually suppose to be nearer than it really is. But they do not attach their faith to a near $\pi\alpha\rho o\nu\sigma\acute{\iota}\alpha$ in such a way that it would be imperilled by disillusionment. On this point I may refer to our previous study of 'the accession-psalms' (pp. 341, 342). Those who are not of the true Israel may perchance 'slip,' but not those who have fully grasped the meaning of the 'covenant.' When doubting thoughts beset them, they either go into the 'sanctuary of God' (Ps. lxxiii. 17) or study the volume of the Torah (Ps. xciv. 12), the temple and the Torah being the two pledges of the promised divine indwelling. By the sure word of prophecy, by the earnests or initial stages of the judgment in history,ˣ and by the sacramental sign of the temple,¹ they know that 'the needy shall not alway be forgotten' (Ps. ix. 19). When Jehovah shall 'find the set time,' he will 'judge uprightly' (Ps. lxxv. 3). The mighty one will 'throughly purge his floor, and gather his wheat into the garner,' as the Baptist said (Matt. iii. 12), alluding to Ps. i. 4. 'Therefore,' as the next verse of Ps. i. continues, 'the wicked shall not stand in the judgment, nor sinners in the assembly of the righteous.' What, then, should be the employment of the waiting Church? The 'Mosaic' Law, according to scholars of Jeremiah, may be far from absolute perfection. But the best Israelites are not unsettled by this. They do not evade any of their religious duties, but strive constantly to 'fulfil all righteousness,' sustained by the thought of preparing the way for redemption. Even the formalists, those tares among the wheat, base upon their own non-moral obedience a claim to share in the Messianic reward.²

Note ᵃ, p. 364.

The chief passages bearing on the question as to the relation of the psalmists to the Law are : Ps. i. ; iv. 6 ; xv. 4 ; xvii. 4 ; xviii. 23 ; xix. 8-15 ; xx. 4*b* ; xxii. 27(?) ; xxvii. 6 ; xxxv. 13 ; xl. 7-9 ; l. ; li. 9, 8, 19, 21 ; liv. 8 ; lxi. 9*b* ; lxvi. 13-15 ; lxix. 31, 32 ; lxxviii. 5 ; lxxxi. 2-6, 17 ; cvii. 22 ; cxvi. 17 ; cxviii. 27 ; cxix. ; cxli. 2.

Note ᵇ, p. 364.

These psalms ought to be studied in connexion with the 'mystic' psalms to which I shall refer later, and which presuppose the sacrificial theory of the more distinctly Puritan school. Pss. v. 4, cxli. 2, may be added to the group, but scarcely iv. 6, li. 21, though Vitringa and Waterland interpret these passages of spiritual sacrifices.

Note ᶜ, p. 364.

This view of the psalms in question is already suggested by Theodoret (on Ps. cxv. 8) : ἔστι τοίνυν καὶ ἐντεῦθεν καταμαθεῖν, ὡς καὶ τοῦ νόμου κρατοῦντος, οἱ πνευματικώτερον τῷ νόμῳ προσεσχηκότες

---

¹ See Ps. lxxiii. 17 (with my note).   ² See Ps. l. and cf. Isa. lviii. 2.

τὰς λογικὰς θυσίας τῶν ἀλόγων προετίμων θυμάτων, τὴν καινὴν διαθήκην σκιογραφοῦντες. The most indubitable record of the 'advanced Puritan section' in early Jewish literature is Enoch lxxxix. 73, 74, which does not indeed assert in so many words that animal sacrifices are wrong, but only that the offerings in the second temple are impure. The writer means, not merely that at different times wicked worshippers or priests (cf. Hag. ii. 14, Psalms of Sol. ii. 3, 4, viii. 13) have vitiated the sacrifices (for there is nothing to justify such a limitation), but that the temple ought not to have been rebuilt before the Messianic era, when, of course, according to later Judaism, all sacrifices but the thankoffering would cease, and sin itself would be no more. May we compare Isa. lxvi. 1–3? At any rate we may appeal to *Assumpt. Mosis*, c. 4; see also Hilgenfeld, *Die jüd. Apokalyptik*, p. 120, and Schürer's review of Lucius on Essenism in *Theol. Lit.-zeitung*, 1881, col. 494. The Essenes, too, must be mentioned in this connexion, if we may accept the account of the attitude of the Essenes towards the sacrificial system in Jos., *Ant.* xviii. 1, 5. The Essenes did not, it is true, according to this passage, reject the principle of a single national sanctuary, for they sent ἀναθήματα to the temple. But they do appear to have gone beyond those psalmists whose spirit (comp. Ps. xv. with the oath of the Essenes, Jos., *War*, ii. 8, 7) they had so thoroughly imbibed, in giving practical expression to their dislike of animal sacrifices. No such were offered by them (Jos., *Ant. l.c.*) 'by reason of the superiority of their own purifications' (ἁγνεῖαι). The 'sacrifices' which they performed by themselves (ἐφ' αὑτῶν) were probably these purifications which were symbolic (comp. Ps. xxvi. 4–7) of the psalmists' favourite sacrifice of obedience and praise. Hilgenfeld infers from this that the Essenes did not possess the 'priestly code' (*Judenthum und Judenchristenthum*, p. 116); at any rate their Pentateuch must have been different from that of the orthodox Jews. The later Nazaræans and Osseni rejected our Pentateuch though, like the Essenes of Josephus, they venerated Moses (Epiphan., ed. Oehler, i. 92, 100). Ἔφασκυν γὰρ πεπλάσθαι ταῦτα τὰ βιβλία, καὶ μηδὲν τούτων ὑπὸ τῶν πατέρων γεγενῆσθαι. Surely a not unnatural inference from Jer. vii. 22, viii. 8.

Note d, p. 365.

See my commentaries, and comp. G. A. Smith, *Isaiah*, vol. ii.

Note e, p. 365.

See Joel ii. 12, 13, and cf. Isa. lviii. (which is more in the manner of Ps. l.). Also Jon. iii. 5–10 (cf. Jon. ii. 10, which has affinities with Ps. l. 14, 15, cxix. 108). The remarks on pp. 450, 451 of Wellhausen's *Prolegomena* apply especially to the writers of such passages. If I have rightly represented Zarathustra, it is no disparagement to the pious men who formed this school to compare them to that holy sage, who is inferior to them, however, in his view of prayer.

NOTE f, p. 365.

This suggests the necessary qualification to a previous remark. It was only too possible that the fear of unconscious transgressions might kill the remains of childlike simplicity in religion. The same fear hung like a pall over the ordinary Babylonian worshipper, at least if the old hymn (No. 4 in Zimmern's *Busspsalmen*; cf. Sayce, *Hibbert Lectures*, p. 349, &c.), which says so much of 'unknown sins,' was heartily repeated by the contemporaries of Nebuchadrezzar. My reference to Rom. vii. 24 may seem too bold to some. But Theodoret has already explained the transition from *v.* 12 to *v.* 13 of Ps. xix. by virtually paraphrasing Rom. vii. 22, 23.

NOTE g, p. 366.

See *Berachoth*, 12, and cf. *Tamid*, 32*b*. This old custom was abolished because the Sadducees asserted that the object of the recitation was to show that the Decalogue was the essential part of the Law (Jost, *Geschichte*, i. 175 ; cf. Biesenthal, *Das Trostschreiben des Ap. Paulus*, p. 145, note).

NOTE h, p. 366.

On this prophet's attitude towards a written Law, see *Jeremiah, his Life and Times*, pp. 107, 119, 120, 157, and cf. my exposition in *Pulpit Commentary*, i. 185, 186. Mr. Ball thinks that Jer. viii. 8 accuses the 'scribes' of the day of putting false glosses upon the meaning of the sacred law. This is hardly enough. But he subjoins this pregnant suggestion, 'It thus appears that conflicting and competing versions of the law were current in that age. Has the Pentateuch preserved elements of both kinds, or is it homogeneous throughout?' (*Expositor's Bible : Jeremiah*, pp. 175, 176).

NOTE i, p. 366.

See my notes on Pss. xl. 7, l. 14, lxix. 32, and introduction to Ps. li. On 'eucharist,' these psalms anticipate Philo (*De Plantat. Noe*, Mangey, i. 348). As to Zoroaster, Dr. Mills remarks that the kind of gifts which are proposed in the hymns called Gâthâs, 'are not sacrificial beasts or fruits, but the actions of the truly pious citizen whose soul is intimately united with Righteousness, the homage of prayer, and the songs of praise' (*Oxford Zendavesta*, part iii., p. 80).

Note ʲ, p. 368.

See those passages in Pss. xxii., xxxv., xl., and lxix. in which the sufferer is distinguished from the church-nation as a whole, and compare especially Ps. xxii. 7 with Isa. xlix. 7, lii. 14, liii. 2, 3.

Note ᵏ, p. 368.

Comp. Wisd. xii. 18, 2 Macc. x. 4. Heracleota in Corderius' *Catena* on Ps. *l. c.* objects to the Septuagint's version; Aquila and Theodotion give ἱλαστής.

Note ᵐ, p. 369.

'No other nation,' says Kalisch, 'had an institution approaching that of the Day of Atonement in religious depth.' Yet even on this holy day the people 'were simply enjoined to keep rest and to fast; no prayer, no confession of sins, was prescribed for them' (*Leviticus*, ii. 340).

Note ⁿ, p. 369.

The later Jewish doctrine of repentance (as described by Weber) is not spiritual enough; but Jewish hymnody reveals a sound devotional sentiment. Comp. the fifth of the eighteen Jewish Benedictions. Through a Jewish Arabian channel the term 'to return'= 'to repent' (Ar. *tāba*) reached Mohammed (see *Koran*, Sur. ii. 51). Zoroastrianism too has a similar expression for repentance; but how formal is its repentance!

Note ᵒ, p. 369.

Among these I do not, of course, include Ps. lxxxvi. 2. St. Augustine may say, 'Hoc vero . . . nescio utrum potuerit forte alius dicere, nisi ille qui sine peccato erat in hoc mundo,' but this is because he adopts Sept.'s mistranslation, followed by Jerome himself and our A. V. Comp. my Study on Ps. lxxxvi. in *Expositor*, Oct. 1888.

Note ᵖ, p. 371.

See Deut. iv. 37, x. 15; cf. Rom. xi. 28. אהבה, of God's love to Israel, often occurs in the Jewish liturgies.

Note q, p. 371.

Hosea and the psalms have already given me occasion as a commentator to speak of חֶסֶד 'duteous love,' as shown (1) from God to man, (2) from man to God, (3) from man to man (especially in Israel). The first and the third of these applications are the commonest; the *loci classici* for the second are Hos. vi. 4, 6, Jer. ii. 2. What follows from the slenderness of the evidence for the latter? That the use is precarious, and that we should seek to explain it away? No; the use of the common adjective חָסִיד presupposes the sense of 'duteous and active love to God' for חֶסֶד. Put aside, if you will, Pss. xii. 2, xliii. 1, Mic. vii. 2, where חָסִיד may mean merely 'trustworthy,' 'upright,' 'humane,' but how many passages remain in which Jehovah Himself is the object of the implied חֶסֶד! The true inference from the rare occurence of the second application of חֶסֶד seems to me to be this—that according to the Hebrew writers we can best show forth חֶסֶד to Jehovah in the persons of our fellow men. For the deeds of חֶסֶד which Jehovah demands are, not sacrifice, but the practice of justice and beneficence. חֶסֶד, as I have said above, is not simply, nor even predominantly, a subjective feeling. We must distinguish it therefore from אהבה את־י'. That phrase emphasizes right feeling towards Jehovah as the root of right action; חֶסֶד, on the other hand, right action as the flower of right feeling (see Ps. xcvii. 10, 'Ye that love Jehovah, hate that which is evil;' i.e. as the next words suggest, show yourselves to be חסידים). Jehovah requires both the feeling (Ex. xx. 6, Deut. vii. 9) and the action (Ps. xviii. 26, Hos. vi. 6). Only once does אֲהָבָה appear to follow instead of preceding חֶסֶד (Ps. xxxi. 24); but there אֶהֱבוּ means 'love Him more warmly and devotedly than ever who gives such proofs of His fidelity.' There are only two passages besides this in which אהב י' occurs in the psalms (xcvii. 10, cxlv. 20), though according to the present text cxvi. 1 is virtually a third. אהב שֵׁם י', however, occurs three times (v. 12, lxix. 37, cxix. 132); רחם י' once (xviii. 2), but the text is most doubtful. The former phrase is valuable as showing (in the light of Ex. xxxiv. 6, 7) the moral grounds of the good Israelite's preference of Jehovah to other so-called gods. Our language, unhappily, fails to supply an adequate equivalent for חֶסֶד; but considering the comparative rarity of the phrase אהבה את־י' (and the like), it involves the smallest loss to translate חֶסֶד 'love' (or, duteous love) and חָסִיד 'loving one' (or, 'duteous loving one'). It was perhaps a similar calculation of gain and loss which led to the Septuagint's occasional rendering of 'ה

by δικαιοσύνη (Gen. xix. 19, xxiv. 27). Of course, as the bond of the covenant 'ח must be righteousness, and yet the Jewish doctors draw distinctions full of insight between 'ח and צדק (see *Succa* 49a; Wünsche, *Der bab. Talmud*, i. 396).

In the Koran not much is said of love to God. Where it is mentioned (see Sur. iii. and cf. xix. 96) it means obedience to God and His apostle. This was not enough for the Sûfîs, to whom God was the All-beautiful, and who devoted the sweetest strains to the raptures of mystic love (*'ishq*). For a monograph on the O. T. conception, see G. Winter's art. in Stade's *Zeitschrift*, 1889, pp. 211–246.

NOTE ʳ, p. 371.

God's covenant-love makes its home upon earth (Ps. lxxxv. 11); it is built up for ever (lxxxix. 2); it toucheth the heavens (xxxvi. 6). Each good Israelite can sing to Jehovah as 'the God of my lovingkindness' (Ps. lix. 18; cf. 11). But 'all things living' have some claim on this gracious attribute (Ps. cxlv. 16, 17, where, as in Jer. iii. 12, Jehovah is called חָסִיד). Once, only once, does the original writer of *Job* speak of the divine 'lovingkindness' as visiting man simply because he is God's creature (Job vi. 10); the author of 'Elihu' follows suit (Job xxxvii. 13).

NOTE ˢ, p. 371.

Of course, it is not denied that the two are closely related (see Hos. ii. 21). But חֶסֶד says far more than רַחֲמִים to those who are in covenant with God. So the great question is, Who *are* in such a covenant?

NOTE ᵗ, p. 372.

One of the later Jewish names for God is רַחֲמָנָא 'the Merciful,' whence the two first of the 'good names' of Allah, *rakhmân* and *rakhîm*, which are not only Islamic but pre-Islamic (see Muir, *Life of Mahomet*, ii. 147, 148). Zoroastrianism has a similar epithet for Ahura Mazda.

NOTE ᵘ, p. 372.

See e.g. Pss. c., cxvii., where universalism and nationalism appear side by side. It was the Gospel which first made it clear that there were no national distinctions in the covenant.

NOTE ᵛ, p. 372.

Throughout the Gâthâs the singer is borne up by the expectation that the end of the present world is not far off.

Note ʷ, p. 373.

Angel-scenes in heaven abound in the Jewish apocalypses; can we help comparing Ps. lxxxii. with these? The rebellion in Ps. ii. (comp. my note on Ps. xlvi. 8) reminds us of Zech. xiv., Ezek. xxxviii., xxxix. The confederate heathen nations, Gog and Magog, were to commit much havoc in the Messianic age according to the Talmud (see *Berachoth*, 7*b*).

Note ˣ, p. 374.

'Initial stages of the judgment.' The teaching of history led the later writers to conceive of the 'Day of Jehovah' as a connected series of divine acts. This idea pervades the (post-Exile) Book of Joel.

PART II.

RISE OF DOCTRINE OF JUDGMENT AFTER DEATH.

A FURTHER question of importance must now be raised, the answer to which will form a suitable close to these Lectures. Had any of the psalmists an intuition of a judgment of individuals, both good and bad, after death, to be distinguished from that great world-judgment of which I have spoken? Doubtless they were not Egyptian theologians; it would be against their manner to describe such a judgment in detail. Nor could we expect them to have one consistent theory, or indeed any logically elaborated theory at all, on the subject. If, however, a judgment, such as I have just described, be a postulate of the moral consciousness, is it not likely that some of the greater psalmists had a real even if somewhat vague presentiment of it? It is probably true that the author of Ecclesiastes, who belonged to the late Persian period, did not hold this belief; but how confined, morally and spiritually, his range of vision was! and how natural it would be that low views like his should have stimulated devout thinkers, by way of opposition, to some bold venture of faith! Why should there not be such a venture in Ps. xlix. 15, 16, provided that parallel passages in nearly contemporaneous psalms point in the same direction? But before reading these verses, let me briefly describe my view of Ps. xlix.,[a] supplementing what has been said already in Lecture IV. (pp. 149, 150).

This striking psalm is primarily no doubt, like Ps. lxxiii., a theodicy. But incidentally it is (as can be shown by the allusions of later writers [1]) a protest against the old Hebrew notion of Sheól on the ground that this notion conduces to the selfish tyranny of the rich by which the psalmist

---
[1] See pp. 412, 413.

and many other good Israelites are sufferers. The rich oppressor does not indeed literally claim to be immortal, but he acts as if he did. His pulse beats so high, and his fortunes are so monotonously fair, that the thought of death but seldom occurs to him (Ps. xliv. 7, 10, cf. lxxiii. 4, 5, x. 6, Luke xii. 19). And when it does (for he must of course hew out for himself a grand sepulchre) he considers that, in a certain sense, his 'glory' will 'descend after him' to that aristocratic department of Sheól where sceptred kings enjoy a majestic repose (Isa. xiv. 9, Job iii. 14).[b] For neither in the upper nor in the lower world can he brook the thought of a judgment. 'How should God know' (Ps. lxxiii. 11)? There is no real distinction either in life or in death save that of rich and poor, strong and weak. But the psalmist rudely awakens the man out of his dream. 'He will not take away all that when he dieth ; his glory will not descend after him.' He will indeed 'go to the generation of his fathers,' but the context implies that, rich and strong as they may have been, their company will not profit him ; in a word, דּוֹר in Ps. xlix. 20 has almost as distinctly an ethical reference as in Ps. lxxiii. 15. And now we can approach the central passage of the psalm (*vv.* 15, 16), which is expressly directed against this 'self-confident' abolition of morality. I venture to quote it in my own translation of a gently corrected text which leaves the 'enigma' in line 4 untouched :—

> Like sheep, they are folded in Sheól ;
> Death is their shepherd, and their frame shall waste away ;
> Sheól shall be their palace for ever,
> And the upright shall trample upon them at dawn.[1]
> Nevertheless God shall set free my soul ;
> From the hand of Sheól shall he take me.

Enigmatical lines, are they not? If we can only explain them, we shall have solved the psalmist's 'riddle' (*v.* 5) ; they will reflect light on the rest of the psalm. They are of course much harder to us than to the original readers, who moved in the same circle of ideas as the author. But is it not

---

[1] Kamphausen's correction, וַיִּרְדּוּ בְמֵישָׁרִים לַקֶּבֶר, has been adopted by Prof. Abbott (*Hermathena*, 1891, p. 72). It means either, 'And they go down to the grave smoothly,' or '. . . justly.' But is either meaning satisfactory? 'Justly' spoils the flow of the description ; 'smoothly' may be supported by the Arabic *yasr* and *yusr* ('ease,' 'gentleness'), but suggests the wrong idea of an euthanasia (Job xxi. 13).

possible to reproduce these ideas by a sympathetic study of contemporary writings, and to prove, following the great Teacher at a distance, in Aubrey de Vere's words,

> that at the core
> Of well-known words to reverent Thought
> There lurks a mine of unknown lore?

The words 'I am the God of Abraham, of Isaac, and of Jacob' were interpreted by our Lord controversially and not critically in accordance with the devout beliefs of His age.[1] The enigma in Ps. xlix. must however be solved by the critic in harmony with the ideas of the age to which both this and the parallel psalms belong, viz. the pre-Maccabæan post-Exile age. For the purposes of the solution we are precluded from noticing the hopes of a later period. To Daniel, to Enoch, to the Essenes I must not refer, though at a later point I may use them in confirmation of my result. But to the surmises of an earlier age I am not forbidden to appeal, for the surmises of one age become the anticipations of the next. Such surmises are possibly contained in Deut. xxxii. 39, 1 Sam. ii. 6,[c] and very certainly in Hos. vi. 2 and Ezek. xxxvii. 1–10 (passages which directly refer only to a national resurrection, but which imply the possibility of the resurrection of individuals), and Isa. xxv. 8, xxvi. 19 (passages in a post-Exile prophecy, referring to the annihilation of death and to the resurrection of dead Israelites in connexion with the Messianic judgment), and with these passages we may group the story of a resurrection in 2 Kings xiii. 21, and the splendid climax of the narrative of Elijah in 2 Kings ii. 11, the latter of which may be illustrated by the account of Enoch in Gen. v. 22. Both the stories in Kings are no doubt pre-Exile, and even if that of Enoch be (as I hold that it is) Exilic,[2] it is at any rate pre-Maccabæan, and the idea which underlies both it and the parallel Elijah-story is genuinely Hebraic. This we can see from the Hebrew account of Paradise. The story of the 'tree of life' (which was probably once supplemented by a story of 'the fountain of life'[d]) attests a belief among the Israelites as well as in Babylon in the possibility of escaping death. It may be objected that Jehovah reserves the use

---

[1] Comp. Mark xii. 26 with R. Simai's proof of the resurrection from Ex. vi. 4 (*Sanhedrin*, 90*b*).

[2] On the Enoch-story, see note ᵗ, p. 432.

of the 'tree of life' for Himself and the Elohim (or 'sons of the Elohim'). But unless there was really a prospect that Adam too, if obedient, might ultimately be allowed to eat of the tree, why did Jehovah place him in his own garden?[e] The same belief also lies at the root of the expectation of a resurrection. Death might be—such was the great surmise—but a temporary or apparent defeat, which would make the final victory all the more glorious. 'Rejoice not against me, O mine enemy.'

Now, assuming, as we must, that the thinkers of the post-Exile Church brooded over these surmises, this was the question which they must have sought to answer, Can an ordinary Israelite who is neither an Enoch nor an Elijah, and is but too apprehensive of 'secret faults,' hope so to walk with God in perfectness of heart that Sheól shall not finally prevail against him? If so, it might be justly said, without implying the Platonic psychology, that, though 'in the eyes of fools such an one seemed to die,' yet 'his soul was in the hand of God, where no torment could touch him' (Wisd. iii. 1, 2). If on the other hand this be impossible, what, it would be asked, is the nature of the life in Sheól? Is it altogether joyless? Is the voice of prayer and praise for ever hushed? Or may it be said of faithful Israelites that 'all they that have gone down into the dust' have the privilege of worship,[f] so that the suffering righteous man need not 'let loose his complaint' like Job, but may 'rest upon his bed' (Isa. lvii. 2), whispering 'Even here doth thy hand lead me, and thy right hand doth guide me'[g] (Ps. cxxxix. 10)? That the thinkers of the Jewish Church had arrived at unanimity upon the subject, cannot of course be affirmed; there are indications of opposite tendencies which have to be patiently followed out. Let us take the gloomier tendency first, and listen to a psalmist who belongs to a very dark part of the Persian period. He is speaking, like the authors of Pss. xxxix. 5, 6 and xc. 10, not merely as an Israelite, but as a man.

> Bethink thee (O Jehovah!) how brief my time is,
> For what vanity thou hast created all the children of men!
> Who is the man that shall live on and not see death,
> Or win escape for his soul from the hand of Hades?

And if we ask how the souls fare in the Israelitish Hades, we are told in a too perspicuous enigma that they 'dwell in

Dumah,' i.e. in (the land of) Silence (Ps. xciv. 17 ; cf. cxv. 17).[h] And who remembers not those comfortless utterances in the psalm (for such it clearly is) ascribed to Hezekiah (Isa. xxxviii. 18), and in Pss. vi. 5, 6, xxx. 10, lxxxviii. 11–13,[1] which make it, I was going to say, so miraculous that even a mustard-seed of faith could exist under such conditions? I know that according to some critics, the speaker in these passages is only the nation personified. For my own part, I do not think so; but even if they be right, such expressions could not have been assigned to the nation, if they had not first been uttered by individuals.

One would have liked to answer the despondent writer of Ps. lxxxix. 49 by pointing to Hos. xiii. 14, which declares that though all the plagues which fill the dark city of Sheól were let loose upon Israel, they would be incapable of destroying Jehovah's 'son.'[2] If these words were possible in the olden days when Jehovah's covenant was with the nation, with equal justice could a psalmist use them (changing 'Israel' into 'each Israelite'), when the covenant had, explicitly or implicitly, been extended to the individual. And happily there were some thinkers who began to feel this. They represent a very different tendency from that just now described, as their works in the Psalter prove, and if in describing them I again have recourse to a modern epithet, I hope not to be misunderstood. So strongly do they realize the hidden and yet revealed centre of the highest spiritual truth that I venture to call them the mystical school.[3] To them belong the psalms which are the chief favourites of the Christian, though passages not less inward occur in several psalms which appear as wholes to be less attractive. Altogether unlike are these writers to other mystics—to Babylonian priests with their litanies of sacred formulæ, to God-intoxicated Persian Sûfîs,[1] and even to their devout but fancy-led fellow-countrymen the later Essenes. Even such high mysticism as that of the Zoroastrian Gâthâs is too much intermixed with superstitious elements to be ranked with theirs. These psalmists are the

[1] Comp. Ecclus. xvii. 27 (on *v.* 30, see Edersheim in *Speaker's Comm.*).
[2] *See* my *Hosea* (Cambridge Bible), p. 124.
[3] Cf. C. G. Montefiore's excellent and profound article, 'Mystic Passages in the Psalms,' *Jewish Quarterly Review*, Jan. 1889, pp. 143-161.

noblest thinkers of an age when the church-nation was still happily free from the moral tension of apocalyptic fanaticism.^{j} They live, not in hermitages, but among their brethren, and their words, which are the free but fervent expression of natural feeling, display a chaste simplicity worthy of classic art. Nor do they represent in Judaism, like the Sûfîs in Islam, an alien type of religion. They are the disciples of a prophet who, though persecuted in his lifetime, acquired after death not less authority in the Church than Ezra himself. I have already referred to the Puritan or anti-ritualistic group of psalmists who derive their origin from Jeremiah. The mystic school is, I think, equally influenced by the evangelical prophet. So far from being opposed to that other group, its members do but give a fuller expression to the underlying thoughts of those brave Protestants. The author of Ps. l. certainly did not mean to assert that obedience and praise were the sum total of religion. They constituted, according to him, the 'body' of true ritual practice ($\theta\rho\eta\sigma\kappa\epsilon\acute{\iota}\alpha$, James i. 27); what was its 'informing soul,' he left for other psalmists to say. How those 'right sacrifices' (Ps. iv. 6) were to be offered by imperfect human beings, whose spirit was not always stable or willing (Ps. li. 14), he did not himself explain. But honest and devout minds could not remain in darkness. They believed in the divine Teacher of Israel, whose law was within their hearts (Ps. xl. 9), and they had the promise of that clear knowledge which was equivalent to prophetic insight (Jer. xxxi. 34; cf. Isa. liv. 13, Joel ii. 28). In short, these holy men, whose monuments are the mystic psalms, had grasped a newer and deeper conception of life, and this they owed to the germs of thought contained in the prophecy of Jeremiah.

Too short is the time that we can spare for the study of these noble singers. Let us at least attempt to enter into their ideas, and not treat them as mere effervescent enthusiasts. It is not enough to say with Bishop Butler [1] that the 'beatific vision' was the object of their hopes. No; they had in some sense attained it. They had won the best of all 'portions,' and 'laid hold upon the life indeed,'^{k} possessing which, they 'desired nothing upon earth.' Or rather, one self-regarding

---

[1] See his 14th sermon.

desire they kept. It was in the temple that they had learned what true life meant, and they still felt towards it like a child towards its mother. Its ministers were their leaders and their friends (Ps. xvi. 3), and their supreme pleasure was to join in its services of praise (Ps. lxxxiv. 5). Had it been possible, they would fain have 'dwelt in the house of Jehovah all the days of their life,' nor was it without a pang that they found themselves on the confines of a higher region of faith.

That they had been guided thither by the Shepherd who supplied their wants, is certain. In proof of this, look at the Guest-psalms[m] (i.e. those which refer to the privilege of dwelling with Jehovah), which may be regarded as a group within the group of mystic psalms. And first of all take the two poetic catechisms in Book I. on the qualities of acceptable worshippers (Pss. xv. and xxiv. 1–6). Can it be only the material temple of which the psalmists speak? Then how is it that sinners do at present 'stand in the congregation of the righteous'? Is Jehovah powerless to drive out the 'guests' who have not 'clean hands and a pure heart'? No; a literalistic interpretation will not meet the requirements of these psalms. May we, then, treat them on the analogy of Ps. i. as virtual prophecies of the Messianic judgment, when the true Israel will be separated from the false, and, if there be a temple at all, its worshippers will be such as God delights in? No; this view not only fails to do justice to the other Guest-psalms, but is inconsistent with the special object of these two. Pss. xv. and xxiv. 1–6 are in fact protests against the heathenish acceptation of the phrase 'Guest of God.' To be the guest of Baal or Ashtoreth or the false Jehovah was to be a frequent visitor to the shrine of the god, to be lavish in sacrifices, and punctual in all ceremonial duties, and the reward of the 'guest' was to have a share of the sacrificial feasts, and a mystic connexion with the deity, which ensured supernatural protection. To be the guest of the true Jehovah was indeed different from this, but still something to be enjoyed, and not merely hoped for. It was to have solved the enigma how it was possible to dwell in Jehovah's house all the days of one's life; it was to present spiritual sacrifices in a spiritual temple. Why should we be surprised at this? If these psalmists have formed the conception of a spiritual Israel, why should they not advance to that of a spiritual sanctuary? If they are followed, as Ps. xxiii. 6 says, by the lovingkindness of their Shepherd, how should they not pass freely into His 'tent'? 'They drank of that spiritual Rock which followed them,' is in the strictest sense true of these noble singers.

Once more, I fully admit the characteristics which the mystic psalmists share with less advanced Israelites. In their keen distress when separated from the temple they are the children of the past. True; but in that independence of the temple which almost against their will they profess, they are the inheritors of the future. Listen to one of them wrestling with the new thoughts which lighten the burden of a grave moral problem. No one, I hope, will suppose that the last distich refers to the psalmist's usual morning visit to the temple!

> Up, Jehovah, confront him, make him bow down,
> Deliver my soul from the wicked by thy sword,
> From men of the world,[n] whose portion is in life,
> And whose belly thou fillest with thy treasure,
> Who are full of sons, and leave their abundance to their children.
> As for me, I shall behold thy face in righteousness;
> May I be satisfied, when I awake, with thine image.
> (Ps. xvii. 13-15.)

Must we not recognize here a faint foregleam of the mysticism of the Gospel and of the First Epistle of St. John?[1] There is indeed one obvious difference, viz. that 'life' in this psalm means, not life eternal, but the life of the senses. But those who are not led astray by terminology will see that the religious theory of the psalmist is the germ of that of the evangelist. 'To see God's face' means to receive from Himself intuitive revelations of His nature and character, so far as these concern Israel and the individual Israelite; it is, in short, to 'know' Him.[2] The psalmist would understand and accept the definition of true life in John xvii. 3, 'to know thee the only true God,' and if he calls the existence of those who are both in and of the world 'life,' he thoroughly agrees with two other psalmists who say that such so-called life is but a

---

[1] See John xv. 18, 19, xvii. 9, 1 John ii. 15, 17, v. 19, &c. (the world); John xvii. 3 (true life); 1 John iii. 2 (vision of God).

[2] See my note on Ps. xvii. 15. For Smend's theory, see p. 426, note ª.

'semblance' (צֶלֶם, Ps. xxxix. 7, lxxiii. 20). The question now arises, Is the psalmist (who, as we know, represents a class) so absorbed in communion with God that he gives no thought to death and that which may follow after death, these being from the highest spiritual point of view mere externals.

A large class of writers reply in the affirmative, either because they have placed this psalm in a period when the idea of a judgment of the individual after death seems inadmissible, or because they regard the notion of compensation in a future life as unworthy of a psalmist. The latter reason may be thought to have influenced Pfleiderer, who, in a very striking passage,[1] treats Ps. lxxiii. 25 ° (that noblest of all the mystical passages in the Psalter) as an expression of indifference to a future readjustment of circumstances to character. The psalmist is, if I do not mistake Pfleiderer's meaning, so absorbed in God that the outward conditions of heaven itself fail to interest him. But even if individuals can at this time have soared so high above ordinary humanity, is it likely that such an expression would have been referred to in a church-hymnal as a realizable object? It appears to me, moreover, that this critic's view would require us to alter the text of the preceding verse, an attempt which has in fact been made, but is arbitrary in the extreme. Nor can I interpret Ps. xvii. 15 from Pfleiderer's point of view. Take either passage with its context, and the only natural deduction is surely this, that to a psalmist of the mystic school the idea of compensation for his afflictions was altogether alien, but that his experience of that lovingkindness, which was better by far than what men call life, being incomplete, he postulated a fuller communion with God after death. Even now he could say that 'nearness to God was his happiness,' but such happiness could not be perfect till he 'awoke' from the sleep of life (so let us interpret בְּהָקִיץ for the present) to a full vision of the divine glory.P What he longed for was not material but moral or spiritual compensation. It is only when he thought of the discords of sin, that outward circumstances formed an element in his

---

[1] *Religionsphilosophie* (1878), ii. 717. Cf. Dr. Martineau's criticism, *Study on Religion*, ii. 361-363. The statement was modified in Pfleiderer's second edition.

view of the future. Not his own outward lot but that of the wicked in the world or age that was to come became the subject of his prophetic meditation.

I cannot indeed prove that Ps. lxxiii. 27 refers to a retribution in what was afterwards called the 'coming age,' though, grouping this passage with others, and taking a wide view of psalm-theology, I believe that it does. But so much, at least, seems indisputable—that the principle of compensation after death (even if only in the moral sphere) is recognized by the authors of Pss. xvii. and lxxiii., and I claim the right to interpret the two last verses of Ps. xvi., the meaning of which is perhaps slightly uncertain,[q] in accordance with Pss. xvii. 15 (as interpreted above) and lxxiii. 24, 25. The enigma in Ps. xlix. 15, 16 I must still leave without a complete solution, but not without having obtained light on the second part of it. Verse 16 is altogether parallel to Ps. lxxiii. 24*b*, inasmuch as it represents departure from this world as an Enoch-like 'assumption' to fellowship with God. Ps. xlix. therefore does contain the idea of the future moral compensation of the good, but we must not affirm as yet that its language is meant to imply a general readjustment of circumstances after death.

Nor could we venture to adopt this interpretation simply on grounds of subjective preference. To justify our finding the idea of a general retribution after death in psalms composed between Josiah's time and the end of the Persian age, we must be able to show, (1) that within this period the Jews were subject to influences which must have strongly favoured its development, and (2) that the subsequent course of Jewish religious thought can be best understood on the supposition that this development actually took place. Let us now approach the first part of our argument, and ask from what source such influences were likely to proceed. Egypt and Greece are excluded[r] because within the period referred to Israel was not in close relations with these countries. But that Babylon and Persia may have deeply influenced the Jewish doctrine of the things after death, will be readily admitted by those who agree with the results of my Sixth Lecture (Part I.). It is not probable that the Jews borrowed such an important idea from a foreign religion, but the germ-ideas which, as we have seen, they possessed even before the Exile, may have been greatly assisted in their development by Babylonian and Persian influences. Let us now consider whether there is reason to think that this was actually the case.

From the Paradise-story of the Yahvist to the Talmudic descriptions of the under-world [s] the Jewish notions of the world beyond nature (if I may use the phrase, to include both 'heaven' and the world of the dead) have a Babylonian or Assyrio-Babylonian tinge. It is evident that again and again, under very different circumstances, the older exercised a fascination over the younger race. To restrict this influence to the imaginative details of the scenery of the spirit-world is unreasonable; the ideas as well as the myths of Babylon must, with the limitation already mentioned, have attracted the Jews. I must however hold myself dispensed from considering at length M. Halévy's theory of the identity of popular Jewish beliefs with 'those which the Assyrio-Babylonians professed relatively to the fate of man after death.'[1] As I have said elsewhere, 'reserves and qualifications have to be made all along the course that M. Halévy has taken.' His conclusions are not without a large element of truth, but as set forth by him are vitiated by his determination to exalt the Babylonians at the expense of the Iranians. It is in the highest degree improbable (see p. 283) that the Persians borrowed any of their distinctive doctrines from the Semites, and I will add that it has not yet been proved that retribution after death was a common Babylonian belief. That there was a notion of the possibility of escape from death, I do not deny, and on a former page I have myself referred to this. I know too that in the Assyrian hymns admission is now and then craved even for private persons to the divine palace in 'the land of the silver sky,' but there does not seem to have been much hope of this boon, nor is it represented as conditional upon character.[2] Professor Sayce, it is true, believes that by the

[1] Halévy, 'La croyance à l'immortalité de l'âme chez les Sémites,' *Mémoires de l'Acad. des inscriptions*, 1882, p. 210 &c.; cf. *Revue archéologique*, juillet 1882, p. 53 &c. In criticism of this paper, see Montet, *Revue de l'hist. des religions*, ix. 319, and my *Book of Psalms* (1888), p. 41.

[2] For a survey of the Babylonian and Assyrian beliefs, see Sayce, *Hibbert Lectures*, p. 365 &c.; Jeremias, *Die bab.-ass. Vorstellungen vom Leben nach*

time of Assurbanipal the doctrine of the immortality of the conscious soul, and with it that of retribution after death, had dawned upon the Assyrian and the Babylonian mind. It would not be surprising if this were really the case. The translation (if the word can be used) of Sit-napistim [t] is not indeed described as the reward of goodness, but we need not assume that the ancient myths expressed the highest beliefs of those who repeated and reproduced them. Nebuchadrezzar's belief in particular was so noble in some respects that we would fain think that it was equally noble in others, and in the Berosian form of the Flood-story a voice from above admonishes those men who are saved but left upon earth to continue in the fear of God, because for his piety Xisuthrus, with his wife, daughters, and steersman, was taken to dwell with the gods. Still I do not see that we can venture to affirm that the greatest of hopes was as yet prevalent, and that Arâlû had ceased to be the 'land from which there is no return.' As Mr. G. A. Smith remarks, 'most of the kings who pray for an entrance among the gods do so on the plea that they have been successful tyrants,'[1] and I see no reason to believe that those private persons who could not afford costly sacrifices or pronounce the most powerful formulæ might make up for ritual deficiencies by what the Zoroastrians called 'good thoughts, good words, good deeds.' So far as the existing evidence goes, the immortality of the crowd must have been problematic in the extreme. It was only upon the mountain-tops of society that the celestial brightness gleamed. The poor and needy, such as the psalms speak of, must have felt themselves practically shut out. Nevertheless it is highly probable that the Assyrio-Babylonian belief in the possibility of escaping death (or, of escaping out of death, for the two ideas were not sharply distinguished by Semitic minds [u]) did encourage meditative Jewish saints brooding over the germs of a higher doctrine in their own religious books. Not to dwell on the legends of epic poetry, both Adar (or rather Ninib) and Marduk bear the titles 'the Merciful One, who giveth life, who maketh the dead to live.' The meaning of these must not be

---

dem Tode (1887); Jensen, *Die Kosmologie der Babylonier* (1890), pp. 212-234; and, with caution, Boscawen, *Transactions of Soc. of Bibl. Archæology*, iv. 267 &c.

[1] *The Expositor's Bible: Book of Isaiah*, i. 411.

rated too low. They express a belief, not merely in the constantly renewed wonders of spring, or in the medical efficacy of incantations, but also in the divine power, which could be set in motion by spells, to restore a dead person to his interrupted earthly existence (cf. 2 Kings xiii. 21). And though on this point we desire fresh evidence, it is possible or even probable that in Nebuchadrezzar's time (i.e. during the Exile) the titles of Marduk, now the head of the Babylonian Pantheon, began to acquire a deeper meaning. At any rate, the emphasis which the Babylonians laid on this attribute of the supreme God must have stimulated saintly Jewish thinkers to ponder over the meaning of similar phrases applied by them to Jehovah. And if, through the impulse derived from Babylon (as a 'second cause' of what was ultimately due to the Divine Spirit) these Jews developed a fuller doctrine of the future life than was known to the Chaldeans, we need not be surprised at this. The Sabæans in S.W. Arabia can be shown to have done so too. It was from the aristocratic immortality which they had learned from the Assyrio-Babylonians that they, alone among the Arabian peoples, developed a definite belief in a happy life after death under the protection of the gods, which was not confined to a few but open to all men.[v] Why should not the more highly favoured Jewish Church have made still greater progress, and why must we suppose that the first signs of this were given in the year 164 B.C. ?

But plausible as this conjecture may be, does it suffice to prove our thesis? Certainly not. A more powerful influence than the Babylonian was required to develop with certainty the doctrine of future retribution from the original Jewish germs. There has been much argument on the absence of a reference to future rewards and punishments in the 'Books of Moses.' And remarkable it certainly is that in the so-called Priestly Code there is no allusion to the doctrine of which we are in search. I do not say that this could not be plausibly explained, even on the assumption that that doctrine was already prevalent in the early part of the Persian period. But it is certainly a simpler supposition that while Persian influence was still weak, it failed to win adherents in the Jewish Church. And now let us turn from Babylon to Persia.

Did the Persian religion, which from the Second Isaiah onwards so greatly interested the Jews, include a belief in retribution after death, and of what nature was this belief, if it existed? The question as to the relation of Iranian to Babylonian beliefs does not concern us now. For centuries before the period of the Psalter, Iranian religion had had its own independent development, and its doctrine of the 'last things,' as you will probably agree, is peculiarly its own. A knowledge of this great religion is necessary to the full equipment of an Old Testament scholar, and this can only be gained from a study of the Zoroastrian Scriptures. How strange it is that these should have been so long neglected among ourselves! If Anquetil Duperron could be roused to a chivalrous self-devotion by a few Zend leaves of the Vendîdâd at Paris, why was no English scholar provoked to rivalry by the complete manuscript of the same Scripture in the Bodleian Library? We may now perhaps hope for better days, so far as Oxford theologians are concerned. It is no longer excusable to study the Old Testament religion without comparing Zoroastrianism, for our own university has given us a trustworthy translation both of the Zend and of the Pahlavi texts, and illustrative works (both translations and critical researches) by foreign scholars are readily accessible.

And now let me take up again a statement made at the end of Lecture VI., Part I., to the effect that the psalms may present affinities to the most spiritual part of Zoroastrianism. I meant that if Mazdeism, or the Zoroastrian religion, is in any high degree a spiritual one, the higher teachers of Israel must have felt an instinctive attraction towards its spiritual elements. For our present purpose, then, we must put aside those reactionary revivals of pre-Zoroastrian Mazdeism by which that noble religion resembled but too closely the cults of heathenism, and seek for the precious essence of Zoroastrianism, that by which it lived and still lives. But where may this be found? In the Avesta, for the objections which may be raised to this are groundless.[w] Not indeed in all parts of the Avesta in equal purity. Just as the essence of Mosaism is more clearly seen in the psalms and prophecies than in the Mishna or even in the Pentateuch, so for the essence of Mazdeism we must refer to the metrical chants of the Zoroastrian Church which bear the name of Gâthas ('songs'). These are, so far as they go, an authentic record of the great reformer of Mazdeism, known as Zarathustra or Zoroaster,[x] whom the Roman Catholic scholar, M. de Harlez, suggestively compares with Moses, i.e. with the Moses of tradition who was psalmist, prophet, and lawgiver in one (cf. p. 76). Would that the Hebrew psalmists could have known them! They would doubtless have recognized their nobility. But to us at any rate the Gâthâs are a repertory of those spiritual elements in Mazdeism, by which this religion must have specially attracted the psalmists. So lofty and so pure is their spirit, and, in contrast to the Vedic hymns, so anti-mythological is their tendency,[y] that at first one can hardly believe that they are ancient, and yet the fall in the tone of the later Avesta makes it still more difficult to believe that they are modern. But granting that Zarathustra was not merely a reformer like Ezra, but a prophet and a founder of a Church like Isaiah, can we not understand the phenomenon? The Gâthâs are 'the utterances of Zarathustra in presence of the assembled Church' (Geldner), and naturally represent a high type of religion; the later Avesta reveals the adulteration which this noble faith could not escape as soon as it became popular. Nor was the founder of this Church entirely without points of contact with the previous age. The Gâthâs, even as they have come down to us, contain a certain number of naïve, childish conceptions, and but for the later editor would probably contain more. That editor appears to have worked in the true spirit of Zarathustra, and to have represented the more spiritual school of thinkers in the religion of Mazda. There were of course other schools, just as we found to have been the case in Mosaism, and we must not wholly neglect the records of these in the Avesta. Nor can we venture to ignore even the very late work called the Bundahis (translated by West from the Pahlavi in the 'Sacred Books of the East'), since though in its present form not earlier than A.D. 651, it contains traditions which must be of very great antiquity. This was long ago pointed out by Windischmann, and it is confirmed by the analogy of the results to which Hebrew scholars are more and more tending in the criticism of the Priestly Code. Dr. West (whose authority is indisputable) speaks still more definitely; he thinks that it may be either a translation or an epitome of the Damdâd Nask, one of the twenty-one ancient Zoroastrian Scriptures.

But before referring to the Zoroastrian doctrine of the 'last things,' I should like to speak of the theory of sacrifice and of morality, since this has an obvious bearing on a group of psalms with which the more mystic psalms are closely connected—I mean the Puritan. Was there any school of Zoroastrianism which held the high doctrine of sacrifice which we find in Ps. l.? Certainly the Gâthâs nowhere sanction the primitive theory of sacrifice denounced in that psalm, and in *Yasna*, xxxiii. 14 we find Zarathustra (or a hymn-writer of his school) offering up his life and all his faculties, 'his obedience to the precepts and all his power,' as the most acceptable sacrifice to Ahura. We cannot however deny that the later Avesta sanctions the gross primitive theory,[2] though more prominence is given to another view, which Zarathustra not improbably sanctioned, and which held the dedication of a small part of a slaughtered animal to a divinity to be a symbolical recognition that the vital force of all good creatures belonged to the good genii. And so far as the sacrifice was concerned, a sacrificial act was of no value, unless coupled with 'good words and deeds and thoughts.'[1] But, it may be asked, may not the word 'good' in this phrase mean simply 'ritually correct'? The supposition is not unnatural. For the greatest friends of Mazdeism must admit that its doctrine of prayer was not nearly as pure as that which is taught in the psalms. The recitation of the Gâthâs and of the Vendîdâd formed the most essential part of the sacrificial liturgy.[2] We may in fact call it, with de Harlez, the ' sacrifice of praise : '—the expression seems to be justified, even if the liturgy in the Yasna be somewhat modern. By offering the right prayers and praises it was believed that both strength and pleasure could be given to the good genii, and that ' the flesh-devouring fiends ' could be

[1] *Yasna*, xxxiv. 2; *Gâh*, iv. 9; *Yast*, xxii. 14.
[2] Spiegel, *Avesta*, Bd. ii., p. lxxvi. ; cf. Bd. iii., p. cxxii., where the influence of the Christian eucharistic service upon the haoma-liturgy is suspected.

held off.[1] Nor was this altogether a later revival of past superstitions; it appears to have had the sanction of Zarathustra himself. So impossible was it even for this Elijah-like prophet to make a complete breach with the past. And yet the supposition referred to just now is erroneous. The moral element in prayer was only overshadowed, not extinguished, by the ceremonial. The foundation of goodness in Mazdeism was, as we shall see, in no artificial sense of the word 'moral.' All good thoughts, words, and deeds, remarks Dr. Mills, culminated in the ritual; 'they were nourished by it and lost in it.'[2] 'L'ordre du monde et du sacrifice,' says M. Darmesteter, ' s'effaça devant l'ordre de la loi morale, les "paroles saintes de la prière, récitées conformément à la règle," se confondirent avec les "paroles de vérité."'[3] Nor can it be denied that the Gâthâs themselves, fairly interpreted, contain specimens of free spiritual communion between the 'Good Mind' of Mazda and the human spirit. The morality of Mazdeism has been lately stigmatized as superficial,[4] and it is true that moral and ceremonial purity are more closely linked together than a Christian can approve. No doubt in course of time ceremonial details were so multiplied as to interfere with the due pre-eminence of what we call moral duties. But upon the whole the ethical standard of the Avesta is not inferior to that of the Jewish Law and of psalms like xv., xxiv. 1–6, cxii.; its regard for the poor is specially remarkable, and must have commended it to the best Jewish teachers, even though they may sometimes have sadly asked why such noble principles were so imperfectly carried out in the policy of their Persian governors (see p. 341). And if we are to confess that ceremonialism in Persia did too often obscure the 'weightier matters of the law,' must we not, to be historically fair, pass a similar criticism upon the Jewish legalism?

Still greater interest will be excited by Zarathustra's profound conception of the rewards of righteousness. It is with some hesitation that I quote isolated expressions from the Gâthâs, and I urgently recommend the student to give a continuous perusal to these poems. I am confident that he will

---

[1] *Yasna,* xxviii. 6; cf. *Vend.* xix. 10. [2] *Oxford Z.A.* iii. 213.
[3] *Ormazd et Ahriman,* p. 17. [4] De la Saussaye, *Lehrbuch der Rel.-gesch.* ii. 42.

then see that I have not imported into Zarathustra's words more than they really mean. There can be but one opinion among those who have thus perused the Gâthâs, that, in the midst of a world almost wholly given up to a gross material eschatology, this ancient Iranian prophet declared the true rewards and punishments to be spiritual. His teaching is based on a distinction, which to the Jews came much later, between the material or bodily life and the mental or spiritual, the latter of which connects us with 'those veritably real (eternal) worlds where dwells Ahura' (*Yasna*, xliii. 3). This distinction did not pass away with Zarathustra; it pervades the Avesta. Here is a prayer in the 'middle Avesta'[1]— 'And now in these thy dispensations, O Ahura Mazda! do thou act wisely for us, and with abundance with thy bounty and thy tenderness as touching us; and grant that reward which thou hast appointed to our souls, O Ahura Mazda! Of this do thou thyself bestow upon us for this world and the spiritual; and now as part thereof (do thou grant) that we may attain to fellowship with thee, and thy righteousness for all duration' (*Yasna*, xl. 1). Another of similar character runs thus,—'And to thy good kingdom, O Ahura Mazda, may we attain for ever, and a good King be thou over us; and let each man of us, and each woman, thus abide, O thou most beneficent of beings, and for both the worlds' (*Yasna*, xli. 2). In short, heaven and hell are not primarily the localities appointed for souls after death; the one is 'life,' 'the best Mental State,' the other is 'life's absence,' 'the worst life,' —a high doctrine, which is embodied in a very noble allegory in the Vendîdâd.[aa]

But can a religion designed like Zoroastrianism for all degrees of moral culture be indifferent to the imperfection of the temporal recompenses of good and evil? By no means. This many-sided religion expressly prophesies a readjustment of circumstances to character, but it views this readjustment not primarily as a compensation of individuals, but as a consequence of that triumph of Ahura which all the powers of evil cannot avert. The prophet himself indeed had no clear-cut eschatological theory. He declined to pry into the

[1] *Y.* xxxv.–xlii. are placed in the midst of the Gâthâs, and are next to them in point of age.

secrets of the future.[bb] He was content with the assured prospect of Ahura's triumph, and to him it is owing that, unlike the Babylonian religion, that of Iran opened immortality to poor as well as rich, on the sole condition of their fighting manfully against evil and the Evil One. And if you ask what 'immortality' means to the prophet, it is not merely deathlessness (the etymological meaning of *Ameretât*), but the perfection of its companion blessing 'welfare' (*Haurvatât*); in other words, it is complete happiness of body and soul, begun in this life and continued in an exalted degree in the next. 'To his kingdom,' says Zarathustra, 'belong *Haurvatât* and *Ameretât*'[cc] (*Yasna*, xlv. 10). With regard to 'the retribution which has been declared a deceit by the daêvas and (perverse) men' (*Yasna*, xlviii. 1), what the prophet tells us is that, when the world was born, Ahura established 'evil for the evil and happy blessings for the good (to be adjudged) in the creation's final change' (*Yasna*, xliii. 5). But this is not the whole of his doctrine. He also speaks in two places of the passage of the Judge's Bridge[dd] (the bridge which joins the two worlds) as the test of the character of a soul, those who pass it reaching the 'Song-house,' those who fall from it (by a mere accident he omits this) attaining as their bourn the 'house of the Lie' (cf. *Vend.* xix. 30). And in complete accordance with this, we find the question 'Where is the rewarding?'—thus answered by a later writer, 'When the man is dead, when his time is over' (*Vend.* xix. 27, 28). There are two judgments therefore, but the first is only an endorsement of the verdict of conscience, according to that saying of the Vendîdâd (v. 62), 'He shall be cast into the place (destined) for the wicked, into the darkness of darkness begotten by darkness. To that world, to the dismal realm, you are delivered by your own doings, by your own souls, O sinners.' Conscience, in fact, according to the fine allegory (see note [aa]), appears to the soul of the deceased man, and conducts it to its place.

This first judgment is in a sense private; the second judgment is public and general. What happens to the souls between them? According to *Yast*, xxii. 15, the righteous soul passes from the Judge's Bridge by four steps. The first places him in the Good Thought Paradise, the second in the

Good Word Paradise, the third in the Good Deed Paradise, and the fourth in the Endless Lights, where is the 'house of songs,'¹ and where, as Zarathustra says, he will 'hear the praises of Ahura's offering saints, who see His face.' The soul of the wicked man on the other hand passes successively into the Evil Thought Hell, the Evil Word Hell, the Evil Deed Hell, and the Endless Darkness (*Yast*, xxii. 33). It would seem, then, as if nothing were left for that universal judgment which is to follow the decisive defeat of Angra Mainyu or Ahriman. This however would be a mistake. A fragment of the Avesta says, 'Let Angra Mainyu be hid beneath the earth. Let the daêvas likewise disappear. Let the dead arise (unhindered by their foes), and let bodily life be sustained in their now mortal bodies.'² Asha, i.e. the Righteous Order, demands that, as a proof of Ahura's triumph, the earth shall be renewed, and the bodies of the faithful be raised to a happier life.[ee] After defeating Ahriman, such was one form of the Zoroastrian belief, Saoshyant (the great hero-prophet, who reminds us somewhat of Mal. iv. 5, 6, but has no analogue in the Psalms) and his helpers shall 'restore the world, which will (thenceforth) never grow old and never die,' and raise the bodies of the dead, who, if pure (or, at any rate, after purification), by drinking the juice of the mythical plant Gaokerena shall attain immortality.[ff] One is grieved to notice this last detail in the description of 'creation's turning.' If it is to be taken literally, Zoroastrianism is here inconsistent with its own principles, and deviates from the lines marked out by Zarathustra. The spiritual elements in its doctrine must to some extent have been neutralized by this reactionary concession to a gross mythology. In Babylonia, indeed, from which the myth of the tree of life probably came to Iran, the belief in the magical powers of this tree can have done but little harm, because it was only a favoured few who could hope to experience them. But in Iran, when Ameretât had been opened to the peasant as well as to the prince, the retention or revival of Gaokerena must have been a real hindrance to spiritual

---

¹ In the Gâthâs, *garô-dmâna* or *dmâna-garô*; elsewhere, *Garonmâna*. Opposed to this is *drûjô-dmâna*, 'the house of the Lie-demon.'

² *Oxford Z.A.* iii. 390, 391.

religion. Still, we must not let this blind us to the moral value of the Persian doctrine of the Resurrection. The Bundahis is thoroughly Zarathustrian in spirit when it states in a remarkable descriptive chapter (xxx.) that the wicked shall be raised as well as the righteous.[gg] Inconsistent as the two accounts of the fate of the wicked may seem, they agree in asserting the strict and awful justice of the divine retribution. And of what sort were the risen bodies of the pure, and perhaps one may add, of the purified? The Avesta contains a remarkable prayer which throws light upon this. It was the pious worshipper's hope that not only his soul but his glorified body might 'go openly' to 'the best world of the saints,' and that there he might 'come round about God, and attain to entire companionship with Him'[hh] (*Yasna*, lx. 11). No longer then would there be a separation between heaven and earth. The sun would for ever shine, and the faithful would enjoy complete and deathless welfare in the fellowship of Ahura and his saints.

And now let me ask, Can the Jewish Church have been uninfluenced by this profound doctrine which came to it from a religion so congenial in some respects to its own? If Babylon stimulated to reflection, must not Persia have suggested or confirmed the only adequate solution of the problems of life? If Talmudic eschatology borrowed something from the less noble parts of the Persian religion,[1] must not the psalmists, with their fine spiritual tact, have welcomed the help of its nobler teaching? Yes, surely. The early revelation to Iranian thinkers of these high spiritual truths, the universal lordship of God and His never-ending relation to the individual, must have had some providential object beyond itself. And I think that we can now see what that object was. The appointed time for the blending of the Aryan and Semitic mind which was to occupy so many centuries, had come. Slowly and cautiously had that blending process to be gone through. Not all the religious writers of Israel were equally prepared to become its instruments; not all clearly saw the task which devolved upon the Church. Some however there were, both prophets and psalmists, who

[1] On the debts of Talmudic eschatology to the later Zoroastrianism, see Kohut, *Z.D.M.G.* 1867, p. 552 &c.

were able to select precisely what was needed to fill up the Church's theology. Prophetic writers eagerly assimilated the belief in a final and complete readjustment of circumstances to character, and psalmists the hope of a nearer sight of God after death. The reader will understand what I mean by assimilation; I have already explained that no important belief of the Jewish Church was in the strict sense borrowed, but that without foreign influence some of its greatest beliefs would not, so far as we can see, have been fully reached. I venture to think that my theory is neither arbitrary nor improbable. So long as the psalms were ascribed not to the post-Exile but to the pre-Exile period, when the spiritual attainments of the Israelites in general were low, and they had as yet no contact as a people with the Persians, it was natural of two possible interpretations of psalm-passages to choose the more meagre. But if it be true that the case has been reversed, it is now equally natural to select the fuller interpretation. Let us then have the courage to read certain Biblical passages in a Persian light. Adoption (in a harmless sense) of Persian ideas there must have been, not always indeed equally full, nor of such a kind as to exclude both vagueness and variety of statement. Such vagueness and variety we find even in the Zoroastrian Scriptures, and are natural in a religion which has not as yet crystallized into dogmatic formulæ.[ii] How then should we be surprised to find them in poetic or semi-poetic utterances like the prophecies and psalms, which spoke not so much to the head as to the heart, and whose readers or singers brought with them the key to their symbolic phraseology?

Let us now turn to some of the Biblical passages which require to be re-read. The one which more immediately concerns us is Ps. xlix. 15, 16, but before returning to this, I would ask leave to consider certain prophetic utterances. (*a*) Isa. xxv. 8, xxvi. 19. The former passage predicts the destruction of death and of the world of death. Instead of swallowing up, Sheól in the Messianic period shall itself be swallowed up. And this prospect concerns not merely the church-nation, but all of its believing members, and indeed all, whether Jews or not, who submit to the true King Jehovah (cf. *v.* 6). Thus the inference which (p. 385) I regretted that the author of

Ps. lxxxix. 49 had not drawn, was to all appearance drawn by the writer of this prophecy. But was he not helped by that religion which had ever placed the destruction of death in the forefront of its system? The companion passage may be said to treat of death under two aspects, the one cheerful, the other depressing. Heathen lords (Nineveh and Babylon) had infringed upon Jehovah's right of sovereignty, and tyrannized over Israel. No human helpers can we mention; 'in thee (Jehovah!) alone can we glory;[1] even in thy name' (cf. Ps. xx. 8). But these enemies—where are they? 'Dead men live not again, shades rise not.' In the course of nature there is no resurrection of the dead; therefore, that there might be no repetition of this tyranny (Isa. xiv. 29), the heathen lords have been swept away: 'thou hast made even their memory to perish' (Ps. ix. 5, 6). Then, after an idealistic outburst the prophet bethinks him of the sad disappointments of the Restoration-period, and, merging his own personality in that of the Church, he utters a grand prayer. Israel's territory has indeed been widened, but it is not in a state of full salvation, and above all suffers from insufficient population. So the Church casts itself upon Jehovah's faithfulness. There is a well-known prophecy which speaks of the revival of the dry bones (Ezek. xxxvii. 1–10). Ezekiel meant by this the revival of the nation (cf. Ps. xxx. 2, 4, and my note), but the prophetic Church-nation (as represented by this nameless prophet) infers from Ezekiel's revelation the resurrection of individuals, not however of all deceased Israelites,¹¹ but of believers, especially perhaps of those who have died for the faith. 'Let thy dead men (Jehovah!) live; let my dead bodies (which have been "given as food to the birds of heaven," Ps. lxxix. 2) arise!' 'Weighty in the sight of Jehovah is the death of his pious ones' (Ps. cxviii. 15). Is it conceivable that those who have been 'faithful unto death' should miss their earthly reward? No; their bodies are a precious seed, which ' thy dew, O Jehovah,' which is the ' dew of lights ' can bring to life. They sleep, but at the call from above will awaken to a new life. 'O might thy dead revive,' is the rendering which in 1870 I adopted from Ewald,[2] and I

---

[1] On this rendering, see note ⁱ, p. 332.
[2] *The Book of Isaiah Chronologically Arranged*, p. 127.

would now ask leave to return to it. It is not a sudden revelation of a new truth which comes to the prophet or to the Church; rather, the Church, among some of whose members the Resurrection-hope is already current, bases a sublimely bold prayer upon this hope. May the Messianic period come, and Judah, which is Jehovah's central dominion, be repeopled by the help of its lost but now restored children! How Zoroastrian much of this is, even down to the singular phrase 'dew of lights!'[kk] Only the Zoroastrianism has been Hebraized, or, more strictly, native Hebraism has grown to maturity under the influence of a congenial though foreign religion. Light, for instance, was always a symbol of Jehovah (see note on Isa. x. 17), but in the special emphasis which the post-Exile writers lay upon this emblem, we may fitly see at once a recognition of the truth and a protest against the error (or the half-truth) of the religion of Mazda.

(*b*) The two passages which we have last studied seem to give this view of the 'last things'—that the faithful Israelites will rise again, and together with those alive in the Messianic period (and the converts from 'all nations') live for ever. The next pair of prophetic utterances (Isa. lxv. 17-22, lxvi. 22) presents a somewhat different picture. The old order of things is to pass away, and, to produce a worthier scenery for the new order, Jehovah will create 'new heavens and a new earth' which unlike the old (Isa. li. 6) shall 'stand perpetually.' But what is the new order to be? We should have expected to be told of the destruction of death, and of the moral regeneration of God's people; in short, something like Rev. xxi. 2-4 would correspond better with Isa. lxv. 17 than the verses which actually follow. Who that, 'according to God's promise, looks for new heavens and a new earth' (2 Pet. iii. 13), can be satisfied with a mere renewal of the idyll of Paradise, which, in seeming contradiction to earlier Messianic promises (Isa. xxxiii. 24, xxxv. 8, cf. Ps. civ. 26), even speaks of sinners in the new Jerusalem? The latter reference is no doubt a slip; the prophet wished to bring out the longevity of the Messianic Israelites, and could think of no better illustrations than those in Isa. lxv. 20*b*. But what a strange slip for any one under the influence of Zoroastrianism to make! At first sight, therefore, Zoroastrian influence seems out of the question, and I still hold, with Matthes, that to regard the conceptions of Isa. lxv. 17 and, still more, of Isa. lxvi. 15 as mere loans from Mazdeism is uncritical.[1] But is it not a striking fact that the first Old Testament writer to employ the phrase 'new heavens and a new earth,' and to give the renovation of the universe a prominent place in his eschatology is this poorly gifted prophet of the Persian period, followed by a writer in the Book of Enoch (Enoch xlv. 4, 5), and by another writer in the not less composite Book of Revelation (Rev. xxi. 1)? Surely it is the easiest explanation of this to suppose that the author of Isa. lxv., lxvi. was stimulated by Zoroastrianism, which from the Gâthâs to the Bundahis so constantly proclaims this doctrine. It is futile to object that if he followed this religion in one point, he must have done so in another; eclecticism is a characteristic of ages of transition. Certainly in his view of death our prophet is peculiar. The writer of Isa. xxv. 8 said, in harmony with Zarathustra death, being an evil, must be abolished. Not so thinks our prophet. Death, according to him, will still be known upon the new earth, but will be deprived of its evil character (Isa. lxv. 20, 22, 23). But how? Not in the sense suggested by the letter of the prophet's description, which rises no higher than the epilogue of the Book of Job. At the time when he probably wrote (see p. 160) the doctrine of rewards and punishments after death was already current among the Jews. To one part of this doctrine he distinctly refers (Isa. lxvi. 24). The souls of rebels, he says, will suffer penal tortures as violent as those which the worm and the fire would cause to their bodies, if consciousness remained (cf. Isa. l. 11 with the Septuagint version). The other part we have to supply for ourselves. Must not the joys of those who rest from their labours be as intense as these tortures? Must not everlasting life (localized, we cannot say how) correspond to everlasting 'abhorrence'? Otherwise the principle of compensation affirmed in Isa. lxv. 13, 14 will be imperfectly carried out. Such thoughts as these must have vaguely stirred in the prophet's mind. Their legitimate and necessary development

---

[1] See *Isaiah*, ii. 120, 126. Comp. Isa. lxv. 17 with Enoch lxxii. 1, xci. 15, 16, v. 20 with Enoch v. 9, and on births in the new earth, *Bundahis* (West), xxx. 26.

is found in the Book of Enoch (see e.g. chap. xxii.). (*c*) Dan. xii. 2. 'And many of those that sleep in the dust of the earth (i.e. in Sheól) shall awake, some to everlasting life (the first occurrence of the phrase), and some to disgrace and everlasting abhorrence.' Here at last we have a definite doctrine of resurrection expressed in a way which shows that it was no novelty. The seeds which Zoroastrianism and some earlier Jewish writers had sown had sprung up. There shall be an awaking from sleep. But not for all men—only for the chosen nation; for there is no natural immortality. And the 'awaking' will not be a boon, even for all Israelites. The writer goes beyond Isa. xxvi. 19, in which there is no distinct reference to any but a resurrection of the righteous. But the difference is only in appearance. The real resurrection is that of the 'just' unto 'everlasting life'[1] (cf. 2 Macc. vii. 14, Luke xiv. 14) upon the renewed earth; the unfaithful Israelites who cannot 'stand in the judgment' (Ps. i. 5) will return to the scene of 'everlasting abhorrence' (cf. Isa. lxvi. 24).

We now return to the psalm-passages, especially (*d*) to our 'enigma,' Ps. xlix. 15, 16, which in fact started us on our long voyage of discovery. How can we be in doubt as to its correct solution? The author was not impelled by dread of an untimely, violent death; he thought of the things after death. And his hope was not merely for a moral compensation of piety (though this ranked highest in his mind), but for a general readjustment of outward circumstances. 'The upright,' he says, 'shall trample upon them (i.e. upon their wasted frames; see p. 382) at dawn.' As for the wicked (i.e. especially the oppressors of the faithful Israelites), 'Sheól is their palace for ever,'[2] and they shall 'for ever be without seeing light.' In this last phrase some may detect an allusion to the new earth—the only one in the Psalter (for Ps. civ. 30, referred to by Grätz, has a different meaning). But it is the context, not the language itself, that suggests this. And what does the 'dawn' mean? It is a figure for the opening of the new

[1] Cf. Ps. Sol. iii. 13–16, Targ. Jon. on Isa. iv. 3, and the Sept. addition to Job, all of which imply a partial resurrection. The Talmud still more distinctly teaches that the resurrection was a privilege of Israel; even imperfect Israelites might hope to attain to it after purification in Gehinnom (Weber, *System*, p. 372, cf. 329).

[2] See my note on Ps. xlix. 15, and cf. Delitzsch.

order of things which later Judaism called 'the coming age.' Rabbi Meir bases an Haggadic interpretation of Ruth iii. 13 upon it,[1] and the Targum of Jerusalem on Ex. xii. 42 says that the fourth of the extraordinary nights is 'when the end of the age shall be accomplished.' But before them both this was doubtless a Zoroastrian image. 'Till the powerful dawn,' says the Zoroastrian when waiting for each fresh day; 'till the powerful frashôkereti' when longing for the everlasting light of the renewed earth and for the resurrection.[ll] (*e*) Ps. xvii. 15. We may reasonably hold that the meaning of this passage is determined by that of (*d*). The awakening probably means the passing of the soul into a resurrection-body. The 'sleep' from which the soul awakens is, in this case, not the sleep of life (see pp. 389, 430), but the so-called 'sleep' of the intermediate state which is not without a quiet and unearthly bliss, and which is described again and again in subsequent literature,[mm] and hinted at, not indeed in Ps. cxlix. 5, but perhaps in Ps. xxii. 30. (*f*), (*g*) Pss. xvi. 10, 11, lxxiii. 24–27. The latter passage is self-evidently of individual application not less than Ps. xvii. 15. With regard to the former, it is certainly possible to hold on the ground of parallel passages (vi. 4–7, ix. 14, xxx. 4) that the speaker is the true Israel. But whatever is said of the true Israel may in some degree be applied to each true Israelite, and a study of the spiritual atmosphere of the psalmist's age leaves no doubt in my mind that Ps. xvi. 10, 11 must have been appropriated without deduction by faithful Jews. I have now to ask, Do the writers, in harmony with (*d*) and (*e*), assume an intermediate state of departed souls? In this case, they leap over the 'sleep,' in their eagerness for the 'awakening.' But in the light of Zoroastrian belief it is permissible to think that the soul, according to these writers, passes directly from this world to the Beatific Vision. It would be absurd to dogmatize on such a point. The latter opinion seems to tally best with the high mysticism of Pss. xvi. and lxxiii., and, in spite of what has been said above, we may, if we will, interpret Ps. xvii. on the same theory. How far it is favoured by the later developments of Jewish belief we must consider later. Still there is nothing in the former theory to

---

[1] Talm. Jer., *Chagiga*, c. 2 (ap. Wünsche, *Neue Beiträge*, p. 377).

which the mystic psalmists might not, in deference to the majority, have accommodated themselves. The world's great change was expected so shortly, that the brief waiting-time might easily be leaped over, and, as we have seen, the interval was not one of gloom and distress for the righteous. The fate of the wicked in both worlds is possibly alluded to in Pss. xvi. 4*a*, lxxiii. 27 ; at any rate, the psalmists must have known that some of their readers would suppose this.

The expressions of the next passages to be mentioned are so vague that we cannot assert that the largest interpretation was that favoured by the author. And yet, considering the currency of advanced eschatological ideas during the later Persian period we may presume that the author both anticipated and permitted the largest view. See, for instance, (*h*) Ps. xxi. 5, (*i*) Ps. xlv. 3, (*k*) Ps. lxxii. 5. The expressions used here may be explained away as mere loyal hyperboles. I have pleaded however in my commentary for a deeper meaning. (*l*) Ps. lxiii. 9, 10. We are not bound to explain this on the analogy of Ps. lxxiii. 26, 27, but many of the earliest readers must have done so. (*m*) Ps. xi. 7 (cf. cxl. 14), where 'beholding' Jehovah's face may simply mean the enjoyment of the divine favour, but may also be interpreted of that fuller communion with God which implies 'everlasting life.' (*n*) Ps. xli. 13*bc* requires a similar comment. (*o*) Ps. xxxvi. 10. Here the 'fountain of life' may mean 'the source of happiness and prosperity' (cf. Jer. ii. 13, xvii. 13), but may also be explained, like the 'river of water of life' in Rev. xxii. 1 (cf. vii. 17 Revised Version), as one of the mythic symbols of immortality.[1] The psalmist virtually says that the true fountain of life is not to be localized by mythic geography, but is with the righteous Jehovah. The phrase took hold of later writers, as we see from 2 Macc. vii. 36 (corrected text), 'these our brethren, having endured a short pain, have now drunk of ever-flowing life.' And similarly the words of the next line, 'by thy light do (or, shall) we see light,' may of course mean only 'to thy favour do we owe all the joys of life' (cf. 'light' in Esth. viii. 16), but it may also be interpreted of the crown of joys—the nearer vision of God.

---

[1] Cf. my commentary on the Psalms, p. 100, and add a reference to Enoch xvii. 4.

So the Septuagint translator took it in the next age (ὀψόμεθα φῶς), and the psalmist who wrote Ps. Sol. iii. 16. And some very early readers of the Hebrew psalm may have explained v. 16 of a Beatific Vision immediately after death.

I have now reached a turning-point in my inquiry. I have endeavoured to show critically that among the religious ideas of the Psalter are those of immortality and resurrection. This result is at once so important and so different from that of much previous criticism, that I am tempted to seek for some external confirmation of its soundness. My search would be a short one if I could, like some critics, recognize either or both of these ideas in the Books of Proverbs and Job, which, with the exception of the three appendices to the former, and the speeches of Elihu in the latter, may not unreasonably be placed before the edict of Cyrus. A belief must have attained a fair amount of currency to be appealed to by the 'wise men.' I cannot, however, satisfy myself that these ideas can be traced either in Proverbs or in Job,[nn] nor can I see how, if they possessed such high philosophic authority, Sirach (more strictly Ben Sira) and the author of Koheleth, in the second and fourth centuries respectively, would have been so reluctant to accept them. For though Grätz is of opinion that there is a reference to the Resurrection in Ecclus. xlviii. 11,[1] and many scholars have held that Eccles. iii. 17, xi. 9, xii. 7, 14, postulate retribution after death, yet there is strong reason to believe that some of these passages have been manipulated and some inserted by a more orthodox later writer.[2] Delitzsch himself remarks of the author of Koheleth, and the same remark is true of Sirach, that the belief in a final judgment is difficult indeed to reconcile with the primitive view of the life of the shades in Hades which he so strongly and so pathetically expresses. We may assume therefore that these two latest of the 'wise men' of Palestine knew nothing of an early acceptance of these ideas by their predecessors. In fact, so far from helping us, the 'Wisdom'-

---

[1] Grätz, *Geschichte*, iii. (ed. 4), 275.
[2] Geiger, *Z.D.M.G.* xii. 536; *Job and Solomon*, pp. 189, 211, 224, 231. Comp. the addition of the Syriac version at Ecclus. xiv. 19 (see Edersheim in 'Speaker'). On the interpolation-theory (Koheleth) see also Driver's criticism, *Expositor*, 1887 (2), pp. 78–80.

literature may be thought to cause us a slight difficulty. If Ben Sira was such a student of Scripture as he makes out, how is it that the higher Scriptural teaching had not penetrated to him? He does not indeed deny in words that others besides Enoch and Elijah[1] may escape the sad life of Sheól; in Ecclus. xlix. 14 he only denies (forgetting Elijah) that any one besides Enoch was translated in his lifetime, and in Ecclus. xvii. 30 that man is naturally immortal.∞ But the whole spirit of his book is opposed to the higher doctrines. The author of Koheleth, too, does not give an absolute contradiction to the doctrine of future retribution and of an everlasting life with God for the good. But what a bitter scoff he utters against those who do hold it (Eccles. iii. 21)! Some may infer from this that the existence of any higher Scriptural teaching is problematical. My own inference is a different one. It is simply this, that if any of the prophecies and psalms which suggest this teaching existed in the times of these writers, they were either not known to them, or, if known, not interpreted in the fullest and most adequate sense. One may hope that there were not many sceptics like the author of Koheleth, who is certainly an abnormal product of post-Exile Judaism. But many old-fashioned, hesitating persons there must have been, who could not get further than Sirach's confident dictum in Ecclus. xvii. 30, and who had this great justification, that the nobler Palestinian teachers spoke seldom on the highest subjects, and mostly $\dot{\epsilon}\nu$ $a\dot{\iota}\nu\dot{\iota}\gamma\mu a\tau\iota$,[2] and that, like Mr. Browning in La Saisiaz, they were somewhat less sure of soul than of God.

We must look elsewhere, then, for the wished-for confirmation of our result, and I venture to think that the Jewish writings of the next age will supply it. I can but take a glance into the large domain which some future lecturer will perhaps occupy. It is to the Apocrypha and Pseudepigrapha that we must chiefly refer, but we must not entirely neglect the Targum and the Midrash, the writings of the New Testament, and the notices which have come down to us respecting the so-called Jewish 'sects.' The question before us is whether the theory to which we have been led will not enable us to

---

[1] See Ecclus. xliv. 16, xlviii. 9, xlix. 14.
[2] 1 Cor. xiii. 12, = בְּחִידָה; cf. Ps. xlix. 5, Num. xii. 8.

account more easily for the later doctrines of the future life. I am well aware that the principle of this argument might be uncritically applied with most unfortunate results. I have no wish for a wholesale introduction of later Jewish doctrines, not all of which are sound historical developments, into Biblical theology. But the essence of my contention is that having offered critical grounds for our theory, we are entitled to inquire whether it does not illustrate and help to explain documents of a later period than the Psalter. And first of all let us turn to the Apocrypha (in a wide sense), not however to the proverbs of Sirach, in which a strong element akin to Sadducæanism cannot be overlooked, but to the Psalms of Solomon and to the Book of Enoch, the former of which may be said to represent the views of the more sober, and the latter those of the more enthusiastic and visionary section of the Pharisaic party.[pp] I give the psalms the precedence, precisely because they *are* psalms, written by ardent lovers of the temple and the synagogues (Ps. Sol. ii. 3, xvii. 18), who may be supposed to have in some points an intuitive comprehension of the older psalmists. 'He falleth,' says one of these writers (Ps. Sol. iii. 13–16), speaking of the 'sinner,' not without a side-glance at the Sadducæan aristocracy, 'yea, evil is his fall, and he shall not rise' [there is virtually but one resurrection]; 'the destruction of the sinner is for ever . . . . But those that fear the Lord shall rise unto eternal life, and their life shall be in the light of the Lord, and shall not fail;' comp. in the canonical Psalter, Ps. xxxvi. 10. 'The life of the righteous is for ever,' says another (Ps. Sol. xiii. 9, 10), 'but sinners shall be taken away into destruction, and their memorial shall no more be found.' The Pharisæan psalmist has been speaking of the *khasīdīm* (ὅσιοι), of those who are in covenant with God, and act up to their engagement, and draws the same inference as the author of our 16th psalm. Those upon whom God bestows such thoughtful discipline (Ps. Sol. xiii. 8; cf. our Ps. xvi. 7*a*) cannot perish. 'Destruction' (perhaps = Abaddon, cf. Ps. lxxxviii. 12) and oblivion (cf. Ps. lxxxviii. 13) are for wilful sinners. And whereas 'the Lord's *khasīdīm* shall inherit life in gladness,' 'the inheritance of sinners is Hades and darkness and destruction' (Ps. Sol. xiv. 6, 7; cf. xv. 11). For 'the sinners shall perish in the day of the judgment of the Lord for ever, ... but those that fear the Lord shall find mercy in that (day), and shall live by the compassion of their God' (Ps. Sol. xv. 13, 15). Can we help comparing the 'enigma' in our 49th psalm? Both psalmists write as (in a good sense) Ebionites; they are tyrannized over by the wicked rich (cf. Ps. Sol. i. 4, 7). Both, too, if I am not mistaken as to Ps. xlix., have a high view of the soul's future, which is unshared (cf. Ps. Sol. iii. 11) by the tyrants. It should also be noticed (1) that these expressions are but a little more definite than those of our 'mystic psalms'—so true it is that dogmatic forms are alien to the best hymn-poetry— and (2) that, like the older psalmists, the writers of these psalms avoid mythological symbols, and found their hopes for the future on the Lord's righteousness and truth. Once indeed we do find a reference to Paradise and to the tree of life; but it is in the very spirit of the older psalmists, and forms a striking contrast to Enoch xxv. 5 (see p. 439, note ^{ff}). To the Pharisæan psalmist, the *khasīdīm* are the 'trees of life' (cf. Isa. lxi. 3). They 'live for ever,' not from tasting of ambrosial fruit, but from 'walking in the law which God commanded us'^{qq} (Ps. Sol. xiv. 1, 2). But to the author of Enoch the tree of life, planted at the holy place (the temple of the Messianic age), is the means of a blessed life to God's elect, and the same conception is doubtless implied in the gloss upon 'as the days of the tree' (Isa. lxv. 22) in the Septuagint and the Targum.[1] Altogether this little Psalter is a fine specimen of the best Judaism of its time, and shows how naturally the ideas of the older Psalter developed into conceptions which some have hastily characterized as new growths.

Let us turn next to the Book of Enoch, which, although a composite work and not without Christian interpolations, is in the main, as some good critics think, of pre-Christian origin; the earliest portion of it, at any rate, may go back to the second half of the second century B.C. That the resurrection-belief is common to all its writers is certain (see li. 1, 2, lxi. 5, xci. 10, xcii. 3), though no distinct doctrine as to the risen body appears anywhere. Let us study the representa-

[1] See the explanation given by Maimun ben Joseph (father of Maimonides), *Jewish Quarterly Review*, ii. 97 (Simmons).

tions of the future life in chaps. xxii., cii., and ciii., which belong to the oldest portion. From chap. xxii. we learn that there are four separate departments in the place of departed souls, two of which seem to be assigned to the righteous, and two to the wicked. Of one class of righteous souls it is stated that they have 'a fountain of water and light.' The wicked, however, those at least who have not been punished in their lifetime, suffer grievous pain, which after the judgment will be heightened. This heightening is significantly described as a putting to death of the souls (Enoch xxii. 13 ; cf. xcix. 11, cviii. 3), and in the Similitudes (liii. 3) we find the torturing function assigned to the Satan, whom, as we have seen, the psalmists appear to avoid mentioning. Not less interesting are chaps. cii., ciii., because in a most vivid style they refute the same false primitive view of Sheól which seems to be attacked in Ps. xlix. Compare, for instance, Enoch cii. 8 with Ps. xlix. 20b; and again, in the earliest part of the book, xcviii. 10 with Ps. xlix. 8, 9, and xcviii. 12 with Ps. xlix. 15 (end). It is difficult to avoid thinking that in the too prosperous 'sinners' who 'deny the Lord of spirits, the last judgment, and the resurrection, we are meant (as in parallel passages of the Psalms of Solomon) to think of the Sadducees.

Now who can doubt either as to the belief expressed or implied in these books, or as to the interpretation which their writers must have put upon our 'enigma'-passage, Ps. xlix. 15 ? The only question is, whether in any of their moods they were tempted to hope for a foretaste of the Beatific Vision prior to the judgment. It is possible to hold that the Pharisæan psalmists had this hope, not only because of the parallelism between Ps. Sol. iii. 16 and Ps. xxxvi. 10, but also because somewhat later it was undoubtedly familiar to the Jews. And it seems to me psychologically probable that the longer the advent of Jehovah or His king was delayed, the more would the faith of pious Jews have sought to beautify the interval between death and the final consummation. But what of the writer in Enoch ? His tone is not that of the psalmists ; what we call the mystic sentiment is but weak in him. He seeks to hasten the day of the Lord, not merely by patient continuance in well-doing, but by wilful and fantastic imaginations. The higher hope is not prominent in the *Grundschrift* ; but neither is it wholly absent. He speaks indeed of the righteous as having nothing to fear even if they sleep a long sleep (c. 5), but 'sleep' is here and elsewhere only a conventional term, which has lost its strict meaning (see p. 441), and in the temporary abode of the righteous (which is not in the underworld, but far away in the west) he places a fountain of water and light. Now what can these be but a reflexion of those highest blessings which are similarly described in Ps. xxxvi. 10? Later on we see that favoured souls, righteous as Enoch and Elijah were righteous, were permitted to live separately from the rest in that earthly Paradise where (see Gen. iii. 8) divine beings 'walked,' and in the enjoyment, equally with Enoch, of the peace of the 'world which is to be.'[1] Obscurely as the writers of Enoch express themselves, one may be sure that they have entered upon that line of thought, the goal of which is the expectation of an immediate vision of God by the departed righteous soul.[rr]

Slowly indeed was that goal reached. Justin Martyr (second cent. A.D.), unconsciously influenced by Judaism, gives the same view of the intermediate state which we have found in Enoch, with the qualification that to martyrs the gates of Paradise were opened directly after death.[ss] This picture of the next life does not come up to the intuition which seems to be vaguely expressed in Pss. xvi., xvii., xxxvi., and lxxiii. Justin does not consider that the martyr-spirit may belong to those who do not die a martyr's death, and that the saying, 'What shall a man do to save his life? Let him slay himself'[2] (i.e. mortify his lusts), indicates a way of being 'faithful unto death' which has the thorough sanction of St. Paul. Jewish sentiment, however, partly coincided with Justin's. Not to quote a Talmudic vision in *Baba bathra* 10*b*, that remarkable homily (see p. 29) which passes as the fourth Book of Maccabees mentions it as a special privilege of martyrs like the 'seven brethren' that they 'live unto God' (4 Macc. vii. 17, xvi. 22), and that they 'now stand before the throne of God and lead the happy life'[tt] (4 Macc. xvii. 18). On the

---

[1] See (in the Similitudes), Enoch lxi. 12, and cf. in a later passage the phrase 'the garden of the righteous' (lx. 13, cf. 8). For Enoch and Elijah, see Enoch lxxxvii. 3, lxxxix. 52, and for the reference to the '*ōlām habbā*, lxxi. 15.

[2] Talm. Bab., *Tamid.* 32*a*.

other hand, another Hellenistic work, the second Book of Maccabees, which approaches much more closely to the Pharisæan theology, seems to adjourn even the reward of martyrs to the resurrection (2 Macc. xii. 43-45). A similar variety exists in the New Testament, which upon the whole, by M. Havet's admission, preserves the character of a Hebraic work. There are five passages which assume that a vision of God is possible directly after death (Rev. xiii. 6, Acts vii. 59, 2 Cor. v. 1-10, Phil. i. 23, Heb. xii. 23), whereas, according to Rev. vi. 9-11, the souls of the martyred righteous remain 'resting' (cf. Rev. xiv. 13) in the underworld, till the great judgment admits them (Rev. vii. 9-17) to the immediate presence of God.[uu] The diversity of view in a single book (Revelation) is specially worthy of notice; the inconsistency of the later Biblical writers is the natural result of the variations of the prophets and psalmists. And must not the same remark be made respecting the Jewish teachers?[1] It was universally admitted that there were two worlds, *'olām hazzeh* and *'olām habbā*, and that the true life was that of the world to come (*Pirqe Aboth*, iv. 21; the figure of the vestibule and the banquet-room), in accordance with the high intuition which, if I am not mistaken, had visited the mystic psalmists. But to the question whether the *'olām habbā* begins for each soul directly after the death of the body, or for all souls together at the resurrection, different answers are given; at any rate, this phrase has sometimes a wider, sometimes a narrower significance. Properly speaking, of course, the 'coming age' began with the resurrection,[2] and there are Talmudic passages which, strange to say, indicate the survival of the old conception of the shades in relation even to great Rabbis. The moral consciousness, however, when strongly developed, could not dispense with a preliminary judgment and recompense (see *Pirqe Aboth*, iv. 27), and, though the language used respecting the latter is by no means always very spiritual, the fact that an 'earnest of the inheritance' was craved brings these

---

[1] See Weber, *System des Altsyn. Theologie*, pp. 158, 326, 327, 331, 373; Geiger, *Lesestücke aus der Mischna*, pp. 41-44; Castelli, *Il Messia secondo gli Ebrei*, p. 248, and 'The Future Life in Rabbinical Literature,' art. in *Jewish Quarterly Review*, July 1889.

[2] I cannot enter into a discussion of the two resurrections.

teachers into direct relation to the mystic psalms. And this is sufficient for our present purpose.

I am now compelled to turn to sources of more mixed value, viz., the Targum and Midrash, and the statements of Josephus on the αἱρέσεις. That the two former in their present form are very late is undeniable,[vv] but having grown out of a much earlier tradition they may supplement older and more precious writings. Of course, they have much to say on the future retribution. Pictures of Paradise and Gehenna abound; in one of them we find it said that the dwellers in Paradise see the face of God. Does the Midrash in this give such a bad exposition of Ps. xi. 7? May it not be allowed to compensate in part for the crudeness of its pictures of the underworld (see p. 401)? And wrong as the Targum may be in virtually denying that Pss. xv. 1 and xxiv. 3 refer primarily to communion with God in this life, must it therefore be mistaken in that which it affirms, viz., that these psalms have a reference to the lot of the righteous in another world? I admit that it is only here and there that its paraphrase can be called suggestive, nor can any one defend the pertinacity with which, like the Targum on Job, it imports a highly developed eschatology into vague and undogmatic utterances.[ww] But we have already found the Targum useful in discussing the national reference of certain psalms, and we must not be deterred by prejudice from availing ourselves of its help in the present inquiry.

There remains Josephus, by his own fault a suspected witness, and yet valuable to those who can pierce through his Græcising phraseology to the underlying Jewish thoughts. I need not attempt a complete study of his descriptions of the three Jewish schools, for I only refer to them upon the special subject of eschatology. First, then, as to the Sadducees and Pharisees.[1] The former, says Josephus, disbelieve in future rewards and punishments and deny the continuance of the soul. Undoubtedly this is correct; the protests against such views expressed in Enoch and the Psalms of Solomon, and implied in the second of the eighteen Benedictions and in the psalm-doxology,[2] and the notices in the Gospels

[1] Jos., *War*, ii. 8, 14; *Ant.* xiii. 5, 9, xviii. 1, 3, 4.
[2] Talm. Jer., *Berachoth*, ix. 5, 9; cf. Derenbourg, *Histoire*, p. 131, Edersheim, *Jesus the Messiah*, i. 315.

and Acts and in the Talmud (see e.g. *Rosh ha-shana*, 17*a*; *Sanhedrin*, xi. 1 = fol. 90*a*) are decisive. The Sadducees lived in the visible present and not in an imagined future. They feared the political unrest which might be produced by a constant looking for the judgment, and disliked the materialism of many Pharisæan descriptions of the future state. In opposition to this, one of the best of the Sadducees insisted that men ought to serve God without thought of reward (*Pirqe Aboth*, i. 3), and the more the Pharisees extracted by an unbridled exegesis from psalms and prophecies, the more their rivals insisted on the significant silence of the written Law. The Sadducees were not, of course, opposed either to the psalms or to the prophecies; the Sadducæan author of 1 Maccabees evidently loved them both. But as practical men, the Sadducees considered that vague poetic expressions should not be treated as *dicta probantia* for doctrine, and in particular were slow to accept even the earliest and best of apocalypses as in the fullest sense a 'holy book.'[xx] That the Pharisees on the other hand believed in all that the Sadducees doubted or rejected, cannot be questioned. Certainly Josephus expresses himself rather oddly—ἀθάνατον ἰσχὺν ταῖς ψυχαῖς πίστις αὐτοῖς εἶναι. In this Josephus may seem to Platonize, but really it is only his Greek way of denying that the life after death is a pale semi-consciousness which no judgment will wake up, just as Josephus's statement that the Sadducees 'take away εἱμαρμένη[yy] entirely' merely means that according to them we are not to sit with our hands folded waiting for the divine judgment, nor yet in a fury of blind fanaticism to pretend to be its commissioned agents. Similarly Josephus's description of the Pharisæan doctrine of the resurrection in *War*, ii. 8, 14, and that of his own belief on this point in *War*, iii. 8, 5 may appear to point rather to transmigration of souls. But in the latter passage he tells us himself that he is 'philosophizing,' and even in *Ant.* xviii. 1, 3 how lightly he touches on 'living again'! Evidently he is afraid to lay too much stress on so unphilosophical a doctrine as that of the resurrection of the body, and uses language susceptible of a twofold interpretation.

It is more difficult to translate the foreign-sounding

account of the Essenes into Jewish terms. Taken as a whole the description cannot possibly be accurate, and yet some of its leading features, critically viewed, may well be genuine, and among these (defending myself for this elsewhere [zz]) I must, in spite of Ohle's criticism, provisionally include the doctrine of the soul. The passages relative to this are important for the illustration both of the mystic and of the Puritan psalms; I will quote the principal parts of them.

Ἐσσηνοῖς δὲ ἐπὶ μὲν Θεῷ καταλιπεῖν φιλεῖ τὰ πάντα ὁ λόγος. ἀθανατίζουσι δὲ τὰς ψυχάς, περιμάχητον ἡγούμενοι τοῦ δικαίου τὴν πρόσοδον. εἰς δὲ τὸ ἱερὸν ἀναθήματα στέλλοντες, θυσίας οὐκ ἐπιτελοῦσι διαφορότητι ἁγνειῶν ἃς νομίζοιεν καὶ δι' αὐτὸ εἰργόμενοι τοῦ κοινοῦ τεμενίσματος ἐφ' αὑτῶν τὰς θυσίας ἐπιτελοῦσι.[1]

Φθαρτὰ μὲν εἶναι τὰ σώματα, καὶ τὴν ὕλην οὐ μόνιμον αὐτοῖς, τὰς δὲ ψυχὰς ἀθανάτους ἀεὶ διαμένειν, καὶ συμπλέκεσθαι μὲν ἐκ τοῦ λεπτοτάτου φοιτώσας αἰθέρος, ὥσπερ εἰρκταῖς τοῖς σώμασιν ἴυγγί τινι φυσικῇ κατασπωμένας. ἐπειδὰν δὲ ἀνεθῶσι τῶν κατὰ σάρκα δεσμῶν, οἷα δὴ μακρᾶς δουλείας ἀπηλλαγμένας τότε χαίρειν καὶ μετεώρους φέρεσθαι. καὶ ταῖς μὲν ἀγαθαῖς, ὁμοδοξοῦντες παισὶν Ἑλλήνων, ἀποφαίνονται τὴν ὑπὲρ ὠκεανὸν δίαιταν ἐπικεῖσθαι, καὶ χῶρον, οὔτε ὄμβροις, οὔτε νιφετοῖς, οὔτε καύμασι βαρυνόμενον, ἀλλ' ὃν ἐξ ὠκεανοῦ πραῢς ἀεὶ ζέφυρος ἐπιπνέων ἀναψύχει. ταῖς δὲ φαύλαις, ζοφώδη καὶ χειμέριον ἀφορίζονται μυχόν, γέμοντα τιμωριῶν ἀδιαλείπτων.[aaa]

There is nothing improbable in this, rightly understood. The Essenes were an offshoot of the Pharisees, and carried the Pharisæan doctrines or tendencies to an extreme. Did the Pharisees say, in opposition to the Sadducees, that 'certain things, though not all, are [entirely] the work of fate' (i.e. providence, or an eternal divine purpose [2])? The Essenes went further, and affirmed that 'fate governs all things, and that nothing befalls men but what is according to its decree.'[3] Did the Pharisees prefer the study of the Law to elaborate sacrificial rites? The Essenes kept up only a formal connexion with the temple, and restricted themselves to a purer worship of their own.[4] Did the Pharisees hold that all souls were immortal, but that even the good would have to wait in the underworld for their reward, viz. the resurrec-

---

[1] Jos., *Ant.* xviii. 1, 5.
[2] Zeno, according to Stobæus, said that we might speak indifferently of destiny, nature, and providence.
[3] Jos., *Ant.* xiii. 5, 9.   [4] Jos., *Ant.* xviii. 1, 5.

tion of their bodies? The Essenes are said to have believed that the spirits of the righteous would no more be burdened with bodies, but would 'rejoice and mount upwards.'[1] But we must not follow Josephus blindly. He either suppresses, or but lightly touches upon, one of the most important Pharisæan doctrines, that which relates to the judgment, the resurrection, and the 'kingdom of God.' Can we hesitate to believe that he deals similarly with the Essenes? There was nothing in the mere belief in immortality (i.e. in future rewards and punishments) inconsistent with the expectation of a grand final judgment, when the soul's happiness or misery would be intensified, and the fact that John the Essene was one of the Jewish generals in the Roman war[2] proves the members of his sect to have been not mere sectarians, but to have shared the popular views on the final or Messianic judgment.[bbb] The acceptance of this belief, if it is indeed a fact, completely separates the Essenes from thinkers like Philo and the author of the Wisdom of Solomon, from whose systems the doctrine of the final judgment is conspicuously absent. And if the Essenes accepted the final judgment, how can we be sure that they did not receive with it some theory of a glorified body? If the pre-existent souls entered into mortal bodies to carry out the first part of the divine plan, why should they not be 'clothed upon' with 'spiritual bodies' to fulfil their service to their Creator?

Let me explain this. The Essenian doctrine of the soul in Josephus, viewed in an Oriental rather than in a Greek light, combines two elements—a Babylonian and a Persian, both Hebraized. The Iranian Scriptures know nothing of the happy island; this is a part of the tradition of the Assyrio-Babylonian poets (see p. 432). But the Essenes whom Josephus describes, being at heart true Israelites, are well aware that not merely to 'brave men called heroes and demigods' (or, in Hebrew style, 'friends of God,' like Abraham) but to all 'good souls' this enchanted ground is open, and though in the apocalyptic style so dear to them they may picture the land of the blessed as Paradise, yet they mean nothing

---

[1] Jos., *War*, ii. 8, 11. On the attitude of the Essenes towards sacrifices, see note °, p. 374.

[2] *Ibid.*, ii. 20, 4; iii. 2, 1.

different from that 'better world of the just' which Zoroastrianism identifies with heaven (see *Yasna*, xvii. 42-44). On the other hand, the description of Hades is distinctly Zoroastrian, and so too is the alternative account which Josephus gives of the lot of good souls, according to the Essenian system. We have in fact in the first sentence of Jos., *War*, ii. 8, 11 a reflexion of the Zoroastrian view respecting the so-called fravashis, those 'guardian angels' which were so linked to men as to form virtually a part of human nature, and which were practically indistinguishable from souls.^{ccc} A fravashi is the man himself as God destined him to become; and without implying the theory of the Mînôkhired (xlix. 22, 23) that most of the constellations are 'the guardian spirits of the worldly existences' (comp. Plato's theory in the *Timæus*¹), one might accurately say (adopting Josephus's words) that the fravashis 'keep coming (to earth) from the most subtle ether,' to which when this life is over they will return. The only discrepancy between the Zoroastrian theory in the Bundahis and the Essenian in our Josephus is that, according to the latter, souls are 'drawn down' into bodies 'by a certain physical enticement,' whereas the former represents the fravashis as voluntarily becoming embodied in order to fight for God and for goodness against the power of the evil one. How shall we account for this? In my opinion, thus. The writer or editor of Jos., *Ant.* ii. 8, 11 has misrepresented the Essenian belief under the influence of Philo, who held, as is well known, that souls descended into the body through being enamoured of corporeal existence. In its present form, the Essenian theory fails to explain either why the unbodied soul should have longed to become embodied, or why, if it instinctively loved the body, it should have rejoiced to 'mount upwards.' Philo does to some extent explain the difficulty by his aristocratic division of souls into two classes —those of the wise (such as Abraham and Moses) and those of the mass of mankind.² But this only in part Philonized Essenism, which knows nothing of Philo's aristocratic theory, gives not even the shadow of a solution. Admit a Zoroastrian

---

¹ See Grote, *Plato*, iii. 262, and cf. Dante, *Parad.* iv. 52-63, 'Dice che l' alma alla sua stella riede,' &c.

² Drummond, *Philo Judæus*, i. 337.

influence upon Essenism, and all becomes clear. The fravashis voluntarily assumed mortal bodies in order to fight for God and for goodness against the power of the evil one.[1] Similar to this, we may reasonably hold, was the belief of the Essenes respecting the 'descent' of the souls—a belief, dependent for its full development upon Zoroastrianism, but not without Jewish germs. For predestination was certainly an old Jewish and indeed Semitic idea (see *The Prophecies of Isaiah*, i. 292), and the psalms themselves cannot be understood without assuming a belief in the ideal (heavenly) as well as real (earthly) existence of God's people Israel. Later on, not only Israel, but Israel's most holy things were represented as pre-existent in heaven; [ddd] so alone, it appeared, was their sanctity inviolable and their permanence ensured. How edifying the idea of the pre-existence of souls (which became a part of Talmudic Judaism) could be made, the student will see from a wonderfully deep poem of Nachmanides freely rendered into exquisite German verse by Sachs.[eee]

And what of the final act which I have ventured to postulate for the Essenian drama of the soul? Is not that also a piece of Hebraized Zoroastrianism? The abolition of the separation between heaven and earth which was an essential part of the Zoroastrian eschatology involves the belief in a transfigured or spiritual body. This, too, is a novelty in Judaism, but is it not foreshadowed in the fiery chariot which bore Elijah up to heaven? And altogether may we not reasonably hold that the statement of Essenian beliefs in Jos., *War*, ii. 8, 11 is probably authentic because it is a natural combination of Hebraized Babylonian and Persian elements?

I am well content if I have done something to show that, although perhaps in some of its details too Zoroastrian, the religious theory of the Essenes was a noble one, and permits us to regard them as true disciples of the Puritan and mystic psalmists. But even without the Essenes (twilight figures, perhaps), it seems to me sufficiently clear that the later developments of Jewish thought favour the view that some of the psalmists had already started in the same direction. But for the necessity of considering a theory opposed to my own, which has some powerful support, I might now close these lectures.

[1] *Bundahis*, ii. 10 (West, *Pahlavi Texts*, i. 14).

I wish to consider it fairly, but before doing so will sum up the results which we have lately gained. The doctrine of an eternal life open to all the righteous, and involving a transfiguration of the body, is neither a mere evolution out of the old Semitic belief in Sheól, nor yet a direct importation from any foreign system of thought. Had it not come into contact with Zoroastrianism Israel would, historically speaking, have struggled in vain to satisfy its religious aspirations. And yet it was not to Persia alone that the Church-nation was indebted for its greatest religious acquisition. In dealing with foreign religions the leaders of the Church exercised a fine discriminating tact, and their followers a singular power of assimilation; or, speaking religiously, God watched over His people, and gave them power to reject any important belief, the germs of which did not to some extent exist in their own religion. Now Jewish religion after the Exile was demonstrably very different in its tendencies from that of the pre-Babylonian period. An incipient dualism existed within it—the dualism of that great antithesis, God and the world, out of which arose by degrees a second, the spirit (or principle of conscious individuality) and the body (with the soul). The first antithesis was clearly recognized by Ezekiel and his successors. The second was far more slowly realized (see Eccles. iii. 21, xii. 7 ?). We find a distinct expression of it, however, in one of the finest of the mystic utterances in the Psalter,

> Though my flesh and my heart should have wasted away,
> God would be the rock of my heart and my portion for ever,[1]

where the 'heart' which will survive the old one is the organ of God-consciousness, or, in St. Paul's phraseology, the πνεῦμα. The 73rd psalm indeed is scarcely older than the last part of the Persian period (p. 148). But the distinction between spirit and body must have begun to grow up long before this, that Jewish religion might be prepared for the moulding influence of a more advanced system of thought. Even if the other mystic psalms were composed as late as the 73rd, they must have been preceded by others of a similar tendency which being less noble have not been preserved.

[1] Ps. lxxiii. 26. See note in my commentary.

And what was this more highly developed system? Zoroastrianism, if the preceding arguments are well founded; but according to a rival theory, Greek philosophy. Consciously or unconsciously, it is said, Greek modes of thought must have begun to modify genuine Judaism from the day that Alexander the Great conquered at Issus. The conclusion of this process in Egypt is seen in the Book of Wisdom and in the works of Philo. That the doctrine of spiritual immortality in these writings is neo-Platonic, is generally admitted; would it not, say our theorists, be reasonable to suppose that any approximation to such a doctrine in Palestine has the same origin? A Jewish scholar assures us that Platonic or Pythagorean speculation dominates the Talmudic doctors of Palestine,[1] while both in St. Paul (once Gamaliel's disciple) and in the school of the Pharisees many Christian writers have found more or less distinct traces of Hellenistic ideas. Dillmann, too, is of opinion that the Book of Enoch may here and there be affected by Greek mythology, though one of its objects is to counteract the far more dangerous influence of Greek philosophy. And a much older book, also of Palestinian origin, that of Ecclesiastes, has been suspected of containing Stoic and Epicurean doctrines, and references have even been found in it to the teaching of Heraclitus.

To this I have to reply that the new and distinctive element in the mental attitude of the later Jews is not so much Hellenism as a half-reluctant openness to foreign ideas, and that Israel's debt to Hellas began, both in Egypt and still more in Palestine, later than is sometimes supposed. Putting Egypt aside, and without repeating my own very definite judgment on the ideas of Koheleth, I will refer the reader to Menzel's painstaking dissertation, *Der griechische Einfluss auf Prediger und Weisheit Salomos* (1889), which shows conclusively that the author of Ecclesiastes is no more a Hellenizer than Sirach is afterwards. With regard to Enoch, the denunciations in xciv. 5, xcviii. 15, civ. 10 may perfectly well refer to a native heterodox literature, an early post-Exilic fragment of which may exist in Prov. xxx. 1–4, and a later one in the meditations, before they were edited, of Koheleth, and to which literature there may be a reference in the

---
[1] Joel, *Blicke in die Religionsgeschichte*, i. 117.

epilogue of our Ecclesiastes (Eccles. xii. 12). I see no necessity for explaining the western situation of Hades in Enoch xxii. 1 (a passage in the oldest part of the book) by Greek mythology; the idea is at home in Egypt, where Amenti, 'the land of the west,' is the invisible lower hemisphere to which the sun appears to descend,[1] and as for the 'Titan-legends' in chaps. liv., lxvii., though Greek influence is not inconceivable, can we not explain even these from Palestinian sources?[2] Of the Pharisees I have spoken above. The view referred to seems to me not only unnecessary but opposed to all that we know of the circumstances of the time. If any one of the three schools had imbibed Greek philosophy, you would expect it to be the Sadducees. But though the Sadducees, like the Hellenizers under Antiochus Epiphanes, borrowed much from Greek civilization in external points, they did not, so far as the evidence goes, incur debts to Hellas, either in religion or in philosophy. What was there indeed in the early Palestinian Greek life to attract a Jew?[3] As to the Talmud, I do not doubt that there is truth in the statement. The opposition of the Rabbis could not permanently arrest the extension of Alexandrinism. Still it will often be difficult to prove a purely Greek origin for Talmudic ideas. The pre-existence doctrine, for instance, which Joel has referred to, might conceivably have developed out of purely Jewish germs, especially when Zoroastrian (not to add, Egyptian) ideas were in the air; the echoes of Platonic psychology which this scholar mentions are equally Zoroastrian. And lastly with regard to St. Paul. Granting that he knew certain Greek phrases which could not but be familiar to Greek-speaking and Greek-reading Jews, does it follow that the ideas which he associated with them were of purely Greek origin? If there was a movement among the Jews towards a belief in spiritual immortality before and during the Greek period, fostered by Persian influences, must not St. Paul have been much more affected by this than by a tincture of commonplace Greek philosophy?[fff]

---

[1] See Brugsch, *Religion und Mythologie der alten Aegypter*, p. 227.

[2] Hellenistic Jews were well acquainted with the Greek story of the Titans. See 2 Sam. v. 18 (Sept.), xxiii. 13 (Sept. Lucian's recension), and cf. Judith, xvi. 7. But see Grünbaum, *Z.D.M.G.* xxxi. 237.

[3] Cf. Morrison, *The Jews under Roman Rule*, pp. 354-357.

When therefore we are told ᵍᵍᵍ (as by Dr. Grätz in 1871 and by M. Montet in 1884) that the doctrine of the resurrection of the body comes from Zoroastrianism and that of the immortality of the soul from neo-Platonism,[1] or (as by M. Montet in 1890) that even the former is 'merely a different reading of the Platonic doctrine of the immortality of the soul,' we are entitled to ask for a revision of these judgments. And we may do so with some confidence, (1) because, among the surprises of the future, it is not likely that we shall see a general adhesion to M. de Harlez's negation of the antiquity of the resurrection-doctrine in Zoroastrianism, and (2) because in asserting that the Jewish belief in immortality comes (in the sense which I have explained) from Zoroastrianism, we do not deny that neo-Platonism helped greatly in strengthening this belief among the Hellenistic Jews. I appeal once more to advanced theological students to follow with more interest the progress of Zoroastrian studies, and as an essential preliminary to acquaint themselves with what has actually been done by the combined labours of critics of different schools. And I think that this interest will be rewarded by fresh insight, not only into the meaning of the Psalter, but also into that of works which stand perhaps even nearer to us Christian theologians, the Pauline and the Johannine writings.ʰʰʰ

My task is for the present at an end. Should I be spared to resume it with the advantage of some years of self-criticism and of helpful intercourse with fellow-workers, I shall doubtless find much to modify or correct in details. But I trust that something permanent has been already achieved by the more consistent application of principles and the fuller combination of results. If I have been able to show that the Psalter is really a monument of the best religious ideas of the great post-Exile Jewish Church, and that from Jeremiah onwards there has been a continuous development, through the co-operation of some of the noblest non-Jewish races and the unerring guidance of the adorable Spirit of truth, in the direction which leads to Christ, I shall feel that I have been privileged to do something, however imperfect, for the best of masters and the greatest of causes.

[1] Cf. also Pfleiderer, *Philosophy of Religion*, iv. 149.

NOTE ᵃ, p. 381.

Are Ps. xlix. and the kindred psalms which will presently be referred to, spoken in the name of the community, or in that of any and every pious Israelite? I have taken the latter view. Smend, however, while admitting that Ps. xlix. 4, 5 can be understood as spoken by the poet, claims the rest of the psalm for the church-nation. Similarly it is the community (*Gemeinde*) whose eternal duration and enjoyment of Messianic blessings is believingly anticipated in Pss. xvi. 10, 11, xvii. 15. On Ps. lxxiii. Smend's remarks are brief, and include no exegesis. Possibly, he thinks, in spite of appearances, it was composed for a liturgical purpose (see *vv.* 1, 28). Klostermann's early work, *Untersuchungen zur alttest. Theologie* (Gotha, 1868) discusses two of these psalms (xlix. and lxxiii.) and in addition Ps. cxxxix. It is, however, arbitrary and unsound alike in its criticism and its exegesis. More help will be got from chap. xlii. of Hermann Schultz's *Alttest. Theologie* (ed. 4), which ably represents a different theory of interpretation from my own.

NOTE ᵇ, p. 382.

In Isa. xiv. two different Semitic beliefs are mentioned respecting the fate of royal personages after death. The king of Babylon expects to join the gods (*v.* 13). But the poet has already expressed the ordinary Israelitish and Phœnician belief, viz. that kings and heroes have their couches of glory in the underworld, probably apart from the vulgar herd (cf. Isa. v. 14). Job, too, is made to express the belief that there are no moral distinctions in the underworld, tyrant-kings and their oppressed subjects being alike 'cut away from God's hand' among the shades. 'Oh that I had died as a newborn child,' he exclaims, 'and joined the great assembly of mankind. I should at least have been no worse off than those kings and counsellors of the earth, who built the ruined cities of the primæval world' (in Job iii. 14 read עֹלָם for לָמוֹ, and cf. Job xxii. 15, Ezek. xxvi. 20). For the Phœnician belief, see Inscr. of Eshmunazar, king of the Sidonians, l. 8, 'let him have no couch with the shades' (משכב as in Isa. lvii. 2, 'they rest upon their couches'); also Inscr. of Tebnêth, Eshmunazar's son, l. 8, 'nor (mayest thou have) a couch with the shades.' The latest monograph on these and other Phœnician inscriptions is G. Hoffmann's *Ueber einige phönikische Inschriften* (Göttingen, 1889); for the inscription of Tebnêth comp. Driver, *Samuel*, Introd., pp. xxvi.-xxix., who is well aware that it illustrates not only the language but the ideas of the Old Testament. It is perhaps allowable to infer from Ezek. xxviii. 13, 14 that the Tyrians also were at one time attracted by the belief expressed in Isa. xiv. 13.

Note ᶜ, p. 383.

The question is, whether 'Jehovah killeth and maketh alive (again)' in 1 Sam. ii. 6 (cf. Deut. xxxii. 39, 2 Kings v. 7) describes what is in the abstract possible, or what He has been known to do or is at least expected to do. I prefer the latter view. In Deut. *l.c.*, 'I kill and I make alive' is parallel to 'I wound and I heal.' Now the healing of disease was a real experience; surely the revival of the dead must have been regarded as such too. Job ix. 5 may of course be quoted in favour of the other view, but even here is it certain that 'which removeth the mountains' merely describes what is in the abstract possible? The phrase may allude to a tradition of what God had once done or to an expectation of what He would one day do (cf. Isa. ii. 19). To 'kill and make alive' is also an attribute of Marduk (see a well-known hymn in Sayce, *Hibbert Lectures*, p. 99, but cf. p. 358).

Note ᵈ, p. 383.

The phrase is found both (see note ⁿⁿ) in Proverbs and in Ps. xxxvi. 10. Comp. the 'water of life' in Babylonian and Egyptian mythology (see next note, and cf. Renouf, *Hibbert Lectures*, p. 141).

Note ᵉ, p. 384.

The Babylonians, like the Iranians, certainly believed that the ambrosial fruit might, under certain circumstances, be partaken of by men. The name of the sacred plant in Assyrian shows this; it means 'in old age the man becomes young (again).' And when Șit-napistim (of whom more later) and his wife were placed in the happy garden and made equal to the gods, it followed that they had free access to the sacred plant and 'water of life' (see Jensen, *Die Kosmologie der Babylonier*, pp. 227, 383; cf. Jeremias, *Die bab.-ass. Vorstellungen*, &c., pp. 89–95). The Hebrew narrative, if we had it in its full form, would probably have made the privilege of eating the sacred fruit conditional on obedience. How skilfully the narrator has given a moral turn to the details of the old story! Contrast the Gișțubar story, where the hero first takes the sacred plant, and then loses it to a serpent. If 'serpent' is correct, here seems to be the original of the serpent-tempter in Gen. iii., as Jensen points out. Whether the Babylonians had begun to allegorize their myth, must be left undecided from want of evidence. Need I say that the 'tree of life' in Gen. ii., iii., has a Babylonian rather than an Iranian connexion? The Gaokerena (see p. 439) of the Avesta may itself be ultimately of Babylonian origin.

Note f, p. 384.

Ps. xxii. 30 (note), which shows at any rate that the departed might be supposed to share in some way in the Messianic hope. This is one of the germs of the beautiful address of the Messiah to God in the Yalkut to Isaiah (359), 'Nor let the living only be saved in my days, but also those who are laid in the dust.'

Note g, p. 384.

It is not unpermissible to compare Ps. xxiii. 4 in this connexion. At any rate, *v.* 4 must be interpreted not less widely than *v.* 6 (see my commentary).

Note h, p. 385.

How forced are the uncritical patristic explanations of these passages! See e.g. St. Cyril (*Catechesis*, xviii. 7), who remarks on Ps. cxv. 17 that those who die in their sins will have, not to praise God for benefits, but to lament; also St. Chrysostom and St. Jerome on Ps. vi. 6.

Note i, p. 385.

Remember, however, there were both orthodox and heterodox Sûfîs. One of the former, Sha'rânî, in a work on the Mohammedan belief, shows that no one can be dispensed from his religious obligations, even if he have reached the high degree of detachment from the world called *al-qurb* ('nearness to God,' cf. Ps. lxxiii. 28).

Note j, p. 386.

The apocalyptic element is weak in psalm-theology (Pss. lviii. and lxxxii. are exceptional). The dangerousness of heathenism must be realized still more vividly and appallingly before the Jewish longing for a complete mundane revolution can become as intense as in the later apocalyptic literature (the germs of which, however, cannot be mistaken in Joel, the second Zechariah, and Isa. xxiv.–xxvii.). Upon the whole, this is the picture presented by the later psalmists —an earnest people devoted to the pursuit of righteousness, and not to be turned aside from it by great difficulties and discouragements. And, from a Christian point of view, the loveliest feature of it is the growth of a mystic and yet not separatistic spiritual religion.

Note k, p. 386.

Originally it was Israel which claimed Jehovah for its 'portion' (Deut. xxxii. 8, Jer. x. 16, li. 19), but in Pss. xvi. 5, lxxiii. 26 a faithful Israelite can make the same high boast (cf. the name Hilkiah). 1 Tim. vi. 19, 'that they may lay hold on the true life,' may be illustrated from an Egyptian hymn, 'Grant to thy son who loves thee, life in truth . . . that he may live united with thee in eternity' (Renouf, *Hibbert Lectures*, p. 230, also from *Korán*, xxix. 64).

Note m, p. 387.

Pss. xv., xxiv. 1-6, xxiii., xxvii. 1-6, which are illustrated by Ps. v. 5 (cf. 12), lxi. 5, xxxi. 20, 21, xxxvi. 8-10, lxv. 5. Within this group the words גור 'to sojourn as a guest,' גר 'a guest' (prop. 'a protected stranger') only occur thrice (Pss. v. 5, xv. 1, lxi. 5), but the idea of 'guestship' is equally expressed in the other passages. That idea has experienced a noteworthy development. It might be thought that the *gēr* or 'guest' of Jehovah would be as fearful and anxious with regard to his future safety as one of those protected foreigners who are called technically *gērīm* in the O. T. And certainly we do find in the passage (Isa. xxxiii. 14) which suggested Pss. xv. and xxiv. 1-6 a speech of certain nominal *gērīm* of Jehovah who apprehend that the 'hearth of Jehovah' may to them be no protection but the reverse. But in the Psalter, putting aside xxxix. 13, cxix. 19, where the state of 'guestship' is viewed upon its less favourable side, to be a *gēr* is to have a joyous sense of absolute security based on the consciousness of a higher and divinely given life (see my note on Ps. xv. 1). Nor can we, I think, duly appreciate the use of גר for 'convert' in new Hebrew (the first beginnings of which are traceable in the Sept. of Ex. xii. 19, Isa. xiv. 1), if we suppose this word in the post-Exile period to have suggested the idea of timidity (see Isa. xiv. 1-3). I venture, therefore, to criticize Prof. Robertson Smith's reference to the phrase '*gēr* of Jehovah' as expressing a timid though earnest legalism (*The Rel. of the Semites*, p. 78). It does express this in the two psalm-passages just referred to (with which comp. 1 Chron. xxix. 15), but not in the other passages, which agree in spirit with the finest utterances of mystic piety. The true *gēr* of Jehovah knows, it is true, that he has no natural right to be on terms of intimacy with his God. He is not like those herdsmen of the desert so graphically described by Mr. Doughty, who explain their often surprising hospitality with the words, 'Be we not all guests of Ullah?' There is a world of difference between his and their religion. The one is supernatural, the other is but natural. Israel was chosen of old by Jehovah with a moral object, and, having forfeited his standing, has been chosen anew (cf. Ps. lxv. 5). In his humility he may call himself a *gēr* or 'protected stranger,' but can he be timid or anxious? Many a psalm returns the answer, No. He is sure that this 'guestship' will last perpetually (Ps. lxi. 5), and sings for joy. And not only faithful Israel has this confidence, but with increasing clearness each faithful Israelite of the mystic school.

NOTE ⁿ, p. 388.

חֶלֶד in Ps. xvii. 14, see Linguistic Appendix. It corresponds exactly to the Arabic *dunyā*. Cf. the saying quoted by Lane (Lexicon, *s.v.*), *bāʿa dunyāhu bi-āḫiratihi*, 'he has purchased his (enjoyments of) the present world at the expense of his (enjoyments of) the world to come.' Of course, this use of חֶלֶד does not imply a recognized and habitual way of speaking. The phrases הָעוֹלָם הַזֶּה and הָעוֹלָם הַבָּא belong to the Hebrew of the Mishna.

NOTE ^o, p. 389.

Wellhausen (followed by Nowack) reads in v. 24*b*, וְאָחֲרֶךָ בְּיָד תִּקָּחֵנִי (*Skizzen und Vorarbeiten*, i. 94).

NOTE ^p, p. 389.

'At the awaking,' בְּהָקִיץ, Ps. xvii. 15, may mean 'when life's short *night* is past;' cf. J. H. Newman's poem, 'Lead, kindly Light, through the encircling gloom.' This is not without plausible support in Ps. xc. 5 (R. V.), 'Thou carriest them away as with a flood, they are as a sleep,' on which Luther remarks, 'Truly our life is nothing else than a sleep and a dream:'—a primitive mystic idea, as we may see in Clem. Alex., *Strom.* v., pp. 599D, 600A (comp. also the Mohammedan saying, 'Man sleeps in life and awakes in death'). We may then interpret לַבֹּקֶר, Ps. xlix. 15, with Card. Cajetan, 'Mortem justorum appellat mane, quoniam in morte incipit verus dies rectorum : sicut mortem impiorum appellavit casum in fovea' (*Psalmi Davidici*, ed. 2, 1532). If we hold Ps. xvii. to have been written before the idea of the resurrection became current, this is perhaps the best explanation (see my commentary). If, however, we place this group of psalms near the close of the Persian period, we shall naturally interpret the 'awaking' of a renewal of the bodily existence, as Dan. xii. 2, cf. 2 Kings iv. 31. For 'thy form,' תְּמוּנָתֶךָ, we might, with Sept., substitute 'thy glory' (cf. Sept., Num. xii. 8).

The correctness of this is shown by the use of כָּבוֹד=the divine glory in the parallel passage, Ps. lxxiii. 24 ; cf. 1 Tim. iii. 16, ἀνελήμφθη ἐν δόξῃ. 'Face,' 'form,' and 'glory of Jehovah' are in fact synonymous expressions for the revealed perfections of God (Ex. xxxiii. 18–20) ; the 'sight' or experience of which gives life and happiness. The fine phrase 'nearness to God' (Ps. lxxiii. 28) seems equivalent to 'seeing God's face.' It occurs naturally to pious mystics in all countries. The Sûfîs often used it (*al-qurb*) to express that degree of blessedness which is only exceeded by intuition (Fleischer, *Z. D. M. G.* xx. 33, and see above, note gg).

NOTE q, p. 390.

According to Riehm (in his edition of Hupfeld's *Psalmen*) Ps. xvi. 10 merely expresses the hope of deliverance from the danger of death. He thinks that the connexion of this and the preceding verse requires this, unless we go so far as to suppose that the speaker looks forward to be taken like Enoch from earth to heaven. But why not? To a mystic (cf. St. Paul's μεμύημαι) there is no death ; what seems so is rather 'assumption.' 'Significanter,' as Cardinal Cajetan says, 'non vocavit eam mortem sed assumptionem ex hac misera in perpetuam vitam' (in the work quoted from above). On Riehm's side it is also urged that in Ps. xxx. 4 (cf. ix. 14) phraseology like that in Ps. xvi. 10 is used of some great danger to which the psalmist is exposed. But it is not a personal but a national danger of which Ps. xxx. 4 speaks ; and of course it is as a faithful Churchman that the speaker hopes for the highest blessings in Ps. xvi. 10, 11. More on this head later.

NOTE r, p. 390.

The coincidences between Egyptian ideas of the soul and those of some parts of the Old Testament need not be denied. They are not however sufficient to prove a direct historical connexion between the religions of Egypt and Judah. Egypt and Babylon may possibly in primitive times have influenced each other religiously (see Jeremias, *Die bab.-ass. Vorstellungen*, &c., p. 93, note [1]), but except in a passage of the Talmud (*Nidda*, 30b, Güdemann, *Religionsgeschichtliche Studien*, p. 7, &c.) Egyptian influence on Jewish ideas of the soul is not clearly visible. The hope of sharing in the divine glory is the privilege of the good in all the higher religions. It could not however wear precisely the same aspect in Egypt as in Judah owing to the fundamental contrast between the pantheism of the one and the pure Theism of the other. On the Egyptian doctrines of the future life, see Renouf, *Hibbert Lectures*, 1879, pp. 179–191; Brugsch, *Religion und Mythologie der alten Aegypter*, pp. 178–180; Maspero, *Rev. de l'hist. des religions*, xviii. 53. Cf. also Lieblein, *Egyptian Religion* (Leipz. 1884), pp. 84, 85, where the doctrine of the fiery tortures of the wicked in hell is represented as distinctively Egyptian. Of Greek influence upon the Jews, more later on.

NOTE ˢ, p. 391.

Among the most widely spread of the later Jewish notions of the underworld is that of its seven gates, which is undeniably of Babylonian origin (there were *twelve* gates, says Brugsch, to the Egyptian Hades). The first Jewish mention of these gates (which imply seven concentric walls, like those of Ecbatana) is in the Sohar; Mohammed adopted the notion from the Jews (*Korán*, xv. 44). The Talmud speaks at any rate of seven parts of hell, the names of which are given in *Erubin*, 19a (cf. *Midrash Tillim*, xi. 7). Probably Dante derived his own sevenfold division of the *Inferno* from his Jewish friend Immanuel (Manoel Giudeo). On the origin of the Babylonian belief, see Jensen, *Die Kosmologie der Babylonier*, p. 175; he connects it with the sevenfold division of the upper world, which we also find in the Avesta. For the later Jewish notions, see the Midrash on the Psalms and the *Pirqe deRabbi Eliezer*, and cf. Wünsche, *Jahrbb. f. prot. Theol.*, vi. 497 &c., Feuchtzwang, *Zt. f. Assyriologie*, 1889, p. 43, Löwy, 'Old Jewish Legends on Hell,' *Proceedings of Soc. of Bibl. Arch.*, vol. x. (1888). The Mandæan doctrine of the underworld has also a large Babylonian element.

NOTE ᵗ, p. 392.

Ṣit-napistim was the name of the hero who with his wife survived the Deluge, and was 'made like to the gods,' and placed in the Babylonian and Assyrian Paradise (see above, p. 427). The words with which the Deluge-story in the Babylonian epic concludes represent this locality as 'far off at the mouth of the streams' (the Euphrates and the Tigris), i.e. probably an island in the Persian gulf (Jensen, *Die Kosmologie der Babylonier*, pp. 212, 383). On the other hand Berosus makes Xisuthrus (the hero of his Flood-story) disappear from earth to dwell with the gods in heaven. This form of the mystic tradition seems more recent; the dwelling of the gods is no longer localized upon earth. It is also the form to which the Hebrew Enoch-story approaches most nearly. Xisuthrus is in fact Noah and Enoch in one, and the story of Enoch is of Exilic origin. Cf. my own art. 'Deluge,' *Ency. Brit.*, 1877, but see also Delitzsch.

Note ᵘ, p. 392.

The virtual equivalence of the two ideas comes out very clearly in the Old Testament. It was favoured by the twofold meaning of מָוֶת, 1. death, 2. the world of the dead (cf. Hos. xiv. 14).

Note ᵛ, p. 393.

Prätorius, *Z.D.M.G.* 1873, p. 645 &c. On the pre-Islamic view of death in Arabia, see Wellhausen, *Reste arabischen Heidenthumes*, pp. 163, 164; Wetzstein, in Delitzsch's *Psalms*, iii. 436. Tradition said that Ḳoss, bishop of Najrân in Yemen, was 'the first who asserted the Resurrection' (Chenery, *Assemblies of Al Hariri*, i. 538).

Note ʷ, p. 394.

There are some possible objections to the use here made of the Avesta. I. It is an undoubted fact that the Avesta, as we now have it, cannot be historically traced beyond the Sassanidæ. The first king of this line made great endeavours to collect the texts of the Avesta, and to secure the traditional exegesis. His successors continued his work, and under Shâpûr II. (A.D. 309-380) the canon of the Avesta was fixed. It is therefore as impossible to be sure that the ancient records have come down to us in their integrity as it is in the case of the pre-Exile portions of the O. T. From this an objector may argue that to use the Avesta as I have done is unsafe, especially as Avesta students have not the ample means of critical analysis which Old Testament critics are fortunate enough to possess. The course which I have adopted is however perfectly justifiable. The existence of a progressive critical analysis of the Avesta cannot be denied. Moreover it is a correct inference from the notices of the classical authors that the leading ideas of the Avesta were prevalent before the close of the Achæmenian period, and if prevalent at all they had doubtless been so for long. It will also be disputed by few critics that in the main the ideas and sacred texts of Achæmenian Mazda-worship are reproduced in the Avesta (see e.g. *Oxford Z.A.* I., Introd., p. liii.).

II. Another objection may be based on the existence of rival schools in Avestic philology (cf. Wilhelm, *Le Muséon*, 1886, pp. 334-358). And obviously there is room for friendly controversy for many years to come. But I may surely hold that the religion of the Avesta can be adequately known from the existing translations. Three of these have lain before me, viz. the recent one in the

Oxford Z. A. by Darmesteter and Mills, and the earlier ones of Spiegel (1852–1863) and de Harlez (1881), against even the later of which (based as it is upon Spiegel) much may be urged, but which is still if rightly used (with the richer German rendering of Spiegel) suggestive, and adequate for all but critical students. I quote it myself for the sake of variety when it does not differ materially from Mills's version. The only doubt can be, whether the Gâthâs are sufficiently well understood to be referred to. Prof. Chantepie de la Saussaye, a thoroughly well-informed historian, though not a Zend scholar, states (*Lehrbuch der Religionsgeschichte*, ii. 23) that, 'even after the translation of Mills, it is for the present the wisest course not to base an investigation of Parsism upon the Gâthâs, on account of the uncertainty of the rendering.' If this be correct, it will be equally imprudent to use these hymns in illustration of the Psalter. But to the opinion of this scholar I would oppose that of a greater authority, also Dutch, Prof. Tiele, who puts his statement aside as an exaggeration. Some parts of the Gâthâs are, as he admits, still very obscure, but entire hymns have been translated in such a way that the general sense may fairly be regarded as settled (*Theologisch Tijdschrift*, 1889, p. 625). Nor does any Zendist think that the difference between translations prevents our getting a clear general view of the purport of most of the hymns. The uncertainty only relates to minute details. I may add that the very passages which I had marked for quotation in Dr. Mills's volume of the *Oxford Z. A.* are for the most part quoted from the original in the same sense and with a similar object by Dr. Hübschmann (no dilettante, but an able specialist) in his important essay in the *Jahrbücher f. prot. Theologie* for 1879.

NOTE ˣ, p. 395.

Much is said of Zarathustra in the Avesta, but legend has for the most part distorted his historical features, substituting a 'fantastic demigod' for the 'toiling prophet.' The exception to this is that part of the Yasna which contains the Gâthâs (chaps. xxviii.–liii.). 'Let the Zendist study the Gâthâs well,' says Dr. Mills, 'and then let him turn to the Yasts or the Vendîdâd; he will go from the land of reality to that of fable.' The observation is just, nor does that cautious historian, Prof. de la Saussaye, deny that in these songs we have a faithful and authentic portrait. Thanks to them, we can form a lively idea of the opposition which Zarathustra's preaching encountered, and of the mighty faith which sustained him under it. Often the prophet himself is the speaker; his family name (Spitâma) is mentioned, as well as the names of several of his relations and friends. Well may tradition expressly ascribe the Gâthâs to Zarathustra. We have next to ask when they were written. To fix the date of the songs is obviously to fix that of the singer. Shall we place it in the 14th century B.C. with Geldner, or, with cautious vagueness, between 1500 and 900 B.C. with Mills? Or shall we, with Spiegel, Justi, de Harlez, and Halévy, bring it down to the 8th century B.C., and suppose a strong Semitic influence on the founder of Zoroastrianism? From the point of view of a critical historian of Israel I must pronounce this to be wildly improbable, and Dr. West (*Journal of Royal Asiatic Soc.*, April, 1890, pp. 508, 509) has produced a noteworthy argument based on the difference between the name of God in the Persian cuneiform inscriptions and those used in the Gâthâs and in the later Avesta, to show that between Zarathustra and Darius we must allow a longer period than the Hebrew-influence hypothesis assumes. 'Thus, in the seventeen hymns of the Gâthâs we find Mazda 98 times alone, Ahura 47 times alone, Mazda Ahura (often separated by intermediate words to suit the metre) 64 times, and Ahura Mazda (often similarly separated) only 19 times, or $\frac{1}{12}$ of the whole number of occurrences. . . . In the later Avesta we only occasionally find Mazda and Ahura alone, or in the form Mazda Ahura, because the new form Ahura Mazda greatly preponderates; still the two words are always independent and separately declined. Turning to the Persian cuneiform inscriptions, we find a further change, as the name of the Supreme Being has become condensed into the single name Aûramazdâ, of which the former component is indeclinable in about 120 instances. . . . There are (only) two instances in which both components are declined . . . just sufficient to show that the old form of the name was not yet quite forgotten.' 'We have to account,' remarks Dr. West, 'for a change which the Avesta did not venture to make in the course of three centuries' (the period allowed on the Hebrew-influence hypothesis for the composition of the Avesta). Dr. Mills's treatment of the question of date is also well worth considering, though his exposition is sadly cramped (Introd. to part iii. of *Oxford Z.A.*). The interesting result follows—that spiritual prophecy is not peculiar to the Semites; Zarathustra was as true and as original a prophet as Isaiah and Jeremiah. The two latter consciously received a call from Jehovah; and so did Zarathustra from the same true God under his name Ahura (*Yasna*, xlii.). His special work was the reformation of the Iranian religion, but he grasped the ideas of his reform so firmly that we may with almost equal justice call him the founder of a new religion. There is philological proof that an organized system of worship had arisen before the separation of the Indian and Iranian peoples, nor can it be denied that the Indo-

Iranian religion contained a latent monotheism and an unconscious dualism.[1] The course of thought, however, was different in India and in Iran. The idea of an all-wise Creator never ripened in India, and consequently no interest was taken there in the moral problem of the origin of evil. A similar apathy was doubtless felt in Iran by the daêva-worshippers whom Zarathustra opposed. The great Iranian prophet developed, or helped to develope, the germs of a higher religion in a distinctly moral direction. Darmesteter indeed holds that Mazdeism pushed this development to an extreme; but it is precisely Zarathustra's consistency which entitles him to our sympathy and admiration. 'His thinking,' remarks Geldner, 'is conservative, self-restrained, practical, devoid on the whole of all that might be called fantastic and excessive.' Why a Christian apologist (Dr. Murray Mitchell) should depreciate the dualism of the Avesta, I do not understand. Speculatively, it is much stronger[2] than the imperfect attempts to grapple with the problem of evil in the O. T., and ethically the Zarathustrian insistence on the ultimate triumph of the good principle stands alone for its boldness and originality. The Gâthâs enable us to form a lively idea of the opposition which Zarathustra's preaching had to encounter from the daêva-worshippers, and of the mighty faith which sustained him under it. For further details, I gladly refer the reader to Geldner's article 'Zoroaster' in the *Encyclopædia Britannica*, which is a good specimen of critical construction vivified by imaginative sympathy.

NOTE y, p. 395.

Prof. de la Saussaye remarks, 'This religion (Mazdeism) had risen above the mythological standpoint, but is it on this account anti-mythological? And if not anti-mythological, must we, with Darmesteter, regard its doctrines as transformed myths? Both questions must be answered in the negative' (*Lehrbuch der Religionsgeschichte*, ii. 27). This seems substantially correct. It is only when we look at the two ends of Zoroastrian development, at the Gâthâs and at modern Parsism, that we can say that Mazdeism was anti-mythological in tendency. Looking at the Avesta apart from the Gâthic hymns, we should hesitate to affirm this. The Gâthâs however *are* anti-mythological in spirit, and in this do they not remind us of the Psalter? Mythic forms of expression may some-

---

[1] *Oxford Z.A.*, vol. i., Introd., p. lvii.
[2] See Mills on *Yasna*, xxx. and xlv. in *Oxford Z.A.*, vol. iii., and cf. West, *Pahlavi Texts*, vol. i., Introd., p. lxix. It should be mentioned that de Harlez ascribes *Yasna*, xxx. and xlv. (xliv.) to 'a poet different from the authors of the other hymns.' The supposition, however, is unnecessary.

times appear, but that does not prove much. How mythic in sound are many Christian phrases! With regard to Darmesteter's view (see *Ormazd et Ahriman*, and the *Oxford Z. A.*, part i.) nothing need be added to what de Harlez and others have said. Probably its gifted author would now express himself somewhat differently.

NOTE ᶻ, p. 396.

See Darmesteter, *Oxford Z.A.*, part i., p. lxviii., and comp. Spiegel, *Avesta*, Bd. ii., p. lxxi. f. ; *Eran. Alterthümer*, iii. 570, 578, 590. The good genii are said to derive strength from the invocation of their names by men and from 'the offerings of Zaothra (holy water) with Haoma (the juice of the yellow haoma) and Myazda (cooked flesh);' see *Yast*, viii. 17 &c. 'Bloody sacrifices are strictly speaking inconceivable on the principles of Parsism.' The tongue, and the left eye, and perhaps the ears, are specified in *Yasna*, xi. 4 as the parts of the slaughtered victim which belonged to Haoma. Strabo (xv. 372) declares that only the soul of the victim belonged to the gods. This however is inaccurate (cf. Herod. i. 132), but the offering of flesh was certainly symbolical, as stated in the text. For a clear description of the parts of the sacrificial service, see de Harlez, *Avesta*, Introd., pp. clxxix., clxxx. With what forms Zarathustra himself sacrificed, we do not know; he speaks in the Gâthâs not as a lawgiver but as a prophet. That he attached value to sacrifice, is certain; that the Gâthâs themselves as inspired forms of prayer and praise had a mystic importance in his eyes, is also certain. But he nowhere sanctions any of the most superstitious ideas respecting sacrifice. It is a misrepresentation when the later Avesta makes him declare the Haoma-offering to be the best means of repelling the evil one; at least, from *Yasna*, xlvii. 10 we may infer that Zarathustra opposed the haoma (or soma) drink of the daêva-worshippers. And if *Yasna*, xxxiii. 14 is not by Zarathustra himself, it is all the more valuable as the record of a school.

NOTE ᵃᵃ, p. 398.

Vend. xix. 27–34; *Yast*, xxii., cf. *Mînôkhired*, ii. 123, 124 (*Pahlavi Texts*, West, ii. 18, 19). The lovely maiden, fifteen years old, who meets the righteous soul at the end of the third night after death, can hardly have suggested to Mohammed the idea of the celestial Hurís (Haug). But at any rate, this Zoroastrian allegory suggested the Talmudic story of the three bands of ministering angels who meet the soul of the pious man, and the three bands of wounding angels who meet the bad man when he dies (*Ketūb* 104*a*).

Note ᵇᵇ, p. 399.

Yasna, xliii. 10, 'Apprends-nous par tes entretiens ce que nous devons te demander' (de Harlez). Or, 'Ask thou (thyself) our questions, those which shall be asked by us of thee' (Mills; cf. his commentary). Zarathustra seems, like the psalmists, to avoid giving scope to the imagination. Nowhere for instance do the Gâthâs speak of the Gaokerena tree, or connect the highest of blessings (immortality) with the drinking of its juice.

Note ᶜᶜ, p. 399.

These words were used in a lower sense afterwards; cf. *Yast*, xix. *in fine*, Plut., *de Iside*, 46, 47. But Zarathustra's idea of heaven survived in spite of this.

Note ᵈᵈ, p. 399.

On the Kinvat-bridge, see *Vend.* xiii. 3, xix. 29 &c., and cf. *Mînôkhired*, ii. 123, 124 (a striking description). The term is not yet a compound in the Gâthâs, see *Yasna*, xlv. 10, l. 13, where Mills translates 'the Judge's Bridge (lit., 'the bridge of the sorter out'). We have the same conception in Mohammed's Sirât, and in the Yorkshireman's 'Brig o' Dread.' Prof. Rhys has pointed out some Irish parallels (*Hibbert Lectures*, 1886, pp. 450, 451).

Note ᵉᵉ, p. 400.

For the teaching of Zarathustra see *Yasna*, xxx. 7–9, xliii. 5. Mills even thinks that there is a trace of the doctrine of the Resurrection in the Gâthâs. In *Yasna*, xxx. 7 he finds a prayer that 'in the future, and possibly at the Frashakard, the completion of progress, the created souls may be restored to a state of sinless happiness, and provided with bodies, as at the first' (comp. *Yast*, xix. 89). But at any rate Zarathustra did not raise the question, 'With what body do they come?'—nor did he transfer to a hero-prophet (Saoshyant) the divine act of raising the dead. He may have had a vague conception of the revival of bodies, but not a theory. Cf. also de Harlez, *Avesta*, Introd., p. clxxxv.

Note ᶠᶠ, p. 400.

In the Gâthâs, Saoshyantô is a name which indicates 'the apostles of the law, those who have deserved well of religion' (de Harlez). But elsewhere Saoshyant is a hero of the latter days, though we also find the name in the plural (*Yasna*, xxiv. 14). See *Yast*, xiii. 129, 'Whose name will be the victorious Saoshyant, and whose name will be Astvat-ereta. He will be Saoshyant (the Beneficent One), because he will benefit the whole bodily world; he will be Astvat-ereta (he who makes the bodily creatures rise up), because as a bodily creature and as a living creature he will stand against the destruction of the bodily creatures, to withstand the Drug (the Lie-demon) of the two-footed brood' (Darmesteter). The Bundahis is much more explicit. In chap. xxx., which probably closed the original work, we read, 'In the 57 years of Sôshyans they prepare all the dead, and all men stand up; whoever is righteous and whoever is wicked, every human creature, they rouse up from the spot where its life departs' (West's translation). Gaokerena is the Iranian 'tree of life,' a white haoma plant reckoned among the chief treasures of Ameretât (see p. 399); *Yast*, ii. 3. It is, so to speak, the ἰδέα of the earthly haoma (the Sanskrit soma), used in the sacrifices, which grows on the mountains (*Yasna*, x. 6–10), and has yellow flowers. Note that Gaokerena is never referred to in the Gâthâs. Zarathustra would not attach the highest of blessings to the drinking of this magical juice (cf. note ᶻ, at end). We can, I think, hardly justify the later Avesta by the analogy of Rev. xxii. 2. The description of which the tree of life forms a part in Revelation is purely symbolical (as *v.* 17 shows), and is more in the spirit of the Psalms of Solomon than of the Book of Enoch (see p. 412), though a still closer parallel is 2 Esdras ii. 12, cf. viii. 52.

NOTE ᵍᵍ, p. 401.

The two accounts of the lot of the wicked after the resurrection in *Bund.* xxx. are as follows. (1) 'Afterwards they set the righteous man apart from the wicked; and then the righteous man is for heaven (garôdmân), and they cast the wicked back to hell.' (2) 'Then all men shall pass into that melted metal (of the hills and mountains) and will become pure. When one is righteous, then it seems to him as though he walks continually in warm milk; but when wicked, then it seems to him in such manner as though, in the world, he walks continually in melted metal' (West, *Pahlavi Texts*, i. 124, 126). The second view is presumably the later. We find it again in the Mînôkhired, which expressly states that the soul of the wicked man 'must be in hell until the resurrection and future existence' (ii. 193), though in another passage the 'destruction and punishment of the wicked in hell' are said to be 'for ever and everlasting' (xl. 31; see however Dr. West's note).

NOTE ʰʰ, p. 401.

Comp. Mills's translation with the more flowing one of de Harlez: 'Afin que nous soyons d'âme sainte, d'esprit heureux; que nos corps soient pleins de majesté de l'éclat du monde meilleur; qu'ils y viennent, ô Ahura Mazda, brillant (de l'éclat) de la pureté parfaite, de la pureté éminemment belle; que nous te voyons, que nous parvenions jusqu'auprès de toi, perpétuellement attachés à toi.' This passage, though ancient, does not belong to the Gâthâs.

NOTE ⁱⁱ, p. 402.

Darmesteter infers from the notices of Zoroastrianism in Theopompus and elsewhere that dogmatic crystallization had already taken place by the end of the Achæmenian period. He admits however that the Zoroastrianism of the Avesta is without a precise dogmatic form.

NOTE ʲʲ, p. 403.

The Septuagint translator however may have taken a wider view of Isa. xxvi. 19. He renders, Ἀναστήσονται οἱ νεκροί, καὶ ἐγερθήσονται οἱ ἐν τοῖς μνημείοις. Equally broad is the statement in the Targum on this passage. Probably however these expressions are not intended to include non-Israelites (see p. 406).

NOTE ᵏᵏ, p. 404.

The idea of the supernatural dew is no doubt Palestinian (comp. Hos. xiv. 5a, with Hos. vi. 2). But 'lights' (אורת, elsewhere only 2 Kings iv. 39, where it means 'herbs') reminds us of the Avesta, where the 'endless lights' are the highest heaven where Ahura dwells. Cf. *Vend.* xix. 118, 119, and cf. Spiegel, *Avesta*, Bd. iii., Einleit., p. xxxix. This Zoroastrian phrase will not however illustrate the phrase 'father of lights' in James i. 17, on which see the patristic passages in Suicer, ii. 1480, 1481.

NOTE ˡˡ, p. 407.

On this formula, cf. Darmesteter, *Ormazd et Ahriman*, p. 239. The term *frashôkereti* means properly the renovation of the world, but afterwards came to be used of the Resurrection. See the *Oxford Z.A.*, and cf. de Harlez, *Les origines du Zoroastrisme*, p. 293, *Avesta*, Introd., p. clxxxv.

NOTE ᵐᵐ, p. 407.

'To sleep' is doubtless a primitive Hebrew phrase for 'to die' (see Job iii. 13, Ps. xiii. 3, Jer. li. 39, 57, and cf. the use of κοιμηθέντες and κεκοιμημένοι for the dead in N. T., e.g. Matt. xxvii. 52, Acts vii. 60, 1 Thess. iv. 14, 15). Its more precise shade of meaning depends on the theological stage of the writer who uses it. It may no doubt imply a scarcely appreciable degree of consciousness, but when moral distinctions have been admitted into Hades, it becomes merely a figure for the state of the soul between the two periods which are closed respectively by death and by the final judgment, and such 'sleep' may be accompanied (as 'Enoch' shows) by great, even though imperfect, joy or pain. We must not, however, with Canon Mason, suppose Ps. cxlix. 5 to represent 'the world with all its political and social forces as helplessly, though unconsciously, enthralled and swayed by the saints at rest' (*The Faith of the Gospel*, ed. 1, p. 217). Alas for a doctrine supported by such an exegesis! Obviously the 'couches' spoken of by the psalmist are not those of Hades (as in Isa. lvii. 2), but either those on which the rejoicing *khasīdīm* reclined at the feast which followed a Maccabæan victory, or those on which these pious warriors had so often sought in vain for sleep, and in subdued accents complained to their God. For the later Jewish views of the 'sleep' of the departed, see Enoch xxii., and a remarkable quotation from 4 Ezra in Drummond's *Jewish Messiah*, pp. 374-377. A noble Protestant view of the subject is eloquently expressed by Maclaren, *Manchester Sermons* (1865), pp. 104-110.

NOTE ⁿⁿ, p. 409.

The chief reward of righteousness, says Ewald, even in the earliest part of Proverbs, is 'the divine life, immortality.' 'As among the Greeks the mysteries encouraged ἡδυστέρας ἐλπίδας,' says Delitzsch, 'so in Israel the Khokma ('Wisdom') appears pointing the possessor of wisdom upwards.' Both critics argue from Prov. xv. 24 that Sheól is in process of becoming Gehenna, and from Prov. xii. 28 that the faith in a higher life was already so definite that a special word אַל־מָוֶת 'not-death,' 'immortality,' had been compounded to express it. Accepting this, it would be useless to deny that the phrases in Prov. ii. 19, v. 6, 'the path (paths) of life' (cf. Prov. x. 17, 'the way of life'), may at any rate include a reference to life after death, and we might then compare Ps. xvi. 11. But this is too bold; a mystical interpretation is not favoured by the contexts. The punishment of the wicked in Prov. xv. 24 (cf. vii. 27, ix. 18) consists in going prematurely to what Job calls 'the house of meeting for all living'

(Job xxx. 23). As for the supposed compound, the combination of אַל with a substantive is without a parallel. We might indeed read עַלְמוֹת (cf. Ps. cxxxix. 24), as Aquila may have read in Ps. xlviii. 15 (see Talm. Jer., *Moed katon*, 83, 2).[1] But the εἰς θάνατον of Sept. undoubtedly gives the better view of the text of Prov. xii. 28 (see *Job and Solomon*, p. 123). I will not deny that an account of Paradise analogous to that in Genesis, with both a tree and a fountain of life, may have been current when the earliest collection of proverbs was made (see Prov. x. 11, xi. 30, xiii. 12, 14, xiv. 27, xv. 4, xvi. 22), but that the 'wise men' before the Exile based any general theory upon this tradition, there seems no sufficient reason to suppose. And what of the greatest of the 'wise men,' whose horizon had been so much extended by the experiences of travel, the author of Job? According to Dr. Grätz, he was acquainted with the new doctrine of the Resurrection, which he represents Eliphaz and Bildad as adopting, and Job himself as repudiating.[2] This again is too bold. All that can safely be found in Job is the idea of 'a supra-mundane justice, which will one day pronounce in favour of the righteous sufferer, not only in this world (xvi. 18, 19, xix. 25, xlii.), so that all men may recognize his innocence, but also beyond the grave, the sufferer himself being in some undefined manner brought back to life, in the conscious enjoyment of God's favour (xiv. 13–15, and possibly xix. 26, 27).'[3] This however is an idea which the speaker caresses, but will not build his faith upon. The famous passage xix. 26, 27 is too corrupt to justify extracting from it the assured hope of immortality, which indeed would be in direct contradiction to Job's own statements in iii. 13–19.

NOTE [oo], p. 410.

'Αθάνατος here is probably a paraphrase. It is noteworthy that in Ecclus. xix. some scribes inserted a passage containing these words as rendered in the Greek (*v.* 19), οἱ δὲ ποιοῦντες τὰ ἀρεστὰ αὐτοῦ, ἀθανασίας δένδρον καρποῦνται, where ἀθανασίας must surely be a paraphrase of חַיִּים 'life.'

NOTE [pp], p. 411.

There may also be in parts of Enoch a dash of Essenism. See p. 449.

NOTE [qq], p. 412.

Cf. the inserted passage, Ecclus. xix. 19, already referred to, also John v. 39 (eternal life in the Scriptures). So too the study of the

[1] The Hexaplar Syriac however does not support this Talmudic statement.

[2] *Monatsschrift*, 1887, pp. 247–249.

[3] *Job and Solomon*, p. 104.

Law is a surer principle of immortality than the eating of the tree of life, according to the Targum of Jonathan on Gen. iii. Hellenistic Jews said the same thing of the practice of the laws of Wisdom (Wisd. vi. 19).

Note ʳʳ, p. 414.

But how strange a picture these writers give! They seem to imagine a gradual progress of the soul towards beatitude. For even the final judgment does not bring the righteous man into permanent bliss. We are told in Enoch xxv. 6 (cf. v. 8, 9) that those who eat of the tree of life shall (not, live for ever, but) 'live long on the earth.' This is through the influence of Isa. lxv. 22, which the writer in Enoch perhaps interprets like the Septuagint and the Targum (notice the allusion which follows to Isa. lxv. 19). The eternal state, then, is still in the future.

Note ˢˢ, p. 414.

See Justin Martyr, *Apol.* ii. 2, ὁ δὲ καὶ χάριν εἰδέναι ὡμολόγει, πονηρῶν δεσποτῶν τῶν τοιούτων ἀπηλλάχθαι γινώσκων καὶ πρὸς τὸν πατέρα καὶ βασιλέα τῶν οὐρανῶν πορεύεσθαι. And for the other part of his view, see *Dial. c. Tryph.*, cc. 5, 80.

Note ᵗᵗ, p. 414.

Comp. this writer's νῦν with the ἀπάρτι of Rev. xiv. 13. In 4 Macc. xiii. 14 we have a parallel to Luke xvi. 22 (Abraham's bosom). Nothing that the author says excludes the resurrection belief; he speaks as of a privilege of martyrs. But nothing that he says directly assumes it.

Note ᵘᵘ, p. 415.

Rev. xiii. 6. Prof. Spitta has made it clear (*Die Offenbarung des Johannes*, 1889, pp. 298,372), that τοὺς ἐν τῷ οὐρανῷ σκηνοῦντας is an editorial insertion—a gloss upon τὴν σκηνὴν αὐτοῦ. For the editor the σκηνή is not the earthly but the heavenly temple, and those who dwell in it are the martyrs. This however conflicts with the intention of the minor apocalypse to which (Revelation like Enoch being composite) Rev. xiii. in the main belongs, and implies a different eschatological conception from that of the writer of Rev. vi. 9–11, in which (cf. Rev. vii. 9) the souls of the martyred righteous are under the altar of the earthly temple in one of those 'storehouses' of which 2 Esdras iv. 41 speaks. That the 'dwellers in heaven' in Rev. xiii. 6 *are* the martyrs is clear from Rev. vii. 15, which the writer must have had in his mind; cf. also Rev. xii. 11, 12. In Heb. xii. 23 there may also be a reference to the martyrs of the Neronian persecution. So at least Renan thinks, but the phrase δίκαιοι τετελειωμένοι may equally well be interpreted like צַדִּיק גָּמוּר 'perfectly righteous,' *Kidduschin*, 40*b* (Wünsche, *Der bab. Talmud*, ii. 107). Psychologically such reverence for the martyrs is very intelligible (cf. Isa. xxvi. 19, Dan. xii. 2, 3). But we must not force allusions to it. Martyrdom may have been in St. Paul's mind when he wrote Phil. i. 23, but hardly when he wrote 2 Cor. v. 1–10. 'Witness-bearing' was surely the principal thing.

NOTE vv, p. 416.

The date of the Targum on the Psalms in its present form is fixed by its paraphrase of Ps. cviii. 11, which explains the 'fenced city' of 'Rome the wicked,' and 'Edom' of 'Kostantina' (Constantinople). The writer lived, therefore, it would seem, before A.D. 476. The peculiarities of this Targum are the same as those of the Targum on Job; note אַנְגְּלֵי, ἄγγελος (elsewhere only in Targum shēnī on Esther). See Bacher's studies on these Targums, Grätz's *Monatsschrift*, 1871, p. 208 &c. (Job); 1872, pp. 408 &c., 463 &c. (Psalms).

NOTE ww, p. 416.

See e.g. the Targum on Ps. xviii. 29, xlix. 10 &c., l. 10, lvi. 14, lxiii. 4, 5, xc. 16, ci. 6, for the recompense of the righteous; and on Ps. xlix. 15, l. 21, lxviii. 15, lxxxiv. 7, cxxv. 5, cxl. 11, for the torments of the wicked. Is the Targumist altogether wrong in his general view of Ps. xlix. 15? It need hardly be added that 'life' is often interpreted as 'everlasting life' (a phrase which first occurs in Dan. xii. 2); see Targ. on Pss. xvii. 14, xxi. 5, xxx. 6, lxvi. 9. Similarly at Ps. lxi. 7, 'generation and generation' becomes 'the generations of this and of the coming age.' Oddly but characteristically in Ps. lxxxix. 49 'death' is paraphrased 'the angel of death.' The dogmatizing exegesis of this Targum may be contrasted with the faithfulness of the Septuagint version. Once, in the heading of Ps. lxv. (lxvi.), it speaks unnecessarily of the resurrection; interpreting the 'refreshment' (ἀναψυχή) of *v.* 12 eschatologically. Also at the end of Ps. xvii. its rendering of תמונתך, τὴν δόξαν σου seems designed to exclude a figurative vision of God in the present life. Notice too the numerous references to a future life and retribution in the Targum on Koheleth, designed, as it would seem, to neutralize the effect of Koheleth's pessimistic tendency.

NOTE ˣˣ, p. 417.

We may infer this partly from Mark xii. 26 (Matt. xxii. 31, 32), and its Talmudic parallel (see p. 383, note ¹), partly from the fact that the author of 1 Maccabees refers (1 Macc. ii. 59, 60) to the stories but not to the predictions in the Book of Daniel, the angelology and eschatology of which were uncongenial to him.

NOTE ʸʸ, p. 417.

It is incredible that the Stoic idea of εἰμαρμένη was current in any Jewish school; even Ecclesiastes does not contain it.

NOTE ᶻᶻ, p. 418.

The criticism of the accounts of the Essenes in Josephus has passed into a new phase owing to the researches of Lucius and Ohle, especially the latter.¹ Both these critics agree that the treatise *De Vitâ Contemplativâ* (a glorification of ' the Ἐσσαῖοι or Θεραπευταί), which passes as Philo's is spurious, and Ohle thinks moreover that sections 12 and 13 of Philo's *Quod omnis probus liber*, which relate to the Essenes, were interpolated by the same hand which had already fabricated the former treatise. As to Josephus, very little indeed is left by this 'vexatious scrutiny' (to use a phrase of De Quincey's). Accepting Zeller's view of the essentially neo-Pythagorean character of the Essenes of Philo and Josephus, Ohle undertakes to show that the accounts of Essenism in *War*, ii. 8 and *Ant.* xviii. 1 are also spurious. Nothing is left in Josephus but a few scattered notices of a very simple Essenism, which may be naturally viewed as a development of Pharisæan piety. Its professors may have formed an עֵדָה קְדוֹשָׁה, like that of which Simon ben Menasya was president, and which devoted one third of the day to the Torah, another to prayer, and another to manual labour (Bacher, *Die Agada der Tannaiten*, ii. 489). Frankel's view, which is rather peremptorily rejected by our lamented Lightfoot, is therefore substantially correct; Essenism is an indi-

¹ Ohle, ' Die Essener: eine krit. Untersuchung der Angaben des Josephus,' in *Jahrbücher f. prot. Theol.*, Band xiv. (1888). See also his *Beiträge zur Kirchengeschichte, Die pseudophilonischen Essäer und die Therapeuten* (1888); and cf. Lucius, *Die Therapeuten und ihre Stellung in der Gesch. der Askese* (1880), and his *Der Essenismus in seinem Verhältniss zum Judenthum* (1881), and cf. Schürer's and Harnack's reviews of these books in the *Theol. Lit.zeitung*. Mr. Morrison duly refers to these books at the end of his excellent chapter on the Essenes in *The Jews under Roman Rule* (1890). Schürer's final opinion will doubtless be given later. Jewish scholars do not seem as yet to have taken notice of Ohle.

genous product, an exaggerated Pharisaism. And if we ask what was the object of the fabricator and the interpolator whom Ohle claims to have brought to light, we learn that it was to promote the interests of a Christian sect or society (De Quincey then was not wholly wrong), strongly influenced by neo-Pythagoreanism.

All this is very plausible. It explains why there is no distinct reference to such a striking organization as that of the supposed Essenes either in the Gospels or in the Talmuds; it is in harmony with the fact that a neo-Pythagorean current became stronger and stronger from Cicero's time onwards, not less than with Zeller's weighty judgment that the accounts of the Essenes have a neo-Pythagorean colour. Still I hesitate to accept such a radical criticism as Ohle's. There is much in Josephus's account of the Essenes which altogether tallies with our previous expectations, and can be explained either from native Jewish or from Zoroastrian beliefs. Josephus may have believed that there was some historical connexion between Pythagoras and the Essenes (*Ant.* xv. 10, 4), just as Diodorus Siculus states (v. 28) that ὁ Πυθαγόρου λόγος prevailed among the Gauls, and Clement of Alexandria professes to know that Pindar was a Pythagorean.[1] This was perfectly natural for such a philhellenic writer as Josephus, but it is somewhat less obvious for us. Why should we refer a theory reported to have been current in Judæa to Pythagoras or to Plato when this philosopher himself most likely borrowed it from the East? Celibacy for instance, which the treatise *Quod omnis probus liber* wrongly ascribed to Philo, but not Josephus, states to have been the Essenian rule,[2] and which may perhaps have been neo-Pythagorean, is certainly not congenial to the Greek nature. True, it is not congenial to Judaism either; 'marriage is honourable in all men' (Heb. xiii. 4) was a sentence which found an echo in all Jewish hearts. Still it *was* a Jewish idea that connubial intercourse was inconsistent with ceremonial purity (see Ex. xix. 15, 1 Sam. xxi. 4, 5, and cf. 1 Cor. vii. 5, Enoch lxxxiii. 2 [3]); a little extremism among some of the Essenes and exaggeration in Josephus will account for the representations of the latter. Remember, too, that Zoroastrianism, though it has no favour for celibacy, represents the procreation of children as ceasing in the coming golden age.

---

[1] *Strom.* lib. v., p. 598B (ed. 1641).

[2] Philo, *Opera*, Mangey, ii. 633, 634; cf. Jos., *War*, ii. 8, 9. The statement in Jos. *l.c.* that the Essenes 'neglect wedlock' is qualified by what is said in § 13. Remember too that the founder of the Elcesaite sect, who represents perhaps an Essenian Judæo-Christianity, is said to have 'compelled marriage' (Epiphanius, ed. Oehler, i. 96).

[3] This passage of Enoch is important because it relates to the conditions of mystic revelations such as were well known among the Essenes.

And above all, the Essenian belief respecting the soul, though it may look neo-Pythagorean, can be adequately explained without the help of Zoroaster's pupil, as Clement of Alexandria calls him, Pythagoras.[1] The amount of reference to Greek mythology is striking, but is of no great significance. The history of the Jewish war was originally written in Hebrew, and Epaphroditus or some other literary friend must have assisted Josephus in the work of translation.[2] To him may be due these excursions into such a very unphilosophical region. It is noteworthy that one of the most characteristic Pythagorean doctrines—that of transmigration of souls—is perhaps (see p. 417) ascribed in Josephus, not to the Essenes, but to the Pharisees.

Lightfoot in his *Colossians* and Hilgenfeld in his *Ketzergeschichte* have argued very ably for a partly Zoroastrian origin of Essenism, and yet I doubt whether all that the former ascribes to Zoroastrianism is really Essenian. For instance, was there ever such a thing as 'Essene worship of the sun'? Our Josephus states, it is true, that before sunrise the Essenes utter nothing of a profane character, but only πατρίους τινὰς εἰς αὐτὸν (sc. τὸν ἥλιον) εὐχὰς, ὥσπερ ἱκετεύοντες ἀνατεῖλαι (*War*, ii. 8, 5). This Lightfoot compares with another passage in the same chapter, which describes how the Essenes carefully buried polluting substances, ὡς μὴ τὰς αὐγὰς ὑβρίζοιεν τοῦ θεοῦ (§ 9). I admit that by τοῦ θεοῦ the sun-god is meant, and I will add that ἱκετεύοντες ἀνατεῖλαι vividly expresses the mythic sentiment of the constantly repeated conflicts between light and darkness, in which human prayers can aid.[3] But surely Lightfoot, who has thoroughly proved this to be the meaning of the phrase, takes both this and the other passage too literally. If it is 'vain to speculate' as to the original Hebrew of the two passages quoted from the *Jewish War*, it is certainly unfair to make Josephus responsible for every detail of Greek phraseology in the translation (which is probably something more than a translation). It seems impossible that any genuinely Jewish sect should have offered worship to the sun even without the Magian rite referred to in Ezek. viii. 17b, or that if it did so there should be no indignant reference to this in the Gospels and the

---

Clement of Alexandria describes both Pythagoras and Plato as τὰ πλεῖστα καὶ γενναιότατα τῶν δογμάτων ἐν βαρβάροις μαθόντας (*Strom.* i. p. 303C), and elsewhere reports the tradition that Pythagoras explained the teaching of 'Zoroaster the Magian, the Persian' (*Strom.* i. p. 304B). In accordance with this view he turns Er, the hero of Plato's famous myth in the *Republic* (Book x.), into Zoroaster. Other writers confound Zoroaster with a Chaldæan wise man, the instructor of Pythagoras (so e.g. Iamblichus, *Vit. Pythag.*, c. 19). Is it possible that there is no kernel of truth in these legendary stories, as Zeller would have us believe? Orientalists will certainly not think so.

[2] See Jos., *Ant.*, Pref. 2.

[3] See Rhys, *Hibbert Lectures* (1866), pp. 295, 296.

Talmud. It is useless to quote later heretical sects (see Epiphanius quoted by Hilgenfeld); we are speaking now of one of the three recognized Jewish schools. I do not however deny that the Essenes may have had a custom which was to a certain extent of Zoroastrian origin. It was a custom which they shared with other Jews, but had adopted with special zest—I mean that of saying the first prayer at daybreak (before the sun shone forth, Talm. Jer., *Berachoth*, i. 2). No one, I think, who reads the blessing יוצר אור will fail to see that it has a reference, partly polemical, to Zoroastrianism ; now it was this blessing and the Sh'ma which had to be recited at dawn (see p. 283) Ordinary Jews, though well aware of this religious duty (see Ps. v. 4, Wisd. xvi. 28), would not be very precise in its performance (see the curious licence granted to royal princes and the like in *Berachoth, l. c.*). But the Essenes, from their habits of early labour, and perhaps (cf. Enoch lxxxiii. 11) from having been instructed in the symbolism of the dawn (see below), would be strict observers of the custom. It would seem as if Josephus's assistant or editor turned this innocent practice, which may have been accompanied by an uplifting of the hands (cf. Ps. xxviii. 2) towards the first streaks of light, into an act of worship which was doubtless common in the east as it is said still to be in India. The biographer of Akbar tells us how his hero 'has been called a Zoroastrian, because he recognized in the sun the sign of the presence of the Almighty,' and we all know how in Tertullian's time a familiar Christian custom received an equally gross misinterpretation.[1]

There remains of course the possibility that this and some other details are merely the romantic inventions of an interpolator. This will have attractions for some readers, but I would warn them not to carry the hypothesis too far. An interpolator would hardly have been so bold if there had not been some *point d'appui* in the genuine Josephus. Indeed, we want the Essenes to account both for certain phenomena of the later sects, and also for some parts of the Book of Enoch and the Book of Jubilees. For the sects, I may refer to Hilgenfeld, *Die Ketzergeschichte des Urchristenthums* ; for the Book of Jubilees to Rönsch's treatise, p. 428. In the Book of Enoch I may mention passages like chaps. vi. (list of angels), lxix. (list of angels again, and a singular passage against written legal declarations), lxxxiii. (notice 1, celibacy in connexion with prophecy, and 2, how Enoch praises the 'Lord of judgment' at the sight of the rising sun, alluding to the symbolical meaning of the dawn, viz. the great final judgment, which had probably something to do with the so-called 'sun-worship' of the Essenes), xcviii. (repugnance to orna-

---

[1] Malleson, *Akbar*, p. 163 ; Tylor, *Primitive Culture*, ii. 387.

ments and to places of worldly dignity), and above all cviii. (love of apocalyptic prophecy, asceticism, Zoroastrianizing phraseology). I have not quoted lxxxix. 73, though it certainly points in an Essenian direction, for a reason indicated already (p. 375). My list of Essenian or semi-Essenian passages is a cautiously brief one ; Oscar Holtzmann, I see, still holds that Essenian passages may be found in what is generally considered the oldest part of the Book of Enoch (*Theol. Lit.ztg.,* Oct. 4, 1890, col. 497). Would it not be better to say, Essenian in tendency? Tideman (*Theol. Tijdschrift,* 1875, p. 261 &c.) actually ascribes the whole of chaps. lxxxiii.–xci. to an Essene. I cannot myself be so positive. But the small esteem in which Enoch was held by the later Jews (see Drummond, *The Jewish Messiah,* p. 72) seems to suggest that this book was felt to contain something out of the line of normal Jewish thought. I presume that Dillmann may be followed in regarding the Ethiopic version, though not made from the original, as for most purposes sufficiently accurate.

NOTE [aaa], p. 418.

Jos., *War,* ii. 8, 11. Observe that Enoch too (xxii. 1) places Hades beyond the ocean in the west.

NOTE [bbb], p. 419.

The Pharisaic and Essenian belief in the judgment may help to account for the ready acceptance of the custom of praying at dawn.

NOTE [ccc], p. 420.

This idea is due to Hilgenfeld, *Die Ketzergeschichte des Urchristenthums,* pp. 146, 147. Very various accounts are given of the fravashis (or, in the Pahlavi Texts, fravâhars). In the later Zoroastrian theology the soul alone seems to be responsible for the man's actions, and to be rewarded or punished accordingly. But in the Avesta (except in the Gâthâs, where the fravashis are not mentioned) the 'souls' and the 'fravashis' are often evidently identified (see e.g. the passage from the Yasna cited above), and in *Bundahis,* ii. 9, 10 it is distinctly implied that assuming a body rendered the fravâhars liable to death. The Bundahis is considered by Dr. West to be a translation or epitome of one of the twenty-one ancient Zoroastrian Scriptures ; it would be hypercritical to reject a statement in such perfect harmony with the idealizing, personifying spirit of Mazdeism. That the fravashis originally meant the spirits of the dead (Lat. *manes*), is certain ; but that this conception early mingled with another— that of the heavenly prototypes of all beings of the good creation, which were objectified and regarded as the Sabáoth or 'heavenly hosts' were by the Jews (see p. 282), is equally certain. The conception of prototypes seems to be of Sumero-Accadian origin; 'my god,' or 'my goddess' in the Babylonian penitential psalms, is to be understood of a guardian spirit, equivalent to the worshipper's 'better self,' or, in other words, of a 'fravashi' (Tiele, *Bab. ass. Geschichte*, p. 554; cf. Ragozin, *Media*, in 'Story of the Nations'). On this subject see further de Harlez, *Avesta*, Introd., p. cxix. &c.; Mills, *Oxford Z. A.* iii. 279; Casartelli, *Philosophy of the Mazdayasnian Religion under the Sassanids*, p. 137, &c.; and cf. Spiegel, *Eran. Alterthumskunde*, ii. 93, Geldner, Kuhn's *Zeitschr.*, 1881, p. 522, &c.

Note ddd, p. 421.

Among the things which the Talmud describes as created before the world was, i.e. as pre-existent in the divine plan, are the Law (cf. p. 358), the throne of glory, the sanctuary, the patriarchs, Israel, he Messiah, and repentance. So *Tanchuma, Nissa*, 11, cf. *Taanith*, 5a, *Baba bathra*, 75a, on the heavenly Jerusalem (cf. p. 274).

Note eee, p. 421.

Die religiöse Poesie der Juden in Spanien, pp. 135–137 (see Hebrew text at end of volume). The 'treasury' spoken of is the storehouse of souls (גוף, see *Yebamoth*, 62a) finely described in *Daniel Deronda*, chap. xliii. On the doctrine of pre-existence of souls, cf. Julius Müller, *The Christian Doctrine of Sin*, ii. 76–78, Delitzsch, *Biblical Psychology*, p. 44. Some have tried, but in vain, to find an allusion to the doctrine in Ps. cxxxix. 15. That it appears full-blown in Wisd. viii. 20 (cf. Farrar's note), and in Philo (cf. Drummond, *Philo Judæus*, i. 336–339)—both products of Hellenistic Judaism—is undeniable.

Note fff, p. 424.

St. Paul's use of the words σκεῦος and σκῆνος for the body, does not prove him to be a Hellenist; a strict Palestinian Jew might have used the same figures. His idea of the future state reminds us rather of the oldest writer in 'Enoch' than of the Book of Wisdom. Nor is there perhaps more than a superficial resemblance between Rom. vii. 24 and Plato's words in the *Phædo* compared by Clement of Alexandria (*Strom.* iii. p. 433A). [But cf. Pfleiderer, *Urchristenthum*, p. 299.]

Note ggg, p. 425.

See Grätz, *Kohélet*; and cf. Band iii. of his *Geschichte*.
I think it fair to add some sentences from M. Montet's essay in

vol. ix. of the *Revue de l'histoire des religions* (1884) :—' Après des siècles d'une douloureuse expérience, je veux dire après avoir constaté les profonds déficits de la religion, après avoir exprimé par la voix de ses penseurs l'angoisse qu'il en ressentait, Israel se trouve en contact avec deux civilisations, dont l'une lui apporte l'idée de la résurrection des corps, et l'autre celle de l'immortalité de l'âme. Voilà les secrets besoins de son cœur satisfaits. Repoussera-t-il les solutions qu'on lui propose, parce qu'elles lui viennent de l'étranger ? Non ; le besoin de croire l'emportera sur le besoin de haïr.'
' Arrivé par les influences étrangères qu'il a subies, par l'idée mazdéenne de la résurrection des corps et la notion grecque de l'immortalité de l'âme, à la conviction qu'il vivra au delà le la tombe, il pense, comme il est chair et qu'à la mort son corps cessera de vivre, que c'est sa chair qui revivra, que c'est son corps qui ressuscitera. Ainsi, lorsqu'on lui dit que la vie est éternelle, il pense au sang qui renferme cette vie, et qui, comme elle, ne périra point. L'immortalité de l'âme, à son point de vue, c'est donc la révivification du sang, c'est la résurrection du corps.'

M. Montet apparently held in 1884 that the germs of a belief in the resurrection deposited in Israel by Persia had to be fertilized by a doctrine derived from another civilization, viz. that of the immortality of the soul, derived from Alexandria. But in 1890, in deference, it would seem, to M. de Harlez, and in opposition not less to Spiegel than to Geldner, he pronounces the antiquity of the resurrection-doctrine in Zoroastrianism as yet unproven. ' As to the resurrection of the body,' he says, ' it is, if we may so express it, a Greek thought in Judaic garb. . . . . The dogma of the immortality of the soul is founded on a dualism—the absolute distinction between the body and the soul—which is quite foreign to the anthropology of the Semitic races. Plato, and after him Platonic Judaism, conceived the soul as an immaterial principle, locked up within the body, and liberated from its prison by the destruction of its mortal envelope.[1] The persistence of life, and its unlimited duration, could therefore only present itself to their minds in the form of the immortality of the immaterial principle in the human person. But the soul was inseparable from the body, to the Jew opposed to Hellenism ; for, though subject in spite of himself—say, unwittingly—to the emancipating and liberal action of the Greek philosophy, he retained with all the force of his will and of his narrow patriotism as much as he could of the spiritual inheritance of his ancestors. Like the Hebrew (? as a Hebrew), he believed in the unity of the human being and in

---

[1] Against the view that the notion, common to Philo and Bardesanes, of the body as the grave of the soul is necessarily derived from Greek speculation, see Gruppe, *Griechische Mythen*, i. 664.

the materiality of his soul; he was convinced of the truth of the formula of the *tōrāh*, "The soul of the flesh is in the blood" (Lev. xvii. 11), "The blood is the soul" (Deut. xii. 23). It is evident that with such an anthropological conception there could be no question of the immortality of the soul, except as a resurrection of the entire individuality, body and soul. . . . . Thus the trust in a life to come, loudly asserted by Greek philosophy, became popular in Israel in two different but closely related forms, that of the immortality of the soul, and that of the resurrection of the body' (*Asiatic Quarterly Review*, Oct. 1890, pp. 337, 338). Over against these statements, so far as they relate to Greek influence on Palestine, I would place a sentence from M. Halévy, with whom I am glad to be sometimes in agreement :—' Les juifs d'Alexandrie, ne pouvant songer à vaincre le paganisme par la force, entreprennent une espèce de transaction avec l'esprit grec, mais avec l'arrière-pensée de l'absorber entièrement un jour ; en Palestine personne ne pensa à transiger : on était ou franchement grec, ou franchement juif.' *Mélanges d'épigraphie et d'archéologie sémitiques* (1874), p. 154.

NOTE hhh, p. 425.

See Preface, p. xxxii. We must remember, too, with regard to Hellenistic literature, that the Judaism carried to Egypt under the early Ptolemies had, according to my theory, been already in some degree Zoroastrianized. No wonder if there are some traces of Zoroastrianism in the works of Philo (Siegfried, *Philo von Alexandrien*, p. 141).

APPENDICES.

APPENDIX I.

LAST WORDS ON MACCABÆAN PSALMS AND OTHER POINTS.

I. It will be convenient to chronicle here the results of some former writers, and then to sum up my own.

The 17 Maccabæan psalms admitted by Theodore are these,—xliv., xlvii., lv.-lx., lxii., lxix., lxxiv., lxxix., lxxx., lxxxiii., cviii., cix., cxliv. Rudinger (Melancthon's former colleague) selects these twenty-four—xliv., xlix., lvii., lx., cviii., lxvi., lxviii., lxxvi., lxxiii., lxxiv., lxxix., lxxvii., lxxx., lxxxviii., lxxxix., xc., cxix., cxx., cxxi., cxxiii., cxxv., cxxix., cxxx., cxxxiv. (he leaves it open with regard to xxvi. and xxviii.). Calvin admits that Pss. xliv. and lxxiv., Vitringa that not only Pss. lxxiv. and lxxix. but also lxxv., lxxx., and lxxxix. are Maccabæan (see Vitringa on Isa. xxiv.). Let us pass to the too brilliant but keen-eyed Hitzig. In his first work on the Psalter (1835-36) he lays down that from Ps. lxxiii. onwards all the psalms belong to the Maccabæan age. In his second (1863-65) he explains that some psalms in Book III. come from the years which preceded the insurrection, and several in Book V. from the times of John Hyrcanus, Aristobulus, and Alexander Jannæus. Olshausen goes even further, and refers most of the psalms even in the earlier books to the Syrian or Maccabæan period (the latest belonging to the reign of John Hyrcanus).

It were unfair not to add a reference to two of our oldest living scholars—Reuss and Grätz. The former, who, veteran as he is, has this year published a second edition of his *Gesch. der heil. Schriften des A. T.*, mentions these as Maccabæan psalms,—xliv., liv.-lvi., lix., lx., lxii., lxiv., lxxi., lxxiv., lxxv.-lxxvii., lxxix., lxxxiii., lxxxvi., lxxxviii.-xc., xciv., xcvi.-cii., cxv., cxvi., cxviii., cxxxii., cxxxviii., cxl., cxlii., cxliii., cxliv., cxlviii., cxlix. Grätz in his commentary (1882-83) gives the following,—xxx., xliv., lxxiv., lxxxiii., cxv.-cxviii., cxliv., cxlviii.-cl. Post-Maccabæan are, cxxxiv.-cxxxvi., (cf. *Psalmen*, Einleit., pp. 48-50). Pre-Maccabæan, but Greek, i., cxix., cxl., cxli., cxlv. ?

The psalms which I have myself ventured to regard as Maccabæan are these,—xx., xxi., xxxiii., xliv., lx., lxi., lxiii., lxxiv., lxxix., lxxxiii., ci., cviii., cxv.–cxviii., cxxxv.–cxxxviii., cxlv.–cxlvii. ? cxlviii.–cl. Those which I have referred to the pre-Maccabæan Greek period are, xvi. ? xlii. and xliii., xlv., lxviii., lxxii., lxxiii. ? lxxxvi. lxxxvii., cxix., cxxxix. ? cxl.–cxliii. ? cxliv.

The importance of our controversy consists in this. We have but one first-class authority for the Maccabæan period,[1] and if we can add to this at least twenty-seven contemporary psalms, our picture of the times will gain greatly in human and religious interest. I indulge the hope that we *may* do so, and that Schürer, in re-editing his survey of the later Jewish literature of Palestine, will be able to include more than the four psalms (viz. xliv., lxxiv., lxxix., and lxxxiii.) on which, when he first wrote, there was 'already a wide-spread consensus.' In the scanty space which remains I wish to examine the external evidence which some have pronounced to make the theory of Maccabæan psalms impossible, and to meet certain objections drawn from the Septuagint Psalter.

1. As to the alleged evidence of the Apocrypha, the real or supposed points of contact between which and the Psalter have been collected by Ehrt (*Abfassungszeit*, &c., pp. 121–132). From the parallelisms in Baruch this writer concludes that the Hebrew Psalter, including Ps. cxvi. (cf. Bar. iv. 20*b* with Ps. cxvi. 2*b*) was already in the hands of the writer (or writers) of Baruch, who lived 'at the close of the Persian rule,' and from those in Ecclesiasticus that the Hebrew Psalter, including Pss. xxxiii., cxv., cxl., cxli., was known to the original writer of the book (i.e. either in 193 or in 173 B.C.), and the Greek to his grandson the translator (i.e. soon after 132 B.C.).[2] It is however in general difficult to show that any particular psalm is referred to, and Ehrt's list requires sifting. Ecclus. xxii. 27 does perhaps allude to Ps. cxli. 3, though not to the Sept. version, and this suggests placing Ps. cxli. before the Maccabæan revolt (cf. p. 66). I am not convinced, however, that Ecclus. xv. 19 is dependent on Ps. xxxiii. 18. The phrase 'His eyes are upon them that fear him' is not at all original; the idea is already found in Prov. xv. 3, xxii. 12. Of course clear allusions to pre-Maccabæan psalms would not surprise me, but I can only succeed in finding one (or, at most, three; see note °, p. 128) in Ecclus. i.–l.; in li. 1–12 (an artificial psalm; see p. 127) there are two. I cannot enter here into the date of Ecclesiasticus and Baruch. Inadequate as Gifford's treatment of the Book of Baruch is (Wace's *Apocrypha*, ii. 251), it is more critical than Ehrt's, but the latter holds a safer view than Edersheim's (*ibid.* p. 9) on the date of Sirach. Nor will I discuss the 'external evidence' adduced

---

[1] On the obscure Talmudic passages, see Derenbourg, *Histoire*, pp. 56–59.

[2] Against the argument based upon Ecclesiasticus, cf. Frankel, *Vorstudien zu der Septuaginta*, p. 22 note, Grätz, *Psalmen*, i. 47.

by Ehrt from 1 Maccabees, for why should one deny that the author of 1 Maccabees can have read the complete Hebrew, and the translator the complete Greek Psalter? See above, p. 58, note [h]; p. 93, note [2]; p. 104, note [n].

2. As to the argument from 1 Chron. xvi. 36*a*, which forms part of the cento of psalm-passages in 1 Chron. xvi. 8–36*a*. It is urged by Ewald and others that since *v*. 36*a* (=Ps. cvi. 48) is the closing doxology of Book IV., the fivefold division of the Psalter had already been made in the time of the Chronicler, after which no fresh psalms were added to the collection. But (*a*) it is not certain that any part of Ps. cvi. is quoted in 1 Chron. xvi.; *vv*. 34–36*a* consist of liturgical formulæ, which were no more composed solely for use in Ps. cvi. than the doxology attached to the Lord's Prayer was originally formulated solely to occupy its present position.[1] It is highly probable that a doxology was uttered by the congregation at the close of every psalm used in the temple service,[2] and there is no reason why not only the doxology in *v*. 36 but the two preceding verses should not have been attached by the Chronicler to the psalm which he had made up simply as liturgical formulæ. (*b*) Even were it otherwise, we are bound to admit that Simon the Maccabee, as high priest, had power to deal as he thought best with the provisionally closed temple hymn-book.

3. The Canon of the Hagiographa (*k'thūbhīm*), it is said, was definitively closed in the time of Nehemiah. In 2 Macc. ii. 13 a tradition is quoted from the 'records' and from the 'memoirs of Nehemiah' to the effect that Nehemiah, when founding a library, brought together in it the books concerning the kings and prophets, and the works of David (τὰ τοῦ Δαβίδ). Well, it is possible that the patriotic governor, in imitation of the Persian kings, and perhaps remembering Hezekiah (Prov. xxv. 1), founded a library, in which he placed such historical and religious documents as he could find. We do not know that he did so; the author of 2 Maccabees was most probably taken in by a mere forgery.[3] But in any case Nehemiah did not thereby 'close the Hebrew Canon,' which was still open in the time of Sirach,[4] and some parts of which were still the subject of discussion at the close of the first century A.D. I shall hardly be

---

[1] See Taylor, *The Teaching of the Twelve Apostles*, p. 116.

[2] See my commentary, Introd., p. xv., and cf. Grätz, *Monatsschrift*, 1872, pp. 482–496.

[3] See above, p. 12, and cf. Rawlinson, *Speaker's Comm. on the Apocrypha*, ii. 116.

[4] This is Dillmann's inference from the Prologue to Sirach. In the book of Sirach itself, however, he can find no testimony to the Psalter, Proverbs, and Chronicles.

expected to discuss seriously the tradition reported by Origen and Hilary,[1] which ascribes the collection and arrangement of the psalms to Ezra; for this is simply based upon the fable in 2 (4) Esdras xiv. 37-50.

More important are the objections drawn from the Septuagint version of the Psalms. It is asked, 1. How are we to account for the fact that none of the psalms are ascribed in this version to the age of the Maccabees? But of course the Egyptian Jewish community received no information on the subject of Maccabæan psalms. It was not the interest of the Jerusalem editors to publish the recent origin of a portion of the psalms. The title of Ps. cx., for instance, shows that the psalm was regarded as worthy of having been written in the Davidic age. One thing the Egyptian Jewish translators do assert, viz. that psalms continued to be composed in the period of the second temple. They do this by ascribing certain psalms (cxxxviii., cxlvi.-cxlviii.) to Haggai and Zechariah, who, as in the Talmud (with Malachi), are symbolic representatives of the earlier period to which they belong.

2. Another Septuagint difficulty is this. How comes it that the Alexandrine translator (on whose date see pp. 12, 83) misunderstands both headings of and phrases in several of those psalms which (according to the hypothesis) belong to the Greek age? Instances of the former case occur in Pss. xvi. and lvi.-lx., and of the latter in Ps. cx. Similar objections may be raised to any historical hypothesis, however probable, and thoroughly decisive answers must be wanting until some private journal of the actors of history is discovered. I do not myself feel the objections to be important. As for the titles, the Jewish scribes themselves may have forgotten their meaning at the time when the temple with its music was reorganized and the Psalter re-edited by Simon (see pp. 9, 11). Nor has it been proved that the complete Greek Psalter was in existence much before the Christian era (see p. 12). And as for the mistaken sense of some passages, how hard it must have been to read Hebrew with accuracy before the square character became general! How incorrectly, as it would seem, even Ben Sira rendered many passages of his own grandfather's work into Greek! Can we be surprised, then, at the occasional ill success of the translator of the psalms, even when he was perhaps a contemporary of some of the psalmists?

Three monographs on Maccabæan psalms may in conclusion be mentioned. De Jong, *Disquisitio de Psalmis Maccabaicis* (Lugd. Bat. 1857). Ehrt, *Abfassungszeit und Abschluss des Psalters zur Prüfung*

---

[1] Origen, ii. 524a, Hilary, 6, and other passages, ap. Lagarde, *Novæ Psalterii Græci editionis specimen* (1887), p. 7.

der Frage nach Makkabäerpsalmen historisch-kritisch untersucht (Leipzig, 1869). Himpel, *Ueber angebliche makkabäische Psalmen*, in the *Tübinger Quartalschrift*, 1870, pp. 403-473.

II. There are still some points of interest upon which, had space permitted, I would gladly have spoken at length in this Appendix. For instance, (1) there is the great question of metre. That there is a tendency to metre in the psalms and in other Biblical books seems to me very probable indeed, and I venture to express the conviction that some writers (notably the learned and acute David Günzburg, *Revue critique*, 24 mai, 1880) have gone too far in the opposite direction to Bickell, whose theory, bold as it may be, has led him to some very acceptable corrections of the text.[1] (2) Then there is the question of the origin and purpose of the psalm-titles. Dean Perowne's quotation from a too little known book, Stähelin's *Specielle Einleitung* (*Psalms*, i. 95), would be a good starting-point for an inquiry. It was certainly not the custom of Arab poets to inscribe their names over their songs, as Keil stated; the songs were transmitted, as has been remarked (p. 210, note g). No such institution as the *rāwī* appears to have existed in Israel. Still there are points of contact between Arab and Israelitish song-writing. It is certain that late Arabic poems were sometimes ascribed to ancient writers with an object, that interpolations sometimes occur, and that the text of famous Diwâns is sometimes preserved in different recensions. 'Dramatic lyrics' (such as Ps. xviii.) are also by no means wanting; 'many a narrator sought to enliven his historical notices by self-composed passages of poetry, which he put into the mouth of his heroes' (Nöldeke, *Beiträge zur Kenntniss der Poesie der alten Araber* (1864), p. x). The Vedic hymns are anonymous; on the Gâthic, see above, p. 434. (3) Later Jewish traditions on authorship. See pp. 190, 207, and cf. Neubauer's article in *Studia Biblica et Ecclesiastica* (Oxford, 1890), pp. 1-58, the fulness of which makes me the less regret my scanty space. The traditions clearly have but the value of conjectures and not very critical ones. With regard to Neubauer's remark that 'the subject has as yet made inconsiderable progress,' I venture to hope that its application may be limited to the study of that part of the psalm-titles which relates to the technical details of the temple-music and singing. Others before me have sought to criticize and account for the ascriptions of authorship in the Hebrew and the Septuagint titles, and I trust that I have

---

[1] The greater simplicity of Julius Ley's system is hardly an evidence that he has approached nearer to the truth. But students of Hebrew poetry will not in fairness ignore this scholar's *Leitfaden der Metrik der hebr. Poesie, nebst dem ersten Buche der Psalmen* (Halle, 1887), nor yet Budde's thorough and important article, 'Das hebr. Klagelied,' in Stade's *Zeitschrift*, 1882, pp. 1-52.

fruitfully continued their work. Among my predecessors I would gratefully mention a Jewish scholar, Krochmal, whose explanation of the mysterious title of Ps. vii. has furnished me with a confirmation of my critical theory (see pp. 229, 243). But the other part of the psalm-titles is, I admit, not always much more clearly understood than in the days of the Rabbis. There is an appearance of better philology in the later theories, but the result remains uncertain. My argument has not led me to discuss this difficult part of the psalm-titles. What success would such a discussion have had, if I am correct in thinking that Jewish music underwent a revolution in the early part of the Greek period? (4) On Asaph, Ethan, Heman, sons of Korah, and other expressions in the psalm-headings (including תְּהִלָּה), see Lagarde, *Orientalia*, Heft 2, 1880. Lagarde connects Heb. *hallel* with Arab. *ahalla* 'to call, cry out,' which is accepted by Wellhausen (*Skizzen und Vorarbeiten*, iii. 107). It is therefore properly the obligatory shouting of the worshipper on a visit to the sanctuary ; the Arabic *tahlîl* consists merely in calling out *labbaika*, 'at thy service, O Lord !' So at least Wellhausen ; the *tahlîl* is usually said, however, to mean the ejaculation, *lā ilāha illā 'llāh*, 'there is no deity but God,' and to resemble the *talbîyah* (see p. 214). The repetition of *labbaika* must be a degenerate substitute for a fuller formula. At any rate, the shouting of the Arabs will help us to realize 'the humble origin of the Hebrew *t'hillah*,' and the 'rough' character of the original 'singing' in the temple (see p. 194). Only by slow degrees did it rise from a shouting like that of the vintage (הִלּוּלִים, Judg. ix. 27, Lev. xix. 24) or of the bridal night (see my note on Ps. lxxviii. 62). Comp. W. R. Smith, *The Religion of the Semites*, p. 411, note [2], where a new and bold theory is started.

APPENDIX II.

THE LINGUISTIC AFFINITIES OF THE PSALMS.

There is no more delicate problem than to select linguistic evidences of the date of a Biblical Hebrew document. Much has been done of late years in this department for the Pentateuch, and a beginning has been made in the critico-linguistic study of some of the prophets. In Job and the Psalms somewhat less interest has as yet been shown, though Budde has given us a careful study of the Elihu speeches,[1] and Giesebrecht a suggestive but too undiscriminating collection of the linguistic evidence for a late date of the Psalms.[2] It is not likely that in an appendix I should do justice to so difficult a subject, or escape making some statements for which scholars will desiderate ampler proof. The reader will see however that what I offer is my own, and that I have written these pages under a sense of the occasional uncertainty of the evidence. I do not myself think that in the case of the Psalms the linguistic argument can be often more than a subsidiary one, and shall be satisfied (though I hope in some cases to have attained more positive results) if I have shown that from the point of view of language no decisive objection can be raised to conclusions based for the most part upon other grounds. The few remarks which follow are intended to forestall criticism or at least to prevent misunderstanding. First, I feel bound to take for granted the same critical results which are presupposed in the preceding lectures and notes. It cannot, in my opinion, be proved that good Hebrew ceased to be written either at the return from Babylon or in the time of Ezra and Nehemiah. But I cast no reflexion on those who may think otherwise, and who study the Hebrew texts from a more conserva-

[1] *Beiträge zur Kritik des Buches Hiob* (1876), zweiter Theil.
[2] 'Ueber die Abfassungszeit der Psalmen; 1. Buch ii.–v.' in *Zeitschr. f. d. alttest. Wissenschaft*, 1881, pp. 276–332. See Driver's art., 'On some alleged linguistic affinities of the Elohist,' *Journal of Philology*, xi. 233, and cf. Kuenen, *Hexateuch* (by Wicksteed), p. 291. Prof. Driver does not assert that the linguistic affinities of 'P.C.' (or the Psalter) are incompatible with a date 'in or near' the Exile, but wishes for a more discriminating collection of evidence. As for myself, I have never dreamed that language would settle critical problems.

tively critical point of view. I will not presume to say that there is but one justifiable method in this or any other branch of Old Testament criticism. I am sure that I could profit much from a similar collection of evidence by Delitzsch or Strack, and I encourage myself with the thought that a scholar like Strack will find some suggestiveness in my own imperfect work. Secondly, let me warn the reader that I rely upon his constant and critical attention. Many necessary or probable inferences I have been compelled from want of space to omit. May I add that the student will be well advised to take the psalms in groups, and work his way backward, as has been done in the lectures? I may perhaps be asked why I have not pursued this method here. The reason is partly that I wished to save space, and partly that it seemed worth while to show that even the psalms most confidently believed to be pre-Exilic present some linguistic phenomena difficult to reconcile with that belief. And next, let me beg the reader to remember the frequent uncertainty of the text. I have several times referred to the possibility of corruption,[1] and repudiated a seeming Aramaism as not in the intention of the writer. If I have not often enough said 'probably' or 'possibly,' let the reader supply this omission. Lastly, a brief answer may be given to the question why some psalms, alleged to be post-Exilic, have so much more literary merit than others. The first point to emphasize is that the circumstances of the nation varied greatly at different points of the long period between the return from exile and the Maccabees. It was always possible indeed to write psalms in a fairly pure Hebrew style, but not always to command spontaneity and vigour. True poets are never numerous, and even these must be depressed by unfavourable circumstances. The next point is, that among the temple-singers analogy requires us to assume different poetical schools. Hymn-writers had to consider both art and popularity; some writers put a higher value on the one and some on the other. There were those who coveted the prize of writing in a style which David might not have disowned, and who therefore cultivated pregnancy and condensation, and interspersed with strict moderation a few archaic forms. There were others in whom a true and deep religious feeling was much in excess of stylistic dexterity. The psalms of the first two books contain most of the best work of the former class, whereas in parts of Books IV. and V. we are conscious that, as Ewald long ago remarked,[2] an 'invasion of popular speech' has impaired the purity of the idiom. How then can we be surprised

---

[1] Cf. Wellhausen, *Prolegomena*, German ed., p. 414.
[2] *Dichter des alten bundes*, i. a, p. 209.

that some psalmists have a much choicer style than others? In the Wisdom-literature there are similar phenomena; contrast the roughness of Koheleth with the comparative elegance of the proverbs of Ben Sira and the masterly genius revealed in Job. And even within the same book, Job for instance or Koheleth, can we not detect differences in the degree of polish?[1] But great as is the variety of style among the psalmists, there is one characteristic which is common to all—a self-abnegation which delights, wherever possible, to adapt the ideas and phraseology of predecessors. If it be strange that the Elohistic writer of Gen. i. should have written in so pure and classical a style,[2] it is at any rate not strange that psalmists, trained up in the traditional processes of hymn-writing, should have composed in a Hebrew which to the uncritical eye passes as that of David. The conservatism of the temple poets was of course not less than that of the priestly legislators, allowing for the difference of their functions; of them both in their various degrees it may be said that they 'came not to be ministered unto but to minister.'

Ps. ii. Post-Davidic, because of אֲדֹנָי (v. 2), which belongs to the prophetic literature; and, if the Aramaic בר (v. 12) be genuine, post-Exile (see Prov. xxxi. 2, which is post-Exile). I confess, however, that the correction adopted in note f, p. 340 appears to me certain; Sept. and Targ. give evidence in its favour, and sense and rhythm are both helped by it. Similarly the Aramaic verb רעע (see Lagarde, *Semitica*, i. 22 ff.) may be safely expelled from v. 9a; read תִּרְעֵם, with Sept. (Pesh. Vulg.) and render, 'Thou mayest shepherd them with a staff of iron' (cf. Mic. v. 6a). There still remains the Aramaizing רגש in v. 1. The noun (masc. and fem.) occurs in lv. 15, lxiv. 3; the verb nowhere else. Aram. הרגשׁ, Dan. vi. 7, 12, 16. רגש and its forms, in the Targums on the prophets and on the Psalms, answers to various Hebrew words, e.g. to המה in xlvi. 4 and lxxxiii. 3, and to רעש in lxviii. 8. May we set against this Aramaism the suffixes of 3 pers. plur. in מו (vv. 3-5, cf. lviii. 7, 8, lix. 12, 13, lxxxiii. 12), which are undoubtedly primitive in type (Olshausen, *Lehrbuch*, § 96a; Gesenius-Kautzsch, § 32, 7), and which Dillmann mentions among the tokens of a high (pre-Davidic) antiquity in Ex. xv. 1-18? Not except under the strict compulsion of internal evidence. These suffixes may be merely employed for rhythmical effect; they are not employed throughout the psalm. Cf. on xi. 7.

[1] Budde, *Beiträge*, pp. 158, 159; Cheyne, *Job and Solomon*, pp. 203-206.
[2] Driver, *Journal of Philology*, xi. 232. It must be remembered that similar difficulties have been felt in admitting the Exilic date of the Second Isaiah. It takes time to familiarize oneself with facts. It is not enough to admit a critical result; you must absorb it.

Ps. iii. 3 and other passages (see Gesenius-Kautzsch, § 90, 2, note ᵇ). The term חָתָּ֗ is not quoted by Dillmann as proving the early date of Ex. xv. 16 ; nor does it prove anything in the Psalter.

Ps. v. 2. הָגִיג or הֲגִיג. Again in xxxix. 4; nowhere else. Is this an Aramaism? Certainly a root *h'gag* exists, by the side of *h'go*, in (Eastern) Aramaic, but if the Aramaic usage in the post-Exile period was the same as in Christian times, the special sense of *h'gag* was 'to imagine,' or even 'to see an imaginary form,' and that of *h'go* 'to spell, read' (cf. Jewish Aram. הֲגָא, new Heb. הָגָה). Had the psalmist no *Sprachgefühl*, no sense of difference of usage? הָגִיג in the sense of 'vain appearance,' would be in place in Ps. xc. 9 (הֶגֶה), but not here. There were therefore probably two Heb. stems הגג and הנה related as שׁגג to שׁגה and שׂגא (see on xix. 13). Cf. on xlix. 2.—
11. The archaistic suffix in מוֹ connects this with several other psalms (see on ii. 3–5, xi. 7).

Ps. vii. is one of the Elyōn psalms (see *v.* 18), and is therefore presumably late (see note ᵘ, p. 83). Once for all, we may draw the same inference for Pss. ix., xviii., xxi., xlvi., xlvii., l., lvii., lxxiii., lxxvii., lxxviii., lxxxii., lxxxviii. (?),lxxxix. (allusion), xci., xcii., xcvii., cvii In *v.* 10 גמר, 'to come to an end' (also, twice, 'to complete'), is clearly a word of the silver age. In the Bible it only occurs in Ps. vii. 10, xii. 2, lvii. 3 (if the text be correct), lxxvii. 9, cxxxviii. 8 ; in the Targums and the Talmud it is of frequent occurrence (also in Syriac, as an intransitive). In *v.* 5 the Aramaizing חלץ should give place to לחץ (see crit. n.).

Ps. viii. 5, ix. 20, 21, x. 18, lvi. 2, lxvi. 12, xc. 3 (?), ciii. 15, cxliv 3. אֱנוֹשׁ here = 'frail (or weak) man ;' so only in Job, Psalms, 2 Isa. (li. 7, 12), 2 Chron. (xiv. 10). Dillmann and Delitzsch would thus interpret Enos (Enosh) in Gen. iv. 26 (Yahvistic), but this name is really only a duplicate of Adam, as Kenan is of Kain ; why suppose a 'Nebenbegriff'? 'Man' or 'ordinary men' is the meaning of 'א in Isa. (viii. 1, xxxiii. 8), Jer. (xx. 10), Deut. (xxxii. 26), and is presupposed by the Yahvist in Gen. *l. c.* But it is also not unrepresented in Job (e.g. xxviii. 13), Psalms (see on lv. 14), and the later parts of Isa. (xiii. 7, 12, xxiv. 6, lvi. 2). These facts on the whole confirm the late origin of Ps. viii., &c. Had 'א conveyed the idea of weakness in Isaiah's time, would he not have used it instead of אִישׁ in Is. ii. 9, 11, v. 15 ?

Ps. x. 7, lv. 12, lxxii. 14, תֹּךְ or תּוֹךְ. Also Prov. xxix. 13 (plur.). A late word. In Jewish Aram. תַּכָּא = Heb. עֹשֶׁק, 1. fine ; 2. punishment (see the verb in Prov. xvii. 26, xxi. 11). In eastern Aramaic *tuko* has, like עֹשֶׁק, an expanded meaning ('oppression') ; it is the rendering of תֹּךְ in Pesh.

II. LINGUISTIC AFFINITIES OF THE PSALMS. 465.

Ps. xi. The form מְנָת (with absorbed ו or י) occurs only in Ps. xi. 6, xvi. 5, lxiii. 11, 2 Chron. xxxi. 3, 4, Neh. xii. 44, 47, xiii. 10. Similarly the form קְצָת (with absorbed ו) is found only in Ex. xxxvii. 8 (kt.), xxxviii. 5, xxxix. 4 (kt.), Dan. (repeatedly, both Heb. and Aram.), Neh. vii. 20, and Ps. lxv. 9. (The first three examples give the plural.) If for other reasons the late date of the psalms referred to and of Ex. xxxv.-xl. (in its present form) is probable, the occurrence of these forms will in a slight degree confirm it. The favourite early forms are קָצֶה, מָנָה. The fact that the latter (with its plur. קְצוֹת) occurs repeatedly in Ex. xxv.-xxix., xxxv.-xl. is no argument against the view here taken. In xi. 7 we find the suffix מוֹ of the 3rd pers. sing., as in Job xx. 23, xxvii. 23, xxii. 2, Isa. xliv. 15, liii. 8. All late passages. Cf. on ii. 3–5.

Ps. xii. נָמַר (v. 2) and זֻלּוּת (v. 9) belong to the Aramaizing period (see above, on vii. 10, and crit. n. on xii. 9). In v. 8 דּוֹר has the (probably) late meaning of 'class of men,' as xiv. 5, xxiv. 6, lxxiii. 15, cxii. 2, Deut. xxxii. 5, Prov. xxx. 11–14. זוּ (for זֶה) is only strange because without an article, in spite of הַדּוֹר (see Ewald, § 293a). Rhythm will account for this, just as the pause accounts for the old term. זוּ in v. 9a (cf. Isa. xxvi. 11). In v. 9, זֻלּוּת (Baer, זֻלֻּת), note the abstract term. וּת, and comp. Talmudic זֻלּוּתָא (crit. n.).

Ps. xiii. 6, גָּמַל with עַל (for לְ), Aramaizing. So ciii. 10, cxvi. 7, cxix. 17, cxlii. 8, Joel iv. 4, 2 Chron. xx. 11. All post-Exile passages. That גמל has not always the same shade of meaning, does not diminish the value of the observation (see my Comm. on Ps. xiii. 6). Not that Ps. vii. 5, cxxxvii. 8, in which different constructions are found, are on this account alone earlier than Ps. xiii. 6, &c. Comp. on lvii. 3.

Ps. xvi. Davidic, says Delitzsch, because of its archaic, peculiar, and highly poetic phraseology. But let us examine the evidence. 1. אֲדֹנָי. If this means 'the Lord' (absolutely), as Del. assumes, the psalm is post-Davidic, if not post-Exile. I prefer 'my Lord,' which is more natural in an appeal for help (cf. xxxi. 15, xci. 2); the suffix has its full force as in xxxv. 23, and prob. elsewhere, see p. 299.—3a. All Ewald's instances of לְ 'quod attinet ad' (Lehrbuch der hebr. Spr., §310a) are from prose-passages, except Ps. xvi. 3, xvii. 4, and one may fairly add Isa. xxxii. 1. But the third of these is undoubtedly and the second not improbably corrupt. הֵמָּה at any rate is superfluous in a relative clause. The text as it stands is therefore neither of the golden nor of the silver age of Hebrew. The two admissible emendations (see my own commentary and Nowack's) both involve placing this psalm in the post-Exile period.—5. מְנָת. See on xi. 6. תּוֹמִיךְ is an impossible form, which Del. should not have

H H

quoted as evidence.—6. נָחֲלַת is no peculiarity of the poet, but, like אֲמָרְתְּ in v. 1, an involuntary Aramaism of the editor. Read נחלתי. But see on lx. 13. שָׁפַר עַל, 'to be well pleasing to,' is probably an Aramaism; cf. Dan. iv. 12.—9. כְּבוֹדִי. See on vii. 6.

Ps. xvii. David, according to Del., has two styles; Ps. xvii. represents the harsh and obscure variety. Hitzig remarks on the rough style which looks to him archaic. But the roughness is intensified by corruption of the text, and the ode in Hab. iii. (post-Exilic) is more abrupt in style than Ps. xvii. Diversities of style existed in the silver age of Hebrew. 3. עָבַר used absolutely for 'to transgress.' The sense is no doubt unique, for 'make to transgress,' which is A.V.'s rend. of the Hifil part. in 1 Sam. ii. 24, will not stand (Klostermann's correction of the verse is probable). But is it therefore to be rejected? 1. It is required to bring out the three classes of sins, 2. we have close by the phrase 'the word of thy lips,' which at once defines the meaning of יַעֲבֹר, and 3. עֲבַרְיָן in Rabbinic means 'a transgressor of the law,' and עֲבֵרָה 'a transgression or sin' (cf. *Yoma*, 86a, עָבַר עֲבֵרָה, 'he committed a sin'). Recollect that after the promulgation of the Law a technical sense like this is to be expected. 4. לְפ׳. The rend. 'as for the works,' &c., is most improbable (see on xvi. 3). Sept. regards the phrase as the object of the verb which it misreads יֹאמַר in v. 3b. Rather it is the accus. to שָׁמַרְתִּי. This is marked by the preposition, to avoid mistakes, as the verb follows at some little distance. The accusatival use of לְ is Aramaizing, and is frequent in Exilic and post-Exilic writings (see Driver on 1 Sam. xxiii. 10; Ewald, *Grammar*, §277e). It occurs elsewhere in the Psalms (see lxix. 6, lxxiii. 18, cxxix. 3). אָדָם '(wicked) men,' as cxx. 2. In lxxiii. 5, lxxxii. 7 the word has a different *nuance*. 10. Suffixes. See on Ps. lxxiii. חֵלֶב here and in lxxiii. 7 is used in a special sense. Generally it means 'fat' or 'fat parts,' but here a particular part of the *viscera* with the accompanying fat. It is in fact a recondite synonym for כְּלָיוֹת (xvi. 7, xxvi. 2), מֵעִים (xl. 9), קֶרֶב (lxiv. 7), קְרָבִים (ciii. 1), all of which, though meaning properly the *viscera* or some part of it, have equally with לֵב received an ethical significance. חֵלֶב must be explained in these two passages by Ar. *ḥilb*, which means either the midriff, or the liver, or the partition between the heart and the liver (Lane). These parts of the body are regarded by the Semites as the seats of the passions. In xvii. 10 pity, and in lxxiii. 7 wicked lusts are thought of as issuing forth from these inward parts. It is important both for the lexicon and for psalm-criticism and psalm-theology to notice the ethical reference which Jeremiah and his scholars give to terms like these. Notice that כָּבֵד (the usual

Hebrew word for liver) is not a member of this group, unless with Halévy we too boldly change כְּבוֹדִי in xvi. 10, &c., into כְּבֵדִי, justifying this step by the Sept. of Gen. xlix. 6, comp. on li. 8. The suffixes in מוֹ and מוֹ֯ are real or affected archaisms. Since the rest of the evidence favours a late date, we may call them affectations (as in lxxiii. 5–7 and especially lxxxiii. 12). 14. חֶלֶד. Only here and in xxxix. 6, xlix. 2, lxxxix. 48, Job xi. 17, Isa. xxxviii. 11 (Cod. Bab.). It is probably a good old Hebrew word although poetic, but except in xxxix. 6 and lxxxix. 48 ('lifetime") and in Job xi. 17 ('a vigorous old age,' cf. Arab. *ḫuld*), the meanings seem to belong to a late stage of thought. Here e.g. 'worldliness' is the sense required (and so Gesenius and Kalisch understand עוֹלָם in Eccles. iii. 11) ; and in Ps. xlix. 2 and Isa. *l.c.* 'time-world.' But as Orelli remarks, ' it is not the way of *the old Hebraism* to view the earth and earthly life as perishable in contradistinction to an eternal, heavenly world' (*Die hebr. Synonyma der Zeit und Ewigkeit*, 1871, p. 45, cf. p. 84). Notice Pesh.'s rend. of αἰών in Eph. ii. 2 '*ōl'moyūtho* (' worldliness ').

Ps. xviii. 2. The Aramaism רחם 'to love' is probably a scribe's error (see crit. n.). If not, the psalm must be very late.—4. מְהֻלָּל. The first of a long series of occurrences of הלל, ' to chant praise to God.' The only very old passage in which הלל has a religious reference is Judg. xvi. 24 (of Dagon), and the only pre-Exilic passages in which it is used of Jehovah are Jer. xx. 13, xxxi. 7 (not counting Isa. xxxviii. 18). It is common in this sense in Chron., and superabundant in the Psalter. But only a very mechanical criticism could make this a proof of the late date of the psalms (see p. 460).—32. אֱלוֹהַּ; again in l. 22, cxiv. 7 (if correct), cxxxix. 19. If this reading is correct (2 Sam. xxii. 32, אֵל), the psalm belongs at earliest to the reign of Josiah, for, as Ewald suggested (see references in my comm.) and Baethgen has carefully argued,[1] אלוה was probably invented as the singular of אלהים by the author of Deut. xxxii. (see *vv.* 15, 17). It occurs twice in the genuine Habakkuk, once in the psalm attached to that book (Hab. iii. 3), forty-one times in Job, once in each of the books of 2 Isa., Prov. (in a very late part), Chron., and Neh. ; also four times in three successive verses of Daniel.—36. עֲנָוָה. Only here and in xlv. 5 (see crit. note), Zeph. ii. 3, and Prov. xv. 33, xviii. 12, xxii. 4. The cognate adjective עָנָו occurs 11 or perhaps 13 times in the Psalter, once or twice in Prov., once in 2 Isa., once in Zeph., once or twice in Amos, twice or thrice in Isa., once in Job, and once in Numbers (k'thibh). But these facts have only an indirect bearing on the date of the

[1] *Beiträge zur semit. Religionsgeschichte* (1888), pp. 296, 297. Lagarde's view that 'א is a broken plural, is difficult.

psalm. It is the prominence given to the virtue of humility in the Psalter (whether עָנִי or עָנָו be the word used, is not very important) which creates a presumption (cf. Isa. lxi. 1) that most of the psalms are post-Exilic. This is a historical but not properly a linguistic argument.—48. דבר in Hifil, only here and in xlvii. 4, in the unusual sense 'to subdue.' Is this owing to Aramaic influence? דָּבַר means 'to lead,' 'govern,' and then (a) 'to guide,' or (b) 'to take,' or 'take away.' Still it is possible that the Heb. Hifil retained a sense which had been lost in Qal and Piel; cf. מִדְבָּר.

Ps. xix. 2, cl. 1. רָקִיעַ. Nine times in Gen. i., four times in Ezek., and once in Dan. But both the idea and root of the word are good Hebrew. See Dillmann on Gen. i. 6, and Driver, *Journal of Philology*, xi. 212.—13. שְׁגִיאוֹת, ἅπ. λεγ., = שְׁגָגוֹת, 'sins of inadvertence;' שְׁגָגָה occurs seventeen times in P.C. (Lev. Numb. Josh.), twice in Eccles., but also in 1 Sam. xiv. 24 Sept. (see Driver *ad loc.*). The latter passage at any rate, if we accept it as genuine, is pre-Exilic. We may assume, therefore, that both שְׁגָגָה and its synonym שְׁגִיאָה are early.—15. הִגָּיוֹן, 'meditation,' again only in xcii. 4 (different sense), Lam. iii. 62, but not therefore late; cf. חִזָּיוֹן. But see on xlix. 2.

Pss. xx., xxi., lxi., lxiii. Use of מֶלֶךְ. The root-meaning is not 'to possess' but 'to give counsel,' 'to decide,' agreeably to the Assyrian and Aramaic usage.[1] מֶלֶךְ can therefore legitimately be used in a wide sense for 'prince' or 'minor king,' as constantly in Assyrian; for general (Job xv. 24, Sept. στρατηγός, cf. Isa. x. 8); and for 'magistrate of the royal house' (Jer. xvii. 19, 20, cf. Jer. xxi. 11, 12). In the post-Exilic period, so largely open to Aramaic influences, the sense of the original meaning of מֶלֶךְ would become strengthened (see Neh. v. 7, and cf. Dan. iv. 24), and a psalmist might all the more naturally apply the term to Simon the Maccabee in the good old Semitic sense of 'consul.'—Ps. xx. 6. דגל the verb, elsewhere only (in participles) Song of Sol. v. 10, vi. 4, 10: the noun, only Cant. ii. 4, and 13 times in Num. i., ii., and x. (a part of the Priestly Code). We cannot however use these facts (even if the reading be correct) until the Song of Sol. has been investigated afresh.—Ps. xx. 9, הִתְעוֹדֵד; cxlvi. 9, cxlvii. 6 עוֹדֵד. Is it at all probable that the author of the post-Exilic psalms cxlvi. and cxlvii. has caught up an archaic (?) word from Ps. xx.? Must not the three psalms be contemporaneous?

Ps. xxii. 2. דּוּמִיָּה. Only here and in xxxix. 3, lxii. 2, lxv. 2. That

---

[1] Friedr. Delitzsch, *Prolegomena* (1886), p. 30; Merx, *Chrestomathia Targumica* (1888), p. 230.

the word occurs nowhere in Job, is strange. If genuine, it is probably a coined word, and bears witness to a period of artificial temple-poetry which cannot be placed early. But is the word genuine? I have accepted it in xxii. 2, xxxix. 3, but not without misgivings (see my crit. note). It is unknown to Sept. and Pesh. in the three latter passages mentioned above, and even if with Hatch we read εἰς ἀνείαν for εἰς ἄνοιαν in the common text of Sept. of Ps. xxii. 2, yet 'the Egyptian' recension, followed apparently by Pesh., reads καὶ οὐ προσέχεις μοι (Baethgen, from Bar Hebræus). See on xxxix. 3.—16. שָׁפָה. A colloquial word (2 Kings iv. 38, Ezek. xxiv. 3), not used in poetry or elevated prophecy, except here and in Isa. xxvi. 12 (in a noble but awkwardly expressed and probably post-Exile passage).

Ps. xxiv. 8, 10. עִזּוּז (again only in Isa. xliii. 17), יְהוָֹה צְבָאוֹת. See pp. 203, 222 (note ᵛᵛ).

Ps. xxvi. 12. מַקְהֵלִים; Ps. lxviii. 27, Num. xxxiii. 25, 26, מַקְהֵלוֹת. Neither form occurs elsewhere, and both Ps. lxviii. and Num. xxxiii. in their present form must be admitted to be late. Still the word is possibly as old as rhythmical temple psalmody. קָהָל (see xxii. 23, 26, xl. 10) would not have suited the rhythm.

Ps. xxviii. 7. יְהוּדָה, as xlv. 18, Neh. xi. 17; cf. יְהוֹשִׁיעַ, Ps. cxvi. 6. The non-syncopation is either an archaism revived under Aramaic influence, or more probably a pseudo-archaism formed on the analogy of really old uncontracted forms (see König, *Lehrgebäude*, pp. 294, 295, and cf. Driver, *Samuel*, p. 113).

Ps. xxix. 10. מַבּוּל, probably a Hebraized form of *abubu*, the Babylonian word for the Flood (properly, a 'destructive storm'); in justification of this see Haupt, in Schrader's *K.A.T.*, p. 66, note ³, and cf. my crit. note on Ps. xxix. 10. 'מ occurs elsewhere only in Gen. vi.–ix. (six times), Gen. x. 1, 32, and Gen. xi. 10. These passages belong some to the Priestly Code, some to the second Yahvist, to whom the Hebrew parallelisms to Babylonian stories are due, and who can hardly be placed earlier than the reign of Manasseh (see p. 280, top). 'מ has no Aramaic affinity; Targ. here has טוּפָנָא (Onk. in Gen. vii., טוֹפָנָא).

Ps. xxxiii. 14. הִשְׁגִּיחַ 'to look at.' Elsewhere only in Isa. xiv. 16, Song of Sol. ii. 9. Probably a late word. In Targ. and new Hebrew. 'prospicere,' 'providere.'

Ps. xxxiv. 19. דַּכָּא. In an ethical sense, only here and in Isa. lvii. 3 (alluded to by the psalmist). Cf. נִדְכֶּה, li. 14. In a physical sense, only in xc. 3; but cf. דַּכָּה, 'crushing,' Deut. xxiii. 2. The root is old Hebrew.

Ps. xxxv. 3. סְגֹר. If this is the Scythian σάγαρις, the psalm belongs at earliest to the reign of Josiah, but is possibly enough post-Exile (see Commentary). Such a loan word would be unique in the psalms, but there are parallels enough in Song of Sol., Eccles., and Daniel.— *v.* 15. צָלַע 'fall.' So xxxviii. 18, Jer. xx. 10. Nowhere else in this sense.

Ps. xxxvi. 2. נְאֻם. Nowhere else in the Psalter except in cx. 1 (of a prophetic oracle); see note below. The metaphorical use of the term here favours a late date.—6. בְּהַשָּׁמַיִם. This retention of the article after the prep. is 'mostly late' (Driver, *Samuel*, page 273, note [1]). In the parallel passage, however (lvii. 11), we find עַד שׁ'; and בה' is probably a corruption.

Ps. xxxix. 3. דּוּמִיָּה. No sign of date. The word is probably a gloss which has slipped in from lxii. 2 (received text). Both rhythm and sense gain by its excision. See on xxii. 2.—4. הָגִיג. See on v. 2.—12. See on vi. 7.

Ps. xlii., xliii. Here we begin to notice a preference of 'Elohim' to the divine name 'Yahveh,' and could we be sure that the psalms which are now Elohistic had not been touched by an editor, we should be entitled to use this fact as a sign of date. It is certain, however, that sometimes, if not generally, 'Yahveh' has been changed into 'Elohim' by an editor (cf. pp. 90, 101, 287), so that we are 'practically debarred from pressing this point' (Toy, *Journal of Soc. of Biblical Literature*, June and Dec. 1884, p. 86).

Ps. xlii. 5. According to Hitzig, the cohortative ה ֫ has here lost its significance. This would agree equally well with Ewald's view of the date and with Hitzig's (for in Jer. iv. 19, 21 both Hitzig and Driver admit this phenomenon). It is however not necessary to hold that wherever the cohort. form occurs in a work which on various grounds is pronounced to be late, it must have lost its meaning (for this is not the case in Jer. iii. 25; cf. Isa. xxxviii. 10). We may, if we will, render, in xlii. 5, 'let me remember . . . pour out,' though a parallel passage, lxxvii. 4, 7, seems to me now against this.—דָּדָה (Piel; see my crit. n.); cf. Isa. xxxviii. 15, where another Levitical poet uses the Hithpael. A colloquialism, and probably late. In Jewish Aramaic it means 'to lead' or 'pull' (of children and young animals) in Pael; 'to hop' (of birds), in Ithpaal, and 'to travel slowly' (of traders). In new Hebrew, 'to lead' or 'pull,' in Piel; 'to hop' (of birds), in Hithpael (cf. מְדַדִּין עֲגָלִין, 'you may lead or pull calves,' and אִשָּׁה מְדַדָּה, 'a mother may lead her child'—viz. on the Sabbath, *Shabbath*, xviii. 2, in Jastrow's *Lex.*). But of course there may be a corruption of the text. In the Talmudic treatise *Shabbath*, 88*b*, it is said, 'Read not (in Ps. lxviii. 13) *yiddōdūn* "they flee," but *y'daddūn*, "they lead them."' A similar view may have been taken of a word in each of the two Biblical passages; Bredenkamp in fact emends in Isa. xxxviii. 13 by introducing the root נדר. But the appropriateness of דִּדָּה to descriptions of religious processions is against this theory, and we may therefore consider the late date of Ps. xlii., xliii., and Isa. xxxviii. 10–20 to be favoured by דִּדָּה. Compare an analogous colloquialism in Isa. xiv. 23 (Exilic).

Ps. xlv. 2. רָחַשׁ, here only. It is probably a colloquialism for הִבִּיעַ and if we could be sure that Lev. i.-vii. did not contain pre-Exilic, we might add that it was probably late. מַרְחֶשֶׁת, 'a kettle,' occurs in Lev. ii. 7, vii. 9, and establishes for Hebrew usage the sense of 'boiling (over).' רְחִישׁ is common in Jewish Aramaic as a synonym of Heb. שָׁרַץ, but not of נָבַע.—מָהִיר. Only here and in Isa. xvi. 7, Prov. xxii. 29, Ezra vii. 6. In Isa. *l.c.* the meaning is 'rapid,' 'prompt' (of a model judge); in the other passages, 'expert' (in some art or business). The latter is also the sense in Aramaic. Note that Prov. xxii. 17–xxiv. 22, according to one theory, was compiled by the author or editor of Prov. i.-ix. (see *Job and Solomon*, p. 138), and that Prov. xxii. 29*b* contains a markedly Aramaizing expression (see Delitzsch *ad loc.*).—5. ענוה. See on xviii. 36.—9. מִנִּי. Some critics compare the Assyrian plural in *i* and the Syriac in *ê* (emphatic state). But the parallels in the Old Testament are very doubtful (see Olshausen, *Lehrbuch*, § 111 *c*). The sense however may be a borrowed Aramaic one ('strings' for 'harp-music;' see my *Psalms*, p. 406, and cf. Payne Smith, *Thes. Syr.*, s. v. *menno*), unless the word is corrupt.—10. שֵׁגָל, only here and in Neh. ii. 6, Dan. v. 2, 3, 23 (Aramaic), unless we may add by conjecture Judg. v. 30 (for שְׁגָל). The verb שָׁגַל is found in Jer. iii. 2, Deut. xxviii. 30, Isa. xiii. 16, and Zech. xiv. 2, where there is a constant euphemistic Q'ri, substituting שָׁכַב. Professor Toy is of opinion that שֵׁגָל was borrowed from Aramaic with the sense of 'queen,' while the native Hebrew verb שָׁגַל, having a low colloquial meaning, became *vox inhonesta*. It is equally admissible to suppose that both verb and noun belong to the old Hebrew vocabulary, but that the Biblical writers deliberately abstain from using the noun of an Israelitish wife. If so, שֵׁגָל is only a guide to the date in so far as it is a guide to the interpretation of the psalm. We have, in short, to seek for a non-Israelitish queen of Israel, and Jezebel, the wife of Ahab, being rejected (see p. 167), we can only find one in the post-Exile period.—18. בְּכָל־דֹּר וָדֹר. The pleonastic כָּל־ elsewhere 'only in very late passages,' such as Esth. ii. 11, 2 Chron. xi. 12 (Ges.-Kautzsch, § 123*d*), to which add Ps. cxlv. 13, Esth. ix. 28. Cf. on lxxxvii. 5.

Ps. xlviii. 14. פַּסֵּג, only here, and, unless corrupt, probably late Hebrew. For the grounds of this, see crit. note.

Ps. xlix. 'Its antique, bold form,' Del.—2. חֶלֶד. See on xvii.

14.—4. חָכְמוֹת. Regal period? See Prov. i. 20, [xiv. 1,] ix. 1, xxiv. 7. תְּבוּנוֹת, as lxxviii. 72, Prov. xi. 12, xxviii. 16, Job xxxii. 11, Isa. xl. 14. הָגוּת. Although the ending וּת is not incompatible with a pre-Exilic date (note גֵּאוּת, חָזוּת, כְּסוּת, and other classical words, mostly from verbs ל"ה), yet the fact that none of the early writers used this convenient word,[1] coupled with the increasing number of forms in וּת in the later period (seven or perhaps eight occur in Ecclesiastes, and there are 'over 100 examples' in Rabbinic [2]), suggests that 'ה is the coinage of a later writer. Altogether the number of rare words from הגה and הגג is remarkable. See on v. 2, xix. 15, xc. 9.—11. בָּעַר. Rare. See xcii. 7, Prov. xii. 1, xxx. 2.—13, 21. יְקָר is not un-Hebraic in form (cf. שְׁאָר). It occurs once in each of these books—Jer., Ezek., Zech., Job, Prov. The psalmist may have selected it for a rhythmical reason. Still the word is as common in Aramaic as כָּבוֹד is in Hebrew; it occurs seven times in the Aram. parts of Daniel, and (through Aram. influence) ten times in the late Hebrew Book of Esther.—12. עֲלֵי־אֲדָמוֹת. A 'bold' but hardly 'antique' expression. This plural form occurs here only.—14. כֶּסֶל 'folly' or 'confidence,' as lxxviii. 7. Twice in Job, once in the Praise of Wisdom (Prov. iii. 26); once in Eccles. A mechanical critic might infer that this use of כ' was distinctively late? But how can it be, when כְּסִיל 'fool' is so common in the older parts of Proverbs? Cf. כִּסְלָה, lxxxv. 9, Job iv. 6.

Ps. l. Its late origin is shown by the names of God in v. 1 (see p. 153) and v. 14 (see above, on Ps. vii.).—10. חַיְתוֹ, elsewhere only in lxxix. 2, civ. 11, 20, Isa. lvi. 9 (twice), Zeph. ii. 14, Gen. i. 24; cf. מַעְיָנוֹ, cxiv. 8, and בְּנוֹ, Num. xxiv. 3, 15. The old case-ending וֹ is one of those archaisms which, partly for rhythmical reasons, the later poets loved. (Cf. on cx. 4.) But if Giesebrecht thinks that it specially favours a post-Exile date of the psalms in which it occurs, he is surely mistaken. Isa. lvi. (probably), Zeph. ii., and Num. xxiv. are all pre-Exilic.—11. זִיז. Elsewhere only in Ps. lxxx. 14 and Isa. lxvi. 11. True enough, the root *is* Aramaic, and from it proceed זֵן 'a bough' and זִיז 'a beam,' and also 'a worm.' The Biblical and post-Biblical Hebrew זִיז might conceivably be of Aramaic origin. But what of מְזוּזָה 'a door-post'? Is not this old Hebrew, and does it not presuppose the same root as the late Hebrew זִיז 'a beam,' viz. זוּז 'to move forward, or backward' (cf. Ass. *za'za'*, 'to move, or shake') or (of things without life) 'to project,' which is guaranteed

---

[1] Convenient; especially because הִגָּיוֹן has two meanings.

[2] Siegfried and Strack, *Lehrbuch der neuhebr. Sprache*, &c., p. 50.

in the former sense for Assyrian by passages in Schrader's *K. A. T.*? Note also that the senses in which זיז is used in the Psalter and in Isa. lxvi. respectively are not Aramaizing senses; the writers have a full consciousness of the root-meaning of the word, and apply this meaning each in his own way. In the Psalter, it is best to render 'offspring;' and in Isaiah, 'udder.' (I have been thus full, because Delitzsch and Dillmann have both missed the point of my crit. note on Isa. lxvi. 11, which is that the sense of 'udder' which the parallelism certainly suggests, is confirmed by the Ass. *zūz*.)—22. אֱלוֹהַּ. See on xviii. 32.

Ps. li. Halévy derives from vv. 4 and 9a a twofold argument for the pre-Exile date of the psalm (*Revue de l'hist. des religions*, 1885, 2, p. 36; cf. 1886, 2, pp. 190–193). כבסני וגו' (v. 4) is, he thinks, modelled on the Levitical formula וְכִבֶּס בְּגָדָיו וְטָהֵר. 'Given that כִּבֵּס means properly "to wash clothes," and that the precept of washing clothes in the rite of purification belongs exclusively to the Priestly Code, must we not see in the expression of the psalmist a poetic idealization of the Levitical formula?' And in v. 9, תְּחַטְּאֵנִי וגו' reminds Halévy that the same word is used of these rites of purification in which hyssop plays such a prominent part (Lev. xiv. 49, Num. xix. 6, 12, &c.). Halévy's only mistake consists in asserting that the phrase כבס מעון is peculiar to Ps. li. 4. We find virtually the same expression in Jer. iv. 14 (cf. ii. 22). But at what period of the higher religion of Israel might not such 'poetic idealizations' of old ritual formulæ have been used? Does not the Second Isaiah use sacrificial phraseology in a figurative sense in Isa. liii. 5, 6, 10?—8. טֻחוֹת partic. of טוּחַ 'to besmear' (with plaster, as in Ezek., or oil, as Talm. Bab. *Nidda*, 24, *ap.* Buxtorf). From the root טח comes probably Aram. מְחָל, מְחוֹל, *ṭ'hōlō, tiḥāl*, 'the spleen,' or (see Payne Smith, s. v. *ṭ'holo*) the kidneys, or even the lungs.[1] Both here and in Job xxxviii. 36 טֻחוֹת means much the same as מְחָל, i.e. the kidneys with their fat (see Lev. iii. 4), or, better, the complex of fat parts in the *viscera*, which the Semites regarded as the seat of emotion. There is nothing remarkable in this usage; what is peculiar is the way in which a group of psalmists pick out a number of words denoting the *viscera*, to serve as symbols of the inner or moral nature. This preoccupation about the moral nature of man *is* late; it marks the post-Jeremian age (cf. on xvii. 10). The author of Job (xxxviii. 36) goes beyond the psalmists, and makes wisdom reside בַּטֻּחוֹת, which is best rendered ἐν φρεσὶ, φρήν and φρένες (cf. Lat. *renes*?) having passed through a similar develop-

---

[1] Suggested by Lagarde's remarks in *Proverbien*, p. 62.

ment to words such as מָחוֹל, מָחַל.—12. ברא. On this word (which, as Barth has made probable, =Ass. *banû*; cf. Ea-bani ='Ea, my creator,' in the Bab. Deluge-story) see Dillmann's note on Gen. i. 1. It supplies no criterion of date.—13. רוּחַ ק׳. A post-Exilic phrase (see Isa. lxiii. 10, 11, and above, p. 162).—Ps. liii. 6. See on lxviii. 31.

Ps. lv. 3, 18. Cohortatives with effaced meaning imply a *somewhat* late date (see on xlii. 5).—4. עָקַת. In the Targum, עָקָא = Heb. צָרָה and מָצוֹק. But the reading is probably corrupt.—6. פַּלָּצוּת. Elsewhere only in Job xxi. 6, Isa. xxi. 4, Ezek. vii. 18. There is no certain pre-Exilic evidence for the word, but an elegiac poet might at any time have coined it. Jer. (xlix. 16) uses תִּפְלַצְתָּ, which occurs nowhere else in the same sense.—12. תֹּךְ. See on x. 7.—14. אֱנוֹשׁ, for an individual, seems late; see Jer. xx. 10, Job v. 17. אָדָם thus limited is also rare (Prov. iii. 13, Eccles. vii. 28).—15. רֵגֶשׁ, see on ii. 1.—22. קְרָב, Aramaic for מִלְחָמָה, a certain sign of late date. It occurs also in lxviii. 31 (plur.), lxxviii. 9, cxliv. 1, Zech. xiv. 3, Eccles. ix. 18, Job xxxviii. 23, not however in the true text of 2 Sam. xvii. 11 (see Driver *ad loc.*).—23. יְהָבְךָ. The verb יהב 'to give' is common in Aramaic, but has gone out in Hebrew except in the imperative. יְהָבָא in Targ. of Ps. xi. 6 = Heb. מְנָת, in Talmudic יהב= 'burden.'

Ps. lvii. 3. גָּמַר עַל. Verb and construction both late (see on vii. 10, xiii. 6).—5. אֶשְׁכְּבָה. See on lv. 3, 18.

Ps. lviii. 'Unparalleled boldness of the style' (Delitzsch). This however is partly owing to corruption of the text (see crit. notes in my comm.). In some minute linguistic points the psalm reminds us of the Song in Ex. xv. 1-18:—notice the repetition (*vv.* 8, 10, five times) of כְּמוֹ, the suffixes in מוֹ (*vv.* 7, 8), the full imperfects in *vv.* 2, 3 (contrast the Chronicler's avoidance of them), the 'defectively' written plural forms in *v. 2* (אלם, which was early misunderstood both in the psalm and in Ex. xv. 10), and, if my suggestion in crit. note (*Psalms*, p. 390) be followed, יָהּ in *v.* 10: If the Song is 'almost certainly post-Exile' (p. 177), it follows that Ps. lviii. is so too.— 5. דְּמוּת occurs once in Dan., once in Chron., 15 times in Ezekiel twice in the Priestly Code, twice in the later parts of Isa., once in Kings. But the root is good Hebrew, and 2 Kings xvi. 10 is pre-Exilic. Even Lagarde only urges that the pointing, not that the word itself, is Aramaic; for דְּמוּת he would substitute דָּמוֹת (*Uebersicht der Nomina*, 1889, p. 148). Cf. Driver, *Journal of Philology*, xi. 216.

Ps. lix. Archaic or archaizing suffixes in מוֹ, as in Ps. lviii. (see on ii. 3-5).

Ps. lx. 6. On the reading cf. p. 108. An Aramaizing *spelling* proves nothing.—13. עֶזְרָת. The archaic form of the fem. (see Olshausen, § 108*d*).

Ps. lxi. 5, lxxvii. 6, cxlv. 13, עוֹלָמִים. Is this plural form the expression of the enlarged later Jewish conception of time? Certainly it occurs in the Exilic and post-Exilic passages, Isa. xxvi. 4, xlv. 17, li. 9, Eccles. i. 10, Dan. ix. 24, and עָלְמִין is frequent in the Aram. parts of Daniel. But it is also found in 1 Kings viii. 12, 13 (=2 Chron. vi. 1, 2), which is no imaginary speech of Solomon, produced in the 6th cent. B.C. by an editor, but a fragment of a genuine Solomonic song (see p. 212), and where the plur. is required by the rhythm.

Ps. lxii. 2, lxv. 2. דּוּמִיָה. See on xxii. 2, xxxix. 3.—12. Note אֲדֹנָי (see on Ps. ii.).—Ps. lxiii. 4, cxvii. 1, cxlv. 4, cxlvii. 12, Eccles. viii. 15, שִׁבַּח, 'to praise.' In Eccles. iv. 2, the same verb means 'to call happy;' in Ps. cvi. 47, 1 Chron. xvi. 35, 'to boast of' (Hithpael). Cf. new Heb. שֶׁבַח 'praise' (*Pirqe Aboth*, ii. 8*b*, Strack). 'Chaldaica est, atque adeo in Davidico contextu barbara. Quippe nulla erat Judæis cum Chaldaicâ [Aramaicâ] gente ac linguâ, Davide regnante, societas.'—Houbigant, ad Ps. lxviii. 18. See however 2 Sam. viii. 6.—11. מְנָת, see on xi. 6.

Ps. lxiv. 3. רגשׁת. See on ii. 1.—Ps. lxv. 9. קְצָוֹת. See on xi. 6.—10. רַבַּת, adverbially, as cxx. 6, cxxiii. 4. Also a Syriac usage; cf. e.g. *rebbath* 'very,' Ephr. *Carm. Nis.* iv. 28, v. 139, *khayyath* 'alive,' Ps. cxxiii. 3 (Pesh.), and other instances ap. Nöldeke, *Mand. Gram.*, p. 201, Wright, *Comparative Gram.*, p. 135.

Ps. lxviii. Of the Davidic age, if not by David (Delitzsch). But what is there in the style which prevents us from accepting the conclusions based upon non-linguistic evidence? The argument for a post-Exilic date derived from the divine names Adonai (*vv.* 12, 18, 20, 23, 27, 33) and Shaddai (*v.* 15) has been set forth above (p. 124, note ᵇ).—7. כּוֹשָׁרוֹת, ἅπ. λεγ. Cf. *kushoro*, Pesh. Ecclus. xxxviii. 31 &c., בָּשֵׁר occurs only in Esther (viii. 5), and Eccles. (x. 10, xi. 6) ; כִּשְׁרוֹן only in Eccles. (ii. 10, iv. 4, v. 10). Aramaic and Talmudic.—18. רִבֹּתַיִם. רִבּוֹ and רִבּוֹת are late Aramaizing forms (cf. Aram. רִבּוֹא, רִבּוּ, *rebbû*), found elsewhere (sing. or plur.) in Jon. iv. 11, 1 Chron. xxix. 7 (*bis*), Ezra ii. 64, 69, Neh. vii. 66, 71, 72, Dan. vii. 10, xi. 12. We must not add Hos. viii. 12, where רבו is an intolerable reading (see *Hosea*, in Cambr. Bible, *ad loc*).—27. מַקְהֵלוֹת. See on xxvi. 12.—31. בַּצֵּר. Only here and in Dan. xi. 24. The ordinary form is פָּז, found in Prov. xi. 24, Jer. iii. 13, Joel iv. 2, Ps. liii. 6, lxxxix. 11, cxii. 9, cxlvii. 16 (Qal, Hifal, and Pual also occurs, but more rarely).

Has the initial פ been changed into ב through the influence of the Aramaic בַּדַּר (which the Targ. gives here)? Or were there from the first two distinct though allied words? At any rate, this word proves nothing.—מְתָרַפֵּס. הִת׳ also in Prov. vi. 3 (pre-Exilic?). רְפַס 'to tread' is Targumic, and occurs also in the Aramaic of Daniel (vii. 7, 19). רָפַשׂ is found twice in Ezek., and once in Hezekiah's collection of Proverbs; מִרְפָּשׂ once in Ezek.; רֶפֶשׁ 'mud' once in 2. Isaiah. Hardly a sign of date.—קְרָבוֹת. See on lv. 22.—36. מִקְדָּשִׁים. Probably *plur. excellentiæ* for מִקְדָּשׁ. So lxxiii. 17, Ezek. vii. 24 (point מִקְדְּשֵׁיהֶם); in Ezek. xxi. 7 the reading is doubtful (see Cornill).—12. חַיָּתְךָ (so point) 'thy clans.' A revived archaism; see 2 Sam. xxiii. 13.

Ps. lxxi. 6. גּוֹזִי, either 'he that loosed me' (as probably Sept.) or 'he that rewardeth me,' in either case an Aramaism [1] (for what reason can there be for resorting to the Arabic *jaza* 1. 'to divide,' 2. 'to requite,' when the Aramaic sense of גְּזָא, 1. to cut off, 2. to repay, is well attested?).—14b. The perf. Hifil of יָסַף is hardly late (as Hitzig), for though it occurs elsewhere only in 1 Kings x. 7, 2 Kings xx. 6, Eccles. i. 16, ii. 9, the parallel passage to 1 Kings x. 7 (2 Chron. ix. 6) changes הוֹסַפְתָּ into יָסְפָה. The Chronicler's alterations of early forms and idioms are so frequent that this must be held decisive.—15. סְפֹרוֹת, ἅπ. λεγ. סֹפֶרֶת, a new formation for מִסְפָּר; cf. on כָּתוֹב, lxxxvii. 6.—21. גְּדֻלָּה. Elsewhere only in cxlv. 6, 2 Sam. (twice), 1 Chron. (four times), and Esther (thrice). The word is uncommon but pre-Exilic (2 Sam. vii. being not later than the time of Josiah).

Ps. lxxii. Solomonic (Delitzsch). But where are the traditionally Solomonic proverbs which have words and phrases like the following?—5. עִם and (so also *v.* 17) לִפְנֵי 'as long as (shall exist).' Rashi points out the late Hebrew affinities of both idioms, comparing for the former עִם הַשֶּׁמֶשׁ ('as long as the sun shall shine'), *Shabbath*, 18a (i. 8 in Strack's ed.), and בִּפְנֵי הַבַּיִת and שֶׁלֹּא בִפְנֵי הַבַּיִת ('while the temple was standing,' 'while the temple was not standing') phrases of frequent occurrence in the Mishna (see e.g. *Chullin*, v. 1). Comp. also עִם דָּר וָדָר, Dan. iii. 33. It is true, בִּפְנֵי is not לִפְנֵי. At any rate, there is no parallel for the psalmist's use of לִפְנֵי in Biblical Hebrew.—6. זַרְזִיף. 'An unique intensive form' (Delitzsch). Rashi and Kimchi both quote *Yoma*, 87a, where the plural occurs. A root זרף (on which cf. Ewald, *Lehrbuch*, p. 133, foot) must be assumed for the Syr. *zorîftô* = זֶרֶם in Pesh. of Isa. iv. 6, xxv. 4. The first

---

[1] See Kohut's *Aruch*, ii. 260, left; Jastrow, *Dict. of the Targ. and Talm.*, p. 229; Payne Smith, *Thes. Syr.*, col. 696.

LINGUISTIC AFFINITIES OF THE PSALMS.

radical is repeated after the second letter as in later Syriac (Nöldeke, *Neu-syr. Gramm.*, p. 191; *Mand. Gr.*, p. 85). The text may however be corrupt (see crit. note).—אֶשְׁפָּר, elsewhere only in Ezek. xxvii. 15.—9. lxxiv. 14, Isa. xxiii. 13 &c., 'wild beasts.' *Post-Exilic?*—14. תּוֹךְ. See on x. 7; we cannot with Hitzig infer a late date from the *scriptio plena*, for though not common in the inscriptions of Mesha and Siloam, nor apparently in the MSS. from which the Sept. was translated, it was evidently not altogether unknown (see Driver, *Samuel*, Introd. pp. xxxii.-xxxiv.).—16. פִּסַּת. In spite of the Talmudic פַּסִּין 'wooden boards.' and Phœn. פס 'a board' (quoted by Mühlau and Volck), I cannot think the sense 'expansion,' 'abundance,' made out thereby. The alleged Aramaism is a corrupt reading. Grätz and Lagarde restore שִׁפְעַת, a good pre-Exilic Heb. word (2 Kings ix. 17 &c.), though of Aramaic affinities.

Ps. lxxiii. An Elyon-psalm (v. 11), and therefore presumably late; this is confirmed by the style. 4. חַרְצֻבּוֹת. A quadriliteral of a specially Aramaic type (see on lxxx. 14). ח occurs only here and in Isa. lviii. 6 (certainly not pre-Exilic). 5-7. Suffixes. See on ii. 3.—6. שִׁית; elsewhere only in Prov. vii. 10. See Nöldeke (*D. M. Z.*, xxxvii. 535), who thinks perhaps שַׁיִת should be read.—7. חֵלֶב. See on xvii. 10.—מַשְׂכִּית 'imagination,' as Prov. xviii. 11 (Græcus Venetus, φαντασία).—8. יָמִיקוּ. הֵמֵק in Zech. xiv. 12 is 'to make to consume away.' The sense required here, however, is 'mock,' which is admittedly an Aramaism.—בָּרֵעַ. Unidiomatic, as Olshausen remarks. Probably the exigencies of rhythm produced the phrase (cf. cxix. 46).—9. תִּהֲלַךְ; only here and in Ex. ix. 23. In both cases, for a similar reason, the sharp sound is pictorial (see König, *Lehrgeb.* § 36, 7a).—12. הַשְׁגּוּ. One of the poetic Aramaisms of the later books. Qal occurs in xcii. 13 and twice in Job; the Hifil of שָׂנֵא, and the adj. שַׂגִּיא, also each of them twice in Job. Aram. שְׂנָא once in Ezra, twice in Dan.; שַׂגִּיא twelve times in Dan., once in Ezra.—17. מִקְדְּשֵׁי. See on lxviii. 36.—18. לָמוֹ. If correct, an Aramaism (see Ges.-Kautzsch, p. 353). But Bickell reads תְּשִׁיתֵמוֹ.—21. The two Hithpaels occur nowhere else. The reflexive and passive forms Hithpael and Nithpael are frequent in the new Hebrew of the Mishna. Note also that חמץ (Pael and Aphel) means 'to cause pain' in Targ. on Prov. x. 1, xxviii. 7.

Ps. lxxiv. 6. בְּשִׁיל בֵּילַפּוֹת (plur.). For both words, only found here, the classical Hebrew is קַרְדֹּם. בֵּילַף (?) seems to be a weakened form of Aram. בּוּלְבָּא, comp. עֵיבָל and עוֹבָל, הֵימָם and הוֹמָם, עֵילוֹם and עוֹלָם. בּוּלְבַּיָּא occurs in Targ. of Ps. lxxiv. 5 for קַרְדֻּמּוֹת just as

בַּשִּׁילִין is given for the same word in Targ. of Jer. xlvi. 22. That *b* and not *ph* is the third root-letter, is shown by the Arabic *kalaba* 'to prick with a spur,' *kullâb*, 'hook, harpoon, spur, saw.'—8. מוֹעֲדֵי־אֵל, a term for places of worship or instruction in the Law. In a parallel poetic description of the desolation of Judah by Nebuchadrezzar the only מוֹעֵד spoken of is the temple (Lam. ii. 6). Hence though the probably Aramaic words in *v.* 6 would allow us to place the psalm in the Babylonian period, this phrase in *v.* 8 points to a later date. Comp. בֵּית וַעַד in the Mishna (*Sota*, ix. 15) for a school of the Law.

Ps. lxxvi. 6. אֶשְׁתּוֹלְלוּ Aramaizing, for השת; similar cases occur in Isa. lxiii. 3, 2 Chron. xx. 35 (both post-Exilic), though in Isa. *l.c.* the text may be corrupt (see Ges.-Kautzsch, p. 147, note [1]).

Ps. lxxvii. 4, 7. See on xlii. 5.—9. גָּמַר, an Aramaism (see on vii. 10).—Ps. lxxviii. See p. 147, and note that עֵזוּז in *v.* 4 and in cxlv. 6 comes from Isa. xlii. 25, and קְדֹשׁ יִשׂ' in *v.* 41 from the two Isaiahs. קָרַב (*v.* 9) and הִתְוּוּ (*v.* 41) are Aramaisms; for the former see above, on lv. 22, and for the latter cf. Syr. *k'vô* 'to feel vexation or repentance' (used in Pael, Pesh. 1 Sam. xxiv. 8).

Ps. lxxx. 13, 14, 16, 17. Peculiar words favouring a late date. אָרָה 'to pluck,' Song of Sol. v. 1; in the Mishna also 'to pluck' (esp. figs). Ethiopic *arara*. It is characteristic of the later period that colloquial words, sometimes perhaps old, find their way into Heb. poetry. כִּרְסֵם 'to gnaw to pieces;' cf. Talm. קִרְסֵם (*Peah*, ii. 7, of mice eating off the ears of corn). The insertion of *r*, in lieu of dagesh, is in no Semitic language so common as in Aramaic (see Porges, *Ueb. d. Verbalstammbildung*, &c., 1875, p. 50). זִיז; see on l. 11. כַּנָּה 'shoot' (see my crit. n.). כָּסַח 'to cut down,' an Aramaism, elsewhere only in Isa. xxxiii. 12 (a late prophecy, at any rate in its present form).—18. אִמֵּץ 'to fix the choice upon,' as Isa. xliv. 14.

Ps. lxxxi. 4. כֶּסֶה; only here and in Prov. vii. 20 (כֶּסֶא). Aramaic.—6. יְהוֹסֵף. An affected archaism. See on xxviii. 7.— 7. סֶבֶל. Again in Neh. iv. 11, 1 Kings xi. 28 (fem. plur. in Exodus). דּוּד 'basket,' as Jer. xxiv. 2, 2 Kings x. 7.—13. שְׁרִירוּת, an Aramaism, = 'firmness.' Eight times in Jer.; and once in Deut. (xxix. 19).

Ps. lxxxiii. Note archaistic suffixes in מוֹ (*vv.* 12, 14), and see on ii. 4, 5.—The appositional locution in *v.* 12 is quoted by Giesebrecht as an Aramaism. But שִׁיתֵמוֹ here has probably been introduced by error from *v.* 14; read שִׁית. With regard to the two parallels to the idiom in the present text in Gesenius-Kautzsch (§ 131, p. 412), Isa. xxix. 23 has probably been interpolated, and in Job xxix. 3 the pointing is doubtful.—2. דֳּמִי 'stillness,' as Isa. lxii. 6, 7; cf. דֻּמִּי, Isa. xxxviii. 10.

Ps. lxxxiv. 4, אֶפְרֹחַ. Again in Deut. xxii. 6 (twice), and in Job xxxix. 30.—11. הִסְתּוֹפֵף, ἅπ. λεγ., from סף; a colloquialism? דּוּר=גּוּר, an Aramaic and new Hebrew word, found (with the cognate noun) repeatedly in Daniel, in the Targums, and in the Talmud (see e.g. *Berakhoth* 8 *a*). דּוֹר in sense of dwelling occurs in Isa. xxxviii. 12 (post-Exilic), and according to De Witt in Ps. xlix. 20; cf. new Heb., מָדוֹר (=מָדוֹר) and מְדָר, Aram. Daniel).

Ps. lxxxv. 9, סָלָה, as Job iv. 6, see on xlix. 11.—Ps lxxxvi. Note the title אֲדֹנָי seven times.—9. כָּבֵד with לְ as Dan. xi. 39, see on xvii. 4. —5. סַלָּח, ἅπ. λεγ. סלח 'to forgive' is a good N. Semitic word (Hebrew, western Aramaic, and Assyrian). In Hebrew, certainly, it is only used in Qal; the Piel (Pael) form which explains סַלָּח is found in the Targums. See, however, on the form Ewald, *Lehrbuch*, § 155 *b* and *c*, and observe that the ordinary equivalent for Heb. סלח in the Targums is שְׁבַק. The other derivative of סלח, viz. סְלִיחָה, is admittedly late (Ryssel quotes שְׁחִיטָה and יְגִיעָה from Chron. and Eccles.). Its form is specially frequent in New Hebrew,[1] and the word itself occurs only in cxxx. 4, Neh. ix. 17 (pl.), Dan. ix. 9 (pl.).—6. תַּחֲנוּנוֹת, ἅπ. λεγ. quoted by Hitzig and Giesebrecht as late. But rhythm might in any age have led a poet to coin this fem. plur., which, with the suffix, gives one more syllable than the corresponding masculine.

Ps. lxxxvii. Written in a harsh quasi-prophetic style, somewhat as Ps. cx.—1. יְסוּדָה, ἅπ. λεγ. A late form, according to Giesebrecht, for the classical form יְסוֹד. But is this at all necessary? See on lxxxv. 6.— בְּהַרְרֵי קֹדֶשׁ; so cx. 3 (best reading). Isaiah (xi. 9) only speaks of the 'holy mountain' of Jehovah. The range of 'holiness' is extending; cf. Baudissin, *Studien*, ii. 129.—5. וְאִישׁ אִישׁ. This locution is only found elsewhere in Esth. i. 8 (אִישׁ וָאִישׁ), and אִישׁ אִישׁ only perhaps in Ex. xxxvi. 4, and fourteen times in Lev. and Num. We cannot argue from this that the ps. must be post-Exilic, for דּוֹר וָדוֹר occurs in Deut. xxxii. 7, and יוֹם יוֹם in Gen. xxxix. 10. But it is a fact that the connexion of the second word in such phrases by *Waw copulat.* is specially common in Chron. and Esther. Dr. Driver gives me the following list of proof-passages, 1 Chron. xxvi. 13, xxviii. 14, 2 Chron. viii. 14, xi. 12, xix. 5, xxviii. 25, xxxi. 19, xxxii. 28, xxxiv. 13, xxxv. 15, Esth. i. 8, 22 (*bis*), ii. 11, 12, iii. 4, 12, 14, iv. 3, 8, 9, 11, 13, 17, ix. 21, 27, 28. See on xlv. 18 and cf. Ges.-Kautzsch, *Lehrbuch*, p. 383. —עֶלְיוֹן. See on vii. 18.—6. כָּתוֹב. Probably here a collat. form of כָּתַב (cf. the phrase in Ezek. xiii. 9), which is a late Heb. formation

---

[1] See Siegfried and Strack, *Lehrbuch der neuhebr. Sprache*, § 47*b*, and cf. Ryssel, *De Elohistæ Pentateuchi Sermone* (1878), pp. 49, 50.

(Ezek., Chron., Ezra, Neh., Esth., Dan.) for the classical מִכְתָּב. The corresponding fem. כְּתֹבֶת occurs in Lev. xix. 28. Comp. on lxxi. 21.

Ps. lxxxviii. 5. אֱיָל, ἄπ. λεγ. See on xxii. 20. The form points to a late age (Ewald, *Lehrbuch*, § 153*a*, 2).—8. סָמַךְ עַל 'to lean upon,' not with the view of getting support, but of causing distress. An unique sense, for which Nestle quotes Syriac parallels (see Nowack *ad loc.*).—13. נָשִׁיָּה, ἄπ. λεγ. Not certainly but probably a late form. The distinction between 'abstract' and 'concrete' ideas cannot be strictly carried out even in new Hebrew (see e.g. יצירה in Buxtorf). 'The land of forgetting' may have been an old name of Sheól, and a *nomen actionis* of the form אֲכִילָה (1 Kings xix. 8) would be the natural term to employ. See, however, remark on סְלִיחָה (note on lxxxvi. 5).—17. בְּעוּתִים. Again in Job vi. 4 (Exilic), which may be alluded to.—צִמְּתוּנִי (so read). The Piel occurs again only in cxix. 139.

Ps. lxxxix. 9. חֲסִין, ἄπ. λεγ; but common in Aramaic (*khasînô*= Shaddai in Pesh. of Job). Cf. חֲסַן; חִסְנָא in Daniel. The root however is proved to be Hebrew by חָסוֹן, Am. ii. 9, Isa. i. 31.—40. נִאֵר, only here and in Lam. ii. 7.—45. מִגֵּר, in its full Aramaic sense of 'throwing down' (2 Kings ix. 33 Targ., for שמטוה). The Qal participle in Ezek. xxi. 17 means 'delivered up.'—48. חֶלֶד. See on xvii. 14.

Here let us pause. Bks. I.-III. contain the psalms which are usually with most confidence assigned to the pre-Exilic period. I have sought to show that there are numerous linguistic phenomena which throw some doubt on this theory, and make the opposite one proportionably more plausible. Had I space, I think that I could prove that Books IV. and V. contain so many unmistakeable Aramaisms, and words belonging distinctively to the later literature, that nothing but the most cogent evidence derived from the ideas could justify us in assigning any of the psalms in these books to a pre-Exile period. I trust that I have shown in the Lectures that such evidence from ideas does not exist. But as a work of supererogation I will devote such space as I can to an examination of some of the most interesting psalms which remain.

Ps. xc. Mosaic (Delitzsch). Can this be? To the phraseological parallels between Ps. xc. and Deut. xxxii. and (perhaps) xxxiii. I have referred already Those most commonly adduced are *v.* 1, מָעוֹן, 'habitation,' used of God, as Deut. xxxiii. 27 (מְעֹנָה); *v.* 2, וַתְּחוֹלֵל of the birth-pangs of creation, as Deut. xxxii. 18; *v.* 13*b*, same phrase as in Deut. xxxii. 36*a*; *v.* 15, שְׁנוֹת יְמוֹת, combined as in Deut. xxxii. 7 (the former only found in these two passages). Of these the only ones which are beyond dispute are the third and fourth. It is the fourth which gives weight to the third, for the phrase in *v.* 13*b* might, if we did not know that the psalmist had some words of Deut. xxxii. floating in his memory, be thought to present a purely accidental coincidence with the 'Song of Moses.' The first and the second depend on the correctness of the text, which, with some other critics, I feel compelled to question. From the fact, however, that in the headings of Ps. xc. and of Deut. xxxiii. alike Moses receives the same high title of 'man of God,' it is not improbable that the reading מָעוֹן (which is a phraseological link between those two songs, as they now stand) already existed when the heading of Ps. xc. was written (see p. 75, foot). Notice in this connexion the old Hebrew verb גּוּז (*v.* 10, Num. xi. 31, and nowhere else); cf. גָּז, common in Aram. in the sense 'to pass away,' 'to vanish.' In the same verse the emphatic but otherwise meaningless cohortative should be observed (see on xlii. 5); in *vv.* 3, 9 the rare words דַּכָּא (see on xxxiv. 19), הָגָה (again in Job xxxvii. 2, Ezek. ii. 10; cf. on xlix. 4); in *v.* 14 the Piel of שָׂבַע (again in Ezek. vii. 19). Comp. הָגָה with הֲגִי, הַגְיָא, 'speech, meditation' (Targ. and Talm. Jer., ap. Jastrow).

Ps. xci. Of uncertain date (Delitzsch; Nowack). Note however the ἀπ. λεγ. סֹחֵרָה (*v.* 4), a synonym for צִנָּה, from סחר in the Aramaic sense 'to surround.' Also that three striking words in this psalm occur in Deut. xxxii., xxxiii., viz. עֶלְיוֹן (*vv.* 1, 9, cf. Deut. xxxii. 8), קֶטֶב (*v.* 6, cf. Deut. xxxii. 24), and מָעוֹן in connexion with God (*v.* 9, cf. Deut. xxxiii. 27). It is true, however, that מ׳ also occurs in Isa. xxviii. 2, and that מָעוֹן may be a wrong reading. A much clearer connexion exists between בִּי חָשַׁק in *v.* 14 and Deut. vii. 7. Lastly observe that the divine names 'Elyōn (*vv.* 1, 9), and Shaddai (*v.* 1) are mostly used by Exilic or post-Exilic writers (pp. 83, 84).

Ps. ci. To the phraseological evidence (p. 67) one would gladly join some more specially linguistic. In *v.* 5 we meet with מְלוֹשְׁנִי (so to be pointed), where the linking vowel is an affected archaism, which justifies us in assuming this psalm to be at earliest a late pre-Exilic work. The same remark applies to a number of temple-songs (see cx. 4, cxiii. 5-9, cxiv. 8, cxvi. 1, cxxiii. 1, Lam. iii. 1, and cf. l. 4, and the passages quoted in the note above). The verb לשׁן (here in Poel) occurs again only in Prov. xxx. 10 (in Hifil). But though אָלְשַׁן and הִלְשִׁין in partic. forms are used in Targ. and in new Heb. for 'to slander,' and on this and other much more important grounds Prov. xxx. is post-Exilic, we cannot argue from this to the post-Exilic date of Ps. ci. Poel is a stem which does not occur in Aramaic, and there is an exact parallel to לוֹשֵׁן, 'to attack with the tongue,' in

I I

עוֹיֵן 'to attack with the eye' (1 Sam. xviii. 9, pre-Exilic). Comp. the Arabic verb *'âna* 'to view with an evil eye,' and *lasana* 'to defame.' Linguistically therefore the psalm may be late pre-Exilic.

Ps. cix. 8. Stade quotes פְּקֻדָּה 'office' as distinctively a late sense, which arose in connexion with the newly organized priestly functions, cf. Num. iii. 32, 36, 2 Chron. xxix. 11 (*Zeitschr. f. d. a. t. Wiss.*, 1885, p. 282). But פָּקִיד='officer' in Judg. ix. 28. שְׁעָטִים, elsewhere only in Eccles. v. 1, does however seem late. 16. בָּאָה has its analogue in Syriac. It occurs in Nifal only here and in Dan. xi. 30; in Hifil only in Ezek. xiii. 22.

Ps. cx. 'Primitive in its vigour and fulness of thought' (Ehrt). Similarly Ewald, who regards it as based upon an oracle of Gad or Nathan. One could certainly imagine that *v. 3b* was 'borrowed from some old poem now lost' (so my commentary admits); but then the text of that clause is liable to suspicion. It is, in fact, the single obscure passage in the psalm, and the Sept., partly supported by two other Greek versions, read differently (מֵרֶחֶם מִשַּׁחַר יְלִדְתִּךָ, the second מִן being used pregnantly, cf. Job xi. 17). In my commentary I have given way to conservative scruples, which in this psalm if anywhere are justifiable. But approaching Ps. cx., as I do now, from a linguistic point of view, I cannot but say that both מִשְׁחָר and טַל seem to me intolerable. Till we know something certain about the Hebrew of the Davidic or pre-Isaianic age, we have no sufficient right to indulge in the conjecture that 'the whole phrase [in *v. 3b*] may be borrowed from some old poem now lost' (so my commentary). Had there really been such a word as מִשְׁחָר ('the early morning sky;' cf. מַחֲשָׁךְ 'a dark place,' lxxiv. 20, &c.), should we not have met with it in some of the many poetical references to the dawn? Philologically the best reading seems to be that of Bickell, מֵרֶחֶם מִשַּׁחַר לְךָ יַלְדֻתֶךָ, i.e. 'from the womb, from the dawn (of life), thy youthful band is (devoted) unto thee.' Bickell too has improved the arrangement of *vv.* 5, 6. The psalm is free from archaisms except that of the linking-vowel (once no doubt a case-ending) in דִּבְרָתִי (*v.* 4). Unless the non-linguistic evidence points decidedly to an early pre-Exilic origin, it must be natural to view this as the affectation of a late poet (see on ci. 5). Note also that no old writer employs the fem. form דִּבְרָה (Job v. 8 is the oldest passage), and that Eccles. is the only book which contains the phrase עַל־דִּבְרַת (Eccles. iii. 18, vii. 14, viii. 2), except indeed Daniel, in the Aram. part of which occurs עַל־דִּבְרַת דִּי. In *v.* 3 we have יַלְדוּת, which is only found again in Eccles. xi. 9, 10, and as the equivalent of מוֹלֶדֶת in the Targums. All that can be done to mitigate the force of these facts has been done by Delitzsch (see his commentary). Note lastly בְּהַרְרֵי־קֹדֶשׁ (see crit. note in my comm.), as in lxxxvii. 1, the idea underlying which is late. Altogether Ps. cx. is a more successful imitation of the prophetic style than Ps. lxxxii., and worthy of being compared with Ps. ii. Among other points of resemblance between Pss. ii. and cx., observe that both contain the post-Davidic divine title Adonai.

Pss. cxl.–cxliii. The three first of these belong, acc. to Ewald, to the time of Manasseh. He admits, however, that this is far from certain. Points of contact with psalms in the first Davidic collection and (cf. Ps. ci.) with Proverbs cannot of course prove the antiquity of these compositions. It is not only those psalms which are imitated, and if Ehrt's list of parallelisms in Proverbs be throughout accepted, it shows that there was already a *Book* of Proverbs in the psalmists' time. חֲמָסִים, which occurs in Ps. cxl. 2, 5, and also in Prov. iv. 17 (and in one of the recensions of our Ps. xviii.; see 2 Sam. xxii. 49), belongs, as Delitzsch remarks, to a more recent epoch, when the plural was substituted poetically for the singular. Note also the numerous ἅπαξ λεγόμενα in these psalms (cxl. 4, 9, 11, 12; cxli. 3, 4, 10; cxlii. 8); especially מַדְחֵפֹת, which must be late.

There are still four psalms of special interest which must not be altogether passed over, though, with one exception, they could not be adequately treated except as members of groups, and indeed of groups which are themselves closely connected by a common linguistic type; these are cxviii., cxxxvii., cxxxix., and cxliv. In Ps. cxviii. notice in *vv.* 10–12 the Hifil (found nowhere else) of מוּל with uncertain meaning, and the Pual (also unique) of דָּעַךְ, a rare word of Aramaic affinities, found four times in Job, once in 2 Isa., and twice in the earliest portion of Proverbs. It is doubtful, however, whether the Massoretic text of *v.* 12*a* is correct (see crit. n.). Observe in passing that psalms belonging to the same group, and for various reasons held to be contemporaneous, do not always exhibit a late date with equal distinctness in their language. In the case of Ps. cxxxvii. a post-Exilic date is assured by the Aram. affix in אֲזַכְּרֵכִי (*v.* 6, cf. ciii. 3, cxvi. 19, &c.), and by the thrice repeated שֶׁ (*vv.* 8, 9). Otherwise the style of the psalm, says Delitzsch, is 'classical,' especially if the text may here and there be emended. Ps. cxxxix. on the other hand is famous for its incorrectness; in it, according to the same scholar, 'the Aramaic-Hebrew idiom of the post-Exile period is taken into the service of poetry.' To me this appears an exaggeration. I admit that the ἅπ. λεγ. רֵעַ in *v.* 2 is an Aramaism, like רְעוּת and רַעְיוֹן (see Delitzsch or Wright on Eccles. i. 14), and that the mark of the accus. in לְרֵעִי is also Aramaic. But in *v.* 3 why should we not emend רָבְעִי into רִבְצִי? רבע

occurs thrice again, it is true, in Lev. xviii.–xx., and, according to Cornill, in Ezek. xix. 7, but there it has a special sense (cf. Levy's *Chald. Lex.* s. v. רְבַע). It seems to me that רִבְעִי is quite intolerable here. And in *v.* 20 are we not justified in correcting עָרֶיךָ into שְׁמֶךָ (see crit. n.)? Comp. Driver on 1 Sam. xxviii. 16, an early passage, which has not escaped the intrusion of the same pronounced Aramaism. The student will of course notice in *v.* 19 the rare form אֱלוֹהַּ; see on xviii. 32. In Ps. cxliv. the linguistic interest centres in *vv.* 12–14, which Ewald regards as a pre-Exile fragment (see p. 66). Here we find, in *v.* 13, the Aramaizing זַן, which occurs nowhere else except in 2 Chron. xvi. 14 (plur.), זָוִית, which meets us again in Zech. ix. 15, and מֶזֶו, apparently a late word for אָסָם.

INDICES.

INDICES.

(The numbers with an asterisk prefixed are those of pages in the second or linguistic appendix.)

I.—NAMES AND SUBJECTS.

ABBOTT

ABBOTT, T. K., 243, 382
Aben Ezra, (on Ps. vi.) 227 ; (on title of Ps. xxx.) 247 ; (on Ps. li. 20, 21) 175
Abraham, (Gen. xiv.) 42 ; (his religious position) 264, 371 ; (in Paradise) xxxiii.
Adonai, 124, 287, 288, **299-303**, 465
Ahab, 167, 179
Ahriman (*angro-mainyus*), 282, 333, 400
Ahura, not historically connected with Adonai, 283
Ahura Mazda, 146, 271, 289, 357, 379, 398 &c.
—— — his spirituality, 282, 283
Akbar, called a Zoroastrian, 448
Akiba, Rabbi, 83, 332
Alcimus, 27, 56, 93, 94, 123
Alexander, Bishop, 116, 264
— the Great, 156, 169, 344, 423
Allegory, Zoroastrian, 398, 399, 437
Amenti, Egyptian Hades, 424, 432
Amos, Book of, 194
Amshaspands, their connexion with archangels, 336, 337
Angels, belief in, 120, 157, 272, 281, 282, 323-327, **334-337**
Anquetil Duperron, 394
Antiochus Epiphanes, 10, 146, 166
— the Great, 69, 114, 115, 128, 166
— Soter, 182
Apocalypse, Persian influence on the, 281
Apocalyptic element in the Psalms, 373, 386

BAUR

Appleton, C. E. A., xii.
Arab song-writing, 192, 210, 459
Arabia, privilege of guestship in, 429
— view of death in heathen, 433
Aristeas, pseudo-, 144, 181, 183
Aristobulus I., 28, 39, 111, 201
— II., 219
Ark, significance of the, 315, 328
Artaxerxes I., 163
— II., 292, 342
— III. (Ochus), 53, 72, 91, 102, 160, 175, 229, 292
Asaph, psalms of, 101, 120, 147, 150, 159
Asidæans, 19, 198 (see also *khasidim*)
Assyrian hymns, 391
Atonement, law of Day of, 161
Augustine, St., 29, 61, 259, 273, 274, 292, 353, 377
Avesta, use of the, 433
— catholic utterance in the, 292, 305 (see also Gâthâs and Yasna)

BABYLONIAN hymns, 65, 194, 213, 267, 268, 278, 279, 376
— influences on Judaism, 391 &c.
— inscriptions, late, 183
Baethgen, Friedr., 31, 123, 137, 178, 217, 244, 467
Ball, C. J., xxiv., 27, 43, 77, 135, 376
Baruch, Book of, xxx., 456
bath qol, 7, 39, 332
Baudissin, Graf, xx., 42, 83, 132, *479
Baur, F. C., 209
— Gustav, 208

BELLARMINE

Bellarmine, Card., 85
Benedictions, the Eighteen, 18, 271, 327, 363, 416
Bickell, Gustav, 157, 182, 207, 459, 477, 482
Binnie, W., 278
Bissell, E. C., xxx.
Boethius, 274
Bredenkamp, C. J., 91, 470
Bridge, the Judge's, 399, 438
Briggs, C. A., xxiv., 7, 304
Brown, Francis, 279
Browne, Sir T., 326
Browning, Robert, 192, 260, 410
Bruce, A. B., 209, 220, 337
Brugsch-Bey, H., 424, 432
Budde, K., 280, 459, *461
Buddhism, 358
Bundahis, Zoroastrian Scripture, 395, 401, 405, 420, 421, 439, 449
Butler, Bishop, 386

CADYTIS, origin of name, 299
Caiaphas, prophecy of, 25
Cajetan, Cardinal, 430, 431
Calamity, Jewish view of, 345, 354
Calendar, Jewish, 68, 80, 184
Caliphs, court-poetry under the, 167
Callimachus, 180
Calvin, 82, 131, 154, 157, 177, 231, 245, 247, 455
Canon, close of Old Testament, 457
Captivity, the third great, 53
Carpzov, J. G., 7, 13
Castelli, David, 53, 415
Cave, A., xxviii.
Chenery, T., 50, 433
Cherub, conception of, 205, 223, 323, 327
Church, germs of doctrine of the, 266, 312
— consciousness in the Psalter, 258
Church, Dean, 370
— Professor, 92, 142
Chronicles, Books of, 298
— their style, 474, 476
Chrysostom, 5, 29, 36, 64, 76-78, 82, 103, 174, 243, 273, 428
Clement of Alexandria, 430, 446
Code, the Priestly, xvii., xxx., 248, 270, 281, 335, 393, 396, *473
Colenso, Bishop, xvii.
Coleridge, S. T., 141
Columban, 253
Conder, Colonel, 195
Cornill, C. H., 106, 128, 185, 301, 476, 484
Cosmogony, Babylonian, 280, 283

DELITZSCH

Cosmogony, Iranian, 283
— Jewish, 272, 280, 283
Covenant, religious conception of the, 345
Cromwell, Oliver, 19
Curtiss, S. T., 43
Cuthbert, St. (Ps. lx.), 96
Cyril, St., 21, 428
Cyrus, 169, 172, 182, 183, 279, 280, 352

DALMAN, Gustav, 213, 299, 300
Daniel, Book of, 15, 25 (note), 35, 37, 94, 105-107, 156, 287, 296, 336, 417, 445
— name of, 106
— Greek additions to, 30
Dante, 94, 96, 98, 232, 265, 274, 337, 420, 432
Darius Hystaspis, 144, 168, 247, 280
Darmesteter, J., 107, 397, 437, 439, 440
David, character and work of, 190-193, 211, 237, 249
— a second, 194
— symbolic use of name, 22, 25, 37, 339
— imaginary psalms of, 205, 206
— ascription of psalms to, 7, 69, 75, 81, 107, 126, 136, 174, 190
Davidic psalms, criteria of, 190, 208
— — relics of genuine, 193
Davidson, A. B., xxiv., 133, 209
Dawn, a religious symbol, 407, 448
Dedication (or, Hanukka), Feast of, 17, 18, 32, 33, 247
D'Eichthal, Gust., 284
Delitzsch, Franz, his *Iris*, 153
— — his argument from colours, 219
— — on Messianic psalms, 260
— — — the Book of Daniel, 106
— — — — — Ecclesiastes, 409
— — — — — Jonah, 306
— — — immortality in Proverbs, 441
— — — Samuel as a psalmist, 210
— — — Davidic psalms, 208
— — — Messianic psalms, 34, 260
— — — Pss. xlii., xliii., 126
— — — — xvi., *465
— — — — xvii., *466
— — — — xliv., lxxiv., lxxix., 93 (cf. 103)
— — — — li. 20, 21, ... 175
— — — — lxxxvii., ... 131
— — — — lxxxviii., lxxxix., ... 129, 130
— — — — cx., ... 34
— — — — cxxii., &c., ... 60 (see also pp. 197, 244, 250 &c.)

DELITZSCH

Delitzsch, Friedrich, 279
Demetrius Poliorcetes, 184
De Quincey, Thomas (on Essenism), 445, 446
Derenbourg, J., 40, 80, 132, 416, 456
De Vere, Aubrey, 204, 382
De Witt, John, 6, 319, 320, *479
Dillmann, Aug., 31, 56, 92, 95, 133, 160, 177, 218, 249, 301, 333, 457, *463, *464, *468
Dorner, Aug., 191
Driver, S. R., xvi., xx., xxi., xxiii., xxiv., xxvi., 57, 182, 298, 304, 409, 426, *461, *463 &c.
Drummond, of Hawthornden, 204
— James, 23, 24, 30, 38, 293, 304, 331, 420, 449
Droysen, 155, 156, 168
Dualism, Jewish, 422
Duncker, Max, 210
Dutt, R. Chunder, xxxiv.

ECCLESIASTES, Book of, 55, 287, 290, 298, 321, 381, 423
— date of, 409
— style of, 463, 472
— not Hellenistic, 423
Ecclesiasticus, Book of, 10, 331
— date of, 123, 409, 456
— appendix to, 127
— not Hellenistic, 423
— Sadducean elements in, 411
— style of, 300, 463
— incorrectness of Greek rendering of, 458
— references to Psalms in, xxx., 117, 128, 456
Edersheim, A., 36, 127, 128, 278, 327, 456
Egyptian influence on Jews, 431
— inscriptions, &c., 181, 304
— religious ideas, 431, 432
Ehrt, C., 49, 78, 104, 456, 458, 483
Eichhorn, J. G., 117, 129, 176
Elijah, story of, 383, 421
Eliot, George, 450
Elmslie, W. G., 158
Eloah, divine name, 205, 206, 467
Elohistic narrative, the, 272, 283, 463
Elyon, divine title, 26, 27, 41, 51, 73, 83, 121, 164, 206, 314, 464
Enoch, story of, xxxiii., 149, 383, 432
— the Babylonian, 432
— Book of, 22, 412, 423
— — — Essenian elements in, 448, 449
— — — Messianism in, 122
— — — view of sacrifices in, 375
Epiphany, Feast of, 32, 34, cf. xxxviii.

GOBINEAU

Essenes, connexion of name, 56
— their belief in angels, 335
— view of marriage, 446
— — — sacrifices, 375
— — — the soul, 418-421, 447
— — alleged sun-worship, 331, 447, 448
Essenism in Jewish Christianity, 446
Esther, Book of, 287, 298
Eternity of punishment, 439
Eupolemus, Hellenistic writer, 13, 109
Eusebius, 103, 185, 273
Ewald, H., xvi., xviii., 21, 32, 35, 38, 65, 91, 97, 102, 109, 114, 135, 146, 158, 162, 165, 167, 176, 179, 190, 191, 217, 245, 249, 299, 328, 457, *462
— — on Davidic psalms, 208
Ezekiel, 301, 321, 353
Ezra, did he rebuild the walls? 71
— his legalism, 358
— was he a psalmist? 253
— did he collect (or complete) the Psalms? 13, 458
— Fourth Book of, 421

FATHER, divine title, 291, 305, 313, 327, 328, 350
Fletcher, Phineas, 54
Flood-story, Babylonian, 392, 432, 469, 474
Forbes, John, 59, 130, 217, 243, 251
Forgiveness, conception of, 54, 347
Frankl, Z., 38, 184, 445, 456
frashôkereti (or *frashakard*), meaning of, 407, 438, 440
fravashis, the, 282, 335, 420, 449
Freudenthal, 13, 29, 109
Fuller, J. F., 38

GANNEAU, Clermont, 181
Gaokerena, 400, 439
Gâthâs, the, 74, 194, 213, 284, 334, 335, 341, 352, 372, 379, 385, 395-398, 436
Geiger, A., 33, 40, 41, 57, 303, 330, 409
Geldner, K., 395, 434-436, 450
Genesis, origin of, 270, 279
Gen. xiv., date of; see Index II.
gēr ('guest'), use of, 429
Gesenius, W., 104
Giesebrecht, Friedr., 111, 180, 182, *461, *472, *478, *479
Gifford, E. H. (on Baruch), 456
Glory, the divine, 331
Gobineau, Count, 13

GOETHE

Goethe, xiv., 367
Goldziher, I., xx., 282, 284
Gore, Charles, ix., xxv., xxviii.
Grätz, H., 13 (Modin), 55 (Purim), 61 (Ps. cxxxiv.), 83 (daily psalms: date of Sept.), 110 & 142 (the 'anāvīm), 125 (Ps. lxviii.), 142 (Ps. lxxii.), 159 (Ps. xlix.), 180 (date of Sept. Pentateuch), 184 (against Josephus), 219 (Simon the Maccabee), 355 & 455 (Maccabæan psalms), 425 & 442 (on the resurrection-doctrine)
Greek influence on Jews, 9, 10, 14, 66, 313, 423–425
Gregory Nazianzen, 29
— of Nyssa, 258
Grotius, 75, 76, 85, 130, 275
Gruppe (on Greek myths), xxxi., 451
Günzburg, David, 459
Guthe, H., 249

HADES, the Egyptian; see Amenti
— — Mandean, 432
Halévy, J., 81, 125, 126, 391, 452, *467, *473
Hallel, the, 18, 32, 49, 50, 57
— origin of word, 459, 460
Hallévi, R. Yehuda, 336, 369
Hamburger, J. (on Jewish parties), 57
Hammond, H., 6, 7
Hannah, Song of; see Index II.
Hannington, Bishop, 234
Hanukka; see Dedication
Haoma plant, the, 437, 439
Hardt, H. von der, 57–60, 253
Harlez, C. de, 85, 157, 213, 282, 395, 425, 438, 440
Harnack, Th., 31
Harrison, Fred., 19
Hatch, Edwin, 12, 469
Haupt, Paul, 61, 469
Havet, M., xxxii., 415
Hawkins, E., 76
Heart, ethical reference of term, 466, cf. 473
Heaven, the Assyrian, 153
— spiritualized or symbolic conception of, 298, 300, 314, 318, 328
Heaven and hell, the Egyptian, 431, 432
— the later Jewish, 391, 416, 432, 444
— the Zoroastrian, 399, 400, 439
Hebrew; see Language
Heman, guild of, 100, 101
Hengstenberg, E. W., 60, 61, 131, 164, 177, 214, 240, 260, 285
Herder, J. G., 326

ISRAEL

Hezekiah, did he collect psalms? 7
— Song of; see Index II.
Hickes, the nonjuror, 327
Hilary, 458
Hildersam, Puritan divine, 174
Hilgenfeld, Ad., 23, 133, 375, 447–449
Hitzig, Ferd., 60, 68, 114, 116, 134, 137, 155, 164, 167, 176, 177, 216, 226, 247, 249–251, 333, 470
— — on Davidic psalms, 208
— — on Maccabæan psalms, 455
Hofmann, of Erlangen, 273, 274
Hoffmann, G., 299, 426
Holland, H. S., xxxiv.
Holtzman, M., 213, 357
Holtzmann, H., 38
— Oscar, 41, 449
Holy and holiness, use of terms, 324, 331
Homer, 37, 184, 198
Hooker, 304
Horace, 273
Hort, F. J. A., 182
Hübschmann, H., Zend scholar, 434
Hupfeld, H., 109, 126, 223
Humility, a note of the true Israel, 98, 110, 171, 468 (top)
Hyde, T., 107, 281
Hyrcanus, John, 13, 24, 25, 39, 93, 96, 143
— II., 26, 146, 154, 219

IDEAL (or, heavenly) existence, 274, 334
Immortality, Babylonian germs of belief in, 391–393
— is the idea in the Psalter? 381 &c.
— Greek belief in, xxxiii.
— Persian belief in, 394 &c.
— Sabæan belief in, 393
— in Ps. xxxvi. 9 Sept., 409
Imra al-Kais, 192
Isaac, St., of Antioch, 29
Isaiah (Book of), higher criticism of; see Index II.
— eschatology of, 402–406
— his literary influence, 162, 164
— was he a psalmist? 214
— founder of Jewish Church, 209
— the Second, his literary influence, 71, 112, 124, 162
Islam, 303, 304, 336, 379
Israel, its receptivity, 267
— late traces of heathenism in, 160, 297
— — missionary function, 292 (see also Judaism)

NAMES AND SUBJECTS.

JACKSON

JACKSON, Dean, 6, 103, 122, 136, 245
Jaddua, 59
Jah, divine name, 124, 300, 301
Jannæus, Alexander, 24
Japanese mythology, 325
Jasher, Book of, 192, 193, 210
Jeduthun, 101, **246**
Jehoshaphat, 177
Jehovah (Yahveh), use of this name in later books, 214, 297, 298–302
— the name, when not pronounced, 301
— Sabáoth, 20, 203, 222, 315, 323, 329
— unique divinity of, 246
— creatorship of, 214, 314, 322
— as Shepherd and Teacher, 249, **343–348**, 352
— humility ascribed to, 224, 343
— prophetic view of, its relation to Nicene doctrine, 290
— may the name be applied to Christ? 222, 305
— objection to Christian use of name, 304
—; see also Kingdom
Jensen, P., 330, 392, 427, 432
Jeremiah, his religious influence, 214, 264
— the evangelical prophet, 316, cf. 425
— school of, 135, 231, 365, 466
— was he a psalmist? 122, 134–136, 230, 242, 247, 250
Jeremias, A., 427
Jeroboam II., 167, 179
Jerome, St., (on Salem) 42, (on anon. psalms) 85, (on Ps. lxxii.) 153, (on old copies of Sept.) 299, (on Ps. lxxviii.) 336
Jewish hymns, 277, 297, 334, 336, 369
Jezebel, (Ps. xlv.) 167, 471
Job, speeches of, 64, 85
— a symbol of Israel, 118, 127
— (Book of), its date, 159, 202, 217, 218, 409
— — — its character, 67, 70, 72, 73, 149, 287
— — — gives the inner experiences of its author, 290
— — — its Babylonian affinities, 266
— — — its mythology, 202, 270
— — — its style, 463
— — — Elihu-section of, 246, 249, 409
— — — epilogue of, 405
— — — Sept. addition to, 406 (note)
— — — monument of a school of poets, 242

LAGARDE

Joel (Book of), xx., 133, 239, 365, 428
— M., 296, 423
Johannine writings, the, 388, 425
Jonah, Book of, 127, 202, 294, 295, 306, 395
— psalm of, its twin brother, 127
Jonathan, the Maccabee, 81
Jong, P. de, 102, 104, 458
Joseph, story of, 158
Josiah, reign of, 91, 205, 215
Jost, J. M., 14, 22, 38, 349, 376
Jubilees, Book of, 448
Judaism, 'duality' of, 296
— later, its view of the heathen, 306
— Egyptian, 423, 452
Judas the Maccabee, 10, 16, 48, 96, 98, 142, 178, 199
Judgment, doctrine of the, 241, 254, 372–374, 387
— on individuals, 381 &c.
Judith, Book of, 25 (note), 37
Justin Martyr, 35, 153, 154, 222, 414, 443

KALISCH, M. M., 302, 377, 467
Kamphausen, A. H. H., 351
Kant, 260
Kautzsch, E., 250, 328, 463 &c.
Kay, W., 6, 90, 134, 221, 226, 245, 347
Kenosis, theological idea, xxv., xxvi.; cf. 344
khasīdīm, the, 19, 27, 33, 48, 49, 56, 57, 92, 93, 98, 117, 119, 129, 150, 195, 247, 364
khesed, or lovingkindness, meaning of, 117, 370–372, 378, 379
Kimchi, R. David, (title of Ps. xlv.) 173, (Ps. li. 20, 21) 175, (Ps. lxv.) 176, (Book of Ezra) 344, (Ps. lxxii. 6) *476
King, E. G., 159
— use of term, 468
Kingdom, the divine, 336, 340, 341
Kingsley, C., quoted, 266
Kohut, A., 282, 401
Korah, psalms of, 100, 101 &c.
Koran, referred to, 65, 69, 325, 333, 377, 379, 429, 432
Kremer, A. v., 167
Krochmal, 50, 58, 243
Kuenen, A., xvi., xvii., xix., 133, 157, 159, 179, 191, 209, 247–249, *461

LAGARDE, P. de, 31, 91, 176, 232, 247, 248, 254, 282, 299, 351, 459, *467, *473

LAMENTATIONS

Lamentations, Book of, 100, 214
Law, preëxistence of the, 358
— imperfection of, recognized, 374
— expansion of meaning, 349, 358
— Levitical, its value, 358, 367
Lazarus, Emma, 18, 104
Leathes, Stanley, 175
Lehrs, K., xxxii., xxxiii.
Lenormant, François, 278
Lessing, his *Nathan*, 335
Ley, Julius, 459
Libations, heathen, 198
Life, Tree of, Babylonian, 400, 427
— — — Hebrew, 383, 412, 428
— — — Iranian, 400, 427
—, Water of, 383, 400, 413, 414, 427, 442
Lightfoot, Bishop, xxix., 56, 209, 447
Lights, Feast of; see Epiphany
Linguistic (cf. App. II.):—
  Value of linguistic argument, xxi., 130, 461
  Is an abrupt style a mark of age? 212, 462, 466
  Scriptio plena, argument from, 477
  Termination *uth*, 472
  Abstract forms in Hebrew, 472, 479, 480
  Aramaisms, presence of, 462, 463, 467, 475, 480 &c.
  Assyrian cognate words, 469, 473, 474
  '*abd*, use of, in Arabic, 303
  Supposed Scythian loanword, 469
  Elohim, Phœnician linguistic parallel to Hebrew use of, 299
Lock, Walter, 277
Lord's Prayer, doxology in, 457
Lowth, Bishop, xii., 7
Luther, 235
Lyra, Nic. de, 253

MACCABÆAN period, greatness of, 15
— — attitude of Jews in Egypt, 38
Maccabee, meaning of, 43
Maccabees, their descent, 27, 32, 43
— — complex characters, 43
— — monument, 13
— — unworthy descendants, 28, 375
— festival of the, 29
— typified by Joshua, 32, 96
— — — Saul, 37, 97
— — — David, 22, 25, 37, 67
— — — Solomon, 37
— first Book of, 56, 298, 300, 417, 456, 457
— second Book of, 38, 39, 56, 137, 345
— fourth Book of, 29

NEUBAUER

Macrobius, 32
Mahdist manifesto, 80
Maimun, 412
Marduk, the god, 282, 392, 393
Margoliouth, D. S., 300
Marriage, Egyptian, with a sister, 183
Martineau, James, 324, 389
Martyrdom, privilege of, 444
Mason, A. J., 441
Mazdeism; see Zoroastrianism
Megillath Taanith; see Calendar
Melchizedek, 26, 27, 42, 99
melekh; see King
Memra, in Jewish theology, 332
Merciful, the divine title, 379
Mercy, use of the term, 371
Merit, later doctrine of, 275, 368
Meru, mount, 330
Messiah, sense of term, 338, 339
— doctrine of, 22, 36, 200, 373
Messiah-Priest, idea of, 22, 36
Metre, Hebrew, 459
Mills, L. H., xxxii., 213, 271, 376, 397, 434, 438, 440
Milne, Bishop, 30
Milton, 108, 221, 276, 320
Mînôkhired, Zoroastrian Scripture, 334, 420, 438, 439
Mitchell, Murray, 282, 436
Mithra, cult of, 32
Moberly, Bishop, 262
Mohammedanism; see Islam
Mommsen, Theod., 184, 219
Montefiore, C. G., 385
Montet, E., 391, 451, 452
Moore, G. F., 85
Morrison, W. D., 424, 445
Moses, his historical character, 85
— was he a psalmist? 74
— Assumption of, 26 (see also Index II.)
Mozley, F. W., 81, 126, 175
Müller, Max, xxxii., xxxiii., 284, 290, 353
Mythology, literary revival of, 202, 270
Myths in the Psalms, 202, 204, 286
— religious value of, xxiii., 286, 326

NACHMANIDES, Hebrew poet, 421
Namelessness, the divine, 289, 304
Names, divine, in various religions, 84, 152, 287 &c., 297 &c., 305, 379
Nebuchadrezzar, character of, 27, 142, 172, 280
— type of Antiochus Epiphanes, 37, 105
Nehemiah, 70, 82, 231
Nestle, E., 105, 106, *480
Neubauer, Ad., 85, 213, 272, 450

Newman, Cardinal, 430
Nicanor, 48, 55
Nicoll, Prof., 142
Noah, the Babylonian, 432
Nöldeke, Theod., xx., 280, 459, 475, 477
Nowack, W., 107, 125, 175

OHLE, R., 418, 445
Olshausen, Justus, 136, 147, 155, 157, 355
Onias, temple of, 12, 14
— II., 127
— III., 123
— IV., 137
Orelli, C. v., 34, 235, 245, 467
Origen, 215, 299, 327, 457
Ormazd ; see Ahura Mazda
Owen, John, xxxii.
Oxford missionaries in Calcutta, xxxiv., 325

PARADISE, Babylonian, 329, 330, 427, 432
— Hebrew story of, 383
Paul, St., his catholicity, 313
— — missionary claim, 306
— — Hellenism and Zoroastrianism in, 424, 450
Paulus, H., 216
Pearson, Bishop, 305
Peele, G., dramatist, 179, 221
Pentateuch, criticism of the, xvii., 6
Perowne, Bishop, 6, 164, 176, 248, 251, 253, 459
Persians, their religious character, 271
— — religious influence on Judaism, 271, 281, 393 &c
— not civilizing agents in Judah, 9
Personification, 274, 334
Peters, J. P., 103
Petrie, Flinders, 9, 10
Pfleiderer, Otto, xxxiii., 389, 425, 450, 452
Pharisees, the, 22, 39, 51, 57, 364, 411, 416-418
Philo, pseudo-, on Essenes, 446
— Zoroastrianism in, 452
Phocylides, pseudo·, 183
Phœnician illustrations, 105, 181 (thrice), 299, 328, 426
Pindar, 178, 180, 273, 446
Plato, his view of the soul, 420, 450, 451
— — myth of Er, 447
Plumptre, Dean, 61, 91, 101, 102, 129, 131, 159

Plutarch, 107, 438
Prayer, doctrine of, in Psalms, 64, 287, 396
— — — — Zoroastrianism, 396, 397
Prayers, Zoroastrian, at dawn, 448
Pre-existence of souls, 421, 450
— — holiest things, 358, 421, 450
Processional hymns, 17, 203
Proselytes, 19, 33, 119, 131, 295
Proverbs (Book of), its date, 409 (on that of the several parts, see Index II.)
— ideas of, 365
— imitated by Sirach, 300
— origin of, 483
— date of Tamil, 80
Prudentius, 329
Psalm-writing, its relation to prophecy, 30
— its long continuance, 30
Psalmody, its humble origin, 194
Psalms, apologetic results of these researches, xxxi.
— should be studied by groups, xxxi., 9
— alphabetic, 51, 228, 243
— daily temple, 72, 83, 157
— of 'Degrees,' 51, 59, 60
— Elohistic, 90, 100, 101, 301 (note), 470
— Guest-, 236, 387, 429
— Maccabæan not *a priori* improbable, 15
— non-linguistic criteria of, 16
— linguistic evidence for, 16 (*cf.* Index II.)
— divine names in, 301
— lost, 107
— 'last words' on, 455-458
— Messianic, 34, 35, 339, 340, 350, 351
— *miktam*, 198
— mystic, 385-388
— mysticism of, 272, 283
— of the night-vigils, 220
— national, 261-265, 276-278, 319
— individualistic elements in, 265, 319
— Puritan, 364-367, 386, 396
— early Christian interpretation of, 33, 259
— magic use of, 279, 284
— not intended only for temple, 363
— theology of, 285, &c.
— traditions on authorship, *459, *460
— (see also Davidic), titles of, not authoritative, 190, 207, 459
Psalter, stages in the formation of the, 11, 12, 100, 201, 241
Ptolemy Soter (or, Lagi), 114, 170, 171, 184

PTOLEMY

Ptolemy, Philadelphus, 144-146, 156, 168-172, 183
— Euergetes I., 127
— Philometor, 180
Purim, Feast of, 55, 229, **243**, 282
Pusey, E. B., 37, 92, 105
Pythagoreanism, 423, 445, 446

RAMESES II., 141
Rashi (Ps. lxxii.) 476, (Ps. lxxvi.) 178, (national psalms) 258
Renan, E., 108, 127, 205, 299, 304, 444
Renouf, le Page, 429, 432
Renovation, Zoroastrian doctrine of, 401, 405
Repentance, 369, 377
Resurrection, Jewish belief in, 402, 406, 440, 444
— Zoroastrian belief in, 400, 401, 438, 439
— when first taught in Arabia, 433
Reuss, E., xviii., 37, 107, 155, 355, 455
Réville, Alb., 283, 358
— Jean, 32
Rhys, John, 438, 447
Riehm, E., 64, 431
Ritschl, Alb., 328
Rudinger, E., 251, **455**
Ruth (Book of), its date and purpose, 306
Ryssel, V., 245, *479

SAADYA, 85
Sachs, M., 421
Sack, Israel, 104
Sacrifices, in Psalms; see Psalms, Puritan
— primitive theory of, 216, 396
— in the Avesta, 396, 437
Sadducees, 51, 57 (name), 411, 413, 416
Salem, the name, 42, 165
Samaritans, the, of Shechem, 232
— their hymns, 30
Sanballat, 232, 233
Saoshyant, Zoroastrian name, 400, 438
Satan, belief in the, 282, 323, 335, 357, 413
Saussaye, Chantepie de la, 282, 397, **434**, 436
Sayce, A. H., xxiii., 65, 268, 279, 282, 323, 376, 391
Scepticism, early Jewish, 410, 423
Schiller, 326
Schleiermacher, Friedr., xvi.

SONG

Schools, Jewish, 348, 349
Schopenhauer, 174
Schrader, E., 208, 268, 279, 323, 473
Schultz, F. W., 175, 208
— H., 297, 307, 426
Schürer, E., 10, 13, 38, 56, 375, 456
Scopas, 114, 115
Scythian invasion, 135, *469
Sennacherib, 165, 216, 217
Septuagint, date of Psalter in, 12, 83
— additional psalm in, 69
— its bearing on the higher criticism, 458
— titles of psalms in, 80, 126, 201, 458 &c.
— view of in Palestine, 172, 184
Serpent, the, in Paradise story, 427
Servant, Semitic use of term, 303
— of Jehovah, 262-264, 275, 292, 293, 368
Shaddai, divine name, 84, 124
Shakespeare, 162
$sh\bar{e}d\bar{\imath}m$, meaning of, 334
Shekina, or divine presence, 40, 331, 332
Sheól, old view of, 381-385
— — — protests against, 381, 412, 413
— light in the gloom of, 384, 407
Shulamith, 273
Sibylline Oracles, Book iii., fanatical, 23, 37
Sidney, Sir Philip, 370
Simon the Maccabee, 11, 23, 24, 26, 28, 39, 147, 173, 199, 200, 457, 458
— — high priest, 26, 41
— — Righteous, 59
Sin, technical words for, 356, 466
— doctrine of, 356, 357, 368
Sirach; see Ecclesiasticus
Sit-napistim, 427, 432
Sleep, uses of term, 389, 407, 430, 441
Smend, R., 57, 127, 133, 175, 180, 277, 350, 426
Smith, G. A., xix., xxiv., 375, 392
— W. R., xxiii., 102, 183, 207, 216, 220, 245, 251, 429, 460
Sobieski, John, 19
Solomon, 141, 153, 173, 210
— did he write any of our psalms? 52, 141
— fragment of psalm of, 193, 212, 475
— so-called Psalms of, 15, 30, 33, 277, 411 (see also Index II.)
— Song of, 167, 179, 273 (foot), 298
'Son of God,' use of phrase, 130, 252, 305 (see also Father)
Song-book; see Jasher

SOPHOCLES

Sophocles, 262, 273
Spiegel, Friedr., 282, 283, 396, 434, 440
Spirit, belief in the, 322, 333, 347
—————Zoroastrian parallel to, 333
Spitta, Friedr., 443
Stade, Bernhard, 131, 136, 154, 157, 218, 249, *482
Stanley, Dean, 48, 126, 295
Stanton, V. H., 36, 38, 99
Stoic ideas, 423, 445
Strack, H. L., 208, 462
Sûfîs, the, 379, 385, 428, 431
Supernaturalism, Jewish, 320, 321
— anti-, charge of, 209
Swete, H. B., 30, 31
Synagogues, 12, 14, 363 (psalmody), 104 (Greek term)
Synesius, 181

TALBÍYA, meaning of, 214, 455
Targum on Ecclesiastes, 444
— — Job and Psalms, 416, 444
— — Isaiah, 440
— of Onkelos, 297
— (shēnī, 'second') on Esther, 109, 444
— on Messianic psalms, 350 (see also Index II.)
Taylor, C., 57, 77, 457
— Jeremy, 297
Tell el-Amarna tablets, 42
Temple, purification of, 10
— music, 9, 11, 13
— singers, 101, 213, 246, 462
— singing, 194, 460
— sacramental view of, 315, 318
— spiritual, 387, 388
Tennyson, 174
Tertullian, 35, 273
Theocracy; see Kingdom
Theocritus, 144, 156, 168, 178, 180, 181, 184
Theodore of Mopsuestia, the 'Interpreter,' 30, 97
——— opinions respecting, 16, 30, 31
——— on prophecy, 273
——— psalm-titles, 207
——— Maccabæan psalms, 455
——— (Ps. ii.) 350, (Ps. vii.) 244, (Ps. viii.) 50, (Ps. xx.) 217, (Ps. xxii.) 245, 274, 351, (Ps. xxxii.) 248, (Ps. xxxv.) 245, (Ps. xliv.) 103, (Ps. xlv.) 179, 350, (Ps. xlvii.) 176, (Ps. li.) 162, 174, 175, (Ps. lii.-liv.) 134, (Ps. lv.-lix.) 123, (Ps. lv. 14) 137, (Ps. lvi.) 30, (Ps. lx.), 107, (Ps. lxii.) 123,

WISDOM

(Ps. lxv., lxvi.) 163, (Ps. lxix.) 245, 351, (Ps. lxxii.) 153, (Ps. lxxiv.) 103, (Ps. lxxv.) 178, (Ps. lxxvi.) 110, 178, (Ps. lxxix.) 30, 103, (Ps. lxxx.) 97, (Ps. lxxxviii.) 129, (Ps. lxxxix.) 351, (Ps. xc.) 84, (Ps. cix.) 63, (Ps. cx.) 350, (Ps. cxvi.) 33, (Ps. cxviii.) 32, 351, (Ps. cxliv.) 67
Theodoret, 33, 58, 77, 79, 85, 103, 107, 129, 134, 136, 175, 178, 181, 207, 217, 223, 273, 274, 353
Theophanies, 156, 344, 353
Thirlwall, Bishop, 156, 185
Tholuck, A., 117, 165, 176
Tiele, C. P., 269, 279, 330, 351, 434, 450
Tiglath-Pileser I., 21
Titan-legends, 424
Tobit, Book of, 30, 307
Torah, meaning of, 355
Toy, C. H., 470, 471
Tradition, poems preserved by, 192, 210

UNDERWORLD, the (see Heaven and Hell and Sheól)
— Babylonian, 432

VARUNA, cult of, 289, 353, 357
Vatke, W., 133, 137, 184, 193, 203, 209, 222
Vedic hymns, 82, 194, 213, 279, 357, 395
Vendîdâd (Avesta), 283, 352, 394, 398, 434 &c.
Venema, 214, 243
Vernes, Maurice, 41, 210, 329
Vitringa, 455

WEBER, F., 334, 335, 337, 377, 406 &c.
Weissmann, S., 154, 184
Wellhausen, Jul., xvii., 39, 57, 81, 128, 154, 212, 216, 219, 351, 329, 376, 430, 459
West, E. W., xxxii., 395, 396, 435, 439
Westcott, Bishop, 179, 181, 182, 209
Wette, W. de, 24, 31, 52, 109, 177, 181, 193
Wiedemann, A., 156, 181
Wilhelm, Eug., 352, 433
Wilson, H. B., xxvii.
Windischmann, Fr., 395
Wisdom, Book of, 423

Wisdom, the divine, 322, 334, 423
Word, the divine, 321
Wordsworth, 222, 274
World, terms for, and their use, 390, 407, 414, 415, 430, 440, 467
Wünsche, A., 56, 407 (cf. Talmud)

XERXES, 181

YAHVEH ; see Jehovah
Yahvist, the, xvii., xviii., 270, 279, 469
Yasna (Avesta), 305, 401, 437 &c.

ZARATHUSTRA, 192, 376, 395 (cf. Gâthâs)
— age and mission of, 107, 434–436
Zechariah, was he a psalmist ? 215
— second part of ; see Index II.
Zeller, E., 445, 447
Zeno, 418
Zerubbabel, 21, 36, 52, 53
Zoroaster ; see Zarathustra
Zoroastrianism, 85, 146, 357, 394 &c.
— Christian influence on later, 396
— names of God in, 288
— modern, 342, 436
Zunz, 55

II.—PASSAGES FROM THE SCRIPTURES AND OTHER ANCIENT BOOKS.

For the pages on which the Koran and the Zoroastrian writings are cited, see Index I.
For Index II. the author is chiefly indebted to the generous help of two friends.

(A) OLD TESTAMENT.

GENESIS.		GENESIS —cont.		EXODUS—cont.	
	PAGE		PAGE		PAGE
i.	76, 149, 272	xxx. 25 (Targ.)	333	xix. 6	216
i.–ii. 4	283	xxxii. 30	289	xix. 15	446
i. 1 (Targ.)	358	xxxiv. 7	356	xx. 1–17	237
i. 2, 3	322	xxxvii. 9	221	xx. 6	378
i. 16	221	xxxix. 3	169	xx. 7	302
ii.	428	xli. 38 (Targ.)	333	xx. 23–xxiii.	237
ii. 14	42	xliii. 14	84	xxi.	250
iii.	427, 428	xlviii. 15	158	xxiii. 13	216
iii. (Targ.)	443	xlix. 6	216	xxix. 6	199, 218
iii. 8	414	xlix. 10	36	xxxiii. 18–20	431
iv. 26	*464	xlix. 22	158	xxxiv. 6, 7	378
v. 22	383	xlix. 24	158	xxxiv. 24	51
v. 24	149	xlix. 37	64	xxxix.	60
vi. 2, 4	324			xxxix. 30	199
viii. 21	321				
ix. 1–17	306	EXODUS.		LEVITICUS.	
ix. 25	64				
xi. 29	183	iii. 1	351	iv. 3, 5	338, 350
xiv.	270	iv. 22	130	v. 4	249
xiv. 1–17	42	vi. 4	383	vi. 8, 9	366
xiv. 18	27	ix. 6	275	ix. 4, 6, 23	353
xiv. 18–20	42, 165	xii. 19 (Sept.)	429	ix. 22, 33	315
xiv. 18–24	84	xii. 42	407	xvi. 2	353
xv. 18	206	xv.	82, 124, 177	xvii. 11	451
xviii. 3	299	xv. 1–3	31	xix. 17	196
xviii. 19	371	xv. 1–18	31, 177	xix. 24	460
xix. 19	379	xv. 2	31, 124	xxii. 32	302
xix. 20	115	xv. 3	222	xxiv. 11	300
xx. 7	155	xv. 6	31	xxiv. 16	300, 302
xx. 9	356	xv. 8	147, 215		
xxii. 18	142	xv. 17	31		
xxiii. 6	219	xv. 16	*464	NUMBERS.	
xxiv. 27	379	xv. 19	178		
xxiv. 45	321	xv. 20	30	i. 10	248
xxvi. 4	142	xv. 21	31	ii. 20	248
xxvii. 41	321	xvii. 16	124	v. 11–29	65
xxviii. 13, 14	206	xviii. 5	351		

K K

NUMBERS—cont.		DEUTERONOMY—cont.		I SAMUEL—cont.	
	PAGE		PAGE		PAGE
vi. 23–27	300	xxxii. 31	205	ix. 6–9	85
vi. 23–26	277	xxxii. 37	205	x. 5	30
vi. 24, 25	124	xxxii. 39	314, 383, 427	xv. 22	210
vi. 24–26	163	xxxiii.	75	xvi. 14–23	192
vi. 25, 26	242	xxxiii. 1	85	xvii. 45	315
vi. 27	302	xxxiii. 2	159, 287	xviii. 18, 23	61
vii. 22–27	315	xxxiii. 5	211, 340	xix. 11	242
ix. 15, 16	353	xxxiii. 11	22	xix. 20	30
ix. 17–22	332	xxxiii. 26	205, 211	xx. 11	192
x. 35	124, 125, 315	xxxiv. 7	75	xx. 29	330
xii. 5	353	xxxiv. 10	85	xxi. 4, 5	446
xii. 7	40			xxx. 1, 2	220
xii. 8 (Sept.)	430	JOSHUA.		xxx. 6	226
xiv. 10	353			xxx. 26	216
xvii. 16	109	i.–xii.	253		
xxiii. 10	211	i. 8	241, 253	2 SAMUEL.	
xxiv. 3	212	v. 14	248	i. 10	218
xxiv. 4	84, 212	x. 1	42	i. 18	210
xxiv. 7	36	x. 12	221	i. 19–27	192
xxiv. 15	221	x. 12–13	108, 211	iii. 3	106
xxiv. 16	84, 212	xiii. 26 (Sept.)	105	iii. 13	245
xxiv. 17	36	xiv. 6	85	iii. 33, 34	192
xxxiv. 28	248	xxii.	152	v. 11, 12	216
		xxii. 22	152	v. 18 (Sept.)	424
DEUTERONOMY.				vi.	20
		JUDGES.		vi. i.	20
ii. 24	366			vi. 2	329
iv. 28	238	iv. 4	30	vi. 5	192, 194
iv. 37	275, 370, 377	v.	125	vi. 13	20
v. 1, 28	250	v. 13	120	vi. 14, 17	20, 203
vi. 1	250	ix. 27	460	vi. 18	20, 203
vi. 6	356	xiii. 18	289	vi. 22	61
vii. 8	370	xx. 1 (Sept.)	105	vii.	60, 117, 206, 212, 238, 251
vii. 9	378	xx. 13	68	vii. i.	206
x. 8	315			vii. 14	239
x. 15	275, 370, 377	RUTH.		viii. 12, 13	107
x. 17, 18	344			viii. 18	21
xi. 21	128	i. 20, 21	84	x. 6	251
xi. 24	206	iii. 13	407	xii. 12	221
xii. 5	328			xii. 13	161
xii. 23	451	I SAMUEL.		xii. 25	173
xiv. 1	130			xii. 28	328
xviii. 18	40	i. 3	222	xxii.	193, 211, 223, 225
xix. 19 (Sept.)	68	i. 13	242	xxii. i.	185
xxi. 5	315	ii. 1–10	57	xxii. 36	225
xxviii. 10	328	ii. 2, 3	178	xxiii. 1	13, 22, 192
xxviii. 56	301	ii. 5	57	xxiii. 1–7	34, 206, 211
xxx. 15–20	356	ii. 6	314, 383, 427	xxiii. 2–7	69
xxxii.	75, 84, 194, 205	ii. 8	57	xxiii. 5	129
xxxii. 4, 18, 30, 31, 37	205	ii. 10	57	xxiii. 5	289
xxxii. 5	236	ii. 24	*466	xxiii. 7	185
xxxii. 8	84, 429	ii. 27–36	128	xxiii. 13 (Sept.)	424
xxxii. 8, 9 (Sept.)	337	iii. 3, 4	332		
xxxii. 11	205	iv. 7	315	I KINGS.	
xxxii. 15	205, 211	viii. 7	341	iii.	154
xxxii. 17	205, 334			iii. 5–14	61
xxxii. 18	205				
xxxii. 30	205				

PASSAGES FROM THE SCRIPTURES, ETC.

1 Kings—cont.	PAGE	1 Chronicles—cont.	PAGE	Nehemiah—cont.	PAGE
iv. 31	129	xxv. 1, 6	246	ii. 10	232
iv. 32, 33	210	xxviii. 3	191	ii. 11–20	70
v. 11 (iv. 31)	102	xxix. 15	429	ii. 18	76
viii.	213			ii. 19	232
viii. 8	317			ii. 20	76
viii. 12	212	2 Chronicles.		iii. 18	244
viii. 12–13	211, 212			iii. 25	235
viii. 14	212	passim	117	iii. 34 (iv. 2)	228, 232
viii. 14–66	213	v. 12	246	iv.	56, 109
viii. 17	328	vi. 40–42	54	iv. 1–8	232
viii. 22	143	vi. 41, 42	52, 60	iv. 2	70, 245
viii. 27–30	329	vii. 21	317	iv. 4, 5	78
viii. 29–30	320	viii. 14	85	vi.	56, 109
viii. 33	212	ix. 23	153	vi. 6, 7	36
viii. 41–43	331	x. 15	298	vi. 14	152
viii. 43	328	xi. 8	109	vi. 17–19	397
viii. 55	143	xv. 9	131	vi. 18	232
xi. 14–25	141	xx.	58, 177	vii. 43–45	213
xi. 34	219	xx. 6	314	vii. 65	36, 40
xii. 4	141	xx. 21	59	vii. 67	213
xii. 15	298	xxviii. 23	337	viii. 10	220
xii. 18	141	xxix. 30	13	ix.	347
xviii. 39	291	xxx. 6–11	131	ix. 33, 34	353
xxii. 17	158	xxx. 16	85	x. 30	220
xxii. 39	179	xxxii. 21 (Sept.)	41	xi. 17	246
		xxxii. 32	117	xii. 24	85
		xxxiii. 11–13	279	xii. 27	50
2 Kings.		xxxv. 15	246	xii. 36	179
		xxxv. 18	341	xiii. 25	78
ii. 11	383	xxxvi. 22, 23	169	xiii. 29	152
iv. 31	430				
iv. 39	440			Esther.	
v. 7	427	Ezra.			
vi. 5	177			ii. 5	229
xiii. 5	167	ii. 40–42	213	ii. 9, 17	181
xiii. 21	383–393	ii. 63	36	iii. i.	97
xviii. 8	251	ii. 65	40	vii. 4, 6	244
xix. 14	217	iii. 1–6	16	viii. 15	218
xix. 35	178	iii. 2	85	viii. 16	408
xx. 13–19	279	iii. 8–13	16		
xxiii. 10	216	iii. 9	244	Job.	
		iii. 10, 11	58		
		vi. 10	156	i. 6	324
1 Chronicles.		vi. 15–18	16	ii.	78, 298
		vi. 16	72	ii. 1	324
ii. 6	129	vi. 22	76, 109	iii. 13	441
iii. 1	106	vii. 6	171	iii. 13–19	442
ix. 16	246	vii. 10, 11	364	iii. 14	382, 426
xii. 27	101	vii. 11 (Sept.)	358	iv., v.	234, 248
xiii. 8	192	vii. 25	348	v. 1	324
xvi. 7	72	viii. 4	235	v. 17–23	73
xvi. 7–36	50	ix.	161	v. 25	142
xvi. 8–36	457	ix. 6, 10–15	353	vi. 10	379
xvi. 34–36	457			vii. 7–10	242
xvi. 36	457			vii. 17	202
xxiii. 5	179	Nehemiah.		ix. 4	371
xxiii. 14	85			ix. 5	427
xxv.	111	i. 1–3	231	ix. 28, 29	346
xxv. 1, 3	30	i. 3	71, 160	x. 6	346

INDICES.

JOB—cont.	PAGE
x. 20–22	242
xii. 9	397
xiii.	307
xiii. 3–4	307
xiii. 4	77
xiii. 6	307
xiv.	354
xiv. 1	82
xiv. 2	78
xiv. 13–15	442
xv. 4	321
xv. 15	324
xv. 16	78
xv. 19	78
xv. 21	78
xv. 23	77
xv. 35	215
xvi. 18, 19	442
xvii. 7	242
xviii. 12	77
xviii. 17–19	77
xix. 19	134
xix. 20	82
xix. 21	355
xix. 25	442
xix. 26, 27	442
xx. 12	78
xxi. 7	242
xxii. 13, 14	321
xxii. 15	426
xxv. 2	340
xxvi. 14	290
xxvii. 14	77
xxviii.	217, 334
xxviii. 28	397
xxix. 12	78, 142
xxx. 22	82
xxx. 23	442
xxxii. 17	158
xxxiii. 14–16	246
xxxiii. 14–30	249
xxxiii. 22	148
xxxiv. 2–4	158
xxxiv. 7	78
xxxv. 10	147
xxxvi. 2–4	159
xxxvii. 13	379
xxxviii. 7	324
xxxviii. 13	78
xxxviii. 22	242
xxxviii. 36	*473
xl. 15	150
xlii.	442
xlii. 10	155

PSALMS.

	PAGE
i.–lxxii.	7
i.–lxxii.	8

PSALMS—cont.	PAGE
i.–lxxxix.	301
i.	190, **238**, **240**, **241**, 251, 365, 373, 374, 387, 455
i. 1, 2	349
i. 1–3	253
i. 2	26, 253, 364
i. 3	240
i. 3, 4	240
i. 4, 5	253, 374
i. 5	223, 406
ii.	36, 190, 208, **238**–**241**, 249, 251, 252, 253, 263, 299, 339, 373, 380
ii.	*463, *475, *483
ii. 1	251
ii. 1	*474, *475
ii. 1–2	251
ii. 2	177, 238, 251, 252
ii. 3	238, 252, 351
ii. 3	*477
ii. 3–5	*474
ii. 4	123, 314
ii. 4, 5	238
ii. 4, 5	*478
ii. 5	251, 252
ii. 6	251
ii. 7	143, 239, 251, 252, 305, 340
ii. 7–9	238, 239
ii. 8, 9	293
ii. 9	251
ii. 12	351
iii.–vii.	226
iii.–xix.	208
iii.	208, **226**–**227**, 252
iii. 1–2	227
iii. 2, 3	226
iii. 2	237
iii. 3	*464
iii. 4	215
iii. 5	227, 320
iii. 7	226, 227, 237
iii. 8	293
iv.	110, 208, 216, **226**–**227**
iv. 1	227
iv. 1 (Pesh.)	242
iv. 2	227
iv. 3	227
iv. 3–6	226
iv. 4	227
iv. 5	227, 242
iv. 6	315, 374, 386
iv. 7	227, 242, 318
iv. 8	227
iv. 9	227, 237
v.	134, 135, 208, **226**, **227**, 233, 242

PSALMS—cont.	PAGE
v. 1 (Sept.)	272
v. 2	*464, *470, *472
v. 4	64, 227, 287, 374, 448
v. 5	236, 429
v. 5-8	236
v. 8	227, 242, 320, 329, 371
v. 9	242
v. 10	242
v. 12	289, 378, 429
vi.	118, 134, 135, 208, 215, **226**–**227**, 229, 233, 234, 242, 247, 277
vi. 1	242
vi. 2	243, 346
vi. 3	228
vi. 4-7	407
vi. 5, 6	385
vi. 6	234, 242, 367, 428
vi. 7	*470
vi. 8	242
vi. 9	243
vii.	77, 78, 91, 109, 134, 196, 208, 220, **227**, **229**, 243, *464
vii. 3	244
vii. 5	*464, *465
vii. 6	234, 244
vii. 7	133
vii. 8	317
vii. 9	196, 370
vii. 9, 10	369
vii. 10	*464, *474, *478
vii. 10, 11	196
vii. 11	215
vii. 13	244
vii. 15	196, 215
vii. 16	243
vii. 16, 17	244
vii. 18	27, 83, 84, 196, 220
vii. 18	*479
viii.	61, 76, **201**, 208, 220
viii. 2	291
viii. 3	201, 220
viii. 4	220
viii. 5	202, 220, *464
ix.	138, 208, 214, 220, **228**–**229**, 342
ix.–xiv.	226
ix.	*464
ix. 3	83, 220, 228
ix. 5, 6	228, 403
ix. 6	228
ix. 6, 7	73
ix. 8, 9	228

PASSAGES FROM THE SCRIPTURES, ETC. 501

PSALMS—*cont.*

	PAGE
ix. 10	243
ix. 12	228, 316, 363
ix. 13	110
ix. 14	407, 431
ix. 16	228
ix. 18	150, 228, 293
ix. 19	374
ix. 20, 21	*464
ix. 21	228
x.	134, 190, 208, 214, 228–229, 342
x. 2–11	229
x. 3–11	228
x. 4	321
x. 6	242
x. 7	*464, *474, *477
x. 8, 9	133, 229
x. 11	242, 321
x. 13	197, 242, 321
x. 14	245
x. 15	254
x. 16	228
x. 18	*464
xi.–xiii.	229
xi.	208, 216
xi. 1	225
xi. 4	205, 314
xi. 6	*465, *475
xi. 6 (Targ.)	*474
xi. 7	408, 416
xii.	197, 207, 208, 227, 229, 356
xii. 1, 2	342
xii. 2	378
xii. 2	*464, *465
xii. 6	227
xii. 8	352
xii. 8	*465
xii. 9	236
xii. 9	*465
xiii.	208, 229
xiii. 3	441
xiii. 6	*465, *474
xiv.	77, 90, 121, 134, 135, 196, 197, 207, 216, 226–227, 301, 342, 356
xiv. 1	197, 242, 321
xiv. 2	314
xiv. 3	197, 342
xiv. 5	197, 239, 352
xiv. 5	*465
xiv. 5, 6	215, 216
xiv. 7	197, 199
xv.–xviii.	208
xv.	197, 208, 236–237, 249, 357, 370, 375, 387, 397, 429
xv. 1	416, 429

PSALMS—*cont.*

	PAGE
xv. 4	236, 374
xv. 11	411
xvi.	196–198, 216, 229, 247, 390, 407, 411, 414, 456, 458
xvi. 2	288, 299, 302
xvi. 3	198, 216, 217, 387, *465
xvi. 4	198, 216, 217, 408
xvi. 5	250, 429, *465
xvi. 6	*466
xvi. 7	411, *466
xvi. 9	*466
xvi. 10	217, 431, *467
xvi. 10–11	407, 426, 431
xvi. 11	441
xvii.	91, 119, 216, 226, 229, 243, 390, 407, 414, 430
xvii. 3	*466
xvii. 3–5	357, 369
xvii. 4	243, 374, *465
xvii. 9–12	229
xvii. 10	*466, *477
xvii. 13–15	388
xvii. 14	229, 430, *467, *471, *480
xvii. 14 (Targ.)	444
xvii. 15	388, 389, 390, 407, 426, 430
xvii. 15 (Sept.)	444
xviii.	67, 70, 79, 107, 136, 142, 185, 193–194, 202, 204, 206, 207, 208, 223, 224, 225, 239, 251, 258, 286, 291, 338, 339, 344, 345, 350, 369, 459, *464, *483
xviii. 1	206, 250
xviii. 2	79, 378, *467
xviii. 3	215, 224
xviii. 4	205, *467
xviii. 5, 6	224
xviii. 7	205, 314
xviii. 8–16	159
xviii. 8–20	205
xviii. 9–13	353
xviii. 10	224
xviii. 10–11	205
xviii. 11	205
xviii. 14	83, 224
xviii. 15	224
xviii. 17	224, 353
xviii. 21–24	238
xviii. 21–28	205
xviii. 21–32	291
xviii. 21–46	206

PSALMS—*cont.*

	PAGE
xviii. 22–24	205
xviii. 23	374
xviii. 25–28	223
xviii. 26	378
xviii. 27	345
xviii. 29 (Targ.)	444
xviii. 31	215, 224, 238, 250, 287
xviii. 32	205, 224, *467, *473, *484
xviii. 33	250
xviii. 34	224
xviii. 35	224
xviii. 36	172, 225, 343, 344, *467, *471
xviii. 38	291
xviii. 42	291
xviii. 44	205, 224
xviii. 44, 45	291
xviii. 44–49	224
xviii. 45	224
xviii. 46	206, *468
xviii. 50	180, 205
xviii. 51	57, 206, 223, 224
xix.–xxii.	208
xix.	197, 202, 207, 208, 225, 244, 349
xix. 1–7	108, 201–202
xix. 2	*468
xix. 2–7	157
xix. 6	221
xix. 8–11	237, 238
xix. 8–15	229, 237, 240, 250, 365, 374
xix. 10	250
xix. 12	356
xix. 12, 13	376
xix. 12–15	276
xix. 13	76, 346, 354, 357, *468
xix. 13, 14	238
xix. 14	55, 225, 250
xix. 15	*468, *472
xx., xxi.	24
xx.	38
xx.	42, 99, 111, 154, 196, 198, 201, 217, 218, 339, 455, *468
xx. 4	374
xx. 6	*468
xx. 7	199, 314
xx. 8	199, 403
xx. 9	*468
xx. 10	341
xxi.	38, 42, 99, 154, 196, 198–201, 217, 218, 339, 455, *464, *468
xxi. 2	111, 350

PSALMS—cont.

	PAGE
xxi. 3	111, 218
xxi. 4	199, 218
xxi. 5	111, 199, 200, 408
xxi. 5 (Targ.)	444
xxi. 6	171
xxi. 7	111, 199, 200
xxi. 8	83, 199
xxi. 10, 11	200
xxi. 14	199
xxii.–xxix.	208
xxii.–xli.	134
xxii.	78, 82, 135, 160, 230–232, 236, 245, 263, 264, 274, 276, 292, 295, 338, 373, 377
xxii. 2	236, *468, *470, *475
xxii. 2 (Sept.)	*469
xxii. 4	231, 298, 327, 331, 334
xxii. 7	264, 377
xxii. 8	232
xxii. 9	234
xxii. 13	232
xxii. 14	232
xxii. 16	236, *469
xxii. 17, 18	232
xxii. 20	*480
xxii. 22	263
xxii. 22–32	298
xxii. 23	231, 264, *469
xxii. 24	295
xxii. 25	248
xxii. 26	231, 250, 264, *469
xxii. 27	374
xxii. 28	306
xxii. 29	315
xxii. 30	407, 428
xxiii.	126, 135, 208, 236–237, 272, 319, 343, 429
xxiii. (Sept. and Targ.)	352
xxiii. 1	158
xxiii. 1 (Targ.)	272
xxiii. 2, 3	250
xxiii. 4	428
xxiii. 5	250
xxiii. 6	237, 388, 428
xxiv.	83, 202, 204, 207, 208
xxiv.	222, 230, 323, 350, 357
xxiv. 1–6	208, 236–237, 249, 387, 397, 429
xxiv. 3	416

PSALMS—cont.

	PAGE
xxiv. 3–6	370
xxiv. 4	248
xxiv. 5	236
xxiv. 6	236, 323, 352, *465
xxiv. 7–10	20, 203–204, 208, 222
xxiv.	8, 10, 203, *469
xxv.	208, 235–236, 248
xxv. 1	248
xxv. 3	235
xxv. 5	347
xxv. 7	235, 353, 357
xxv. 8–9	347
xxv. 10	345
xxv. 14	345, 347
xxv. 15	235
xxv. 15–16	235
xxv. 15–22	235
xxv. 22	235
xxvi.–xxviii.	135
xxvi.	126, 127, 208, 230, 233, 331, 455
xxvi. 1–5	369
xxvi. 2	*466
xxvi. 4–7	375
xxvi. 6	370
xxvi. 12	*469, *475
xxvii.	208, 250
xxvii. 1–6	208, 236–237, 429
xxvii. 3	237
xxvii. 4	237, 331
xxvii. 5	237, 250
xxvii. 6	374
xxvii. 7–13	230, 233
xxvii. 7–14	233
xxviii.–xxx.	208
xxviii.	127, 230, 233, 248, 331, 455
xxviii. 1	234
xxviii. 1–6	111
xxviii. 2	320, 329, 448
xxviii. 6	250
xxviii. 7	215, *469, *478
xxviii. 8	233, 350
xxix.	201–202, 208, 221, 325
xxix. 1	101, 324
xxix. 1–2	202, 221
xxix. 2–10	202
xxix. 9	203, 314, 331
xxix. 10	*469
xxx.	18, 30, 135, 208, 216, 227, 234, 247, 455
xxx. 2, 4	403
xxx. 3	247
xxx. 3–5	234

PSALMS—cont.

	PAGE
xxx. 4	234, 407, 431
xxx. 5	247
xxx. 6	32, 234
xxx. 6 (Targ.)	444
xxx. 7	247
xxx. 10	227, 234, 385
xxx. 12	32, 102, 234, 247
xxx. 13	234
xxxi.	135, 208, 230, 233, 245, 246, 247
xxxi. 4	250
xxxi. 11	346
xxxi. 15	*465
xxxi. 20	250
xxxi. 20–21	429
xxxi. 21	237
xxxi. 22	232
xxxi. 23	247
xxxi. 24	247, 378
xxxii.	208, 214, 235–236, 276, 346
xxxii. 1, 2	356
xxxii. 1–5	346
xxxii. 3–4	236
xxxii. 3–5	354
xxxii. 5	236
xxxii. 6	236, 248
xxxii. 8	236, 347
xxxii. 10	214
xxxii. 11	214
xxxiii.	190, 195, 201, 214, 215, 248, 455, 456
xxxiii. 1	195, 214, 215
xxxiii. 2	79
xxxiii. 5	214
xxxiii. 6	321, 322
xxxiii. 7	215
xxxiii. 9	215, 322
xxxiii. 10, 11	322
xxxiii. 12	215
xxxiii. 14	*469
xxxiii. 15	319
xxxiii. 16, 17	195, 199
xxxiii. 16–18	215
xxxiii. 17	199
xxxiii. 18	456
xxxiii. 20	79, 195, 215
xxxiii. 20, 21	318
xxxiv.	208, 235, 245, 248
xxxiv. 5–7	235
xxxiv. 8	235, 323
xxxiv. 14	356
xxxiv. 19	*469, *481
xxxiv. 23	235
xxxv.	78, 82, 122, 135, 225, 230–233, 245, 366
xxxv. 3	*469

PSALMS—cont.	PSALMS—cont.	PSALMS—cont.
xxxv. 5 323	xl. 7–9 374	xlv. . 25, 62, 147, 155,
xxxv. 5, 6 235	xl. 8 365	156, 166–174, 178,
xxxv. 10 . . 81, 246	xl. 9 . . 366, 368, *466	179, 180, 183, 185,
xxxv. 11 232	xl. 10 . 234, 246, *469	217, 276, 291, 296,
xxxv. 12–15 . . . 232	xl. 13 244	339, 350, 456
xxxv. 13 374	xl. 13–18 230	xlv. 1 (Sept.) . . . 173
xxxvi. 15 232	xl. 14–18 . . 90, 135	xlv. 2 . 171, 180, *471
xxxv. 15 . . . . *470	xl. 18 . . 81, 101, 243	xlv. 3 . 179, 199, 408
xxxv. 23 .299, 302,*465	xli. . 208, 230, 233, 248	xlv. 3–8 180
xxxv. 27 225	xli. 2–4 246	xlv. 4 . . . 171, 179
xxxvi.–xxxix. . . . 208	xli. 6 246	xlv. 5 . 169, 225, *467,
xxxvi. . 207, 208, 225,	xli. 10 . 133, 134, 233	*471
414	xli. 13 408	xlv. 5–6 179
xxxvi. 2 . 227, 323,*470	xlii.–lxxxiii. . . . 90	xlv. 6 171
xxxvi. 2–4 207	xlii.–xlix. 90	xlv. 7 . 181, 182, 185
xxxvi. 5 227	xlii.–xliii. 276, 456, *470,	xlv. 7 (Sept.) . . . 182
xxxvi. 6 . . . 379,*470	*471	xlv. 7–8 . . . 169, 171
xxxvi. 6–13 . . . 207	xlii. . 69, 78, 99, 110,	xlv. 8 . 101, 171, 179,
xxxvi. 7 225	114–115, 120, 126,	180, 338
xxxvi. 8–10 . . . 225	147, 228, 231, 273	xlv. 9 . . 179, *471
xxxvi. 10 408, 411, 413,	xlii. 2 126	xlv. 10 . 168, 173, 181,
414, 427	xlii. 4 126	*471
xxxvi. 12 207	xlii. 5 . 114, *470, *478	xlv. 13 171
xxxvi. 26 250	xlii. 7 . 110, 115, 317	xlv. 14 179
xxxvii. 77, 234–235, 248	xlii. 8 115	xlv. 15 173
xxxvii. 1 234	xlii. 9 14, 110, 114, 126,	xlv. 16 179
xxxvii. 7 234	147, 221, 366	xlv. 17 . . 169, 180
xxxvii. 21 234	xlii. 10 110	xlv. 18 . 180, *469,*471,
xxxvii. 25 235	xliii. . 69, 114, 228, 239	*479
xxxviii. . 135, 230, 233	xliii. 1 . 227, 342, 352,	xlvi. . 148, 162, 163–166,
xxxviii. 1 242	378	176, 177, 239, 249,
xxxviii. 1 (Targ.) . . 272	xliii. 1 (Sept.) . . . 126	*464
xxxviii. 2 346	xliii. 2–3 80	xlvi. 3–4 162
xxxviii. 5 353	xliii. 3 . 110, 126, 128,	xlvi. 5 . . . 83, 164
xxxviii. 18 . . . .*470	322	xlvi. 5–6 318
xxxix. . 101, 110, 134,	xliii. 5 101	xlvi. 7 . 162, 165, 252
135, 158, 230, 233,	xliii. 9 80	xlvi. 8 . . 177, 380
246, 276	xliv. . 91–93, 95, 96, 98,	xlvi. 11 . . . 163, 199
xxxix. 2 356	102, 103, 287, 298,	xlvi. 12 177
xxxix. 3 . 233,*468,*469,	356, 368, 455, 456	xlvi. 15 80
*470, *475	xliv. 4 32	xlvii. . 71, 158, 163, 176,
xxxix. 4 . . *464, *470	xliv. 5 185	177, 350, 455, *464
xxxix. 5 233	xliv. 6–7 95	xlvii. 2–3 292
xxxix. 5, 6 384	xliv. 7 . . . 195, 382	xlvii. 3 . . . 83, 164
xxxix. 5–7 . 233, 235	xliv. 7–8 . . 92, 108	xlvii. 4 . . . . *468
xxxix. 6 . . . . *467	xliv. 10 . 95, 102, 382	xlvii. 4–5 165
xxxix. 7 389	xliv. 11–17 91	xlvii. 6 . 176, 203, 317
xxxix. 9–12 . . . 233	xliv. 16 108	xlvii. 9 315
xxxix. 12 . . . .*470	xliv. 17 . 102, 103, 201,	xlvii. 10 . . . 176, 292
xxxix. 13 429	220	xlvii. (xlviii.) 14(Sept.) 158
xl. . 135, 136, 230, 244,	xliv. 18 345	xlviii. . 83, 114, 148, 162,
245, 368, 377	xliv. 18–19 . 90, 91, 196,	163–166, 176, 177,
xl. 1–12 . . . 153, 234	369	249, 319, 363
xl. 2–4 234	xliv. 21–22 92	xlviii. 3 . . 164, 317
xl. 2–12 364	xliv. 21–23 90	xlviii. 4 126
xl. 4 234	xliv. 22 196	xlviii. 5 . . 165, 252
xl. 5 234	xliv. 23 299	xlviii. 6 252
xl. 6 247	xliv. 24 286	xlviii. 11 164
xl. 7 376	xliv. 25 . . . 95, 321	xlviii. 13–14 . . . 164

PSALMS—*cont.*

	PAGE
xlviii. 13–15	. . . 319
xlviii. 14	. . . *471
xlviii. 15	 442
xlix.	. **149–150**, 158, 198, 229, 381, 383, 390, 412, 413, 426, 455
xlix. 2	. *467, *468, *471
xlix. 2–5	 158
xlix. 4	. . *472, *481
xlix. 4–5	 426
xlix. 5	. . . 73, 382
xlix. 8–9	 413
xlix. 8–12	 159
xlix. 10 (Targ.)	. . 444
xlix. 11	. . *472, *479
xlix. 12	. . . . *472
xlix. 13	. . . 149, 150
xlix. 14	. . . . *472
xlix. 15	. xxxviii., 413, 430
xlix. 15 (Targ.)	. . 444
xlix. 15–16	. 381, 382, 390, 402, 406
xlix. 16	 149
xlix. 20	. 382, 413, *479
xlix. 21	. . . 149, 150
l.	. 90, 124, **150–153**, 158, 159, 162, 176, 234, 344, 364, 373, 374, 375, 386, 396, *464
l. 1	. 132, 152, 156, 273, 298, *472
l. 2	. . . . 159, 365
l. 3	 164
l. 4	. . . . . *481
l. 4–5	 159
l. 5	. . . . 150, 345
l. 7	 159
l. 10	. . . 225, *472
l. 10 (Targ.)	. . 444
l. 11	. 159, *472, *478
l. 14	. . 83, 376, *472
l. 14–15	. . 176, 375
l. 16	 345
l. 21	 444
l. 22	. 152, *467, *473
li.–lxx.	 90
li.	. 130, **161–162**, 173, 174, 175, 208, 230, 234, 235, 245, 370, 376
li. 3–19	. . 175, 364
li. 4	. . . . . *473
li. 6	. . 161, 175, 357
li. 7	 357
li. 8	. 347, 356, 374, *467
li. 9	. . 162, 374, *473
li. 12	. . . . . *474
li. 13	. 322, 333, 347, *474
li. 14	. 356, 386, *469

PSALMS—*cont.*

	PAGE
li. 16	 370
li. 18–19	. . . 162
li. 19	. . 369, 374
li. 19–20	. . . 175
li. 20	. . 162, 175
li. 20–21	. 82, 162, 175, 365, 367
i. 21	. . 315, 374
lii.–liv.	 134
lii.–lv.	 134
lii.–lix.	 121
lii.	. 55, **121**, 134, 136, 208, 248
lii. 1	. . . 107, 123
lii. 3	. . . 121, 197
lii. 4	 133
lii. 10	 133
lii. 11	 133
liii.	. **90, 121**, 133, 134, 135, 197
liii. 2–3	 245
liii. 6	. 121, 215, 216, *474, *475
liv.–lvi.	 455
liv.	. **119, 121**, 134, 136, 208, 277
liv. 5	. . . 131, 133
liv. 6	 133
liv. 8	. . 133, 289, 374
liv. 9	 133
lv.–lvii.	 121
lv.–lix.	 123
lv.–lx.	 455
lv.	. 78, **122–123**, 126, 133, 135, 136, 208, 246, 276, 342
lv. 1 (Sept.)	. . 272
lv. 3	. . . . *474
lv. 4	. . . . *474
lv. 6	. . . . *474
lv. 7	 134
lv. 7–9	 137
lv. 11	 133
lv. 12	. 133, 134, *464, *474
lv. 13	 123
lv. 13–15	. 121, 123, 133, 134, 233
lv. 14	. . 137, *474
lv. 15	. . . . *474
lv. 16	 121
lv. 18	. . 136, *474
lv. 19	 227
lv. 22	. 121, 133, *474, *476
lv. 23	. . . . *474
lv. (lvi.)	 30
lvi.–lx.	. . 134, 458
lvi.–lxiii.	. . . 208

PSALMS—*cont.*

	PAGE
lvi.	. **121**, 133, 136, 198, 208, 333
lvi. 1	 134
lvi. 1 (Targ.)	. . . 272
lvi. 2	. . 133, *464
lvi. 3	 227
lvi. 5	. 133, 322, 332
lvi. 7	. . 133, 229
lvi. 8	 133
lvi. 10	 133
lvi. 11	. . 322, 332
lvi. 12	 133
lvi. 14 (Targ.)	. . . 444
lvii.	. 55, **121**, 133, 134, 136, 207, 208, 455, *464
lvii. 2	. . 133, *464
lvii. 3	. 67, 83, *474
lvii. 4	. 126, 133, 322
lvii. 5	. . 133, *474
lvii. 6	. . 199, 314
lvii. 8	 47
lvii. 11	. . . . *470
lvii. 12	. 47, 199, 314
lviii.	. 78, **120–121**, 133, 134, 137, 207, 325, 428, *474
lviii. 2	 324
lviii. 5	. . . . *474
lviii. 7–10	. . ! . 121
lix.	. **121**, 132–136, 196, *474
lix. 2	 273
lix. 4	 133
lix. 5	 133
lix. 6	. 101, 132, 133, 164, 222, 323
lix. 7	 133
lix. 8	. . 121, 133
lix. 9	 123
lix. 11	. . 133, 379
lix. 12	. 121, 123, 215
lix. 13	 234
lix. 14	 133
lix. 15	 133
lix. 18	 379
lx.	. 93, **95, 97**, 98, 99, 100, 102, 107, 194, 198, 277
lx. 2	. . 107, 273
lx. 3	 95
lx. 3–6	 96
lx. 6	. . 108, *475
lx. 6, 7 (Targ.)	. . 275
lx. 7	 97
lx. 7–14	 47
lx. 8	 107
lx. 8–10	. . 96, 108
lx. 8–11	. . 108, 208

PASSAGES FROM THE SCRIPTURES, ETC. 505

PSALMS—cont.	PSALMS—cont.	PSALMS—cont.
lx. 11 108	lxv. 3 . . . 169, 292	lxviii. 30–32 . . . 124
lx. 12 . . . 102, 107	lxv. 5 . . . 429, 430	lxviii. 31 . 47, 113, 125, *474, *475
lx. 12–14 95	lxv. 6 225	
lx. 13 . . *466, *475	lxv. 8 162	lxviii. 34 125
lx. 14 333	lxv. 9 . . . *465, *475	lxviii. 36. 199, *476, *477
lxi. . 99, 110, 134, 199, 200, 208, 237, 276, 455, *468	lxv. (lxvi.) 1 (Sept.) . 444	lxix. . 65, 77, 78, 82, 91, 118, 134, 135, 147, 156, 230, **231–232**, 236, 245, 263, 264, 272, 274, 377, 455
	lxvi. . 90, **162-163**, 177, 276, 455	
lxi. 1–9 111	lxvi. 1–4 176	
lxi. 3 110	lxvi. 6 176	
lxi. 3, 4 134	lxvi. 7 . . . 163, 340	lxix. 2, 3 236
lxi. 4 110	lxvi. 8 176	lxix. 4 236
lxi. 5 . 236, 429, 430, *475	lxvi. 9 (Targ.) . . . 444	lxix. 6 . 102, 236, 332, 353, 354, *456
	lxvi. 10–12 176	
lxi. 6 111	lxvi. 12 . . 444, *464	lxix. 7 222
lxi. 6–8 111	lxvi. 13–15 . 176, 374	lxix. 8 102
lxi. 6–9 99	lxvi. 18, 19 . . . 176	lxix. 8, 9 233
lxi. 7 . . . 199, 200	lxvii. . 90, 124, **162-163**, 242, 292	lxix. 10 102
lxi. 7 (Targ.) . . . 444		lxix. 13 233
lxi. 7, 8 . . . 111, 350	lxvii. 5 . . . 292, 305	lxix. 21 233
lxi. 8 . . . 110, 322	lxvii. 7 101	lxix. 26 233
lxi. 9 . . . 110, 374	lxvii. 12 (Sept.) . . 185	lxix. 31, 32 . . . 374
lxi. 10 111	lxviii. . 84, 112, **113-114**, 124, 125, 147, 455, 456, *469, *475	lxix. 32 376
lxii. . 101, 110, **121**, 123, 134, 208, 227, 233, 242, 455		lxix. 36 232
		lxix. 37 . . . 289, 378
	lxviii. 2 . . . 126, 135	lxx. . 90, 101, 135, 147, 156, 230
lxii. 2 . 175, 233, *468, *470, *475	lxviii. 3, 4 125	
	lxviii. 4 124	lxx. 6 101
lxii. 3 134	lxviii. 5 124	lxxi. . 90, 134, 135, 147, 176, **230**, 245, 455
lxii. 5 227	lxviii. 5, 6 344	
lxii. 7, 8, 9 . . . 134	lxviii. 5–7 246	lxxi. 6 . . . . . *476
lxii. 8, 9 110	lxviii. 6 317	lxxi. 14 . . . . . *476
lxii. 9 . . . . 64, 287	lxviii. 7 . 114, 124, *475	lxxi. 18 244
lxii. 10, 11 . . . 233	lxviii. 8 125	lxxi. 19 246
lxii. 11 . . 227, *475	lxviii. 9 101	lxxi. 20 (Sept.) . . 12
lxii. 12 . . . . *475	lxviii. 11 125	lxxi. 21 . . *476, *480
lxii. 12, 13 . . . 246	lxviii. 12 . . 125, 246	lxxi. 22 331
lxiii. . 99, 110, 126, 134, 199, 200, 208, 237, 455, *468	lxviii. 13 . . . . *470	lxxi. 24 156
	lxviii. 14 135	lxxii. . 13, 90, **141–147**, 156, 168, 173, 180, 184, 185, 217, 244, 291, 296, 339, 350, 373, 456, *476
	lxviii. 14–19 . . . 208	
lxiii. 2 101	lxviii. 15 124	
lxiii. 3 236	lxviii. 15 (Targ.) . . 444	
lxiii. 4 . . . . *475	lxviii. 15, 16 . . . 116	
lxiii. 4, 5 (Targ.) . . 444	lxviii. 16 316	lxxii. 1 . . 143, 144, 156
lxiii. 5 110	lxviii. 17 . 124, 316, 317	lxxii. 2 . . 143, 145, 169
lxiii. 7 110	lxviii. 18 . 125, 351, *475	lxxii. 5 . . 36, 408, *476
lxiii. 9, 10 . . . 408	lxviii. 19 . 124, 163, 203, 317	lxxii. 6 . . . 155, *476
lxiii. 11 . . . . *465		lxxii. 7 36
lxiii. 12 . 99, 111, 134, 200	lxviii. 20 . . 113, 125	lxxii. 8 . 142, 154, 169, 171
	lxviii. 20–24 . . . 113	
lxiv. . 78, **121**, 208, 455	lxviii. 20–28 . . . 113	lxxii. 8–11 . . . 145
lxiv. 3 . . . . *475	lxviii. 21 . 124, 125, 314	lxxii. 8–14 . . . 155
lxiv. 7 . . . . *466	lxviii. 22 125	lxxii. 9 . . . . *477
lxiv. 10 . . . . *475	lxviii. 25 . . 125, 203	lxxii. 11 143
lxiv. 11 134	lxviii. 25–28 . . . 113	lxxii. 12 . . 142, 145
lxv. . . 162, 176, 292	lxviii. 27 . *469, *475	lxxii. 12–14 . . . 143
lxv. 1 (Sept.) . . . 272	lxviii. 28 148	lxxii. 14 . 144, *464, *477
lxv. 2 . 175, *468, *475	lxviii. 28, 29 . . . 113	lxxii. 15 . . . 143, 155
lxv. 2, 3 176	lxviii. 29 125	lxxii. 16 . 142, 155, *477

INDICES.

PSALMS—cont.

	PAGE
lxxii. 17	142, 145, 154, *476
lxxii. 19	8, 13
lxxii. 20	7, 8, 154
lxxiii.–lxxxiii.	90
lxxiii.	67, **148–149**, 150, 158, 198, 276, 381, 390, 407, 414, 422, 455, 456, *464
lxxiii. 1	92, 352, 370, 426
lxxiii. 2	356
lxxiii. 3	149, 234
lxxiii. 4	*477
lxxiii. 4, 5	382
lxxiii. 5	*466
lxxiii. 5–7	*467, *477
lxxiii. 6	*477
lxxiii. 7	*466, *477
lxxiii. 8	*477
lxxiii. 9	*477
lxxiii. 11	83, 321, 382, *477
lxxiii. 12	*477
lxxiii. 15	236, 305, 352, 382, *465
lxxiii. 17	227, 356, 373, 374, *476, *477
lxxiii. 18	149, *466, *477
lxxiii. 20	110, 389
lxxiii. 21	*477
lxxiii. 22	150
lxxiii. 23	149
lxxiii. 23, 24	149
lxxiii. 24	319, 430, 431
lxxiii. 24–25	390
lxxiii. 24–27	407
lxxiii. 25	389
lxxiii. 26	422, 429
lxxiii. 26, 27	408
lxxiii. 27	111, 390, 408
lxxiii. 28	149, 426, 428, 431
lxxiv.	**91, 93, 95, 98**, 102, 103, 148, 455, 456
lxxiv. 1	95, 158
lxxiv. 3	103, 149
lxxiv. 3–7	94
lxxiv. 5 (Targ.)	*477
lxxiv. 6	*477, *478
lxxiv. 7	102, 103
lxxiv. 8	93, 104, *478
lxxiv. 9	35, 40, 94, 97, 104
lxxiv. 10	94
lxxiv. 12–17	103
lxxiv. 14	105, *477
lxxiv. 18	197
lxxiv. 20	94, 104, 105, 345, *482

PSALMS—cont.

	PAGE
lxxiv. 23	105
lxxv.–lxxvii.	455
lxxv.	99, **148**, 149, **165**–166, 177, 178, 455
lxxv. 1	166
lxxv. 2	177
lxxv. 3	342, 374
lxxv. 4	165, 177
lxxv. 5	149
lxxv. 5, 6	166
lxxv. 6	178
lxxv. 8	177, 342
lxxvi.	99, 110, **148**, **165**–**166**, 177, 178, 455
lxxvi. 1 (Sept.)	110, 165
lxxvi. 3	42, 165
lxxvi. 3, 4	110, 178
lxxvi. 4–7	178
lxxvi. 6	*478
lxxvi. 9	165
lxxvi. 12	165, 178
lxxvi. 13	178
lxxvii.–lxxxi.	99
lxxvii.	66, 99, 101, 110, 115, 130, **147**, 158, 246, 273, 276, 455, *464
lxxvii. 4	*470, *478
lxxvii. 6	66, *475
lxxvii. 7	126, 147, *470, *478
lxxvii. 8	299, *465
lxxvii. 9	*464, *478
lxxvii. 10	345
lxxvii. 11	83
lxxvii. 16	148
lxxvii. 21	158
lxxvii. 37	345
lxxviii.	99, **147**, 157, *464
lxxviii. 4	*478
lxxviii. 5	374
lxxviii. 7	*472
lxxviii. 9	*474, *478
lxxviii. 13	147
lxxviii. 17	83
lxxviii. 25	324, 336
lxxviii. 35	83
lxxviii. 37–39	371
lxxviii. 41	331, *478
lxxviii. 49	147, 157, 335
lxxviii. 52	158
lxxviii. 56	83
lxxviii. 60	223
lxxviii. 65	222
lxxviii. 69	212, 317
lxxviii. 72	*472
lxxviii. (lxxix.)	430

PSALMS—cont.

	PAGE
lxxix.	18, 27, 91, 92, 93, **94, 95**, 97, **98**, 102, 103, 104, 142, 277, 455, 456
lxxix. 1	70, 93
lxxix. 1 (Sept.)	352
lxxix. 2	56, 66, 93, 403, *472
lxxix. 3	93
lxxix. 4	104
lxxix. 5, 6	95
lxxix. 6, 7	307
lxxix. 8	104
lxxix. 8, 9	353
lxxix. 10	126
lxxix. 13	95, **158**
lxxx.	95, 97, 99, 102, 132, **147**–**148**, 455
lxxx. 1	312
lxxx. 1 (Sept.)	110, 178
lxxx. 2	148, 158, 159, 334
lxxx. 4	318
lxxx. 5	101, **132**
lxxx. 6	126
lxxx. 8	101, 132
lxxx. 13	148
lxxx. 13, 14	*478
lxxx. 14	159, *472, *477
lxxx. 15	101, 132
lxxx. 16	158, 350
lxxx. 16, 17	*478
lxxx. 18	*478
lxxx. 20	101, 132
lxxxi.	83, 99, 110, **147**–**148**, 157
lxxxi. 2–6	147, 374
lxxxi. 4	*478
lxxxi. 6	148
lxxxi. 6, 7	*478
lxxxi. 6–17	147, 159
lxxxi. 9–11	356
lxxxi. 11	159
lxxxi. 12–17	341
lxxxi. 13	*478
lxxxi. 14	356
lxxxi. 17	374
lxxxii.	83, 99, 110, **120**–**121**, 132, 134, 221, 325, 335, 337, **342**, 352, 373, 380, 428, *464, *483
lxxxii. 1	130, 322, 336
lxxxii. 5	342
lxxxii. 6	83, 121, 130, 324
lxxxii. 7	120, *466
lxxxiii.	59, 95, **97**–**98**, 109, 177, 238, 239, 455, 456

PASSAGES FROM THE SCRIPTURES, ETC.

PSALMS—cont.	PAGE
lxxxiii. 2	*478
lxxxiii. 3	97, 251
lxxxiii. 4	97, 251
lxxxiii. 5	252
lxxxiii. 6	251
lxxxiii. 9	109, 110, 184
lxxxiii. 10	93
lxxxiii. 10–13	47
lxxxiii. 12	*467, *478
lxxxiii. 14	*478
lxxxiii. 17	98
lxxxiii. 18	251
lxxxiii. 19	83, 98, 121
lxxxiv.–lxxxix.	90
lxxxiv.	90, 119, 126, 132
lxxxiv. 2–8	120
lxxxiv. 4	11, *479
lxxxiv. 5	349, 387
lxxxiv. 7	344
lxxxiv. 7 (Targ.)	444
lxxxiv. 8	120
lxxxiv. 9	101, 131, 164
lxxxiv. 9, 10	132
lxxxiv. 10	119, 159, 199, 233, 338
lxxxiv. 11	120, 295, *479
lxxxiv. 11 (Targ.)	275
lxxxiv. 12	132, 305
lxxxv.	90, 102, 119, 126
lxxxv. 1	274
lxxxv. 6	*479
lxxxv. 9	119, 159, 199, 287, *472, *479
lxxxv. 10	332
lxxxv. 11	28, 36, 379
lxxxvi.	47, 90, 119, 129, 131, 217, 279, 455, 456, *479
lxxxvi. 1	119, 129
lxxxvi. 2	117, 119, 377
lxxxvi. 5	296, 369, *479
lxxxvi. 6	*479
lxxxvi. 8	246
lxxxvi. 9	119, 130, *479
lxxxvi. 9, 10	296
lxxxvi. 10	129
lxxxvi. 13	129
lxxxvi. 14	131, 133
lxxxvi. 15, 16	302
lxxxvi. 16	131
lxxxvii.	90, 118–119, 131, 269, 296, 456, *479
lxxxvii. 1	*479, *483
lxxxvii. 2	329
lxxxvii. 3	80
lxxxvii. 5	83, 317, 330, *479
lxxxvii. 6	*479

PSALMS—cont.	PAGE
lxxxviii.	90, 102, 117, 118, 129, 227, 272, 287, 455, *464
lxxxviii. 3	129
lxxxviii. 4	118
lxxxviii. 5	*480
lxxxviii. 7	129
lxxxviii. 8	*480
lxxxviii. 11	129
lxxxviii. 11–13	385
lxxxviii. 12	411
lxxxviii. 13	411, *480
lxxxviii. 15	321
lxxxviii. 16	129, 273
lxxxviii. 17	*480
lxxxix.	52, 53, 90, 102, 116–118, 129, 130, 175, 206, 233, 238, 246, 339, 455, *464
lxxxix. 1	101
lxxxix. 2	67, 379
lxxxix. 2, 3	130
lxxxix. 3	128
lxxxix. 6	324
lxxxix. 6–9	130
lxxxix. 7	324
lxxxix. 7, 8	337
lxxxix. 8	212, 324, 336
lxxxix. 9	*480
lxxxix. 10, 11	130
lxxxix. 11	*475
lxxxix. 18	129
lxxxix. 19	117, 129, 332
lxxxix. 25	129
lxxxix. 27, 28	143, 305
lxxxix. 28	83, 130, 252
lxxxix. 30	128
lxxxix. 39	338
lxxxix. 41	130
lxxxix. 41, 42	148, 350
lxxxix. 45	*480
lxxxix. 46	117, 130, 293, 350
lxxxix. 48	117, 233, 293, *467, *480
lxxxix. 49	385, 403
lxxxix. 49 (Targ.)	444
lxxxix. 50	224
lxxxix. 51	293
lxxxix. 52	338, 350
xc.–cl.	8, 301
xc.	47, 63, 69, 73, 74–76, 84, 89, 455, *480
xc. 1	86, 354, *481
xc. 1–4	354, 355
xc. 2	*480
xc. 3	*464, *469, *481
xc. 5	430
xc. 5, 6	354

PSALMS—cont.	PAGE
xc. 7	354
xc. 7–12	354
xc. 8	76, 346, 354, 357
xc. 9	*464, *472, *481
xc. 9, 10	73
xc. 10	75, 354, 384, *481
xc. 11	355
xc. 13	*480, *481
xc. 13–17	76
xc. 14	*481
xc. 15	*480
xc. 16 (Targ.)	444
xc. 16, 17	85
xc. 17	76
xci.–xcii.	51
xci.–c.	63
xci.	72, 73–74, 83, 84, 124, 234, *464, *481
xci. 1	73, 83, *480, *481
xci. 2	*465
xci. 4	*481
xci. 6	*481
xci. 9	83, *481
xci. 11	323, 335
xci. 14	*481
xcii.–xcviii.	69
xcii.	72, 73, 76, 83, 158, *464
xcii. 1	246
xcii. 2	83
xcii. 4	79, *468
xcii. 5–7	76
xcii. 7	*472
xcii. 8	73, 93
xcii. 10, 11	76
xcii. 12	133
xcii. 13	*477
xcii. 14	133
xciii.	71–72, 132, 144, 157, 158, 163
xciii. 1	342
xciii. 2	318
xciii. 2, 4, 5	318
xciv.	72, 123, 158, 455
xciv. 4	133
xciv. 6	342
xciv. 10	305, 306
xciv. 12	348, 373
xciv. 17	385
xciv. 22	72
xcv.–c.	71, 158, 163
xcv.	71–72
xcv. 1	72
xcv. 7	158
xcvi.–cii.	455
xcvi.	71, 202
xcvi. 1	71, 195
xcvi. 1 (Sept.)	72
xcvi. 2	246

INDICES.

PSALMS—*cont.*

	PAGE
xcvi. 3	228, 294
xcvi. 3, 4	292
xcvi. 7	221
xcvi. 10	228
xcvi. 13	292
xcvii.	71, 83, 344, *464
xcvii. 1, 2	292
xcvii. 7	221, 341
xcvii. 9	83
xcvii. 10	368
xcviii.	71
xcviii. 1	195, 332
xcviii. 9	292
xcix.	71
xcix. 1	334
xcix. 1–3	292
xcix. 3.	289, 298, 301, 332
xcix. 5	298
xcix. 6	83
c.	71, 379
c. 1	292
c. 3	151
ci.	63, 67–69, 208, 249, 339, 456, *483
ci. 1	67
ci. 2	67
ci. 5	*481, *482
ci. 6 (Targ.)	444
ci. 7	99
ci. 8	68
cii.	63, 70–71, 231, 264, 277, 287
cii. 5	78
cii. 5, 6	78
cii. 6	82
cii. 7	78
cii. 10	78
cii. 11	82
cii. 12	78, 354
cii. 14	71
cii. 16–18	295
cii. 20	314
cii. 24	78, 82
cii. 25–29	78
cii. 26–28	82, 298
cii. 28	82
cii. 29	319
ciii.	63, 208
ciii. 1	*466
ciii. 3	*483
ciii. 10	357, *465
ciii. 11	248
ciii. 13	248, 305
ciii. 14	357
ciii. 15	*464
ciii. 17	248
ciii. 18	345
ciii. 20	324
ciii. 21	323

PSALMS—*cont.*

	PAGE
ciii. 22	366
civ.	58, 63, 201
civ. 3	314
civ. 4	323
civ. 11	*472
civ. 20	*472
civ. 24	322
civ. 26	404
civ. 30	322, 406
civ. (cv.) 45 (Sept.)	68
cv.–cvii.	63, 147
cv.	50, 58, 157
cv, 1	228
cv. 8	345
cv. 10	345
cv. 16–22	158
cv. 44, 45	351
cvi.	8, 50, 58, 89, 157, 457
cvi. 4, 5	276
cvi. 6	353
cvi. 16	83
cvi. 37	334, 335
cvi. 45	345
cvi. 47	*475
cvi. 48	457
cvii.	8, 50–51, 58, *464
cvii. 2, 3	51
cvii. 3	150
cvii. 11	51, 83
cvii. 20	321
cvii. 22	374
cviii.	47, 455, 456
cviii. 11	444
cix.	47, 63–65, 77, 82, 98, 208
cix. 2	77
cix. 2–5	65
cix. 3	77
cix. 6	335
cix. 6–15	77, 78
cix. 6–19	77
cix. 6–20	63, 64, 65
cix. 7	78
cix. 8	*482
cix. 11	77, 78
cix. 13	77, 246
cix. 16	78
cix. 18	78
cix. 21	64
cix. 22	78
cix. 23	78
cix. 24	78
cix. 26–31	65
cix. 28, 29	78
cix. 28–31	78
cx.	20–29, 34, 35, 36, 47, 49, 67, 68, 69, 75, 89, 96, 143,

PSALMS—*cont.*

	PAGE
	200, 203, 208, 217, 238, 239, 301, 339, 373, 458, *479, *482
cx. i.	35, 37, 47, 200, 251, 299, 458
cx. 2	26
cx. 3.	20, 25, 36, 49, 238, *479, *482
cx. 4.	21, 25, 52, 57, 99, *472, *481
cx. 5	49, 212, 251
cx. 5, 6	251, *482
cx. 5–7	24
cx. 6	28
cx. 6, 7	212
cxi.	50–51, 240
cxi. 1	211
cxi. 5	345
cxi. 9	289, 301, 345
cxii.	50–51, 240, 397
cxii. 2	352, *465
cxii. 5	234
cxii. 9	*475
cxii. 12	236
cxiii.–cxviii.	18, 19, 49, 50
cxiii.	49, 127
cxiii. 3	177
cxiii. 4	327
cxiii. 5–9	*481
cxiii. 6	343
cxiii. 7–9	57
cxiii. 9	57
cxiv.	49
cxiv. 7	*467
cxiv. 8	472, 481
cxv.–cxviii.	32, 47, 49, 455, 456
cxv.	18–19, 50, 131, 455, 456
cxv. 2	126
cxv. 3	314
cxv. 8	374
cxv. 9–11	195
cxv. 9–13	19
cxv. 11	296
cxv. 12	295
cxv. 13	19
cxv. 17	385, 428
cxvi.	18–19, 33, 119, 206, 455, 456
cxvi. 1	82, 378, *465, *481
cxvi. 2	456
cxvi. 3	224
cxvi. 6	*469
cxvi. 9	19, 314, 328
cxvi. 15	19
cxvi. 16	131, 273

PASSAGES FROM THE SCRIPTURES, ETC.

Psalms—cont.		Psalms—cont.		Psalms—cont.	
	PAGE		PAGE		PAGE
cxvi. 17	374, *465	cxxii.	. 52, 54, 55, 276,	cxxxiii. 3	. 319
cxvi. 19	*483		319	cxxxiv. . 53, 61, 220, 455	
cxvii.	19, 53, 379	cxxii. (Sept.)	60	cxxxv. 1	. 61
cxvii. 1	475	cxxii. 4, 5	60	cxxxv.–cxxxviii.	456
cxviii.	16–18, 22, 33,	cxxii. 5	60	cxxxv.	. 50, 53, 58, 59,
	50, 131, 203, 234,	cxxiii.	. 55, 455		61, 70, 455
	301, 455	cxxiii. 1	314, *481	cxxxv. 2	. 58
cxviii. 2	372	cxxiii. 2, 3	302	cxxxv. 3	. 289
cxviii. 2–4	19	cxxiii. 3 (Pesh.)	.*475	cxxxv. 5	. 220
cxviii. 4	296	cxxiii. 4	.*475	cxxxv. 6	. 314
cxviii. 5	287, 301	cxxiv.–cxxix.	54	cxxxvi.	. 50, 53, 58, 59,
cxviii. 6	133	cxxiv.	. 52, 54, 176		61, 70, 371, 455
cxviii. 7	133	cxxiv. (Sept.)	60	cxxxvi. 1	214
cxviii. 10	98	cxxv.	. 54, 455	cxxxvi. 4	178, 345
cxviii. 10–12	17, *483	cxxv. 1, 2	318	cxxxvi. 5	322
cxviii. 14	215, 301	cxxv. 3	55	cxxxvi. 10–18	178
cxviii. 14, 15, 16	31	cxxv. 5	55	cxxxvi. 26	328
cxviii. 15	57, 195, 403	cxxv. 5 (Targ.)	444	cxxxvii.	. 69, 80, 81, 162
cxviii. 15, 16	17	cxxvi.	54	cxxxvii. 1 (Sept.)	. 69, 80
cxviii. 17	19, 296, 307	cxxvi. 1	54	cxxxvii. 5	128
cxviii. 18	234	cxxvi. 5	234	cxxxvii. 6	.*483
cxviii. 19	57	cxxvii.	. 52, 54, 55, 212	cxxxvii. 8	128, *465
cxviii. 19–20	203	cxxvii. 1	32, 54, 61,	cxxxvii. 8, 9	483
cxviii. 20	. 57, 195		154	cxxxviii.–cxlv.	. 63, 65
cxviii. 21	17	cxxvii. 1, 2	237	cxxxviii.	. 67, 80, 208,
cxviii. 21–22	17	cxxvii. 2	61, 62, 173		455, 458
cxviii. 22	17, 61	cxxviii.	. 54–55	cxxxviii. 1 (Sept.)	. 66
cxviii. 25	17	cxxviii. 5, 6	320	cxxxviii. 2	320
cxviii. 26	17	cxxix.–cxxxi.	276	cxxxviii. 3	67
cxviii. 27	17, 273, 372,	cxxix.	.54–55, 176, 277,	cxxxviii. 6	343
	374		455	cxxxviii. 7	. 79
cxix.	. 51, 202, 240, 278,	cxxix. 3	.*466	cxxxviii. 8	. 67, *464
	348, 364, 365, 374,	cxxx.	54, 175, 273,	cxxxix.	. 67, 72, 89, 123,
	455, 456		277, 455		277, 278, 286, 291,
cxix. 17	.*465	cxxx. 2	54		426, 456, *483
cxix. 18	321, 348	cxxx. 4	.*479	cxxxix. 1	196
cxix. 19	429	cxxx. 7	54	cxxxix. 1 (Sept.)	. 66
cxix. 41–46	295	cxxx. 8	346	cxxxix. 2, 3	.*483
cxix. 54	51	cxxxi.	. 51, 52	cxxxix. 7	322
cxix. 55	221	cxxxi. (Sept.)	60	cxxxix. 10	.79, 384
cxix. 62	221	cxxxi. 3	54	cxxxix. 14	332
cxix. 81, 82	150	cxxxii.	52–54, 60, 72,	cxxxix. 15	.79, 450
cxix. 84	293		102, 117, 203, 229,	cxxxix. 16	. 79
cxix. 96	356		238, 339, 455	cxxxix. 18	. 319
cxix. 101	243	cxxxii. 6	52	cxxxix. 19	.*467, *484
cxix. 104	243	cxxxii. 8	25, 52	cxxxix. 19, 20	148
cxix. 105	348	cxxxii. 8–10	. 52, 54, 60	cxxxix. 19–21	67
cxix. 108	364, 375	cxxxii. 9	52	cxxxix. 19–22	. 79
cxix. 113	51, 55	cxxxii. 10	199, 350	cxxxix. 23	196, 370
cxix. 114	215	cxxxii. 12	345	cxxxix. 24	442
cxix. 130	321	cxxxii. 13–18	53	cxl.–cxlii.	65
cxix. 132	378	cxxxii. 14	317	cxl.–cxliii.	. 66, 69, 456,
cxix. 139	.*480	cxxxii. 16	52		*483
cxx.–cxxxiv.	51	cxxxii. 16, 17	25	cxl.	. 66, 77, 78, 455,
cxx.	. 55, 455	cxxxii. 17	60		456
cxx. 2	.*466	cxxxii. 18	60	cxl. 2	.*483
cxx. 6	134, *475	cxxxiii.	.52, 53–54, 55	cxl. 4	.*483
cxxi.	54, 276, 455	cxxxiii. (Sept.)	60	cxl. 5	.*483
cxxi. 1	59	cxxxiii. 2	237	cxl. 8	. 66, 79

PSALMS—*cont.*		PSALMS—*cont.*		PROVERBS—*cont.*	
	PAGE		PAGE		PAGE
cxl. 9	*483	cxlvi. 6	*468	xiii. 12	442
cxl. 11 (Targ.)	444	cxlvi. 8	79	xiii. 14	253, 442
cxl. 11, 12	*483	cxlvi. 9	199, 468	xiv. 27	442
cxl. 14	408	cxlvi. 10	199, 352	xv. 3	456
cxli.	66, 78, 79, 455, 456	cxlvii.	49–50, 56, 162, 215, *468	xv. 4	442
cxli. 2	374	cxlvii. (Sept.)	58	xv. 8	365
cxli. 3	356, 456	cxlvii. 1	215	xv. 14	220
cxli. 3, 4	*483	cxlvii. 2	50	xv. 24	441
cxli. 4	66, 198	cxlvii. 5	220	xv. 33	225
cxli. 4, 5	198	cxlvii. 6	199	xvi. 6	365
cxli. 4–7	66	cxlvii. 10	199	xvi. 22	442
cxli. 7	66	cxlvii. 10, 11	215	xvii. 26	*464
cxli. 8	79	cxlvii. 12	*475	xviii. 12	225
cxli. 10	*483	cxlvii. 13	50	xix. 7	134
cxlii.	66, 81, 127, 455	cxlvii. 15	321	xix. 21	154
cxlii. 2	287	cxlvii. 16	*475	xix. 25 (Sept.)	253
cxlii. 8	*465, *483	cxlvii. 18	321	xx. 27	348
cxliii.	78, 119, 455	cxlvii. 19	349	xxi. 3	365
cxliii. 2	119	cxlvii. 19, 20	50, 215	xxi. 24 (Sept.)	253
cxliii. 5	66	cxlviii.–cl.	49, 456	xxi. 27	365
cxliii. 10	322, 347	cxlviii.	48, 56, 58, 215, 455	xxii. 4	225
cxliv.	66, 206, 224, 344, 455, 456	cxlviii. 5	215	xxii. 10 (Sept.)	253
cxliv. 1	*474	cxlviii. 9, 10	69	xxii. 12	456
cxliv. 1, 2, 3	79	cxlviii. 14	48, 49	xxii. 19	*471
cxliv. 2	215	cxlix.	20, 47–48, 56, 98, 455	xxiv. 9 (Sept.)	253
cxliv. 3	220, *464	cxlix. 1	48, 195, 364	xxv. 1	13, 154, 457
cxliv. 4	79	cxlix. 1–5	49	xxvi. 2	64
cxliv. 5	220	cxlix. 5	52, 407, 441	xxviii. 4, 7, 9	253
cxliv. 5–7	79	cxlix. 6	47, 48	xxviii. 14	365
cxliv. 8	66	cxlix. 7	49	xxix. 18	253
cxliv. 9	79, 195	cxlix. 9	47	xxx. 1–4	321, 423
cxliv. 10	66, 81	cl.	49, 56, 455	xxx. 4	287
cxliv. 12	66	cl. 1	314, *468	xxx. 5	224, 287
cxliv. 12–14	66, 79, *484			xxx. 9	302
cxliv. 12–15	79, 208	PROVERBS.		xxx. 11–14	236
cxliv. 15	79			xxxi. 2	*463
cxlv.–cxlvii.	456	i.–ix.	159, 198, 217, 218, 365	xxxi. 10–31	55
cxlv.	47, 66, 69, 279, 455	i. 1	154	ECCLESIASTES.	
cxlv. 4	*475	i. 7	365	iii. 11	*467
cxlv. 6	*476, *478	ii. 19	441	iii. 17	409
cxlv. 8, 9	296	v. 6	441	iii. 21	410, 422
cxlv. 10	66	vii. 27	441	iv. 1–3	121
cxlv. 13	66, *471, *475	viii.	217, 218, 334	v. 6	335
cxlv. 14	79	viii. 22–31	322	v. 7	144
cxlv. 15	79	ix. 18	441	vii. 16	129
cxlv. 16, 17	379	x.–xxii. 16	190	vii. 28, 29	197
cxlv. 17	296	x. 1	154	xi. 9	409
cxlv. 20	378	x. 11	442	xii. 1	355
cxlvi.–cxlviii.	458	x. 17	441	xii. 7	409, 422
cxlvi.–cxlviii. (Sept.)	58, 215	x. 21	352	xii. 11	352
cxlvi.–cl.	49–50, 69, 90	x. 22	62	xii. 12	424
cxlvi.	49, 56, 66, *468	xi. 17	236	xii. 14	409
cxlvi. 4	58, 93	xi. 30	442	SONG OF SOLOMON.	
cxlvi. 5	79	xii. 28	441	i. 4	179
cxlvi. 5–9	246	xii. 28	442	ii. 4	*468

PASSAGES FROM THE SCRIPTURES, ETC.

Song of Solomon —cont.		Isaiah —cont.		Isaiah —cont.	
	PAGE		PAGE		PAGE
iii. 8	179	xviii. 7	131, 328	xxxviii. 20	157, 242
iv. 7	179	xix. 18	42, 170	xxxix.	279
iv. 14	179	xix. 18–25	131, 184	xxxix. 6–7	131
v. 13	179	xix. 21	172	xl.	125, 130, 131
v. 16	179	xix. 23–25	170	xl. 3	124
vi. 7	169	xx.	131	xl. 9	274
vi. 8	169, 173	xx. 5	219	xl. 11	158
vii. 5	179	xxii. 13	*477	xl. 13	333
viii. 6	124, 298	xxii. 15	159	xl. 14	336
viii. 13	179	xxiii.	131	xli. 2	37
		xxiv.–xxvii.	120, 125, 133, 428	xli. 4	82
Isaiah.		xxiv. 4–13	133	xli. 8	371
		xxiv. 5	306	xli. 14	245
i. 15	370	xxiv. 21–23	120	xlii. 1	252
i. 25	42	xxiv. 23	82	xlii. 1–4	292
ii. 2–3	315	xxv.	277	xlii. 1–7	274
ii. 3	357	xxv. 1	247	xlii. 4	275, 293
ii. 12	336	xxv. 6	402	xlii. 7	124
ii. 19	427	xxv. 8	383, 402, 405	xlii. 8	217
iv. 1	328	xxvi.	203, 277	xlii. 10	195
iv. 3 (Targ.)	406	xxvi. 4	124	xlii. 10–12	214
iv. 5	330	xxvi. 12	*469	xlii. 10–31	71
v. 14	426	xxvi. 13	302, 333, 341	xlii. 21	217
vi.	203	xxvi. 19	383, 402, 406, 444	xliii. 17	178, 222
vi. 2	221			xliii. 21	367
vi. 3	203, 331	xxvi. 19 (Sept.)	440	xliii. 23	365
vi. 5	341	xxvi. 29	125	xliv. 2	211
viii. 7–8	248	xxviii. 6	333	xliv. 5	131
viii. 9	239	xxviii. 9–10	348	xliv. 8	224
viii. 12, 16	210	xxviii. 16	318	xliv. 21	263
viii. 13	178	xxviii. 26	357	xliv. 22	369
ix.	338	xxix. 6	323	xliv. 23	214
ix. 5 (6)	305	xxx. 7	131	xlv. 1	338
ix. 6	336	xxx. 20	357	xlv. 3	169
ix. 6–7	142	xxx. 21	348, 352, 355	xlv. 7	269
ix. 7	128	xxx. 27	177	xlv. 8	214
ix. 8	321	xxx. 29	194	xlv. 12	324
x. 17	404	xxxi. 4	203	xlv. 14	124, 131
xi.	338	xxxii.	249	xlv. 15	314
xi. 1	128, 154	xxxii. 1–8	249	xlvi.	279
xi. 5	154	xxxii. 9–20	249	xlvii. 4	288
xii.	31, 176, 214	xxxiii.	177, 237, 249	xlviii. 8	371
xii. 1–2	277	xxxiii. 11	178	xlviii. 11	217
xii. 2	31, 124	xxxiii. 12	478	xlviii. 13	82
xii. 4	228	xxxiii. 13–16	249	xlix. 1–9	274
xiii. 16	84	xxxiii. 14	429	xlix. 6	275
xiv. 1 (Sept.)	429	xxxiii. 15–16	237	xlix. 7	245, 264, 377
xiv. 1–3	429	xxxiii. 22	177	xlix. 9	124
xiv. 9	382	xxxiii. 24	404	xlix. 14	299
xiv. 12	36	xxxiv.	65, 120	xlix. 14–19	274
xiv. 12–15	181	xxxv. 8	404	xlix. 21	57
xiv. 13	329, 426, 427	xxxv. 10	124	l. 4–9	274
xiv. 13–14	317, 326	xxxvii. 36	178	l. 11	405
xiv. 14	84	xxxviii.	118	li. 5	293
xiv. 29	403	xxxviii. 10–20	210, 214, 247	li. 6	82, 404
xiv. 31	177			li. 9	131
xvi. 5	171	xxxviii. 11	124	li. 9–10	130
xviii. 5	178	xxxviii. 18	13, 367, 385	li. 10–11	124
				lii.	273

ISAIAH—cont.		ISAIAH—cont.		JEREMIAH—cont.	
	PAGE		PAGE		PAGE
lii. 1	80	lxv. 65, 153, 217, 234,		xi. 15	173, 185
lii. 7	71		329, 405	xi. 20	196, 245
lii. 7–9	274	lxv.–lxvi.	159	xii. 3	242
lii. 13–liii.	263, 274	lxv. 3–5	160, 397	xii. 6	137, 250
lii. 14	245, 377	lxv. 5	65	xiii. 17	158
liii.	264, 273, 275	lxv. 11	198, 397	xiv. 7–9	214
liii. 2–3	377	lxv. 13–14	405	xiv. 9	328
liii. 2–9	264	lxv. 14	217	xiv. 19–22	214
liii. 3	264	lxv. 15	65	xv. 16	328
liii. 5, 6, 10	*473	lxv. 17	404, 405	xvii. 5	92
liii. 8	245	lxv. 17–22	404	xvii. 5–8	240
liii. 10	367	lxv. 19	443	xvii. 6	240
liv.	273	lxv. 20	404, 405	xvii. 7–8	13
liv. 1–3	57	lxv. 22	405, 412, 443	xvii. 8	240
liv. 4 (Sept.)	212	lxv. 23	405	xvii. 10	196
liv. 7–8	234	lxvi. 65, 153, 160, 234,		xvii. 12–13	182
liv. 13	386		329, 405	xvii. 13	318, 408
lv. 3	22, 129	lxvi. 1–2	152	xvii. 14	247
lv. 4–5	292	lxvi. 1–3	375	xviii. 20, 22	195
lv. 5	224	lxvi. 3	153, 160, 217,	xx. 12	196
lv. 7	368		365	xxii. 15	170
lv. 11	321	lxvi. 5	65	xxii. 16	170
lvi. 1–8	294	lxvi. 6	197	xxiii. 24	314
lvi. 7	14, 328	lxvi. 6–24	165	xxiv.	230
lvii.	353	lxvi. 11	*472, 473	xxv. 4	294
lvii. 1	135	lxvi. 15	405	xxv. 25–26	232
lvii. 2	384, 426, 441	lxvi. 17	160	xxvi. 8, 11	137
lvii. 7	176	lxvi. 21	160	xxix. 4–7	266
lvii. 15	343, 344	lxvi. 22	404	xxix. 8	116
lviii.	127, 375	lxvi. 24	160, 405, 406	xxx. 19	192
lviii. 2	130, 374			xxxi. 4	192
lix. 123, 134, 137, 161,		JEREMIAH.		xxxi. 10	158
	162			xxxi. 13	247
lix. 3	370	ii. 1	321	xxxi. 33	356
lix. 14	133	ii. 2	378	xxxi. 34	386
lx. 14	80	ii. 13	408	xxxiii. 3	64
lxi. 1	124, 338	iii. 4	305	xxxiii. 11	214
lxi. 3	171, 412	iii. 12	379	xxxiii. 21	207
lxi. 6	366	iii. 16–17	315	xxxv.	230
lxii. 3	218	iii. 16 (Targ.)	329	xxxvii.	247
lxii. 4	217	v. 1	197	xxxvii. 5	125
lxii. 6	274	v. 6	232	xxxviii.	247
lxiii.	147	v. 16	242	xxxviii. 6	136
lxiii.–lxvi.	160	v. 23	197	xlii. 11 (Sept.)	110
lxiii. 1–6	203	vii. 4	329, 330	xlv. 3	242
lxiii. 7	130, 175	vii. 10–11	328	xlix. 1	232
lxiii. 7–lxiv. 118, 130, 156,		vii. 12	328	l.–li.	8
	160, 162, 175	vii. 22–23	151, 366	l. 19	158
lxiii. 9	248	viii. 8	151, 366	li. 19	429
lxiii. 10	333	viii. 22	313	li. 34	127
lxiii. 11	272, 345	x. 1–16	333	li. 39	441
lxiii. 16	305	x. 7	340	li. 57	441
lxiii. 17	357	x. 12	333	li. 58	8
lxiii. 18	130	x. 16	429	li. 64	8
lxiii. 19	130, 328, 340	x. 21	197		
lxiv.	161	x. 23	346	LAMENTATIONS.	
lxiv. 5	130	x. 23–25	214		
lxiv. 10	130	x. 24	242	i.	277
lxiv. 11	103, 130	x. 25	197	ii. 6	*478

PASSAGES FROM THE SCRIPTURES, ETC.

LAMENTATIONS—cont.
	PAGE
ii. 7	194
ii. 15	164
iii. 122, 136,	277
iii. 22–23	334
iii. 35, 38	83
iv. 20 (Sept.)	305

EZEKIEL.
i.	327
i. 24	84
viii. 17	107, 271, 447
x.	326
x. 5	84
xii. 10	219
xiv. 14	106
xiv. 15	335
xxvi. 7	141
xxvi. 20	426
xxviii. 2	219
xxviii. 3	94, 106, 107
xxviii. 13–14	330, 427
xxviii. 14	317
xxxii. 29 (Sept.)	110
xxxiv. 11–16	158
xxxiv. 24	219
xxxvii. 1–10	383, 403
xxxvii. 25	219
xxxviii.	165, 380
xxxix.	165, 380

DANIEL.
iii. 26	320
iii. 33	66, *476
iv. 24 (27)	278
iv. 31	66, 332
iv. 31–33	267
vi. 11	320
vii. 7 (Sept.)	38
vii. 8, 11	166
vii. 23–24 (Sept.)	38
vii. 26	49
ix.	161, 298, 301
ix. 16	104
ix. 20	236
ix. 24	*475
ix. 25	41
ix. 26	123, 350
ix. 27	105
x. 13, 20, 21	120
xi.	34
xi. 14	114
xi. 22	219
xi. 31	105
xi. 33, 35	348
xii. 2	406, 430, 444

DANIEL—cont.
	PAGE
xii. 2–3	444
xii. 3	348
xii. 11	105

HOSEA.
i. 10	305
ii. 21	379
iii. 5	128
iv. 4–5	277
vi. 2	383, 440
vi. 4, 6	378
vii. 8–9	277
viii. 1	329
viii. 12	*475
ix. 7	116, 118
xi. 1	130
xiii. 2	245
xiii. 14	345
xiv. 5	440
xiv. 14	433

JOEL.
i. 15	84
ii. 11	123
ii. 12	295
ii. 12–13	375
ii. 28	386
ii. 28–29	40
iii.	160
iii. 2	165
iii. 11	120
iii. 17	25
iv. 11	324

AMOS.
iii. 5	179
iii. 7	106
v. 21–23	194, 195
vi. 4	179
vi. 4–5	167
vi. 5	192
vi. 10	297, 301
ix. 11	128
ix. 12	328

OBADIAH.
verse 7	134

JONAH.
ii.	61, 206
ii. 2 (1)	127

JONAH—cont.
	PAGE
ii. 2–9	126
ii. 3	127
ii. 10	375
iii. 5–10	375
iv. 2	295

MICAH.
iv. 2	357
iv. 10	131
vi., vii. 1–13	224
vii.	277
vii. 2	135, 378
vii. 14–20	224
vii. 17	206

NAHUM.
i. 2–10	228

HABAKKUK.
ii. 1	64
iii.	125, 156, 210, 214
iii. 1	14
iii. 2	125
iii. 3	287
iii. 6, 7, 8, 9, 10	125
iii. 12	125
iii. 13	125, 175, 350
iii. 14	125
iii. 19	157, 224

ZEPHANIAH.
ii. 3	225
ii. 8	232

HAGGAI.
ii. 7	21
ii. 20–23	36

ZECHARIAH.
ii. 4	71
ii. 4–5	231
iii. 8–9	36
iv.	36
v. 8	323
vi. 9–13	21
vi. 9–15	36

L L

ZECHARIAH—cont.		ZECHARIAH—cont.		MALACHI.	
	PAGE		PAGE		PAGE
vi. 11	21, 218	ix. 16	218	i. 6	152, 305
vi. 13	21, 36	x. 6	157	i. 10–11	364
vii. 9–10	249	xi. 8	158	i. 11	169, 176, 292
viii. 16–17	249	xii. 7	329	ii. 10	305
viii. 22–23	131	xii. 8	181	iii. 1	67
ix.–xiv.	7, 133, 154, 239, 428	xiv.	160, 380	iii. 3	175
ix. 4	171	xiv. 2	165	iii. 4	364
ix. 8	248	xiv. 3	107	iii. 15	149, 234
ix. 9	143, 171, 179	xiv. 5	324	iii. 17	288
ix. 10	142, 171, 252	xiv. 9	82, 169, 342, 352	iv. 5–6	40
ix. 13	137	xiv. 21	160, 329		
		2 Zechariah	239, 428		

(B) NEW TESTAMENT.

S. MATTHEW.		S. JOHN.		1 CORINTHIANS.	
ii. 1–12	281	i. 11	334	ii. 8	222
iii. 12	374	i. 18	327	vii. 5	446
xi. 21–23	64	iv. 22	290	xiii. 12	410
xi. 25, 27	327	v. 39	442	xiv. 26	30
xiii. 35	284	x.	319, 343	xv. 25	34
xvi. 27	336	x. 16	352		
xviii. 10	335	x. 22	32	2 CORINTHIANS.	
xxii. 30	336	xi. 51	25	v. 1–10	415, 444
xxii. 31, 32	445	xii. 31	337		
xxii. 41	34	xii. 41	222	GALATIANS.	
xxiii. 23	150, 159	xv. 18, 19	388	ii. 8	293
xxiii. 37, 38	64	xvi. 13	352	iv. 26	274
xxvi. 24	63	xvii. 3	388	vi. 16	266
xxvi. 30	33	xvii. 5, 6	313		
xxvii. 35	284	xvii. 9	388	EPHESIANS.	
xxvii. 52	441			iii. 15	302, 327
xxviii. 18	222	ACTS.		iv. 12–16	266
		ii. 34–36	34		
S. MARK.		vii. 59	415	PHILIPPIANS.	
i. 11	252	vii. 60	441	i. 23	415, 444
iii. 5	98	xii. 15	335	ii. 7	344
xii. 10, 11	33	xiv. 15, 16	306	ii. 11	305
xii. 26	383	xvi. 25	363	ii. 2	17
xiv. 26	32, 33	xvii. 30	306	iii. 20	274
S. LUKE.		ROMANS.		1 THESSALONIANS.	
i. 9–11	39	i. 19–21	306	iv. 14, 15	441
i. 67	30	vii. 22, 23	376		
ii. 11	305	vii. 24	376, 450	1 TIMOTHY.	
ii. 14	334	viii. 15	288		
ii. 26	305	ix. 6	342	iii. 16	431
ix. 26	305	x. 12	313	vi. 15	153
xii. 19	382	xi. 28	275, 377	vi. 19	429
xiv. 14	406	xii. 16	353		
xvi. 22	443				
xxii. 25	39				

PASSAGES FROM THE SCRIPTURES, ETC. 515

TITUS.		JAMES.		REVELATION.	
	PAGE		PAGE		PAGE
i. 12	271	i. 17	440	i. 4	335
		i. 26	366	iii. 12	274
		i. 27	386	vi. 2	179
HEBREWS.				vi. 9–11	415, 443
				vii. 9	443
i. 1	124	1 PETER.		vii. 9–17	415
i. 7, 8	179			vii. 15	443
i. 8	182	ii. 9	367	xii. 4	273, 274
i. 14	324	ii. 25	353	xii. 11, 12	444
ii. 5	325, 337	iii. 15	273	xiii.	443
v. 6	34	v. 4	353	xiii. 6	415, 443
vii. 1–10	27			xiv. 13	415, 443
vii. 3	42			xv. 3	340
vii. 17, 21	34	2 PETER.		xvii. 14	153
x. 1, 2	354	iii. 13	404	xvii. 17	408
x. 1–10	367			xix. 12	259
x. 13	34			xix. 16	153
xi. 10	274	1 JOHN.		xxi. 1	405
xi. 34–38	29			xxi. 2, 10	274
xii. 18	337	i. 8	369	xxi. 2–4	404
xii. 22	274, 337	ii. 15, 17	388	xxii. 1	408
xii. 23	415, 444	ii. 16	355	xxii. 2	439
xiii. 4	274, 446	iii. 2	388	xxii. 16	36
xiii. 20	353	v. 19	388	xxii. 17	439

(C) APOCRYPHA AND OTHER ANCIENT WRITINGS.

1 ESDRAS.		vi. 3	331	xliv.–l.	128
		vi. 19	443	xliv. 5	11
iii.	52	viii. 20	450	xliv. 16	410
iv.	52	xii. 16	372	xlv. 1	76
		xii. 18	372, 377	xlv. 12	199
		xii. 19	352, 369	xlv. 24	42
2 ESDRAS.		xiv. 16–20	181	xlv. 26	42, 128
		xvi. 12	321	xlvii. 1	60
2 Esdras, book of	441	xvi. 28	448	xlvii. 3	244
ii. 12	439	xviii. 15	321	xlvii. 11	60
iv. 41	443			xlvii. 14–17	153
viii. 52	439			xlvii. 22	60
xiv. 37–50	458	ECCLESIASTICUS.		xlviii. 9	410
				xlviii. 11	409
		i. 13 (Pesh.)	128	xlix.	52
TOBIT.		xiv. 19	409	xlix. 14	410
		xiv. 20, 21	241, 253	l. 15	314
xii. 15	335	xv. 19	456	l. 18	13
xiii. 11	328	xvii. 17	337	l. 24 (Pesh.)	128
		xvii. 27	385	l. 26	232
		xvii. 30	385, 410	li. 1–12	127
JUDITH.		xviii. 21	369	li. 5	127
		xix. 19	442	li. 6	118, 127
xii. 2, 13	195	xxii. 27	66, 456	li. 10	327
xvi. 7	424	xxiii. 1–4	327		
		xxiii. 9	300		
		xxiv.	334	BARUCH.	
WISDOM OF SOLOMON.		xxiv. 6	296		
		xxxvi. 15	40	i. 11	156
iii. 1, 2	384	xxxvi. 15–16	25	iii. 23	97
v. 15	331	xxxix. 1–11	241	iv. 20	456

INDICES.

1 MACCABEES.		1 MACCABEES—cont.		2 MACCABEES—cont.	
	PAGE		PAGE		PAGE
(Syriac)	43	xii.	37, 297	xv. 22	178
i. 24	166	xii. 10	297	xv. 36	48, 229
i. 24, 30	94	xiii. 14	50		
i. 33	80	xiii. 27–30	14	4 MACCABEES.	
i. 37	93, 104	xiii. 39	39		
i. 57	94	xiii. 41–42	200	Maccabees, Fourth	
ii. 1	32	xiii. 42	39	Book of	29
ii. 27	95	xiii. 42–47	199	vii. 17	414
ii. 29	57	xiii. 47–50	80	xiii. 14	443
ii. 42	56, 364	xiii. 51	40	xvi. 22	414
ii. 43	49	xiii. 51, 52	11	xvii. 18	414
ii. 44	48	xiii. 52	26		
ii. 59, 60	445	xiv.	23, 38	ENOCH.	
ii. 62	93	xiv.	23		
ii. 63	58, 93	xiv. 7	50	v.	414
iii. 24	125	xiv. 8–11	24	v. 8, 9	443
iii. 41	98	xiv. 9, 43	23	v. 9	405
iii. 45	18	xiv. 11	50	vi.	448
iii. 46–60	94, 95	xiv. 13	24, 50	x.	221
iv. 1	199	xiv. 14	28, 68, 80	xiv. 9–23	314
iv. 6–11	104	xiv. 15	11	xiv. 22	336
iv. 28	199	xiv. 27–46	26	xvii. 4	408
iv. 30–33	17	xiv. 36	68, 80	xxii.	406, 413, 441
iv. 30	66	xiv. 41	22, 35, 40, 200	xxii. i.	424, 449
iv. 33	48	xiv. 47	26	xxii. 13	413
iv. 37–59	16	xiv. 51	41	xxv. 5	412
iv. 46	22, 40	xv. 3, 21	253	xxv. 6	443
iv. 54	18	xv. 26	48	xxxix. 1	336
v. 1, 2	98	xv. 27	48, 79	xlii. 1, 2	334
v. 35	105			xlii. 1–3	323
vi. 28, 54	92	2 MACCABEES.		xlv. 4–5	405
vi. 62	79			li. 1, 2	412
vii.	27	i. 1–36	38	liii. 3	413
vii. 9	123	i. 9	33	liv.	424
vii. 10	79	i. 18	32	lx. 8, 13	414
vii. 12, 13	56	ii. 1–18	38	lxi. 5	412
vii. 14	27	ii. 13	457	lxi. 12	414
vii. 16–17	93	ii. 14	12	lxvii.	424
vii. 26	197	iii. 4–7	123	lxix.	448
vii. 33	156	iv. 34, 35	123	lxxi. 15	414
vii. 34	166	v. 11–16, 26	94	lxxii. 1	405
vii. 39	98	vi.–vii.	93	lxxxiii.–xci.	449
vii. 40–43	178	vi. 2	105	lxxxiii.	448
vii. 40–44	197	vi. 18	66	lxxxiii. 2	446
vii. 49	48	vii.	29	lxxxiii. 11	448
viii.	37, 92, 297	vii. 14	406	lxxxvii. 3	414
ix. 9–16	94	vii. 36	408	lxxxix. 52	414
ix. 18	93	ix. 4	166	lxxxix. 73	449
ix. 19–21	37, 108	x. 1–7	16	lxxxix. 73–74	375
ix. 23	68, 93	x. 4	377	xc. 9	24
ix. 26, 28	56	x. 6	33	xci. 10	412
ix. 27	35, 40, 96	xii. 35	109	xci. 15, 16	405
ix. 73	68	xii. 37	48	xcii. 3	412
x. 21	68	xii. 43–45	415	xciv. 5	423
x. 46	79	xiii. 13–17	93	xcviii.	448
x. 61	253	xiv. 6	56	xcviii. 10, 12	413
xi. 53	79	xv. 12–16	96	xcviii. 15	423
xi. 58	23	xv. 16	98	xcix. 11	413
xi. 60	98			c. 5	414

www.ingramcontent.com/pod-product-compliance
Lightning Source LLC
Chambersburg PA
CBHW071133300426
44113CB00009B/959